MIGHTIER
than the
SWORD

MIGHTIER
than the
SWORD

A Kyokushin Karate Coming of Age Story

by Nathan Ligo

LIGO INK
DURHAM, NORTH CAROLINA

Mightier Than The Sword was written in 2006 and 2007, and edited to its current form in 2008, 2009, and 2010. It is a work of nonfiction, i.e. it is a true story in that it relates actual events to the best of the author's ability to recall them years after they occurred. All accounts of events should therefore be regarded as the author's recollection and/or interpretation of actual events. Although the names of people who might be considered well-known have not been changed, other names and descriptions have been changed to conceal actual identities. Any
resemblance, therefore, between these fictitious characters and actual people, whether living or dead, should be taken to be purely coincidental.

Cover photograph by Mims Copeland. Jacket design by David Christie. Book production by Carol Majors. Back jacket photograph by Amy Kirshner.

The opinions expressed in this manuscript are solely the opinions of the author and do not necessarily represent the opinions or thoughts of Ligo Ink or its board of directors. The author has represented and warranted full ownership and/or legal right to publish all the materials in this book.

Mightier Than The Sword
A Kyokushin Karate Coming of Age Story
All Rights Reserved.
Copyright © 2011 Nathan Ligo
V2.0 R1.0

This book may not be reproduced, transmitted, or stored in whole or in part by any means, including graphic, electronic, or mechanical without the express written consent of the publisher except in the case of brief quotations embodied in critical articles and reviews.

LIGO INK
www.budokaratehouse.com/LigoInk
ISBN: 978-1-4327-6920-8

Ligo Ink and the Ligo Ink logo are trademarks belonging to The Society for the Betterment of the Human Condition through the Training, Instruction, and Propagation of Budo Karate, Inc.

PRINTED IN THE UNITED STATES OF AMERICA

For Helen

And in loving memory of *Shihan* Jacques Sandulescu
who died November 19, 2010

PREFACE

MIGHTIER THAN THE SWORD emerged from a single chapter called "Davidson" in a broader twelve-chapter book outline. Although other episodes of my story may turn out to be more conventionally marketable – the time I spent training in Japan in daily contact with Mas Oyama, for example! – it was this chapter that developed a life of its own and demanded a more immediate treatment. I was, in that sense, waylaid by my muse, and it is this chapter of my life experience that comes now to fruition.

The result is a book that I am content to share, but not completely without reservation, since it represents a small part of a much bigger story, and is not completely representative of the character described. *Mightier than the Sword* is the story of a turbulent coming of age, and some readers may be struck by one or two of the controversial truths that its young protagonist holds to be self-evident. Rebel though I most certainly was at the age of 21, 22 and 23, I feel compelled to emphasize here that much of the seventeen years since have been dedicated to bringing my adult life into a better cadence with the human herd in terms of how I choose to express the particulars of my ongoing and ever-evolving rebellion.

With regard to Kyokushin, this is a partial story of one Kyokushin karateka, and not necessarily a treatise on what Kyokushin Karate is meant to be. Kyokushin Karate, as a life-governing discipline, is practiced by many thousands of people worldwide – twelve million at the time of Mas Oyama's death! – and one of the reasons why it remains so powerful is that its practice can mean different things to different people. *Mightier than the Sword* describes Kyokushin Karate as what it meant to me during my own coming of age, and that meaning was certainly at least as much a result of the unique circumstances of my adolescence as of any teaching inherent in Mas Oyama's Kyokushin.

My editor encouraged me to mention here that the timeline of the story is NOT linear. My motivation in writing was to reveal certain elusive truths, and the structure of the retelling might best be described as "a corkscrew, tightening in on a series of revelations" (my editor's words) that I felt I could only approach in this manner. The book's event progression is layered. Each section takes the reader further into the story chronologically, and, at the same time, deeper into the persona and closer, therefore, to those elusive truths. The book is nonfiction, it is a true story, and with several specific exceptions, names have not been changed.

I could not have brought this work to completion without the heroic dedication of my editor Annie Gottlieb. Her willingness to press forward, revision after revision, particularly in the final sections, finally achieved a result that had seemed at times unattainable. It gives the two of us no small satisfaction that, through our combined labor, we were able to retain portions of the book's original content that had been deemed unmanageable by several of the manuscript's early readers – including Annie herself!

To my first writing teacher, now-retired Davidson College Professor of English, Tony Abbott, I owe yet another debt of gratitude, since it was he who read the manuscript and told me that I'd finally written a book. This was enormous in the context of our shared history, since he'd condemned so many of my earlier attempts. Without this one key piece of encouragement, I wonder if this book, too, wouldn't have remained shelved alongside all the others.

Finally, I'd like to express a word of thanks to *Shihan* Michael Monaco who came to my rescue and supplied, at the last minute, several photographs that I've used to replace ones I had to remove because I could not contact the original photographer to secure permissions.

All proceeds generated by the sales of this book will go towards supporting the nonprofit organization that I have founded and made my life's work. Readers may find information about The Society for the Betterment of the Human Condition through the Training, Instruction, and Propagation of Budo Karate (d.b.a. Budo Karate House and Ligo Dojo of Budo Karate) online at www.budokaratehouse.com. Any additional contributions made will go directly to help make self-esteem–

and discipline-instilling karate training available to young people who might not otherwise be able to participate. At the dojo, we teach karate and karate alone. In accordance with Mas Oyama's teaching, it is best through hard physical training that the greater truths of life will emerge; we provide the hard physical training, and hope that each individual will discover those greater truths that will be important for their own lives in the future.

> ... Sato's gift, a changeless sword,
> By pen and paper lies,
> That it may moralise
> My days out of their aimlessness.
> A bit of an embroidered dress
> Covers its wooden sheath.
> Chaucer had not drawn breath
> When it was forged. In Sato's house,
> Curved like new moon, moon-luminous
> It lay five hundred years.
> Yet if no change appears
> No moon; only an aching heart
> Conceives a changeless work of art.
>
> — W.B. Yeats

> ... in solitude, or in that deserted state when we are surrounded by human beings and yet they sympathize not with us, we love the flowers, the grass and the waters and the sky. In the motion of the very leaves of spring in the blue air there is then found a secret correspondence with our heart. There is eloquence in the tongueless wind and a melody in the flowing of brooks and the rustling of the reeds beside them which by their inconceivable relations to something within the soul awaken the spirits to a dance of breathless rapture, and bring tears of mysterious tenderness to the eyes like the enthusiasm of patriotic success ... So soon as this want or power is dead, man becomes the living sepulcher of himself, and what yet survives is the mere husk of what once he was.
>
> — P.B. Shelley

FOREWORD

AT THE TIME of Masutatsu Oyama's death in 1994, he was regarded by many as the world's greatest living *karateka*. His Kyokushin Karate had spread to 133 countries around the world and was reputed to have touched as many as twelve million students.

Forty years earlier, the Korean-born "Mas" Oyama had, himself, become a virtual revolution in the world of Japanese karate, in that it was he who introduced stone- and therefore bone-breaking power to the highly stylized traditional forms of karate that had come to exist in Japan. Kyokushin Karate became known for its no-nonsense practicality, its fearsome physical power, and a theretofore unseen degree of spiritual strength conjured through a revival of Japan's do-or-die samurai personality.

Once Kyokushin exploded to such incredible proportions, Mas Oyama took on only a very few students that were his own, that he himself guided, day by day, in an attempt to ensure that his teaching would endure. *Uchi deshi* literally means "live-in disciple;" it is the opposite of the *kayoi deshi* or "commuting student," who merely visits the dojo regularly for training. Mas Oyama's *uchi deshi* program was a one-thousand-day monastic karate program for his small group of personal students who lived in the Young Lions' Dormitory, a small building attached to his world headquarters dojo in Tokyo.

PART I

ONE

RETURNING TO MY HOME town of Davidson, North Carolina following my failure to complete Mas Oyama's *uchi deshi* program – having run away without a word to my teacher after less than 600 of the 1000 days required for graduation – I was convinced that karate was a thing of my past. Having been there at the heart of it all, and then having thrown it all away, how could I ever go back?

I was not yet 21 years old.

There was no question in my mind that I would resume my education at Davidson College. Homesick in the Young Lions' Dormitory in Tokyo, I'd often longed to be back there. My memories of my freshman year, beginning at age seventeen, were nothing but electrifying. For the first time in my life I'd discovered the thrill of learning for the sake of simply knowing.

How selfish I believed it to be to devote all of one's energy to the betterment of self!

I would go back to school. But first I had a higher priority, one that I hadn't allowed myself, probably ever. It was nearly December when I came home from Japan. I'd come home just in time for the spring semester, but I decided to wait until August and fall semester in the name of a truly rare cause.

After seven years I had left my obsession with karate behind. Leaving Mas Oyama's *uchi deshi* program in disgrace, and in the process severing my relationships with both Mas Oyama and his nephew Seong Soo Choi who had sent me to him, was the single most heartbreaking experience of my life. How ironic, in the light of that heartbreak, to have found a sense of freedom I'd never before experienced!

Yes, I'd failed, but I was also free.

Ever since I was fifteen, I'd been so single-mindedly devoted to following Master Choi's advice in the hope of making it to Japan, and then so single-mindedly devoted to succeeding once I got there, that it felt as though my entire life had consisted of nothing but hard, hard work.

Don't you think you deserve to just relax for a while, take it easy and enjoy? I asked myself. *Don't you deserve to live life like everyone else for a change? Like all these normal people who lack missions of life-and-death importance?*

The answer that came back was an unequivocal "Yes!"

At the age of 20, I felt I had already lived an entire life. Squeezed into seven years – success or failure set aside – I had spent an entire life's worth of energy in devotion to a cause that I now found myself suddenly free of. I looked around me and beheld other 20-year-old Americans working meaningless part-time jobs or beginning their junior years of college . . . and I saw children! 20-year-old children who hadn't even begun to live!

I wondered if they could handle sinking their teeth into life's veins as I believed I had. Many of them, I thought, lost in pursuit of an education without direction, would likely never come close to experiencing what I had already squeezed into a tiny fragment of my own life. I compared myself to them and felt like I had all the time in the world.

I set out to relax and have some fun.

I moved into an apartment with several roommates who had no ambitions or inhibitions. I bought a car and spent hours fixing it up just for the fun of it. I pulled my father's boyhood electric trains out of the attic and set them up to scream on their tracks around the perimeter of my room. I pursued women for the sake of sex and somehow managed to catch up to a few of them. I was strong enough to keep a gorgeous underage girl, who wound up intoxicated in my bed after a party, sleeping peacefully at arms' length even though I barely slept a wink, knowing that she was available to me and that I wouldn't have been her first. I was weak enough to make a fool of myself by falling momentarily in love with a first cousin of mine I'd been attracted to since we were kids. The weatherman announced a tornado warning, and I set out on the highway with a friend to try to see it. For a brief period, I lived just on the safe side of being a hazard to myself.

It was then that I began writing. After all, I had all the time in the world.

I had already decided that I would write the story of the past seven years, culminating with my experience in Japan as a personal student of

Mas Oyama. Karate was a thing of my past – yet the pursuit of it had been so incredibly powerful that I believed the story had to be told. After the near-utopian first ten years of my life ended with the breakup of my father's second family, I became the undeniable proof of a past my father wanted desperately to leave behind. By the time my mother dissolved *her* second marriage four years later and began a succession of fresh starts in which there was less and less room for me, I had long since developed into an unhappy, unhealthy, and weak adolescent, and had finally gotten my feet under me again thanks to Master Choi. I had found some balance, but only after putting myself through seven years of hellish training and study, chasing a dream that most people my age wouldn't have been able to fathom. And even though the pursuit hadn't turned out as I'd imagined it would – I'd failed in Japan, after all! – there was this incredible feeling of liberation, of rebirth, of joy!

It hadn't turned out as I'd struggled to make it, yet it had somehow brought me where I so desperately wanted to be.

I'd started out weak and abnormally unhappy. I'd then spent years trying to make myself into a titan in order to stamp out a sense of personal weakness that seemed only to intensify the harder I fought to correct it. In the end I'd failed – I was no titan – but the result was one I hadn't expected. For the first time in my life I found myself simply normal and content, if not actually happy. What a bizarre twist of fate that failure in a single-minded pursuit could result in such a sense of liberation!

I reveled in the realization that I'd failed with a clean conscience, because there wasn't any more that I could have given in the attempt.

No, it needed to be written. It needed to be told. I was certain that if I could tell it in the right way, it would be of value to other young Americans who struggled to find their way safely past the pitfalls of adolescence with their identities intact. That was what I believed myself uniquely to have done, and that was what I felt compelled to share.

Sadly, I could barely find words to describe my experience to anyone, let alone write it. I didn't have the slightest idea how to write beyond a high school level. Yet I started anyway, armed with a feeling of invulnerability stemming from the conviction that I'd already lived, endured, and sucked the marrow dry from an entire life. I humored myself to believe that I was at least better off than writers who know how to write but have no story to tell.

"I'm going to start with the end because it's still so fresh in my mind," I wrote, and with this line, still six weeks before my 21st birthday, I began a several-page, for me heart-wrenching account of my then only two-week-old escape from Mas Oyama's *uchi deshi* dormitory.

I began to tell a story that I had no idea I hadn't even yet begun to live.

* * *

I'd known Professor Tony Abbott, chairman of Davidson's English Department and one-time nominee for a Pulitzer Prize for poetry, ever since I was a small child. His older children babysat for my brother and me once or twice, and his house in the center of Davidson, which he rented out summers while he and his family were at the lake, was one of several that I'd lived in with my mother during the first two years after her separation from my father when I was five.

A decade and two stepmothers later, in a bid to get me out of my father's house as soon as possible, the second one did me the greatest favor imaginable by using her position in Davidson's admissions office to arrange for me to leave public school a year early and move into one of Davidson's dormitories as a freshman, and Dr. Abbott had played an unknowing role at that time. My stepmother arranged for me to take several samples of my eleventh-grade writing to him over the summer, so that he could offer his opinion on whether I could handle Davidson classes without first completing twelfth-grade English. Somehow Dr. Abbott gave his blessing and, although I'm quite certain my writing was atrocious, I made the connection with the man who would teach me the principle that keeps me writing to this day. Although others would follow, it was the basic freshman composition course I took from Dr. Abbott that first fall semester that was the most significant of my writing education. It was in that class that I learned that I could write, even though I then had no clue that I'd ever really want to.

I returned from my Japan experience nearly three years later resolved to study English instead of the math and physics I began before going overseas. It was to write autobiography that I wanted to study English, and it was to my first composition teacher, Tony Abbott, that I turned for guidance.

Little more than a hedonist at the time – during those first months *back from the monastery* in Japan, it's fair to say that all I cared about was the pursuit of women I might lure into my bed! – I contacted Dr. Abbott to ask if he would help me shape my writing into an independent study so that I could benefit from the regular critique of a qualified reader. From the common-use computers at the college on which I wrote my first few pages, I moved first to a small apartment over the Soda Shop on Main Street with my father's older, already obsolete word processor. There I spent many hours writing with my feet propped on the windowsill overlooking the sidewalk, my keyboard in my lap and a mostly unlit cigarette dangling from my lips. Two months later I moved into the only college dormitory available to students while the college was shut down for the summer, and there I lived in a two-bedroom suite with nothing in it but a mattress and my computer.

Each time I delivered another chapter to Dr. Abbott, I'd come into his office a day or two later naïvely expecting to see the same excitement in his eyes that I felt just below the surface of the words I put on paper. Each time I was disappointed to see in his eyes that what I had written was little more than dribble, a few more pages of what might have to be many, many more than I ever imagined before my story might ever be read.

"You have to figure out why anyone is going to care," Dr. Abbott told me.

"People read autobiographies because the people who write them are people of some notoriety who interest them. The average Joe on the street could write down his life story, but who would care unless the writer had done something noteworthy? What is it about the story you want to tell that's going to make it matter to your chosen audience? In terms of the writing and learning to write well, you have to simply keep writing. Write regularly, keep trying to iron out the technical problems – learn to spell! – and don't quit. Whether or not anyone's ever going to care enough to pick up your book in the first place is another story altogether . . ."

His commentary wasn't meant to be disheartening, but I was disheartened. I'm sure partially as a result, there were some weeks at the end of the summer, as the fall semester approached, during which I spent many hours in front of the computer and failed to write. But what was disheartening to hear was also starkly real and brutally educational. Dr. Abbott was right, and in little ways the accuracy of his observation settled in to hold hands with my unwavering conviction to form the principle that keeps me writing to this day. There was an important story in me to tell if I could ever get it correctly told. Momentarily deadlocked or not, it was on that new, adjusted foundation that I would push forward into the future.

Never quit and good writing will come.

Live whatever life becomes necessary to make sure someone will take notice and, when the time finally comes, it will be published.

And then, someday, the world will finally know.

* * *

Seven months after my escape from Japan, seven months during which I accomplished little more than putting thousands of poorly combined words to paper, I began training again. My karate training began in a way that I never would have expected. I had actively resisted the temptation.

Back in the spring, a Davidson student from Africa named Anthony Mubiru had heard that I'd had some kind of unique overseas training experience. He tracked me down to ask if I'd teach him. He desperately wanted to learn karate, he told me, and in the tiny town of Davidson, with its student body of 1500 and its similar-sized permanent population, there was no karate class that he could join. North Carolina's largest city, Charlotte, was just a half-hour drive away, but as an international student he didn't have a car, and there was no public transportation

"I'm sorry," I told him, "I've retired. I'm no longer practicing karate."

I used the term *retired* with some discomfort, because it generally denotes retirement due to age after a long career. How was I to explain that having run away from the world's most famous karate teacher, there was no way I could bring myself to continue?

I literally had no desire.

Anthony was persistent, though. He asked again some days later. I was moved by his belief that he could change my mind after I'd told him so unequivocally *no*, and finally I resolved to test his determination. I invited him to join me on Davidson's track and football field the next morning.

Anthony met me and I took him through a standard Young Lions' Dormitory first-year student's morning training session: a fast six-kilometer run followed by three sets each of rope-jumping, jumping squats, knuckle push-ups, and sit-ups. Three or four months out of training at that point, my stamina was much less than it had been, but my body remembered the motions, and Anthony struggled to keep up. I told him if he could hang with that training for a while I would begin to teach him the kicks and punches of karate. He thanked me for the workout, and we agreed to meet at the same time the next day.

I was there, early the next morning, but Anthony didn't show up. I don't know if he was sore from the day before or whether he failed to wake up like he'd planned, but my attitude was a relieved "To hell with him! I didn't want to teach this guy in the first place!" He called me a number of times after that to try to arrange a make-up date, but I didn't return his calls.

That summer I was working as an assistant manager at the Davidson College dining service, a position that I held from almost the first November day I returned to America until the following August, when I'd finally resume my college education and trade that job for one more compatible with an academic schedule.

My boss had a hit list of changes she wanted made in her new position, and she used me and my energy to break down a few walls in her way. In fact, one day she asked me to get a sledgehammer and literally pointed to a few walls she wanted knocked down. It was during the time when I was living in Duke Dormitory, trying to write for Dr. Abbott and suffering from writer's block. Swinging that hammer felt altogether too much to me like swinging an ax, and there had been an earlier emotionally charged, transitional event in my life during which I'd swung an ax for the spiritual benefit of the sweat spilled.

After work I drove to the hardware store and bought quite a nice one. I'd never used an ax with a double blade like that one before, but I tested its balance there in the aisle next to the gardening tools, compared the way it felt in my grip to its single-bladed counterpart, and had no doubt which one would better serve my purpose.

I already had a few trees in mind.

In the massive forest ravine behind the house in which I'd grown up, one that my father built and then left behind when he divorced my first stepmother, a hurricane named Hugo had sent several tornados roaring overhead three years earlier and toppled several massive beech trees. I'd gone to the house in search of that second ex-wife of my father, since she and I had had a particularly close relationship when I was a child, and instead I found those trees down on her property. They insulted the memory of my childhood playground, fallen across the creek with their massive red-clay-packed root clusters torn upwards towards the sky, and I'd already fantasized about having the time to remove them. An artist photographer and professor of photography at the University of North Carolina at Charlotte (UNCC), Martha was in the Florida Everglades with her camera again – gone back to the swamp for the summer – and I went to work in the forest in which I used to play as a child.

I would exercise there for an hour or two every day for the rest of the summer and into the fall.

I didn't even consider it training at first. My body just hungered for the workout. I wanted to sweat. But before I knew it, I was becoming aware of the technique of swinging the ax. I was paying attention to my breathing, to my stance, my grip, to the path the ax blade followed through the air, and the relation of the blade's angle of impact to the amount of damage inflicted on the wood. In short, I was applying my adolescent understanding of karate to an entirely new set of techniques, in a completely unrelated, yet in some key ways similar pursuit.

I humored myself to evoke the training of Yoshikawa's Miyamoto Musashi,[1] who gave an entire season to the study of cutting rocky soil with a spade in order to deepen his understanding of grip, of the swing, and of the cut. Of course, I was far from a Musashi, and I understand the risk I take of coming across as a dreamer, since I was never a champion. Had my one-time *uchi deshi koohai*[2] Nicholas Pettas gone out and spent half a year training with an ax, recognized parallels between the activity and his karate, and maybe even learned something that he could carry back into the K-1 kickboxing ring that made him for a time one of the most famous names in Japanese pop culture, that would have been a different story.

Not only was I just me, but I was only twenty-one and I shudder to think how little I knew. Nevertheless, young and naïve as I was, these were

---

[1] Miyamoto Musashi (c.1584-1645) is Japan's most famous samurai-era swordsman and author of *A Book of Five Rings*. His life story was immortalized in the semifictional book *Musashi* by Eiji Yoshikawa (1892-1962).

[2] *Koohai*, "junior," is the opposite of *sempai*, "senior." Anyone who has seniority either in terms of current rank, or in terms of who began training earliest, is referred to by his juniors as *sempai*. On one's first day of training, therefore, everyone else in the dojo is one's *sempai*, and should be remembered as such even when the newcomer progresses faster through the ranks.

the thoughts I entertained. The activity did sneak up on me and become training, and from it I did learn lessons that I would carry into my karate in the future.

As my power increased, I sheared off my first ax handle. I was upset because it meant that I had to cut my training short, but after another trip to the hardware store the next day, I found myself trying, this time intentionally, to achieve enough power to once again embed the double-edged ax head in a downward swing into a horizontal tree trunk and to be once again rewarded by the sound of cracking hickory, the sudden weightlessness of the handle in my grip, and the dull thud as the splintered ax handle crashed harmlessly into the peat.

In a quest ultimately for mastery, I'd temporarily turned my back on efficiency and set off in search of physical power. The result was another broken ax handle and a hunger for more.

By the time I bought two axes on my next trip to the store, I had already been training my one-handed swing. First my right hand for ten swings, then my left. I knew from karate that training with a handicap would improve the technique once the handicap was removed. The damage inflicted on the three-foot-diameter trunk that I spent sometimes days in a row cutting through just once was not only proportional to the power and the focus of the impact, but also to the angle at which the blade struck the grain. As any one training session drew on, the burning in my forearms intensified and, as a result, the angle of the ax handle in my grip became harder and harder to control. Swinging an ax with one hand therefore trained that control of grip, so that the next time I used two hands, the control would increase more than just twofold. I sacrificed power, of course, when I started using two axes at once, one in each hand, swinging sometimes outside to inside, right hand and then left, and sometimes crossing my body each time, swinging from inside to out.

The enhancement of technical ability once I went back to using one ax in both hands, however, was starkly apparent.

On the whole, I was a fairly weak 21-year-old. Unlike Nick and Judd and Sandor in the dormitory in Japan, I had been beaten in the dojo far more often than I beat my opponents. Yet I had been an *uchi deshi* of Mas Oyama for nearly six hundred days, and I'd spent six years training before that to prepare for them. I knew three hundred knuckle pushups in one session, I knew fifteen hundred consecutive jumping squats in a single set, I knew thirty consecutive one-minute rounds of full-contact, bare-knuckle *kumite*,[3] and I knew two hours of *kihon* and *iddo* and *kata* [4] performed in front of Mas Oyama at the intensity that only his watchful eye could instill. I was far from the strongest one at *Honbu*,[5] but after that experience I was no pushover either, and I'm sure that I must have been a sight to behold at my peak, training in the woods in nothing but shorts and sockless work boots, an ax in each hand, shifting my weight into a forward-leaning stance as I swung, first from a right back-leaning stance and then from a left one, focusing my breathing from my *tanden*[6] to the best of my barely dawning understanding, sweat and woodchips flying, snarls liberally employed.

Having been out of training for half a year, I was far weaker when I entered the woods with my ax than I had been when I left Japan.

Five months later, I was far stronger.

I had also changed.

I understand the risk of telling such a story, having had no one there to bear witness. But whether the force that drives me is spiritual strength or violent denial of intolerable weakness, let the story I am only just beginning to tell of the choices I would make in the subsequent sixteen years be evidence of the change that occurred within me during that return to training: I began to hear my conscience calling to me so strongly that had it called any louder I'd have feared for my sanity. Whether the call I responded to was vision or fantasy, my path changed direction during that training in the woods onto the course that I still struggle to follow today.

For the entirety of my adolescence, I'd done all that I'd done to bring honor to my first teacher, Master Choi, the man I credited with saving my life. I'd given it a pretty good shot – I'd fallen short of the mark, but the

---

[3] *Kumite* is practice fighting in the dojo which often in Kyokushin Karate resembles more "fighting" and less "practice".

[4] *Kihon*, *iddo*, *kata*, *kumite*: the four basic divisions of karate training. *Kihon* involves the practice of stationary techniques; *iddo*, moving ones; and *kata* a prearranged series of movements performed with the intent of mastering an understanding of their applications during fighting.

[5] "General Headquarters." Mas Oyama's dojo in Tokyo was referred to as *Honbu Dojo*, the headquarters of the *International Karate Organization*.

[6] Physically this might refer to the diaphragm although in the Eastern sense this is the spiritual center of one's being, from whence *chi* energy originates.

result was that I'd found my life worth living for the first time. But there in the woods with that ax, swimming perhaps in an inflated sense of my own power, with no witness or opponent to put me in my place, I became awestruck by the drive to transform myself that I'd somehow conjured up from within.

I'd once carried a barbell equal to my body weight across my shoulders to the top of a mountain to raise money for charity out of an altruistic notion that I could also show the newspaper-reading public that even *normal people like us* could break out of our comfort zone to achieve for the greater good. With bleeding feet I'd once walked forty miles to make an apology to Master Choi for overstepping my bounds. I'd endured nearly 600 days secluded in a grueling karate program that no foreigner had ever graduated from – me, Nathan Ligo, the weakest, smallest kid in every peer group or academic class I'd ever been part of. Sure, I'd been beaten, bruised, broken, and knocked down time after time, but I'd dished out my own fair share of beatings, too. Japan Champion, Masuda Akira, had knocked me out during a full-contact 90 seconds because I'd knocked him around enough for the first 85 that he had no choice but to beat me, when he'd rather have paced himself just a little bit further into the 100 consecutive fights he completed that day.

But far greater than any physical feat, I found myself in those woods – bug-bitten, blistered, and dripping with sweat – suddenly in awe at what I'd achieved in terms of a remaking of self.

Having been through all that you've been through, I asked, *how can you justify not making an effort to show other young people the way?*

You are the only American student of the world's greatest living karateka!*[7] How can you possibly justify not carrying forward that which he handed you? You have seen what you can endure, all for someone else. You have experienced, firsthand, the empowerment of at least believing all that you do is self-sacrificial, done for the sake of another. How can you possibly live with yourself if you sit by and do nothing in a world where so many need the doors to their own innate spiritual strength opened for them, a world where so few teachers and role models are even aware that we all have such doors within us just waiting to be opened?*

The answer that came back was unequivocal and terrifying.

Maxed out with my ax, blinded by the physical strain, I'd nearly crawl up the slope out of the forest. With my forearms so wrecked that I could

---

[7] Practitioner(s) of karate.

barely close my fists, my arms so tired I could barely lift them, my body so dehydrated I could barely see, I must certainly have been out of my mind.

And it was then that the answer rang out so clearly.

It was the kind of dream that all of us have when our self-image is at one of its extremes, when we imagine the ways we might rise above ourselves and achieve something spectacular, something that those who think they know us couldn't even imagine. But I was supposed to dismiss it like everyone else. I was supposed to allow the constraints of reality to come rushing in to the rescue and reveal the fact that I was just as helpless as the rest, and that my vision, my image of what I might achieve, was only a fantasy; it could never come true.

This time, however, something — mountains of wood chips, maybe, marking how far I'd come — made me confident enough not to dismiss the fantasy as nonsense. Master Choi had always told me that completing Mas Oyama's *uchi deshi* program would be like getting a magic ticket for success in life. "Succeed there," he said, "and there's nothing you won't be able to do." I had not succeeded, yet somehow I was reaping benefits that shouldn't have been mine. Somehow just pushing myself to the extreme that I had in the attempt had shown me to be strong enough to set myself free. And there I was with my ax, pushing myself beyond exhaustion yet again, and I realized that if I was willing to go that far, and to keep going that far day after day, I just might have a chance of actually turning the fantasy into reality.

Is it vision that drives me, or is it fantasy?

Throughout this chapter of my life — and onwards into the future — that question would haunt me. But the answer always came back: *It's up to me!*

I *can* decide whether it's going to be vision or fantasy. The deciding factor is how far I'm willing to push myself towards the extremes of exhaustion in the pursuit of artistic creativity.

Do what it takes to keep your eyes seeing eyes, Nathan! When in doubt, drive yourself to the point of collapse where everything is so clear. Maintain like this and you can pound the fantasy into the here and now.

Is it far-fetched?

Is it crazy?

Is it more likely to fail than to succeed?

Of course it is. But what chance is there if I don't try?

Who else is going to take the risk?

Who else has been shaped by his life up to this point into one who can not only see the path but also dare to take it?

What right do I have to turn my back and cower?

I've got just this one life, and in a sense I've already lived it. What right do I have not to give myself over to the experiment?

To hell with it . . . Rot!

Push forward.

Never quit.

Be willing to let it kill you and you might have a chance.

Are you willing?

Hell, I'm halfway there already.

TWO

It took me the rest of that first year back at Davidson to draw that kind of thinking out of the valley of my childhood and into my daily life, where I might put it into practice.

My classes would start at the beginning of September, and having lived on campus already for the second half of the summer, I knew that with the resumption of normal college life my daily trips to the forest were going to be hard to continue. And yet, those echoes of conscience had begun to nag me. Mas Oyama's intention in inviting me to Japan had been that I would return to America and teach Kyokushin[8] to Americans. *Why not at least give it a shot?* I wondered.

And then, as if on cue, the summer wound down, and three or four potential students started to crawl out of the woodwork. The African Anthony Mubiru called again.

Like with Mubiru, I'll take them out on the track and run 'em to death, I thought. *I'll make them suffer, and they won't hang with it for long. If they can stick with it, then I suppose I'll have to teach them.*

Why not see what comes of it?

And so it began.

Nathan Ligo, one-time *nidan*[9] of Master Choi's Carolina Martial Arts Club in Chapel Hill and failed brown belt *uchi deshi* of Mas Oyama, believing he'd irrevocably cut his ties to both, began teaching Kyokushin Karate anyway. I asked my first four prospective students to meet me on the track at seven a.m., six days per week, Monday through Saturday. I

---

[8] A proper name. "The way of the ultimate" or "the ultimate way."

[9] *Shodan, nidan, sandan, yondan*, Japanese for "first, second, third, fourth grade black belt". *Dan* means "grade" or "class".

assured them that if they didn't show their desire by being there every day, I'd lose interest. "Wear sweats, running shoes, and a plain white T-shirt," I told them. "If you can endure the morning trainings for a while, I'll start to teach you karate."

One guy nearly passed out on his first day. Another threw up on his second. *They won't last the week,* I told myself.

And I didn't much mind.

My academic courses started awkwardly. It had been nearly three years since I'd been a freshman at Davidson, I was a newcomer in that the classmates I'd spent my first year with had graduated at the beginning of the summer, and it took some effort to get back into the routine, certainly given my attachment to the extracurricular. A course on the writings of the 14th century poet Geoffrey Chaucer, in which we read all of his work in the barely readable precursor to modern English, would be the bear of my semester. My American literature survey would turn out to be the most meaningful. I would get very little other than practice out of the writing seminar I took, because I wasn't allowed to write what I was passionate about, and in the end I wound up failing Economics 101, which, as taught by that particular professor, about required a PhD just to comprehend the lectures.

Davidson is a private liberal-arts college, which means that students study a wider range of courses beyond their majors than university students routinely do, a practice designed to provide a deeper foundation to one's education in the arts and humanities than schools with nonacademic career-track focus. Davidson was consistently ranked as one of the top ten private colleges in America, and although it wasn't Harvard or Princeton, the standard of learning was far above average. Unlike at many public universities, you couldn't pass your economics course if you weren't able to demonstrate a reasonable grasp of the subject matter. Davidson did not have a graduate school, but it was known for sending a large percentage of its graduates successfully on to receive higher education elsewhere, and many graduates were known to go on to places like Harvard or Princeton to study medicine or law, or to follow scholarly pursuits in greater depth.

At the invitation of one of my professors, Nobel laureate Seamus Heaney sat in for a question-and-answer session with the nine members of my modern Irish poetry course one day during my senior year. The following year, Pulitzer Prize-winning poet Philip Levine stopped by for a reading. In short, I reaped the benefit of a relatively high-level education, and I was well aware that I was lucky to be where I was. Perhaps I even had a better appreciation than some of my extremely bright classmates who took it for granted or, conversely, were upset that they hadn't gotten into Harvard.

I was especially appreciative of the high-level education I was getting when I was being soundly beaten, either by my economics course that first semester, or by the Chinese history class that similarly defeated me in the last semester of my last year at Davidson.

On the extracurricular front I was maxed out. Those three or four guys who began training with me every morning somehow refused to quit, and their number soon increased to as many as six. I was obliged to start enhancing their morning conditioning workouts with afternoon karate training, which sometimes eventually had as many as nine participants. Several of the guys were actually an inspiration to me in their desire to learn, given my still uncertain recovery from having abandoned karate altogether.

One morning about two months in, I decided to enlighten them as to how much more capable the human body is than we give it credit for, and showed them they could all do 500 consecutive jumping squats after our run. Six of us stood in a circle together, and each person counted ten reps, for a total of sixty repetitions by the time we worked our way around the circle once, and we went on around eight and a half more times. I was truly dumbfounded when all five of them, one by one, separated by a hundred or so repetitions, staggered away from the circle to throw up. Each one took only a couple of minutes to spit the taste out of his mouth before jumping right back into the circle. One of them even went back for seconds, having failed to empty his stomach completely the first time. And yet none of them quit! – and I was left to marvel that even though I was much stronger than they were then, they were so much stronger than I'd been when just starting out.

I was the physically inferior Beta returned from the trenches of trying to make myself a titan, and I was shocked to find myself setting the pace for a group of Alphas.

One afternoon during class in the mirrored dance studio I used as a dojo, I challenged my student Trip to trade increasingly powerful uppercuts to the stomach with his roommate Thad, who had also become my student, until one of them quit. Once again I was rendered speechless to watch as both of them refused to be beaten. They couldn't possibly have had enough of an understanding of technique yet, of course, to know how to control the depth of impact so as to stun the diaphragm and make it fail. But what they lacked in technique they more than made up for in spirit.

For what seemed like an eternity they used their entire might to punch each other in the gut, finally at the end nearly lifting each other off their feet with the impact, only to brace themselves for the answering blow. I finally had to stop them after it became clear that neither one of them was going to quit. In an inspiring demonstration of one of the benefits of real karate training, they left the dojo better friends than they had been when they came in, and I found myself surprisingly hopeful for a future of real karate in America.

I left my job at the Dining Service in the final week before classes started to become the night and weekend manager of the café in the Student Union, and I spent much of my time there studying in my office, cursing the interruption whenever work responsibilities broke my chain of thought. My penchant for chasing women to make up for lost time hadn't quite been dispelled, and my third significant extracurricular activity was the mostly nighttime hours I spent thus engaged. I have a particularly painful memory of being torn from the warmest and most comfortable of beds by a girlfriend's alarm clock at 6:00 in the morning in time to drag myself out into the cold to meet the guys for morning training. I have an even more painful memory of leaving a party at that same off-campus house just a handful of days later with yet a different young woman who was to become the most significant of my year.

In the midst of all that, one of my roommates, who'd also become my student, pointed out an advertisement in *Black Belt* Magazine for a Kyokushin Karate tournament in Rochester, New York, at which Mas Oyama was to be the honored guest.

Mas Oyama is to be the honored guest.
At a tournament.
In Rochester.
In America.
In MY country!

Time ground to a halt. My world stopped spinning as I struggled to process the news I'd just learned.

I had zero intention of returning to Kyokushin, to Japan or to Mas

Oyama. In fact, I had no notion that I'd ever even see Mas Oyama again. I was too ashamed. Yet raw, unadulterated Duty hit me in the gut like a freight train, and I knew that as painful as it was going to be to face him, the rest of everything I was doing in my life and everyone breathing in it could go to hell, but I would be damned if Mas Oyama was going to set foot in MY country without my being there to open the car door for him, carry his bag, make sure that he was safe, and look under every stone for ways that I might make his visit as comfortable and successful as possible. I was still his *uchi deshi*. I was blown completely over by the notion, I was at once terrified and devastated, yet there was no other alternative.

I felt as though if I'd been dead my body would have clawed its way out of the ground to stagger its way to Rochester without me.

* * *

My student Dave and I made the drive, Friday after class and all night long, thirteen hours to Rochester. I hadn't even remembered Kyokushin's Rochester branch chief [10] Michael Monaco when I called him, but he figured out right away that I was the one who had helped him past the guards at the Tokyo Budokan[11] at the Fifth World Open Karate Tournament the previous year. He would be happy to arrange for a place for me and my student to stay for free once I arrived, he told me. I'd just need to call him once I was in town, and he'd "put me up" with one of his students.

Dave stayed with me for the first seven hours of the drive, but by the time two a.m. became three, he was out cold in the passenger seat beside me. On one particularly bleak stretch of highway I hit a possum on the interstate doing seventy-five. I saw the red of his beady little eyes shining the reflected light of my own headlights back at me only after it would have been catastrophically dangerous to swerve. I braced myself for a bump when he went under my front right tire, but there was only a *swoosh* as the tire stretched his body out into a fifteen-foot smear on the highway.

The next morning, high as a kite on coffee and not having slept a wink, I pulled into a parking lot to change clothes out of sight of the hotel

---

[10] Official position within Mas Oyama's International Karate Organization given to instructors entrusted with developing the organization in their general geographical area.

[11] The "Madison Square Garden of Tokyo," a superdome, where all the biggest fights are held.

where I knew the tournament delegation was staying. I left Dave sleeping in the car and walked out into the open to smoke the only one of a new pack of cigarettes I'd smoke before throwing the pack away. I smoked it in a bid to quell the stir of the bat-sized butterflies in my stomach.

Less than 600 days into my training in Japan, I had broken under the pressure of a program in which I was the only American — and not a very strong one at that! — and in which full-contact, bare-knuckle fighting was a daily part of the routine. I hadn't seen Mas Oyama since the morning ceremony that last day before I ran away in the night, and facing him, I knew, would be one of the hardest challenges of my life. I was so afraid and strung out on caffeine when first I lit that cigarette that the fronts of my thigh muscles shook on my thighbones and nearly cramped in an apparent attempt to run away without me. I changed my pants there in the wide-open of the parking lot, slid into a pair of loafers, and pulled on a white shirt, tie and jacket. Ten minutes later, I washed the smell of cigarette smoke off my hands and face in the men's room off the lobby of the Airport Holiday Inn. The lobby was full of Kyokushin people, and there was even a table set up to welcome fighters who hadn't spent Friday night.

Someone told me that Mas Oyama was in the restaurant having breakfast, and one minute later, from the café doorway I saw him sitting near the window at a table for ten. He looked remarkably well, remarkably like himself, and remarkably human. He is one of the people that you meet, if you've ever had a chance to meet such a man, who is so powerful and so well known that it's almost shocking to behold him in person and realize that he is indeed made of flesh and bone like the rest of us. Spend time separated from him, however, and by the time you see him again, you will as likely as not have been overcome by his enormity and have all but forgotten that he is just a man after all.

I'd never loved another man like I loved that grandfather-age titan there across the room — save perhaps for my first teacher, his nephew, but then, that love was really one and the same. For me that day, however, Mas Oyama might as well have been the most vicious of bloodthirsty beasts for how afraid I was to face him. I stepped into the restaurant just far enough to see him across the room, and there I backed towards the wall just inside and stood in *fudo dachi* [12] like a gargoyle flanking the door. My

---

[12] Most basic of karate stances, indistinguishable to the untrained eye from a simple standing posture with equal weight on both feet, feet parallel within one's shoulder

fists, although clenched, I lowered a degree from the norm to my sides so as not to draw attention to myself. A hostess asked me if she could seat me and I told her no, thank you, I was waiting for someone.

The position and location that I'd assumed next to the door, with equal weight on both feet and my back as straight as the wall six inches behind me, was the *uchi deshi* standard. I was terrified to be doing so once again, but I was discovering that with Mas Oyama in the house, *uchi deshi* had never merely been something I'd done. It was what I was.

David Bunt was there with Mas Oyama and so was Cameron Quinn. Bunt, an American, had been an office worker at Mas Oyama's *Honbu* when I was an *uchi deshi*. He was also my *sempai*,[13] since he was already a *shodan* when I arrived there to discard the belt I'd received from Master Choi and don a white one instead. His Japanese was far ahead of mine, and I could tell that he was translating for Mas Oyama as he had on so many occasions when I was in Japan. Cameron Quinn, a branch chief from Australia who'd authored a well-known book in the English-speaking Kyokushin world, *The Budo Karate of Mas Oyama*, was actually far better at Japanese than David, and he was there as well. With the exception of Michael Monaco I didn't recognize the other half dozen figures at the table, and quite frankly I didn't pay much attention. I realize now, they must have been the rest of the motley crew of North American branch chiefs.

Twenty minutes later Mas Oyama – *Sosai*[14] as we only ever referred to him – rose, said his thanks for the breakfast, shook a few hands, and headed towards the door and therefore directly towards me. As he neared, I bowed, and issued an "Osu!" that was the restaurant's loudest that day.[15] I didn't care. Like I said, the rest of the world could go to hell, as much as I had thought I wasn't any more, I was Mas Oyama's *uchi deshi*, and I greeted him in the only way I knew how.

---

width. Basically it's how karate people "stand at attention" in the dojo awaiting instructions.

[13] "Senior," opposite of *koohai*, "junior."

[14] *Kancho* means "chairman" or "president". *Sosai* is a more honorific term adopted within Kyokushin for Mas Oyama after he got older and his organization became so huge.

[15] A one-syllable Japanese oath (long *o*, silent *u*) used in the dojo along with a bow as a salute, or in conversation to mean "yes!" or "yes sir!" or "understood!" The term is actually best translated as, "I will persevere in the face of any hardship," or perhaps "I will stop at nothing to learn what it is that you're teaching!"

I was a bit surprised when he looked straight at me and summarily passed right by me without saying a word, although I realized later that he would have never seen me with hair and in a jacket and tie before. He barely got two steps, though, before David Bunt turned to him and said, "That was Ligo, your *uchi deshi* at *Honbu*." Mas Oyama stopped in his tracks, turned, and looked not merely *at* me this time, but also *into* me. Recognizing me then, he did little to conceal his surprise.

"Ah, Ligo," he said, approaching and extending his hand. He had a reassuring twinkle in his eye. He would have been able to see my fear. "You come to my room," he said. I was always surprised when he spoke English, because he was insecure with the little bit of English he did speak, and he almost never tried.

"Osu!" I said again at full volume, bowed and shook his hand with both of mine. His hand released, I raised my eyes again to find he'd already turned his away to go. Still petrified, I stood rooted to the floor for a long moment before I realized I was being left behind by the half-dozen or so who were accompanying *Sosai,* and I jumped to fall into formation. The *Power Karate Magazine* photographer, Kobayashi Yo, who was one of several Japanese traveling with Mas Oyama, recognized me, smiled, and put a hand in the middle of my lower back to kindly shove me past the two or three people between me and *Sosai*, reminding me that as an *uchi deshi* my place was a step behind and a step beside my teacher. I remember that friendly shove for the very first time today as I write this, I can feel his hand in the small of my back as if it was yesterday, and I realize now this it was that helpful nudge that broke my spell and pushed me back onto the path that I remain on to this day.

I *was* Mas Oyama's *uchi deshi.*

It didn't matter if I was nervous or afraid, or strong or weak, or whether I'd graduated or not. Duty took over and rendered the *me* part of that equation irrelevant. Only service was important. My God, was I Mas Oyama's *uchi deshi*, and by God, was I back to stay!

Months later I would read a letter that *Sosai* had already written to Master Choi, my first teacher and his nephew. It was written during my first months back in North Carolina after failing in Japan, and several months before I'd even picked up my ax. It was still ten months before Rochester.

Mas Oyama had written:

International Karate Organization *Honbu*
Kyokushinkaikan
Director Mas. Oyama

January 11, 1992

Dear Mr. Choi,

    Thank you very much for the Christmas card you sent me. I have to apologize to you because I could not answer the phone when you rang. I am very sorry but I was very busy.

    I am planning to visit USA in the spring. Your two cousins (my daughters) and aunt (my wife) are staying in NY now, and I am going to visit them. So, I could visit your place together with Mr. Bunt from New York, who speaks Japanese, at that time.

    Also, I would like you to visit Tokyo when you will go back to Korea. In February, probably I will be busy with the *dan*-promotion test for my students but I will arrange my schedule if you let me know yours.

    Regarding Mr. Ligo, I regret that he dropped out from *uchi deshi* like that. I was considering to give him 2nd *dan* and a graduation certificate of *uchi deshi*, as a special case, if he had tried harder and made his best. You know, smart persons do stupid things sometimes, making a fool of himself.

    I will consider about your two training halls and I think that we should discuss about that matter as well.

    I wish you a happy new year and good health.

Yours sincerely
Mas Oyama

As far as Mas Oyama was concerned, I must have been all but lost to him then.

THREE

ONCE IN *SOSAI'S* SUITE, which included a large sitting room, I was told to sit, and I waited uncomfortably in a corner chair. As *uchi deshi* in Mas Oyama's company, we only ever sat bolt upright with our feet planted firmly on the ground, our fists planted firmly on our hips, and without leaning our backs against the backs of our chairs. We generally didn't even look right or left unless our attention was required elsewhere. *Sosai*, translated by David Bunt, spoke with two or three others before summoning me.

"Osu!" I stood up and bowed, and approached the chair to which I was ushered. Mas Oyama was tying that bandana around his head that he often wore when he was feeling parental. I was reminded of an earlier time when he'd worn it under similar circumstances.

As a skinny, weak 19-year-old first-year *uchi deshi*, I'd endured months of hazing by a French-Algerian *sempai* of mine named Mocaram – my only *gaijin* [16] *sempai* – who was in his second year. At that time in the dormitory, fear and intimidation was a key tool employed by our *sempai* to keep us walking the path they wanted us to, and although *Sosai* would finally put his foot down and instigate change, at that early time our *sempai* could basically abuse us even for no reason other than to entertain themselves. The abuse that I took at the hands of the Frenchman was employed regularly and ruthlessly to show off to the other two foreign members of my class, one-time Australian lightweight champion Judd Reid and several-time Hungarian lightweight champion Sandor Brezovai.

Mocaram was certainly not a champion, but he was anxious to be perceived like one.

---

[16] *Gaijin* is short for *gaikokujin* or "foreigner." The original (historic) connotation was of one who was unwelcome in Japan.

Sandor was far stronger than the Frenchman, Judd was edging up on being at least as strong, but I was definitely far weaker. Within my first week, Mocaram latched on to the fact that I had been a student of Mas Oyama's nephew for six years before coming to Japan, and he decided that meant I must think I was something special and, as a result, degraded me at every possible opportunity for the months that followed. I imagine that he had been treated fairly harshly by his *sempai*, and knowing them – they were my *sempai* too! – I suspect their treatment of him had been much more abusive than his of me.

The abuse that the 75-kilogram Mocaram directed towards me in those first months, as my new training routine and diet whittled away my own weight to a very lean 65 kilos, took various exclusively nonphysical forms, of which making me wash all his laundry by hand every day – regardless of whether it was already clean – was the one I hated most.

We washed all our clothes in our first year, and well into our second, in a washtub, with cold water, under the outdoor spigot in the street in front of *Honbu*. The only way to dry the clothes was to hang them in the dormitory, since the clotheslines in the sun in front of *Honbu* were reserved for our *sempai*, and clothes very often – particularly in winter – took days and days to dry. It was summer when I arrived in Japan, Tokyo's summers are so hot and humid that we often couldn't stand the contact of our futons' fabric against our flesh in the night and sometimes opted to sleep directly on the *tatami*,[17] and even after a full day of hanging in the stagnant air of the dormitory, our clothes were typically still damp. Time and time again Mocaram would order me to take down all his clothes from where they were still hanging in the second-floor *obiya*, the *big room*[18] where eight to ten of us slept each night – and hung our laundry! – to take them back outside to wash them again, even though I'd already washed them the day before.

To have any chance of drying, of course, wet clothes would have to be very thoroughly wrung out, and since we didn't have any kind of wringer, the routine was to fold over and twist the garments tighter and tighter

---

[17] Straw mat used as flooring in traditional Japanese homes.

[18] The large room upstairs in the dormitory where all the first-year *uchi deshi* slept was big enough for twelve futons, two end to end, times six, side by side. Twelve of us occupied this same room, but one or two on lobby guard duty actually slept, each night, just inside the main doors to *Honbu Dojo*.

until we'd squeezed as much water out as possible. This we'd have to do to wring out the soapy water, again to wring out the first course of rinse water, and again for the second. Mas Oyama reminded us regularly in our *uchi deshi* trainings that we should always wash our *dogi* [19] by hand in this fashion to increase the power of our grip, and I imagine that this was one of the excuses, both by which Mocaram justified making me wash his clothes, and by which Mocaram's *sempai*, the third-year guys, denied us the use of the washing machine and centrifuge on the first floor that they used without inhibition.

Mocaram's second favorite weapon was simply to abuse me verbally. We weren't allowed to talk back to our *sempai* with anything but "Osu!" and we were, of course, required to stand when spoken to. There were many times upstairs in the *obiya* that Mocaram would sit on his futon while I stood on the opposite side of the room in *fudo dachi* beside mine, as he challenged himself to find as many ways as he could to call me weak and worthless and then concurred with my agreement when I answered in the only way I was allowed, "Osu!"

All of this was for the benefit of Judd, and particularly Sandor, so that Mocaram could show them how powerful he was, and they were very often a reluctant audience for the sick charade. In the beginning Judd had endured the same abuse, but Judd was stronger than I was, and once he'd made Mocaram feel his growing strength in *kumite,* the Frenchman backed off. His M.O. was to abuse the weak in order to prove that he was stronger than, I guess, *someone*. Mocaram *was* far stronger than me. He bashed me in *kumite* with his year ahead of me in training and his ten-kilogram weight advantage, all while pretending it was no effort for him to do so. He never had a harsh word for Sandor, because he knew Sandor could crush him. As the weakest of the foreigners in the dormitory, I was the obvious target.

Of course I hated him with a passion, and I wasn't raised to be capable of even thinking about other people in such terms. The few times in my life I have fallen prey to feeling that way, it was a result of long-term undeserved punishment from which I could not escape, due to the relative power and proximity of the abuser. My second stepmother certainly, one particularly snotty Alpha male classmate of mine in junior high school, and Mocaram might be the complete list of those who have drawn out that kind of worst in me. I often stood there in *fudo dachi* imagining how I

---

[19] Karate uniform.

might rush Mocaram like a wild animal, rip his eyes out of their sockets, and tear the jugulars out of his neck. But even if I had thought I might be able to take him in a surprise attack, there was a feeling in the dormitory at that time that to fight one *sempai* was to fight all of them, and that was a battle I most certainly could not have won.

I learned later that Mas Oyama probably would have approved if I'd pounded Mocaram's brains out with one of the many half-baseball bats in the dormitory left over after *tameshiwari* [20] demonstrations – if I hadn't been strong enough to do it with my fists. But, in the absence of that understanding, any uprising in the dormitory was unthinkable, and I could only endure. Mocaram was so childish that he'd blow his nose in a tissue, drop it on the *tatami* beside his futon, and summon either Judd or me to come get it and put it in the trash can next to the door.

"Ligo!"

"Osu!" I'd shout, and jump, sometimes even out of sleep, into *fudo dachi*.

"Throw away that tissue."

"Osu!" and I'd jump to do so. I was in Rome doing as I believed Romans were supposed to do, and there was no precedent for insubordination no matter how ridiculous the command.

Another day he'd finish eating a doughnut and throw the wrapper on the floor next to him. "Jad-do!"

"Osu!" Judd would leap to his feet.

("Jad-do," was the best pronunciation of "Judd" the Japanese could handle given the limited number of possible syllables in the Japanese language, and Mocaram used it condescendingly to show he was just as superior as his own Japanese *sempai*.)

"Throw away that trash," he'd say. "Hurry up!"

"Osu!" Judd would comply.

That routine didn't actually last very long, because one of the higher-ups caught word of what was going on, and Mocaram was told in no uncertain terms by his third-year *sempai* never to tell us what to do in the dormitory again. We were told in equally clear terms not to pay any attention to Mocaram's orders. The Frenchman was miserable in his life in

---

[20] Literally "stone breaking," but denotes the practice of breaking inanimate objects such as boards, bricks, concrete blocks, baseball bats, and Japanese roofing tiles with karate blows to improve and/or demonstrate technique.

Japan, and he started to really hate me then, because he took for granted that I'd reported him to his *sempai*.

Learning patience, forbearance, and self-reliance was a very strong part of our training in the dormitory. We wrote daily journal entries to Mas Oyama, which he read every day for the entirety of our time there, but we were almost never allowed to address him directly. The point was to learn how to choose our words carefully, how to, in other words, ensure that our relationship with our teacher would be as deliberate as possible, never taken for granted or off the cuff. Likewise, we were trained to keep our mouths shut and endure to the extent that it was reasonably possible in order to avoid troubling Mas Oyama with our petty-by-comparison concerns. Mas Oyama was the director of a twelve-million-member organization. He managed the dozen or so of us, his personal students, but he also of course managed the International Karate Organization, and Kyokushin-kaikan.[21] It was our job to endure. *To persevere*, after all, is the meaning of *Osu!* Mas Oyama always told us that we should think of him like a father and that if we had problems we should come to him. But there was also an unspoken understanding, promulgated by the Japanese, that we weren't actually ever to do so.

Interestingly, this flew directly in the face of Master Choi's advice to me concerning his uncle. "If there's something important that you need, or if you have some kind of problem, you have to go to my uncle and tell him," he told me. "Of course, don't bother him with unimportant things, but if you go to him when you need him, he will remember you above the others, and in the end he'll love you for it."

After a half year or so of tolerating my *sempai*, Mocaram, I finally had enough, and I broke with dormitory tradition in accordance with my first teacher's advice and took my troubles to *Sosai*. Mocaram was no longer abusing me directly by then, but he finally drove me over the edge in his continued bid for attention, by taking to bad-mouthing *Sosai* himself. Judd and I couldn't believe it when Mocaram started talking about how Mas Oyama was fat and lazy and how he didn't teach us when he didn't feel like it. Of course our shock encouraged him all the more, and I'm sure he didn't mean it – Mocaram loved *Sosai* just like the rest of us – he was simply immature and restless in the dormitory, and he wanted to shock

---

[21] Japanese name for Mas Oyama's Kyokushin International Karate Organization headquarters.

us and show us, I suppose, that he was tough enough even to talk badly about Mas Oyama.

I wrote a journal entry that week in Japanese, in my journal that *Sosai* read every day, one that I was mortally afraid one of my *sempai* might discover and read. I wrote that Mocaram was a bad person and that he most certainly was not my friend. I wrote that he was abusive of his authority and that he even said bad things about *Sosai* behind his back. "Presumably," I wrote, "this guy will go out into the world after he graduates and represent Kyokushin. I simply wanted to make sure that *Sosai* knows the kind of student he has in his dormitory." [22]

Mas Oyama was clearly angry the next morning in the morning ceremony, and as soon as it was over, I asked the English-speaking secretary to ask *Sosai* for permission to talk with him in private about something I'd written in my journal.

Two hours later, *Sosai* called the dormitory on the intercom phone and asked that I be sent to his office. I was, of course, as terrified then as I was upon meeting Mas Oyama in Rochester two years later. I was doing something for which, as far as I knew, there was no precedent. None of my peers had ever gone to talk to Mas Oyama about a personal issue. To my knowledge, none of my peers had ever instigated a conversation with Mas Oyama about anything, ever.

I arrived in *Sosai's* office and followed like a ghost as he took me and his interpreter back out, into the stairwell, and up to his fourth-floor apartment. When Mas Oyama was younger, he had lived there with his family on the fourth floor of *Honbu*. It was his private area, and I'd never been higher than the third floor. As far as I knew, none of my *uchi deshi* roommates had either.

Sosai gestured to a soft chair in the living area of a very humble apartment, and told me in Japanese to sit.

"Osu! *Shitsurei shimasu!* (Excuse me for sitting!)" I said and did as I was told, bolt upright with my fists on my hips, my stomach quivering with fear.

Mas Oyama sat opposite, with the secretary between us, and unbuttoned his fly for comfort. I waited while he tied that fatherly bandana around his forehead.

---

[22] One never addresses one's seniors in Japanese with "you." The third person is always used.

Unfortunately, I was too frightened to do a very good job of presenting my case concerning Mocaram. I nearly stuttered, and I was deeply ashamed afterwards of my inability to talk to *Sosai* in a normal way. Mas Oyama used to yell in frustration, *"Kami-sama jaa nai, Watashi! Ningen da yo!* (I'm not a god! I'm just a man like you!)" whenever people treated him as such – which I dare say most people did most of the time, except for his closest confidants. He was a god for me (I had no confusion that in a literal sense he was just an extraordinary man, of course), and it was very hard to talk to him as if he was simply ordinary.

Mas Oyama, center, with most of the author's class of 1st year *uchi deshi*. From left to right that's me, Yamakage, Judd, Kato, *Sosai*, Komukai, Sandor, Ishida, and Suzuki. Mocaram was for some reason absent. Oshikiri was in the hospital with a broken rib. Kuruda was downstairs on lobby guard duty.

To the best of my ability, I did proceed in spite of myself to tell Mas Oyama, very politely and very fearfully, about all that I'd endured at the hands of Mocaram. You might imagine my dismay when, the further I got into my description, the less concerned Mas Oyama seemed to be. I kept waiting for my last translated line to be the one that would get a rise out of him, but time and again, it didn't. Even when I told him Mocaram was talking badly of him personally, he didn't react as if it was a matter of concern. Of course he was very patient and kind, and seemed to be concerned about me, but I kept expecting him to get angry about Mocaram's behavior, and he never did.

Finally out of desperation I told him that Mocaram was shoplifting from local shops. Only then did Mas Oyama display a glint of anger.

He leaned forward in his chair. "He's stealing from neighborhood shops?" he asked the secretary to make sure that she'd interpreted correctly.

She asked me again and I confirmed that she'd heard me right.

"What is he stealing?" *Sosai* asked.

His interpreter asked me and, embarrassed, I told her truthfully that Mocaram had been shoplifting the type of soft porn magazines those shops carry.

Sosai understood my English, slapped his armrest, and laughed. He picked up the intercom phone next to him and dialed the extension for the dormitory. I heard one of the Japanese answer, "Osu, Suzuki here!"

"Suzuki," *Sosai* boomed.

"Osu!!!" *Sosai's* voice was unmistakable and our *Osu's* were particularly loud when addressing Mas Oyama.

Sosai asked to speak with *Ryoobo-san*,[23] the old woman who worked in the dormitory dining room preparing our lunches and dinners, Monday through Saturday.

Ryoobo-san came to the phone and *Sosai* asked her to join us on the fourth floor of *Honbu*. We waited for an excruciatingly long time for her to arrive.

I was surprised by the familiarity with which *Sosai* interacted with *Ryoobo-san*, although I'd never seen them together outside of the dormitory before. He stood up when she arrived — of course I stood up when he stood up — and he sat her down next to him, smiled affectionately and put his hand on her hand as he spoke. They were similar in age, and it struck me that they were interacting as dormitory father and mother. There were great smiles shared between them, and it was apparent that they held each other in high esteem.

Once pleasantries had been exchanged, *Sosai* asked *Ryoobo-san* to go to Mocaram's box sometime when he was out training, and look to see if the items he had there were new and if they cost more than the money he was known to have. The interpreter explained to me what was being said.

---

[23] Literally, "Dormitory Mother." The *san* (Mrs.) makes the term honorary.

"I've heard that Mocaram might be shoplifting," *Sosai* explained.

Ryoobo-san smiled and, "Oh, is that all?" she said. "But there's no reason for me to look in his room. I know that he's been stealing."

"Is that so?" *Sosai* said, straightening in his chair, surprised.

The interpreter translated.

"Yes, he's stolen a few items a few times. I know because the shopkeepers saw him stealing. They came to me and told me afterwards and I paid them for what he stole with my own money. I didn't want to bother anyone about it, so I just paid them. The items were not expensive."

"Oh, is that so?" *Sosai* scolded her in a "wow, what an admirable thing you did!" sort of way. He went on to talk with her for a few moments in a very familiar and friendly tone on other unrelated subjects, and the interpreter did not translate.

"Good!" *Sosai* finally said with finality, leaning forward and planting his hands on his armrests in preparation to stand. "Is there anything else Ligo wants to say?"

The interpreter asked me and, still uneasy with how the conversation had gone, I told her that that was fine.

"What's your weight now, Ligo?" *Sosai* asked me directly in Japanese once we'd stood.

"Osu! It is sixty-seven kilograms!" I answered in Japanese, stretching the truth by probably a kilogram.

"Ah, that's not so good! You have to eat more and become strong," he said.

"Osu!" I responded.

"*Gambatte*! (Persevere!)" he said.

"Osu!" I responded again.

Rochester, two years later, was much like round two of the same conversation. *Sosai* sat across from me, concerned, attentive, kind and terrifying. I was so nervous I could barely speak.

"I'm very happy that you look very well," *Sosai* began. David Bunt was translating. "We were all very worried when you left the dormitory. For two days until we received your letter, we worried, and all the *uchi deshi* looked for you."

"Osu! *Shitsurei shimashita!* (I was very rude.)" I said. My shame was utter and complete.

"People steal for all kinds of reasons," *Sosai* said. "For example, one might steal because he's hungry and can't feed his family, and we cannot blame him too harshly in this situation."

"Osu!" I answered, confused about why he was talking about stealing. It was only later that I realized that in my desperation to escape from the dormitory I had left with a handful of pocket change, probably about 3000 yen (thirty dollars), that I'd borrowed from a short-term Australian roommate, an *uchi deshi* under Cameron Quinn named Wally who'd come to spend just a few weeks in the dormitory. I wondered if *Sosai* had misunderstood and thought that I'd stolen money and that's why I'd run away, rather than that I'd run away for another reason and the money, which I did in effect steal by not returning it, had been the means with which I'd run. As was fast becoming my norm, I was inclined not to clarify when only my own reputation was at stake, and I let it go without dispute. I wondered if David Bunt had translated incorrectly, but even if I hadn't been in agony for the conversation to be over, I wouldn't have spoken up. To do so would have been selfish.

"Osu!" was all that I could say. "I will try harder in the future."

"What are you doing now?" *Sosai* asked.

"Osu! I'm a university student again. I'm studying writing because I want to write a book about my experience in Japan. And I'm teaching karate at my college."

"Oh, is that so?" *Sosai* asked, "How many students do you have?"

"Less than ten," I told him. I incorrectly used the word *deshi* (disciple) rather than *seito* (student), and *Sosai* scolded me sharply.

"They are not your *deshi!*" he told me. "They must be your *friends* first! *That* is the most important thing. Train with them as friends and you will be successful."

"Osu!"

"Well, I'm happy to see that you're well," he concluded. "You should make close friends here among these Kyokushin branch chiefs in America. Soon you will be among them if you can make wise choices."

"Osu!" I said again, and that was the end of my personal conversation with *Sosai* on the occasion of our reuniting in Rochester. Soon afterwards, the entire group of us left the hotel for the convention center where the tournament was to be held.

* * *

I spent the rest of the weekend playing bodyguard and personal assistant to *Sosai*. I did my best to never leave his side. I opened doors for him, I carried his bag, and I practiced crowd control when he got swamped by fans wanting his autograph.

In Japan, it was well accepted that one of our roles as *uchi deshi* was to be *Sosai's* bodyguards, even though we lived in an era when there was no longer much need. Nevertheless, during the *kumite* part of day-long gradings[24] at *Honbu*, we were often stationed in a full-squat position at the front corners of the head table where *Sosai* sat to protect him and his guests from potential injury should bodies go flying in their direction. Probably it was childlike and naïve, but I spent the entire tournament watching the crowd for that one American lunatic who might want to do an important person harm. Mas Oyama was in my country – I was his only *uchi deshi* in America – and if anything was going to happen to Mas Oyama on American soil, it was going to be over my dead body.

A staff member of *Shihan* Michael Monaco's took this photograph of *Sosai* at the head table (top left) at Monaco's 1992 tournament in Rochester, and inadvertently took a picture of me (second suit from right) watching the crowd for that random nut case who might want to do an important person harm. The blond kid in a suit to my left is my student and roommate Dave.

---

[24] "Grading" or perhaps, "exam." Gradings for promotion to a higher belt at *Honbu* always included the most grueling of bare-knuckle full-contact fighting.

I commented to Michael Monaco on his placement of the head table on an elevated platform against the wall, overlooking both the crowd and the tournament with a clear line of sight – and therefore a clear line of fire – from nearly everyone in the room. I didn't allow myself to be put at ease by Bill Scott and John Farrell (two massive US branch chiefs I met that day), who sat on either side of *Sosai* throughout the tournament even though Bill Scott's day job was in law enforcement, and it was obvious that the pouch he wore around his waist contained a none-too-small firearm.

I alone detected *Sosai's* frustration when spectators and *karateka* alike walked so frequently between him and the action without so much as ducking their heads as they passed. It disturbed me that, because of the setup, so many of them were allowed to approach him to push items in his face that they wanted signed, many of them without so much as an "Osu" or a "thank you." Finally I positioned my student Dave at the front right corner of the table and myself at the front left, and we stood there for the rest of the day, blocking that corridor and redirecting foot traffic around the long way that didn't go directly in front of *Sosai*.

During a lunch break in a suite at the hotel attached to the convention center, *Sosai* called my name towards where I stood in *fudo dachi* against the wall just inside the door. He was sitting in a large armchair, at the end of a coffee table lined by sofas and opposite a television. On one of the sofas to *Sosai's* left sat a humongous grey-haired man in an official yellow Kyokushin blazer that would have swallowed me completely. I could have put both of my feet, it occurred to me then, inside just one of his gigantic sneakers. Next to this humongous man was a tiny grey-haired lady in glasses that must have been his wife. The giant was *Sosai's* age and the three of them seemed remarkably relaxed in each other's company.

"Osu!" I leapt forward when *Sosai* called my name, to learn how I could be of assistance. He had not spoken to me since our meeting that morning except to say *"Arigatoo!"* on one or two occasions as I performed some service for him.

Sosai gestured for me to sit next to him on the other sofa to his right, and he introduced me to the couple with whom he'd just shared his lunch. "This is Ligo," *Sosai* said in English with a thick accent. "He is *uchi deshi* in Honbu."

"Osu, *Shitsurei shimasu!"* I answered as I sat. ("I'm going to be rude by sitting!")

"This is *Shihan* Jack and Annie," *Sosai* said. "My friends in America." [25]

"Osu!" I said again, this time to Jacques Sandulescu as I stood up and shook his hand and his wife Annie's for the first time. My hand felt like that of a child in Jacques' grip. It wasn't that he was exceptionally tall; it was rather that his bones were huge. *Twice the width*, I thought, *of any normal man*.

"How . . ." *Sosai* began. "Your age. What is your age?"

I was a bit in awe because I had never heard *Sosai* attempt so much English before that morning. "Osu, I'm twenty-one," I said in Japanese. I'd been in situations before where *Sosai* was introducing me to some associate or another. He had been clearly proud of his foreign *uchi deshi* in Japan, and particularly proud of our varying ability to speak Japanese. I answered in Japanese because it was clear to me that that was what *Sosai* wanted.

"Ah, twenty-one," *Sosai* said in English. "He's twenty-one."

Sosai stood up and gestured for me to take his chair so that I could sit next to Jacques. "You have to be friends with Jack," *Sosai* said, and I could tell that he was making an introduction that was important to him.

"Osu!" I answered and reluctantly took the seat where I'd been told to sit with another *"Shitsurei shimasu!"* *Sosai* excused himself and walked back to a smaller, harder chair against the wall. I stood again when he sat down.

I exchanged small talk with Jacques and Annie – where I was from, how I ended up in Japan, etc. – but I'm sure I wasn't a very good conversationalist. I was made too uncomfortable by nearly having my back to *Sosai* and by knowing he was sitting in a smaller, harder chair, with his back against the wall. I was sitting with my back straight, of course, and both of my feet were flat on the floor. I was not leaning back, and I did have my fists planted firmly on my hips.

Jacques startled me at one point by issuing a "Nathan!" that was a bit louder and more abrupt than I was used to in such close quarters.

"Osu!" I said with a start. Apparently his tone had had the desired effect.

---

[25] If *sensei* means "teacher", *shihan* would mean "master instructor" or "teacher's teacher." Traditionally a body of students would address their teacher as *sensei* to show respect and *shihan* to show a greater level of respect once their teacher aged or advanced to higher levels of accomplishment. In a later attempt at standardization within the IKO, *sensei* was arbitrarily assigned for use with instructors of 3rd or 4th *dan*, while *shihan* was used for instructors of 5th *dan* or higher.

The first of four substitute images with which I have had to replace photographs by Kobayashi Yo because he could not be located to obtain written permission. Original photo showed Mas Oyama having lunch with Jacques Sandulescu and his wife Annie just moments before he introduced them to me for the first time. "I could tell that [*Sosai*] was making an introduction that was important to him." This photograph by Michael Monaco, taken in Tokyo, shows Jacques's enormous stature. That's Mas Oyama, of course, in the foreground.

"Relax!" he said. "You're too tight! Take it easy."

"Osu!" I said, and did the best I could.

Annie asked me if I'd ever heard of Jacques' book *Donbas*. I hadn't, I told her, and she said they'd send me a copy. Apparently it was something about Jacques' escape from a prison labor camp in Soviet Russia as a teenager.

After a few minutes, the room fell back into silence. I glanced up at some kind of nature show that was on the TV, playing in a muffled tone. Suddenly I became aware in my peripheral vision of *Sosai* craning his neck to see the television around a lamp on an end table that was in his way. I leapt for it with a start, lifted it gently off the table, and started to set it on the floor. "Oh, Ligo, *arigatoo!*" *Sosai* laughed. "That's okay. That's okay," he gestured for me to leave the lamp where it was. He made no effort to hide the fact that he was grateful that I'd noticed his discomfort.

"Osu!" I answered, and "Osu! *Shitsurei shimasu!*" when I bowed and sat back down again. I felt no more awkwardness by that time in *Sosai's* company. For the time being, I'd escaped the "*Sosai* as god" trap once again, and with a long silent sigh I realized that I felt much relieved.

The next morning after breakfast, the tournament behind us, *Sosai* hosted a meeting of North American branch chiefs in the hotel conference room, and one of the interpreters told me that *Sosai* wanted me to be there. Everyone present, I presumed, was my *sempai* – they were certainly all older than me – so I sat intentionally at the far end of the table, with my back straight and my fists on my hips, and merely watched and listened.

I don't recall much regarding the specific topics discussed that day, but impressions remain, and I do remember noticing that more than several of the branch chiefs didn't seem to get along well with one another. Several were plainly competing for *Sosai's* attention in a way that I, probably alone, could tell displeased him. I'd come to suspect during

Kobayashi Yo's picture of me sitting bolt upright with my fists on my hips during the 1992 North American branch chief meeting in Rochester has been replaced by this staff photo of Michael Monaco's. Here, Mas Oyama and Jacques sit at the head table watching the tournament. Coincidentally – since I write of knowing *Sosai's* facial expressions better than some of the others present – this particular image shows Mas Oyama exasperated at some unknown occurrence, and Jacques struggling to contain himself because he'd clearly rather be giving whoever caused *Sosai's* frustration a good thrashing.

my six years of training, studying *Sosai's* nephew, that maybe Koreans in general, but more likely my teacher's family, or maybe even Koreans from their particular region of the country, possessed an ability to read far more from people through eye contact and body language than we Americans can comprehend. Just like that lamp in *Sosai's* way that no one else would have noticed, I was acutely aware of watching the branch chief gathering, and the individuals present, through *Sosai's* eyes, and I wondered at the irony that several of the suits there seemed to have no clue either that they were being watched, or how they were being seen.

I wondered at the extent of the education Mas Oyama's nephew had given me beginning when I was a very young thirteen, entertaining thoughts even then of me as the son he never had, and knowing by the time I was fourteen that it was my ambition to one day become his uncle's student. "You have to keep your mouth shut and your eyes open," he told me then. "You can learn more by watching my uncle's eyes than other people can teach you with all their words in their entire lifetime." Indeed, I had come to have that same impression watching Master Choi's eyes when he taught. More than just a few times, he would be lecturing a dojo full of us when his eyes would stray across mine, my gaze would reach out into his, desperate to learn, and he would realize that according to his own advice I was looking *into* him for lessons deeper than the words he spoke. And he would encourage me. With an alarming frequency, he'd leave his gaze there, focused gently on mine, as if to invite me to see what I could find.

I loved Master Choi so intensely by the time I was seventeen that there came to be a sensation that he was opening himself up to me in such a way as to make me feel completely welcome and completely trusted, even in the most inner reaches of whatever that is within each one of us that defines us as what we are. On occasions when he lectured for as long as fifteen or twenty minutes in the middle or at the end of a training session, his eyes would drift into and remain locked in mine sometimes for half or more of the entire lecture, as if for those cherished minutes I was the only student in the room. All I had to do was blink or turn away or change the focus of my eyes, and I could break the connection, and he'd return to scanning the eyes of his other students, perhaps in search of that same glint of reception in someone else.

Two decades later, I remain one hundred percent certain that the optical communication that happened between me and Master Choi was real and not imagined. In an attempt to understand, I'd even go so far as to test my notion that I could manipulate that connection with tiny machinations of the focusing muscles in my eyes. "Okay," I'd tell myself, "To test whether the sensation is real or imagined, I'm going to catch Master Choi's gaze when it crosses mine and then hold it until I'm ready to let it go." I'd then flex my eyes – or was it that I relaxed them? – in the way that opened the doors to him, and sure enough, there he'd remain for minutes on end as if there was no one else in the room. "Okay," I'd then tell myself, "that's enough. The other students will wonder why he favors me," and I'd then make whatever the adjustment was that would let him know that I'd seen enough for one day. Sure enough, without missing a beat, he would move his gaze on to the other students.

The author with Master Choi ten years after the events of this book. This photo was taken in Korea at the top of a small mountain near Mas Oyama's birthplace called, in Japanese, *Garyu* or "Reclining Dragon." Mas Oyama's parents are buried here (two earthen mounds, right and left, encircled by stone), beside Master Choi's father, who was Mas Oyama's eldest brother. It was to the top of this mountain that, according to legend, Mas Oyama, the boy, is reputed to have run in order to shout, "One day my roar will wake this sleeping dragon!"

Master Choi had to be aware. It was as if he chose to allow the exercise to continue, since he certainly could have put a stop to it at any time. "Of course you're seeing exactly what you believe you're seeing," it was as if he said with his eyes. "Trust your ability to see it." Like his uncle, Mas Oyama's nephew was an uncanny teacher. He taught even when he wasn't teaching, and he taught lessons buried under the other lessons that you had to look for to see. I know it was the love I felt for him that opened the doors to my benefiting from those lessons, and I felt sorry for the other students who weren't ever aware.

Master Choi's English could be fairly atrocious, and even students that had been his for years used to get frustrated and ask, "What did he say? I can't understand him. Was that English?" Thanks to what Master Choi taught me on another level, however, I came to understand not only all the English, but also something like an entirely separate and unspoken language that existed in the background. Other students wondered how I knew where he wanted me to be, or how he wanted me to adjust a certain technique, given the words – or lack of words – that he used. "Open your eyes, stupid," I wanted to say in response to their frustration, "he just told us. Didn't you see it?"

I would be lying to suggest that I shared more than just a few such moments with *Sosai*.

The social divide between him and me was too great: Where I might have been something like a son to Master Choi, I was merely another grandson-aged student to Mas Oyama. With his 133 countries and twelve million students, he rarely diverted his energy to playing such games with me. I'm sure that he could see through me if he chose, but he was so much older, perhaps, that it was beneath the dignity of his position to allow me to read him as Master Choi had so often invited me to read him in the name of my education.

In a future book, I'll describe in more detail how – hungry to comprehend – I once foolishly crossed a line with *Sosai* and looked into him as his gaze met mine during a lecture, and how he was not only immediately aware but even responded outright with anger. I was one student in a lineup of a dozen, *Sosai's* eyes met mine, he alone would have seen my attempted trespass since it was all in my gaze, and he scolded me with a sharp *"Nani yatte-n da!"* ("What the hell do you think you're doing?") that would have left the others in the room completely clueless, since all eyes were on him.

Nevertheless, I did receive some strong signs of approval from *Sosai* during the time that I was in Japan, and the reason went beyond mere tangible facts such as that I was his Korean nephew's student or that I was his first foreign *uchi deshi* ever to write daily journal entries for him in Japanese. (After the morning ceremony, when Mas Oyama lectured us alone sometimes for as long as thirty minutes each day, he'd approvingly bring up something I wrote in my journal – or maybe it was simply the fact that I wrote one – often enough that I'd wish I had a rock to crawl under and hide.) It didn't escape *Sosai's* notice that, more than the others, I knew when I was being watched. I often knew better what *Sosai* wanted to see in me at a particular moment. And as often as possible, I watched the world – and particularly myself – through Mas Oyama's eyes. Then as now, at the branch chief meeting in Rochester, I knew when he was annoyed with someone's behavior even when he chose not to let them know. I had developed a sense that Mas Oyama approved of me because of the times he knew that I was aware.

My Australian roommate Judd gave me the nickname "Knoll" once in the dormitory when we were trying to find derogatory nicknames for each other.

"Why Knoll?" I asked.

"Know all," he said, "It's because you know it all, all the time."

FOUR

DURING SIX YEARS as Master Choi's student in Chapel Hill, I listened at least a half dozen times as he recounted one particular episode of the Mas Oyama legend in order to emphasize the strength of character that could be developed through karate training. The story involves a young Mas Oyama killing a hoodlum with a single punch in a bar fight and then swearing never to use his karate again, having realized that the man's death was unnecessary.

Although the story was presented as fact, I always wondered to what extent it was true.

In his youth, Mas Oyama fought and killed bulls with his bare hands in his quest to become the world's strongest fighter. After emerging from two years of isolated mountain training, during which he aspired to train more hours a day than he slept – and by the end of which the trees around his cabin, on which he practiced thousands of punches a day, finally withered and died – he was frustrated to be unable to find another man against whom he could test his strength, and he turned his training towards bulls marked for death at slaughterhouses. Mas Oyama knew that butchers used a heavy hammer with a sharp point to slaughter bulls: They would strike the bull with a powerful blow to the forehead, the point would penetrate the bull's skull, and, depending on the butcher's skill, the animal would drop dead with minimal suffering.

"I ought to be able to make my fist as powerful as a butcher's hammer," he reasoned. "I've already made my fist similar to a stonemason's mallet, slicing the mountain stones around my cabin for practice."

We can read Mas Oyama's own account of how his first attempt to kill a bull with his bare fist failed, and how the bull was enraged and tore apart the stall in which it was held. We can assume the account to be true, since we've seen the actual flickering black-and-white movie that made Mas Oyama famous. A documentary producer heard about his exploits and filmed a barehanded battle on a beach, man versus bull, that raged on for forty-five minutes, finally ending when Mas Oyama toppled the exhausted bull and chopped off one of its horns with the edge of his hand.

The most significant of the photographs I replaced because I could not obtain rights showed a young Mas Oyama holding a bloody bull horn which moments earlier he'd triumphantly sliced off the bull's skull with his *shuto* (knife-hand strike). The reader may find it online with a simple Google search. This photo, by Michael Monaco's staff, shows Mas Oyama's amazing profile. His other ear (not visible) was badly scarred from fighting ("cauliflower ear"). It's easy to imagine a man who looks like this going head to head with a raging bull.

We know from Mas Oyama's own accounts that when it was his goal to break his opponent's ribs but his opponent's arm was in the way, his philosophy became to break both the ribs and the arm that protected them. We know that Mas Oyama approached *tameshiwari* with a similar philosophy: "Either the stone will break, or my hand will be broken. Either way I will strike the stone with all of Heaven's might!" It's not hard to imagine, therefore, that Mas Oyama possessed the power to kill a man with a punch.

According to the story his nephew told, Mas Oyama was distraught over the suicide of a beloved but unruly student whom he'd had to expel from his dojo, and he happened into a bar and intervened when he saw a gangster harassing a young woman. When the ruffian attacked him with a knife, Mas Oyama blocked the would-be lethal thrust and struck his attacker with a single, devastatingly powerful barehanded blow that killed him. Mas Oyama was arrested, but then released from jail once the police determined that he had acted in self-defense. Upon encountering the dead man's widow and orphaned son, however, Mas Oyama was overcome with grief, realizing that the death was unnecessary. "Superhuman power must be accompanied by superhuman responsibility," he told himself. He swore to the ruffian's family that he'd never use his karate again, and that he would instead dedicate his life to farming their meager fields, since he'd killed the man who'd provided for them.

According to the story, Mas Oyama followed the dead man's family to their farm and worked their land despite their scornful attempts to run him off. One day the young son of the slain man told his friends that a lunatic had taken to living in the shed behind his house and was harassing his mother. The boys armed themselves with heavy sticks and came in a band to chase the crazy man away. Mas Oyama refused to defend himself, however, and he was beaten severely. One of the boys recognized him: "Isn't that the karate master who kills bulls?" The boys fled the scene, leaving Mas Oyama unconscious and bleeding.

Three days later, when Mas Oyama awoke from a coma, he found the dead man's wife and son at his bedside and it was their turn to beg for his forgiveness; they'd seen his sincerity, and they begged him to return to his life of karate. According to my first teacher, the temporary bouts of partial paralysis that his uncle experienced throughout his life were a result of that beating that he'd taken all those years earlier when he refused to defend himself against a band of boys.

Although I'd heard the story told many times, I finally wrote it down for the first time soon after returning to Davidson from Rochester. Dr. Abbott had told me that getting even small pieces of writing into print would create a track record that could be advantageous once I had a finished book. It was for that reason that I pursued, and finally achieved, the publication of an article that I wrote about Mas Oyama and Kyokushin Karate in *Black Belt* Magazine. At that early stage I had no real awareness of any reason for wanting to publish the article beyond the largely selfish desire to kick off my own writing career. Obtaining Mas Oyama's permission to publish that article, and obtaining sufficient assurance that he clearly understood what I'd written, would turn out, however, to be the ordeal that ultimately tipped the scales and carried me back to Japan, and back to Mas Oyama's *Honbu*, for the first time since I'd run away in the night eighteen months earlier – I was of course wary of publishing a story about Mas Oyama killing a man if he didn't want it made public.

Even though I still had no idea what role, if any, Kyokushin would play in my future, my relief at being welcomed so warmly by *Sosai* in Rochester had at least cleared the way for my giving in to an impulse that had been clawing at me for some time. My *uchi deshi* classmates would be graduating that March – seven Japanese and one Australian, presuming they'd all made it – and, as hard as I knew it would be to be there and be the only one who had failed, I felt driven to attend.

Certainly the drive to use what I had learned in Japan was already beginning to boil up inside me. Indeed, it was nearing the point where it would finally burst out into the here and now. Yet at the time, I couldn't have put into words any motive for wanting to travel to Japan other than to congratulate my one-time roommates upon their graduation – that and to face on my own two feet the scene of my life's greatest defeat.

I was stunned to find a personal letter in my Davidson mailbox from Mas Oyama less than a month after meeting him again in Rochester.

> Dear Mr. Ligo,
>
> I hope that you are in good health. After I came back from New York, I have been and am still very busy with the work for Kyokushin. So I am sorry for my late reply. It was nice meeting you again in New York and I was relieved because you looked very fine. I hope that you would remember the Kyokushin spirit as well, and that you would do your best in the future, too. Wish you the best,
>
> Mas Oyama

The signature was unmistakably his. I was extremely humbled – one doesn't find personal letters in one's mailbox from Mas Oyama every day – but even so, the gap between my failure in Japan and the notion that

I might ever have anything of significance to offer the Kyokushin world seemed unbridgeable.

Sure, I was writing a book about my unique experiences in Japan; I was teaching karate classes and teaching them well. Sure I had a line on publishing an article about Kyokushin. But Dr. Abbott's words rang in my ears and put me in my place:

"You have to ask yourself why anyone's going to care."

I did ask, and the answer that came back to me all too often then was *no one probably ever will.*

No one's going to care about the guy who failed.

At the very least I have to go back and face it. I have to prove to myself that I can. I have to go and see if all that was there is really gone for me after all.

Japan wasn't exactly the average weekend destination for a Davidson College student. In fact, I'd need a couple of days more than a mere weekend, and I had to fight with one of my English professors to reschedule a midterm exam that was meant to be taken that Friday.

"Why should you be a special case?" Dr. Thomas asked. "You're a college student, and taking this exam is your job. Why would you even consider going overseas at a time like this?"

"I know," I said, "but I have no choice. Going to this graduation in Japan is more important to me not only than this whole class, but also than this whole semester. I know it will be an inconvenience, and I'm sorry, but I have no choice."

In the end, I traveled to Japan without letting anyone there know I was coming. I was so close to talking myself out of it, and I wasn't about to give anyone else a chance. One thousand dollars was no small amount of money for me to come up with, and who travels halfway around the world for a weekend to attend a graduation for a program he failed to complete? I would arrive the day before the graduation ceremony – without notification or invitation – and ask the first floor reception staff to notify *Sosai* that I'd come to congratulate my former classmates, and ask for permission to spend those three nights in the dormitory. It was a gamble whether I'd have enough money to keep myself off Tokyo's streets if the answer was no. But I figured that it was less of a gamble whether *Sosai* would take me in.

Once when I was in my second year in the dormitory, *Sosai* caught word that a young Frenchman was sleeping on a bench in the park, having spent all his money on membership fees at *Honbu* so that he could attend trainings for the few weeks he was in Japan. *Sosai* insisted that the stranger be brought into the dormitory and given a place to sleep and meals to eat. It wasn't that I took for granted that I'd be welcomed; certainly nobody at *Honbu* owed me. It was rather that I had faith that I would be welcomed because of the very same Kyokushin brotherhood for which I was traveling to Japan in the first place. My gesture of brotherhood would be met with brotherhood, that's all. "Always ask Mas Oyama," his nephew told me. "He will remember you more than the rest and in the end he will love you for it."

When the bus dropped me at the Metropolitan Hotel just three blocks from *Honbu*, my stomach was already tied up in knots. I'd walked there so many times in among the businessmen in suits, a bald underweight white *uchi deshi* in sandals and the same hand-washed sweat pants I wore every day that month, on the way to use the bank of phones from which I could make international calls, or to the gift shop off the lobby where I could buy chocolate. The whole *uchi deshi* experience had passed like a dream. Just as Mas Oyama had a tendency to slip into the more-than-human category in my mind after not having seen him, my dormitory experience was so completely separated from the norm of my life in America that rolling up to the Metropolitan Hotel, for the first time since I'd left Japan six months earlier, crashed in on me like an avalanche.

Oh, but of course! It wasn't all a dream after all, was it?

My *uchi deshi* experience at *Honbu* had most certainly not been a dream, and a few head-spinning minutes later I found myself back in Mas Oyama's dormitory for the first time since I'd left it in the night, sixteen months earlier.

* * *

My classmates' welcome exceeded my wildest expectations. Of course everyone was already exuberant and celebratory because they were graduating, but I was particularly moved that the Japanese received me as if it was Christmas and I was their Christmas present. Judd and Nick wanted to know, of course, what had happened to me and why I'd left and what I'd been up to. They hadn't heard anything about me, they said, until *Sosai* came back from America and told them that he'd met with me and that I'd been "very helpful to him." I skirted the question of why I'd run away from the dormitory, and instead changed the subject to the fact that I was in college and teaching a small karate class of my own.

Unless I imagined it, by the time I ran away I had developed a somewhat closer bond with my Japanese classmates than had Judd, Mocaram, Sandor, and even Nick. Of course, in the end Judd and Nick lived there in the dormitory for much longer than I. In the beginning, however, I was the most like my Japanese compatriots. I began at the beginning with a white belt like they did, I wasn't already a champion like Judd and Sandor, and I made a constant effort to communicate with them in Japanese.

Photo taken in front of *Honbu* the day after my classmates' graduation. That's Kuruda on my right and my Australian friend Judd Reid on my left. Nicolas Pettas is standing over my right shoulder (with scarf) as he entered his third and final year in the dormitory, and that's his only remaining classmate Mahashi to his right. To Nick's left are my classmates Kato (baseball cap), Komukai (glasses), Yamakage (fur-lined jacket) and Oshikiri (black jumper). Suzuki and Ishida were both present that day but somehow absent from this photo. The tall Australian (Papua New Guinean, actually) in the very back row is Wally, from whom I borrowed $30 on the day that I ran away from the dormitory 16 months earlier. Also present are three of Nick and Mahashi's *koohai* (two standing in the back row, and one squatting beside Judd), and my *sempai* Houssain, a general *Honbu* student from Iran, in the gold jacket, top right.

Once, when I was still living in Japan, we sensed trouble one late evening in the street outside *Honbu* after the dojo was closed. Judd – maybe Nick, I suppose Mocaram – and I sat up with a start from where we'd been reading, sleeping or writing in our journals, and pricked up our ears to the sound of Japanese being shouted in a guttural tone that could only mean a fight. As the shouts became louder, we cautiously but briskly exited the dormitory and rounded the block through the narrow streets to the front of *Honbu*.

Five or six of our seven Japanese classmates were gathered there, and Suzuki and Komukai were on the verge of exchanging blows. More accurately, Suzuki was on the verge of bashing Komukai. Apparently there was a dispute over the equal sharing of tasks around the *Kaikan*,[26] it was believed that Komukai hadn't been holding up his end, and Suzuki had become the spokesman for the group. He was laying out their grievance in no uncertain terms, and Komukai must have known his situation was precarious.

Judd's nickname for Suzuki – one of the taller, skinny ones, with a slender face, black-rimmed glasses, and a receding hairline (which we only discovered after we actually started to have hair in our second year) – was Batman, because he was a bit of a control freak and he had a tendency to get a little psycho when pressed. We half expected him one day to take up one of the dormitory's half bats and go to work on whoever was making his day go badly. I'm not sure why he eventually became just about my best friend among the Japanese – it wasn't that I let him beat me at *shogi*.[27] I think it was rather because he was such a genuinely nice guy under the tough façade, and because he and I communicated well despite our lack of a common language. I suppose it could have been partly because of what happened that night when he was gearing up to fight with Komukai.

The two remained locked in a shouting match for what seemed like an eternity. Judd and the others left at some point, leaving me alone with the Japanese. Suzuki finally decided that Komukai sufficiently understood the point, and he turned away, having made up his mind that it wasn't worth it. Suzuki was not one to back away from a fight – I think his common sense just got the better of him and he let it go. Yamakage, however, the Gangster – Judd's nickname again, since it seemed like all he ever wanted

---

[26] Short for *Kyokushinkaikan*, the main building containing the dojo and *Sosai*'s office and apartment. *Kaikan* could be used interchangeably with *Honbu*.

[27] Japanese chess.

to be was a kneecapping *yakuza* – didn't feel like letting it go. Almost as soon as Suzuki turned away, Yamakage grabbed the collar of Komukai's T-shirt. With the fabric stretched to nearly tearing, he took to the high curb in order to gain a height advantage – he was significantly shorter than Komukai – and from above, punched Komukai in the teeth with a blow that makes me shudder to this day.

Komukai, who had not defended himself, went down to his knees, bleeding the thickest, blackest blood I'd ever seen out of his mouth and down the front of his T-shirt to spatter onto the street. It was soon after that that I lost my head and piped up in my best Japanese, and scolded the whole bunch of them for fighting over nonsense.

"*Kenka wa dame da yo!* (We're all brothers here!)" I told them, "*watashitachi wa mina kyodai da yo!* (What the hell are you fighting with each other for?)"

It's very possible that I didn't clearly understand the situation, and that therefore my scolding was out of place. And it's equally possible that they didn't understand what I was going on about, since my Japanese was so rudimentary. They might have just thought I'd gone crazy; they'd never seen me that outspoken before, let alone in partially coherent Japanese. Nevertheless, for a few valuable moments I had the undivided attention of at least a significant few of the mob, and they stood there and listened like they understood what I was saying. Perhaps they were just shocked that I'd made my voice heard, since I was usually the meek one who was smart enough not to make any waves.

Particularly I remember Suzuki's gleaming eyes, listening, comprehending, still angry (not at me), and sympathetic to my emotion, even if my interference was off base. Komukai, recovered but bleeding, listened as well, probably relieved that I'd drawn the attention off of him. I'd be curious to know if they even remember. I have a hunch that that night, and over time, my Japanese roommates came to feel that I cared about them, and about us, and about the dormitory as a family unit, in at least a little bit more of a genuine way than the other foreigners did.

There's no question that some significant elements of our lives as *gaijin* at *Honbu* had absolutely nothing in common with theirs. As *uchi deshi*, they were the dogs of the dojo. We got treated like dogs a lot too, but when it came down to it, we were the guests of the dojo as well. Mas Oyama insisted that we be treated like guests since, he said, as foreigners we would have concerns and hardships that the Japanese would never have to deal with.

We certainly shared in the responsibilities of maintaining the dormitory; we cleaned all the nooks and crannies and commodes of *Honbu* every morning just like the Japanese. But on the other hand, there was a whole list of awe-inspiring tasks that they were responsible for, in terms of maintaining *Honbu*, that we were never asked to perform. Two Japanese *uchi-deshi* were stationed on lobby guard duty on rotating shifts twenty-four hours a day, seven days a week: Two of them stood at attention in *fudo dachi* in four or six-hour shifts all day long during business hours, and two of them slept each night on futons right inside the front entrance after the building was closed. We foreigners were never asked to participate – except, in my case, for one shift during the Fifth World Open Karate Tournament, when I was not only left alone on lobby guard duty, but also asked to answer the telephone, which rang off the hook as fans and newspaper reporters called to ask for results.

"Osu! I don't speak Japanese fluently but I can at least tell you who won the tournament," I told the callers in Japanese over and over again.

There was a divide, therefore, between the foreigners and the Japanese, but I'd managed somehow to bridge the gap to some extent. I had a distinct impression, upon returning to *Honbu,* that I had been missed, and that a good few of the Japanese were genuinely happy to see me. It's hard to remember specifics. We went out one night to eat near *Honbu* to celebrate their graduation. There was lots of beer, Suzuki and Yamakage were smoking, and, becoming drunk, I joined them for at least one celebratory cigarette.

Sosai ate dinner with us that Saturday in the dormitory as he had nearly every Saturday during the time that I lived there.

I remember being a little bit uncomfortable in *Sosai's* presence. He'd welcomed me, but I had not called or written ahead to gain his permission, and the real issue, I suspect, was the question mark as to what I was doing there at all. "What future does this American who didn't graduate have with Kyokushin?" *Sosai* might have been asking himself. "His behavior certainly leaves something to be desired. He leaves the dormitory a year ago without notice. He treats me so well when I visit Rochester, but then he shows up here without notice again, and without any clear indication of what his intentions are."

He must have had his doubts whether I would ever be of any value.

Sosai sent Komukai to South Africa for a year that night at dinner in the same tone that he might have asked someone to pass the tea. Along with Ishida, Komukai was one of the dormitory's oldest – he'd been in the army before becoming an *uchi-deshi* – and like the rest of them, I suspect, he didn't have any clear plans for his future after graduation. *Sosai*, at least for Komukai, solved that problem that night.

This picture of the author was taken with my camera that night in Ikebukuro when we went out to celebrate my classmates' graduation. This is clearly NOT a picture from dinner with *Sosai*.

"Komukai," he said, after finishing his dinner and passing off those dishes of our enormous Saturday night feast that he didn't want to eat to the skinniest first-year students at the table.

"Osu!" Komukai leapt to his feet and turned to face *Sosai* at his end of the table.

"I want you to go to South Africa next week."

"Osu! *Wakarimashita!*" Komukai said "I have understood." As far as I could judge from everyone's reaction – which of course was all in the eyes, since no one would have reacted otherwise in front of *Sosai* – no one had known that *Sosai* was going to send Komukai to South Africa, least of all Komukai.

"The branch chief there wants a Japanese instructor in his dojo for a year. He will take care of you," *Sosai* explained.

"Osu! *Wakarimashita! Arigatoo gozaimashita!* (I have understood! Thank you very much!)"

Judd and Nick made me laugh later that evening in the dormitory. "Poor bastard," Judd said. "He was just about to be free and *Sosai* sends him to Africa. What the hell is he going to do in Africa? He'll probably find himself living in a grass hut, and his wife will be out hunting for his dinner with a spear!"

"Yeah," Nick said, "he'll probably wish then that he was back in the dormitory."

I remember sitting at the table in the dormitory that night across from Yamakage, because his jaw was broken and wired shut and he struggled to open his lips wide enough to sip tea while the rest of us were eating.

The same night as the previous photo, at the same table. From right to left, that's Suzuki (who gave me the cigarette), Wally (on a later trip to Japan; I'd left the dormitory sixteen months earlier owing him 3000 yen), Judd and a *Honbu* student I didn't know. Standing behind is an *uchi deshi koohai* of Nick and Mahashi whose name I can't recall, but who appears later in this book in a photograph with world champion Midori Kenji.

Sosai scolded him for the injury.

According to Judd, Yamakage had put two guys in the hospital over on the more metropolitan side of Ikebukuro Station near Sunshine City. One of them had broken his jaw. He'd been walking and saw a big rugby player-looking white guy treating a Japanese girl roughly. He'd stepped in, in the way I can only imagine Yamakage the Gangster intervening, but unbeknownst to Yamakage the white guy's friend was witnessing the whole scene from the sidelines. Yamakage grabbed the jacket of the guy who'd been fighting with the girl – much, I suppose, as he'd grabbed Komukai's T-shirt – and the guy's friend charged in from across the street and sucker-punched Yamakage from the side, shattering his jaw.

That angered Yamakage, of course, and he got up and beat both foreigners until they were sprawled out in puddles of blood on the concrete. I'd been punched by Yamakage, at least in the body, and it's a none-too-pleasant experience. He's got a malformed fist from a previous injury so that his first knuckle protrudes an easy centimeter beyond the second one, and when you get punched by him, you get hit with just that one knuckle, and it smashes into you like a ball-peen hammer.

It was that knuckle that had broken Komukai's teeth that night in front of *Honbu*.

Sosai scolded Yamakage because he'd suffered the injury and was unable to eat. "If you can't eat," *Sosai* said, "you can't get stronger, and training is your first responsibility."[28]

"Osu! *Shitsurei shimashita!* (I was very rude!)" Yamakage said though the wires that held his jaw together.

"What about the guys you were fighting with?" *Sosai* asked.

"Osu! They are still in the hospital," Yamakage managed without moving his jaw.

"*Subarashii!* (Wonderful!)" *Sosai* said. "If you're going to fight, make sure that you win!"

"Osu!" everyone answered.

"And if you have to get injured," he continued, "you have to make sure that the other guy's injuries are twice yours!"

"Osu!" we answered again.

"*Subarashii!*" *Sosai* said again to Yamakage. "Sit down. Eat!"

"Osu! *Itadakimasu! Shitsurei shimasu,*" Yamakage managed once again, and he took his seat.

Sosai gave me one of his two cakes that night when it came time for

---

[28] It's noteworthy here that *Sosai* was coaching Yamakage about the importance of his *ongoing* training, since it was *on the eve of Yamakage's graduation*. The completion of *uchi deshi* training was to mark *the beginning* of our life of training, not the end of it.

dessert. "Osu! *Itadakimasu!* (I humbly receive what you've given me!)" I responded according to the tradition, but I wasn't proud to receive it. *What have I done to deserve Sosai's generosity?* I asked myself as I continued like the rest to eat in silence.

* * *

Perhaps the best news of the weekend was that a year earlier, the previous spring, just four months after I'd run away in the night, *Sosai* had kicked out the French-Algerian Mocaram once and for all, just three days before he was meant to graduate. Judd and Nick told me the story on a cross-Tokyo train. I was baffled because they actually seemed a bit sympathetic. Mocaram's abuse of me had finally stopped as I entered my second year and started to get a bit stronger, but I apparently hadn't forgiven him, and I wasn't above hearing the story of his demise with some satisfaction.

"He wasn't training," Judd said. "He was just sitting around on his futon, getting fatter and counting the days until he graduated. Someone told *Sosai* that he wasn't going to morning training and wasn't going to the dojo, and *Sosai* threw him out."

"Really?" I asked. "Just like that?"

"Just like that," Nick said. "*Sosai* called the three of us, and we ran around the block and up to *Sosai's* office. We said 'Osu, *shitsurei shimasu!*' when we entered and stood there in *fudo dachi* just inside the door like always. *Sosai* was doing paperwork, and he didn't even look up when we came in. He just sat there shuffling his papers around and organizing his desk. By the time twenty minutes passed, we started to get really nervous because it was obvious that he was angry. Every once in a while, he'd look up at us and sigh angrily, we'd say 'Osu!' and he'd go right back to his papers."

"Jesus Christ!" I said.

"Yeah, tell me about it! Finally he looked up and told Mocaram to pack his bags and get out of the dormitory immediately and never come back. That was it."

"Fair dinkum, Ligo," Judd said, "we were scared to death!"

"Mocaram was crying and begging *Sosai* and asking him what he did wrong. *Sosai* told him to shut up and get out, and Mocaram cried all the way back to the dormitory. *Sosai* left us standing there for ten more minutes. He didn't say a word to either of us. He just sat there doing paperwork again. He'd look up and we'd say, 'Osu!,' and then he'd growl like he does and go back to his newspaper."

"God, I bet you were crapping in your pants," I said.

"Yeah," Nick said, "my knees were shaking. We were sure our turn was next."

"Finally," Judd chimed in, "*Sosai* looked up, we said, 'Osu!' and he told us to go back to the dormitory. We did, and then . . . Jesus, twenty minutes later, he called us again! 'Oh-oh, it's our turn,' we thought. We ran all the way back to his office and said, 'Osu! *Shitsurei shimasu!*' again when we went in. *Sosai* was still angry, he didn't even look up, but finally he did, we said, 'Osu!' and I was sure that he was going to kick us out then, but he didn't. Instead he told us to keep our noses clean, to go back to the dormitory, and train hard."

"You mean he called you all the way back to his office just to warn you again?" I asked.

"Yeah, scare us to death again is more like it," Judd said. Nick was laughing.

"Sorry I missed it," I said. "Holy shit, fucking guy got what he deserved!"

"I guess so," Judd said. "He actually got better after you left, though. In the end he wasn't such a bad guy. He was just lazy and childish."

"Yeah, I guess so," I said, replaying the events that had just been relayed and placing them on my own timeline. I'd run away just four months before Mocaram's expulsion. *Sosai's* entire perception of Mocaram would have been colored by that conversation we'd had in his fourth-floor apartment a year earlier when *Ryoobo-san* confirmed that he'd been shoplifting. I knew that *Sosai* favored me for my intelligence, for my Japanese, and for the fact that I was his Korean nephew's student. *I wonder*, I thought then, *if* Sosai's *throwing Mocaram out had anything to do with me?* Did he somehow blame Mocaram for my loss?

A darker thought occurred to me. *Sosai* sponsored me to the tune of over $6000 of dormitory fees during the nearly two years I was in Japan, and I ran away without mention of whether or not I'd pay it back. His secretary wrote to me twice in Davidson before the Rochester tournament and told me that *Sosai* wondered why I'd left like that, but ordered her not to press me for the money. She added that *Sosai* hoped I was going to be successful in whatever I decided to do with my life and, she added, I could pay back the money whenever I could. "There's no hurry," she said *Sosai* had told her to tell me, "but," she said, *she* wanted me to know, and she knew I "would do the right thing."

With a nervous knot in my stomach, I wondered if my betrayal had made things harder for the other foreigners in the dormitory. *Sosai* had been sponsoring Mocaram as well, just like he was sponsoring Judd and Nick. Maybe *Sosai* was thinking, "I support these guys and this is how they thank me! Maybe they're all going to run away like Ligo!"

I consoled myself that that theory didn't really fit. By throwing Mocaram out once and for all, *Sosai* ensured that Mocaram would never pay him back, and Mocaram must have owed *Honbu* far more than I did since he was about to graduate. No, it looked more as if *Sosai* was trying to use him as an example to keep Judd and Nick walking a straight line. If anything, it was more like "I don't care about the money. Only correct behavior is important."

Mocaram had been just three days away from becoming the first foreigner to graduate (out of 120 who'd tried, and failed, to complete either the full program or the amount of time they'd committed themselves to). Being the first would have been an extremely honorable position to hold. Perhaps in the end *Sosai* questioned Mocaram's character enough that he didn't want him to hold that honor. Judd would have been a year away then, and it was Nick who was really the budding star of the dormitory's small foreign population.

I supposed I'd never know. Maybe *Ryoobo-san* had simply caught him shoplifting again.

* * *

On the day of my departure, I asked the secretary to tell *Sosai* that I'd be leaving that day to go back to college and to ask him if I could meet with him before I went. Permission was granted, and the conversation that I had with *Sosai*, as translated by his secretary, was brief. If *Sosai* favored me at all then, he didn't show it. He asked me what I was studying and how many students I had. The answer was, "Nearly twenty, if I include the women's self-defense course I'm teaching" – by then I'd arranged for students at Davidson to get physical education credit for taking my classes.

I made the mistake one more time of using the word *deshi* (disciple) instead of *seito* (student), and *Sosai* was angry once again. I hadn't clearly understood the first time, and *deshi* was still the only word for "student" I knew. *Sosai*, however, remembered that he'd already corrected me once, and responded crossly, reminding me that friendship was the most important thing, and that in the beginning the contemporaries I taught had to be my friends first, and my students second.

"Osu! *Wakarimashita* (I have understood)," I answered. I was still aware of not fully understanding *Sosai's* advice, but I let it pass, not wanting *Sosai* to think me stupid. *I will remember what Sosai said*, I consoled myself, *and I'm sure his meaning will reveal itself to me in time.*

I explained through the secretary that I'd written an article about *Sosai* and Kyokushin, and that I had an opportunity to have it published in an American magazine. "I just wanted to make sure that it's a *true* story," I told *Sosai,* once I'd given him a three-sentence description of the story in which he'd killed a man with a punch. I explained that I'd been told it many times by his nephew.

Mas Oyama laughed. "It is a *good* story," he answered, "you have my permission to have it published as long as it represents Kyokushin in a positive light."

Sosai gave me permission to publish the story so quickly that I still couldn't help but worry that perhaps he didn't understand all that I meant to tell. I had learned very well, however – beginning in my boyhood relationship with his nephew in North Carolina – that once Mas Oyama had spoken there was no "but . . .", no going back to beg for clarification once he'd made up his mind.

"Osu!" was the answer I gave, and once I'd spoken it, my path was set.

With a growing sense of awe, I realized on my way out of his office that Mas Oyama had just given me his entire take on the Mas Oyama legend, one certainly based on truth, but also undoubtedly blown out of proportion by the many books, movies, and even comic books that were produced in Japan to celebrate the exploits of the world's greatest living karate legend. Sonny Chiba had played Mas Oyama in a trilogy of films loosely based on real events, and the ten-year-long comic book series, *Karate Baka Ichidai*, celebrating Mas Oyama's exploits spanned something like ten thousand pages.

Was it out of humility that Mas Oyama had called my story a "good" one rather than a "true" one? I'm sure my Japanese readership, with access to the many histories and fictions about Mas Oyama written in Japanese, will know far better than I. I left our meeting that day, however, with a whole new perspective on the Mas Oyama story:

Sosai was immortal, and in a sense, where truth in biography ends and fiction begins is irrelevant in the case of someone like that. The important thing for him was his living legacy – the march of Kyokushin across the globe, strengthening individuals and improving the bonds of friendship between them for the sake of a better world. What mattered, therefore, wasn't whether it was a true story, as I had been told, or whether it was merely a good story based on truth. What mattered was that it would serve to propagate the Mas Oyama legend, and therefore Kyokushin itself, even after he was gone.

Those of us who fall short of legendary status, I realized in the light of my own autobiographical writing, are stuck with the plain truth, and the truth I left *Honbu* with that morning was that if I truly was stumbling back into the Kyokushin world, I had my work cut out for me.

* * *

Quite literally the entire dormitory walked me to the Metropolitan Hotel to see me off, and I was extremely humbled. We snapped a few pictures with my camera of the group of us in front of *Honbu*, and a couple more at the Metropolitan in front of the parked airport bus. The eight members of my class, Judd, Suzuki, Kuruda, Komukai, Yamakage, Ishida, Oshikiri, and Kato, and the two members of Nick's class, he and Mahashi, and even several members of their *koohai's* class, all walked with me, not letting me carry my own bags, and insisting on waiting until the bus pulled out of the lot before they started back to *Honbu*.

My head still spinning from the warmth of my former classmates' reception, I was left to wonder what role Kyokushin would have in my future. As it turned out, I left Mas Oyama's office that day with something far more important than mere permission to publish the article I'd written for *Black Belt*. I can't remember how I happened to see a typed list of the names, addresses, and contact information for all of the world's then-existing IKO branch chiefs, or why it dawned on me to ask for a copy of the North American pages. I was, however, to discover that it was a fairly rare document, *Honbu's* official and updated record, and that it was not one distributed among world branch chiefs. It wasn't secret; it just wasn't readily made available, and no one was likely to ask for a copy if they didn't know it existed. It was the fact that it was a complete list that made it rare. It was information, that's all, but it was *Honbu's* information, and I was about to get my first lesson in the strategic advantage of having more complete information than the majority was privy to.

On the bus leaving *Ikebukuro* I studied the twenty-five names on the North American list.

How humbling that the entire *uchi deshi* dormitory – every single resident! – walked me to my bus at the Metropolitan Hotel on my return to America the day after my classmates graduation! If that wouldn't make a young man want to return to Kyokushin, I don't know what would. – Of particular interest here, note Yamakage's swollen face, his jaw wired shut (in patterned jacket to my right), Suzuki's broad smile with his arm across my shoulder, Komukai (in glasses at rear) waving as if already on his way to Africa, and my own face, looking pale, exhausted, bereaved. I was the one who'd failed, after all.

Several of them I recognized from the branch chief meeting five months earlier in Rochester. There was Jacques Sandulescu, of course, at the top of the list; there was one of Mas Oyama's first *uchi deshi*, my *dai-sempai* Seiji Kanemura, whom I'd met once as a teenager in New York City (and who'd told me flat-out that I was too small and weak to be successful at *Honbu* as an *uchi deshi*) [29]; and there was Rochester's Michael Monaco, Quebec's André Gilbert, and British Columbia's Stuart Corrigal. Randy James of Brooklyn, Tom Flynn of Massachusetts, Leslaw Samitowski of Chicago, Henri Orlean of Queens, John Farrell of Pennsylvania, Bill Richards of Binghamton, Bill Scott of somewhere else in New York, and Michael Lorden of Orlando were other names I recognized as those whom I'd met for the first time in Rochester. Of course, David Bunt's name was on the list too. Bobby Lowe in Hawaii was certainly a name I had heard – he was apparently the first Kyokushin instructor in a dojo established by Mas Oyama outside of Japan – and although I was surprised to find his name there, Guam's Paul Alfred had taken me and the other foreign *uchi deshi* out to dinner in Tokyo on at least one memorable occasion.

And then there were other names I didn't recognize. Who, for example, was this California crowd, including Mickey Tuck, Jimmy Nishimura, and Joe Hamamoto?

And there were a few others.

What we really need, I said to myself, *isn't articles published in* Black Belt Magazine.

What we need is our own publication!

And just like that, I realized exactly what a North American Kyokushin magazine-by-subscription would look like – one that instructors and students would buy, perhaps even pre-order, because pictures and stories of their own dojos would be in it, along with technical, historical and other valuable information about Kyokushin. *If just a third of North America's Kyokushin students would place advance orders,* I reasoned, *surely such a project could generate enough money to cover its cost . . .*

I was fairly satisfied with the article I'd written for *Sosai,* but I was utterly dismayed at having to publish it in *Black Belt.* Though it would certainly further Kyokushin's notoriety in America as well as, I believed, my own budding career as a writer, I couldn't shake the notion that it would also risk potentially belittling both Mas Oyama and Kyokushin by association, by portraying them side by side with examples of the calamity that was the American martial arts scene.

---

[29] The prefix "dai" means "great", hence "great-*sempai*" indicates a *sempai* so far ahead of me that we were of different generations. *Dai-sempai* tend to be both highly respected and old enough to be one's parent.

I couldn't understand how any self-respecting magazine could run pictures on its covers of out-of-shape–looking guys in blatantly staged action poses, complete with blatantly fake facial expressions of either pain or jubilation, depending on which role in the mock self-defense mêlée each model played. A Japanese Kyokushin magazine might show a fighter getting knocked out, and it would be clear that the blow delivered was a real one, thanks to the sweat, and the blur, and that impossible-to-fake look on someone's impact-distorted face at the moment the lights go out. *Black Belt* was accustomed to showing fat guys posing in multicolored karate uniforms, one snarling with his fist touching the other guy's face, and the other imitating the facial expression of someone getting punched. For me, having been there at the heart of it all, *Black Belt's* content was a laughable symptom of the fantasy-based American martial arts embarrassment.

A magazine based on Kyokushin Karate, I reasoned, *could lay the foundation for a new generation of quality martial arts instruction in the U.S. Maybe in time other martial arts would be able to compare, but in the meantime a purely Kyokushin magazine just might fly!*

American Kyokushin as well, it occurred to me then, needed work. It should have been distinguishing itself from all the other crap, but somehow it was not. *People should hear the name* Kyokushin *and realize that it is something else*, I thought. *Comparing Kyokushin to American martial arts is like comparing apples to oranges. The problem is, American Kyokushin fits in all too comfortably with the oranges!*

No, America needed to see the real thing. The perception needed to be changed. The standard needed to be raised. Bring Japanese or European Kyokushin to the US, and the American martial arts scene would never be the same.

Make a magazine, I thought, *and it will start to change that perception.* With a magazine, one could present American Kyokushin side by side with its international counterparts, and the examples that weren't up to par would be exposed. That tiny percentage that did measure up would be pushed to the forefront as the example to aspire to, and those that had the potential to rise up and meet the world standard would be forced to do so in order to survive. Americans would be shamed and electrified as they began to realize what could be achieved, both through Kyokushin as a movement on a national scale and, in terms of the individual, through a higher standard of Kyokushin training.

"The pen is mightier than the sword," the old adage goes.

"The way of the warrior is the twofold way of pen and sword, and he must have a taste for both ways," Miyamoto Musashi wrote in his *Book of Five Rings*.

Why not test it? Why not try an experiment? At the very least, it would be a way to give the most that I could to Kyokushin while I'm still in college.

Budo Karate Illustrated! I thought.

The cover and dedication page of the first volume of *Budo Karate Illustrated*, designed and published in 1994 by the author with the intent of creating an ongoing periodical publication for the Kyokushin International Karate Organization in North America. Mas Oyama in front of Niagara Falls during his 1992 trip to Rochester can be seen at left. The aging building, bottom right, is *Honbu* Dojo, the Kyokushinkaikan, which *Sosai* dreamed of rebuilding before his death. The sign in the foreground on the construction barrier announces his intent to do so

In the end, Kyokushin was just the name of a style. *Budo* karate, however – budo being the would-be qualifier for all of Japanese karate were it to be brought more into line with the traditional, do or die warrior tradition of Japan – was the karate that Mas Oyama had sought to define through the creation of Kyokushin.[30]

---

[30] *Budo* means "martial way" or "military way" but should be differentiated from the terms "martial arts" or "martial way" used by other cultures because of its strictly Japanese

Budo karate, taught correctly, can redefine lives. It can open minds to better ways and deliver spiritual strength to those who follow them. It can empower free thinkers to take the risk to make a difference in a world that will increasingly need a difference made by free-thinking individuals. Of course it was my duty to Mas Oyama to propagate Kyokushin, but it was also my moral obligation to the world to try to make it a better place if I could see a way.

Was it far-fetched that I, at twenty-two, might launch a magazine to rival *Black Belt*? Wasn't it more likely to fail than to succeed?

Of course it was.

But who else was going to take the risk?

Who else had been shaped by his life into one who could not only see such a path, but also dare to take it?

I've got just this one life, I thought on the bus back to Narita. *Hell, I've already lived and thrown away the one I was entitled to by failing in Mas Oyama's program!*

What right do I have NOT to let myself go to the experiment?

Whether or not in the end the vision would be exposed as fantasy, I allowed the *Budo Karate Illustrated* picture to simmer there on the airport bus and on the plane back to North Carolina. I turned it around and around in my head with a nervous excitement that, too much like caffeine, kept me agitated, restless and squirming on the edge of my seat.

Budo Karate Illustrated.

Okay, let's give it a shot!

---

character grounded in the warrior tradition of Japan. I.e. "Martial Way" as translated from Korean or Chinese is significantly different from "Martial Way" as translated from the Japanese. *Kendo, Judo, Aikido, Karate-do* and *Iaido* are all examples of Japanese *Budo* arts.

FIVE

A YEAR PASSED, and I woke with a start when another plane, this one taking me back to Japan for the third time in twelve months, touched down on the tarmac at Narita. I had slept so desperately for the thirteen-hour passage that I could recall literally only two waking moments during the entire flight.

I fell asleep while the plane was still on the ground in New York, I woke up just briefly when the flight attendant asked me to put my seat back into a full upright position for dinner, and I woke up one more time when the air conditioning conspired with the slow trickle of drool that had been oozing past the corner of my mouth to leave my chin painfully chafed. Apparently when I put my seat back upright I simply fell forward, face first, to sleep with my forehead against the back of the seat in front of me, my neck bent at an impossibly uncomfortable angle for the remainder of the flight. I had no meals, no beverages. I was so exhausted that I closed my eyes in America and when I opened them again, we were on the ground in Japan.

The flight attendant told me she resorted to shaking my shoulders to wake me at mealtime, but that I refused to wake up.

I was arriving in Japan for my *nidan* grading – twenty consecutive full-contact fights against rested black and brown belt opponents, my first full-contact fights since I fled Mas Oyama's dormitory two years earlier. I'd have just three nights to try to pull myself together in advance of what I feared would be the most severe physical beating of my life. The year that I'd lived since my classmates' graduation – a year that passed very much unlike any other year of my life – left me so accustomed to relying on bursts of adrenaline-fueled creative energy to blast my way through the haze of exhaustion brought on by the demands of the *Budo Karate*

Illustrated project that my survival instinct pushed me in a direction that for most people wouldn't have made sense. I should have gone directly to the travelers' inn in Ikebukuro where I planned to stay to get as much rest as I could, but instead it was towards a certain mountaintop overlooking Tokyo Bay and Mt. Fuji beyond that I was drawn.

Two days of rest wouldn't have made a difference at that point. The alternative that I sought, however, would carry me through.

In the midst of all the work I was doing in Davidson, *Sosai* had ordered me to come back to Japan to take my *nidan* grading. He'd surprised me with the invitation when I met with him at *Honbu* ten weeks earlier – on my second return to Japan since reuniting with *Sosai* in Rochester – on a mission to pull together additional material for the first volume of North America's new Kyokushin magazine, *Budo Karate Illustrated*. I suppose he had no idea that I was enrolled in twelve courses that year, rather than the expected eight, and that I'd taken four additional courses during the summer session when other students were on vacation. *Sosai* was certainly aware of the work that I was doing for Kyokushin in America, and he knew that I was an active college student, but I'm sure he had no idea just what kind of college student I'd become.

He would have had no idea of the extremes to which I'd had to reach to make it all possible.

It was clear that *Sosai* was intensely proud of me by then, that he was pushing me to achieve a status from which I could put all that I'd learned from him in Japan to use in America. Kyokushin had become so far reduced in the United States that even my incomplete education at *Honbu* must have made me look like I could develop into a star. In the dormitory for yet another Saturday night dinner with *Sosai* in the first week of January – with Judd, Suzuki, Kuruda and the rest all long gone, and Nick and Mahashi, this time, only three months from graduation – *Sosai* asked me if I could come back to Japan in March for *Honbu's* annual *dan* grading.

I had a 1st *kyu* [31] brown belt at the time, the same one I'd left the

---

[31] Traditionally in Kyokushin Karate there are ten *kyu* levels which count backwards from ten, from white belt to brown, before reaching first *dan*, the first black belt level of which there are also ten. (Only Mas Oyama had ten stripes on his black belt at the age of seventy; five and six were exceedingly rare – Jacques had six – and only Bobby Lowe and perhaps one other person ever had more than six.)

dormitory with when I ran away. I was flattered, but uncertain that I'd be able to endure the ten full-contact fights. Yet it was *Sosai* who was telling me to grade and there was only one possible answer. "Osu!" I answered, and just as *Sosai* had dispatched Komukai to South Africa ten months earlier with the nonchalance of a dinner guest asking for the salt, he told me that I should do twenty fights instead of ten and test directly for my *nidan* instead.

"Osu!" I said, "*Gambaremasu!* (I will persevere!)"

And so upon arrival at Narita on the occasion of a *nidan* grading that might as well have been a death sentence for how sure I was that I would be severely beaten, instead of taking the bus to Ikebukuro, I went to the tourist information desk and used my imperfect Japanese to ask how best to travel to Tateyama in Chiba Prefecture, where I'd traveled twice before for *Honbu's* annual summer camp. It was a site chosen by *Sosai* originally because it was where he'd battled that bull for a documentary producer's camera so many years earlier. When I was nineteen and twenty, young and naïve enough that the lines between fantasy and reality were still naturally unclear, I'd made friends there with a Zen monk named Nagare, and had unintentionally become a momentary student of his teacher, a Tai Chi and Zen master named Yamaguchi. It was in their company that I believed I'd have the best chance at finding the power that I'd need to face the challenge immediately ahead.

Three years earlier, when I was still an *uchi deshi*, Yamaguchi *Sensei* had taught me the proper method and position for Zazen[32] practice; performed a ceremony on my behalf that I understood to be inducting me as a Buddhist layman; and assigned me a Zen *koan*, the answer to which I was to search for throughout my life. But it was really the place and the personalities that had made the experience a spiritual one. As a teenager desperate to remake myself through karate training, at times when I found myself overwhelmed by just how hard the road ahead would be, I'd dreamt of a way that I might withdraw from the world into what I perhaps naïvely perceived to be the peace and tranquility of isolated ascetic practice. Nagare-*san*[33] and Yamaguchi *Sensei*, when I met them, stuck me as the epitome of that lifestyle that I could have stepped into so easily if I hadn't already found my life's work in Kyokushin.

---

[32] Seated Zen meditation.
[33] The suffix "san" means "Mr.", "Mrs." or "Miss."

My apologies to Mr. Nagare, seen here extreme left, whose image was damaged by an accident of photography. Yamaguchi *Sensei* is to my left, seen here on my first trip to Tateyama when I was a first-year *uchi deshi*. When I met these men in 1990, I was startled to find Mr. Nagaoka, extreme right, smoking so many cigarettes between his sometimes as many as sixteen daily half-hour sessions of *Zazen*. Apparently he had only recently renounced his life as a *salaryman* to become a monk.

"Karate *is* Zen," Mas Oyama wrote. He argued that the mental state that one has no choice but to achieve in battle was the same mental state that the Zen monk sits and waits for throughout a lifetime of meditation. He taught that while of course there's no shortcut to liberation, the ultimate solution can be better found through the rigors of grueling physical training than in the idleness of seated Zen. Mas Oyama himself was a practitioner – surely he would not have been able to defend his "karate is Zen" principle had he not been – and on top of the natural attraction I'd always felt, I believed it my responsibility to endeavor to know what my teacher had known in order to better understand his teaching.

From Narita I took a bus to Tateyama, once again not knowing where I would stay or whether or not I would be received. I'd exchanged letters with Nagare-*san* since I'd been back in America, writing in my rudimentary Japanese. To demonstrate that he and his compatriots were in my thoughts, I even once sent them a gift of three pairs of leather work gloves.

I had been inspired to learn on my first trip to Tateyama with *Sosai* that those three monks were tunneling through their mountain with hand tools, carving a spiral staircase straight through the solid rock of the mountain from the temple at the base all the way up to the temple and meditation hall at the top. Nagare-*san* told me that they managed about fifteen meters per year, and when I asked him how long he thought it would take them to finish, he laughed and assured me that he would never see the project's completion.

I remembered the worn cloth work gloves in which they worked and thought that they would appreciate the gloves that I bought for them at the same hardware store in Davidson where I bought my ax.

Nagare-*san* was surprised to see me approaching that week of my grading, but pleasantly so. When I explained to him why I was in Japan, and that I'd come in search of a moment of peace in advance of the slaughter I knew my grading would be, he told me that he would ask Yamaguchi *Sensei's* permission for me to sleep in the small quarters on top of the mountain adjacent to the temple, where visiting monks slept.

I practiced *kata* alone on the manicured lawn in front of the temple overlooking the Pacific that afternoon. In the evening, Nagare-*san* and his wife fed me the same Japanese curry rice that we'd eaten in the dormitory for lunch every Thursday following our special *uchi deshi* training with *Sosai*. Nagare-*san* and I meditated together for a twenty-minute session the next day, and then he left me alone so that Yamaguchi *Sensei* could come to critique my technique and discuss my progress. I was ashamed that I had not practiced for some time, except, of course, through Mas Oyama's radical definition of Zen.

Nonetheless, if it was peace and a renewed sense of power that I'd come for, at the very least it was peace that I found. That afternoon I said my many thanks to my friends at Tateyama and set off with open eyes towards the pending doom I sensed ahead at my *nidan* grading. In Ikebukuro, I spent the longest twenty-four hours of my life stretched out alone on the *tatami* mats at the *Kimi Ryokan*.[34] Still exhausted, I tossed and turned, frustrated that images of what lay ahead kept me far too agitated to sleep.

* * *

As I expected, the grading almost killed me.

I was disappointed that *Sosai* was not present. I didn't worry when I heard that he was in the hospital; I was accustomed to his going to the hospital every once in a while for several days at a time for "rest and recuperation," and he'd looked so well just ten weeks earlier when we'd met just after Christmas. Yokomiso *Shihan* sat in *Sosai*'s chair and presided over the exam, with Ishida *Sempai* administering.[35] Perhaps only sixty brown and black belts were grading. Comparatively few that year were testing for higher *dan*.

One month earlier I'd been surprised once again to find a letter in my Davidson mailbox from *Honbu*:

Dear Mr. Nathan Ligo,

Today I am writing to you to let you know that you have permission from *Sosai* to promote to *shodan* provided you are recommended by a branch chief. As you may have known already, *Sosai* has asked Mr. Michael Monaco to do it for you. Now *Honbu* has received his recommendation for your *shodan*. As soon as payment of $150.00 is confirmed, your *shodan* certificate will be issued accordingly. Please send two photos (4 x 5 cm) of yourself and the belt size.

The date for the dan-promotion test has not been announced yet, but most likely the last Sunday in March.

Thank you for your prompt attention.

Sincerely, Taiko Watanabe

---

[34] *Ryokan* means "travelers' inn". They are generally of a traditional Japanese style and attract traveling students and young tourists.

[35] Yokomiso *Shihan* was a kind grey-haired gentleman who taught the seniors' class on Friday nights at *Honbu*. Ishida *Sempai* was an *uchi deshi sempai* of ours four or five years graduated by the time my class entered the dormitory. After his first two years, he ran away in the night and *Sosai* told him he could re-enter the dormitory only if he began the program again from day one. This Ishida *Sempai* apparently did. He lived in the dormitory for a total of five years, and we always thought him to have been a little bit "affected" because of it.

It remains interesting to me today that *Sosai* – who could have overruled any one of his organization's policies he'd wanted to – still took the time to go through the motions of having me promoted so that I would be wearing a *shodan* when I came to Japan to test for my *nidan*, rather than the brown belt that I had worn for so long.

Sadly, the crisp new black belt with its one golden stripe didn't make me feel any more powerful, and the beating I took was indeed a severe one. Once the *kihon*, *iddo* and *kata* part of the grading was over, I managed to fight six individual fights as part of other students' consecutive twenties or thirties, and, as was the custom, those six counted as six of my twenty. It was therefore, in the end, just fourteen that I had to do consecutively.[36]

It's difficult to recall specifics beyond the general impression of the entire experience, but there are several moments of the fighting session that will likely remain with me forever.

The first was when Ishida *Sempai* cautioned everyone who was participating to do their best to prevent whoever was attempting his required number of consecutive fights from succeeding. He told us that we would not be promoted ourselves if we were perceived to be doing any less when we fought than trying to break our opponent so that he would not be able to continue. All that was a euphemism, of course – and you only had to know Ishida *Sempai* to know it – for telling us that he expected us to murder one another. "*Sosai* couldn't be here today," Yokomiso *Shihan* added, "so you have to fight your best to honor *Sosai*, and that means fighting like every fight is your last."

That was, it occurred to me, both the old man's and young man's version of telling us that the expectation was that we do our best to live up to the spirit of *kill or be killed*.

And of course, this is as it should be. *Sosai* had said the same thing to us when Japan Champion Masuda Akira fought his 100 consecutive fights. But interestingly, on that occasion many people had *not* tried to stop Masuda. This time was different. Ishida *Sempai* must have said something that struck a chord, because the fighting at my grading was particularly brutal.

As was the trend during that era at *Honbu*, ever since Judd and especially Nick began to introduce the Japanese *dojosei*[37] to the power of

---

[36] At *Honbu* we fought ten consecutive full-contact fights against rested black or brown belt students per *dan*, i.e. ten for *shodan*, twenty for *nidan*, etc.

[37] Dojo students.

the foreign fighter, it was the foreigners who truly bashed me that day. The Japanese wore me down fight by fight, of course, but it was the foreigners who beat me half to death.

    A tall, blond, lightweight Danish kid from Nick's teacher's branch dojo in Denmark nearly killed me during his own *nidan* grading with a series of devastatingly powerful kicks to my head that, had any one of them landed, would most surely have injured me beyond any ability to continue. They weren't merely KO techniques; they were skull-breaking techniques. Perhaps three times during the sixty seconds I fought him, the creative sense of survival I'd developed over two years at *Honbu*, almost always fighting people bigger and stronger than me, kicked in and revealed to me on an instinctive level how not to get maimed, though I most certainly did not win. The kicks came at my head so fast and so powerfully that I doubted whether I'd be able to stop them, even if I was correctly positioned to block – and I wasn't, because he was so fast. Instinct made me simply drop so that they'd whistle by harmlessly overhead through the space where my skull had been a split second earlier. Twice I even cheated by just letting my legs go out from under me to drop my body like a sack of potatoes onto my back on the dojo floor. The kicks came at me so fast that I couldn't even duck in any kind of controlled way. I certainly am not proud of surviving that round in that way, but at least I protected myself from being severely injured, and that, I suppose, indicates that I had at least learned something during all the fights I'd fought as an underdog at *Honbu* over the years.

    It was the Russian brown belt ex-boxer who was then staying in the dormitory for a short term, however, who really took me to within inches of my life. I fought him about halfway through my fourteen consecutive fights, and his punches were so unbelievably heavy I felt certain my ribs would crack. After taking a dozen of them, there was quite literally nothing left that I could do to defend myself, and he continued to pummel me around the room for the remainder of the fight. In advance of delivering the most dangerous blow I took that day, he drove me right over the row of our compatriots seated cross-legged against the wall (all of the day's fighters in waiting sat like that, knee to knee, all the way around the perimeter of the room), and down the wall into a corner, where I became pinned between his fists and the wood paneling. I couldn't block, I couldn't fight him off due to exhaustion more than anything else – my arms weren't working the way they were supposed to – and, to my dismay, no one was stopping the fight. I remember thinking in a detached way, *I thought when someone gets driven out of bounds, the referee was supposed to stop the fight and bring the fighters back to the center of the room.* Ishida *Sempai* made no move to intervene, however, and I'd taken all I could. I slid down the corner of the room as the Russian continued to pound my body towards the floor, blow after bare-knuckle blow, with everything he had.

The last punch, the one that really did me in, was one of those he threw from above, still standing as he punched down, attempting to hit my sternum as it slid below his own waist level. The last such downward punch grazed my Adam's apple, my throat swelled shut, and all of a sudden none of the pain to my ribs mattered anymore. My windpipe was completely closed and I could not inhale. My throat felt as if it had been crushed beyond salvage.

These screenshots are from the author's fight, two years earlier, with Japan champion, Masuda Akira. This was Masuda's 7th fight out of 100, and I was defeated by TKO (an incapacitating *chudan mawashi geri*[38] to my solar plexus 87 seconds into the 90 second round). I include these photos here because it is the same dojo and the same kind of crowd that existed at my *nidan* grading.

---

[38] Roundhouse kick to the midsection.

Writhing in panic on the floor, I struggled to massage my Adam's apple as I had seen other fighters do when accidentally struck in the throat. Suzuki, my second, who'd been wiping the sweat from my brow between rounds and helping me to stand towards the end when my body wasn't working properly, saw that I couldn't breathe and took over massaging my Adam's apple. Several excruciatingly long moments later, with a hoarse gasp I managed to suck in my first breath of air in three quarters of a minute. After a few more choking gasps, I began to breathe again somewhat normally, given the extreme demands of the circumstances.

Another time I saw the dojo floor closer than I ever had before, my face smashed into the spinning hardwood as I struggled to peel myself up off the floor. Once I hesitated to return to the center of the dojo when Ishida *Sempai* called me up to resume a fight. "*Dekinai* (I can't do it)," I said under my breath, so only Suzuki could hear past all of the shouts of encouragement from the spectators. "*Dekimasu yo,* Ligo-*san!*" he said, massaging my shoulders from behind and preparing to shove me back into the center. "Of course you can, Ligo! *Gambatte!* (Go on!)"

Sure enough – always loyal – Suzuki slapped me on the back and pushed me right back into combat, where I took care of the business of defending myself because I had no other choice.

Finally, I did do some damage to several of my Japanese opponents. In one particular round towards my last when my arms wouldn't work properly for punching, I hit this poor kid over and over and over again with my front forearm elbow strikes. I hit his upper arms, I hit his chest – I missed when I tried out of desperation to hit his jaw! – I issued a *kiai* [39] at the top of my lungs when the fight started to go my way. The crowd was cheering. I'd found my second wind and was able, at the very least, to slug it out again after several rounds during which I was simply beaten. I think in the end I probably won six or eight fights, lost three or four, and Ishida *Sempai* had generously deemed the rest of them draws. There's no question that the only full-time college student in the room took one of the most severe beatings of the grading that year.

I probably could have staggered back to my hotel room that night, but I opted not to, because it was nearly impossible to walk. There were sharp pains in my chest when I inhaled, my legs moved but not the way my brain told them to, and I kept being overcome by fits of vertigo. Just

---

[39] "Spirit shout," to accompany karate techniques during training or *kumite*.

up the street from *Honbu*, I staggered past the entrance to a 24-hour bath, leaned on a light post to think about it for a second, and then staggered in and paid my admission.

The bruises all over my chest, arms and thighs hadn't turned purple yet. They were still red welts, some of which looked like scores of tiny little dots of blood just under the surface of the skin, as if the blood vessels within had simply exploded. In the mirrors at the bath some of the wounds looked like I was actually bleeding, and I caught myself trying to wipe the blood away. There were fifty or so men there, bathing. I would have stood out in the crowd as an American even if I hadn't also been beaten to a pulp.

The next day I went with Mahashi, who was just then graduating along with Nick, to see *Sosai* in the hospital. Mas Oyama was sitting up in bed with that bandana tied around his head when I stepped in with a bow and an "Osu!" He looked remarkably well. His wife was next to him. I didn't have a translator.

Sosai spoke to Mahashi first. I didn't understand what was being said, and I couldn't comprehend why Mahashi was crying.

When my turn came, I spoke to *Sosai* in a painful raspy whisper. The blow to my larynx had not only completely robbed me of my voice, it had also permanently torn one side of whatever the connective bands are that keep one's Adam's apple in place. (To this day I can hold it gently with my hand and move it aside with a clicking of cartilage, far further to the right than I can to the left.) My ribs hurt badly to breathe, but I had been able to stamp out my inclination to stagger into the room. I was presenting myself to Mas Oyama.

Sosai asked me about the grading. I told him that it had gone as well as could be expected, given that most of my efforts were then going into my studies, rather than into training. I apologized for the fact that I had no voice. *Sosai* asked me about the *Budo Karate Illustrated* book (the forerunner of our new Kyokushin magazine would be a hardcover book). I told him that it would be ready very soon.

"Yes, but when?" *Sosai* asked. "I want to see it as soon as possible."

"Osu!" I said and apologized. "It's being printed as we speak. They tell me that perhaps even two weeks from now it will be ready. It's mostly out of my control, but I will try to hurry them."

"Thank you," *Sosai* said, "I really want to see it."

I was too stupid to understand his sense of urgency.

Sosai asked me next what he could do for me in an official capacity. It was pretty clear that the reason he had pushed me to grade for my *nidan* was that he intended to make me the youngest American ever to receive a branch chief certificate from *Honbu*, since according to IKO regulations, *nidan* was the minimum requirement. More than just a few of the branch chiefs in America were challenge appointments: *Sosai* had challenged them to establish a branch by awarding them certificates. My *sempai* David Bunt, for example, had been made a branch chief by *Sosai* so that he could participate in the North American organization on a developmental level, even though he didn't have his own dojo.

"No thank you," I rasped. "I have nothing to ask you for at this time. It can wait until you're out of the hospital. I was worried because you're in the hospital, but now that I see how well you are, I'm no longer worried. There will be plenty of time later." I believed that asking him for a branch chief certificate would have been selfish at a time like that. Besides, I was so undeserving. I could barely walk for the severity of the beating I'd taken the day before.

My head spins when I recall *Sosai's* response; it somehow burned itself into my memory even though I completely failed to understand its import at the time. *"Shimpai shite imasen,"* I said. "I'm not worried."

"Shimpai-yo!" Sosai said sternly. "You should worry!" He turned down the corners of his mouth, rolling out his lower lip and drilling me with his eyes in an attempt to make me understand what I was so clearly missing.

"Osu!" I said stubbornly. "Thank you, but I will wait until you're better."

Sosai heaved a heavy sigh and asked me one more time what he could do for me before finally giving up. He looked frustrated, like he wanted a translator and like I hadn't said the right thing, and I couldn't tell why. My Japanese was insufficient for handling the situation. I was nervous, injured, and at a further disadvantage because I could barely talk. It's quite clear, I suppose, that I was in total denial of what was just before me to see. I had absolutely no comprehension of the fact that that would be the last time I would see *Sosai* alive.

So proud I am at times in my life of my ability to see, and of having seen in *Sosai* what Master Choi had taught me to see in his uncle, and yet that day I was completely blind. Perhaps I was watching myself too intently through *Sosai's* eyes, wondering why this meek little American could possibly be deserving of a branch chief appointment.

Perhaps I was watching myself so intently that I failed even to see Mas Oyama.

* * *

Later that afternoon I attended the opening ceremony for World Champion Matsui Shokei's[40] new branch dojo at Asakusa in Tokyo, and participated to the best of my ability in the training that followed. Ten weeks earlier, when I visited Japan during my winter vacation to gather additional material for *Budo Karate Illustrated*, I'd met with Matsui and shot a wildly successful series of photos for the first volume. For my camera he had demonstrated the before and after positions of the entire set of Mas Oyama's *kihon*.[41]

Somehow I'd gathered courage beyond what should have been mine and called Matsui from Davidson out of the blue one evening that December. I reminded him who I was and asked him if he remembered my face, and he told me that "of course" he did. I went on to tell him that I was designing a book on the state of the American Kyokushin organization, and I asked if I could meet with him that January, prior to the meeting I'd already scheduled with *Sosai*. He agreed, and once I arrived in Tokyo he met me and took me to eat or drink something that I can't for the life of me recall. The meeting was simply too important, and it took everything I had just to communicate in Japanese without an interpreter.

I wanted to ask *Sosai* on that trip for permission to make the book that I was then designing the first issue of an ongoing periodical publication. Of course that had been my vision from the start, but my one-time *Honbu sempai*, David Bunt, for one, had recommended, when I'd first sought support from the American Kyokushin establishment, that I begin with a yearbook on Kyokushin in the U.S. rather than

---

[40] Matsui Shokei, winner of the Fourth World Tournament in 1987, would become *Kancho* (chairman) of the Kyokushinkaikan and IKO after Mas Oyama's death. *Shokei* is an alternate reading for *Akiyoshi*. Mas Oyama always referred to him as Matsui *Akiyoshi*. Matsui always preferred *Shokei*.

[41] Sequence of basic techniques formalized by Mas Oyama, composed of open and closed fist strikes, blocks, and kicks.

launching into a periodical project that I might or might not be able to continue. Since the chances to communicate directly with *Sosai* were so few and far between, and since one's words have to be so carefully chosen during those limited encounters, I'd only ever written to *Sosai* about a one-time publication.

Sensei Matsui Shokei teaching his ceremonial first training of the year in early January of 1994, ten weeks before the opening of his branch dojo in Asakusa that March. This photo was taken by the author on the evening of our first meeting about *Budo Karate Illustrated,* when Matsui agreed to become the magazine's official "technical advisor."

"I wanted to ask you for your help," I boldly told Matsui that January night in Tokyo. "I want to ask *Sosai* tomorrow when I meet with him for permission to make my book the first issue of an ongoing magazine. I'm afraid, actually, that he won't say yes, because I'm so young and inexperienced. I thought maybe if you would agree to support the project by acting as technical advisor – if I could include in the magazine photos of you demonstrating correct technique – then perhaps *Sosai* would be more inclined to support my endeavor."

Matsui not only agreed, but he invited me to come by his dojo later that week for his dojo's ceremonial first training of the year, so that I could take pictures of him performing – as I'd suggested – the movements of Kyokushin's *kihon*. The day after my meeting with Matsui, *Sosai* agreed to support the project as an ongoing magazine, and when I contacted Matsui ten weeks later at the time of my grading, he'd once again told me to come by for another official event he was hosting so we could discuss a second photo shoot.

This time, he was hosting the opening ceremony for his new branch dojo at its new Asakusa location.

The guest list that day included a Who's Who of the Kyokushin world. As I waited in the tiny elevator for the doors to close I was caught off guard by Kurosawa Hiroki, who stepped into the elevator just on my heels, accompanied by one other. Surprise combined with my instinct to say "Osu!" and get out of my *sempai's* way, and I actually sprang back out of the elevator to the best my stiff legs would allow, bowed, and hissed "Osu!" through my still so recently crushed throat. To my embarrassment, I actually missed the elevator when the doors closed without me in it.

Like many Kyokushin *karateka* of my generation, I was a little bit in awe of Kurosawa. At the 1990 Osaka tournament I fought in, I watched in amazement as Kurosawa got his fist tangled with my *uchi deshi sempai* Shichinoe's *dogi* sleeve or incoming punch, and nearly ripped the two middle fingers off his hand. Initially I'd thought that it was a compound fracture, but it turned out that when the fingers were laid backwards against the back of his hand, the bones ripped through the skin at their base rather than actually breaking. As I remember it, without so much as flinching, he used his other hand to roll those two damaged fingers back into a fist, and went right on punching Shichinoe as if nothing had happened.

The video that they'd produced about Kurosawa had deemed him "the fighting machine." I'd been told that *Sosai* disapproved of him because he'd once walked off a tournament mat without bowing when he disagreed with the judges' call.

I won't attempt to list who was at the new Matsui Dojo that day, but it was just about everybody who was anybody. Masuda Akira was there, and

I wondered if he remembered me from his 100-man *kumite*. Noticeably absent was *Sosai*, of course, as well as any of my *gaijin* friends. Nick's teacher, Shihan Butz, was there from Denmark – he'd brought Nick's *koohai*, the blond kid who'd just about killed me, to Japan for the grading and wound up, perhaps by default, at Matsui's reception. After a long speech, preceded by several other speeches from Kyokushin dignitaries, Matsui changed out of his suit into his *dogi* and broke two baseball bats in an amazingly short, sweet, and successful demonstration. The first bat he broke was vertical and anchored only at the base, and he broke it with a *gedan mawashi geri;*[42] the second he broke – much to my amazement – with a downward *shuto*,[43] the bat having been laid horizontally across two chair backs at waist level. I'd broken bats with my shins by then, but I couldn't, and can't to this day, imagine breaking one with my *shuto*. In the years since I've heard that it's possible to buy special *tameshiwari* bats in Japan – bats designed to be a little weaker specifically for karate demonstrations – but at the time I hadn't heard of such a thing, and I took for granted that the bats he broke were of the same quality as the Louisville Sluggers I'd bashed my shins on in America so many times.

At what I mistakenly thought was the end of the day's events, I waited for an opportunity and asked Matsui, in the same raspy whisper with which I'd addressed *Sosai* that morning, when he and I might talk about a second photo shoot. He asked me if I planned on attending his training, which was to immediately follow the ceremony.

"Osu! I just completed my *nidan* grading yesterday," I told him, "so I'm not sure how well I can do, but I will do my best," and, "oh, but . . . is it possible to purchase a uniform? I didn't know there was a training, and I didn't bring my own."

Matsui asked me what size I needed, and then flattered me by handing me a new *dogi* and telling me that I could have it as a present, since I'd just completed my *nidan* grading.

I knew it to be a $100 gift.

Needless to say the training was painful – happily it did not involve *kumite* – and I was able to arrange a photo shoot with Matsui for the following day.

---

[42] Low roundhouse kick, usually shin to thigh.
[43] Edge of hand: the proverbial "karate chop."

SIX

DURING THE TWELVE MONTHS that separated those two trips to Japan, I had undergone one of the most significant transformations of my adult life.

The underlying feeling I'd been doing my best to deny ever since I began training again with an ax in the forest of my childhood had finally burst forth into my life's here and now. The *Budo Karate Illustrated* vision provided the catalyst. *Maybe, just maybe, I can achieve something for Kyokushin worthy of Mas Oyama's investment in me after all!*

Just a year and half earlier, I'd convinced myself *fresh out of the monastery* that life's indulgences were mine by right. I'd worked so hard for so long, why not be like everyone else, make up for lost time, and reap the pleasures I'd denied myself during my eight-year, single-minded and selfless pursuit of bringing honor to my first teacher?

But then the voice of Conscience piped up and started to pollute what could have been such a pure pursuit of self-gratification. Yes, life's most intense passions were mine for the taking, but what greater passion could there be than the ultimate appeasement of conscience? *To live from the heart is to live without regret. What greater high might I steal from life? Certainly not the fleeting physical pleasures that are available to me just because they are to everyone else?*

It's no wonder that it was the middle third of my Part Two British literature survey course that was the most enticing of my second semester back in school. I struggled with the older material of the Part One survey, but the British Romantic poets of the mid- to late portion of Part Two were the ones with whom I came to feel the most affinity.

I was a little bit slower academically than most of my peers – my natural strength is for numbers, not words – but I made up for it with appreciation for the education I was reaping. The vast majority of my peers studied to get grades, to get into better graduate schools, to get better jobs. Like them, in the beginning I opted for economics, thinking I might like to be a businessman and make lots of money. I took Constitutional Law that second semester because I knew lawyers' salaries to be at the higher end of the spectrum. But by the middle of that same semester, I was starting to find new purpose for my education: I would be one of the most highly educated students of Mas Oyama. I would use what I'd learned to give back to the Kyokushin world. I went to class the way the devout go to church. I looked for meaning in the lectures, the readings, and the coursework that I could apply to the ever more undeniable course of my own life, one that was finally starting to come into view.

I wasn't the best of students because I never worked for the grade. I tended to downplay the importance of material that I merely had to learn to pass the course, while at the same time searching between the lines for meanings that I felt I would need for my future. My Davidson education is one of the two most valuable of my life, side by side with my *uchi deshi* training, because, like Musashi's *pen and sword in accord,* they are the two equal parts of the education that make me what I am.[44] Davidson was a liberal arts college, which means that I was afforded the academic freedom to pick and choose, shape my own education and follow my interests in the direction that most appealed to me.

The British Romantic poets sang to me songs of gnawing the marrow out of the very bones of life, savoring every morsel as if there would only be one chance. That notion fused with a Confucian concept that was the most meaningful of my earliest round of Davidson coursework: according to the Confucian scholar Mencius, despite the challenges that arise when men combine into societies, mankind is, at its core, fundamentally charitable, and fundamentally desiring to live in such a way as to make the world a better place. This teaching appealed directly to the entire impression of my childhood, which was all but utopian for my first decade, until my mother's and father's lives went awry. I came back from

---

[44] Master Choi drove me to concentrate my energies on academics, never believing me physically strong enough to ever become a champion in Japan. "Have you read Musashi? Good, read it again! Make sure you get at least a 3.5 grade point average again this semester!"

Japan, and started training with my ax, and my heart started to speak to me in words I could almost hear, telling me to risk it all to give it all. And finally, like the last piece of the puzzle, here were the Romantics, affirming the notion I was already entertaining that living life to its fullest just might mean having to savor it, not just for its pleasures, but also for its pain and anguish. The Romantics encouraged me to let go.

Why flinch, I asked, *from the notion that pulling out all the stops in the process of following my conscience might mean for me a life sentence of pain and disappointment in the pursuit of a maybe-someday ultimate fulfillment?*

Isn't even that part of human life – suffering! – life to be celebrated, nevertheless?

I could no longer deny a growing sense that to give my all to the vision that was forming within me would mean steering deeper into the abyss than even the misery of my adolescence had taken me. One possible future that I could see was of my simply withering away under the enormity of the endeavor. I looked into the future and shuddered to see myself dying under its weight. But while the notion scared me, the Romantics comforted me with their avowal that it would be that exact willingness to charge into the abyss if necessary that would make my life the most meaningful in the end.

Within a month after returning to Davidson from my classmates' graduation in Japan, I wrote to the two senior members on *Honbu's* North American branch chief list: Jacques Sandulescu in New York and Bobby Lowe in Hawaii. Seiji Kanemura was for some reason not in contact with *Honbu*. He hadn't been at the meeting in Rochester, and it was clear that it was with Jacques and Bobby Lowe that the influence in North America lay. With their support, I dared to believe I'd get Mas Oyama's backing, and if he was on board, I could be certain that the rest of the American branch chiefs would follow.

"We need our own English-language publication," I typed in a three-page letter to both Jacques and Bobby Lowe, "and with all the U.S. branch chiefs selling issues through advance orders to their students, we'll be able to fund it. I have the time and the energy to put it together. With your support, we can gain *Sosai's* backing. The magazine will work to bring us all closer together – to try and bridge the gap between the squabbling U.S. branch chiefs. It will help to make the organization stronger, and American Kyokushin stronger in the process. If there are any additional proceeds we can donate them to help with *Sosai's* dream of building a new *Honbu* Dojo during his lifetime."

I had plenty to do while I waited for their responses. My impatience for the project's acceleration – one that by the middle of the next spring's semester would be hungrily consuming every calorie of my pitifully overburdened existence – was sidelined for the moment by the demands of my two British literature surveys, another writing seminar, constitutional law, and the English department's senior colloquium, in which we were meant to begin to integrate and assimilate all that we'd learned in preparation for graduate school. Add to that my near full-time responsibility of managing the Union Café (concentrated mostly into night and weekend hours) and teaching karate classes six days a week, and I was blissfully just a little bit too busy to dwell on the acceleration I could feel looming just around the next corner.

Since my father was a longtime Davidson College professor, up to four years of my education was paid for by Davidson. That means I had exactly eight semesters to finish an eight-semester education. I'd completed two my freshman year at Davidson, but unfortunately for my current situation, I'd then opted to transfer to the University of North Carolina at Chapel Hill, a much larger school of lower academic standard, for my sophomore year, in order to study Japanese and train with Master Choi. Even though Davidson had paid for two semesters at UNC, I'd dropped out in the middle of the second one to go to Japan, and two of the four courses I had completed didn't transfer credit because they weren't part of Davidson's curriculum. Consequently, after being out of school for two years, I found myself with only two years in which to finish nearly three years of schooling. Neither I nor my family could have afforded Davidson's tuition for even one additional semester beyond the eight that I was allowed through my father's employment. As a result I opted to take five courses instead of the standard four that second semester (the one during which I went to Japan for my classmates' graduation), and the following year I would take six classes per semester, significantly more than the normal Davidson course load.

Three years of college in two years. The full-time job of managing the Café at the same time. Teaching my karate classes. Single-handedly creating a new magazine for the future of Kyokushin in North America.

No problem.

I am Mas Oyama's only American uchi deshi, *after all. What else should I take on?*
Is it dangerous to thus fill my life so close to the bursting point?
Sure it is, but so be it!
Celebrate even the collapse if it comes to that!
Who needs sleep, anyway? Who else is going to try?

Bobby Lowe's response to my first letter was disappointing. I couldn't tell if he'd misunderstood what I wanted to do, or if he was politely trying to tell me that he didn't think it could be done. I'd written him a detailed three-page letter about how I planned to organize, fund, design, market, and distribute a magazine for U.S. Kyokushin, and his response was vague enough to make me wonder if he'd even read my proposal. Buried within a multi-page letter about the summer seminar he was organizing for Kyokushin, he wrote:

"In reference about raising funds for the building of a new *Honbu*, this has truly been *Sosai's* dream of a lifetime. However, we are talking in the millions of US dollars and whether we can raise this hefty amount of money is very questionable. But I will do everything possible to help with this project in making this dream a reality."

Of course I'd only "mentioned about" contributing any magazine proceeds to the new *Honbu* fund to make it clear that I wasn't motivated by money. The benefit of the project that I imagined was the magazine itself, and *Shihan* Lowe didn't seem to see any value in that. Even if I had envisioned the project as primarily a fund-raiser, I would never have suggested that it could raise *all* the money needed to build a new *Honbu* for *Sosai*, but *Shihan* Lowe seemed to dismiss my idea as if I'd approached him with just that lunatic notion.

Shihan Lowe went on to tell me that his fighters "took first places in the Senior Black Belt and in the Color Belt Open" divisions as well as the "most spirited fighter award trophy" in a recent tournament in Vancouver. The whole tone of the letter rang to me of, "I'm sure you're not capable of doing what you want to do, but meanwhile here are my accomplishments."

Oh well, I thought, *at least he did say he'd do anything he could to help. At the very least he's not objecting to what I want to do. We'll see what Shihan Jacques has to say.*

With Jacques, I had an advantage called *Donbas*.

Donbas was the first of three autobiographical books he'd authored, the one that his wife Annie had asked me if I'd read when *Sosai* introduced us in Rochester. The book was some years out of print, but I managed to hunt down a copy through an interlibrary loan program at the Davidson College library. I felt compelled to learn who I was going to be petitioning for support, and reading Jacques' book became my first significant diversion of time and energy in the name of the *Budo Karate Illustrated* project.

I was house-sitting over a long holiday weekend for a professor of mine who was out of town, and I had coursework to do, but I spent a full day and night reading *Donbas* anyway.

After fighting his way out of a slave-labor camp in Stalin's USSR, Jacques fought his way to American citizenship as a professional boxer. It was a boxing promoter circa 1950 that helped the monstrous "Jack Herman", the name under which he boxed professionally, to immigrate to the US from Canada where he'd temporarily landed after his years in a displaced persons camp in Germany following the war.

It turned out that the Donbas was the barren coal-producing region of Ukraine where Jacques was taken as a teenager by the Soviet troops who'd occupied his native Romania. Sweeping through his village one day, they rounded up anyone who looked tough enough to mine coal, and shipped them off in boxcars, innocent villagers plucked right off the streets and made slave laborers in support of Stalin's war machine. Jacques spent two years of his life, from age 16 to 18, in a slave labor camp where the Soviets routinely worked, starved, or froze laborers to death because it was cheaper to round up replacements than to keep the current ones alive. *Donbas* was the story of Jacques' struggle there to survive. Jacques, I learned, became one of the few, crawling out of the frozen USSR and into the West.

By his second year in the Donbas, Jacques was completely surrounded by death. Everyone was starving and, one by one, the prisoners around him succumbed to despair and died. In one particularly harrowing account, Jacques wrote of a woman who became too sick to work and finally could not even be roused from her blank-eyed trance. When Jacques and her other bunkmates noticed teaspoon-sized globs of lice falling from under the rags with which she'd bound her hair, they removed them and found that her head was a half-inch thick living mass of lice. When they cut her hair and scrubbed what was left with kerosene, they found her flesh so badly ulcerated that it was as though they were washing away her scalp as well. The woman recovered for a time, but many hundreds of others were not so lucky. As Jacques' second winter approached, he fought to be reassigned back underground into the mines. They'd had him working above ground and exposed to the elements, tipping over wheeled carts of rock onto an ever more mountainous heap near the mine entrance. He feared that he would freeze to death as the winter approached, and he lucked into another year of life when he took advantage of some rapport he'd built with the Russian miners to get himself sent back underground.

The following winter, however, his luck ran out.

The mine in which he was working collapsed, and he was buried alive in a pitch-black tomb no bigger than the breath before his nose. He could not move but knew that something was terribly wrong with his legs. Six hours later, Jacques' closest friend in the camp, a fellow Romanian youth of similarly giant stature and character named Omar, frantically digging, uncovered the tips of Jacques' boots. When one of the toes moved, he redoubled his efforts and found Jacques pinned there, injured but alive. Jacques' friend had refused to quit digging for him even after others had called off the search. Jacques was transported to a hospital outside the camp, where his legs swelled to twice their original thickness, then burst open and drained foul-smelling pus. Jacques spoke Russian by then, and he soon understood with horror that his legs were to be amputated. That night, Jacques wrapped them in bedsheets and wires torn from his mattress and, by sheer force of will, dragged himself out of the hospital and across town into the train yard, where he climbed the ladder of an open-topped coal car on a track pointed west, and buried himself in coal and ice.

It was that ice, and perhaps the lice in his bandages, that saved Jacques' legs as he lingered between starvation and hypothermia for days, crawling from train car to train car, stealing food whenever he could, and finally making his way to American-occupied Germany. When he met Mas Oyama in the sixties in New York City, he was a nightclub owner and a retired professional boxer, and the two found immediate friends in one another, each able to see in the other an element of their shared giant-like character that could only have come to be through the survival of such hardship.

This man and I have a thing or two in common, it occurred to me when I first read *Donbas,* but what a disaster it would be to try and describe for him why! If only my father could have stood, for even one moment, in Jacques' father's shoes!

On the day of his abduction, Jacques looked for his father in the frantic crowd outside the freight train into which the Soviet troops were packing prisoners. They were packed so tightly, several hundred to a car, that they wouldn't even be able to sit down for the several days they survived without food or water, nor would they have wanted to, since by then they were standing in a slick of each other's filth. Jacques saw his father for the last time through the small window of his boxcar, a proud aristocratic German Transylvanian who had served in the First World War, fighting back tears as he frantically searched for a last glimpse of his only son.

The Soviet-backed Romanian government stripped Jacques' father of everything over the next several years while Jacques fought for life in the Donbas, and his father eventually died once the Communists' "interrogation and reeducation" sessions began to rob him of his dignity as well. I, on the other hand, had fallen victim to my father's unintentional, ten-year-long, piece-by-piece abandonment as he discovered, day by day, that there was no place for me in his third life with his third wife and their children, and, although no one was beating me or depriving me of food, my teenage years had seemed every bit the same kind of prison. Jacques lost his father, and his home and his family, in a single instant that had passed like a blur; I'd lost mine day by day, in a ten-year-long succession of days that left me feeling every bit as torn.

I knew my father to be a good man at heart, and for ten long years I went back and forth between believing it was spiritual weakness that he had fallen prey to, and at other times, blindness. The answer to incorporating me happily into his new family was right in front of him; was he just not strong enough? Or was he simply blind? Could it just be that it was beyond his ability to see outside the 50-year-old iron box he'd built for himself, a box of "this is the way a family is supposed to be, and I'm too old to risk looking for a better way?" Either way, I suffered bitterly as a result of his life hardening onto a path that had no room in it for me. I'd come back from Japan intent on writing that story, and the story of how Master Choi and his uncle in Japan had unknowingly corrected a young life that had been so hurt by that abandonment. But then I read *Donbas* and I found myself ashamed. How could my story be worth recording beside the story of the hardship Jacques had endured?

Shihan Jacques lent his support to my book project in a brief but powerful telephone exchange, and in April, just one month after my return from my former classmates' graduation, I wrote a second letter to both Jacques and *Shihan* Lowe, thanking them for their support and asking if they would each write a letter of support on official letterhead, letters that I could first show *Sosai* to ask his permission, and later distribute, along with a proposal, to the rest of the US branch chiefs.

Still waiting for responses in May, I wrote to *Sosai's* secretary at *Honbu* to impress upon her, once more, the importance of translating for *Sosai* exactly what was in my *Black Belt* Magazine article about his killing a man, so that I could be sure that he approved. He'd told me in Japan that as long as it painted Kyokushin in a positive light, I had his permission to publish, but since then I'd spoken both to *Shihan* Jacques and my *sempai* in New York, David Bunt, and confessed my concern about *presuming to know better than Sosai* whether my story would paint Kyokushin in a positive light or not. Of course, it seemed to me that it did – for me, that story had always been the one that best exemplified Mas Oyama's strength of character! – but this was Mas Oyama in the flesh that we were talking about, and I was just me, the 22-year-old lightweight American kid who'd failed to graduate.

How catastrophic it would be if I misjudged!

Days passed while I waited for a response to that letter as well.

Participation in my karate classes dwindled as final exams neared. I secluded myself to prepare for my own exams in the library of the forest house in which I'd grown up. My stepmother Martha was mostly away, finishing up her own classes at the university in Charlotte.

I opted to memorize large chunks of the mostly Romantic poems that appealed to me from part two of my British literature survey, rather than studying the critique-packed course notes I'd written down from my professors' lectures. I did well on that exam, but my performance was far below average on the older literature from the survey's Part One. I'd found it quite a challenge to get through the pages and pages of U.S. Supreme Court opinions I was required to read for my constitutional law course – reading them was more like learning a foreign language than reading Chaucer's Middle English had been – yet my professor, known to some as "Scary" Mary Thornberry, proved to be a lot less scary than her nickname when she took pity on me and gave me a passing grade on an exam that I knew to be a degree or two less than satisfactory.

I fought bitterly with my father over my decision to use up what was left of the little bit of money my mother, his first divorced wife, had set aside for my education, to take summer school courses at Martha's UNCC, thirty minutes by car from Davidson. By taking a science course, a course in writing poetry, a Brit. lit. survey course that focused specifically on the Romantics, and History of Western Civilization, all of which would transfer to Davidson, I'd be able to graduate by the end of the next year within the bounds of the free tuition that I received as his son. The alternative would have been to prolong my college education by at least a semester and go into some significant debt.

The whole concept must have been truly dismaying for my father. Not only was I opting to use my mother's tuition money, over which he had no control, to do something he and his third wife didn't want me to do – he certainly would have exercised purse-string control had my going to summer school at UNCC depended on his money – but I had also made plans to live for the summer with my girlfriend in the house that he'd built and then given up when he left my first stepmother. Martha was going to be away for the summer again, back in the Florida Everglades with her camera, and she needed someone to watch over the property and feed the cats. I'd stay there rent-free in exchange for keeping an eye on the property. I'm sure my father objected to me living with a girlfriend, but it really must have irked him that by living in Martha's house I'd be, in effect, supporting the stepmother I'd loved since childhood rather than the one he was married to. The most important issue for him, though, it came out finally, was that he wanted me to take a summer off from college and work so that I could pay him rent to live in the backyard cottage he'd originally refurbished for me, he claimed, to appease his conscience, since there was no longer room for me in his house.

For a decade already I'd been doing my best to bite my lip and support his third marriage, but by the end of my junior year of college the chinks in my armor were starting to show. My stepmother's subtle but relentless esteem-eroding treatment as she tried her best to shame and degrade me into relating to her the way she thought I should, and my father's inability to intervene on my behalf, had long since been robbing me of the respect that I ought to have felt for my father, and the love that I had for him had now begun to suffer. In support of his fantasy that he might force the actual family he had into the conventional mold of his family tradition, he had taken to issuing statements of blatant denial such as "I was never married to Martha," apparently to help him cope with what he considered to be earlier, unspeakable failures.

There has to be something wrong with a man who looks his adult son straight in the eye and tells him that he was never married to a woman who had been that son's stepmother for six years and whose wedding ceremony that son had attended. "You mean you don't consider yourself to have been married to her because you weren't married in a church?" I'd ask. "No," he'd respond, "I mean what I said. I was never married to her." He'd then go on to explain something about the fact that, since he'd acted as both minister and witness at their courthouse ceremony, the marriage had never been a legal one, somehow as if that technicality mattered in the context of the conversation. My father had been trained and ordained to be a Presbyterian minister, but had only worked in the profession for a short time before going back to graduate school to study art. His denial clearly went beyond merely trying to fill me in on a legal detail I'd never known.

"But she was my stepmother for six years," I'd say. "I was at the courthouse with you and Aaron, and Tom, and Nancy, when you got married. You introduced her to your parents as your wife, and you lived with her as husband and wife and referred to her to as your wife to everyone you knew, didn't you?" It made me ill to realize that he wasn't going to budge. It was as if he was begging me to just agree with him and help him make his past go away, and with no other choice, I'd let the subject drop.

With the corners of his graying moustache twitching with rage, my father would tell me how he was "working his fingers to the bone" to pay for my college education, when, in fact, the money actually came from Davidson College, the employment benefit of free tuition that didn't alter his salary one bit. Of course, he did spend some of his income to pay for half of my room and board in college (while my mother paid for the other half), but the reality was that he had borrowed a huge amount of money in order to restore the house that he lived in with his new family, and he had come to resent having to divert any of his monthly ability to pay it off towards the support of a son from a prior marriage, who, for some reason, couldn't seem to let him pretend that he hadn't had any.

It had already been a year since my father left me speechless by coming straight out and telling me that he didn't believe he'd ever see me again after I got what I wanted and graduated from college. I was shocked because up until then I was still fighting tooth and nail to rescue him, and abandoning the attempt hadn't even occurred to me. My father had become all about closing his eyes to certain blatant realities in order to make the outward appearance of his life fit into tradition's mold, and my decade-long concerted effort to save him had been about using the open eyes that he'd given me, after all, to keep his eyes pried open. He'd say something like "I was never married to Martha," and I'd consider it my duty, out of love for him, to expose the fact that he was lying to himself.

"Leave me alone! Let me close my eyes so I don't have to be tormented," his choices implied, and "No way," came my response, "if you close your eyes to the truth I'll lose respect for you, and once respect is gone, love will follow, and then I'll lose you completely." For him, our ten-year-long conflict had been about my refusing to accept his current wife. But on that topic, I'd always bitten my tongue. For me, that battle was ninety-nine percent internal, and was all about not becoming an orphan, since the original love I felt for my father was so great. Out of love for my father, I'd endured his wife's unnecessarily condescending treatment of me with lips sealed shut for ninety-nine out of the hundred times I'd felt stung. It was to that extent that I tried – for my father's sake! – to be the mature one and create a space in which mutual feelings of respect might develop, but finally, ten whole years had passed, and my stepmother's negativity was starting to be too much to bear. My father loved me. Of that there was no question, but he seemed so pitifully confused: it was as if ever confronting his wife was more dreadful for him than watching his son painfully erased.

I was 22 then, however, at the end of my junior year, and I suppose it was because I was finally starting to grow up that I chose to use the summer to achieve something for my own future – and for Kyokushin's! – rather than risk being consumed for yet another year by the effort to rescue someone who didn't want to be rescued.

And so it was into my childhood home that I moved that May, despite my father's bitter protest. I had four summer-school courses to take, an ambitious self-training routine in mind, and a naïve notion that I might finally get over the hump and bring all the work I'd done that year on my autobiographical book closer to completion.

I embarked on the summer with an intense feeling of optimism and excitement. I was moving into the home in which I'd lived first with my own mother, and then later with my father's first replacement for her, Martha, whom I'd come so similarly to love. Family for me most certainly wasn't in my father's new house across town. Martha would be gone for the summer, so it wasn't exactly in my childhood home either; nevertheless, it was to at least the remnants of the warmth and comfort of family that I moved into Martha's house. My girlfriend Lissa would be moving in with me, and I was on the verge of considering her the family of my future anyway.

I spent Martha's last week in North Carolina working with her to shore up a foundation leak that was letting water into the basement and painting the basement floorboards with polyurethane to protect them from any future leakage. But then Martha left, my courses at UNCC got underway, Lissa moved in, and I spent many hours in front of my computer, mostly failing to write. One of my karate students who was staying in Davidson for the summer trained with me off and on. My student Rafael joined us a few times.

On June 15, I received a letter from *Sosai's* assistant:

Dear Mr. Nathan Ligo.

Thank you for your letter of May 25th addressed to *Sosai* and me. As requested, I have translated this story for *Sosai*, and here is his comment on this. "The story seems fine with me. Once somebody said I have killed 57 people. Then Kyokushin Karate was forbidden by the British Government once. I can not stop people from talking about me."

Sincerely, Taiko Watanabe

I wasn't exactly sure what to make of that. I chalked the ambiguity up to meanings lost in translation, however, and took it as final permission to publish the story I'd written. I was a bit embarrassed that I'd troubled *Sosai* yet again when he'd already given me his answer, but I was consoled to recall Master Choi's advice that Mas Oyama would love me if he remembered me and that he would remember me if he was given opportunities to do for me, so I shrugged it off and notified the *Black Belt* editor that I'd gotten *Sosai's* final blessing.

I was nagged by a sense that my correspondence with *Sosai* had been somewhat dishonest. I had been holding off telling him what was really foremost on my mind: that I was 100% engaged in laying the political foundation for an all-Kyokushin magazine project that would depend on his endorsement. Yet since I wasn't ready to ask him for that endorsement – I didn't yet have the official letters I'd requested from Jacques and *Shihan* Lowe – perhaps on some level I knew it worked to my advantage to keep myself "remembered" to *Sosai* in the meantime. Ultimately I dismissed my unease. As soon as I had my official responses from Jacques and *Shihan* Lowe, *Sosai's* desk would be my project proposal's first stop.

On June 29th, Jacques wrote the letter I'd been waiting for:

Dear Branch Chief:

> I support Nathan Ligo in his project to create an American Kyokushin Yearbook for all of us. I urge you to add your support and your dojo's stories and pictures.
>
> We in the US Organization desperately need to come together, both to help each other in promoting *Sosai* Oyama's magnificent Karate, and to show *Sosai* that we have the basis for building a strong organization. Mas Oyama's Kyokushin is the strongest, most spiritually serious karate in the world. It should be a leader of the US martial arts. It's long past time for us to get to know each other, pull together, and start to present a united front.
>
> I see the *American Kyokushin Yearbook* as one place to communicate about our individual dojos and events and to show our combined strength. Nathan Ligo is a serious student of Kyokushin who has trained at *Honbu*. Because he is young, he has the energy and courage – and the time – to undertake this project, which can benefit us all. He has made it very clear that he wants all of you to be active participants and to make the Yearbook yours, not his.
>
> I have agreed to advise and guide Nathan on this project. I expect you to join in and look forward to knowing more about you, your students, and your contributions to Kyokushin.
>
> Osu! Jacques Sandulescu

I waited a few more days after receiving Jacques' letter before calling *Shihan* Lowe in Hawaii, since I had received no further word from him. "I was hoping to have a letter of support from you as well," I reminded him.

I can't remember the exact words *Shihan* Lowe used to deny my request, but I vividly remember a sensation of disappointment and diminishing respect.

What motive would this guy have, I wondered, *to refuse to help me with a project that is for the good of all of us?* Was it possible that, as I sensed, he felt competitive, and therefore defensive – the great Bobby Lowe, *Sosai's* first overseas instructor? *He's already made Kyokushin history,* I thought. *Why would he want to stand in the way of the next generation's trying to keep it alive and strong? Had he somehow thought my request rude?*

It was pretty clear that the relationship between Jacques and Mas

Oyama was significant enough that *Sosai* was likely to support my idea with only his endorsement.

There was only one way to find out.

Within twenty-four hours of receiving *Shihan* Lowe's denial of support, I attached Jacques' letter to one that I'd written to *Sosai's* assistant and dropped it in the mail to *Honbu*, asking that she translate these two paragraphs directly for *Sosai* even if she decided, in the interest of time, to paraphrase the rest:

> Dear *Sosai*,
>
> Osu! I know that this may seem to be a very bold endeavor for someone of my age and experience, but I know in my heart that it can become successful. In my opinion, the most important result of this project will be that it will help to make the Kyokushin instructors in America understand the need to work together. If the project earns money for *Honbu*, that will be wonderful. However, even if the project earns only a little money, it will still be greatly beneficial to American Kyokushin.
>
> As I spend more and more time isolated from Kyokushin, I realize more and more that my life is incomplete without it. In ten months I will graduate from college with a degree in English literature (with a focus on writing). I am already exploring means by which I will be able to return to Japan after my graduation. *Shihan* Lowe mentioned to me on the phone that you were considering beginning again to print the English Kyokushin Karate magazine. I wonder if I could use my writing skills to assist you? I look forward to hearing your opinion concerning the *American Kyokushin Yearbook* and I look forward to seeing you at *Honbu* soon.
>
> Sincerely, Nathan Ligo

After holding my breath for nearly a month, I received a fairly disappointing, albeit preliminary, response from Tokyo:

> Dear Mr. Ligo.
>
> Thank you for your letter dated July 6, 1993. As requested I have translated your letter for *Sosai*, but he has been busy and may not be in mood of making any comments on this matter. I will of course let you know as soon as I get any response from him. Thank you for your patience and cooperation.
>
> Sincerely, Taiko Watanabe

It was as a result of this letter that I visited *Shihan* Jacques and his wife, Annie, at their Greenwich Village apartment in New York City for the first time. I had only one week before classes would start again at the beginning of fall semester. Evidently *Sosai* wasn't sure yet if he approved of my proceeding. If his thinking teetered one way, he'd tell me to go ahead, but if it were to tilt the other way, the project would be dead. Remember that there was no "but . . ." when dealing with *Sosai*. "Osu!" was the only possible answer, and there is no *but* in *Osu!* In case he was gearing up to put an end to my project due to my age and inexperience, I figured a face-to-face meeting with Jacques would be the best way to head him off at the pass.

I was so sure of the value the project could have for Kyokushin in America that I was confident that *Sosai* would be sure, too, if he could stand where I stood. It was my responsibility, I believed, to make him see what I saw, so that he would have the tools he needed to make a decision that could only in the end have been his.

But there was more to it than that.

There was another, riskier notion boiling up in me. It boiled up like a distant growl that I wouldn't then have dared to put into words.

Sosai hadn't yet seen – he couldn't possibly have seen – exactly what kind of weapon he had in me to make his work happen in America. He hadn't seen me for what I believed myself to be becoming. He hadn't seen what I knew I was capable of if I pulled out all the stops. He hadn't yet seen the success of the effort both he and his nephew before him had put into shaping me as an instrument for the future of American Kyokushin. He hadn't seen my true face, but I had decided to show it to him.

Over my dead body if necessary, I was going to show him.

I suppose I was insane to think such a thing.

SEVEN

Sosai's "not being in the mood to make a comment on the matter" caught me off guard.

The way I was coming to operate, I tended to see my work's finished product not just in terms of an imagined possibility, but rather as a foregone conclusion. In my exhaustion, when I looked into the future and saw, it was as if what I saw *was* the future. Such was the force of my optimism. It's why I use the word *vision* rather than *plan*. The vision came into being in finished form, and it was with a resolute *it's just a matter of time* that I beheld it as something that was going to happen. Of course there would be obstacles to overcome, and of course there was no way of knowing what they would be, but by giving in to the vision as a foregone conclusion, I knew I'd maximize my ability to plow through whatever challenges I might face.

I was well aware of the risk. If I moved forward as if it was going to happen at all costs, and then it started not to happen, I could imagine that those costs – costs to my own well-being – could become significant. Being willing to do anything to make it happen would maximize the project's chances of success, but how badly, I wondered, could that *anything* hurt me?

But "So be it!" was the answer I always fell back on. Who was potentially going to get hurt by launching towards a foregone conclusion of success with such reckless abandon? Only me, of course. I would be the one at risk, and so be it! I'd already lived the life I was allotted by making it to Japan and throwing the opportunity away by failing. If my second chance was going to drive me into a premature grave?

So be it!

I was going to celebrate it!

I was going to fill my life with it! I was going to revel in the pursuit of it, even as it drove me into the ground.

The story of my trip to Japan for my *nidan* grading – six months after the end of that summer I spent at Martha's – provides a literal example or two of how the project could have killed me.

The date of the grading, as it happened, was the same week as Davidson's midterms. Before leaving for Japan, I had to complete my Chinese History and Art History exams, and had to reschedule with my professors to cram them into the Monday and Tuesday of that week before my Wednesday departure for *Honbu's* weekend grading. (Happily, my modern Irish poetry professor – the same Harry Thomas whom I'd argued with to go to Japan the year before – wasn't giving an exam that semester.) The Saturday before exam week, Kyokushin branch chief Henri Orlean was hosting his tournament all day in Atlantic City, and many of the North American Kyokushin principals would be there. Jacques and Annie would be, they'd become my closest connection to a community in which I was otherwise somewhat of an outsider, and I could not pass up the chance to further *Budo Karate Illustrated*.

I left Davidson at about dinnertime to drive all night, nine hours north to Atlantic City, alone and without proper sleep for several days. Around three o'clock in the morning I took the wrong exit off the highway, and opted to cover fifty or sixty miles of my journey on back roads that seemed, as the crow flies, more direct. Traveling sixty-five miles per hour on a dark country road in a car with one headlamp out, I came to a place where the road curved sharply to the left. There were no lights along that stretch of road, only reflector posts positioned every thirty feet around the outside of the curve to warn motorists.

Unfortunately, right at that curve, a dirt road exited off the paved one, straight ahead in the exact direction I was traveling. At that spot, instead of every thirty feet, there was a 100-foot gap between reflector posts. I caught just a glimpse out of the corner of my eye of the curving row of shimmering orange lights diminishing off to my left, with an involuntary gasp as my vehicle left the pavement and went airborne at sixty miles per hour, off into the blackness. The dirt road dropped sharply below the raised outer edge of the paved curve, and continuing straight off the concrete at sixty felt like flying off a ramp in a car show.

Okay, there went the road off to my left, I thought calmly. *None of my* tires are touching pavement. *Now I'm going to die.* My one headlight, pointed skyward, didn't reveal that I was flying straight along the course of a smooth gravel road that would catch my car a moment later like a jai alai scoop. As far as I knew, I was flying off into forest, and I'd be stopped cold by the nearest tree trunk and killed.

Close calls happen to motorists all the time, of course. The point is, however, that driving forward with such resolve, especially given the limited resources I had at my disposal, sometimes more than bordered on reckless. I didn't have the time or money to repair my headlight, I didn't have the luxury of sleeping like a normal person, but I did have the conviction to drive all night long and alone to Atlantic City. I didn't sleep except for ninety minutes upon arrival, in the back seat of my car in the parking garage at the Taj Mahal Casino and Convention Center, where the tournament was to be held. It was the foregone conclusion of success that carried me forward, and foregone conclusion doesn't leave much room for sensible precaution when approaching the limits of what might actually be achieved.

Ironically, I sensed no danger at the tournament itself.

My determination to barrel ahead at all costs was only boosted by the accomplishment of my various magazine-related missions: among other indications of coming success, Chicago's Leslaw Samitowski took me to his room and handed me $2100 in cash as an advance order for 90 copies of *Budo Karate Illustrated* when it was ready!

Even the day's one sour note caused me no significant alarm. Sosai had appointed a new branch chief in New York City, he was at the tournament that day, and he seemed overly proud to have been admitted to a group to which he too was a newcomer. Was it the fact that he was Japanese? Was it possible that he subscribed to the racist opinion that only Japanese people could understand real Japanese karate?

Even Jacques seemed altered by his presence.

That was when most of us met Katsuhiko Horai for the first time, and I was intrigued some years later to read the letter of introduction that Mas Oyama had written to Jacques regarding Horai, at nearly the exact time of my grading in Japan:

> Dear Mr. Jacques Sandulescu,
>
> As you may have known already, I have appointed Mr. Horai as a new branch chief in New York. He is very reliable, smart, and

responsible. Most of all he comes of a good family. Of course I do not know him that well. It usually takes a long time to know a person well. Both Shigeru Oyama and Tadashi Nakamura used to be very reliable to me and then things turned out badly. Anyway, I want to believe that he is loyal to me and will be. He is a good *karateka* and he was a prize winner at the 15th All Japan Tournament. I hope you can support him fully. Your understanding and cooperation is highly appreciated.

Sincerely, Mas Oyama

The effort that Mas Oyama put forth in this letter to convince himself to feel comfortable with someone about whom he so plainly had doubts is remarkable, given what we would all come to know about Horai over the years to come. *Sosai* starts out by comparing him to two students who ultimately betrayed him, and then goes on to say, "I want to believe that he'll be loyal" which implies "but I'm not sure I do," and then "I hope you can support him," which likewise implies "but I'm not sure that you'll be able to."

Blissfully unaware that Horai, himself, would one day pose one of the greatest threats to the success I was blindly putting myself at risk to achieve, I got back in my car and drove all night again, back to Davidson. I slept only a couple of hours Sunday morning, then launched into a frantic, sleepless three-day study and exam-taking session before boarding the plane for Tokyo. The thirteen hours of sleep I got on the plane were the most significant of my week, and the most I would get for some time to come.

If I had been killed at my grading by that blow to my throat, I would have been the first and only one ever killed at a *Honbu* grading. People were sometimes seriously hurt – even the Japan Champion I fought, Masuda Akira, after his 100-man kumite, was hospitalized – but an accidental death at a grading was unheard of. Nevertheless, to attempt a 20-man *kumite* when I did, lacking the experience of a *shodan* grading's 10-man *kumite*, and being far less tough than I'd been as an *uchi deshi*, was, to say the least, risky. I could have been badly injured. But once *Sosai* ordered it, my grading became a means to the vision's end, and there was no question in my mind that I would charge forward, no matter what the risk.

But then, I was never really concerned about being physically undone by any such accident. It was rather that as I made an ever stronger emotional commitment to bringing about a desired end for which I believed myself on certain fundamental levels to be inadequate, I became increasingly unable to shake the feeling that one possible outcome could be my own eventual *internal* undoing. I was staring into a future that I believed might unravel me at the core, and yet I knew that I would not turn away.

Compensating for my lack of ability would take a certain kind of creativity. I knew I had it in me; I'd tapped it once before as a teenager.

Jacques can be seen here in the background (c. 1970) at JFK, welcoming *Sosai* to New York. This is a remarkable photo because of the other personalities present. *Sosai* is addressing Tadashi Nakamura, who was the first "Young Lion" *Sosai* entrusted with introducing Kyokushin Karate to America. When Nakamura abandoned Kyokushin, *Sosai* was forced to replace him with American Kyokushin's second director, Shigeru Oyama (right, foreground, no relation to Mas Oyama), who would finally break from Kyokushin as well. It was this pair of painful splits that would result in *Sosai's* deep mistrust of the American system so often inhospitable to the Japanese *budo* spirit. Behind *Sosai* is Seiji Kanemura, who was still on the IKO's branch chief list when I first saw it in 1993. I have heard these three called Mas Oyama's first three *uchi deshi*, although I have only been able to verify that Seiji Kanemura actually lived in the same dormitory where I would live twenty years later. The other two were instructors at *Honbu* before being dispatched to America.

But what kept me on edge was that I also knew all too well where that creativity came from. It had been born of near emotional destruction during an adolescence that had beaten me down so low that I'd not only come to feel dead on the inside, but also to fear that physical death might be close on the heels of the spiritual one.

That was what scared me.

Could pursuing success at all costs push me once again to those limits? Now that Mas Oyama was in the picture, would it not push me beyond them if the vision started to fail?

Hopefully it won't come to that, I consoled myself. *With a little luck – and a little support from my friends, Jacques Sandulescu and Masutatsu Oyama! – I should be able to pull it off without having to turn to such desperate means.*

Within moments of receiving Mrs. Watanabe's "*Sosai* might not be in the mood" letter from *Honbu*, I called Jacques and Annie and asked them if I could drive up for the weekend to talk to them about what I should do next. "Nathan!" Jacques boomed, "If anybody in all of Kyokushin gives you any problem, an-nee-body, you lemme know. I'll straighten 'em out, understand?"

"Osu!" I said, wondering if that even applied to *Sosai*.

"When are you going to be here?" Jacques asked.

"Osu, I should be there late tonight," I told him.

"Good. Drive safe. Call Annie when you get close and she'll give you directions."

"Osu!" was all I could say, and I left North Carolina indulging in a sense of excitement that nonetheless struck me as dangerous. I was driving to meet the survivor of *Donbas* for the first time since *Sosai* had introduced us – and for the first time knowing what he'd actually been through – and if *Sosai* was indeed teetering, I figured there was no better person on the planet to help ensure that he teetered the right way.

There was only one way to find out.

* * *

I was already up and dressed the next morning in Jacques' second apartment when I heard his door slam. In two small apartments side by side, Jacques and Annie had an assortment of what turned out to be SEVEN monstrous cats. One of the three on my side sat bolt upright and stared at me like an alley cat ready to fight for the small piece of real estate in which he'd finally found a home, and it occurred to me that if the neighboring apartment doors, which didn't quite fit in their frames after fifty years of settling, were not kept closed, the cats would probably wonder off. I was standing a moment later when Jacques turned the key in the lock of my door and walked in wearing a red Hawaiian print shirt, no shoes, and a pair of boxer shorts.

"Osu!" I bowed in the Japanese fashion.

"OSU," Jacques growled as he scooped up one of the cats. "You sleep O.K.?" he asked.

"Osu!" I responded.

"Hey, Nathan. Don't say *Osu!* to me all the time. Sit down! YOU'RE MY FRIEND. Call me JACQUES!"

"Osu!" I said, not knowing how else to respond. Behind me on the wall was a massive framed photograph of my teacher Mas Oyama. It was signed by him in bold permanent marker, and the inscription read "To my best friend, Jacques and Annie, 1976."

"Relax!" Jacques said, "Don't be so nervous!"

"Osu!" I said. I could feel Sosai's eyes burning through me. Jacques had ducked and rolled his shoulders forward to enter the apartment as I might have had to step through a miniature door on a playground.

"Are you hungry?" he asked as he brushed away a small gathering of Manhattan cockroaches and poured more food than a large dog would eat into the cat bowl.

"Osu. I could eat," I answered.

"Wait here. I'll bring some food."

"Osu!" I said, and he slammed the door behind him. A second later, again, SLAM! I heard his apartment door close. I only had enough time to say good morning to the one of the giant cats I could actually approach before Jacques came back. SLAM!, his door, and SLAM!, mine.

"Can you cook?" Jacques asked.

"Osu . . . actually, I have to," I said, "I manage a café, and I have to cook almost every day."

"GOOD!" Jacques boomed with a twinkle in his eye. "Everybody should know how to cook!" Jacques handed me a badly mangled ounce or so of butter that he held between his thumb and forefinger by the twisted wrapper the way one might hold a dead fly by its wings. He positioned his

The most painful of the photographs lost to ownership issues was a scan of the actual image of Mas Oyama that hung in Jacques's dining room. *Sosai* had inscribed it, "To my best friend, Jacques and Annie, 1976." This one, substituted, shows Mas Oyama in front of Niagara Falls in 1992 during the weekend of the Rochester tournament. Luckily, Kobayashi Yo wasn't the only photographer taking pictures that day. This one is by Michael Monaco's staff photographer.

other hand, which was clenched into a fist, palm down over the counter. When he opened his hand and removed it, four eggs magically appeared. Four eggs in one fist! "Here, cook these," he said. "What do you cook in your restaurant?"

"Eggs, actually . . . eggs, bacon, ham and hamburgers," I answered. "It's a fast-food sandwich shop for the students at Davidson.

We make everything to order. It's not that bad . . ."

"Do you like fried chicken?" Jacques asked as he lit a gas burner on the stove and discarded the wooden match.

"Osu," I said.

"Good. Tonight, I'll cook fried chicken . . . Do you want bagels?"

"Osu." I said, feeling a bit awkward for lack of a good English word to use in place of the "*Itadakimasu!*" I would have used in Japan,[45] and wondering where a New Yorker from Transylvania had learned to cook fried chicken.

"Good. Wait here."

"Osu!" I stood up again as he went out. "OSU," Jacques growled into the stairway, and SLAM! I began melting the butter in a frying pan.

A few minutes later, I'd finished cooking the eggs, put them on a plate, and sat down at the table in front of four toasted bagels and a purring cat. "Osu!" I stood when Jacques entered again.

"I brought you some coffee," he said. He handed me a four-cup glass measuring cup filled to the four-and-a-half-cup brim with thick black steaming liquid.

This guy's a true giant! I thought. *Only a giant would serve a breakfast like this one!*

Jacques sat down and devoured half a New York bagel in one chomp. He was tall enough sitting down that I felt like I was looking up into the eyes of someone standing on the other side of the table.

"I wanted to talk to you about the book," I said.

"Just say the word," Jacques said. "What can I do for you?" His eyes had become deadly serious.

"I finally got this letter back from Tokyo." I pulled Mrs. Watanabe's

---

[45] "I humbly receive your offering" is actually a far more standard expression in the highly polite Japanese language than a non-Japanese might think upon hearing its translation. It's used like "thank you" any time one receives food from a senior person. There are a handful of Japanese expressions that don't exist in English that English speakers who spend some significant time there tend to miss dearly upon returning to their English-speaking countries.

letter out of the stack of papers on the chair and handed it to him with two hands. He read it in a glance.

"What kind of answer is that? *Sosai* might not be in the mood? This lady needs to tie him down and ask him the question!" Jacques exclaimed. "Hey, Nathan!"

"Osu!" I responded, thinking, *Oh-oh, here it comes.*

"MAKE THE BOOK! I told you, youthful energy is priceless. If anybody gets in your way, they just need to be straightened out. All you have to do is tell me, and I'll take care of it. Do you understand?"

"Osu!" I said. "But what if *Sosai* doesn't support it?"

"Don't worry. *Sosai* will support it."

"Osu," I said incredulously, wondering if that meant that I should just proceed.

I had come all the way from North Carolina to ask for Jacques' opinion on *Sosai's* letter, and in thirty measly seconds I had fulfilled the entire purpose of my trip. No discussion. "MAKE THE BOOK!" That was it. With Jacques, too, there was no *but* in *Osu!*

Unresolved but not wanting to look weak, I changed the subject and asked Jacques how he first met *Sosai*. His answer wasn't at all what I had expected.

We don't have any pictures from my earliest trips to Shihan Jacques and Annie's Greenwich Village apartment. This one was taken there nine years later.

"A friend of mine played the guitar here in the Village," Jacques explained. "He showed me *Sosai's* book, *What is Karate?* This guy Augustine wrote a letter to *Kancho* in Tokyo – he was called *Kancho* then – and found out that he was actually planning to come to New York. Augustine asked me if I wanted to come with him to meet him."

Jacques rolled his eyes toward the ceiling and made a pleading, two-handed, palms-turned-up gesture that said, "Why such a stupid question?"

"So I said to him," he went on, "'You crazy bastard! Of course I want to meet him!' You see pictures of this guy in his book smashing bricks with his bare hands and chopping the horns off bulls. He's the strongest karate man in the world!

"We met him on a Sunday afternoon in the lobby of the New Yorker Hotel. I saw him sittin' there: He was wearing dark sunglasses, but I could tell by the way he sat that this was the same guy that I had read about . . . that had spent two years alone on top of a mountain practicing karate. In his book, he wrote that when he came down from the mountain he punched a telephone pole, leaving knuckle-shaped dents in it. The wires swung back and forth, and he knew he was the strongest man in the world. And he set out to prove it.

"We had dinner in Chinatown that night, and the next day we started training: six hours a day for six months. There was nothing like that training! That was when I learned the importance of repetition. We did every technique over and over . . .

"Before *Sosai* went back to Japan, he did a show at the Garden. He broke fifteen boards with his fist and let members of the audience hit his knuckles with a hammer. The audience went crazy, and the next day, the *New York Times* called him the strongest man in the world. Anyway, that's when we became friends. He didn't have any money. I helped him out a little . . . bought him a coat and some food . . ."

Suddenly Jacques stood up. "Hey, Nathan. Did you read *Donbas?*"

"Osu," I said with a sigh, thinking of my own book I was writing.

"Did you like it?"

"Osu." *What kind of question is that coming from the man who wrote it?* I thought. *God, it's amazing!*

"Good. I'll be right back." SLAM!, the door closed behind him.

I sat back down and went to work on the last bagel. One of the cats rubbed across my shin. SLAM! a moment later I heard Jacques' apartment door, and he came back in and handed me an inch-thick stapled stack of legal-sized paper.

"This is *Hunger's Rogues*," he said, "the next book after *Donbas*. What time are you going home tomorrow?"

"Osu, probably around eleven. It's a long drive back to North Carolina."

I was thumbing through the pages of Jacques' second book. Each legal page had two facing photocopied pages of text on it. Apparently it was out of print too, and even they didn't have an original copy. The entire book was longer than three hundred pages.

"Good. You can read this before you go home."

"Osu!" I said, suddenly dismayed at the task I'd been assigned. I had twenty-four hours to read the book, and my eyelids were already heavy from the long drive and the sounds of the nonstop Greenwich Village night. I realize today that if I hadn't had my *uchi deshi* experience in Japan, I wouldn't have taken his assignment literally. I was probably the only 22-year-old American alive who would visit someone's home and then not sleep in order to read, cover to cover, the book that his host ordered him to read upon arrival.

Jacques started to leave, but he turned back and said, "Hey, Nathan, Annie and I go to the health club at two to train. Did you bring your *dogi*?"

"Osu," I said.

"Good. We'll come get you before two."

"Osu," I said, and "Osu!" again as he stepped out.

"OSU," he growled, and I had a sense that the pit from which he conjured that one syllable was deeper even than the five-story stairwell that echoed it. I waited for the second slam. I was still standing, feeling the weight of the pages, and it came: SLAM!, and I sat back down at the table and got to work.

Hunger's Rogues picks up where *Donbas* leaves off. Again it describes a portion of post-World War II European history with which most people are unacquainted. Instead of being in a prison camp in Russia, Jacques was in a DP (displaced persons) camp in West Germany. It wasn't safe to go back to Romania, so he was stranded along with thousands of others in a foreign country, a country that was in ruins, and a country under occupation at that. These people, refugees really, were packed into fenced-in camps, only different from prison camps in that "DPs" could check in and out with the guards at the gate whenever they wanted to come and go.

Like *Donbas*, *Hunger's Rogues* is a story of survival. Due to the economic chaos that followed the war, German currency was worthless. In an attempt to feed its people, the occupation government issued everyone, citizens and DPs alike, ration cards that could be exchanged for portions of bread, butter, potatoes, cabbage, and other staple necessities. Unfortunately, it wasn't ever enough, especially not for the DPs, and certainly not for the six-foot-three Jacques, who was making up for two years on slave labor rations of wormy bread and gruel.

The result for Europe was a thriving black market. Commodities such as sugar, coffee, and meat were used instead of money. Virtually anything was obtainable for the right price. Interestingly, the cigarette, especially the American cigarette, was the most stable and therefore the most valuable form of "currency." Cigarettes were both hard to get and one of the very few indulgences available to people who had lost almost everything.

It was in this world, the black market of postwar Europe, that Jacques had adventures you'd have to read about to believe. At one point, Jacques teamed up with one of his German friends and a retired Russian officer and drove a canvas-covered military truck illegally some 2000 miles into Bulgaria, to buy cigarettes at a plant behind the Iron Curtain where they were abundant and cheap. The three million cigarettes they bought for a sack full of black-market gold watches were worth a fortune in western Europe. They packed the cigarettes into empty fifty-five-gallon fuel barrels: a layer of cigarettes (loose, no packages) and then a sheet of thick paper, another layer of cigarettes, another of paper, until ten barrels were filled. The trio then turned around and drove all the way back through Germany into France, where they knew they could offload their cargo easily for French francs, one of the few forms of cash still relatively stable in Europe. They sold the cigarettes to Algerian black marketeers in Paris for more money than any of them had ever seen, and they were in the midst of a celebration in the finest hotel in Paris when they received a startling tip from an unexpected visitor. It seems that the barrels in which they packed the cigarettes had had enough of a trace of gasoline in them that their cigarettes had been contaminated. Everyone who smoked them became violently ill.

Needless to say, the Algerian black marketeers were out for blood! But that wasn't the full extent of their troubles. When the Algerians learned that their cigarettes were worthless, they dumped them on the market, instantly reducing the value of the black market cigarette to zero. Nobody would buy cigarettes. Nobody would take them in trade. Not only were these Algerian black marketeers gunning for Jacques and his companions, therefore, but so was every criminal, mobster and black marketeer in Paris who had based his fortune on the cigarette. Watching the road behind them over their shoulders, Jacques and his companions fled back to Germany.

Ironically, the safest possible place for Jacques was back inside his DP camp. After all, the camp had guards, and strangers were not allowed inside.

That afternoon at two, I joined Jacques and Annie for their regular workout. I was impressed. Jacques was sixty-five years old, and Annie was no teenager. I, on the other hand, had been a student for two years in the most rigorous karate training program in the world, and these two worked me to death! Like *Sosai* when I knew him, Jacques didn't kick much anymore. — When he was a kid, his legs had been crushed in a coal mine cave-in, for Heaven's sake! — But, also like *Sosai*, when Jacques threw a punch, the mere sight of it was enough to make you cower. Tiny little Annie, on the other hand, threw head-level kicks that I wouldn't want to get hit with. When we trained together, Jacques led the count. He was sixth *dan*; Annie was first. We worked our way through ninety minutes of *kihon*, *iddo* and *kata* that Jacques had originally been shown by Mas Oyama thirty years earlier, and that they both had refined under the guidance of early Japanese students of Mas Oyama such as Tadashi Nakamura and Shigeru Oyama who came to New York.

I found myself asking, *Why karate? What's the attraction of karate for a man like Jacques? He's huge; he doesn't need it for self-defense.* The answer began to come to me that afternoon after the workout. Jacques and I were in the locker room getting dressed.

"Jacques."

"Eh."

"You know the book that I'm writing . . . my story?"

"Yeah, what about it?"

"Well, after I read *Donbas*, I almost stopped writing it. I was ashamed.

I've always considered my story to be about suffering: the suffering that a young American can go through in today's screwed-up society where people have so much, they can't figure out how to act towards one another. It's about how much karate did for me. But what I call 'suffering' in my book is nothing compared to what you went through. How can my story have any meaning next to yours?"

"Hey, Nathan!" Jacques' eyes drilled me so hard that my own felt beaten out of focus. "Physical hardship can make you dead, but growing up in America can make you WISH YOU WERE DEAD. Write the book! Understand?"

"Osu," I said.

That was when I first saw the heart of the giant. That was when I saw an undeniable sign of the same understanding, spirit, and compassion for *the little people* that I had seen so many times demonstrated by Mas Oyama. And it was this capacity that both Jacques and *Sosai* possessed that made me understand why Jacques must have practiced karate.

I ceased to wonder what karate has for Jacques. I wondered, instead, what everyday life in America could really have for Jacques without karate. Life in America must pale next to life in the Donbas and in postwar Germany. Sure, those times represent great hardship and pain, and life here in America is relatively carefree, but that's just the point:

Life in America is easy.

Before, fighting for survival, those must have been the times life was made of for Jacques!

Those were the times he must remember as when he was truly alive, times when he had no choice but to activate all of his senses, to utilize every scrap of his strength and ingenuity, simply to survive. In order to wrap his own infected, subhuman, condemned legs with wire and bed sheets and drag them, without food or shelter, to safety across hundreds of miles of enemy territory . . . to do all this, Jacques must have had to evoke every morsel of life-energy that he had at his disposal. How can someone who has actually lived the life of a giant, the life of a character in a novel – even if that time was so miserable! – ever really be content with everyday life in the aftermath?

To survive for two years in the Donbas, Jacques must have clenched his fists, gritted his teeth, and demanded that his mind be lord and master of a world that was trying its best to kill him. Jacques demanded that all outward sense, sense that brought to him the potentially devastating agony of life under those conditions, be the obedient servant of his mind's will. Does it not make sense that Jacques would embark on the path of a discipline that teaches that the mind must be lord and master over a body that doesn't always want to do what the mind demands of it, simply to maintain what he at one time learned? [46]

Here in America, would Jacques not find true camaraderie only among those who undertake the quest for truth and understanding through the deliberate pursuit of hardship? Why would Jacques not have unending respect for a man who deliberately exposed himself to two years of isolation and cold and tireless, agonizing physical exercise? Does it not make total sense that Jacques would understand, better than the rest of us, how Mas Oyama, during his mountaintop ordeal, would find the strength to dent telephone poles with his fist and battle bulls barehanded? What do we, the little people, have to offer a giant like Jacques? How can people who have never known suffering ever really understand a man like him? Is this not why Mas Oyama and Jacques became lifelong friends?

In *Donbas*, Jacques writes of his friend Omar:

> One of the Russians asked Omar and me to help set up a supply tent next to the mess hall. They had already started driving in the posts, but the ground was rocky and frozen under the snow. The fourth post would not go in at all. The Russian who was swinging the sledgehammer grew more and more tired with each blow. Then another Russian, a blacksmith, grabbed the sledgehammer and started swinging as hard as he could. At the second blow the handle of the sledgehammer cracked. There was a rail tie from the mine track lying nearby. Omar picked it up and walked to where the fourth post was to be placed. He looked toward me, but I was already walking in his direction. I held the post. Omar swung the heavy tie with anger. With each blow the post went into the ground

---

[46] From Wordsworth's Prelude: *There are in our existence spots of time, / That with distinct pre-eminence retain / A renovating virtue, whence — depressed / By false opinion and contentious thought, / Or aught of heavier or more deadly weight, / In trivial occupations, and the round / Of ordinary intercourse — our minds / Are nourished and invisibly repaired; / A virtue, by which pleasure is enhanced, / That penetrates, enables us to mount, / When high, more high, and lifts us up when fallen. / This efficacious spirit chiefly lurks / Among those passages of life that give / Profoundest knowledge to what point, and how, / The mind is lord and master — outward sense / The obedient servant of her will.*

about half an inch, and after about fifteen blows it was in far enough that I no longer had to hold it for him. I let the post go and stepped back to watch. The Russians had gathered to see the spectacle, too. And it was a real show. Back home, people paid money to see such a performance. The Russians wouldn't even have thought of using the tie; normally it was carried by two men. Yet this giant was using it as a sledgehammer by himself.

For me, to hear Jacques describe someone else as a giant was beyond my comprehension. Jacques described his father similarly:

> I remembered a giant of a man who had shaken his fist at a gathering storm and had me, a small boy, half believing he could stop the rain. Who could put vast amounts of food in his mouth at one time – I loved to watch him eat – working it around with his tongue, the powerful jaw muscles grinding then swallowing with deep grunts of satisfaction, washing the food down with heroic swallows of wine. And suddenly laughing at something that had happened days, weeks, or months ago – laughing till the rafters shook, pounding his fist on the table for the sheer joy of it. I remembered him standing on the station platform, head and shoulders above the crowd of screaming, crying people, visibly fighting back tears, while I stared out of the tiny window of the boxcar that would take me to Russia.

"My father was the only man in the Romanian army who could lift a cannon by the spokes of its wheels," Jacques told me. I thought of Jacques in the Donbas: He and Omar were the only men in the camp who could dump the coal car at the top of the tower all by themselves.

Both Omar and Jacques' father were giants. At least, this is how Jacques remembers them. Sadly, it seems for the most part that men like this live only in the past: Jacques' father and Omar are gone. Jacques, however, like *Sosai*, I realized, remained a giant among giants.

"Osu, *Shihan*," I said in one of our final conversations that weekend. "What's that scar? It looks like a bullet hole." Jacques' apartment was sweltering in the Manhattan summer, and Jacques was sitting there in his boxers like a mountain.

"Oh, that," Jacques said, "That's where a Russian soldier shot me."
"Really? You're kidding?"

"Yeah, but that's another story . . . hey, Nathan, do you have a girlfriend?"

"Osu," I said, marveling at how close the gunshot scar was to the centerline of his chest.

"Is she a nice girl?"

"Osu. She is, she's a very nice girl . . . We were actually fighting just before I came up here."

"What's her name?"

"Osu. Her name is Lissa," I said.

"Hey, Nathan!"

"Osu!" he'd made me jump again.

"DON'T FIGHT with her if she's such a nice girl! What's the matter with you? Life's too short!"

"Osu," I said, wondering if it was really possible just not to. "I'll do the best I can."

PART II

EIGHT

I COULDN'T POSSIBLY do justice to a telling of my return to Kyokushin – and to Mas Oyama! – without broaching the subject of romantic love.

Two women played roles significant enough to demand mention. The first one, Lissa, with whom I shared a short but passionate relationship, is primarily significant because of the way its crushing demise left me emotionally vulnerable to falling in love with the second. To try to tell the story without mention of Helen would be to tell a story so far separated from the truth that I could no longer with a clear conscience call it my own.

I'd always had a penchant for women, although for long periods of my life that penchant far exceeded any success I had getting close to one. When I was still a 17-year-old freshman at Davidson College, eighteen months before I went to Japan for the first time, a 21-year-old senior French literature major I'd been tutoring in physics took me back to her dorm room one evening after a study session in the library and gave me an education of her own. She and I probably only spent four or five months together in all, yet it felt like a lifetime because she was my first, and because I never once slept anywhere but in her bed for the rest of the semester. At the end of the year, she graduated and went on to graduate school at the Sorbonne, and I left Davidson for the University of North Carolina at Chapel Hill to study at least one semester of Japanese before leaving for Japan.

Before that, however, I had endured an excruciatingly long ten years of falling in love with girls when I was a child, and young women when I was a little older, who were always out of reach, since I was cripplingly shy and almost always physically inferior to all those who might have been my competition.

The fracturing of my parents' first attempt at family – the one that produced my brother and me – resulted ultimately in our being bussed back and forth across North Carolina in the name of dividing our time as equally as possible between two households. For several significant years of our childhood they even had us alternating school years between Davidson, where my father remained, and Chapel Hill where my mother had moved in with the man who would later become my stepfather. During the school year, we would spend every other weekend with the parent with whom we were not living, and if we ever lived in one place for more than a year, we would spend that year's summer vacation with the other parent.

The undeniable positive result of my being bounced back and forth like a tennis ball was that I always felt close to both of my parents. They were desperately afraid that the breakup of my childhood home would rob me of the stability of what *home* was meant to be, and they compensated individually by making sure that I never felt a want of parental attention. The greatest negative result, however – and for me it was crushingly negative – was that I never integrated socially with the new groups of peers into which I was thrown after each migration.

My classmates went to the same schools and played the same weekend games and attended the same summer activities for the entirety of their twelve years of public school. I was forever cursed to be the newcomer.

Not only did I suffer the dual disadvantage of being on the one hand a little bit brighter than most – certainly in terms of the artistic creativity that my parents had so encouraged – and, on the other hand, inferior physically – many of the kids a year, and even two years, behind me were bigger – but I was also introduced, year after year, to a new group of classmates as *the new kid who will be joining us this year*. After meeting with my parents and, I can only imagine, being subjected to the full force of their guilt, my teachers would always make a special case of me, and encourage my classmates to include me and make me feel welcome as if I were somehow disadvantaged beyond the reality of my situation.

Admittedly, the tragedy of my public-school experience was partially a side effect of advantages that I wouldn't trade even if I could go back and stamp out the painful loneliness of my inability to fit in. I attended three years of preschool in one that was actually founded by my parents and the parents of two or three of my earliest classmates, in an attempt to educate their children in the way that theory taught that group of ex-hippy college professors would give us the best chances of growing up into well-rounded, enlightened adults. We were kept very close to our teachers, usually no more than ten of us in a class with both a teacher and an assistant teacher. We were introduced to math and reading and writing, but these conventional subjects were never forced upon us as they might have been in public school.

Instead we were taught artistic creativity, freedom of expression, and freedom of emotion. If we exhibited some talent or interest, we were encouraged to pursue it even at the risk of being different. Likewise, if we exhibited some weakness – in my case, athletics and, initially, reading and writing! – we were not muscled into trying to catch up. We were given no religious instruction, and we were not taught to see the world as anyone else told us it was meant to be seen. Instead, our innocent assertions became objects of the greatest praise whenever it became clear that we were looking at the world with our own two eyes, and searching for our own understanding of why things were the way that they were. We were taught to express ourselves openly and freely. If we were sad or hurt, we were not discouraged from crying; if we were angry we were welcome to express our anger rather than stifling it; if we were afraid we were allowed to be, but were gently urged to see if we couldn't overcome whatever it was that scared us.

Once I was moved into public school, it took me some years to figure out that I was supposed to behave in a certain way, and not to behave in other ways, to be accepted. My instinct was to trust and become close to my teachers, and I was slow to learn that most of my peers saw that as an attempt to gain special favor. My classmates saw me pleasing my teachers both because I knew the answers better than most, and because I was closer to being on my teachers' wavelengths than on my peers'. I had been taught to get along with adults, not to try to get away with mischief behind their backs; I was naturally inclined to anticipate what my teachers wanted and give it to them before they asked for it, and I was innocent of any inhibitions against doing so. In the eyes of my peers, however, the favor that I received from my teachers could only mean that I thought I was better than them. Add that to my striking physical inferiority, a rosy-cheeked baby face, and feminine deep-brown eyes that tended to charm the socks off all of my teachers, and the result for me, socially, was devastating.

My childhood came to be characterized by an intense loneliness that increased year by year, until, by the time I was first introduced to karate as an early teenager, I had been spiritually reduced to enough of a shell of a boy that it had resulted in chronic physical illness. The nausea and pain in my stomach was finally diagnosed when I was eighteen as reflux, at a time when doctors were hesitant to prescribe medication because the condition was only then coming to be understood as something more than simple indigestion. In eighth grade I missed forty days of school, and brown-bagged Pepto-Bismol for the rest of it in an effort merely to make it through my days. Ninth grade taught me some balance of having to either manage or endure the pain, but even the next two years of my life after that were characterized by a battle of having to desperately manage what I ate or suffer the consequences.

Early in second grade – when I was just seven – I developed a crush on a little blonde girl named Erin whom I rarely even had the nerve to approach. In my relative isolation, it became easy to dwell on thoughts of her, and since I was too shy to share them with anyone, least of all her, it was only natural that I allowed my longing for her to intensify into something all-encompassing, maybe even more than real love ever could have been. On the very last day of the year – just one year after my parents separated and I started going home one week to one parent's home and the next week to the other's – the teachers at my elementary school hosted a celebration filled with the kinds of games, outdoor art projects, delicious foods, and other such activities that excite children, and in one dance we all stood in a circle and held hands, boy, girl, boy, girl. I broke more than once into the circle to hold this little girl's hand, and she finally asked me innocently, "Why do you keep holding my hand?" I was too shy to respond with anything more than an excuse and a stammer, and I never saw her again, as that day was the last I would spend with that peer group before being whisked away to another one.

The next year, in third grade in Chapel Hill, I repeated the exact trend with a beautiful but somewhat nerdy girl named Emily, who wore glasses and was the constant companion – for the whole year! – of another boy who somehow managed to monopolize her attention. Fourth grade, back in Davidson at yet another school – since for second grade my parents had bussed me to nearby Charlotte – was an especially bleak school year, during which I stood out so far ahead of my peers, particularly in math, that the teacher often excused me from class altogether to work on special projects in the library. The punishment I received from my peers on the playground was particularly brutal. Alternating team selection by class Alpha team captains was especially painful for the regularity with which I was left to be the last pick and even sometimes left out completely if there was an odd number of players. Worse, there wasn't a single girl in my class who attracted my affections, denying me even that excuse to lose myself to daydreaming! Happily, in fifth grade back in Chapel Hill and in yet another peer group, there was Wendy, followed in rapid succession by Jenny in sixth, both of whom I loved nearly all year long with an intensity that finally drove me to confess it to them in small, humiliating ways, reminiscent of getting caught holding Erin's hand during that dance in second grade.

And the trend continued into middle school.

A dark-haired, dark-eyed girl named Jessie was the heartthrob of my eighth grade year. We didn't have any classes together and I rarely spoke to her. In the end I only expressed my love with my eyes, and that probably just enough to confuse her. With Karen in ninth grade, I became fairly good friends – I tutored her in math – but we could never have shared a romantic relationship, as others our age were by then beginning to do, because she stood a full five inches taller that me. I was still the shortest 15-year-old in my class. Middle school was the time when I took the first steps towards ultimately breaking the trend, in that I did share immature and experimental relationships with several girls who were not the ones for whom I was so desperate.

I was literally tortured in high school by a tall blonde named Katy, whose father paid me to teach her math. Yet by this time I was becoming passionate about my karate training, and I took another step towards breaking the trend of falling victim to annual star-crossed loves by almost ceasing to be interested in women at all. Certainly by eleventh grade, I didn't care about anything except training and studying so that I could make it to Mas Oyama's Japan, a drive that continued into my freshman year of college, when Dillon, the aforementioned senior French literature major, became at once the first woman I slept with and the first one I would fall in love with even though I hadn't first loved her from afar.

At UNC in Chapel Hill, I had a couple of other fun but largely meaningless affairs before I left for Japan, and in Japan, as an *uchi deshi*, I didn't cross paths with any women often enough to even notice them, let alone fall in love. I do have a vivid memory of training one night in a class for black- and brown-belt students at *Honbu*, taught by Mas Oyama, to which he brought his 18-year-old daughter, Kikuko. I had spoken with her already once or twice in passing, since she spoke English and had spent some time living in America. I was somewhat amused to realize that for the first time since I'd come to Japan, there was someone in the dojo whom I wanted to impress more than Mas Oyama himself. Another time, one Saturday evening, he brought her to have dinner with us in the dormitory, and Mas Oyama complimented me in front of everyone for the vigor with which I scraped all the edible fruit from the rind of the watermelon he had bought us. I was distinctly more pleased to be complimented by him in front of her than if it had been only Mas Oyama and my *uchi deshi* peers, as it was every other Saturday night.

The sense of liberation I experienced upon returning from Japan resulted in a smattering of largely meaningless romantic flings, until I was back in school full time. I've mentioned how for a short time I became emotionally entangled in a one-sided way with a first cousin, somehow convincing myself in the whirlwind of my newfound freedom that even a relationship largely forbidden by our society could have been possible.

And then, soon afterwards, there was the all-pivotal Lissa.

I was twenty-one when I met her. I walked her home one late night from a weekend party at my girlfriend Sara's house where, as I mentioned earlier, I had sometimes torn myself painfully from the warmest of beds, two hours earlier than I would have had to for class, to go meet my earliest karate students for morning training. Lissa worked for me at the Café. A senior, she was one of the returning students who'd already worked part-time during previous years before I took over the post of night and weekend manager. I'd called her at her parents' home in Atlanta before school even started, just as I'd called all the others, to introduce myself and to schedule student workers to cover the first night and weekend shifts once students began to return.

So Lissa apparently worked for me. I must have known her already for several weeks. Somehow I hadn't noticed her, though, until that night at the party. She looked at me with a pair of deep green eyes that made me inadvertently stop in my tracks, straighten my spine, and redistribute my body weight so that each of my legs supported exactly half of it. Without being aware that I took a deep breath, I realized that it was because of her that I'd taken it, and when it was time to go I offered to walk her home.

I was a long-time worshipper by then – in a bit of a desperate way – of the beauty and majesty of the natural world. It had probably begun as an escape from the darkest period of my life, when circumstances beyond my control pounded me down towards a feeling of emptiness and despair. Starting in my thirteenth year, the resultant physical illness weakened me day by day. Everything that I ate or drank burned my stomach in a way that made my head spin; I'd lose balance, and it would hurt to move. Finally I learned to cope, but I was plagued by having to cope *or else* for four more years. Perhaps my excessive, sentimental appreciation for life and the world in which we live was a byproduct.

Perhaps I needed something that beautiful to hold on to.

My father was raised by his parents to be a preacher. He attended seminary at Princeton to become a Presbyterian minister and worked in an American church in Paris for a year before deciding that it was more his parents' calling for him than anything that came from within. He went on from there to the opposite extreme and studied art and art history at UNC–Chapel Hill, and it was at the start of his subsequent decade as artist-scholar that I was born, in the first year after he became a professor at Davidson. As a result, I never had even a moment of Christian education. I am grateful that my parents encouraged me as a child to see the world as I saw it, to ask questions and seek the answers to them with my own experience and my own experimentation, rather than telling me that I was supposed to see the world in any particular way. I was thus spared having to ever see the world through the Christian filter of *God made this, God made that*, and I can unequivocally state that I have never entertained even a moment's belief in what has always seemed to me so man-made a concept as the Christian God.

It was perhaps out of desperation, therefore, that in the throes of my struggle to escape from the relentless nausea and vertigo of my mid-teenage years I came to behold the world, and life itself, in a way that bordered on worship. For me there was no divinity about it. There weren't spirits in the birds and stones and trees, like there were for the American Indians or for the Japanese in the Shinto tradition. Nevertheless, I came to behold the birds, and the stones, and the trees, and above all else the air and the sea and the sky, as so incredibly beautiful that they might as well have been divine. Desperate for some reason to want to live intensely enough to drag myself out of my despair, I began a practice — at the North Carolina coast in front of crashing waves, or on the peaks of Grandfather Mountain surrounded by so much of the world all at once — that I would carry forward into my adult life.

The routine was first and foremost *to notice* the natural impulse to be moved by beauty, to catch the impulse before the concerns of life could trample it, and to pause to revel in it, to savor it, before letting it get away. The pause and the reveling always took the same form. I would allow the scene, or the sound — or the scent! — to stop me in my tracks, I'd shift the balance of my weight to both feet, straighten my spine, and behold that which had moved me one more time before taking in a deep breath of the world around me. That breath came to embody life for me. Starting at the very bottom of my lungs like Master Choi had taught me, I would draw it in slowly and steadily, a single inhale, until my chest swelled to capacity. When it was time, I'd let it go again in a long steady exhale like it was the most precious substance on earth, the embodiment of the heart-stopping beauty both of the natural world and of life, which for me, became one and the same.

Remember that I was raised to be a particularly sentimental child, and I came almost religiously to indulge in an emotional response to any scene that moved me to an awe-filled realization of how beautiful life was, a response so powerful that it would take my next breath away. I didn't have to, I suppose, but I often allowed it to stagger me. I allowed myself to be blown away. I allowed my head to spin momentarily with the additional blast of oxygen brought in by the inhale, and I associated that head-spinning euphoria with the emotional response to beauty as much as with its physiological cause. I allowed myself to feel the impact in my eyes, which would inevitably burn in the start of the tear reflex. I'd stand in a wide-open area where there was as much of the sky available to me as possible, take my single rejuvenating breath of life, my eyes would fill with tears, and sometimes, when I was alone, one would even break free and tickle its way down my cheek. That sensation, too, I came to associate with the power and beauty of this world in which we live.

"My god, it's so unbelievably beautiful!" I'd whisper to myself, understanding completely then how earlier people without the benefit of scientific understanding came to deify various elements of the natural world.

My god, I can see how people come to believe there is a God!

And with that, I'd wipe the tear from my chin and continue about my business, usually no more than a handful of seconds since I'd paused to revel in the moment for the duration of that single deep breath. I'd go about my business feeling stronger than I had moments before.

I have vivid memories of anticipating the agony of my morning trainings in Japan, and deliberately dispelling the fear with single deep breaths of the Ikebukuro morning. To this day, when I walk past the park at *Sosai's Honbu* where we trained every morning, it is first and foremost the scent of it that blows me away, and brings it all back, the virtual lifetime that I lived there all compressed into less than two years. It's the scent of the place that brings it all back because it was the scent with which I filled my lungs, sometimes every single morning, to come to grips with the fact that I was finally actually in Japan and, more than that, to convince myself that I'd be able to survive it.

The eyes are amazing instruments, not just because they bring us sight, but also because they bring us communication on a level beyond words. Scientific evidence suggests that even as humans, the most developed mammals on Earth, we too can smell each other's emotion. Like beasts far more wild than ourselves, we can smell sexual attraction, we can smell fear, and we can smell aggression. I know beyond a shadow of a doubt that in each other's eyes, we can see these things as well. And with practice we can see even more.

I've written of Master Choi's eyes, and Mas Oyama's. Next to my worship of life and nature, the second most beautiful discovery of my adolescence was love, and having lost it momentarily at home – having some degree of love for oneself is certainly a prerequisite to being able to feel love of, and for, others! – I have no doubt that I saw it for the first time again in the eyes of my first karate teacher, Mas Oyama's nephew, Master Choi.

There is a related, though different, kind of communication that happens within the gaze of lovers, just as there's a third that occurs within the gaze of combatants. There is no question that in the majority of the fights I fought at *Honbu*, I was beaten. I did have some heroic moments as well, however, and there was one in particular in which I humiliated an obnoxious but dangerous *sempai* of mine in *kumite* in front of *Sosai* by beating both of his eyes into purple, swollen slits with *jodan mawashi geri*[47]

---

[47] High roundhouse kicks.

that stopped just short of knocking him out. I'll tell the story later in more detail – since I have so few victorious moments to recount, I might as well get all the mileage I can out of the few that I have! – but I have no doubt that the way I used my eyes during that bout is what won it for me.

Not every fighter is susceptible. Or maybe it's that I never learned how to see into just anyone so that I might defeat them like I defeated my *sempai* that day. *Sosai* had been so angry with me when I gave in to my curiosity one morning in Japan and looked *into him* in a way that crossed a barrier I should never have crossed. But just as in *kumite* there are opponents who are vulnerable to a certain kind of gaze, I have also encountered women into whom I've been able to look, and share something quite the opposite of that which I've used on occasion to so unnerve my opponents.

One afternoon in 1995 or 96 when I was writing alone in a coffee shop near Kangnam Station in Seoul, a young Korean woman who passed by the window outside at once stunned and flattered me by not only exchanging with me a spontaneous, unspoken and purely optical dialogue, but also confirming in a very clear way, plain for all to see, that the communication had indeed occurred.

"Wow, you're really beautiful, aren't you?" I told her inadvertently within my glance the moment our eyes met through the glass. "Why, thank you very much," her eyes said in return, as she actually physically bowed ever so slightly and embarrassed herself by reflexively positioning her mouth to utter the first syllable of *Kamsahapnida!* [48] just as she disappeared from view. She hadn't broken her stride, and our eyes just met for that millisecond, but when I turned in my chair to watch her go, I noticed that she'd lightened her step. She was truly beautiful, and like most truly beautiful women, she had been touched by the compliment.

My cousin, the one with whom I momentarily became infatuated during that period of my life *fresh out of the monastery* in Japan, had similar eyes. I'd loved her all my life, of course. She was my cousin! My parents and hers were not close, however, and our paths had crossed only a half dozen times in our lives before they crossed for the first time as adults without our parents present when we were both twenty. In my newfound hunger to savor life, I could not conceal the fact that for the past three of the six times our families had brought us together, I had entertained feelings of being in love with her.

---

[48] "Thank you" in Korean.

She was stunningly beautiful, she was brilliant, she was graduating that year with a degree in English literature, she was my type. We spent twenty-four hours together in South Carolina; her brother, a first-year Davidson student, was present, as were a handful of her friends, and the six or seven of us all shared a room that night, safely camped out together on the sofas and on the floor. But it was on the walk that she and I took alone that evening that an exchange occurred that would cross the bounds of propriety in our day and age, here in Christian America.

We walked hand in hand and then made the mistake of stopping to look into each other's eyes. "My god, you're so incredibly beautiful," I told her. Her eyes and mine tripped into one another, she kissed me, the sexual tension that I had tried and failed to stifle all afternoon broke free, and I reciprocated without inhibition. I feel certain to this day that an optical communication occurred, and that it was the only reason why she dropped her guard and made a choice that *for her* was so far out of character. "I love you like life, Kristen, and my god, do I love life!" would have been the subtitle for the scene of that silent movie. It was 100% pure, 100% genuine, and 100% from the heart, and I am sure that's why she let me kiss her.

I have tried to figure out what came over me during that month or two when I was infatuated with a first cousin of mine who almost immediately came to her senses, stamped her foot, and went back to walking the straight line that she's always otherwise walked. I was definitely attracted to her physically, but I'm also certain that, far more than that, I was drawn to her because she was family. It was as if she became for me the embodiment of the family I was just then in the throes of losing. During that very year, I was on the cusp of finally turning away myself after a decade of being step-by-step abandoned by my own parents. As clear as it was that I would eventually have to turn my back and move on to escape the unrelenting heartbreak of being thrown away, how desperate I must have been to hold on!

After my father divorced Martha when I was eleven, he made it impossible for me to see her, and I didn't until I became a freshman at Davidson and tracked her down when I was seventeen. She and my father came to represent family for me after my first one dissolved, and when my father left Martha, not only was she torn from my life abruptly, she was also torn from it entirely. My biological mother, to whom I've devoted very few words, was married from the time I was eight until I was sixteen to a man in Chapel Hill who had six daughters. They were my stepsisters for those seven years of my life, and we spent holidays together, vacations together, and dinner together every night for years on end. After some years of struggling to integrate, I came to love them too. More than that, I came to depend on them to complete my picture of what functional family was meant to be.

I suppose my mother couldn't have known that I'd inherit that part of my father's personality that would leave me so ill-equipped to maintain ties with my stepsisters after her own midlife crisis resulted in her leaving my stepfather and, in one fell swoop, assuring that my stepsisters and I would never again come home to the same house.

So not only was it Martha – the surrogate mother that had come in my world to epitomize family – but also no less than six sisters who were there one day and gone the next. All that had happened already by the time Kristen's and my paths crossed so inappropriately when we were twenty, and it wouldn't take Sigmund Freud to point out that I'd fallen in love with the only remaining female member of my family just as I was about to lose the last shred of it!

I've described that brief era of my life as hedonistic, and there have certainly been other occasions in my life when I've pursued women purely for sexual gratification. But in my defense, I don't even tend to be physically attracted to women I don't respect. Unlike other college boys whose paths I crossed during the seven long years it took me to finally graduate, I was never one to pick up drunken girls passed out on sofas towards the end of fraternity parties. Sara was brilliant, Kristen was brilliant, Lissa was brilliant, Dillon was off the charts. It's important to know that I pursued this type of woman – even when my top priority was to catch up to and make love to one or two of them – because of their intellect, because of their compassion, because of their capacity to love, and because I respected them for who they were.

I have no doubt that the optical communication that I would resume a year later with Lissa – and multiply in her case tenfold! – began in the throes of that brief love affair with my first cousin. But it was Master Choi, and his uncle Mas Oyama, who had shown me the way. They were the ones who taught me to look into people's eyes and to believe that there was something all-important to be found there. Lissa and I fell into each other's eyes from the first moment we took a second glance at each other. We fell in a second time in the doorway to her dormitory twenty minutes later. It was all both of us could do some minutes after that to pry ourselves out of each other's arms in an attempt to catch our breath and say good night. The passion that I found there rocked my world in a way that it had never before been rocked. Indeed, if my reaction to Lissa that night runs contrary to the tough-guy karate fighter image, then so be it! I have no choice but to tell it.

I got halfway down the hill from Duke Dorm, where Lissa lived, on my way back to my room – where within the previous week I'd shared a night with Sara – and a cool October breeze whipped past. I shivered, crossed my arms, and paused to look up at the moonlit sky.

I was moved and, in accordance with my habit, I stopped.

I shifted my balance to two feet, rocked my head back, closed my eyes, and drew in a long, deep breath of life.

There were wispy white bands of mist that night, which rushed past the moon on a breeze that ran perpendicular to the breeze at ground level. Somehow the moon fought its way through the clouds with all of its glory, and the entire sky glowed. Its aura crashed down on me with a weight that I suddenly could not withstand, and with a sudden jolt my stomach muscles locked, pulling my forehead towards the ground. The concrete cut into the knuckles of my left hand, my other shot out instinctively to catch my fall, and the palm of it ground into the sidewalk. For a handful of moments I couldn't see and I couldn't breathe. I'd allowed my eyeballs to roll upwards into the backs of my eyelids, and there they quivered as I struggled to bring them back into line with my skull.

"Stop it!" I growled, and fought my way back to my feet. My stomach muscles relaxed, and with the next inhale, my eyes dropped back down to let the moonlit scene in.

Balance returned.

What in hell was that? I scolded myself angrily as I started back down the hill, wiping a tear from my cheek. *Have a little fucking dignity, will you!*

But Jesus, what the hell was it?

It started with the moon.

Innocently, I looked up again – and again I was overcome. It was all I could do to stagger the rest of the way down the hill like a drunk. *My god, it's so unbelievably beautiful, this life, this world!*

My god, what did that woman do to me?

Moonlight through Trees, borrowed from an earlier period of my life when I was experimenting with Zen and Japanese ink painting (and, more specifically, with Zen mindlessness, and the search for how one might mindlessly — and therefore expertly — realize an inner image through art). This was painted when I was 18 and still six months away from going to Japan for the first time. Moments earlier, I was moved by this exact image as I passed a moonlit forest.

NINE

IT WASN'T THAT I LOVED LISSA that made our relationship such a passionate one. It was that I loved her without inhibition.

She fit the bill perfectly: just like all the women I had loved in my life from afar, she was unattainable. She was engaged to be married to a Davidson alum who had graduated the year before and moved to Texas for graduate school. She was not only unavailable, therefore, she was also forbidden, and the combination echoed to a T the degree to which my lifetime's worth of star-crossed loves had been so painfully out of reach. Yet somehow, this time, when I looked into Lissa's eyes, I watched her resolve crumble – she was mine because she loved me too! – and I came to love her without inhibition.

Through Lissa, I would come to realize that I'd never let myself go to unadulterated romantic love before. The women with whom I'd shared relationships – and there were several – I would not let get close to me beyond a certain point. With Dillon I'd come the closest. I most certainly loved her, but in the name of karate and my pursuit of becoming the first American to complete Mas Oyama's *uchi deshi* program, I'd always held a part of me back. As a freshman at Davidson, I was still deep in the throes of my initial remaking of self through karate training and study, and I considered falling in love to be a threat to achieving all that I hoped to achieve. "Don't love me, Dillon," I told her when I was just seventeen. "I'm only going to leave you. My life will take me to Japan and once I'm there, I'll need every scrap of energy, every ounce of creativity I have. If you love me, I'll only hurt you in the end."

It wasn't until I was actually in Japan that I came to love Dillon without inhibition. For weeks of nights on end, sleeping alone in Mas

Oyama's dormitory, I dreamt of the warmth and closeness I'd come to associate with her. I'd reach out for her in my sleep, and open my eyes with a start, only to curl back into myself, aching with the realization that she wasn't there. Lissa came into my world engaged and therefore forbidden. I wasn't allowed to have her. Yet, in my newfound freedom, it was all mine, was it not, all that life had to offer, mine then for the taking?

I was desperately overcommitted that first year back at Davidson — more classes than I was meant to take, the beginnings of the *Budo Karate Illustrated* project, the karate classes that I taught every day, and my full-time job at the Café. But now I had found the one extracurricular activity that would come to be equal in its enormity to all the rest.

Lissa.

I have a record of the entire relationship. It's what's left of a book in which I at first, and then Lissa and I together, glued scraps of the evidence of the life we shared. Glued to one page are the dry, crumbled fragments of leaves from the leaf pile that we jumped in, playing for just those few moments like kids the day after we realized what we'd found in each other. Glued to another are the petals from the rose to which I taped an address label and a stamp, and asked the mailman to put it in her mailbox, unwrapped, so it would be there for her when she came in with her key. There's the label of the tequila bottle we drank from together at Martha's house during the summer that we lived there, and the ticket stubs to the movies, plays, and concerts we went to, all marked with the dates that we went to them. There are matchbooks from the restaurants where we ate, paper targets we shot at in the woods with the .22 on a study break, and a photograph of us together on the way back from Grandfather Mountain in the snow. There are the notes we left to let each other know when we'd be back from the library, or that I'd be out late closing the Café; the grocery list in Martha's unmistakable handwriting when she sent us to the store to get something for dinner the week that her father died; and no less than eight tear-soaked fragments of the tissues that scattered the floor around Lissa's chair the night she struggled for hours on the phone to know what to tell Bryan, her fiancé in Texas, while I read Chaucer in the next room.

In our first week, we sat on the grass in a little-traveled area of campus, holding one another, our knees tucked, Lissa leaning on the fronts of my thighs, me leaning on the fronts of hers. We spent those two hours studying each other's eyes. Barely blinking, I told her the entire story of the book I was writing, the saga of Master Choi and his prodigal student Nathan Ligo who went to Japan to study under his legendary uncle Mas Oyama. She was awed by the story the way I'd always wished Dr. Abbott would be when he read my chapters, and I know now that the difference was in the way we looked at one another. I hadn't yet learned to record the emotion on paper, but as I told the story in person without inhibition, Lissa read the rest in my eyes. Struggling to write the story in the years to come, I'd lament the fact that I didn't have a tape recorder that day because I knew I'd never told it so successfully. Ultimately I realized that it wouldn't have made any difference: The success of the telling wasn't in the spoken word.

Lissa accused me of "Ninja mind games" for the way that I managed to get inside her with my eyes. "You've got me in an eye-lock again," she'd say. "How do you look into me like that?" she'd ask me another time, flabbergasted. "What are you doing? How do you get inside me like that? Why can't I stop letting you?"

"It's because I love you," I told her. She was still, that day, resisting me, still struggling to hold on to Bryan.

Martha's father, Cliff, died the day Lissa and I jumped in the leaf pile, our first day together. He was eighty-nine and one of the freest souls I'd ever met. Although I remembered him telling me bedtime stories when I was a child, and though he awed me with his joviality whenever our paths crossed, he and I were no longer particularly close, as I'd been separated from Martha for so many years. My heart ripped open nevertheless when I heard that he'd died, and I rushed immediately to find Martha. I knew how hard it would hit her, Cliff's only daughter, his protégé in savoring life, and I loved Martha like life.

Somehow sadness isn't the first thing I feel when people die – not yet, anyway. Death seems to me to be such a natural thing. People die, and once they do they don't feel any more pain. Isn't it selfish of us to feel sorry for ourselves for the loss of them? I could imagine Cliff's belly shaking with laughter as he said, "Don't sit around moping! Go live!" It was that "Go live" that made me run to Martha because I loved her. It was that "Go live" that made me bring Lissa with me on what became our first date: the funeral and wake of Martha's father.

Martha's mother was Catholic, and for her we held the service in a Catholic church. I held Martha's hand. She held her mother's. I was a bit mortified that my father showed up and sat in one of the back rows, the ex-son-in-law from a decade earlier who'd been loved like a son by Cliff, but who'd then abandoned not only Martha and her folks, but also virtually all of the friends that had been his, too, during the years that they'd been married. At the wake in the forest we remembered Cliff by drinking potent drink, eating delicious food, and dancing like bohemians into the wee hours of the morning. Lissa and I spent that night together in one of the guest beds in the studio, fully clothed under the blankets, with no choice but to hold each other for how cold it was that October without heat.

Lissa and I were already building the foundation for becoming the legends of *carpe diem* that we would become – at least in our own minds – over the months that followed. Davidson students self-schedule their exams during a one-week period at the end of each semester. Three nights into that week, without a single exam taken yet, I planned a midnight study break with Lissa to drive into Charlotte in search of one of North Carolina's last Krispy Kreme doughnut shops. We were spending most of our nights together by then, but we'd tear ourselves apart and challenge ourselves to stay in opposite corners of the campus for two-, three-, or four-hour blocks, so that we could concentrate enough on studying to actually have a chance of passing our courses.

"Come rescue me," Lissa had said, ". . . in a couple hours. Shall we say around midnight?"

"What are we going to do?"

"I don't know," she said. "Let's go for a drive. Let's get off campus. I suppose we should find something to eat, if we're not going to sleep again tonight."

By then I had pages of Whitman, pages of Emerson, and pages of Poe torn from my textbooks and pasted to the condensation on the walls of one of Duke Dorm's shower stalls. The dormitories had an endless supply of hot water, and standing under the shower in the wee hours of the morning kept me alert as I read the writing on the walls. Afterwards I'd lay the pages out on the tiled floor to dry before consulting my notes and tearing out a few more pages. In this way I fought, without sleep, to get myself where I needed to be for my first exam the next day. Lissa and I had plans to drive home to her parents' house in Atlanta as soon as our exams were finished. We wanted to get them over with as soon as possible.

On the way back from Charlotte at one A.M. – my car didn't have heat, either – Lissa huddled next to me, wrapped in a blanket, and told me she didn't want to go back to school.

"But what about our exams?" I asked.

"I know," she said, "I just don't want to go back yet."

"What do you want to do?"

"I want to play in the snow . . . I want to make snow angels."

"But there's no snow," I said.

"Well," in frustration, "let's find some!"

"We could drive to the mountains," I said. "There'll be snow on the Blue Ridge Parkway."

"Okay," she said. "Let's go."

"Are you serious? It'll take all night!"

"We only live once," she said.

I laughed to myself – at Lissa's turning the tables on me! – and when we reached the Davidson exit, I kept on driving.

Boone, the home of North Carolina's Appalachian State University, was silent and covered in a three-inch dusting of fresh snow as we drifted into town after three A.M. The streets were empty; my car's tracks were the only ones on the main square. Lissa and I took turns flopped out on our backs in the snow, flapping our arms and legs in slow motion to leave the impression of skirted, winged angels. We clambered carefully to our feet so as not to disturb our creations, and we argued over who made the better snow angel.

I drove Lissa past Grandfather Mountain in search of a view, and shivered because in the moonlight I could see the torrents of windblown snow swirling past her peaks. In silence I thought of Mas Oyama's mountain training and of a life-changing night I'd spent shivering alone on that ridge near the summit on my eighteenth birthday. The terrible beauty of that image took my breath away because I could still see myself in it.

My god, I thought to myself, *have I really escaped after all?*

The gates to the Parkway were closed due to the snow, but we parked anyway, and walked several hundred yards towards the portion of that ridgeline highway that's cantilevered out over the valley below. The snow was biting our faces then, the wind fought its way through the clothing that we'd chosen merely to go out for doughnuts, and we paused to look off into the moonlit foothills to the east.

"There's a photograph up at the visitor's center that Hugh Morton[49] took of the Charlotte skyline from the peak up there with a telephoto lens," I said.

"You mean we can see Charlotte from here?"

"On a clear day, with a telescope we could probably see the Chambers dome."[50]

"Where do you think it is?" Lissa asked, peering off into the darkness.

"I don't know for sure," I said. "I suppose that glow on the horizon is Charlotte. That streak's probably the highway we came in on. See it?"

"Oh yeah," she said. "It's funny to see stars below us like that, rather than above." She was referring to the thousands of lights of the houses and cities stretched out before us. There were no actual stars in the sky.

The entire state glowed white in the moonlight below us. I shivered.

"I suppose we should go back," I said.

"Is Chaucer calling?"

"I guess so," I said, "We might have to delay our trip to Atlanta for a day."

"Maybe two," she said.

"One," I said.

"Okay, one."

"I love you today," I said.

"Love me tomorrow," she responded.

"We'll see. I think I'm just going to love my bed more than anything else tonight."

"I know. But if we sleep, we're liable to miss some of it. Life, I mean. It's better this way."

I laughed. "You're right. When did you become such a good student, anyway?"

"*Osu!*" she said with a smile, but I winced as I turned toward the mountain. Moonlight glowed on one of Grandfather's icy faces. The *nebulous luster!* I thought.

Those WERE *the days when my heart was volcanic!*

---

[49] White-haired Hugh Morton inherited Grandfather Mountain, the highest mountain in the Blue Ridge mountain range and one of the highest peaks east of the Rockies, and made it into a park and nature reserve. His brother inherited the smaller mountain opposite, shaved off the top, and built an ugly multimillion-dollar ski resort in plain view of Grandfather.

[50] Chambers is the largest academic building on the Davidson College campus.

I struggled to conjure the Poe I'd need for what was now that same day's exam. I laughed when more of it came to me. *Volcanic*, I thought, *as the scoriac rivers that roll, as the lavas that restlessly roll, that groan as they roll down Mount Yaanek, in the realms of the frozen pole, roaming with Psyche, my soul.* [51]

Lissa and I fought with gnashing teeth and full-contact blows for the freedoms we enjoyed, but it wasn't until our whirlwind relationship was finally dying out during the end of that next summer at Martha's that we started to fight against each other. Our snow-angel flight in December of 1992 happened within two months of my getting kicked so hard in the gut by Duty and driving all night to Rochester to watch over Mas Oyama's visit to America. When I traveled to Japan for my former classmates' graduation five months after that, I was still uncertain what role, if any, Kyokushin would play in my future. I was making the transition from hedonist to Romantic and finally back to disciple again, and the steps that Lissa and I took together on the path of that transition were often violent.

I've boasted of Lissa's and my ability to break the bonds of convention in an unprecedented celebration of freedom. Looking back, however, I realize that the freedoms in which we indulged were actually more like training exercises for the greater freedom we were struggling to achieve than a celebration that we'd actually found it. Lissa and I were both far from being free emotionally, and it was with full-contact blows and gnashing teeth that we fought to tear down the walls that each of us threw up in the defense of emotional safety.

"Love me," I'd tell Lissa, half pleading, as often as I told her that I loved her.

"I love you today," she'd respond, half the time joking, teasing, laughing with me at the irony. It was our joke together: we understood it perfectly; we were on the same page. Yet I kept asking, because at least we could laugh together, and because, once in a blue moon, she'd respond,

---

[51] Paraphrased from "Ulalume" by Edgar Allen Poe. Walking at night in the *ghoul-haunted woodland of Weir*, the poet ignores the dire warnings of *Psyche, his soul*, and discovers beneath (or within) the beautiful *nebulous luster* of a brilliant constellation, the tomb of his *long lost Ulalume*, the lover (perhaps a personification of the beauty of the natural world) that became the source of his creative power. Was it *embracing* her that created the violent schism within himself that meant he could walk, and have a conversation, with himself, i.e. both he AND his soul, *Psyche* (his own excessive consciousness), or was it his subsequent *scorn for her* that created the rift?

"Oh, but I do love you, Nathan", and I'd allow myself to buckle under the weight of it.

We'd come to omit, but we were both well versed in the implied Part Two of that that sentence. "I love you today," it went, "but I just don't know if I'll still be able to love you tomorrow. I don't know if I'll still have the strength to keep it up. Perhaps I'll retreat once again to the untouchable personality I spent my adolescence constructing in the name of this relative safety."

"Love me," Lissa would tell me another time, turning the tables and challenging me this time to love her as I so desperately wanted to.

"I do love you," I'd say, "I don't have a choice. It's beyond my control."

"And tomorrow?" she'd ask.

I'd laugh and half-jokingly confess, "Tomorrow's beyond my control, too, dear. Shall we settle for today?"

How easy it is in middle-class America to succumb to such decadence!

I wasn't Jacques Sandulescu, I'd never been arrested and tortured, and imprisoned and starved, and shot and forced to work to the very verge of death. I was from America, land of the free, home of the credit card and the second mortgage, home of Disney World and the almighty hamburger! In other corners of the world, large swaths of humanity fight for survival, they fight for their next meal, and they fight because adjacent swaths of humanity are swarming over their borders to kill them with AK-47's, land mines, and blood-borne diseases. How truly privileged we must seem to other, poorer people in the world, to be free to devote so much energy to the kind of internal battles I fought with Lissa!

If we were dodging bullets or scrounging for food, wouldn't we just take the fact that we loved each other for granted?

Yet by the time Lissa entered the scene of my twenty-first year – and Jacques reminded me in New York that "growing up in America can make you wish you were dead!" – there wasn't a single love-based relationship in my life that wasn't bleeding. My mother was too busy remaking her own life to be much aware of mine, the stepmother I'd come to love like my own had been torn from me along with the sisters I'd finally made mine, and my own father, the one who was meant to love me unconditionally, was instead driving me out in the cold in a cowardly attempt to erase history and force the reality of his world to match the fantasy that might replace whatever his own parents had denied him.

Both Lissa and I, it seems, had come to see unconditional loving as a threat – Lissa for her own set of reasons carried over from her adolescence. Together we came to realize it, and together we came to wage war on the artificial defenses that blocked true freedom to seize the days of our lives and live them as we so strongly believed it was our right to do.

Live for the day, love for the day? That's not good enough. There's more. Love for tomorrow and always as well!

The leaf piles we jumped in, the snow angels we made, the mementos we saved, the tequila shots we drank, the bullets we shot, the love we made – all of it was a quest to love without inhibition. *If we can break convention's mold, surely we can break through all of fear's walls as well!* That was what we fought for, and that, in the end, is where we failed.

More than a decade later I took the pages of the book that Lissa and I had made together out of a mildewed manila folder in which they were all crumpled and out of order. In one particularly fierce battle with one of the walls Lissa had thrown up in retreat, I tore them all out, every single page of the book, and scattered them one by one on the floor around the weeping and terrified woman I loved. She'd shut me out one day, that day had become a week, I could see in her eyes that that particular wall was one of her highest and strongest, and with everything I had – with full-contact blows and gnashing teeth – I fought to break it back down, because I loved her.

"Rescue me!" she'd say, because even when she was resisting, her perception – and our pact! – was that resistance was wrong.

"I'm trying with everything I have," I'd respond.

On other days it was Lissa who gnashed her teeth for me. She and I were on the same page. We were fully aware of our defenses, why they were there, and what they blocked us from, and we had agreed together to fight through them because we wanted so badly to be together. It was for the survival of us that we fought. It was to rescue one another, for the sake of us, together.

On one page of our book I'd pasted a fragment of a journal entry.

"I started to leave. I didn't look into her eyes," it began. "'Where are you? You left me,' she snapped, stamping her foot. 'You just went stoic on me again. Look at me! Where did you go?' I looked back into her eyes again. 'God, she's so incredibly beautiful! What in the hell am I doing? I'm leaving another one. Ten minutes ago I was head over heels and now I'm ready to turn tail and run. Let it go. Love her for another day!' When I hugged her, her feet left the ground. 'Jesus,' she said, since I'd squeezed the air from her lungs. 'I will love you tomorrow,' I told her, 'So help me, I will!'"

* * *

It was during my first semester back in school that I began my study of English with Chaucer and the American literature survey, it was then that I drove to Rochester to meet Mas Oyama, and then that I fell in love with Lissa. It was during the following semester that I took both parts of the British literature survey simultaneously, and traveled to Japan for the graduation ceremony of my former *uchi deshi* classmates.

At the beginning of that second semester I moved out of the on-campus senior apartment that I shared with three seniors – my student Dave and his two roommates turned out to be drunks too much of the time – and moved back into Duke Dorm where Lissa lived, and where I'd written for Dr. Abbott alone the summer before.

How incestuous a tiny community like Davidson's can be!

Fate had put Lissa in the very same room where the Residence Life Office had put me the previous summer! It was in what was to become her room, therefore, that I'd suffered from writer's block, from there that I'd gone out in desperation to pick up my ax. It was the same room where Lissa littered the floor around her chair with balled-up, tear-soaked tissues, talking on the phone with her fiancé in Texas, while I read Chaucer in the next room.

So for her last semester at Davidson, Lissa, no longer engaged, technically lived on the first floor of Duke, while, technically, I lived on the third. For all intents and purposes, however, we shared a life completely together. I suffered the indignity of telling my father in an off-the-cuff sort of way that I imagined Lissa and I were headed towards marriage.[52] It was with mild hangovers and celebrative smiles – including one particularly broad one at the shenanigans of the night before – that I

---

[52] In the end, Lissa and I were never, of course, to be married, and since my father, by that time, commended me for so little, I came particularly to loathe any situation in which I'd fail to fulfill any ambition I'd been weak enough to confess to him in the name of trying to get him to finally approve of me *for something!*

sat with Lissa's parents during graduation while she marched across the stage to receive her diploma. I moved into Martha's house a few days later amidst a torrent of my father's objections, and Lissa joined me there after spending the first couple of weeks after graduation with her family in Atlanta.

Already by then the *Budo Karate Illustrated* project's first letters had been written and sent. I'd received the first round of responses, and I'd sent off the second round of follow-ups. It wouldn't be until the end of summer, though, that the acceleration would begin:

Having fought my way to Japan for Master Choi as a teenager, I already believed that I knew a level of selfless pursuit that no one I'd ever met could possibly comprehend. Little did I know that once I'd succeeded in directing that same type of energy towards doing for Master Choi's far greater uncle, the endeavor would balloon outward into something that I never could have imagined.

TEN

It was with such feelings of optimism that I closed the book on my first year back at Davidson, and began a new chapter at Martha's!

This was finally going to be the summer that I'd bring my autobiographical book closer to completion. My computer was still set up on a table in the library from when I'd used it to hack out my final writing assignments during exam week. Martha would be gone again, but I was home, back in my real home for the first time since I was a child. Power pooled like primordial soup all around me there in the valley of my childhood, and the four classes that I was scheduled to take at UNCC posed no threat to my vision of that summer as an unprecedented orgy of creative production.

All of a sudden, however, there was water in the basement apartment. The house's foundation had sprung a leak. Martha and I went to work with two shovels, a pickax, and several five-gallon buckets of masonry sealant in an effort to save the basement's floorboards. Martha was desperate to get out of town and begin her own summer of artistic production, and although I became exhausted by the morning-to-night digging, I didn't mind. Like Hurricane Hugo's trees toppled in the ravine down by the creek, water leaking into the basement insulted my memory of what my childhood home was meant to be. My father was no longer there to take care of the house, and responding once again to Duty, it was actually *I* who began the project by digging a seven-foot-deep pit behind a stone retaining wall at the lower end of the foundation to clear a drainpipe that had become clogged during the two decades since the wall was built.

Martha joined the project at that point, however, and decided that the foundation at the front end of the house might have to be dug out as well, that the inside of the concrete block walls needed to be sealed, and that the floors had to be repainted with polyurethane. I reminded myself that I would be living in the house for free over the next ten weeks, but by the time six full days of work spilled over into the seventh, I began to lament the lost time that I'd planned to be writing. My first two classes in Charlotte were about to begin, and I was feeling farther than ever from a finished manuscript.

Finally, the basement was sealed and Martha was gone – my classes began – and I sat night after night in front of my computer, but failed to produce anyway. A Davidson College student named Jeff, who'd been Martha's basement tenant for the year, wouldn't move out for two more weeks, and somehow I couldn't settle into a productive routine for the fact that he was there too. In desperation I recounted several autobiographical episodes in long letters to Lissa in Atlanta, but soon after that, Lissa moved in and I no longer had even that excuse to write. My classes at UNCC were some of the most enjoyable I'd ever taken, but part of the reason why was that they were a vacation from Davidson's higher academic standard. The poetry-writing seminar nearly defeated me because it required so much creativity, and mine was all tied up – literally! – in my other writing project. In Martha's kitchen I wrote a few lines of personal value nevertheless, and filed them away for future use.

Lissa and I celebrated our reunion by protecting the living-room carpet with beach towels in front of a five-foot-tall inferno that we built in the 200-year-old red-brick fireplace, and by doing shots of tequila while we smeared each other with as much olive oil as we dared steal from Martha's kitchen. Weeks passed, and we became domestic together for the first time. We did a lot of cooking in the nude.

The laundry started to pile up in the back bedroom.

Lissa started to withdraw.

I suppose it was doomed from the beginning. Our relationship couldn't have lasted. Our passion was too powerful. It came on too strong.

And my transformation had begun.

When Lissa and I began, I was bridging the gap from Hedonist to Romantic. The only mission that I had was to live life, celebrate it – revel in it! – and get as far ahead as I possibly could. But even before I met Lissa, I'd awakened the voice of Conscience, training there in the valley of my childhood with my ax. It slept a little again after that, but then a trip to

Japan showed me that there was still a future for me there, that my energy might in fact still be put somehow towards positive use in the world. I was corresponding by then with Jacques Sandulescu, Bobby Lowe, and Mas Oyama, letters from New York, Honolulu and Tokyo showed up in my post office box, and I became that guy on campus that not only had his hands in everything, but also pulled it all off, and seemed to have such a good time doing it, all at the same time. I became the guy on campus who annoyed everyone else in conversations about their futures because I knew exactly what choices to make and what lay around the next corner. Most seniors at Davidson still had no idea what they wanted to do with their lives. By then, I was starting to see my own future with such clarity that the events that befell me ceased to surprise me anymore.

In short, I was freeing myself from the lure of living a life merely to steal what pleasures I could, and my old self started to reemerge – newly educated, stronger, more confident, and better prepared to move forward. What greater pleasure could there be, after all, than living a life of value to someone whose teaching meant so much to so many thousands of people? What greater appeasement of conscience could there be than making myself, in the years to come, into just such a teacher?

That emerging personality must have terrified Lissa.

She came back to Davidson to live with me – she came back because of me – and took a job at a local coffee shop in order to support herself and her life with me. Meanwhile, I drove forward a thousand miles an hour into pursuits that I believed to be of earthshaking, large-scale importance. Lissa's walls started to fly up. "What's to stop me," she asked, "from just getting caught up in the support of you? What happens to my dreams?"

"What are your dreams?" I'd ask.

"I don't know," she said. "But how am I ever going to know if so much of my energy is tied up in you and your work? I spend all my time rooting for you, and I realize that I'm no closer to knowing what's best for me!"

"But isn't that okay?" I'd ask:

"If your path hasn't revealed itself yet, how is ceasing to live in the meantime going to reveal it to you any faster? Don't you love me?"

"Yes, of course I love you! I've loved you harder than I've ever loved anyone else, but that's the point! I love you so much I feel like I'm lost. What happened to *just live for today*?

"When did you get so tied up in the future?"

By the end of the summer I no longer looked forward to coming home from Charlotte. I started rather to fear what I'd find there. I found myself regularly engaged in conversations like this one with Lissa, and part of me knew that I was losing her. I began to lament the fact that my writing wasn't getting done. I was spending so much energy trying to rescue Lissa for the sake of us together, and it occurred to me that I had lamented the same kind of loss when Martha and I were sealing the basement.

It didn't take much longer after that for despair to set in. Lissa pulled back completely — she closed her eyes to me — and I came to feel as though my chest had been run through by a fence post. I'd let myself so free to love this woman! I'd folded her so masterfully into my vision for the future. I'd spent a year proving to myself, and to her, that I was finally free enough to love her that way. But the second I trusted that she would be there to love me in return, the second I diverted some of my creative energy towards what might become my life's work, she started to shut me out.

Mas Oyama said time and time again how bad a recipe for life it can be if a man alters his course for a woman before he's secure enough in his own path. Of course it would never have occurred to *Sosai* to reverse *man* and *woman* in that sentence. He was a product of another society in another era, when women were the keepers of their husbands' houses. And I'm sure his scenario still applies in many cultures around the globe today. Some women feel trapped being supporters of their husbands' goals, and long desperately to escape to their own devices, but others, I'm sure, are completely content. Neither is wrong, and many have the best of both worlds. Lissa's problem was that she didn't know yet whether or not she was willing to lose, or possibly even find, herself in the support of me. *Man* and *woman* don't fit into Mas Oyama's sentence anymore, here in present-day America. Ironically, Lissa was following *Sosai's* advice . . . and I told her so!

I wouldn't have wanted her to lose herself. She needed to figure out what she wanted for her own future, and I wouldn't have dreamt of standing in her way. The problem was that she didn't know yet what *her way* was. She was afraid that the confidence and power with which I began to pursue my goals would eclipse her chances of ever discovering her own.

Of course, I didn't help myself much.

She started to shut me out, the sensation was physically painful – like my rib cage being crushed – and I responded physically. She pulled away farther than she ever had, and I grabbed hold of her in a desperate attempt to keep her loving me. She and I had conditioned each other to do it, of course. It was our unspoken contract with each other. With full-contact blows and gnashing teeth we expected each to come to the other's rescue to do whatever was in our power to tear down both our walls. Of course it never came to actual blows, but at the end of that summer, when she pulled so far away, twice I responded half impulsively and half exactly as she'd trained me to respond: I reached out and grabbed her by the elbows in a dangerous and futile attempt to keep her from throwing us away.

Both times Lissa crumpled into a puddle of tears, terrified, I think, more of my resolve than of my physical strength. And both times, like a child who'd unknowingly grabbed a red-hot pot on the stove, I pulled back, realizing only after it was too late that a line had been crossed from which we'd likely not be able to recover.

And we did not.

The sensation that my rib cage had been run through didn't go away. For days I carried it with me every waking moment. In the night I reached out to Lissa, begging her to love me, but even her sympathetic embrace failed to make the hurt go away.

I loved Lissa like life. I loved her with everything I had. But everything I had wasn't enough. She had been my exercise in loving free when so many of those that I'd loved had been torn from me that I no longer considered it safe. And now I was losing her too. Like a burn on your hand so painful that you want even the hand to be gone, I wished for the amputation of my whole chest. The heartbreak became a dull physical ache that made me want to leap out of my body and leave it behind.

I'm sorry, Jacques, but that's where Lissa and I were when I first visited you in New York and you scolded me for fighting with my girlfriend . . . That's where Lissa and I were when my stepmother Martha rolled into town at the end of the summer like a white angel of mercy.

My father's ex-wife Martha remains to this day my closest living family member. My love for her is unconditional, and the relationship that we share is the only one, in my world, that remains unaltered since I was a child. There is no question that when my father left her, all feelings of warmth and comfort I associated with *home* came to an abrupt end. Martha is an extremely warm, contact-oriented person, and so she was that kind of stepmother. Sadly I was to learn of my father that he had been, too, mostly by virtue of being married to Martha. As soon as he left her, and began a life with a third wife who was quite opposite, he shut down the warm part of his personality as well.

My stepmother Martha in the snow at the log house overlooking the woods where I played as a child. The photograph was taken by Michael Mauney some years after the events of this book.

Years went by, but I never stopped believing that the warmth that was missing from my family had somehow been left behind in the log house with Martha. When I was seventeen and a freshman at Davidson, still eighteen months before I'd travel to Japan for the first time, I gathered my nerve and – without saying anything to my father – drove out to Martha's house for the first time in five years. And my intuition was correct. After not having seen her since I was a child, I fell into her arms, and it was as if I had finally come home to what home was meant to be. Just as Judd Reid, Sandor Brezovai, and I share a sacred bond that very few others can grasp – thanks to the *Wakajishi-ryo* [53] experience that only the three of us have in common – Martha and I shared the bond of having our lives painfully disrupted at the same exact instant, and by the exact same circumstance. Just like me, she was an unwilling participant in that second rupturing of my father's family. We were both victims of the same tragedy, and even though we'd been pried apart for six long years, the love we had for each other remained untainted.

In exactly the same way, my stepsisters – my mother's stepdaughters – became unwilling participants in a family split that none of us either chose, or precipitated, or had the slightest bit of control over. We sat down together to the seventh year or so of shared family dinners one day, and the next day we no longer had a common house to come home to. I was living in Davidson with my father for high school when the fracture occurred, and by the time I finished my first year and a half of college, and two more years in Japan after that, so much time had passed that trying to pick up those torn threads of family was the furthest thing from natural. A handful of times in the decades that followed I dreamt of encounters with my stepsisters, and woke up in the night feeling horrible loss.

As I write this, I haven't seen either of my biological parents for more than a decade. Of course I did feel loss for them. Devastating heartbreak is more accurate. But at least in their case that loss was spread out over a decade into a piece-by-piece abandonment after both their second attempts at family collapsed and each failed to fit the adolescent sons from their first marriage into their third tries. In their times of turmoil and transition, I became in the case of both of them the responsibility of the other parent, yet since their turmoil and transition often coincided, family faded out for me, day by heartbreaking day, in both households.

When I dream about my biological parents today, I wake up relieved that they exist only in my dreams.

My love for my stepmother Martha, however, remains unaltered.

---

[53] *Wakajishi-ryo*, "Young Lions' Dormitory." Although there were other foreigners in the dormitory during the two years I was in Japan, the three of us entered the dormitory at virtually the same time, and thus experienced life there in a way, particular to that specific era, that no one else could possibly grasp, having not been there.

Our relationship is the one I share today with a parental figure that I know I can rely on. Sadly, though, in mid-August of 1993, she returned to my childhood home to find Lissa and me in the final, violent throes of our year-long love affair, and it was a bit too soon after our reunion for the two of us – Martha and me – to take that love for granted, given our common history of abandonment.

By the time I was returning home from my final classes at UNCC, Martha was spending full days with Lissa at home, and it became immediately apparent that she'd been fully appraised of the negative turn Lissa's and my relationship had taken. Lissa had confessed to Martha that I'd scared her – physically – and suddenly, the reality of her devoted adopted son was eclipsed by the image of the ex-husband who'd abandoned her. I was not guilty of my father's crime, yet I saw in Martha's eyes that she not only suspected me capable, but had also passed judgment, and decided I was culpable.

I had not neglected the maintenance of her property that I'd agreed to take on for the two months Martha was gone, but I hadn't taken care of it to a level that met with her approval, either – and suddenly I found myself in my father's shoes for that reason too. When he moved out, Martha made a desperate and daring decision to keep the house even though it wasn't finished. She'd spent years on her own, therefore, pushed to the edge of exhaustion maintaining her professorship while finishing the house all by herself. My leaving some gravel unraked and the hillside unmowed must have echoed my father's abandonment perfectly.

How could she possibly have known what effect her choice of action would have?

Emotionally, I'd been driven from my father's house across town by his decision to charge me rent to live in the cottage behind the house which he'd been steadily excluding me from ever since I was twelve. Now, my last remaining parent in my newly rediscovered childhood home – Martha – decided to charge me rent too, retroactively, for the months I'd lived there, since I'd failed to live up to her expectations regarding property maintenance:

I who had tackled Hugo's trees!

I who'd volunteered my full days to seal the basement!

I who'd spent the summer in the throes of healing from the same wound that she and I shared! Martha who loves me like her son, Martha who loved me then too, but must have told herself that she was teaching me responsibility by charging me rent to stay in my childhood home!

She couldn't possibly have known, of course, the effect her failing to trust me would have.

"Pay me or get out," she told me in effect, and I had no choice but to go. Worse, I had no place to go except the backyard cottage of my father's house across town.

White angel of mercy!

Heartbreak compounded heartbreak. Martha's inadvertent driving me out of the home I thought I'd found combined with Lissa's banishing me from the refuge I thought I'd found in her to create the catalyst for the most extreme course change of the third decade of my life. A growl was forming within me like lava building up in the deepest recesses of my being, and at the end of that summer a new Nathan Ligo took his first steps out into a world that would never again be the same.

* * *

Two months later, two months into my living alone in the cottage behind my father's house, my latest, borderline impossible, six-course class schedule was in full swing. Mas Oyama's permission had been granted and the production stage of the *Budo Karate Illustrated* project was underway. Lissa was still at Martha's house, momentarily lost, and I – the guilty one exiled – had not spoken to either of them. In late October, Lissa sent me the page of our book from our day one, when Cliff died and she and I jumped in a leaf pile. Only crumbs of one of those dry leaves remained, stuck to the page with a wide, clear piece of packing tape.

On delicate paper, in a beautiful hand Lissa wrote:

Dear Nathan,

I've forgotten how many nights it's been that I've come home hoping that the little red blinking light on my phone will deliver a message from you. But the little buttons go, and the machine whines and beeps, and your voice is not there. I stopped counting the nights. Counting was something we did together – we marveled at the way time passed for us: now slow and luxurious, and then, wham! it's been four weeks, fourteen weeks, seven months . . . We counted and we documented. We kept scraps of proof of how outrageously we were living and how insanely we kept loving each other. Why did you start it? You and your books, I think; perhaps you set your story too far aside while you were compiling ours.

Well, it's day 368 according to my records. On October 18, Cliff died and we jumped in a leaf pile. Today I send you that page from the book, I wonder what you will feel when you open it? Will you throw it away? If you do, I suppose it's a good thing I sent it: it shouldn't mean anything anymore.

What has happened? When was the last time we loved each other? When did we stop trusting? When did we get confused about taking it a day at a time? What went wrong?

Have we been wrong for each other all along?

I think of your eyes. The smell from this candle at my side reminds me of your room in the dark with Sinéad and the almond oil. Same candle, same smell. We made love, ate dinners, studied together, talked, watched movies, listened to Prince — all with the candle burning at one time or another. The scent brings it all back.

What went wrong?

I think of your eyes. I think of how far away you seem to me now. How removed. Your soul seems all closed up to me anymore. Makes me realize how unguarded you really were when you told me to "keep 'em coming" a year ago. You wanted to love me then. You told me how different it was; that you had nowhere to go, no plan except right now going to school. Your dreams stretched out like a highway and you were enjoying the fast cruising, not just covering miles to the next landmark along the way. So you seemed to me. To live for the day, you said, is all you can try to do. A day at a time (and you checked my hand for the ring). You wanted to love, and you wanted to risk being loved. You told me I wasn't strong enough to resist loving you.

You were right, goddamn your ego! I did love you. You were everything loose and confident and daring. You were every unconfined element that I yearned for in Bryan and could not find. You were dangerous to love from the beginning for that very elusive looseness that I was drawn to. Live for today? Don't worry? Don't plan? Just drink it all in? And work, work, work for the someday goals? God, who wouldn't fall in love with you?

You taught me to relax. You reminded me of spontaneity. You laid me out naked in the sun, gave me cigarettes late at night, made snow angels, brought banana splits and pansies in little paper cups of water. You tucked me in, and waited till I slept, standing on the dresser and holding me from the edge of the loft. You woke me up wanting to make love. I loved you for building fires for Martha and for holding me tight while we warmed up the futon with tequila in our bellies. I loved you for telling me I was beautiful with your mouth and your eyes and your hands on my body in the night. I loved you for reading Frankenstein *to me in the car on the way back from Atlanta. I loved you for setting the mousetraps. I loved you for Greek food in the mall on Sunday afternoon, and for topless pizza, and for Crispy Scallion Chicken cravings after great sex. I loved you for doing katas on the grass and showing me how to make a good fist, and I loved you for being hurt when I punched you too. I loved you for sushi and beer and dancing and swimming and snuggling . . .*

I think of your eyes and I have a hard time not crying again.

I've never stopped crying since I met you. You held me and collected my tissues when I hung up the phone and was trying to let go of Bryan. I still cry — sometimes for Bryan, when I miss him — but now for you, mostly.

I feel loss.

When Bryan and I were over, I felt fear and uncertainty and shame for backing out. But I knew in my heart that I had pulled out and I had wanted to.

Now there is no fear, no uncertainty in my soul, and no shame. I just feel loss. What I had believed in, what I had trusted in, what I had hoped for was not that we would always do well together, not that we would always be happy, and not that we would even always work it out — but that, at the core, we loved loving each other.

I've never been so violent or miserable or angry with anyone but you. I've never cried or yelled or struggled against anyone as I have with you. I've never given so much of myself to the risk of you. Yet I've never felt such abandon, such a willingness to let life take me where it should. I've never felt so tightly held, for who I am, in all the instability and insecurity: we clung to each other more than once. It's never been so wonderful to be in someone's arms and fall asleep, knowing that tomorrow will be more of the same devilish roller-coaster.

Maybe that was the problem, after all. Our extremes were so damn broad. It was either wonderful or hell. So many people just shook their heads. How could it last? It must've burnt out.

But still, I've never felt so vital, so crisply and newly alive.

It's late and I'm lying here wondering if Jeff hated us for making love just on the other side of that wall. I've been sleeping alone for so long now I don't even turn in my sleep. The covers are always on me and I wake in exactly the same spot and position as I crawled into the night before. Mornings, I hear Martha move around upstairs in the kitchen. I lie here and think of coffee. And in those moments I imagine that I will walk into the kitchen and you will be sitting there. I imagine that everything could be perfect and you could come home with me for Thanksgiving and Greg and Julie could visit and you could read to me and we could dance and smoke and sauna and watch movies and go out for sushi and scallion chicken and make snow angels and take bubble baths and jump in leaf piles all over again . . . And then I want to cry because it's really just morning and my body is sore and I have to get up and go to work and nothing's perfect except for my bed which is never even rumpled.

I feel loss. You are gone from me and somehow I was part of making you go and I am sad for what is gone with you. I'm sad a lot because my love for you is not gone at all. Now it's day 369 and I miss you.

L.

I skimmed Lissa's letter and then laid it aside.

I didn't answer it.

I didn't call.

A week later Lissa sent me a shoebox containing all the other torn pages of our book. Apparently she'd gathered them up when I'd scattered them around her on the floor of her dorm room. I'd mailed the book to her once, when she was still struggling with her decision whether or not to break off her relationship with Bryan.

With it, in a second letter, she wrote that she assumed that if none of it meant anything to me any more, I'd probably just throw it away.

I didn't respond, but I did pack the pages away in a manila envelope for future use. Already I knew that with Lissa I'd lived an important chapter, even though it was starkly clear to me that that chapter was through.

"Why did you give up?" Lissa asked me in that final letter as many times as she told me in the first one that she thought of my eyes.

Why did I give up, Lissa?
Oh, but it wasn't I who gave up.
I merely altered course.
Life is too short to surrender.
I fell in love with Helen.

ELEVEN

DURING SIX YEARS as Master Choi's student before leaving for Japan, I attended four annual summer camps at the North Carolina coast with the students of his CMAC.[54]

In the greater Kyokushin world, summer camps and seminars tend to offer easier training than what we do in the dojo on a daily basis. As an *uchi deshi* I looked forward to the summer camps we attended each year at Tateyama because, with the exception of the ten-kilometer road race, those three two-hour trainings a day, mostly *kihon*, *iddo* and *kata* on the sand, paled in comparison to the grueling day-in and day-out of *uchi deshi* life. *Honbu's* regular students, unused to training more than once a day, were usually worn out by the end of the camp, but my classmates and I felt rejuvenated, having gone three days without our standard morning training. It was that set of daily body conditioning exercises that left us in a constant state of exhaustion, through which we had to struggle to make it through our regular dojo trainings at *Honbu*.

Master Choi's summer camps were the opposite. We were accustomed, then, to dojo trainings four times a week. At the beach, however, we'd train four times a day in the hot sun, on sand that was sometimes so hot that we preferred to stand on patches of sharp broken shells. Often the last half-hour of our two-hour workouts was done in waist-deep water, practicing kicks and sprints against the current, and even downward knife-hand strikes against the incoming waves.

It was great fun for a teenager, but it was also exhausting, and sometimes even daunting.

One particular personality-shaping event occurred on the second day

---

[54] Master Choi's Carolina Martial Arts Club at UNC–Chapel Hill.

of the fourth and final CMAC summer camp I attended before leaving for Japan. I was 18 years old.

Much of North Carolina's coast is made up of barrier islands, and during our beach camps we often ran the length of whatever island we were on and back again. That last year we were at Sunset Beach, the southernmost barrier island of the North Carolina coast, and we ran from the pier all the way down to the jetty at the far end of the island to practice *kihon*, *kata* and *iddo kekko* [55] before turning around to run back again.

The round-trip distance is less than seven miles.

I can't imagine what training I had been doing, or failing to do, during the final days of my freshman year at Davidson, but for whatever reason – and much to my horror! – I turned out to be the one who was physically unprepared for the run that day.

Although Master Choi went to great lengths to make sure I wasn't allowed to congratulate myself as such, there's no question that I had become something like a son to him. I'd fought my way up to *nidan* since I began as a white belt at the age of thirteen, the only child in a class of university and graduate students, and it was a well known, although mostly unspoken, fact by then that Master Choi and I held a special relationship. He was grooming me to enter his uncle's three-year program in Japan, although in accordance with his wise policy of keeping me humble, Master Choi rarely admitted that he was thus preparing me. It was rather I who wanted to go, and *maybe* he'd "recommend me" to his uncle if I were to "train hard and become strong."

By the summer of 1989, however, I stood out in another way. I'd organized my own karate club at Davidson College and run it throughout the previous academic year.[56] It's true that I only averaged five or six regular students at a time, but they were the first ones that were my own, and I'd already taken them twice from Davidson to Chapel Hill, three hours northeast by car, to test for their first *kyu* promotions under Master Choi. Thus ten of Master Choi's students – and two of my own! – attended the camp that year at Sunset Beach, making me the first of Master Choi's students ever to bring students of his own to a CMAC summer camp.

---

[55] *Kekko* is Japanese for "training", or "practice." *Kihon, iddo, kata, kumite*: the four basic divisions of karate training.

[56] This was my *first* round of teaching at Davidson, as a CMAC *nidan* under Master Choi, having not yet been to Japan.

As the ranking member present, I'd actually run all the trainings on the first day. Master Choi had been delayed in Chapel Hill, and didn't arrive until late that first evening.

With my back to the ocean, I took this picture of the members of Master Choi's CMAC at our 1989 camp at Sunset Beach. That's Master Choi, third from right. My students from Davidson College can also be seen here. Stan Armistead (extreme right) and Andrew Peery (in a dark T-shirt with a circular emblem on Master Choi's right) became that year the first students to attend one of Master Choi's camps that were the students of one of his students, rather than his own.

For all of these reasons and more, it was particularly ironic that it was I whose legs started to fail on the island-length run the second day of the camp. On the first day, leading the workout myself, I set out with the students to cover a full mile's worth of *iddo kekko* techniques in *zenkutsu-dachi* [57] in one long uninterrupted set. That's a fair number of techniques in a long deep stance, and I felt particularly pressured never to skimp on one of my stances since I was the one asking everyone else to do something so daunting. Had I failed to eat enough protein once that training was through? Or was I just that far out of shape at the end of my first year in college?

---

[57] *Iddo kekko* means "movement or transfer training" and refers to performing basic techniques in long, deep stances forward or backwards, covering ground with each technique. *Zenkutsu-dachi* is one of our longest, deepest stances.

Whatever the case, I can still feel the dull ache of failure in my thighs from the run that next day.

We ran in our *dogi* in a double file line with the senior belts at the front and the beginners in back. We followed the line defined by the diminishing waves as they rolled in as far as they were going to make it before sinking into the sand. If we ran too close to the water, our feet would sink in the sludge, but at just the right distance from the sea, the sand was packed hard like a tennis court, and it was on that line that we preferred to run.

As the senior student for the first time, I was running beside but an inch or two back from Master Choi at the front of the pack. Three-quarters of the way down the island, Master Choi and I exchanged a nearly silent communication.

"Sir," I said so that only he could hear. He looked at me out of the corner of his eye. Nobody spoke during the run, so until that moment the only sounds had been the wind and the dull thunder of breaking waves. "What is it?" he asked with that glance.

"My legs are failing," I told him.

The pair of runners just behind us might have heard through the Atlantic's muffled roar. The ones behind them surely did not. I'd spoken just barely loud enough for Master Choi to understand what he in any case would have read in my eyes.

My apology for the failure was conveyed optically, and I knew right away that he'd seen it. He was concerned because it was uncharacteristic for me to be the one to fall out of training, and he actually turned his head towards me so that he could see both of my eyes with both of his own. He evaluated what he saw there – he saw that the success of his training was my first concern, that I wasn't exaggerating my condition, and that I was surprised, too. He all but nodded his understanding, all contained within that same momentary glance, and in a way that told me that he was grateful to have been apprised of the situation.

Some minutes passed. We continued to tread our way down the length of the island. The Atlantic breeze filled our *dogi* like sails. Without missing a stride, and in a way that none of the students would be aware that it had anything to do with me, Master Choi gave the command for us to rotate 180 degrees in place and start running backwards. We often ran backwards or sideways for segments of our beach runs to work different leg muscles, and I was grateful for Master Choi's genius when I realized that by turning us backwards, he was giving my failing forward-moving leg muscles a chance to recover. Of course, running backwards made our progress slower, and we couldn't keep it up for long, so a couple hundred yards later we turned forwards again. At least Master Choi had bought me a little more time.

I barely made it to the end of the island without giving away my deteriorating condition to the rest of the students. We trained there for an hour before starting back. Master Choi and I both hoped that the break from running would lead to sufficient recovery, but by the time the hour had dragged past, I was sure I was in for a rough return. My thighs shook as they struggled to support my body weight in the deep stances in which we practiced our basic techniques.

That's me with my back to the camera, leading a *kata* workout. Different students of different levels are performing different *kata*, hence the lack of synchronization.

On the return, I only made it about one-quarter of the way before my legs gave out and I could no longer keep up. It was particularly frustrating because if my head, heart and lungs were my motor and my legs merely my wheels – as my high school cross-country coach had so often suggested – it was my wheels that gave out, but my motor was fine. The muscles in my legs simply failed. In utter shame, I dropped out of formation and let my *koohai*, one by one, move ahead of me. Over the next 500 yards or so I watched as the double-file line of *karateka* ahead of me got farther and farther away. Meanwhile, my legs got worse and worse. By now I was staggering with stiff legs that barely bent at the knees.

That's when Master Choi's genius showed itself again.

I couldn't hear anything but the wind and the droning waves – the pack was too far ahead for me to hear anything of them – but apparently Master Choi gave the command and, once again, everyone turned and started running backwards. Before, when I'd been at the front of the formation, turning us backwards had merely given my legs a second chance. But this time, his turning everyone around to run backwards had an entirely different and unexpected effect.

He turned everyone's eyes towards me.

Everyone knew, of course, that I'd fallen out of the lineup, but at least once they'd passed me I could maintain an illusion that perhaps they'd forgotten. Master Choi turned them around, however, and all of a sudden there were a dozen steadily gazing witnesses to my failure. It was more than I could bear. What happened next happened all on its own.

With strength that I couldn't even imagine I had, I lowered my body weight, howled internally with rage, and charged forward like a demon possessed. Of course, the muscles that one uses to sprint are slightly different than the ones used for long-distance running, so from a physical standpoint, it makes some sense that I was able to find strength to carry me forward on legs that had seemed useless a moment before. What caught me off guard, however, was that the sprint was the fastest of my life. Somehow I'd conjured it up from my reserve when there shouldn't have been any. The eyes of my *koohai* bugged as I roared in on them like a kamikaze pilot and then soared past with only my toes cutting the sand, as if my billowing *dogi* top carried me on the wind. I witnessed Master Choi's tacit approval as I regained my position at the front of the line-up.

As if on cue, he gave the command, and everyone started running forwards again.

Of course, I didn't last long. Back at the slower pace of the group, my legs stiffened up, and now it had to be clear to everyone present that I was having major difficulty. I fought to keep up. My legs wouldn't bend and I had no choice but to compensate by allowing my heart and lungs to go into overdrive. Keeping up just wasn't in the cards for me that day.

Once again I fell out, and once again I suffered the indignity of watching the group move farther and farther ahead. *That's it,* I thought, *no way can I catch up with them again.* We were only halfway back to the pier, and I had no choice but to face the fact that everyone would be done, and I would stagger in alone and in shame twenty minutes later.

But then, lo and behold, Master Choi came to my rescue again. As was his way, he came to my utter education. He turned the group around one more time, again I found myself looking into the eyes of my *koohai*, and again I could not control my response. I let a roar break past my lips, and charged forward at a suicide pace. Once again I regained the group, and once again Master Choi turned them around to join me.

The third time we repeated the cycle I didn't stop sprinting when I reached the front of the formation. I knew I was just going to fail again once I dropped my pace down to a jog, so I kept right on going. I doubled the length of my sprint and ran 150 yards on ahead of the group. There I turned around 180 degrees and started running backwards – and discovered, once again in awe, that Master Choi had turned the group around as well. Once again I was facing everyone. Only now, they were running forward and it was I who was running backwards.

It was then that I felt the full impact of Master Choi's improvised solution to my dilemma. Master Choi knew that if he turned the class's eyes towards me, I would be able to conjure power that I didn't otherwise know existed. In this way he not only kept me moving, but he taught me something on a completely different level from what the rest of the group got that day. The experience was a pivotal one for me because of where the power came from. It came from shame, it came from rage, it came from passion, it came from loyalty, and it came from love. It certainly did not come from anything like I'd ever before imagined when Master Choi spoke of "tapping into one's spiritual power," but there's no question that what I had conjured was raw, unadulterated spirit. The power did not come from the muscles in my legs. But nor did it come from some kind of mystical, elusive, monk-on-a-mountaintop cosmic power. It was more like it came from the roar that had wanted to break loose from my midsection when first Master Choi turned my *koohai's* eyes toward me. It came from within me, but what surprised me was that it was born of a perspective, a platform perhaps, an attitude that I'd never before imagined part of my repertoire.

I learned that when we are in desperate need of power, it's there for the taking far more often than we think. More than that, though, I learned that to assume that the only place we're going to find it is where we're accustomed to looking is to limit our true potential. If we open our eyes to the existence of alternate sources of power that we may never have considered — and that we may not discover until the hour of our greatest need — we just might surprise ourselves with what we actually can do. Decide resolutely to succeed and, with an open mind, alternate sources of power just might reveal themselves as you approach what you perceive to be your limits.

Close your eyes to the possibility of such alternate sources, on the other hand, and it's much more likely that you'll fall short of your true potential.

* * *

The last weekend before classes started for my final year at Davidson, I found a letter in my mailbox on *Honbu's* unmistakable stationery. It was the same week that I moved out of Martha's house and into the one-room cottage behind my father's, and just a handful of days after returning from Jacques and Annie's in New York. I held my breath as I ripped open the envelope.

The letter was signed by Mas Oyama himself.

"Dear Mr. Nathan Ligo," it began. "With many thanks I have received your letter dated July 6, 1993. Regarding *American Kyokushin Yearbook*, I have no objection to your project. I hope that you will be successful in this. As you said in the letter, I believe this yearbook will benefit all of American Kyokushin."

"Sincerely," it was signed in his bold, graceful hand, "Mas Oyama."

And, with that, the floodgates opened.

I wasted no time moving my base of operations — course work for my SIX classes included — into my manager's desk at the Union Café. It was my responsibility to schedule student workers to cover all the night and weekend shifts from the first day back. Many of my last year's crew were returning to campus, but some weren't — Lissa, for one, had graduated! — and a percentage of my efforts had to be devoted to recruiting, hiring and training new employees. I'd already made arrangements with the physical education department so that Davidson students could fulfill one of their two athletic course requirements by attending my karate classes, but now I reserved a dance studio in the new sports complex for two hours every evening starting at 7:00, and began posting fliers around campus to recruit new students as well.

Davidson allocates two or three days at the beginning of each semester for students to choose and sign up for classes. I spent some time struggling with the process. There was a course on the eighteenth-century novel that I wanted to take above all, but it was only offered once a week during a peak class time, and that made it difficult to fit in a couple of the other classes I needed to take. In the end, I wound up enrolled in a Shakespeare course, Chinese politics, intermediate Japanese (which Davidson students were allowed to take as a one-on-one tutorial for the first time that semester), a design course offered through the art department (two art classes were required for graduation), French (two foreign language credits were also required) and, of course, The 18th-Century Novel. Assuming I'd pass all those and add them to the four credits I'd earned over the summer, I'd be able to graduate after just one more semester, and therefore within the bounds of the free tuition benefit I received because of my father's employment.

My *Budo Karate Illustrated* letter-writing campaign, originally limited to Jacques, *Shihan* Lowe, and then *Sosai* while I waited for that all-important endorsement from the top, now suddenly exploded: There were twenty-six branch chiefs and dojo operators to correspond with in all corners of the country, from Orlando to Massachusetts, from Chicago to California, and even to Hawaii and Guam. I created a multipage packet of information that included a written description of the book I planned – I was still calling it the *American Kyokushin Yearbook* – and I sent one to each of twenty-six names on my list. Enclosed was a copy of *Sosai's* letter of permission, Jacques' letter of support, and a self-addressed, postage-paid survey card on which I asked a handful of questions designed to further evaluate how the project would be received.

"Are you willing to support the project by submitting material?" I asked. "Are you willing to market copies to your students through advance orders at $20 per book plus shipping? At that price, how many do you imagine you will be able to sell?"

There were other questions as well, but they were mostly smokescreen for the above all-important ones. If the individual branch chiefs weren't going to support the project, I might as well hang it up. If they didn't think they could sell copies in advance of printing, I'd have to seriously reconsider my plan. Their estimate of the demand for the book in their dojos would help me forecast how many copies to print and what my budget would be.

I did some significant research on how to lay out and print the book I'd envisioned – I'd never done anything like this before, so I had to learn everything from scratch. I all but decided upon a company in Montgomery, Alabama that specialized in high school and college yearbooks. They were accustomed to working with young, inexperienced staff and getting books produced by an end-of-the-school-year deadline that worked well with my timetable. They only made hardcover books, which wasn't how I'd envisioned *Budo Karate Illustrated*, but a key point of their production procedure actually rendered them cheaper than any soft-cover option I could find.

Instead of doing a color separation for each photograph and sizing and cropping them individually, they were accustomed to creating physical layouts with actual-size photographs, cropped by hand and pasted to the page with a spot of glue. They would then photograph the entire spread, and save money by having to do only one color separation per spread. They probably had to do it that way to remain competitive since, as a yearbook company, they were accustomed to dealing with 60, or even 100, photographs per page. To charge by the photograph as other printers did would have been cost-prohibitive.

As the first couple of weeks of the semester passed, I came to the eventual estimate that I'd be able to print 2000 books at a cost of about $19 each for a total of $38,000. Four dollars would cover the postage, so I'd sell them for a total of $24 each, $19 plus $4 for shipping and $1 for good measure. I estimated that I'd be able to break even, even if I didn't manage to sell every single copy. This was more money, of course, than as a 22-year-old I'd ever dealt with in my wildest imagination. $40,000 would have bought me nearly two more years of classes at Davidson and paid for my entire *uchi deshi* experience seven times over. For a mere $1000, I'd bought the old, beat-up Ford Fairmont that would take me back to Michael Monaco's annual tournament in Rochester, for the second time, later that semester, and then on to Henri Orlean's tournament in Atlantic City in the days before my *nidan* grading in the spring.

My research led me to Pagemaker, a computer program designed for creating book and magazine layouts, and I learned how to use it the hard way. I did some research into copyright law, thinking I'd want to keep exclusive rights to the name *Budo Karate Illustrated*. Somehow I failed completely to figure out that I should have incorporated to protect myself financially should the magazine fail.

Having given in to the foregone conclusion of success, there was really no reason to prepare for the project's failure.

I'd spent many hours during the summer at Martha's writing and rewriting – and writing again! – an application for a $10,000 grant from a nonprofit foundation called the Thomas J. Watson Foundation, which gives this sum of money to sixty or so graduating seniors each year, nationwide, to pursue a research project of their choice overseas during the year following their graduation. The types of projects for which grants were given were reputed to be fairly outlandish, and I'd been told that from four finalists selected each year by Davidson faculty, the Watson Foundation almost always awarded fellowships to either two or three of them. Davidson was a small school, and usually twenty or thirty students applied. I imagined myself using $10,000 to return to Japan to pursue writing associated with Kyokushin, and therefore considered it obligatory that I not only pursue, but also secure, one of those positions. I knew that my preestablished relationship with Mas Oyama would make my application a uniquely appealing one to the Watson people, and it was therefore with a high level of confidence that I applied, and became a finalist, for the $10,000 grant.

In my most recent letter to *Sosai* I'd written that I was "already exploring means" by which I would be able to return to Japan after graduating from college. The Watson Fellowship was the "means" to which I referred. I couldn't think of anything I'd rather do after graduation than return to Japan to resume my training while putting my Davidson education to work for Kyokushin. Back in Tokyo, I would work on the second issue of *Budo Karate Illustrated* and on what was quickly becoming my dream project, an English-language biography of Mas Oyama.

How incredible it would be to work on such a project in close proximity to the man himself, to have firsthand exposure to his stories! How vital I believed it to be that such a work be done sooner rather than later!

Not even giants live forever.

The first stage of the Watson application process was to write a proposal, attach recommendations, and submit them to a faculty board at the beginning of that fall semester. I'd shared multiple drafts of the proposal I'd written over the summer with a Davidson professor Dr. Abbott recommended who'd participated several times in the selection process. She gave me advice and criticism, and I went home and applied the recommended changes. Jacques and Annie wrote a second official letter for me, one of two required recommendation letters, and Dr. Abbott wrote the second.

The next stage of the process was a faculty interview in which each of a dozen or so selected applicants would be required to present his or her proposal, verbally, to a board of Davidson professors — nearly twenty of them, if I remember correctly — one lone applicant at the end of a long conference-room table pitted against a significant cross section of Davidson's faculty. It was this faculty board that would choose four finalists, and the Watson Foundation, then, would dispatch a lone representative to Davidson in the spring to interview the four one more time, before making a final selection.

Not unlike the *kamikaze* charge I ran on the beach with Master Choi in 1989, this second stage of the Watson application process four years later was to become a powerful transitional event in the education I acquired while at Davidson that had little to do with the academic education I simultaneously pursued.

TWELVE

I'D RETURNED FROM JAPAN two years earlier overbrimming with confidence. I'd failed, but I'd also given my all in the attempt. My all hadn't been enough, but knowing that I had given so much had set me momentarily free. I felt as though the world was mine and I could do with it as I pleased. There did exist one nagging side effect, however, to my collapse in Japan that threatened to hold me back as I fought to live the life of self-entitlement I perceived so many others my age to be living.

I'd always been nervous having to stand up and speak in front of large groups of people, but after Japan, that anxiety grew into a larger issue that came close, at times, to rendering any such attempt impossible.

Time passed, and it became more and more difficult to explain to those around me the enormity of the experiences I'd had in, and leading up to, Japan. Unable to share that ultimate truth of who I was, I came to feel as though I was lying, simply going through the motions of being a normal college student. I came to see myself from the outside interacting with those around me as vividly as I saw the people with whom I interacted. I would watch myself, say, tell a story to a group in a social setting, and I'd lose my train of thought. In the worst cases, it would occur right in the middle of a critical sentence, and I'd fumble over my words for an excruciatingly long moment that would force me to imagine myself giving up entirely and fleeing the scene in embarrassment.

Happily, it never came to that. It was almost as uncomfortable, though, to stammer for that long moment, clear my throat painfully once or twice, and then have to confess that I'd lost my place. I can only think of one occasion when that embarrassing confession didn't turn out to be the exact mechanism that brought me back to my train of thought. I was, in all cases but one, at least able to finish what I'd started.

This newfound and infuriating fear hit me most often when reading passages aloud in class – which we had to do all the time as English majors. One of my professors asked me to read the first lines of Chaucer's *Canterbury Tales* out loud one day – he knew I'd already completed the Chaucer course, in which we read so much of the entire work in its original Middle English. That was about the first day of class, since the Brit lit. survey doesn't go back much before Chaucer, and one poor freshman girl was almost in tears for fear that she'd entered a class – or even a college! – that was going to be too difficult for her. "What did he just read?" she asked in a panic. "How did he know how to pronounce the words like that? Am I supposed to be able to know how to do that?"

I laughed to myself. Her outburst had diverted attention from me!

Apparently I'd made it through with some semblance of fluency, but it was a miracle, given how I felt. Sweat had broken through the pores at my hairline, my heartbeat had jumped to an alarming rate, and I'd lost the ability, entirely, to judge when to pause during the reading to breathe.

Most of the time, I was able to hide my handicap. Other times it felt as though I didn't even have one. Perhaps it was chemical. Maybe if I'd eaten differently that morning, or slept better the night before, it wouldn't even have happened. There were certain situations that I came to avoid, however – because I felt so incredibly miserable when such attacks occurred – and on days when I felt particularly susceptible, I would dread upcoming tasks of public performance that I knew I could not avoid.

Of course, it could have been simple exhaustion.

There's no question that the further I pushed myself, the less sleep I got, and the worse my susceptibility became. We read something like eight complete plays by Shakespeare that semester; for my Chinese politics course, there were often entire books that we were required to read, cover to cover, for just one week's discussions; and I don't think I ever read more pages for a single course at Davidson than I did for "The 18th- Century Novel." All that work had to be done outside of class, and those were just three of my six classes; hiring, firing, scheduling and training in the Café generally kept me up half the night anyway; and if it hadn't been for the workouts of the daily karate classes I taught, I might have collapsed completely as the time requirements of the *Budo Karate Illustrated* project increased.

Budo Karate Illustrated had become the engine that drove all the rest. I'd given in, remember, to a foregone conclusion of success. *Budo Karate Illustrated* wasn't merely going to succeed, it was going to succeed just as I envisioned it succeeding. Letters from giants like Mas Oyama and Jacques Sandulescu arrived periodically in my mailbox to affirm the notion I struggled to beat down: that I, too, was living the life of a giant by doing, like these figures I idolized, things that the average people around me would never consider. I was probably insane to think it, but I looked into the future and saw myself altering the course of Mas Oyama's Kyokushin in America, in a small way, yes, but in just a big enough way that, if I played my cards just right, America's future itself just might take a significant turn for the better.

Wouldn't my own passion, after all, be enough to enact change? Wouldn't others be motivated by my half-blind response to Duty? Wouldn't they be moved by my sacrifice once they saw, through my writing, what I was all about? Jacques said if we could bottle it we'd make a fortune, and whether I was delusional or not, I believed it to be the case because I'd never met another in the North American Kyokushin world who worked even a fraction as hard as I did. It wasn't, after all, the results of the work that were necessarily so important.

It was setting the example of being willing to make personal sacrifice in the attempt.

Photographs, biographical sketches, and article submissions from dojos across the country were arriving daily in my post office box. I was leaping hurdles every day, learning how to process a photograph in this way or that, or how to send text coursing through a magazine layout as if on its own with Pagemaker. Tom Flynn, Mas Oyama's branch chief in Massachusetts, told me, "In all my years of practicing Kyokushin in America, I've never seen anyone put together a project that's achieved support from all the players involved. If you need *any* help with *anything,* all you have to do is say the word and help will be on the way."

"Use my name like a battering ram!" Jacques told me. "If anyone gets in your way, just let me know and I'll straighten 'em out!"

Far from reducing my ability to succeed on multiple fronts, the enormous creative demand of the magazine project fed a creative fire that pushed me through all the rest. I was passing all my courses, I was on track to graduate in six semesters rather than eight, my students were getting stronger and more numerous, my Watson proposal had been one of the dozen selected for the second-stage faculty interview, the article I'd written for *Black Belt* was finally going to be published, and even when I had to interrupt it all to go down to the basketball court to fire the worker who had called in sick (and was subsequently seen playing basketball), the Café ran like clockwork. At midsemester, I visited Davidson's best-known photographer, tested his confidence in his ability to shoot high-speed photographs, and, convinced, hired him to do a photo shoot for the magazine in which I leaped to new heights and performed the best *tameshiwari* of my life thus far. I broke two wooden baseball bats with a *gedan mawashi geri* for the first time, and like William Tell, split an apple balanced on a student's head with a jumping, spinning kick that would have broken his skull had I been off my mark. Afraid that the photographer might miss *his* mark, in fact, I performed the stunt twice more, each time with an identical result: We stood at the end of Davidson's new basketball court and I hit my targets so hard that chunks of apple flew horizontally like clusters of buckshot the entire length of the court before spattering on the wall at the far end of the room. I was on fire. I was unstoppable. I had become a machine of production for Kyokushin. I, who had failed to graduate, was becoming, or so I believed, the embodiment of Mas Oyama's intention for the graduates of his *uchi deshi* program.

Through the haze of my exhaustion, I'd smile at the private joke and liken myself to the mythological Greek king, Midas, who had the power to turn everything he touched into gold. Midas was emerging at the end of that last summer that Lissa and I spent together. With a sharp-toothed smile I was starting to see the future, it scared her in the face of her own uncertainty, and she closed her doors to me and ran.

And the loss of Lissa, wasn't the only unfortunate side effect.

The impact on my ability to relate to my peers in social situations was devastating. I was already dumbstruck by the inability to share with anyone the experiences I'd had in Japan, and now the experiences I was currently having, right there in their midst, began to make all that had gone before pale in comparison. And still I was powerless to make anyone understand.

"You have to ask yourself why anyone's going to care," Dr. Abbott told me. "You have to ask yourself who's going to pick your book up off the shelf, instead of one of the ones next to it."

Midas's version of William Tell's splitting an apple with an arrow as it balanced on his son's head. The impact of this kick was so powerful that fragments of the split apple hit the wall at the opposite end of Davidson's basketball court. In order to miss my student's head, the impact also had to be so completely horizontal that the fragments hit that opposite wall at head level, having traveled down the LENGTH of the court like a tight cluster of buckshot. (Note from this, and the book's other photographs, that I was clean-shaven at the time of my classmates' graduation March '93, and again in December '93 when I visited *Sosai* at *Honbu*. The beard came and went in the nine months in between, and might, therefore, be considered Midas's beard.) Photographs by Bill Giduz.

Not only, therefore, was I continuing to write my story, but Midas started to live it again. He started to live a life that, so help him, people were going to care about, because even if it killed him, he was going to realize achievements in his lifetime that people would have no choice but to notice. Midas knew it was going to happen that way because, with a secret smile and surrender to the foregone conclusion of success, he saw it as if it were a snapshot image of the product of his life's work, already in finished form.

And in something like perpetual awe at what I'd become, it became all the more difficult to finish telling my stories in social situations, and to read my assigned passages aloud in class without losing my train of thought. I crashed the hardest I'd yet crashed in the North American branch chief meeting, held once again in Rochester the morning after

Michael Monaco's tournament, one year to the day after my reunion there with Mas Oyama. I drove all night again, twelve hours to Rochester, leaving Friday after class, to attend that meeting and present, in person, to so many of the people I'd already corresponded with, my vision for an *American Kyokushin Yearbook*. The year before I'd been a mere bystander in the meeting, and *Sosai* had told me to sit in because I'd be "among them one day soon." This year, *Shihan* Monaco pulled the rug out from under me by yielding the podium to me the instant the meeting got

This was the first time I tried to break two wooden baseball bats with my shin. It took me three whacks, but I finally got the job done. The sequence shown is not an actual sequence, but rather a "piecing together" of shots from the three attempts. The look on my face in the first shot is clearly the result of my having already kicked the bats and failed to break them. My *dogi* pants leg is rolled up to show that my shin is not protected.

underway. "Yours is the most exciting point to bring up this year, Nathan," he told me, "so why don't you start the meeting by talking to everyone about your project?"

"Osu," was all that I could say and, having been up driving all night, I launched into a presentation of the vision that I could see so clearly. It's no wonder, I suppose, that I started what I had planned to say, got two lines in, and froze. All I could see was myself from the outside, failing so utterly to show them the full scope of what I could see that I felt as though the whole thing was a lie. The pores at my hairline cracked open to allow tiny beads of sweat to leak through. My heart raced to an extent that would have set off alarms had I been in a hospital in intensive care.

And at that moment I wished that I was.

This photo was omitted from the *Budo Karate Illustrated* book. One might note that it was one of the few stunts performed that day that the photographer missed, although the truth of the matter was that I missed it, too. The boards did not break.

The secret motive of the project, of course, had been to expose American Kyokushin to the best that *international Kyokushin* had to offer, thereby revealing America's weaker links, knowing that they might not recover. The Terry Garinis and Mickey Tucks would take major blows when they had no choice but to compare themselves not only to the Michael Monacos, Tom Flynns, and Randy Jameses, but beyond that to the Japanese, the Australians, the Brazilians, and the Europeans, who made the whole lot of them in America look like charlatans. The project was one that everyone would support – I knew they would because I could see the project's future! – and yet at the same time, the rug would be pulled out from under a good several of them when they saw how terrible their karate was. When international Kyokushin was placed side by side with the substandard American version, the Monacos, Flynns, Samitowskis, and Jameses would adapt and grow stronger.

But the rest would get burned, and several of the rest were present that day in Michael Monaco's branch chief meeting.

In their case, my entire presentation was a lie. I watched myself from the outside as I started to tell it, and my presentation barely got off the ground. Jacques' wife Annie, the Harvard grad with whom I could have about the easiest conversation of the bunch, told me afterwards that it wasn't even noticeable. "Yeah, you got a little flustered," she said, "but in the end you got your point across, so who cares? Just chalk it up to experience, and be a little bit better prepared next time. It's clear that just about everyone plans to submit material and sell copies to their students. What else do you want?"

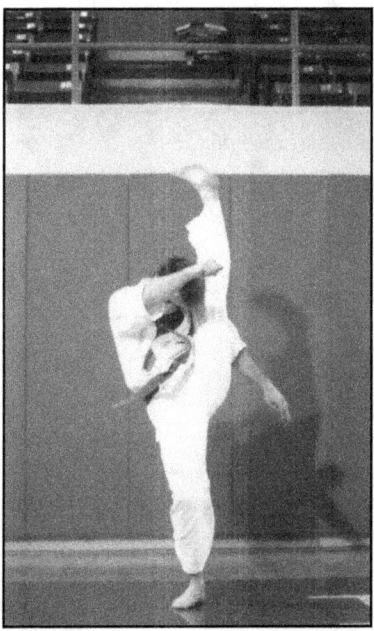

Bill Giduz's timing was truly spectacular that day as he caught with his camera technique after technique at the best possible moment.

And so I left Rochester to drive all night back to North Carolina for classes Monday morning, ashamed of my weak performance but successful.

Of course the project was going to succeed!

Mas Oyama was behind it. Jacques was behind it. *Shihan* Lowe had decided that he'd better get on board and submit material or he was going to get left out. By the time I got back to North Carolina, Midas's secret, knowing smile had returned. *Maybe it's precisely because I fumbled over my words so badly that everyone's going to support it! If I'd shown them the strength and confidence that I really feel, wouldn't I have come across as threateningly precocious? Wouldn't I have been overstepping my bounds in the face of the Shihan Lowes and Michael Monacos there that day?*

Why do the U.S. branch chiefs squabble among themselves?

Because they don't want to be outdone! If I'd come across as strong as I feel, the only non–branch chief invited to the North American branch chief meeting, if I'd come across as Nathan Ligo, the only American to have been as close to Mas Oyama as a personal student since Mas Oyama lived for five months with Jacques in New York in the 60's, wouldn't my proposal have met with opposition? Instead, I tripped over my own tongue like an idiot and came across as someone who was totally unthreatening. Isn't that, in fact, exactly why they're all still on board?

Is it really that I can see the future?

Or is it rather that I know that I'll do whatever it takes when the time comes to ensure that the future I envision will come true?

Could my resolve have become so primal that it would reach out and take over, dashing even my public demeanor if necessary, to carry me safely past a potential pitfall I hadn't even considered?

* * *

Try as I might to deny my embarrassing failure to simply talk to a group of people in Rochester, it was that same kind of collapse that I feared would ruin my faculty Watson interview.

Only this time, such a result would be catastrophic.

I'd get in there and have just ten minutes to show that cross-section of Davidson's more eminent professors how confident and capable I was. There were only 150 professors at Davidson. The twenty in the room would be more than a tenth of the entire faculty. None of them were lightweights; none of Davidson's professors were. Their fields spanned the entire scope of Davidson's course offerings. *This one's for* Sosai, I told myself. *This one's for Kyokushin. It could bring me back to Japan to research Sosai's biography before he dies. I have to succeed in this presentation at all costs. If I get tongue-tied like I did in Rochester, it'll all be over. Failure is not an option.*

And so I had my suit cleaned and pressed – the same one I'd worn in Rochester the week before – but instead of wearing it for the fifteen-minute walk across campus to Chambers, I emerged from the one-room cottage in my father's backyard wearing sweats and running shoes. My suit was draped over my shoulder, still in the cleaner's packaging. My dress shoes I carried in my other hand, as I set out deliberately towards campus, ninety minutes early.

When I was an *uchi deshi*, our *sempai's* torture instrument of choice had been the jumping squat. We averaged only 150 or so each morning in morning training, but if we were ever in trouble, or if our *sempai* got angry at us, the number of consecutive jumping squats we could be ordered to do – often under threat of violence – reached into the high hundreds. One morning in my second year in the dormitory, when the lot of us overslept our alarm clock and were fifteen minutes late for morning training, the dormitory chief ordered us to complete fifteen hundred consecutive jumping squats – 100 for every minute we'd been late.

At the time I thought he was insane. *There's no way we can do 1500 nonstop repetitions when three sets of fifty burn our muscles so badly every morning!* But of course we said *Osu!* and started anyway. Moving down the line, each of us counted ten, we'd shout a *kiai* on the tenth count just as we always did, and then the next guy would count ten more. *Surely someone's going to drop out eventually,* I reasoned. *Someone's muscles are going to fail, and then someone else's, and then I'm sure mine will. I'll just keep going until someone else drops out. I'm sure as hell not going to be the first!*

Unfortunately, however, everyone else must have been thinking the exact same thought. No one was going to be the first – and so no one dropped out! We completed 1500 consecutive jumping squats, and my perspective was forever changed. The pain, of course, had been significant. At times I wondered if I might not rather be dead than do another hundred. My thigh muscles were pushed to beyond failure. My lungs were exploding. I looked forward to the end so that I could puke. I longed to be on Sunset Beach again, with Master Choi there to turn my *koohai's* eyes towards me to give me that second wind.

But no second wind came. And yet, like the others, I completed the entire 1500 repetitions in a nonstop fifty minutes. In a state of disbelief, I found that I could walk back to the showers and then to the dormitory once it was over.

The next day, of course, none of us could bend our legs. We staggered up and down the stairs as if we had wooden legs without knees. It wasn't until a week later, when the pain had subsided, that I realized the extent to which Minami *Sempai,* our dormitory chief at the time, had empowered my future by showing me, once again, how the limits to what we believe ourselves capable of are so often only perceived ones after all.

I knew that all too well by the time of my Watson interview. And alone during the hour beforehand, in what had been my dojo in Johnson Gym my freshman year (and Davidson's wrestling room before that), I began to do jumping squats. I wasn't after a reaffirmation of the knowledge that we're far more capable than we believe ourselves to be.

I was after the torture.

There alone with no one to bear witness, I drove myself through 1000 consecutive jumping squats in the last hour before the interview. I wasn't averaging 150 each morning, like I had been in Japan. I was a full-time college student and only a part-time karate teacher, and I knew 1000 repetitions would be like 2000 had I still been training like an *uchi deshi.*

And I was right. It about killed me. My legs hit what I perceived as failure after only 200 reps, and still I charged forward. My lungs were exploding by 500, and by 600 I started trying to talk myself out of the rest by asking if that wasn't enough already.

But it wasn't, and I knew it.

I growled, I howled, I gnashed my teeth, and I fought forward to 700, to 800, and beyond. At the end of 1000, I checked my watch. There was no time for a shower, but I'd brought a towel. I shed my sweats and shoes right there in the puddle of sweat that had formed around me, toweled myself dry, and stood there naked for a few moments as I demanded control of my breathing in order to lower my body temperature.

What a sight I'd have been if someone had chosen that moment to walk in!

Moving to the other side of the room so as to no longer be standing in sweat, I got dressed except for my top button which I left unbuttoned, my collar which I left turned up, and my tie which I left untied. Slowly and deliberately, I walked across campus to Chambers with my jacket folded neatly across my arm, and my arms held slightly out from my body so that sweat wouldn't form on the front of my shirt beneath the weight of my arms. Midas smiled wide as I found that I could barely bend my legs to walk up the dozen stone steps between Cannon Dorm and Chambers, knowing that no one in the interview chamber would have a clue.

I smiled again at the uselessness of my legs when I reached Chambers' marble stairs.

Just like one year earlier, when I'd stepped into the men's room of Rochester's Airport Holiday Inn to wash the smell of cigarette smoke off my hands and face in preparation for my reunion with *Sosai*, I stepped into the men's room in the main hall of Chambers to button my top button, tie my tie, and turn down my collar. With a brown paper towel that smelled like cardboard I wiped the beads of sweat from my face and forehead. That same sweat held my hair in place as I pressed it with my fingertips. The coarse red beard that I'd allowed to come in since the summer was just long enough to grab in a handful, and thinking back to when my father had one – he was my hero then, high on the roof at the log house, driving nails into row after row of cedar shingles – I tugged it to a point and, for a fleeting moment, imagined my kilted forefathers in the hills of Scotland.

I checked my watch and took a deep breath. All I needed was ten minutes. I couldn't let myself sweat for ten more minutes.

After that I could collapse.

Somehow I managed to knock twenty professors out of their conference-room chairs that morning. None of them knew who Mas Oyama was, but they'd all been introduced to him by reading my project proposal. They knew that I'd had some kind of unique karate experience overseas. After sitting down at the head of the table in the chair I'd been offered, I smiled, looked them all in the eye, wished them a good morning, and thanked them for granting me the opportunity to share my idea with them in more detail. Then, knowing the podium was mine, I stood up and explained that the best way to show them the intensity of the life I had experienced in Japan was to show them how I spoke with Mas Oyama – the founder of Kyokushin Karate, a teacher of twelve million worldwide.

At that, I slid the chair out of my way, shifted my weight equally to both feet, and with my hamstrings flexed and my weight imperceptibly shifted forward to the balls of my feet, I raised my white-knuckled fists to face forward just in front of my hips to assume *fudo dachi*. After hesitating for only a moment to gather power in my low belly, I crossed my arms to bring my fists close to my opposite ears, I visualized *Sosai* walking into *Honbu* like he did every morning of my second year as I cleaned the dojo's *shinzen*,[58] and I brought my fists down to their original position with an atom-splitting intensity as I bowed and issued the thunderous "OSU!" that only a *Honbu uchi deshi's* encounters with *Sosai* could engender.

Twenty professors at the table involuntarily straightened in their chairs, a third of them jumped, and one or two swallowed nervous lumps. I had the eyes of all twenty of them simultaneously; I had their eyes the way I wanted to have them, and I knew from that instant that the day would be mine.

For the next ninety seconds I visualized *Sosai* before me and spoke to them *in Japanese* in the thunderous tone of the *dojo kun*,[59] or of the Japan Champion reciting his oath at the opening ceremony of the next year's All-Japan Tournament. "Osu, I am the American *uchi deshi*, Ligo!" I swore as if *Sosai* himself were my audience. "I've come here to Japan to work for Kyokushin! I've come to finish what I failed to finish before and continue my training! I've come to make the second issue of the magazine that I've created for the future of American Kyokushin! I've come to write a biography of Mas Oyama! I've come to sacrifice my entire life, my every breath, my every drop of blood for the future of Kyokushin if necessary to ensure that your legacy is carried proudly into the next generation! I spill my blood for you and I spill it with pleasure because I know that your work is one and the same as my own, that to achieve for Kyokushin is also to achieve for me, and that through this work, I might achieve a position in life from which I can make the world a better place for everyone, not just those who practice karate!"

The poor girl waiting outside in the hall for the next interview must have been terrified as the chamber door shook on its hinges. The professor teaching in the classroom above must have paused in his lecture to try to identify a sound the likes of which that building had never heard. And just as smoothly as I'd transformed myself from just another unassuming college student to the monster that took over the building, a moment later I relaxed my fists, my diaphragm, and my hamstrings again, smiled, softened my eyes, and morphed gently back into the baby-faced 22-year-old college kid who'd entered the room. I moved my chair back into place to take my seat, eight more minutes passed in the interview, and I can't remember a lick of it except that it wouldn't

---

[58] Altar at the front of the dojo, arranged by rules associated with Japan's Shinto tradition.
[59] Dojo Oath.

have mattered what was said at that point. I knew the nomination was mine.

For a mere ninety seconds, and for the first time ever in the two years since my return from Japan, I had been completely honest with Davidson. I had opened the floodgates and showed them what I'd been carrying inside. There was no conflict then, there was no cause for insecurity or doubt. I'd let the beast out of its cage, I'd showed them Midas's sharp-toothed grin, and then showed them how smoothly, how masterfully, I could bottle it all up again and blend into the crowd. I'd shown them not only that I was uniquely qualified – that no other American could possibly achieve what I set out to do – but also that my confidence and my passion to do it were insurmountable. Not only did I receive the nomination, but I heard from other professors in passing that they'd heard about my interview and that I was considered a shoo-in for the $10,000 grant.

Midas gnashed his teeth as he walked down the hall of Chambers that day, loosening his tie, and forgetful of the numbness in his thighs. He laughed at the fact that the Japanese he'd used had been far, far less than the meaning he'd conveyed with his tone, with his stance, and with his eyes, and that since none of the professors present that day spoke Japanese, they had no idea. In being completely honest with Davidson for the first time by revealing what was inside him struggling to break free, Midas had lied completely about his ability to speak fluent Japanese.

Midas could have told them, "The elephant had pink and green stripes and it laid a beautiful golden egg on the moon" in the tone he'd used, and they'd still only have heard, "The world is mine! Get out of my way before you embarrass yourselves."

THIRTEEN

IN EARLY DECEMBER, I called *Honbu* and found myself inadvertently having a conversation with Mas Oyama.

I had received all the *Budo Karate Illustrated* submissions I was going to get from the U.S. branch chiefs. The entire floor space of my one-room cottage was littered with stacks of photographs: a stack from Rochester, one from Chicago, one from Guam, and all the rest, twenty-two piles in all. My six classes had driven most of the remaining work of laying out the book into the upcoming four weeks of my winter vacation. I feared that I would not get much sleep during what was meant to be a period of rest, but I was chomping at the bit to get the project underway.

I thought of the star-packed sky that became my quiet companion so many nights when I was the last one to walk across campus after the Café closed at one, and I smiled to myself to realize that I was even further conditioned for sleeping just three or four hours a day by the nearly sleepless exam week I'd just finished. – A year had gone by since Lissa and I drove past Grandfather Mountain in the snow, and I felt as if I hadn't had a full night's sleep since then.

After checking yet again to make sure I'd calculated the time difference correctly, I called *Honbu* from the cottage in my father's backyard to try to arrange a meeting with *Sosai* before school started again in January. I hadn't spoken with Sosai in person since my classmates' graduation nine months earlier, and it was still three months before the *nidan* grading I didn't yet know Sosai would ask me to take that coming spring.

Ten o'clock at night in Davidson was 11:00 a.m. Tokyo time. I had multiple book-related motives in mind for one more trip to Japan, but there was one mission, above all others, that I considered paramount: I would ask *Sosai* for permission to turn what had only ever been presented to him as the *American Kyokushin Yearbook* into the first issue of an ongoing English-language Kyokushin magazine, called *Budo Karate Illustrated*.

David Bunt, my *sempai* in New York, had advised me way back in June to start by asking *Sosai* for permission to make a one-time publication. When Jacques and Annie seconded his advice, that's the course I took. Now, however, it was clear that we really did have a chance to create a North American Kyokushin magazine – the first issue was going to succeed – and now it was time to share the idea with *Sosai*.

Master Choi taught me that showing sacrifice was the best way to ensure a positive result in a negotiation with his uncle, and what better way to show sacrifice than being willing to cross the Pacific to meet with him? Needless to say, calling *Honbu* terrified me. The call would be as important as my Watson interview, only this time, my Japanese would have to be correct.

As it turned out, I was able to identify myself, relatively smoothly, as Ligo, the former *uchi deshi* from America, when *Honbu*'s first-floor receptionist answered the phone. I could tell from her voice that she remembered me, I knew who she was too, and I was ashamed that I had never learned the names of those Japanese ladies who stood in the back of the dojo every morning during our morning ceremony. She connected me upstairs to Mrs. Watanabe, who caught me totally off guard by handing the phone directly to *Sosai*.

I didn't even have time to panic.

"I wanted to ask *Sosai* if I could meet with him in the first week of January," I told her in English.

"Oh, I see," she said, "why don't you ask him yourself? I'm sure he would be very happy to hear from you."

I didn't have a chance to protest. I'd called to arrange a meeting with *Sosai*, through his assistant. I'd never spoken with Mas Oyama on the phone before. No one I knew ever had. No one I knew spoke Japanese.

A moment passed. I nearly choked trying to regulate my breathing. *Sosai* picked up the phone. "*Hai*," he boomed ("Yes?") in his unmistakable baritone. I imagined Mrs. Watanabe having just told *Sosai*, "Mr. Ligo from America wants to talk to you. I'll put him through."

Damn her! I thought.

I hadn't spoken with *Sosai* since my classmates' graduation, and if he hadn't sounded so incredibly *genki* [60] that morning, I would probably have fallen right back into the *Sosai as God* trap, and the pressure would have doomed the conversation before it even began.

"Osu! *Amerika no Ligo desu! (Osu!* It's Ligo from America calling!)" I responded in the only way I knew how. My volume was a degree less than the shout with which I had shaken my professors in their seats, but I wouldn't have been surprised if *Sosai* nevertheless moved the telephone receiver half an inch further from his ear.

"*Hai, gokorosama desu!* (Thank you for all your hard work)," he said. "*Genki desu ka?* (Are you well?)" *Sosai* was speaking to me deliberately and slowly in Japanese that he knew I'd understand.

"Osu! I am well," I said, pausing uncomfortably before asking, "And *Sosai*, are you well?"

"I'm fine, thank you," he said. "What can I do for you?"

"Osu! I would like to meet with you at *Honbu* in January, if possible," I said. "*Yoroshii desu ka?* (Would I be permitted to do so?)" Although *Sosai* had done much to put me at ease by his manner, I could feel my Japanese fluctuating dangerously near the limit of my ability.

"*Hai, yoroshii desu yo* (Yes, of course)," he said. I barely had time to react to myself, *Wow! That was easy!*

"*Osu, arigatoo gozaimasu!*" I said. "*Ano . . . Honbu e iku-toki ni, ryoo-ni nettemo yoroshii desu ka?* (Oh, and sorry, but when I come to Japan, is it possible that I might be permitted to sleep in the dormitory?)"

"*Hai,*" he said, "*itsu kimasu ka?* (When are you coming?)" He was using language a bit more formal than he would have with someone my age had I been Japanese. Although *Sosai* almost never spoke English, he was no stranger to having to interact with foreigners with less than a language in common. Apparently he knew my Japanese ability, and I was flattered that he was willing to use that polite form with me, because it would be easier for me to understand.

"Osu!" I said, "January . . ."

And the conversation broke down. For all the times I'd reviewed the Japanese counters for days of the month (the first, the second, the third, etc.; they're all irregular and none of them sound like the corresponding numbers), I suddenly couldn't conjure up the appropriate one to tell *Sosai* what date I would be arriving. All I could do was stammer, and finally try to

---

[60] High-spirited.

rescue myself by asking awkwardly if I could speak once again to his assistant.

Sosai laughed in a friendly way, but I could tell he was displeased that I'd revealed how nervous I was. Mrs. Watanabe came back on the line a moment later, and she and I arranged a meeting for the day after my scheduled afternoon arrival in Tokyo during the first week of January. We exchanged formalities, and the call came to an end.

Midas's smile wasn't enough then to rescue me from the shame I felt, having just spoken with Mas Oyama on the phone. *Who the hell am I to be granted an individual audience by Mas Oyama, and in his own language?*

I wondered if I'd dreamed it.

My every bit of energy for the months that preceded that call had been tied up in doing for that giant with whom I'd just spoken. If the widening rift in my personality between me and the monster Midas hadn't already begun to compensate for the extreme demands of my imposing list of responsibilities, I'd have long since failed out of my classes, lost my job, and probably, for all intents and purposes, been reduced to a babbling idiot. Instead, the fracture had somehow given birth to an alternate consciousness which could focus entirely on the *Budo Karate Illustrated* project every moment of every day, even as I went through the motions of everything else.

Already for weeks by then, I'd found that I could function as Nathan Ligo, the normal, albeit overcommitted, college senior, even though my every moment of conscious thought – and social interaction! – was overshadowed by the enormous creative processing demand of *Budo Karate Illustrated*. It didn't even leave me while I read. Whether I was reading Jane Austen for my eighteenth-century novel course or yet another play by Shakespeare, some significant portion of my brain was chugging along in the background – like a computer program running offscreen. I knew it was there because every couple of pages, that more important window would pop up on its own, whenever that greater task required some deliberate action on my part to keep the creative process grinding forward, and the process always seemed to be a step ahead of where it had been the last time, as if it had still been happening without me. I woke up in the night, during the few hours I slept anyway, from dreams in which I was having conversations with key players in the *Budo Karate Illustrated* progression, or composing letters, or text, or even arranging photographs in the layout. I'd wake up and remember vividly what I'd dreamed, and smile to myself when I realized I'd had original thoughts in my sleep that were actually applicable to the real-world development of the vision.

Other mornings, I'd wake up and lie there struggling to remember what that Eureka!-like solution was that I'd figured out in my sleep. I'd curse myself the mornings I couldn't remember: *Damnit, there's no excuse! I knew I should have gotten up to write it down!*

Through it all, Mas Oyama had been behind me, looking over my shoulder, encouraging me to fight forward. He stood there with his brow wrinkled, the corners of his mouth turned down, his fists on his hips. The ends of his belt beyond the knot were several inches shorter than they had been in years past, but his eyes shone piercing and bright. I could feel his pride as I drove myself beyond exhaustion. All of the work was for him, all of it was supported by my sense of him watching over my shoulder. I'd played and replayed conversations with him while walking across campus, while in my shower until the hot water tank ran dry, while reading Dafoe or about China's Cultural Revolution, and even in my sleep. I formulated Japanese conversation after conversation to test whether or not I'd be able to get my point across when next we spoke.

And then, to so suddenly hear his voice like that, like he was right there beside me, had all but blown me away.

Sosai wasn't an easy man for someone my age to talk to, especially not for one who had been his *uchi deshi*. In Japan, we weren't even allowed to speak to him unless he spoke to us first. All things considered, I couldn't believe how smoothly the conversation had gone.

I took a deep breath and, growling to myself, dug through papers on my shelves to find the necessary phone number, and dialed the dojo of Kyokushin's most recent World Champion, Matsui Shokei.

Setting up a meeting with *Sosai* had only been Part One. Mas Oyama's agreeing to see me was the prerequisite for half a dozen other arrangements that needed to be made. The first was to dare to arrange a meeting with Matsui for the night before my meeting with *Sosai*. I had a favor to ask of him as well.

* * *

It took nerve to call Matsui and ask him to meet with me – given how famous he was and how much of a nobody I was – but the notion of meeting him alone despite my limited Japanese wasn't completely far-fetched. I had held my own during short but significant conversations with him twice before, the first time much, much earlier, when my Japanese was far less than it had become by that December of 1993.

In fact, one of my first-ever successful conversations in Japanese had been with Matsui.

Less than a year into my training in Japan, some fifty members of *Honbu* went out together after training to wish a happy, healthy *sayonara* to a dojo *sempai* of ours who was moving to Australia. I always got Oota *Sempai* and Watta *Sempai* mixed up. They were both big guys who were so far ahead of me in rank that I never had much of a conversation with either one of them, and that early into my time in Japan, I was still having difficulty with Japanese names. I believe it was Oota *Sempai* who lost his temper when I kicked him in the head once during a *kumite* training in preparation for the Osaka Weight Category Tournament in 1990: He took me out of training for a week by lifting me up and throwing me, spine first, into the sharp corner of the plywood box that covered whatever kind of machinery was in the corner of the first-floor dojo at *Honbu*. It's always easier to remember the names of those that beat us up! If I'm not mistaken, though, that would have been after this *sempai* of mine for whom we had the *sayonara* party left for Australia. So maybe it was held in honor of Watta *Sempai*.

I can't be sure.

At any rate — whichever one of my *sempai* he was — he was one of *Honbu's* old guard, who may even have been senior to my graduated *uchi deshi sempai*, Yuhi and Ishida. Of course, as time passed and I grew up a little bit, I would come to know that *Honbu's* significant *sempai* went a lot farther back than those that were regular faces in the trainings when I was an *uchi deshi*. At the time, however, Matsui — the Champ, as we called him, thanks to Judd's habit of assigning nicknames to all the Japanese — came by to teach training every once in a while, and certainly he was the *sempai* of about everyone I knew. (Matsui had become World Champion two years earlier.) There were a couple of old men around, such as Yokomiso *Shihan* who taught the seniors' class on Friday nights, but other than that, most of my "high-level" *sempai* at *Honbu*, I would learn, were high-level only in my limited understanding, because they were enough bigger and stronger than me to seem untouchable, rather than because any of them had much real seniority in the greater Kyokushin world.

That nearly every *sempai* I knew was Matsui's *koohai* meant that the crowd I thought of as *Honbu's* senior echelon was really little more than a group of youngsters. Matsui then was only 28 or 29.

Vast amounts of beer were consumed that night. We ate – but mostly drank! – at two different establishments, since the first one closed and threw us out before we'd had our fill. There followed an exciting half hour or so while the fifty of us wandered through the streets of Ikebukuro drunk, searching for a second establishment that could accommodate all of us and would stay open long enough. It was exciting because as *uchi deshi* we rarely had opportunities to walk through Tokyo streets at night, certainly not with a beer buzz, and walking with us was none other than Kyokushin's world champion!

Several places denied us entry, even though we could see that there were tables open, before we found one that would serve us. My Japanese was far from fluent, but I got the distinct impression that fifty drunk Kyokushin *karateka* were more of a liability than they wanted to risk inviting into their establishments at that late hour of the night.

As first-year *uchi deshi*, we didn't have many opportunities to drink alcohol, but two of the times that we did, our immediate *sempai* – the third-year guys who lived like kings with us in the dormitory, with their washing machine and their own separate rooms – tortured the lot of us by making us drink massive quantities of beer until everyone threw up. So it wasn't exactly with eager anticipation that we realized we were going to be in another beer-drinking environment with our *sempai*. Judd and I tended to see beer and *sempai* together in the same room as dangerous, and any time we were offered beer we deliberately drank as little as possible. We knew well that as the evening matured, the chances that we'd be able to escape drinking much more beer than we wanted would decrease exponentially.

The drunker everyone got, the more dangerous the night would become.

Somehow that night did not become dangerous, though, perhaps because of Matsui, who, although surrounded by drunks, didn't have a single drop to drink all night. I watched him turn down beer that he was offered time and time again. I idolized him then, of course, and the fact that he wasn't drinking made me respect him all the more. When my *sempai* offered me beer – and almost everyone there was my *sempai* that night – I was required to answer, "Osu! *Itadakimasu!*" ("Thank you for your kind offering!") and empty my glass, whether I wanted to or not, so they could refill it for me. The fact that Matsui didn't drink meant that no one there was his *sempai*. What was so special about Matsui that even when Yokomiso *Shihan* offered to fill his glass, he was able to say, "No thank you, I'm not drinking tonight"?

It was as though he was above it all, and everyone allowed him to be.

My conversation with Matsui happened at that second pub we went to. Unlike the first one, in which we'd had one large open banquet room all to ourselves, this one was more of a traditional restaurant-style drinking establishment with low Japanese tables with cushions for sitting cross-legged on the floor. Somehow I was placed next to Matsui, and I was drunk enough by then – though not by choice – to feel more excitement than the stress I probably should have felt at finding myself sitting right next to the Champ.

Matsui was at the end of the long table, I was to his right, and Judd was at my other elbow, if I remember correctly. Yokomiso *Shihan* was across the table from me with one other elder *Shihan* whose name I can't remember, and a second Australian short-term *uchi deshi* named Rod was beside them.

Rod – otherwise known as "Roddo" because the Japanese have a hell of a time pronouncing any one-syllable word that ends with a consonant other than "n" – had been recommended to the dormitory by Cameron Quinn, and he was the only *uchi deshi* I ever saw *Sosai* kick out with such complete disdain. We were all assigned some area of the *Honbu* building to clean every morning after breakfast and before the morning ceremony, and Rod was supposed to be helping one of the Japanese clean *Sosai's* office – a very honorable duty, I thought. Mas Oyama came in early one morning, and found Rod rocked back in the secretary's chair reading a magazine with his feet up on the desk. He hadn't even noticed that *Sosai* had walked into the room! So of course he hadn't made the slightest move to stand up and say *Osu!*

Sosai kicked Rod out that day, if not in fact that very moment. Rod had only been in the dormitory for several weeks, and I was never happier. I disliked Rod immensely because he was rude, immature, and didn't seem to appreciate in the slightest the privilege that had been bestowed upon him. He was one of those young foreign lost souls that always seem to congregate and become all the more lost in Asian capitals – and I have met several! Rod knew Judd somehow, thought what Judd was doing sounded pretty cool, and wrote to his former karate teacher, Cameron Quinn in Australia, to ask him for a recommendation. Within a grand total of about three weeks from the time he first heard of Mas Oyama's *uchi deshi* program, Judd and I were going across Tokyo by train to help him move more bags full of belongings into the dormitory than all the rest of us had put together.

It had taken me, remember, six years of shedding blood, sweat and tears under the tutelage of Mas Oyama's nephew in North Carolina to make it to Japan. That Rod might be admitted to the dormitory on a whim was insulting enough to me already, even if our personalities hadn't combined explosively. I can't remember exactly what he said or did to upset me one day in the dormitory, but he was nearly a year my *koohai* and, like Mocaram before him, it seemed he needed someone to disrespect in order to assert the fact that he wasn't weaker than everybody else. He said something rude and obnoxious that one simply doesn't say to his *sempai* and, bowing to the pressure of what had become the trend there for awhile in the dormitory, I'd told him that we'd solve the problem "next time we met in the dojo." What that meant, of course, was that we would solve it with our fists next time we fought. Unfortunately, I wasn't raised to be much of a *solve it with my fists* kind of guy, and I was completely unprepared when Rod came storming downstairs five minutes later to call me outside shouting, "Come on then, Ligo! We'll solve it right now!"

In the street outside the dormitory, Rod backed me into a corner in front of my classmates. I realized then I couldn't escape without fighting, so I kicked him in the balls with all my might. Unfortunately, under duress, my aim was imperfect, and my *mae geri* [61] landed ineffectually in the crease of his leg. He punched me in the face twice, which resulted later on in some swelling of the bridge of my nose – which Judd laughed at me for – but no blood. Somehow in the process I had gotten hold of Rod's neck or collar, and about the time Minami *Sempai* (our dormitory chief) came running out of the dormitory yelling frantically in English, "No fighting! No fighting," I managed to wrestle the top half of Rod down so his head was on the pavement below me with my right hand cocked back to throw a punch. We stopped then – the two-way ineffectual nonsense that our little

---

[61] Front kick.

brawl had been – because Minami *Sempai* had ordered us to. It remains a source of shame to me to this day that I didn't pound Rod about the face and ears a couple of times while I had such a clean opportunity.

Sosai would likely already have been apprised of the fact that Rod had disrupted the peace and order of the dormitory by the time he came in to his office and found Rod with his feet up. It does occur to me that that makes two foreign dormitory residents that *Sosai* kicked out who had, at one time or another, problems getting along with me.

But it would be dangerous to read too much into what was probably just coincidence . . .

Rod was across from me at the table next to Yokomiso *Shihan* when I had my first conversation with Matsui, and I only bring him up now to emphasize how intoxicated I must have been when I found myself suddenly able to communicate so fluently in Japanese. Rod passed out about an hour into our sitting there, his head pitched over backwards, and he started gurgling in an unmistakable announcement that he was about to vomit beer all over everything and everyone within a five-foot radius. Yokomiso *Shihan* noticed it before I did and yelled at me in Japanese across the table.

"Ligo!"

"Osu!"

"Take Rod to the toilet right away!"

"Osu! *Shitsurei shimashita! Dekimasen!*" I responded. ("I'm very sorry, but I cannot!")

"Ligo, hurry up! *Abunai!* (It's about to get dangerous!)" he said.

"*Shitsurei shimashita! Dekimasen!*" I repeated. Judd was howling with laughter. Somehow I managed to congratulate myself for maintaining composure next to the young giant on my left, even though it was because I was so drunk myself that I'd declared my incapacity to carry Rod to the toilet.

"Ligo, Jaddo, *hiyaku!* (Ligo, Judd, hurry up!) Roddo's going to puke!"

With no one who cared enough to rescue him, Rod went ahead and puked all over himself, and Judd and I had no choice, in the end, but to pick him up and haul him off to the toilet.

My response to Yokomiso *Shihan* was significant because we never, ever said "No" when one of our *sempai* told us to do something. Responding with "I cannot," when I most certainly could have in at least some fashion or other, was completely unheard of. It demonstrates how much I disliked Rod: I'd refused for the first and only time an order I'd been given by a *sempai* – and Yokomiso *Shihan* was a very high-level *sempai* indeed!

I carried that ungrateful slob's luggage all the way across Tokyo so that he could move in and make a mockery of uchi deshi life, and now I'm supposed to carry his fat ass to the toilet so I can watch him puke? I don't think so! If he's going to make an idiot of himself by throwing up all over himself, to hell with him!

Surely I owe Yokomiso *Shihan* an apology, even though he, too, had finally succumbed to laughter. "Osu! I cannot!" was outrageous enough, all by itself, since "Osu!" and "I cannot!" are an exact contradiction. "Osu," after all, means "I will press forward in the face of any hardship."

I really did feel pretty big that night, talking to Matsui.

I'd grown up a student in Master Choi's CMAC watching blockbuster documentaries from Japan of Mas Oyama and his students performing the most amazing feats. It wasn't until the end of my time with Master Choi, however, that I learned that the videos I watched revealed only a miniscule part of the full scope of "modern" Kyokushin Karate. The only videos I'd seen – and I'd watched them over and over again – were of the first and second world tournaments back in 1975 and 1979. I saw Sato Katsuaki, for example, awarded a victory against Royama Hatsuo in the final fight of the First World Open. I knew well the American champions of that earlier era, Willie Williams and Charles Martin, and I knew how Willie had finally fallen to the bare-knuckle blows of the Brit, Howard Collins. I knew Oishi Daigo and Ninomiya Joko. I even knew the Thai kickboxers, and those sad little Chinese kung fu fighters who got so badly beaten by the Japanese.

But what I hadn't seen, ever, was the fruit of another decade of evolution of Kyokushin tournament fighting, which resulted in the type of speed and finesse for which Matsui had become so well known.

It wasn't until many more years later that I would come to understand what was lost during that decade of rapid evolution.[62] When face punching and defense against punches to the head were phased out of tournament

---

[62] During this era, young aspiring fighters inspired by tournament champions trained in the dojo to do what they saw their heroes doing. Since their heroes weren't throwing punches to the head, or blocking punches, the next generation largely failed to learn how to defend their heads from hand techniques. What the young generation failed to realize was that the first generation of Kyokushin fighters acquired their prowess by using these more dangerous techniques in the dojo, while only setting them aside for competitions in the name of safety.

fighting, however, what Kyokushin fighters learned to do with their bodies in terms of high kicking speed, accuracy and lethality was nothing short of amazing. It was during that pivotal four-day summer camp on the beach with Master Choi in 1989, in fact, that I watched the first new Kyokushin videotape I'd seen in several years. It was Matsui's 100-man *kumite*, and I'm not ashamed to say it brought tears to my eyes.

Nowadays, when there is more anti-Matsui sentiment than pro, his political opponents like to bring up the fact that many of the hundred he fought that day weren't really qualified to fight an All-Japan Champion. Sure, it's a great feat to fight one hundred consecutive bouts against rested opponents, but while his critics are right that many of his opponents were well below his level – no one was at his level, after all! – his jaw-breaking finesse was incredible.

Watching Matsui's 100-man *kumite* for the first time, it was all I could do not to panic. I was on my way to Japan within the year, I'd studied the giants of the first and second world tournaments, and I'd been warned that I was physically too small ever to be able to compete with them. And in my understanding of what Kyokushin tournament fighting was, that made total sense to me. The fighters of the first and second world tournaments were giants in stature, as well as in character. They were huge! I was preparing to go to Japan at five-foot-nine and 155 pounds, and it was easier for me to relate to the Chinese kung fu guys who got crushed than to the Kyokushin giants who won. Matsui's tape, however, caught me totally off guard. It was the most amazing thing I'd ever seen. It was like Hollywood's kung fu movies that were so obviously fake, only Matsui's blows were all real! At the end of his techniques was real impact that knocked his challengers out, one by one, like rag dolls. And worst of all – the reason for my panic, and perhaps even for my tears – was that I realized that someone my size, in the modern Kyokushin era, had broken through and shown that a level of technical skill could be developed to where the giants could be beaten. And that meant that I would have to change my conception of what I, too, could achieve through my training. It had been so much safer to believe I could never be like them. Now, suddenly, I realized that I would be expected to try!

And I told Matsui so, that night at my *sempai's sayonara* party in Ikebukuro, in the first ever successful conversation that I held completely in Japanese. "When I saw the videotape of your 100-man *kumite*," I told

Matsui, "I cried." What I wanted to say was that it brought tears to my eyes, but I didn't know how to say that in Japanese. In fact I didn't even know the word for *to cry*, but with a fingertip tracing the path a tear would follow down from my right eye, I made him understand the missing word.

"*Naita?*" he said. "You cried? Why?"

"Osu," I said, "because I never saw technique like that before."

"Why did you want to learn karate? What do you want to do with your future?" the 28-year-old Matsui asked the then 19-year-old me.

I had already explained that I was the student of the Korean nephew of Mas Oyama. I knew Matsui to be Korean, and I knew, therefore, that he would be interested to hear of my Korean roots. He was curious to hear about Mas Oyama's nephew, since Master Choi was a figure completely unknown to the Japanese world of Kyokushin.

"Osu, I want to teach Kyokushin in America," I told Matsui.

"Why?" he asked. "Can you make money teaching karate in America?"

"I don't know," I explained. "But I desperately want to teach karate to Americans to try to make America, and the world, a better place."

"How can you do that?" he asked.

"America has many problems," I told him. "Of course it's one of the strongest countries in the world, but its people also have some of the world's greatest problems."

"What kind of problems?" Matsui asked.

"*Amerikajin wa kokoro no mondai ga iroiro arimasu,*" I said. "American people have all kinds of problems of the heart."

"*Soo desu ka?* (Really?)" Matsui asked. "*Tatoeba?* (For example?)" Perhaps I was naïve, but for the life of me, I'd have to say that Matsui was genuinely interested in what I was telling him. And I'm certain that, because I had his eyes, he understood even a little more than the literal meaning of my limited vocabulary. At the very least he would have understood the truth behind the words.

"Weakness," I told him.

"Weakness?" he asked.

"Osu, weakness. Karate training can make Americans stronger spiritually. Of course I would only be able to teach a few of them, but in that way, over time, I would help to make America a better place. Life is too easy in America. Americans tend to take the easier course when faced with difficult choices. Karate's spiritual strength can change that for some of them." Whether he understood my every word or not, Matsui – perfectly sober – gave me 100% of his attention that night. I had the distinct impression that he grasped the meaning I was trying to convey, and more than that, that he was moved by my candor and by my motivation for wanting to practice karate.

That was why, longer than two years later, I felt confident enough to telephone Matsui from North Carolina to arrange a meeting. It was for that reason, also, that I would feel all the more betrayed, and disappointed in Matsui, years later when he and Katsuhiko Horai would stand, personally, in the way of my teaching Mas Oyama's karate in America.

That January, however, three weeks later when I met with Matsui in response to my telephone call from Davidson, he far from stood in my way. It was with genuine kindness, interest and encouragement that he welcomed me and my plans.

I rode in his car – he drove – from his dojo, where we'd met. He took me to a small restaurant and we ordered food. I had brought visual aids, photographs mainly, and I used them to supplement my limited Japanese as I described for him my vision for *Budo Karate Illustrated*.

The first part of my presentation was about carrying a barbell up Grandfather Mountain.

How ironic it was – looking back – that I led off by telling the future failed chairman of Mas Oyama's IKO an anecdote about how *budo* and morality had proven to reign supreme over the standard principles of business when it came to the development of a karate school!

How ironic that he agreed with me, that he was impressed, and that he did little to conceal the extent to which he was moved!

"You have lots of talent, Ligo," he would tell me five years later in Budapest and it was crystal clear to me then that he remembered at least the impression that he got from our conversation that night in Tokyo, when I told him how I had carried a barbell equal to my body weight to the top of Grandfather Mountain. I had done it to raise money for charity, yes, but even more than that, I'd done it to rescue Master Choi's two ailing dojos and to promote Mas Oyama's *budo* karate as a means of doing good for the community, rather than simply glorifying violence, making money, and propagating the fantasy notions of karate students' abilities that tend to thrive in the closed circles of America's non-contact martial arts schools.

In 1991, home from my *uchi deshi* experience in Japan, I carried this barbell equal to my body weight to the top of Grandfather Mountain to raise money for area charities and popularize my teacher's dojos. It was a triumph of *budo* over business, and it was with the story of this event that I convinced Matsui of the value of the *Budo Karate Illustrated* project.

In short, I set out to give Matsui an understanding of my entire concept of conscience-born *vision*, which was just then coming so clearly into view. My idea of carrying a barbell up a mountain to popularize

Master Choi's dojos had been the first example. I hadn't planned the barbell stunt, or contemplated it, or thought of it in a casual sort of way and then put it on a back burner to simmer before deciding that it would work. Instead, presented with the heart-wrenching dilemma of how to set Master Choi's schools back on the right track, it had dawned on me, from the very first moment, as foregone conclusion: *That's the way! That's the answer! There is no better, and it will work to fulfill the current need!* All I'd needed do was catch hold of the impulse, in as close to its original form as possible, and act on it like there was no other way.

The proof of the vision's validity had been the multileveled successes that it engendered.

Master Choi and I started with barely forty students in two dojos, and we were losing the battle: Our student body wasn't growing fast enough and the bills weren't getting paid on time. After my barbell stunt generated nearly a dozen newspaper articles across North Carolina, however, suddenly we had more than a hundred students in each school! More than that, though, I had shown some significant segment of the community not only that karate could be used for the betterment of the human condition, but that we as individuals – even those of us who had started out weaker than the rest! – could be at the forefront of such a charge. We had directly raised money for needy causes, but I knew even then that I had also indirectly set an example of what karate in the human community can be all about. Allow the hard physical training of karate to instill spiritual strength in the individual, and that individual will be better prepared to make hard decisions for the betterment of everyone, rather than just selfish ones for the betterment of his or her own financial or social position.

The point I made to Matsui that night – and I could see that he understood – was that I had an instantaneous gut feeling about how successful the barbell project would be for all of those reasons, some of them obvious and others harder to see, and that I'd had the exact same sensation at the moment the *Budo Karate Illustrated* vision was born.

"This magazine *will* be successful," was the point I sought to make. "I know that it will be successful because I can see it. I can feel it! It will be successful in a multifaceted way that will make that barbell stunt look like an exercise, like a mere warm-up for the real thing!"

I didn't have the Japanese, of course, to explain all the benefits I could see. The ongoing project would raise money for *Honbu*, and maybe create a future position for me with a salary that I could use to help fund my own dojo: That part was easy to explain. It would make Mas Oyama's karate better known in North America: That part was easy, too. Much as Michael Monaco's tournament had, it would show the U.S. branch chiefs what could be achieved if we all worked together: That part was a little harder to explain, but I got my point across.

What my Japanese was not up to explaining was, "It will expose the charlatans as charlatans, it will expose the fakes as fakes, it will focus the spotlight on those that need to raise their standard closer to the international norm. The influx of information from overseas and the in-your-face comparison of the weak ones to the strong will either break the weak ones or force them to get with the program." This, the most deeply entrenched motive of the project, was very much on my mind that day, but it stayed, in the end, on my side of the language barrier.

"*Sugoi!*" Matsui exclaimed when the impact of my barbell vision dawned on him. "Wonderful! Great!"

"*Sugoi!*" he exclaimed when I told him how our student body had jumped overnight to greater than 200 students.

I could see in his eyes that he'd gotten exactly the point I'd set out to make, and it was that night in Asakusa that Matsui himself became the fulfillment of the next step in the vision's realization. "I'd like to introduce a photo essay in every issue of the magazine of Japanese fighters demonstrating the latest developments in Kyokushin techniques and their applications," I told him. "In this way, we can work to raise the technical standard of North American Kyokushin by showing everyone the latest that Japan has to offer."

"I was hoping, in fact," I went on to explain, "that you would be the subject of the first such photo-essay, and that you would agree to become a technical advisor for the magazine project, to oversee an article like that in every issue that we print on into the future. That's why I asked to meet with you tonight, in advance of my meeting with *Sosai* tomorrow. I have come to Japan to ask *Sosai* for permission to convert this one-time hardcover book into the debut of an ongoing periodical publication. With you in my corner, supporting the project as its technical advisor, *Sosai* will be more likely to approve."

Matsui didn't even have to pause to consider. His answer was the unequivocal *yes* that Midas already knew it would be.

But I had one final favor to ask.

"I suppose it's very rude to suggest," I asked Mas Oyama's heir-apparent that night, "but do you think you could call *Sosai* on my behalf . . . to tell him that you and I have discussed the project and that it seems like a viable, valuable project to you?"

"You want me to call *Sosai* for you?" Matsui asked.

"Osu, *onegaishimasu*! (Please do this favor for me!)" I used a full array of the tools Master Choi had taught me to convey, above and beyond the spoken word, that I was uncomfortable asking him to do such a favor for someone as unimportant as me, but that I believed it to be of such importance to the development of *budo* karate in North America that I was going to dare to do so anyway.

This time, he did hesitate. I held my breath.

"Very well," Matsui said finally, "I will call him."

With something quite the opposite of joyous celebration, it dawned on me that every single one of Midas's ambitions was coming true. Jet lag, perhaps, chose that exact moment to catch up with me. I looked into the future and beheld the work that had yet to be done, and the thought of it knocked me, internally, to my knees.

Matsui drove me to *Honbu*.

"Osu!" I saluted, and bowed as he drove off around the park where the blood from my knuckles, too, shed during a virtual lifetime's worth of morning trainings, must still have been mixed in with the soil. Until that moment I'd forgotten about my sore throat. It was dark and cold, and after a brief assessment, I realized that I probably still had a fever. I was back at the dormitory again, for the first time since my classmates' graduation nine months earlier, and I was so tired tears came to my eyes.

To this day, I have no idea whether Matsui called Mas Oyama on my behalf. It was that weekend, however, that *Sosai* asked me how many days I'd resided in the Young Lions' Dormitory. "Osu! Longer than 500 days," I'd told him, and he ordered his secretary to prepare a graduation certificate for me even though I hadn't completed the program.

"You may not have stayed for 1000 days," Mas Oyama told me with this gesture, with his manner, and with his eyes, "but through your choices, you've shown me that you are embodying the purpose for which I support my dormitory and exert so much effort for this random assortment of misfits that pass through my life.

"Take Kyokushin and run with it, Ligo. Remember what I've taught you, fight to make Kyokushin in America stronger, and use it to make the world a better place."

FOURTEEN

MY TRIP TO JAPAN was a success on all counts, even though, out of a lingering youthful stupidity, it nearly killed me.

I was ill when I left North Carolina – sick with a chest cold and a sore throat – but by the time I abused myself for the several days I stayed in Japan, living the life of the protagonist in this twisted story of ambition and transformation, I had recovered to some extent. Perhaps I kept myself so occupied that my cold finally just went away.

I was traveling on almost no money. The cheapest flight to Tokyo that I'd been able to find on such short notice left me overnight in Toronto for a change of airlines. I arrived in Toronto after dark in a fever-induced stupor. It was pouring down snow. As in most airports, there was a wall of direct-line telephones to an assortment of hotels, and I scanned the accompanying placards for the one that appeared to be the cheapest.

I'd actually planned to sleep in the airport lobby – I'd once spent two nights in the airport at Narita, so I knew that I could endure a single night in Toronto! – but once I arrived, I was so sick and tired that I resolved to find the cheapest possible accommodation with clean sheets and a hot shower. I was surprised to find that a YMCA was advertised among the Hiltons and Holiday Inns. I'd never stayed in one before. Where I come from, YMCAs are for exercising, not sleeping, but I'd heard that historically they existed as cheap accommodation for young people, so I decided to give it a shot.

Maybe they do things differently in Canada, I thought.

I picked up the receiver and spoke with a male voice that told me there were indeed vacancies for the night. He told me that there was a bus I could take to a subway station, and then a subway I could take to the Y – or maybe it was the other way around. At any rate, it was a bit of an ordeal to get there, but I decided to go anyway, despite my fever and more luggage than I would have liked to carry that far. I was carrying a laptop computer that I'd borrowed from the college through my stepmother's office (and this was back when laptops weren't all that small), a camera bag, and a briefcase, in addition to my garment bag, which contained a suit, my *dogi*, and several other changes of clothes.

Ninety minutes, a train, and the last possible bus I could have taken later, I arrived at the address, stepped out into the snow, and staggered up a deserted street, barely able to carry all my luggage. I read the addresses on the building fronts in search of the right one. Moments later, the public transportation that had brought me there long gone, I found the correct address and walked up to the door of the YWCA.

What the . . . ?

YWCA stands for Young *Women's* Christian Association! Somehow I found myself, at midnight, in a snowstorm, in a foreign city, with a fever and a sore throat, two hours from the airport and in the hours after all public transportation had shut down, standing outside a travelers' inn that was only open to women!

What the hell have I done? I asked in disbelief. *Did I read the sign wrong in the airport?* Could I have been that stupid? In America every community has a YMCA (Young *Men's* Christian Association), but for the most part there were no longer YWCAs. Could I have seen the sign, recognized those familiar letters, and just taken for granted that it said Y*M*CA?

I wanted to smack the guy working at the counter. "Couldn't you tell on the phone when I called that I wasn't a woman?!" I pleaded. Apparently he'd just thought I was a woman with a deep voice, since what man would be stupid enough to try to book a room in a YWCA? He was at least able to call a cab for me, and I spent the sixty-five dollars that I would have spent for my clean sheets and hot shower on taxi fare back to the airport so that I could sleep on a bench in the departures lobby.

By the time I got there, it was two a.m., and I was beside myself. By 3:00 I'd decided that the floor against the wall was more tolerable than the rows of bucket seats that made up the airport benches. I don't remember much after that. That sleep, plus the sleep on the eleven-hour flight to Japan, must have done me some good, because I didn't feel so terrible by the next night when I met with Matsui. I'm sure that adrenaline took over to mask the symptoms of my cold.

For the next two nights, I slept in the dormitory for the last time. Nick and Mahashi were only three months away from graduating – they'd graduate about the same time as my *nidan* grading. Nick had two *gaijin koohai* living with him in the dormitory at that time (both two- or three-month visitors to the dormitory as Sandor had been), Rodney from South Africa and the blond Danish kid whose name eludes me, but whose *jodan ushiro mawashi geri* [63] would so nearly remove my head from my shoulders at my grading two months later. I'd been at Judd's graduation nine months earlier, and he was out of training, living out his own hedonistic rampage in Tokyo, but he had heard that I would be in town and he'd come by the dormitory to visit.

That's me in the dormitory, clean-shaven and rosy-cheeked, and thus looking remarkably young for twenty-two, in the back row on the left next to Judd, whose graduation I'd attended nine months earlier. In the front row, that's Nick (left), just three months before his own graduation, and two short-term dormitory residents, Rodney (center) from South Africa, and Nick's *koohai* from Denmark whose name has escaped me, but who would come so close knocking my head off my shoulders at my *nidan* grading less than two months later.

Nick and Judd were interested in the work I was doing on a magazine in the US, and in the fact that I'd just met with Matsui and would be meeting the next day with *Sosai*. Nevertheless, I had never in my life felt

---

[63] Back spinning kick to the head.

more the Beta in a room full of Alphas, and I suspected that any one of those four guys could have crushed me in *kumite* without breaking a sweat.

What business do I have here in this place? I asked myself as I fell asleep that night on the same futon in the same spot where I'd slept for nearly two years of my life. *This is Mas Oyama's Young Lions' Dormitory! It is a place for champions. And what am I?*

> *I'm a nobody. I'm a quitter. I'm a loser.*
> *Look at my condition now.*
> *Weak! Weak! Weak!*
> *A fish out of water.*
> *Fool!*

Sosai welcomed me to Japan the next morning in the morning ceremony at 9:30, and by 10:00 I was meeting with him upstairs in his office. The *piéce de résistance* of my entire trip to Japan was his signature on an official letter that I'd boldly written for him, defining *Budo Karate Illustrated* as an official ongoing periodical publication of his International Karate Organization, me as editor, Matsui as technical advisor, and Jacques and Annie as advisors. I was acutely aware of how bold it was to ask him to sign something that I'd written, so I only offered it to him to save his staff the labor of writing it once I'd gone through its content with him piece by piece. I shuddered – and Midas sneered! – to have already written Matsui in before leaving North Carolina even though I hadn't spoken to him until the night before.

Much to my relief, *Sosai* agreed with every point, including the one I'd come to Japan for: Without batting an eyelid, Mas Oyama put his stamp of approval on my changing a one-time yearbook into a magazine that I then believed would become a large part of the work I'd do for the rest of my life: The *American Kyokushin Yearbook* officially became *Budo Karate Illustrated*.

International Karate Organization *Honbu*
Kyokushinkaikan
Director Mas. Oyama

Budo Karate Illustrated is an official periodical publication of the *International Karate Organization* and the Kyokushinkaikan. Its purpose is to establish an official, direct line of communication between the World Headquarters of the IKO in Japan and the various branches of the IKO located in countries around the world.

Its goal is to help prevent misconceptions of the true nature of *budo* karate as taught by *Sosai* Masutatsu Oyama from arising due to the vast spatial separation between Japan and the world branches.

President Masutatsu Oyama will have final word in all issues of organization, staff, and subject matter. However, due to the language barrier, President Masutatsu Oyama and the Kyokushinkaikan cannot be held responsible for any conflict arising due to any included material.

Every issue of *Budo Karate Illustrated* will be read and approved by U.S. and European Advisor, *Shihan* Jacques Sandulescu before printing.

All features generated in Japan concerning technique will be supervised by Kyokushin Karate Technical Advisor, *Shihan* Akiyoshi Matsui.

The Editor, Nathan Ligo, takes full responsibility for any conflict arising due to any included material.

Budo Karate Illustrated will be printed once in 1994, biannually in 1995 and 1996, and quarterly starting in 1997. All generated proceeds will be used or distributed by the Kyokushinkaikan as it sees fit in order to further the propagation of Kyokushin Karate.

[Signed] Masutatsu Oyama
Chairman, IKO *Honbu* Kyokushinkaikan

I'd never seen *Sosai* so relaxed and unceremonious as he was with me that day and the next day, when I met with him again in his office. I was accustomed to being intimidated by his strict manner. This time, however, when he spoke with me, when he took out photo albums to show me photographs that I might like to use in my layout, or when he made suggestions of material he'd like to see included in the first book, his manner was more that of a gentle grandfather than I'd ever seen it. I was used to experiencing him as, in a word, piercing. That weekend, however, he let down all his defenses and treated me like family.

"I tend to treat my *uchi deshi* like sons because while they're here, I have to be their family," he told me as his assistant translated. "In your case, however, I also think of you as a son, but I've always also thought of you as a grandson first, because you were my nephew's student before you became mine. He is the one that would have been like your father. I hope that you will remember what I have taught you, and what he taught you before that, and do your best to live accordingly."

I wasn't sure exactly how to respond. All I knew with *Sosai* was, "Osu! *Wakarimashita!*" ("I have understood!"), so that's about all I said. *Sosai* asked me how many days I'd resided in the dormitory, and when I told him, "longer than 500 days" (I didn't know the exact count because I'd been home for three months in the middle of it helping Master Choi; it was probably more like 600, start to finish), he told me that it was an admirable achievement, since no foreigner had ever completed the program at the time when I began. He ordered his assistant to have a graduation certificate prepared, and to strike through the "one thousand days" part of the text and write in "500 days" instead. It was done very professionally, and March 15, 1993, the date of my classmates' graduation nine months earlier, was written in. I was sent several blocks away to acquire a passport-size photo, and *Sosai* signed the ledger-size document himself right there in front of me, and sealed both his signature and his alteration of the printed text with his *hanko*.[64]

Sosai seemed to me that day to be the epitome of power, of course, as he always was, but more than that, he seemed to epitomize health and, dare I say it, he also epitomized love. I'm not sure exactly what it was that I interpreted as health, except perhaps for how warmly and gently he interacted with me. He seemed to me actually to be exuberant, as if he'd woken up that morning and said, "What a beautiful day to be alive!"

The father of modern karate, *Sosai* Masutatsu Oyama, would be dead less than four months later. Cancer, that day, must already have been eating him alive. Although I'm certain that he must have known, I had no idea. He looked to me that day like he would live forever.

He definitely gave me the impression that I would never again be without him watching over me.

Sosai epitomized love for me that day because he left me feeling, unequivocally, that he approved of me, that he was proud of me, and that he felt some sense of accomplishment having been my teacher. The gesture was an uncommonly loving one coming from a man like Mas Oyama. He autographed a copy of Cameron Quinn's book, *The Budo Karate of Mas Oyama,* and gave it to me that day – it was the only book written in English that he had new copies of in his office. He accommodated every request

---

[64] Traditionally wooden, a unique red-ink stamp historically used in lieu of a signature on official documents in Japan.

that I had concerning the *Budo Karate Illustrated* project. He awarded me an honorary graduation certificate from his *uchi deshi* program in front of everyone in the morning ceremony on my last full day in Japan. But none of that could ever possibly compare to the greater gift he gave me that day — and in his final days after that:

Sosai bestowed upon me a stamp of approval that only *Sosai* could give. "I approve of you, I am proud of you because I know that you will continue to work hard for Kyokushin, and I know you will work hard to become a valuable member of society," were the gesture's unspoken words.

Of course, I remain devastatingly humbled. I'd already developed a heightened sense of conscience, but by leaving me in the way that he did, *Sosai* gave me a heightened sense of responsibility as well. *I damn well better get it right!* I have reminded myself daily since *Sosai's* death. *He approved of me because of how hard I was working, and because of how hard I was working to listen to my heart. I'd better keep listening, and I damn well better stay on my guard to prevent that channel from becoming clouded. His approval was a great gift, but it wasn't a blank check. It will be a lifelong struggle to keep myself walking the path that will allow me to continue to draw on it!*

At dinner in the dormitory that Saturday night with Nick and Mahashi, and my other would-be *uchi deshi koohai*, *Sosai* asked me in front of everyone what my plan was for the future.

"Osu! I will teach karate in America," I said.

"Where in America?" he asked.

"Osu, I'm thinking about Atlanta," I said. "It is the largest city in my area." I also knew Atlanta was a city with which he was familiar.

"*Subarashii!*" he said. "Wonderful! You should be like . . ," he paused to conjure the right name, as he did some days when all foreigners' names were running together for him. "Cameron!" he announced. "You should be like Cameron from Australia, and teach karate and write many books."

"Osu! I will do the best that I can."

"Are you coming to *Honbu* for the grading in March?" he asked.

"Osu," I said "I will do the best that I can." This time I answered with less confidence, both because I wasn't sure I'd be up to a *shodan* grading and because I couldn't imagine how I could afford to come back to Japan in less than three months.

"*Subarashii!*" he said again. "But you should test for your *nidan* instead."

"Osu, *Wakarimashita!* (I have understood!)" My stomach did a triple somersault as I processed internally what *Sosai* had just told me to do. *He just told me to test for my nidan in two months. That means a twenty-man kumite. My god, it'll kill me!*

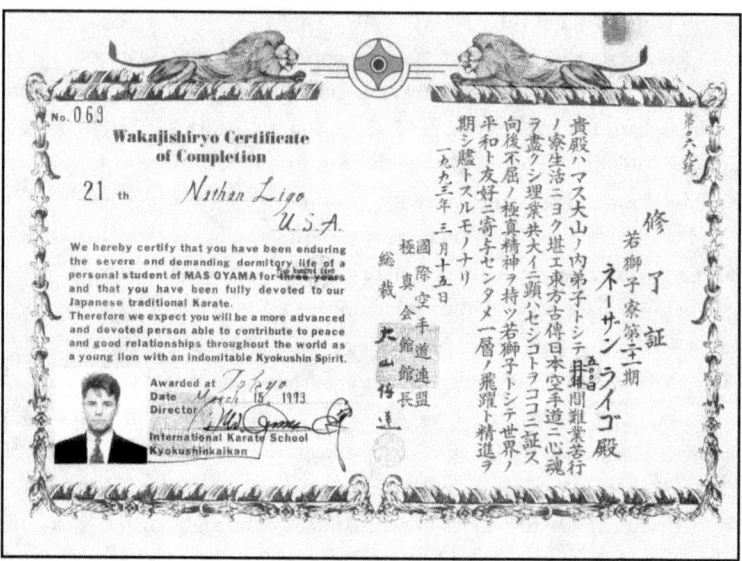

Mas Oyama ordered his assistant to have a graduation certificate prepared, and to strike through the "one thousand days" part of the text and write in "500 days" instead. It was done very professionally. I was sent several blocks away to acquire a passport-size photo, and *Sosai* signed the ledger-size document himself right there in front of me, and sealed both his signature and his alteration of the printed text with his *hanko*.

"When will you graduate from college?" *Sosai* asked. Now he was asking, I was sure, for the sake of the other *uchi deshi* present. He was leading up to speaking to the others about me. I'd told him already that morning that I'd be graduating in May.

"Osu, I'll graduate this year in May," I said.

"Very good, Ligo," he said, "*Gambatte!* (Persevere!)"

"Look," he was suggesting to the others, "this small American guy managed to become a *budoka*! He even learned Japanese in the process and now he's going to devote his future to Kyokushin!"

"Osu!" I said. "*Gambaremasu!* (I will persevere!)"

"Ligo was here in the dormitory for 500 days," *Sosai* said to the other *uchi deshi*. "He trained very hard, and now he is working very hard to support Kyokushin in America."

"Osu!" everyone responded through their mouthfuls.

"I have decided to give him a graduation certificate as a special case even though he did not complete the full program."

"Osu!" everyone answered again, and I was utterly ashamed.

For all of the Saturday dinners I'd had with *Sosai*, he'd never spoken that many words to me before. He rarely spoke that many words during dinner to anyone! Dinner in the dormitory was for eating, it was for eating a lot, and if he said anything at all during dinner, it was usually very brief and to the point:

"Komukai, go to South Africa."

"Osu!"

"Yamakage, you shouldn't have gotten injured when you fought!"

"Osu!"

"Judd, what's your weight now? . . . Excellent! You should eat more . . ."

"Osu!"

Short, direct questions or statements were usually all that he said while we concentrated on the enormous task at hand, which was to eat, to eat a lot, and to eat non-stop until *Sosai* decided we'd had enough. I was utterly ashamed that he had used an already unprecedented conversation with me to announce to my *koohai*, who were fighting their way through a program I'd failed to complete, that he was going to be giving me a graduation certificate "as a special case."

Of course it was *Sosai* speaking, and there is no "But . . ." with *Sosai*, so everyone just said, "Osu!" and kept right on chewing.

Way back in the beginning, Sandor, Judd, Mocaram, and I had shared the dormitory for six weeks with a Ukrainian named Stanislav who knew absolutely nothing about karate when he arrived. At the end of his six weeks, *Sosai* tested him for his black belt and sent him back to Ukraine to establish the very first foothold of Kyokushin Karate in that country.

Today, there are tens of thousands of Kyokushin *karateka* in Ukraine as a result of that daring first step.

Sosai, I think, was no idiot.

FIFTEEN

JUDD AND I WENT OUT on the town one night that week, and there was no ambiguity about our intention to pick up girls and get laid.

I'd been all but celibate since Lissa, so overcommitted for months now that I wouldn't have had the time or energy even if I'd been trying. In Japan for the next couple of days, there was little more I could do to further the project except work on an article I was writing about Jacques. I'd gotten it well underway on the plane on the laptop computer that I'd brought along for that purpose, and I'd even done some additional work on it at night in the dormitory. I consoled myself that there would be time to finish it on the plane on the way back, and I decided to give myself a night off to hang out with Judd for old times' sake.

Judd was fresher *out of the monastery* than I was – he'd graduated just nine months earlier – and he'd wasted no time finding a job as a bouncer in a club in Roppongi, and an apartment nearby where he could systematically drive three years of celibacy out of his system, one-night stand by one-night stand. Judd's blond hair and blue eyes were in fashion among a certain type of Japanese women that frequented Roppongi nightclubs – a class of women that were generally not my type – and over my next several visits to Japan, I would watch in awe the ease with which Judd brought new Japanese girlfriends home, night after night.

My business with Mas Oyama was nearly complete. The last item that I had to take care of before returning to America was my scheduled meeting with Matsui at his dojo for the photo session he'd agreed to do. I went out with Judd, therefore, aware that I wouldn't be back in the dormitory that night and a little bit nervous about making my 9:00 appointment with Matsui the next morning. The club scene wouldn't even be getting started until midnight, and Tokyo trains are all still by one a.m.

We only live once, right? Shouldn't we live life to its fullest every chance we get? Judd and I had lived an earlier lifetime together in Tokyo under the constant watchful eye of our *sempai*. We'd never once in two years been out on the town, just us, completely free to do as we pleased.

We started the evening at an upscale, discothèque-like club with dance floors on two levels made up of three-foot glass squares that alternately lit up in different primary colors. The club's female patrons plainly put some significant effort – and money! – into dolling themselves up. As nightclubs go, it was a classy one. I laughed to myself: the Japanese men, too, were drinking dainty, colorful cocktails with umbrellas and citrus wedges! I spent fifteen minutes or so talking to a beautiful young Japanese girl in a knee-length white dress. She seemed flattered to have caught my attention and excited to be talking to an American.

Fifteen minutes, however, was long enough for me to start to fret.

Dammit, Nathan, you're too nice! I was telling myself. *And now your Japanese is running out! Pretty soon you won't have anything left to say!* I looked up and scanned the dance floor for Judd. He and an American guy he knew were standing on either side of a less-pretty but shapely girl at the edge of the room. Judd was laughing and running his hand down her thigh while his friend distracted her by admiring her earrings. *Look at them over there!* I thought. *Pros! And here I am asking this sweet, innocent girl how many brothers and sisters she has in basic Japanese! She's far more beautiful than the one they're with, but isn't she hanging out with me because I'm SAFE?! Is the trick to picking up girls in bars just to be cocky and aggressive?*

I looked back over towards Judd a moment later, but the three of them had disappeared. Suddenly, Judd's American friend was beside me.

"Hey!" he said, "What did you say your name was? Leego? Hang out here for just a second, okay? Guard these stools! Don't let anyone take our table!" I didn't have a chance to argue: I didn't understand exactly why he was asking me to stay, so I didn't quite understand, either, when he said something in excited, hurried Japanese to the girl I'd been talking to, grabbed her by the arm, and led her towards the door.

What the hell? I thought.

I looked around, in vain, for Judd. *What did this jerk of an American friend of Judd's just say to this girl I've been talking to for the past fifteen minutes? Was it that he wanted to show her something?*

Twenty-five minutes passed. I was embarrassed for fifteen of them and pissed off for the last ten. There I was, Judd was gone, his friend was gone, the girls were gone, and I was alone, sitting there like an idiot, guarding the stools!

When the four finally came back in, Judd, the American, and the girl Judd was with had looks on their faces and springs in their steps that suggested Santa Claus had come early. The girl in the white dress – who did not look quite so joyous – diverted her eyes when I reached out to her with mine. I realized that she'd recently tried in vain to wipe smeared lipstick off her face. Her eyeliner had been imperfectly repaired. Could she have been crying? Her mouth looked like it hurt.

What the . . .?

I turned my eyes towards the American. He was still laughing, but now he'd turned his back on the girl he'd taken outside, ignoring her. *Asshole!* I thought. He was saying his good nights to Judd.

"Later, Leego!" he said. "Enjoy your stay in Japan!" He set off, alone, towards the door. I turned back towards the girl in the white dress and our eyes met for the first time since she'd come back inside. I was ashamed that there was something there that made her no longer seem so appealing. It was like all her beauty had been stripped away. She turned and ran off towards the bathroom.

"What the fuck happened, Judd?" I asked.

"Whatta'ya mean, Ligo? Nothing happened. We took those girls outside, that's all."

"But that one doesn't look too good," I said.

Judd laughed. "I don't know what they did," he said. "They were on the other side. David can be a bit of a prick. I wouldn't be at all surprised if she didn't know why he was taking her outside."

It took me some minutes after that to get the wind back into my sails. *But couldn't you see that I was sitting here talking to her?* I thought, but I didn't say it.

"Yeah, well, you clearly weren't getting anywhere," I could imagine Judd saying.

I wasn't being much of a good drinking buddy – Midas wasn't any help picking up girls in bars, apparently – and I was angry.

I started to regret that I'd missed the last train.

Upstairs some minutes later, a group of women beckoned us into a private room. Judd and I were both pretty desperate, by then, for any kind of diversion – including especially from one another! – and we allowed ourselves to be drawn in.

Out of the frying pan, into the fire! I thought: there were more sets of perfect breasts at that one round table than I'd ever seen in one room before. The women were a little bit older, there were nine of them, they were Asian but not, I thought, Japanese. They squeezed us in among them, on plush, upholstered wall-lining bench seats. One of them put her arm around me. Another asked us what we wanted to drink.

None of them spoke Japanese.

They were from Singapore or Malaysia, if I remember correctly – somewhere I'd never been and knew little about. We spoke with them in English, which most of them handled pretty well. Judd was a bit drunk, and he was complimenting one of them on her perfect breasts – even reaching out to examine one when she warmed up to his compliments and offered him a squeeze. "I had them done in Hong Kong," she was telling him proudly. It was about then that I began to get uneasy about the big strong hands on these dainty little women. Their long, beautiful, brightly manicured nails weren't enough to hide the fact that the one across the table from me on the other side of Judd looked like she had the grip of a lumberjack.

I scanned the table, looking at hands and Adam's apples. Half of them had their necks hidden by scarves or high collars. *Oh shit,* I realized. *These women aren't women!*

In our defense, they were quite well done up to hide their "imperfections." They really did have perfect breasts, and plenty of cleavage exposed to reveal that their breasts were real. *Definitely not falsies,* I thought. *How do they do that? Hormones? Surgery?*

Neither Judd nor I had ever encountered such creatures before.

"Judd, I don't think these women are women," I said to him across the table in Japanese.

"Ah, come on, what are you on about, Ligo?" Judd said, just then, at the end of his sentence, realizing what I had said. He looked around the table once again.

"Fair dinkum, Ligo! Are you serious?" he blurted out in English with his thick Brisbane accent. "How can you tell?"

"Look at their hands," I said, once again in Japanese.

Judd was actually holding the hand of the lady next to him who'd let him examine her breasts. He lifted it up to take a closer look. He peered at the hand, he looked at me, and he busted out laughing.

"Fuck, Ligo," he said in English, reaching out to take another squeeze of the breast nearest him, "but they've got such perfect tits! How do they do that?"

I squirmed in my seat, because Judd – in typical Judd fashion – had started talking, right out in the open, about the ladies at our table. The ladies pretended well, but I watched their eyes, and it was plain to see that at least several of them were on to the fact that we were on to the part of them they most wished they could conceal.

"Don't you think we should go, Judd? It's getting late, isn't it?" I said in English, acting.

Judd was laughing. He'd put down the lady's hand he'd been holding.

"Oh, don't go!" The lady nearest me began to overplay the feminine dismay of a jilted lover. She grabbed my forearm as I started to rise. This one did, indeed, have the grip of a lumberjack.

Judd was also having difficulty getting out, since he was all the way at the back of the room. The ladies were doing their thing, I realized, playing their game, tearily acting the part of women who were being abandoned. I'm sure they congratulated each other later for the good fifteen minutes that they'd kept us fooled.

"But you can't go, Darling! We were just starting to have such a good time!" the one next to me was saying as I tried, unsuccessfully, to peel her fingers off my arm.

Judd was still laughing, but I could tell he was about ready to walk across the table smashing glassware, to start throwing punches if necessary, to get back outside. Innocent Beta that I was, I was trying to talk my way out.

"I know," I said, "I'm sorry, but we really have to go. We have an appointment. We have a meeting really, please . . ." The unfinished part of the sentence, which then made me laugh too, was " . . . please, don't make me have to give you a big *hiji*.[65] I might get blood on your dress."

That was funny to me because of course we were in no danger – they were just putting on a show – and I had no impulse whatsoever to hit anybody. I laughed, because it would have been the dumb American

---

[65] Nose-smashing elbow strike.

jock thing to do. If I'd been the aggressive jerk that lied to get the girl out into the alley, I'd also likely be the one that started throwing unnecessary insults when cornered by such creatures.

"But you can't go, Honey!" the "girl" next to me was saying. "Okay, if you truly have to go, give me a kiss first?"

Oh, Jesus! I was thinking. *Forget it!* Maybe the *hiji* wasn't such a bad idea.

Perhaps she saw that desperation in my eyes, and gave me the out that I needed: "Just one kiss," she said, "just a little peck on the cheek." She turned her cheekbone towards me. "Just a *little* kiss," she said.

Ah, what the hell, I thought, and I gave her a peck on the heavily powdered cheek. She pretended to blush and released her grip.

"Oh, you're such a dear, sweet boy!" she said, touching the corner of her eye with her handkerchief and reaching out to touch my face with her white silk glove.

"Yeah, well, I'm sorry," I said as Judd finally extricated himself and pushed past me towards the stairs. "Thank you so much for the drinks, ladies," I said, stepping backwards, "but we really must be going."

They were all waving goodbye as I turned toward the stairs. The one closest to me waved with her handkerchief. Overacting the female part was her game, and she was good at it.

Judd and I didn't stop running when we got to the bottom of the stairs. "Jesus Christ!" I said.

"Ligo! Was that for real? Where those really men?"

"I think so. I think it's time to leave! They seemed like they were getting pretty attached to us."

"Yeah! Let's get the hell out of here!"

We were playing of course then. They weren't going to come after us, but the notion of what we'd just escaped gave us good cause to laugh. Escaping danger through laughter was one of the things Judd and I did well together – we'd done it for two years in the dormitory – and I welcomed the laughter this night too: It helped me forget how pissed I was that Judd had left me there alone while he went outside with his American rapist friend.

I welcomed the laughter for another reason, too. I was embarrassed not to have played more the Alpha, breaking free from the trannies upstairs with a rude gesture and an insult. It was me, opting not to throw the extra punches after I had Rod's head pinned on the pavement, all over again. Twenty-four hours had not passed since Mas Oyama expressed his intent to make me the only American, and one of only two non-Japanese in its 30-year history, to hold a graduation certificate from his *uchi deshi* program. (Nick would join Judd and me by graduating three months later.) In spite of even an honor like that, I'd been unable to escape my nice-boy breeding.

And at the time, I cursed myself for it.

"I can't believe you kissed him," Judd laughed.

"Yeah, well, he did have beautiful tits," I responded with a wisecrack to make the shame go away, and we both laughed.

We'd decided to try one more time in Roppongi — Judd had some knowledge of the Tokyo streets, so I'd resolved to tag along wherever his instincts told him we would find our best chance of picking up girls we could take home. *Am I to give up entirely and leave the evening to finish on such an uncomfortable note?* I thought. *Should I just quit with such an unpleasant taste in my mouth?*

Interestingly, it was that next half hour that came so close to killing us.

Perhaps I should have learned not to trust Judd's judgment, given the past couple of hours we'd spent together, but it was already pushing two a.m., Tokyo's public transportation had shut down, and I couldn't have gotten back to Ikebukuro if I'd wanted to.

And so, Roppongi it was.

Tokyo's dive.

The night scene where East met West, where there were as many foreigners in the clubs as Japanese. The place where Japanese who wanted to meet foreigners went, and therefore the place Western men go to have the easiest shot at picking up Japanese women who want to be picked up by Western men.

I'd only been there once before, and only for a few minutes. It was during the chaos surrounding the 5th World Open Tournament in 1991. Technically we weren't allowed out of the dormitory on our own, but there were so many foreigners crowding *Honbu* just then, any one of whom could have invited us out for dinner — and we were allowed to go out with foreign branch chiefs when they asked us. We'd used that fact as cover, and went out AWOL to steal a glimpse of how the other half lived, staying only long enough for a brief look, and then turning back so as not to miss the last train.

Interestingly, about the first person we saw that night in Roppongi was Dolph Lundgren. He had been a Kyokushin European champion before he became the actor who played the Russian guy Rocky Balboa beat up in *Rocky IV,* and he was there in Tokyo, having been invited by Mas Oyama to support the tournament. I suppose he was the modern-day version of Sean Connery, who had been a guest of Mas Oyama during an earlier era. All those ninja in the James Bond movie *You Only Live Twice* were Mas Oyama's students. Mas Oyama supported Sean Connery's movie, which was filmed in Japan, and in exchange Mas Oyama invited Sean Connery to *Honbu* and gained some publicity for Kyokushin.

I hadn't been to Roppongi since I'd run into, and then escaped from, Dolph Lundgren there two years earlier, so I was very much at the mercy of Judd's experience.[66]

Judd hitched us a ride with a 6-foot 2-inch Middle Eastern man in a kimono driving a tiny red sports car with two Japanese girlfriends. It was only moments after we'd escaped from the transsexuals, and I just assumed Judd knew what he was doing when he asked this perfect stranger if he could drop us off at Roppongi. Judd would eventually become fairly financially able living on his own in Tokyo, but at that time he was only nine months out of the dormitory, he and I were both on the same shoestring budget, and we were both willing to risk asking someone we didn't know for a ride to save having to pay Tokyo's exorbitant taxi fares.

All of us *gaijin* had at least that in common.

This giant Middle Eastern guy, who looked totally insane anyway to be roaming the city in a kimono – at least it was a man's kimono! – told us we could have the back seat, and we climbed in. As it turned out, his tiny little two-door sports car's back seat was so tiny that it probably wasn't really a seat at all. There was no floor room. If you had small children, you could probably only stuff them in there in the correct position if they had no legs. The only way Judd and I could get in was to climb in while the front bucket seats were forward, and then hug our knees to our chests, right up to our chins, so that the driver and his two girlfriends could lock their seatbacks upright.

Only then, when it was too late, did it become clear that our driver

---

[66] We were AWOL that night, and not anxious, therefore, to run into any Kyokushin people, and when we ran into Dolph – almost literally; it was a near collision – we diverted our eyes and walked away as quickly as possible.

was extremely intoxicated. No doubt he'd been drinking, but there was something about his eyes that made him look like he was hyped up on something a little more potent as well.

"Where are you from?" I asked him, trying to be polite.

"Tripoli," he responded, "Libya. Where are you guys from?"

It had only been a couple years since Ronald Reagan had sent a squadron of F-14's screaming down from Europe across the Mediterranean to blow up several of Qaddafi's children in one of his palaces, and I suddenly found more cause for unease. The car had no back doors. I couldn't have gotten out if I'd wanted to.

"I'm from Australia," Judd said, "And he's from . . ."

"I'm from Australia too," I cut in. It was about then that our driver realized that his wallet was missing.

The scene was about to take a significant turn for the worse.

Apparently the Libyan was convinced that one of his Japanese girlfriends, the one who was sitting on the emergency brake and straddling the gearshift, had stolen his wallet. They started to argue, and I started to fear for her safety. The lunatic behind the wheel looked like he was going to beat her up right then and there – he was that irate. There was a lot of shouting. By that time everyone was looking for the wallet, and not a moment too soon it turned up in one of the front floor wells. So now the Japanese ladies were angry that their boyfriend had accused them of stealing, and a verbal fight continued in Japanese. The Libyan punched the dashboard. He was still in a red-faced rage by the time he cranked the engine.

He was that worked up, he was drunk, and probably high, and he hadn't even begun to drive.

The Libyan slammed the car into first gear and mashed the accelerator to the floor, spinning the car's wheels in place, and somehow allowing the car to travel only the eight inches to the bumper of the car parked in front of us before slamming on the brakes and throwing us all forward. He then cranked the wheel as far as it would go, and slammed the car into reverse with an anger that made me think he was visualizing beating up the shouting Japanese girl beside him. He stamped the accelerator to the floor again, screeching the wheels this time in reverse, and traveling again the foot and a half that he could before squealing to a stop just short of crashing into the car behind us. In this way, in a temper tantrum that came close to causing us all whiplash, he inched his car back and forth out of its tiny parking place, and finally adjusted the car's angle so that on the next lurch forward, he kept the gas pedal mashed all the way to the floor and peeled out into the street.

None of the three of them had stopped yelling at each other during the ordeal. Judd was poking me in the side and laughing at "the wog" [67] in the front seat. He was drunk – so was I, a little bit – and he was saying something about how he thought the Arab guy was going start "bashing" the girls in a second. I was amazed that Judd didn't sense the danger we were in as our driver angrily slam-shifted his way through five gears until the speedometer topped out at something like 160 kph.

And he was hurtling through the narrow Tokyo streets!

He ran two red lights and swerved into oncoming traffic to pass cars in our lane that were traveling at the legal limit. He passed them as if they were standing still.

"Awwlllll right!!!" Judd was howling in excitement in my right ear, while the driver and his two dates continued to scream at each other in the front seat and our driver continued to travel at lethal speeds. He turned onto a ramp that led to a two-lane section of raised highway that apparently allowed motorists to drive up out of the city and cover several blocks without having to stop at all the lights. Tokyo is one of the most amazing cities in the world in its cleanliness, and especially in its lack of noise pollution – it's full of quiet little neighborhoods right next to huge thoroughfares – and that type of raised highway with high walls must have been one of the ways city engineers managed to get automobiles and trucks up out of the way of all the quiet pedestrian and bicycle traffic for which Tokyo is famous.

The Libyan took this particular ramp at 160 and barreled towards the rear end of a truck that was in our way like a skydiver whose chute hadn't opened. I only realized that I'd buried my fingernails in the back of his seat when my fingertips started to burn. The ramp not only had no shoulders, but it was lined by high walls that ran right up next to our side mirror, so we couldn't even see around the bend as the road started to curve. As we

---

[67] An Australian, derogatory (and probably racist) slur for a Middle Eastern or Mediterranean person. I'd never heard it before and only learned it from Judd, but for nearly two years it was our nickname for our French-Algerian *sempai*, Mocaram, who made us wash his clothes and get up even from sleep to throw away his trash.

roared in on the truck in our path at a relative speed difference of about 90, the centrifugal force pinned me between Judd's body weight and the left side of the car.

I braced myself for the collision.

Our driver's foot never left the gas pedal as we came within inches of rear-ending the truck in front of us. Much to my momentary relief, he jerked the wheel at the last moment, bumped over the soccer-ball-size concrete domes that ran up the center of the road to warn motorists if they accidentally crossed into the wrong lane, and barreled around the blind curve past the truck.

Judd was my best friend for the time I lived in the dormitory, and although there are a few things we don't have in common, I still consider him a friend of near brotherly proportions. I was angry at him that night, however, for laughing like an idiot, as if it was the most exciting ride of his life, while I, next to him with my life passing before my eyes, could only imagine what would happen if a car came up around the bend. There would be no way to get out of its way, and we would collide head-on and be killed.

The Japanese ladies had stopped yelling.

One of them had involuntarily braced her palms against the dashboard. The Libyan had won their fight by terrifying them into silence. Perhaps he suspected that I was an American and was taking his revenge for Qaddafi's kids.

Somehow we got past the truck at the last possible moment, and our terrorist driver bumped the car back over into our lane again as an oncoming, wide-eyed motorist instinctively smoked his brakes in front of us. Sadly, the ordeal wasn't quite over. We were still traveling at 150, and the ramp started to curve down again, apparently taking us back down to street level. At the bottom of the ramp, there was a stoplight – which was red and facing us – and I could see cars crossing back and forth in both directions through the intersection at the opening of our high-walled ramp. For a moment I was relieved, because I figured our driver would finally have no choice but to stop.

But he didn't.

We flew blindly through the red light at about 80 into a random gap in traffic, and the Libyan jerked the steering wheel to ninety degrees, sending the vehicle into a screaming spin. Through a cloud of white burning rubber,

I watched as the back end of our vehicle spun all the way around 180 degrees to backwards, before the front tires grabbed the concrete and we swung 90 degrees back around again to forward. Without missing a beat, Qaddafi Jr. stamped on the accelerator again and took off along with traffic, at a right angle to the direction we'd emerged from the ramp.

And almost immediately after that, it was over.

Seconds after spinning into traffic, he cut off into a side street, slammed on his brakes, and slid into a parking space against the curb. The Japanese ladies dove out of the car, and I was right on their heels.

"That was awesome!!" Judd was shouting. "Can we do it again?"

"No, Judd, you freakin' idiot, come on, get out of the car! You're drunk and that psychopath's going to kill you!" I got hold of Judd by the jacket and pulled him out of the car.

"Where are we?" I asked.

"Roppongi," Judd said, still turned and laughing, looking back at the sports car as I dragged him away.

"Well, thank god for that!" I said, as I turned back too, for just the moment necessary to catch a glimpse of the license plate. I did a double-take.

"DIPLOMAT," it said, in addition to a letter and just a few numbers.

"Son of a bitch!" I said aloud. *That guy IS one of Qaddafi's people! He's a diplomat! Above the law AND insane!*

What a day that would be! I thought to myself. *Mas Oyama gives me a graduation certificate from the most prestigious karate program in the world and, on that very night, I go out and get myself killed trying to get laid!*

Judd and I had a couple of drinks at a little bar on the corner, and within about a half hour we'd picked up two women and taken them "for a walk" in the park. One was tall and questionably pretty; the other was short and stocky, and I wondered how old she was, or rather, how young. I never would have left with her, except that the two of them were together, and the pretty one would never have left with Judd unless we brought her younger friend along too. She was cute, though, in her own way, and I was drunk enough, and I'd been celibate for long enough, that I could have made do. We loaded them into a taxi and took them back to Judd's place. Judd's one-room apartment was big enough for two futons side by side, and he had two. The apartment smelled like the dishes in the sink and the sex of the girl he'd had there the night before.

I spent the last three hours of the night there under the blankets with my date, whose name I'm not sure I caught the first time, trying unsuccessfully to seduce her. Judd's older, more experienced date disappeared under his blankets almost immediately and never came up again for air, but it was clear that the girl in my bed had never done the things her girlfriend was doing, and after some minutes of trying my best to convince her that she might like it, I realized that it wasn't going to happen. She seemed awfully middle-school to me, age-wise, and while Judd used her older girlfriend next to me in ways I can only imagine – she was his second for the night – I wound up lecturing my date on how she shouldn't allow herself to be picked up by strange foreign men in bars in Roppongi unless she was prepared for things to happen to her, at the hands of the next guy, that she might not want to happen.

"You'd better just not go to Roppongi at all," I told her. "It's not safe."

In the end I was afraid to sleep for the half hour I could have, for fear I'd sleep through my meeting with Matsui. It was already daylight, and at seven I got up to shower. Judd took advantage of my getting up to throw the girls out so he could get some sleep, and they were gone by the time I was dressed.

On the train platform, I had a serious talk with myself about the choices I had made that got me where I was that morning, feeling like I did. I was so sleepy I couldn't see straight. I'd been guzzling water ever since I woke up to combat the queasiness in my stomach, and I was walking a fine line between being utterly ashamed and afraid I'd screw up my meeting with Matsui, on the one hand, and dumbfounded that I'd met with Mas Oyama the day before and was on my way to meet Matsui now, given what had transpired in between.

I can't stop it, no matter how hard I try, I marveled. *Like an avalanche has no choice but roar down its slope once it's started, no matter how bad I screw up, there'll be no changing the vision's course now!*

Midas was taking over in response to my depleted physical state, and I let him, because I knew he'd have the best shot of pulling me out of my predicament in one piece. I was fighting up from the bottom again, and I wondered if that wasn't where I was at my best: beaten to the ground, fighting to clamber to my feet, and refusing to be defeated. Of course, in this case, it was my own choices that had driven me down. I wondered about the vision and its uncanny ability to drive me through to its inevitable conclusion with or without me. Midas was better equipped to handle the challenge of the day than I was without him. The choices I'd made during the night had ensured that I hit the physical rock bottom where Midas's defiance would be sure to make itself known.

Stepping off the train in Asakusa at 8:45, Midas gnashed his teeth at one of Tokyo's gigantic squawking ravens. *Good for you, Nathan!* he said. *Fill life to the bursting point!*

Doing so, after all, was the drug that kept Midas kicking.

"Learn to bottle it!" Jacques told me, ". . . and we could all make a fortune."

SIXTEEN

It's no wonder that I have so little recollection of my meeting with Matsui. The photographic record remains, however, so I know that I was there.

There are thirty-two techniques in Mas Oyama's *kihon* series, and I nailed every single one as Matsui performed them for my camera. He demonstrated *fudo dachi* and how to assume *sanchin dachi*, and from there he demonstrated each of the *seiken* and *uraken* techniques, all of the *shuto* techniques, the blocks, the two techniques we do from *kiba dachi*, and of course all of the kicks.[68] Kyokushin's most recent world champion posed for me in before, during, and after positions for each motion, and somehow I returned home with a flawless set. I even caught the high kicks at the exact instant when they reached their maximum height.

Mas Oyama taught that all of karate must be built upon a foundation of these most basic, stationary techniques, and he emphasized the strength of his belief by insisting that every training at *Honbu* begin with thirty-six repetitions of each and every one (six reps to refine technique, and thirty more performed at maximum intensity). It was therefore with *kihon* that I began what I hoped would unfold from there to become a series of demonstrations of Japan's technical ability to American Kyokushin enthusiasts by means of photo essays in *Budo Karate Illustrated*. Of course Matsui had much more exciting things to offer than *kihon*, but I believed myself then to have plenty of time. He had agreed to be the magazine's

---

[68] *Kihon* means "basic techniques"; *fudo dachi* is our basic "standing at attention" stance between exercises; *sanchin dachi* is the basic pigeon-toed stance in which we practice all of the upper-body *kihon* techniques. *Seiken* means "forefist"; *uraken*, "back fist"; *shuto*, "knife-hand"; and *kiba dachi* is our "horseback riding" stance.

technical advisor, and I knew that I could count on him for additional material for additional issues in the future. Indeed, the day after the *nidan* exam that would beat me so badly ten weeks later, I'd ask him in a painful, raspy whisper to meet with me to pose for a second set of photos, and then, too, he would agree with apparent pleasure.

A portion of one of the actual physical layouts of the *Budo Karate Illustrated* book showing my photographs of Matsui performing Mas Oyama's *kihon*.

Crossing Matsui off my to-do list, I stashed four rolls of newly shot 35mm film in my inside jacket pocket, where I would keep them, reassuringly pressed against my body until I had them safely back in North Carolina. At the train station, I had two rice cakes and a bottled green tea for breakfast. I came a little bit back down to Earth once the food hit my system, and I realized how tired I was. I thought of Judd in his futon, peacefully sleeping his life away.

I had to meet with Mas Oyama one more time before leaving Japan.

Sosai had arranged for me to meet with the editor of Kyokushin's Japanese-language *Power Karate Magazine* earlier in the week, so that I could ask him for permission to use photos of Mas Oyama's recent trip to Rochester. I'd already met, therefore, with one Mr. Inoue at the *Power Karate* office – I knew his face from nearly two years of morning ceremonies at *Honbu* – and he'd referred me to the magazine's star photographer, Kobayashi Yo, the same *samurai* cameraman who'd given me that helpful shove back into place behind *Sosai* fourteen months earlier in Rochester. At his studio, in yet another Tokyo neighborhood, I met with Mr. Kobayashi and received a solid gold set of photographs, including especially the one of Mas Oyama at Niagara Falls that would become the cover shot of the first issue of *Budo Karate Illustrated*. The photographs that he'd taken in Rochester fit perfectly into my *American Kyokushin Yearbook* format, since they showed *Sosai* on his most recent visit to America.

One of the photos taken in my second photo shoot with Matsui, this one ten weeks later, the day after the ceremony held to mark the opening of his new "Matsui Branch Dojo," just after my *nidan* grading at *Honbu*.

The day before the tournament, Michael Monaco and several other branch chiefs, including Cameron Quinn and David Bunt, had taken

Sosai to Niagara Falls on a sightseeing excursion. I'm almost glad I wasn't there to see the 70-year-old *Sosai* jump over the safety railing and stroll confidently out onto a tiny outcropping of rock over the falls to pose for photographs. He didn't have a *dogi* with him, so Cameron lent him his, and one of my challenges in the cover design of my book became to figure out how to erase Cameron's name off his belt (in the days before digital photo editing) lest I print a photo of *Sosai* for all to see, so obviously wearing someone else's belt.

Mr. Kobayashi graciously agreed to let me use his photographs; *Power Karate* had only used a few, so many of them had never seen the light of day. Of course I promised to credit him for any photo that I used. I hadn't yet seen how well my photos of Matsui would come out, and I wasn't very confident that they would come out at all. I believed, therefore, that Mr. Kobayashi's photos would become the book's most important ones, and I thanked *Sosai* in that last meeting with him for arranging for me to acquire them.

Sosai's bestowal of the honorary graduation certificate he gave me in the morning ceremony on my last morning in Japan was about as unceremonious as it could have been. He called me to the front of the lineup, held the document at arms' length to read it aloud, downward through his reading glasses, handed it to me, and shook my hand. The experience was a blur. I was highly self-conscious, and ashamed to receive the certificate in front of my *koohai* – including especially Nick and Mahashi – who were still struggling towards the expected, full-term completion of the program. I watched the whole event painfully through their eyes, and I don't remember it clearly. *Sosai* would have told me, "*Gambatte!* (Persevere!)" and I would have responded, "Osu! *Gambaremasu! Itadakimasu!* (I will persevere! I humbly receive what you've given me!)" Of course I would have bowed to receive the document with two hands. When *Sosai* extended his hand, I would have shaken it with both of mine.

I'd somehow managed to deny my cold away, but I received my graduation certificate nevertheless exhausted, jet-lagged, and hung over.

I did some last-minute running out from *Sosai's* office to a photo lab later that morning to make high-quality copies of a couple of old black-and-white photographs he'd offered me to include. I made copies of a couple of pictures of Jacques that were in *Sosai's* photo album, which Jacques later forbade me to use. They were shots that had been arranged by the flamenco guitarist and *karateka*-wannabe who'd arranged Jacques' first meeting with *Sosai* in New York City. Apparently this guy had prepared some *Black Belt* Magazine-style photos of himself and Jacques in karate-like poses, before either of them had practiced karate, thinking that it would make him look impressive in *Sosai's* eyes to seem to be fighting with someone so huge.

"If you publish them I'll kill you," Jacques would tell me in the weeks to come, and of course I would not.

The next two weeks of nearly nonstop work began the moment I got on the bus at the Metropolitan Hotel to take me to Narita. *Sosai* had asked me how many pages the book was going to be. "Osu! It will be eighty pages," I'd told him, but he'd frowned and said, "No way. It's impossible. You must make it at least one hundred pages!" There was no "But, I . . . " when speaking with *Sosai* – there is no "but . . ." in *Osu!* – and all I could say was, "Osu! *Wakarimashita!* (I have understood!)," all the while thinking to myself, "Good! At least the effort of creating twenty more pages than I'd planned will kill me, and I won't have to worry about getting killed fighting twenty full-contact fights at the end of March!"

None of *Sosai's* students' ambitions were ever big enough for him.

"You want to design eighty pages? Good, make it 100! You think you can take your *shodan* grading? Good, why don't you take your *nidan* grading instead?" None of these were really suggestions, of course. They were what *Sosai* expected. Through challenges like these, he constantly sought to show us how we can achieve so much more than we take for granted, and there was never any acceptable answer other than, "Osu! *Gambaremasu!* (I will persevere!)"

By asking *Sosai* that week if I could make the *American KyokushinYearbook* the first issue of *Budo Karate Illustrated*, I'd hinted that my ambition didn't stop at the low marks David Bunt and Jacques and Annie had advised me to set. I wonder today what he would have said if I'd revealed the true extent of my ambition. The *Budo Karate Illustrated* project existed in my mind by then as a mere experimental first step out of 100 I could see myself taking in my lifetime of both working for Kyokushin, and struggling to make a difference in the world beyond Kyokushin through its teaching. If I had told him what I could see, I wonder if he'd have thought me insane.

Without Midas there with me, there was no way I could have been convincing.

The printer in Alabama told me back in the fall that if I didn't deliver my finished layout by the third week of January, there would be no guarantee they could keep it at the top of their spring production schedule, where I'd insisted it remain. May, the end of the school year, would be crunch time for them, since they were contracted to deliver yearbooks to high schools and colleges before the start of summer vacation. If I could get them the layout by January 20th, however, there was a good chance I'd be able to see the finished product by the end of March. That was an immense amount of work to complete in a very short time, but I recognized the deadline's collateral benefit:

My classes would be starting on the 15th, and I really did need to have the book layout behind me as much as possible. I was teetering dangerously on the brink of my critical final semester of college, and the closest thing I'd had to rest over my winter vacation had been pretending to be engaged in my father's family Christmas celebration – that and romping around Roppongi with Judd.

For ninety minutes on the bus on the way to the airport, I feverishly ground away on my laptop, composing the second half of my article "A Giant Among Giants," about Jacques. Another ninety minutes after that, after checking in and waiting through the excruciatingly long passport line, I resumed my writing, cross-legged on the floor and plugged in to an outlet next to a wide-screen TV in the departures lobby. The TV was airing loud sumo wrestling matches, and it must have been a popular event since nearly everyone in the room gazed in my direction, breaking into occasional fits of raucous cheering. I felt as though they were watching me write – at the very least aware of me, there on the side, ignoring their popular pastime in the name of trying to make a difference for their futures, too. I believed myself to be leaving a fingerprint on a page of history, and the thrill of it propelled me forward.[69]

Twelve hours passed. My laptop battery was long since dead, and the

---

[69] This article, "A Giant Among Giants" exists almost verbatim as Chapter Seven in the current volume, a noteworthy fact given my reliance on the foregone conclusion of success, and the vision that developed for me during that time that included a snapshot picture of my completed autobiographical writing. Interesting that the same voice carries; interesting that I wrote a chapter *then* for a book that I wouldn't write until thirteen years later; interesting that the passage I quoted from *Donbas* about Omar driving a tent stake into the ground contained both a split sledgehammer handle and an unspoken optical communication that occurred between Jacques and Omar.

article still wasn't finished as we touched down in L.A. The shoestring budget to which I'd held my travel agent had me following a different route home than the one I'd taken overseas, and I was shocked to behold the silhouettes of palm trees painted against grey, rainy California skies. Afraid to part with them for even an instant, I had those four rolls of film, plus now the thirty color slides that Mr. Kobayashi had given me, tucked safely into my inside jacket pocket. I believed myself to be carrying the most valuable pocket contents of my life, and although I was careful to pass the rolls of high-speed film around the X-ray machines at the security checkpoints, in my inexperience I still feared that there could be some damage to the film from the close proximity to X-rays.

Just after *Sosai* told me that I had to make the book at least 100 pages, he asked me, "Have you included a history of Kyokushin?" When I told him that I had not, he gave me a hot-off-the-press, ten-page, New Official Kyokushin Timeline in neatly-typed Japanese, and told me in no uncertain terms to translate it and include it in the book. "Osu, *wakarimashita!* (I have understood!)" was of course my response, and I spent my first full day back at my father's house in Davidson in an all-day jamboree translating session at my father's dining room table with a Japanese friend of mine from UNCC whom I'd once tutored as he struggled to learn English. He read the lines aloud, following our old routine since it was good practice for him too, and I typed in English, editing in real time as we went.

For the layout itself, I commandeered an 50-foot hallway in Davidson College's Computer Center and lined one entire wall with actual-size, two-page spreads fresh off the printer, switching them out with revised copies every time I edited and reprinted a page. I hired a college girlfriend of mine named Lisa – not to be confused with Lissa – who I knew to have a nearly perfect eye for catching spelling, grammar, and formatting errors, and she and I worked together for several days straight, taking turns at the one computer terminal there that had Pagemaker, and running back and forth to our hall-length design table to rearrange the actual photographs that we were by then starting to lay out in their actual locations. I was in sometimes hourly contact with Jacques's wife, Annie, who was the book's official copy editor, working on draft after draft of the book's text-heavy portions. If there were mistakes to be found, she would be sure to find them. Annie had written an article of her own about Rose James, America's long-time women's heavyweight champion.

Somehow we got it done. My classes had already begun, and the Café was open by the time I sent off the first complete draft to Annie in New York for a final copy edit. Four days later, by the time I got it back marked in red ink, I already had my first writing assignments due for my classes. Of course there had been a moment of celebratory relief upon sending off the completed project to Annie: now there was nothing I could do for the project but wait for the edited pages to come back. Into those four days of would-be peace, however, I'd had no choice but to pack the business of getting my last semester as a student underway at a breakneck pace. If I didn't, surely the precariously stacked pieces would come tumbling irreparably down.

The bear of my semester would be my father's Survey of the History of Art in the Western World. My father had been teaching art history at Davidson since the year before I was born, and I signed up for his class because I knew it would be my last chance to take one of his classes – not to mention, I feared, a last chance for me and my father as well. I'd taken his History of Modern Architecture my freshman year, when I was just seventeen, still two years before becoming an *uchi deshi*, and it was one of the best classes I took at Davidson. I knew my father to be a very strict professor, and I knew – mostly from living with him for twenty years and hearing his classes described – that passing this harder course would depend on getting to a point where I could look at any piece of art created in the history of Western civilization and identify the period in which it was created, the likely artist, the date of its creation within a reasonable margin of error, and at least one fact about the work that made it significant. "Oh yeah, that's the *Mona Lisa*," for example, "painted by Leonardo Da Vinci during the Italian Renaissance. It was painted in 1503, and there is some controversy over who the model was, including whether or not the artist used his own face to arrange the facial proportions." Of course the *Mona Lisa* would be easy for most of us to identify, but there were several thousand images in our textbook that we would be responsible for, most of them not as well known. My father had thousands of slides – including multiple angles of building facades and pieces of sculpture that didn't appear in our textbook – and all those images would be fair game as well. My father's course, I knew as I signed up for it, would be the one most likely to make me feel like I had to learn a whole new language just to make it through.

In addition to art history I'd take a course on the history of China (which, it occurred to me, when added to the courses I'd already taken in Chinese politics, Japanese language, and East Asian philosophy and religion, would nearly qualify me for a second major in East Asian studies, had a double major option existed at Davidson). There would also be the modern Irish poetry course I've already mentioned (the one that Seamus Heaney crashed one day), a final semester of Japanese as an independent study, and another independent study in writing that Dr. Abbott had helped me organize to get academic credit for all the writing I was doing for *Budo Karate Illustrated*.

The Café would still be my responsibility, but I made the cold, calculated decision to cancel my karate classes that last semester and concentrate on my own training for my *nidan* grading. I'd be returning to Japan for a year as a Watson Fellow following graduation, I reasoned, and there wasn't really any future for my small group of karate students anyway, either in itself or for the future development of American Kyokushin. As much as I'm sure they had learned about *budo* karate in the total of fifteen months that I'd been teaching this go-round, they would scatter to all corners of the country after graduation, and their level was not such that many of them would likely continue training, much less be motivated or able to introduce Kyokushin to their new communities. If I'd known from the beginning that developing Kyokushin in America was going to be my future, perhaps I'd have made a few choices differently. As it was, however, I felt as though I'd basically become an athletic instructor for a handful of hobbyists, and I let it fade away.

I had ten weeks to prepare for my *nidan* grading, and I took that challenge as the matter of life and death that I literally considered it to be. I trained twice a day, and concentrated all my energy towards an attempt to regain some semblance of the power-stamina I'd had at my strongest as an *uchi deshi*. Man-sized (and man-weight) punching bags are extremely rare in the Unites States, and I didn't have one. Training on the football field, however, it had struck me how similar in size and shape were the vinyl-covered foam-rubber cylinders that protected football players from injury when colliding with the goalposts, and I was pleasantly surprised when I started pounding on one. It was two feet in diameter, six feet tall, and a bit spongier than a good heavy bag, but since the eight-inch iron core was unyielding, it was actually quite a good substitute. Mornings therefore were for running, push-ups, sit-ups, jump rope, and jumping squats, and afternoons were for stamina training on the bag. The iron posts of the basketball goals adjacent the football field were the same diameter as the goalposts, and I moved a goalpost pad there each day so as not to be so much the center of attention. On numerous late afternoons I'd tape my knuckles, the flesh there softened from months of hacking away at my PC, and drive myself to the limits of my endurance, punching and kicking the bag into the early hours of the night.

Annie's editing came back four days after I'd sent it off, and then came the flurry of activity required to make the necessary changes and send the pages off again, this time along with the hundreds of original photographs, to the printer's in Alabama. At one point I'd naïvely believed that once that carton was mailed off, I'd finally be able to heave a sigh of relief and concentrate my energy on other things.

The opposite, however, turned out to be the case.

Sure, there was a momentarily feeling of freedom once the first issue was completed. Once again there was nothing I could do until the publisher's proofs came back. But what I hadn't counted on was that once that parcel was mailed and the $20,000 down payment made, developing the vision from a single book into an ongoing magazine multiplied tenfold the project's required creative demand. In the short term, it was time to start gathering material for Book Two, and of course I still had to concentrate on sales so that there would be enough money to make Book Two a reality.

In an unprecedented gesture of *budo* brotherhood that caught me totally off guard coming from an American-made *karateka*, Mas Oyama's branch chief Tom Flynn in Massachusetts made good on his earlier promise to make any resource available to me I needed to bring my project to fruition. When I finally reached my $20,000 deadline with the printer, I only had $17,000 in hand. All I probably needed to do was stall for a few days, and the cash would have arrived, since money was still trickling in, but I made up my mind anyway, perhaps in the spirit of Master Choi's "better to ask for it so he'll remember you" philosophy, to go ahead and ask Tom Flynn for the cash. *Test the project's momentum*, I told myself. *Reaffirm just how unstoppable it is!*

I called Tom Flynn on a Tuesday and he wired the $3000 to me by Wednesday, no questions asked. *My God, the* budo *spirit does exist in America!* I thought. *Perhaps making Mas Oyama's Kyokushin widespread on* this *continent* too – his karate founded on the fortifying of human relationships through hard physical training – isn't going to be as impossible as I thought it would be!

Midas was gnashing his teeth again, and as you might have begun to suspect, Midas, and the sense of borrowed power that he represented, had long since begun to draw me towards a level of self-confidence that bordered on dangerous. *No matter what happens,* I'd decided, *the project is going to barrel through any obstacle in its path. With or without Nathan Ligo, the silly expendable vessel that sustains it, the vision is going to roll through like a river of lava into the exciting realms of the future. The poles would have to tip off their axis, hell would have to freeze over, Mas Oyama would have to die – God forbid! – for anything to even come close to shaking its momentum!*

As far as I was concerned, however, hell wasn't going to freeze over, the planet wasn't going to tip, and Mas Oyama wasn't going to die. With him as eagerly behind *Budo Karate Illustrated* as he had shown me he was, there would be no end to the project's success. I had just six weeks before the tournament in Atlantic City and my grading in Japan. I trained hard, studied hard, and stayed on top of my classes. The Café continued to run as it was supposed to.

But the alternate consciousness born of the vision's creative demand had made a gentle shift.

Before, it had existed in the background, I went through the motions as college student, karate teacher, and café manager, and the processing demands of the vision only interrupted to take over every once in a while. Now, however, even Tom Flynn had teamed up with Jacques Sandulescu, who'd told me to use his name like a battering ram. The two of them teamed up with Mas Oyama, Midas, and Matsui, and joined hands not only with the book's now unstoppable reality, but also with the delayed, earthshaking realization that *Sosai* had made me the only American to hold a graduation certificate from his *uchi deshi* program; that the Watson for which I was considered a shoo-in would be on the way; that I would soon be graduating from Davidson; and that if the grading didn't kill me, my *nidan* certificate would be on the way as well.

Mas Oyama ordered Mrs. Watanabe to write to me promoting me to *shodan*, her letter explaining that fact arrived, and suddenly it dawned on me. *Sosai* intended to make me a branch chief!

He was going to do it to challenge me to establish my own dojo, and so, in accord with his creed, challenge me beyond the limits even of my own ambition. Why else would *Sosai* insist that I test directly for my *nidan*, since I was so clearly below *Honbu's* standard in terms of preparedness? *Sosai* had made David Bunt a branch chief to challenge him to establish a branch as well, but no one in America, ever, would have been issued a branch chief certificate at such an early age as me.

The effect of the simultaneous realization of all that Midas was turning to gold knocked me into a constant state of disbelief at what had become of me. Like my vision of carrying a barbell up a mountain to save Master Choi's schools, the *Budo Karate Illustrated* vision, with all of its facets and underlying motives, had been born in a single life-changing moment that I'd somehow managed to grab hold of before it slipped away. I didn't plan it, or scheme it, make it up, or wish for it. Rather, it had dawned on me like, "Of course! Why didn't I think of it before? It is the only way. It is the best way, and there is no other option!"

And now, all of it was falling into place to prove it. All of it was turning to gold. And I was staggered by the realization.

The daunting part – the part that took my breath away – was that I could still see all the rest as well. The vision came to me like a snapshot and included *Budo Karate Illustrated*, but it never stopped there.

The magazine was just the beginning!

I could still see far into the future beyond *Budo Karate Illustrated*, the college diploma, the *uchi deshi* graduation certificate, the *nidan*, the branch chief certificate, and the Watson. I could see not just one dojo, but one hundred dojos opened by the graduates of the *uchi deshi* program that I'd create in America. I could see the influx of spiritual strength into the hearts and minds of American young people that a small army of such role models could inspire, and the potential results of that influx, the results I could see, were earthshaking.

I looked into the future through the all-focusing lens of my vision and I saw all people – and, yes, especially non-*karateka!* – just a hair more open-minded, just a hair more *seeing,* just a hair stronger spiritually, and therefore just a hair more willing to sacrifice their own blood, sweat and tears for the common good, rather than just for themselves and their own social and economic advancement. I saw people looking back and realizing just how small a shift it had required, how stupid they'd been not to recognize that it had been right there within reach all along – that gentle shift towards seeing the world and all of its people as things to be cared for and sustained, rather than used or, worse, used up!

I saw people opening their eyes to the fact that the way we as a people currently live does amount to stealing in so many ways, both from the planet on which we live and from the majority of its people with whom we can so easily pretend to have no connection. I saw people everywhere willing, with newly opened eyes, to alter their own individual paths through life just enough to alter the trend. I saw people taking for granted that not only do we not know all the answers, but that we'd better figure out that we don't know any of them before it's too late for us – not because we're completely clueless, but because realizing how little we know, rather than congratulating ourselves on how much, is the only way to unlock our potential to learn as much as we will one day need to know to avoid unraveling ourselves completely as our populations continue to boom.

I shuddered at the image of people respecting laws and understanding the need for them, but also taking for granted that the laws we have – our legal codes, religious laws, social laws, moral laws, the laws of tradition, the laws of habit, and most importantly our perceived laws of personal limitation – are far less than the life-governing laws that might yet be found. I saw people knowing that the laws that we have now are insufficient, and that our survival just might depend on our willingness to break them if necessary to find better ones.

I saw people accepting the fact that societies have lives of their own, and that trends that the majority follow are very often not the best ones, and that any single decision to defy those trends can affect the whole in lasting ways. I saw people knowing that social trends are shaped by human weakness and vice at least as much as by human virtue and strength. I saw them therefore questioning society's every single directive, questioning every "this is the way you're supposed to live your life" by subjecting it to the scrutiny of their own conscience, their own education, and the wisdom born of their own personal experience, before jumping to the conclusion that people in numbers must know better than they do.

I saw people, on a vast scale, waging war against their own perceptions of personal limitation. I saw them knowing that what they believe themselves capable of is only a fraction of what they actually might achieve, and I saw them knowing that it is their human responsibility to hold on to that knowledge, whatever the extent of their success or failure, since the only way to achieve more is to know in one's heart that there is more that one can do.

I saw people questioning whether wisdom and creativity are transcendent and innate, whether all of the past wisdom and creativity of humankind might not in fact already exist within each one of us, not out of a complacent refusal to learn and study, but because believing the answers lie within us – not only in the history books – removes the single most significant roadblock to finding them there.

I saw people taking for granted that it is our duty to become educated, and that education doesn't just come from Ivy League schools, and that it doesn't necessarily depend on having enough money to pay for it. I saw people understanding that education is everywhere and that most of it is free and in front of us for the taking. I saw people understanding that the greatest education that can be gained derives simply from experiencing new things, becoming acquainted with new and different kinds of people, embracing them for their positive attributes and trying to carry those attributes back into our own lives. I saw people understanding that education should never be reduced to being only about a paper, a title, or a qualification that gets us to a better-paying job, that it must not merely be about making the circumstances of our own, individual lives better, but that it must rather be about making better the one life that all of us share as co-inhabitants of this same, gently turning rock.

I saw people understanding that education derived from one single source is tantamount to anti-education, and that there is no greater crime than to shut out learning from multiple sources in defense of the authority of any one source. I saw people taking for granted that the greatest ideas born of man so far to explain the world in which we live can't hold a candle to the ideas that might yet be born in our own hearts. I saw people believing themselves capable of overcoming all odds as long as they're willing to make the appropriate sacrifice. I saw them taking for granted that no one was going to do it for them, that the sacrifice has to be theirs, not someone else's, and that it has been their responsibility to try to make a difference all along. I saw people believing that the greatest trespass they might commit is to put their fate and the fate of mankind in the hands of another and merely wait for the answers to be delivered.

I saw people understanding that all humans are born wanting to do good, and that if they turn bad it's only because the world into which they came made them that way, and that nevertheless, somewhere inside, their original nature is still alive. I saw people taking for granted that all people's original nature – starting first and foremost with their own! – must still exist no matter what traumas and disappointments and mistakes – no matter what repression! – may have obscured it along the way, and that that original nature might be tapped, the doors to it might be reopened, at any time, to render their lives, the lives of all people, and of the world itself, happier, healthier and truer to humankind's actual potential for greatness.

I saw people figuring out that as complicated as all of that might sound – as daunting to enact in its entirety – it takes only one single change of attitude or thinking to embrace the whole; that all of those values might come to the individuals who embrace them in one single wave; and that society might, by that single change in attitude, alter its course away from the catastrophic, global dangers that all of us face, rather than charging – so boldly! – directly into catastrophe's jaws.

I saw this earthshaking image as the 100th step of which my diploma, my graduation certificate, and my book project were just the first three, I saw the 100th step as clearly as I saw the first, and the first steps were all coming true to prove not only themselves but also the rest, since they were all part of the same undeniable vision. The realization drove me into a perpetual state of awe that took my breath away and made my head spin. I found myself precariously balanced on a precipice between ultimate artistic creativity on one side – as if it was right there within my reach – and incapacitating overload on the other. Having seen what I'd seen, I was convinced that the greatest sin imaginable would be to quit somewhere short of draining every drop of my own blood if necessary to make it come true.

Success or failure aside, I realized that the path of my life was set, and come hell or high water, I'd have no choice but to follow it.

And I was terrified.

And ten weeks passed.

I kept one nostril above water: I stayed on top of my classes, I trained twice a day for my grading. I got the proofs back from Alabama and made my last corrections. I planned feature articles for Book Two. I sold more copies of Book One. I drove to Atlantic City to share my ideas with the

U.S. and Canadian branch chiefs. Katsuhiko Horai was there for the first time, and I sensed an accompanying sour change in the air, but it didn't intimidate me. Chicago's Leslaw Samitowski took me to his room and handed me twenty-one hundred dollars cash from under his mattress for 90 advance orders of *Budo Karate Illustrated* and Michael Monaco explained that people of his generation from Poland had cause to be skeptical of banks. I sat for my midterms without sleep, boarded a plane for Tokyo, and then a bus for my Tateyama mountaintop to visit Yamaguchi *Sensei* and Mr. Nagare before retuning to Ikebukuro for my grading. I barely survived that crazy Russian's blow to my throat. I met with Matsui the next day to ask for permission to shoot a second round of photos, and that favor was granted. In a painful, raspy whisper, I spoke what would turn out to be the last words I ever spoke to Mas Oyama, in his hospital bed, with his wife at his side, and Mahashi crying.

Sosai's last words to me were, "*Shimpai-yo!*"

He drilled the back of my skull with his eyes as if there were stones between him and me that needed to be smashed. "No, you should worry," he told me.

"You should worry," he told me, and I was too staggered under the weight of all that I carried to comprehend the simple truth he was trying to make me understand.

PART III

SEVENTEEN

LISSA MAILED ME the torn pages of our book and, with them, a letter in which she wrote that she thought I'd probably just throw them away, that I'd probably think they didn't matter anymore. Three times in the same letter she wrote that she thought of my eyes. "I think of your eyes," she wrote, "and I have a hard time not crying again. Why did you give up?"

Why did I give up, Lissa?

Oh, but I never did. I changed course and kept right on moving forward. Life is too short to surrender, remember?

I fell in love with another.

I'd fallen in love already months before my work took me to Japan to meet with Mas Oyama and photograph Matsui at New Year's.

I fell in love with a woman with whom I never shared a romantic relationship; in fact, I almost entirely kept her at a safe, professional distance to hide the fact that I loved her. She was older than me by four or five years, she was married, she was one of my professors. She was beautiful, brilliant, and blissfully unavailable.

Sadly, she was exactly my type.

The episode marks the chapter of my story that I am most ashamed to tell, and yet it is beyond my power to omit, because her presence in my life was so integrally tied to the rise and fall of my manic alter ego Midas that to pretend it never happened would be to render the entire story untrue.

Her name was Helen Ecks, and although it would become something of a twisted joke for me to refer to her as *Dr. Ecks*, I almost only ever did.

Dr. Abbott introduced her to me in a chance encounter at the Café. It was during that same spring semester when I traveled to Japan to attend my *uchi deshi* classmates' graduation. Lissa and I were all but living together in Duke Dorm, and I was simultaneously enrolled in both sections of the introductory British literature survey. The English department interviewed several candidates that year for two faculty openings, and part of the routine, apparently, was for the prospective new hires to give a single lecture to English majors with the rest of Davidson's English faculty in attendance. The course designated for them to visit that year was my senior colloquium, and Helen was one of four recent PhDs to lecture, once each, during the semester.

Dr. Abbott – the department chair – was showing her around campus in the hour before class, and I ran into them by chance. He introduced us, and I immediately hoped that she would be one of the two hired, but it wasn't until the middle of the next hour that I realized why. Her lecture was on Milton's *Paradise Lost*, and when she was done and opened up the forum to questions, I asked her a fairly stupid one, more out of interest in her than in Milton. As she answered my question, I had the chance to look her in the eye for more than just a fleeting moment, and it was then that I realized she was a *seer*.

Like Lissa, like my cousin Kristen, and like that young Korean lady I complimented through a coffee-shop window one day in Seoul – and like Master Choi! – she had eyes that I fell into as if that was where I was always meant to be. If I didn't dream it, that quality in her was much stronger than anything I'd ever encountered before. She spoke to me and I squirmed in my seat, suddenly so utterly aware of my classmates watching us that even in simply listening I could hardly function.

Can they see it? I wondered. *Did anyone else see what just happened?*

I was dangerously in love with Lissa at the time, and she and I were obsessed with trying to understand what it was about the way her eyes and mine fell into one another's to create the sensation that communication happened there beyond words. I noticed Helen, therefore, that first day, and I immediately felt drawn to her simply because I wanted to know more.

I wanted to understand.

I hope she gets the job, I thought when she'd moved the class's attention on to answering someone else's question. *Good God! Whatever class she teaches next semester, I'm sure I'll be in the front row!*

I didn't mention her to Lissa. The sensation was new and elusive enough that it was easy to believe it had been my imagination. I even forgot about it at first, dismissed it as nothing and let it go. Over the next several months, however, I was just enough haunted by what I had seen in Helen to remember, sometimes, and to look forward to the next semester for a reason that I never had before. I was distracted in a way that felt like I'd better not mention it to Lissa. Half the time I feared I would reveal something hurtful with my eyes if I told her. The rest of the time I dismissed it as silly and figured there wasn't anything to mention.

It pains me to realize that the first words I spoke to Helen alone outside of class were a lie, because over time I would develop something like a friendship with her, and lying is an awful way to try to be someone's friend. It was evening at the very beginning of the following semester, and I called her name – Dr. Ecks, of course – out of the gloom of the ghostly and deserted third floor hallway of Chambers, just as I caught a glimpse of her disappearing into a stairwell. I hadn't seen her since the day of her lecture, but by that time she was very much on my mind.

Lissa had left me just a matter of days earlier, and I'd already moved out of Martha's house and into the cottage in my father's backyard. I'd just recently come back to Davidson after meeting Jacques and Annie in New York for the first time, and if I hadn't yet received Mas Oyama's letter granting me permission to open the *Budo Karate Illustrated* floodgates, I would be receiving it within days. The only class Helen was teaching that I could take was on the eighteenth-century novel. It was offered at the worst possible time considering the other classes I wanted to take, and the practical reason why she was on my mind was that I was trying desperately to repair a six-course schedule that had been thrown all out of whack once I signed up for hers.

Meeting with Dr. Abbott to discuss my course choices for the semester, I asked, "What the hell is an eighteenth-century novel anyway? I didn't know anyone read novels in the eighteenth century."

"Oh," he said, "She'll be teaching Jane Austen, for example, from right at the beginning of the 19th century, and, before that, Samuel Richardson, Daniel Defoe . . . You know *Robinson Crusoe*, of course, *Pride and Prejudice*, *Sense and Sensibility?*"

"Oh, I guess so. I read a Robinson Crusoe comic book when I was a kid," I said, wincing as I realized how stupid that must make me look to a man who was once nominated for a Pulitzer. "Anyway, this eighteenth-century novels class seems like one I'd like to take. I'd better take it if all I've read of that period is a comic book! I'm trying to fit these other courses in around it. What do you think about this Shakespeare course?"

I lied to Helen later that same day in the entrance to the stairwell on the third floor of Chambers. "I've got to sign up for a sixth course," I told her, "and I was thinking about trying to take yours."

The truth, of course, was that her class was the first one I'd signed up for. It was all the others that I was having trouble fitting around it. Hers was the only course I gave a damn about, and I felt obliged to dumb down my desire to "maybe I'll take it if I can fit it in" because I couldn't reconcile how badly I wanted to take that course with my lack of interest in the subject matter.

I did not enroll in Helen's class in order to pursue her. I don't remember when I learned that she was married, but it wouldn't have made any difference. The initial pull that I felt towards her was not a romantic one. I simply wanted to understand why I felt so strongly pulled. I felt drawn to her in a way that made me desperately want to succumb.

"Six courses! Why so many?" she asked.

"Money," I said. "I've got to finish college this year and get outta here, unfortunately. I've got eight semesters of free tuition because my father is a professor here, but I made some bad choices and wasted some of it early on, and now I've got no choice but to graduate this year. So it's gotta be six classes this semester, and maybe even six again next time. What's the work load like for The 18th-Century Novel?"

"Fairly heavy, actually," she said, "certainly in terms of reading. I'm not going to ask you to take any exams, but there will be several papers due, and it will take some effort to stay on top of the reading. We're reading the abridged *Clarissa*, but it's still nearly a thousand pages, and we'll only have about two weeks to get through it."

"*Clarissa?*" I asked.

"Yeah, it's this massive 1500-page novel that English students always dread reading."

"And this is how you try to sell your course?" I asked, smiling, and both of us laughed. She'd realized how she must have sounded and laughed first with her eyes, at herself, and that broke the ice and left her open to be toyed with in the spontaneous way that I had.

It was during that moment of laughter that I dared to reach a little farther into her, and suddenly I found myself squirming again, just as I had in my seat the previous spring. The sensation was not of merely falling into her gaze, as I had with Lissa, but of being entirely enveloped by it. It wrapped all the way around me and touched me on all sides with a warmth that crept towards the void that had been torn wide open again upon losing both Lissa and Martha, and my childhood home, just one week before. It was a wave of warmth reminiscent of being held as a small child, and it took my breath away. I suppose I was a fool not to walk away right then and there, and never look back.

How could this ten-times-Lissa have possibly been safe?

At the very least, I knew for certain that I had been right – the young Dr. Ecks possessed that same quality for which I was so desperate. She was a seer, I knew it then unequivocally, and I pulled my gaze back as quickly as I'd first stepped in.

"I guess we'll see what happens," I said, taking an actual step back. "I'd really like to take the course . . ." I was aware then of complimenting her with my eyes and I could see that her step had lightened. ". . . I'll have to see if I can make my schedule work."

"Good," she said, "So I guess I'll see you in class, or not – either way I'll see you around. Davidson's a pretty small place."

"Yeah, it is," I said. "Welcome on board! I'm glad you got the job . . . Oh, and that's the stairwell to Perkins over there." A moment earlier she'd been lost, trying to find her way to a faculty orientation in Perkins Auditorium, the fourth-floor classroom under the Chambers dome – the stairwells from the ground floor of Chambers stop at the 3rd floor, and one has to take a second stairwell to the top.

"Thanks," she said, "I'm sure I'll figure this place out eventually."

We parted ways, and I cringed. *Why would you be so glad she got the job, you idiot?* I scolded myself. *Say stupid things like that and you're going to give yourself away.* I took a deep breath to shake the embarrassment and regain balance.

God forbid she noticed!

Classes started two days later, and by then so had the *Budo Karate Illustrated* acceleration. The coming Watson interview was already weighing heavily on my mind, and I spent my nights in the Café office, studying Japanese and reading books on Chinese politics and plays by Shakespeare. Helen's course kicked off with Defoe's other most significant novel, *Moll Flanders*.

The amount of reading required was truly daunting, and it was no surprise, therefore, that The 18th-Century Novel was the least popular literature course offered that semester. It was common at Davidson to have less than twenty students in a class, or even as few as a dozen. Helen looked on the bright side when only four students signed up, and expressed her delight that two of them were male, since the novels of the eighteenth century tend to be fairly girlish. Once it became clear that the class wasn't going to be canceled, however, I worried for her morale. The eighteenth century was Helen's primary field of interest – she'd written her dissertation at Berkeley on Jane Austen – and for her sake I hated the fact that there weren't more Davidson students tough enough to brave the course that was closest to her heart. She also taught a survey course, and maybe even freshman comp, and those classes were always jam-packed.

In our tiny little upper-level literature class, however, I had her almost all to myself.

It took me half the semester to understand that I was in love with her. It didn't make the least bit of sense, so, for a while, it was easy to dismiss. *How could I possibly be in love with someone I only know from arm's length? One of my teachers, no less! How stupid is that, anyway! How juvenile! When was the last time, eleventh grade? Before that, third? – How could I love someone for something inside her that no one else can see, that I fear even having to try to explain? It's a fantasy, isn't it, this being able to see into someone else? Isn't it just something that I've conjured up to cope with some deficiency that's too frightening to face?*

I must be insane to even think it!

Even reaching forward into Helen with my gaze turned out to be a dangerous double-edged sword. As with Lissa, I had the sensation that I could see into her – and see in her exactly what was so intoxicating to me – but the flip side was that doing so made me feel completely exposed. I couldn't look into her without feeling that I was revealing my innermost reaches, and one of the things hidden there was the fact that she'd rocked my world. I was so afraid that I'd give myself away, I fought the temptation to reach out to her at all. Sometimes I must have resorted to shutting her out completely. I remember being afraid that she'd think I didn't like her very much.

Perhaps it wasn't that she was in any way susceptible; maybe it was just that I'd finally met my match.

Helen was living alone in Davidson that year. Her husband Jack

– another brilliant doctor of English literature out of Berkeley – had followed his own first job offer somewhere else. If I understood the situation correctly, they would spend that year making the decision whether he would relocate to Davidson for her career, or she to wherever he was. I'm sure it would have been challenging for them to find jobs at the same college, as they were both rising stars in the same field. The smaller the school, the harder it would be to find places for both of them, and Davidson was awfully small.

The fact that she was living alone in Davidson, and that her husband was halfway across the country, was maddening, of course. Lissa's fiancé Bryan had been halfway across the country, too. In the case of Helen, however, I became steadfast, early on, in my resistance to any such temptation. I'd told Lissa that she wasn't strong enough to resist loving me, and she'd damned my ego for it, because she had, in fact, loved me. With Helen, I all but hid under the table in an effort to make sure she didn't even know I'd noticed her.

Certainly I was very much on the rebound. Post-traumatic stress might even be an appropriate term for what I was experiencing then, given my past, having for the first time in my life let myself love someone so completely as I had Lissa, and then having lost her so completely in almost the same instant when the mother figure I most associated with the warmth and comfort of childhood so coldly drove me out of that childhood's home. I'd spent a lifetime before Lissa bottling up my love for women I could never be with, on the one hand, and keeping at emotional arm's length those who could have been mine, on the other, out of an instinct, most likely born of so much loss, to keep myself safe. With Lissa I'd found the freedom that I'd always secretly longed for only to be shut out again in the end.

Was it in self-defense, therefore, that I mounted such a titanic effort not to open the floodgates of my own gaze and reveal to Helen that I loved her?

Or was it the defense of her well-being that kept me in my place?

"My God, you're so incredibly beautiful," I told my cousin Kristen that fateful afternoon in South Carolina, and she melted like I'd never seen another woman melt.

Her mother, my father's younger sister, looked me straight in the eye when I was eighteen and preparing to go to Japan, and told me to "beware of the demons you might encounter in foreign lands, and how they might sway you to evil ways." I didn't know exactly how to respond, because it sounded almost as if she was warning me of actual demons, some kind of evil, pointed-eared monsters that were lurking in the shadows waiting for their chance to lead me astray. I was grateful for her concern, and I trusted unconditionally that she loved me as much as any aunt could, but her warning struck me as one of the most preposterous things I'd ever heard.

Later that afternoon, out bowling with Kristen's two younger brothers, I asked the older of the two, "Did you hear what your mother told me . . . about demons lurking in the shadows?"

"Yeah, you better be careful!" he told me.

And he was deadly serious.

My head spun with the realization that a family so close to me, biologically, could believe in the literal existence of angels and demons. I was eighteen years old and it was the first time I'd ever encountered educated, well-to-do people who looked and acted normal, but took such things literally. It seemed so medieval! I had thought such beliefs were limited to isolated mountain people who jumped up and down in church, spoke in tongues, and brought poisonous snakes in to be part of their services. Yet Kristen had graduated from Bowling Green with a degree in English literature, and the next oldest one, Mark, was considering Davidson! Kristen's father is a minister – much as my own father had been raised to be; I wondered with amazed disbelief how the way my father had raised me – to see the world through my own eyes, to ask questions, and to look for, and rely on, my own answers – could be so completely opposite to what my cousins had been taught by my father's sister and her husband.

Kristen, at the time our paths crossed in such an "inappropriate" way, had recently broken off an engagement of her own to a man a couple of years her senior who'd proposed to her in front of hundreds at a missionary convention, and who was then in his final year of training to become a minister. Indeed, Kristen had taken up her relationship with him again almost immediately after her encounter with me, so fresh out of my own monastery, and I had been heartbroken – twice! – when she wrote to tell me that she'd merely been "overcome by a moment of passion," and to ask me not to come to her wedding once they'd made their decision, again, to marry.

I must seem fickle describing the Kristen, Lissa, Helen progression, but the fact is that I was very much in love with Kristen two years before Helen – I loved her as family, and I was in love with her, too! – and it was an earlier, lesser version of the double heartbreak I was to suffer at the loss of both Lissa and Martha to be informed that I'd lost the woman I loved *and* yet another piece of my family, both in one fell swoop.

Thinking back, it was remarkable the way Kristen crumbled when I opened my eyes to her – I invoked her God, for heaven's sake! – and told her that I was blown away by how beautiful she was. In accordance with her upbringing, she was the last person on earth who would have thought herself capable of a romantic entanglement with her own cousin! Whether you call that incest or just kissing cousins, isn't that one of those cardinal sins that Christians are always dodging their demons to avoid?

"Goddamn your ego!" Lissa wrote, referring to the time when her resolve crumbled, when in the doorway to her dorm room after I walked her home from Sara's that night and found her to be the seer that she was, I summarily opened my eyes to her and invited her own closeted capacity for love to rush in, in the form of romantic passion.

"You're not strong enough to resist loving me," I told her, and in the end she did. She loved me harder, and stronger, and more desperately than she'd ever loved another. With gnashing teeth and full-contact blows she'd loved me – and in the end, I'd watched her devastated because of it.

She wrote that she "felt loss," that "her blankets were never even rumpled any more", and that she cried when she thought of my eyes, and none of that compared to what I felt in her when I grabbed her by the elbows in a desperate effort to keep her with me, and she collapsed into a crying pile at my feet. I imagined Kristen collapsing, too, as she confessed what had happened between us to her fiancé. I'd lost Kristen and now I'd lost Lissa, somehow I'd hurt both of them, it felt as though I'd somehow drained both of them of something vital, and with those memories still so raw, I found myself in love with Helen in a way that grew day by day and made all that I'd experienced before pale in comparison.

How can it be love to subject anyone to such risk? I asked myself, forsaking my newly found *carpe diem* creed for the sake of this woman I loved, even for her marriage, because it, too, was part of who she was.

I am ashamed now to have flirted then with the belief that had I opened myself to Helen, she too would have fallen. At the time, I was caught up in the power of it all. Lissa called it ego, and she was right. Why would someone I held in such high esteem as I did Kristen fall so hard when I reached into her with my eyes? Why would Lissa? It wasn't that I had made a pass at either one of them that made them momentarily mine. I'd always been the Beta who couldn't pick up girls for the life of me, and women susceptible to sexual advances weren't my type anyway. It was somehow rather that I opened myself up to them, and when I did, I stumbled upon a way to convert one of the weaknesses I hated most about my personality into a terrible strength.

I looked into these women and demanded that they love me, and they did. That was Midas at his most vicious. In his world, the world was his – he was unstoppable – and that applied as well to the women that he wanted, provided they were women who could see into that specific world that was his. Through their eyes, Kristen, Lissa and Helen had all visited Midas's world to varying degrees. In the same way that I bowled a score of Davidson professors out of their conference-room chairs in my Watson interview – by being brutally honest with them and revealing what was inside me for the first time since I'd returned from Japan – I was routinely honest with Kristen, Lissa and Helen in a way that people who rely merely on words for communication can't possibly understand.

I never really knew Helen well – certainly not in terms of the tangible. I do feel like I got to know Lissa. But in my decade-long quest to understand exactly what transpired between me and Helen, and how it became so powerful, I find myself returning to what I know for sure about Kristen.

She was raised to be a healer.

Demons and angels aside, I can imagine that the one instinct her missionary background instilled in her more strongly than any other was an instinct to heal.

And in that, Kristen would have had a much more powerful tool at her disposal than any ideological training could have given her.

For my own part, I had become so aware of Conscience that I could sometimes hear my own like a speaking voice telling me to sacrifice for the young people of the future. Such a heightened awareness had to have come first from my parents, since such things can only be instilled by the earliest training. At least half of that influence must have come from my father, and my father and Kristen's mother grew up in the same household! I can only imagine that Kristen, therefore, would have been raised to possess a similar sense of compassion.

Does it not seem possible, then, that what I saw in Kristen's eyes as "so incredibly beautiful" was not only her ability to see, but also her instinct to heal, all that she would have seen in me as such desperate need? Reeling as I was just then from the final blows of my parents' decade-long, piece-by-piece abandonment – contrary to the tough-guy karate-man image or not! – might that experience not have left an emotional vacuum in me that any instinctive healer would feel compelled to rush in and fill?

Master Choi taught me not only how to look into other people's eyes, but also how to project myself into the eyes of others, and falsity was something that medium just wouldn't convey. He taught me to reveal, in a glance, the ultimate truth of who I was to those who could see it, the good and the bad, the strengths and the weaknesses. With Kristen, and with Lissa, when I looked into their eyes, the ultimate truth of what I was feeling at those exact moments was that I wanted them more than I wanted every subsequent breath of my life. "My god, you're so incredibly beautiful," I told Kristen, and she responded with passion. I looked into Lissa's eyes and she too responded with passion. But it's impossible for me to reconcile my looking into them in that way with something as rude as a sexual advance.

The sensation of desire soared right past – and denied! – the stereotypical hormonal reaction of physical attraction, although in the case of Kristen and Lissa that reaction certainly followed. After my first encounter with Lissa, I'd staggered away drunk – the power and beauty of the night sky had been the trigger – and it was all I could do to catch my balance and maintain composure.

As time passed, the sensation of desire that overcame me when I looked into Helen's eyes was the sensation of wanting to consume or devour, make mine forever, and throw away the key.

Kristen fell.

Lissa fell.

But I wasn't going to let that happen with Helen. I took a physical step backwards. I shut down the gaze. I closed the doors.

And I ached.

EIGHTEEN

It was during the long weekend of our Thanksgiving vacation that Helen spilled out of the four or five scheduled hours per week that I spent in her company to fill every corner of my world. Dr. Abbott asked me to stay in his house to walk the dog for several days while he went out of town to visit family, and he didn't even have to finish his sentence before I knew I would, no matter what the favor entailed. I had a paper to write – for Helen! – and the alternative would have been to spend those days at home.

My stepmother had long since seemed to me a little bit too satisfied that the cottage where I lived behind my father's house was in the backyard "like the doghouse." A self-congratulatory twinkle in her eye arose whenever the topic came up, which spoke of her resentment of my being in her life in the first place. I wondered if she thought she was fooling anyone with her "I care about you so much" mask, or whether she in fact knew I could see right through it. The delight she took in anything that came up that could be degrading of me or my morale was so blatant that I wondered if she wasn't daring me to try to prove it.

Of course I wouldn't have been able to. She'd have denied it and condescendingly called me "angry" – absolving herself by suggesting that I was "chronically angry and therefore maladjusted" – and reveled in yet another victory won in her decade-long struggle to make me go away.

"I would be very grateful," Dr. Abbott explained. "About the only thing Kayo lives for anymore is getting a chance to go out for walks so he can experience the world through all the exciting smells he can't find at home." I remembered Kayo as a puppy from when I was five. Eighteen years later, he was nearly blind, and so stiff I was relieved to discover that he could actually walk at a fairly decent clip, provided he was allowed to stagger for several initial steps to build up momentum.

I was relieved not to have to spend four relatively free days under the same roof as my father, as well.

The grief, watching him struggle to deny his wife's overt resentment, was particularly painful, since winning that battle meant convincing himself that abandoning me to my stepmother's abuse was the correct course for his wife, life, and future. I was old enough to remember a time when my father's shoulders weren't always curved forward and his tail wasn't always between his legs in his own home, and the worst part of being there was watching a man I'd once held in such high esteem apparently choosing to remain in that state.

Dr. Abbott and I were not close when I was a child – his kids were much older – but I did remember him from when I was that young, and he represented for me something of my utopian childhood in Davidson. His home seemed more welcoming than my own father's did, certainly if I also wanted to get any work done – or, God forbid, allow myself any moments of rest! In what felt like a blink, therefore, I was leaving my toothbrush next to the sink in Dr. Abbott's guest room, and setting myself up at the computer in his study with Jane Austen's novel *Persuasion*.

Like the town of Davidson with all its students gone, Dr. Abbott's house was utterly quiet.

My resolve had broken down a week earlier, and in the most subtle of ways I'd crossed the line from professional to personal and asked Helen out to lunch. We agreed to meet at one of Davidson's few off-campus restaurants, and the rendezvous became as much a date, I suppose, as a student could have with his married and unavailable professor, having resolved to keep the love that he felt for her bottled up in an attempt to make her a friend.

During the semester, I encountered Helen semi-regularly in the Café, where I spent my lunch hour most days and she came for lunch sometimes, and two or three times we even sat down together in passing. To me, she had become a confidante to an extent that I'm sure she never knew. During the middle of that semester there was only one thing in my life, and that was the *Budo Karate Illustrated* acceleration. I was fighting my way back to Mas Oyama and Kyokushin, and the battle consumed every calorie of my pitifully overburdened existence. I was enrolled in six classes, and somehow I went through the motions of all of them. I taught karate every day, and those motions too were so automatic as to happen nearly without me. The Café was supporting me as much as I was supporting it, meals were free for me there, and I was allowed to all but make up how many hours each week I was going to pay myself for.

And I paid myself well.

I was almost always there, though, or just moments away, nights and weekends when the Café was my responsibility. As with all my other responsibilities, I'd figured out how to give it 100% of my attention while simultaneously committing 100% of my attention elsewhere, and the operation ran so smoothly that my boss always initialed the totals I wrote on my timecards without question.

One side effect of channeling 100% of my attention in five different directions – somehow adding up to nearly 500% energy exerted! – was that I became fairly withdrawn. For the entire previous year, and until just three months earlier, I'd spent nearly every waking moment in Lissa's company when I wasn't otherwise occupied. Now, not only was I suddenly without that constant companionship, but I considered myself so duty-bound to succeed in my all-but-impossible endeavors that I had no inclination to try to replace it. My life had become like a perpetual exam week, and with pages of literature pasted to the walls of shower stalls to keep me awake, I struggled to keep even part of one nostril above water so that I could breathe. I solved problems in my sleep and woke with a start to record the solutions for fear I'd forget them by morning. Midas was rising to force – it was his blind confidence that opened the floodgates to the necessary creativity to stay on top of it all – and Nathan Ligo all but gave up trying to explain himself to those around him. What would have been the point? How could I possibly have described what was really going on in my life to those with whom I had only Davidson in common? Without the ballistically brutal communication I'd unleashed – even for just a minute or two – on my professors when they elected me a shoo-in for the Watson, or the beyond-words communication that I'd shared in a prolonged eye-lock with Lissa, how could anyone even begin to relate?

That's where Helen became, for me, confidante. She was the only one I talked to about any of it. Of course I couldn't possibly have visited her every day at her office, or called her on the phone every evening to share with her what I so desperately wanted someone to understand. To do so would have crossed the line that with gnashing teeth and full-contact blows I'd sworn to defend. I was so afraid that I would give myself away that I limited myself to chance encounters, and then, further, only to those opportunities in conversation that didn't make me look like I was too desperate to share. My confessions, I restricted to the realities of the *Budo Karate Illustrated* project, and to that topic alone. How ridiculous I'd have seemed if I'd explained that my silly little karate yearbook was to become the first step of a hundred that would one day change the world for far more than just American practitioners of karate!

I'm going to publish this book, I could have explained, *that's not only going to be the forerunner of a magazine that we'll see on newsstands within the next decade, making America's existing martial arts magazines look like the garbage that they are, but the project will also be the first step of several significant ones taken in a lifetime of steps that just might open the eyes of enough people in this country to have a lasting, trend-correcting influence on American society itself.*

Cannot one teacher, I asked, *influence thousands in a lifetime?*

And if his students become teachers themselves, mightn't they, in turn, influence hundreds of thousands who wouldn't otherwise have been touched?

How insane I'd have sounded!

So of course I didn't try. I restricted my conversation to *Budo Karate Illustrated* and graduating from Davidson. The fact that there was so much more to it, I left up to Helen's intuition and the line of wordless communication that I dared to believe she and I shared. She'd see the energy behind the drive and know that it was something different . . . something more.

I've described how, in a spontaneous moment of humor, Helen's laughing at herself had provided the opening, and how I'd reached forward ever so slightly with my gaze to find out if my suspicions about her being able to see were true. I've described how, bowled over by what I found, I immediately drew back, afraid that I'd crossed a line that might have disrespected her – or worse, revealed myself to her!

Such exchanges accompanied nearly every conversation that Helen and I shared, and no one ever knew.

I can't even be sure of the extent to which Helen was aware.

It was never anything so rude and transparent as trying to convey something with a glance. In *kumite* at *Honbu* with that *sempai* of mine whose face I pounded to a pulp in front of Mas Oyama, I didn't look at him and make a face that announced, "Now I'm going to beat you." On the contrary, I was utterly terrified that the opposite would be the case. I was terrified that he would beat me in front of *Sosai*, and the survival instinct drove me to turn over every stone in search of a weapon I could use to protect myself. In doing so, I must have discovered something planted there by Master Choi and, somehow, I managed to produce a gaze that subliminally danced in past my *sempai's* defenses and so unnerved him that he had no idea what hit him until he was in the corner of the dojo a half hour later using ice packs to keep his black eyes from swelling shut.

By the time Helen's and my paths crossed, I was frighteningly aware of that one particular wavelength of optical communication that I'd learned might be used to convey such a wide range of thoughts and feelings, from "My god, you're so incredibly beautiful," in the case of a lover, to "Now I'm going to break you," in the case of an opponent. What I never knew for sure was to what extent those I've here called "seers" were themselves aware. Lissa certainly was! Was it not therefore reasonable to assume that the others were too? It was very conscious for me – often during that time I would lose the words of conversation completely and just rely on gaze, since what it conveyed seemed to be so much more authentic – but I have no idea if those who could see, as I believed Helen could, saw consciously, or if they merely processed what they saw on a level akin to intuition.

How can I possibly describe the delicacy with which I dared to interact with Helen during the months when we saw each other regularly?

Instead of barreling in like a linebacker, as I routinely did with Lissa, I would dance gently around the edges of the possibility of doing so, then reach forward to meet her in the middle as mere punctuation to a verbal exchange – and then only at the depth to which she herself invited me. With Kristen and Lissa, the emphasis had been on penetration and possession – I was so hungry then, and there was nothing in me that encouraged restraint. With Helen, restraint was where I began.

How audacious that I even allowed our eyes to meet!

Through them I fed to relieve a desperate hunger. It was a hunger for companionship, for camaraderie, and for understanding. It was a hunger to not be so alone in what I alone seemed to be able to see. It was a hunger to fill the void left by Lissa, Lissa who had momentarily filled the void left by all that had gone before. In Lissa's case, I fed by having. In Helen's, I fed by not having, by denying myself her for her sake, and by flattering myself that she had to be aware on some level.

Could she have known?

Surely she'd have seemed conflicted – hesitant perhaps! – in our daily interaction.

But it was with the warmest admiration, acceptance and compassion that she met me, and it was that with which I struggled to fill the void. And on most days it even seemed to suffice. Was I tempted to take more? Of course I was. Was I infuriated by what I couldn't have? Unbelievably so. Yet, somehow, I managed to find just what I needed to make it through my days, while not risking that which would have put an end to it all.

"How truly wealthy a person might consider himself to be!" I marveled, ". . . to be considered a friend by this woman!"

There were moments in Helen's tiny classroom when I felt like a vampire lusting for blood, as if I could somehow sink my fangs into that which I found so intoxicating and drink until there was nothing left. These were the times in her company that I won my greatest battles by not simply getting up and walking out of the classroom, never to return. If Helen was ever aware, she must have been equally aware of that battle I fought to restrain it, because she never once withheld from me the warmth of her friendship.

It must have been the confidence she thus inspired in me that convinced me I'd be able to handle taking her out to lunch.

The notion wasn't, of course, in any way far-fetched. Davidson was a small place, professors and students often shared meals, and the only thing that might have rendered our one off-campus lunchtime meeting out of the ordinary was that Helen was living in Davidson without her husband for the year, and I was in love with her. Hopefully no one knew that, though – even I was often able to convince myself that it was nonsense! – and no one would have given the two of us a second glance, even at an off-campus restaurant.

I'm not sure how it was that Helen and I wound up sharing a table that day with two or three other junior members of Davidson's English faculty. It may have just happened by chance. The alternative that occurred to me was too frightening to contemplate. *Had Helen worked behind the scenes to ensure that her lunch with me would be chaperoned?*

Could I have been that transparent?

As concerned as I was initially, however, that our lunch for two was turning into a lunch for several more, it wound up feeling completely natural. The mix of personalities present that day was certainly a riot.

Most notably, my American literature survey professor from the year before, David Strom, was there. His presence was ironic for two reasons. The first was that I'd written a journal entry for one of his classes two semesters earlier that was supposed to be a response to a passage by Walt Whitman, but in which I'd strayed into writing about my relationship with Lissa. I had been embarrassed almost from the moment I turned it in – I don't think it was exactly the kind of response he'd expected – and I wondered if he remembered. To his credit, "Thank you for sharing," he'd written at the bottom of the page, "but is that kind of passion sustainable?"

The real irony of Dr. Strom being there, though, was that he was engaged to one of his students – who was my age – and it was widely rumored that he'd tragically sacrificed his job at Davidson because of it. Like Helen, he was a tenure-track professor, meaning that Davidson hired him with the understanding that if things went well in his first two years, they would make his employment permanent. At about the same time that it came out that he was engaged to one of his former advisees, however, Davidson decided to deny him tenure. For obvious reasons, it is considered an ethics violation for professors to have romantic relationships with their students. Dr. Strom claimed that the relationship hadn't begun until the student in question was no longer one of his, and I never knew her or the specifics of their relationship. Nevertheless, he was denied tenure, and it was widely believed that he had been passed over for at least the appearance of wrongdoing.

It was Dr. Strom's last year at Davidson, and by then he would already have been looking forward to his next teaching position somewhere else.

Shireen Carroll arrived with Dr. Strom. Like Helen, she was fresh out of graduate school. In addition to two new tenure-track literature professors, one of them Helen, Dr. Carroll had been hired that year to start a creative-writing program at Davidson. I'd dog-sat for Dr. Carroll once already as well – the big scary one was named Toto, and the little white poodle was named Thor! Apparently I'd developed a reputation for being willing to stay in professors' houses to watch over pets and such while they were away. Her presence was ironic because she was the Davidson faculty member that year most commonly mentioned by male students as the one they wished they could get to know a little better outside of class.

My friend and student Rafael was a big fan of Dr. Carroll.

If Sarah Beasley, my Shakespeare professor, wasn't there that day, it isn't surprising that I find myself superimposing her presence among those that were. She was the other new, not-yet-tenured member of Davidson's English Department, and the three of them – the three women hired that year – were very often together. Professor Beasley looked so young that she was sometimes mistaken for a student, and she was even guilty of insisting at times that we call her Sarah, which further complicated the distinction. Come to think of it, she must not have been there: It was in her presence that I had committed the most painful Freudian slip of my life – one that had involved Helen – and if she had been there I'm sure I would have remembered squirming in my seat.

Three of us, students in Professor Beasley's Shakespeare class, had been riding in her car to Winston-Salem, a small North Carolina city about ninety minutes from Davidson, to watch a live production of *The Merchant of Venice*. From the back seat an hour into the journey – overtasked and exhausted to the verge of blindness as was my norm that semester – I leaned forward out of my gloom with the intention of calling out "Sarah," to ask her some question I can't recall.

Somehow I called out "Helen" instead.

There was a sudden silence. Everyone in the car turned towards me, wondering what the hell I was talking about, since there wasn't a Helen in the car. Professor Beasley glanced up in her rearview mirror.

I'd bottled my feelings for Helen so tightly that I never even allowed myself to utter her name out loud in anything but a professional context. Although she'd been "Helen" to me almost from the very beginning, I'd never even once spoken anything other than "Dr. Ecks." It took me, therefore, an excruciatingly long moment to recover, and that moment was one of the most painful of my year.

No one treated me like I was out of place as the only nonprofessor at lunch that day, however, and no one gave the slightest indication that they suspected me of harboring any affection for Helen beyond that of a student who appreciated his teacher enough to ask her out to lunch. I can't remember much of the discussion; I wonder if I'd turned the task of making small talk over to that part of my fractured personality that could handle such situations more smoothly without me.

It did occur to me that the entire crowd was Dillon's age, plus perhaps only a year or two. My first lover Dillon had been a senior when I skipped twelfth grade and started college as the youngest member of my freshman class. I'd spent many hours hanging out with Dillon's crowd, and so the age difference between me and my lunch companions that day was nothing out of the ordinary: Dillon would have just received the Sorbonne's equivalent of a PhD in French literature, and she would be taking her first teaching position at a college in the U.S. in the coming year. These young Davidson professors were the most nonjudgmental crowd imaginable, and I found myself completely at ease.

Once we'd each picked up our separate checks, Helen suggested that the two of us walk up the street for ice cream. *Could it be charity?* I wondered. *Is she aware? Did I fail to hide my disappointment when her colleagues showed up?*

We spoke as we walked, and I took a long, deep breath that I apparently hadn't allowed myself during lunch. Equilibrium was returning, my concerns draining away. This was the kind of one-on-one time I'd hungered for with Helen, and if she was in the least bit uncomfortable, she didn't show it.

Over ice cream, alone and at the other end of Main Street, Helen and I skirted literature and *Budo Karate Illustrated* and talked about my history and her future. She and Jack were still trying to decide where they would settle, and she wanted to hear the pros and cons of growing up in Davidson from someone who had. She wanted to know if it had been a good place to be a kid. I told her that it had been for me, because of the families and the Children's Schoolhouse that my parents had founded, and because of the tiny close-knit community in which everyone knew everyone. I told her I'd heard that Davidson's elementary school had been much improved since my one miserable year there. I described my high school experience as a positive one, even though Davidson faculty brats had become such a minority among the children of the builders and bankers who'd come in and bought up the highly coveted properties around Lake Norman.

It was crystal clear that the reason why Helen was asking was that she and her husband were planning a family of their own. As counterintuitive as it may seem, I was completely at ease with that notion, because I had zero intention of pursuing her romantically. Respecting her was where I took my greatest pleasure, and as long as it seemed to me that it would have disrespected her to pursue her, I remained steadfast in my decision not to. Of course I wonder what would have happened if she had even hinted that she was unhappy in her marriage. I wonder if I'd have taken society's law against pursuing a married woman and trampled it with the same disdain I'd showed one or two of society's laws before in the name of gobbling up the days of my life. Would I have rolled the dice to find out what would come of opening myself to her as I had to Lissa?

I didn't have to consider it, though, and I certainly never dwelled on the idea. Not even the tiniest possibility of romantic involvement with Helen ever presented itself.

At one point our conversation turned to the recent demise of my relationship with Lissa. I had Helen's eyes then, and if there'd been even a hint of trouble in paradise, I'm certain I'd have seen it. The only hint of discontent I gleaned, in fact, was that she and her husband weren't living in the same city. That fact made it easy for me to do what I'd been doing all along:

I struggled to normalize the feelings I had for her. If I couldn't make her a lover, I would be damned if I wasn't going to do everything in my power to make her a friend!

I had first been attracted to Helen by a single elusive quality that made my projects the realest thing in my world that year. In search of creativity, I'd barreled through Reason and looked past intuition to my heart as the source of answers to carry me through my day-to-day. Psyche mistrusted my entire endeavor, too,[70] and I constantly had to deny Reason to keep moving forward. The idea that I might do all that I was trying to do seemed so preposterous, even to me, that my denial of reason regarding Helen made total sense. Reason couldn't explain what I saw in her, just as it couldn't explain how I could see what I saw in my future. I saw both of them with the same eyes – one was like an exercise for training myself to see the other – and to deny one would have been to deny the other as well.

And that, Conscience wouldn't allow me to do.

How perplexing it was to sit there with Helen and be completely in

---

[70] From Poe's "Ulalume": *But Psyche, uplifting her finger, / Said-"Sadly this star I mistrust-/ Her pallor I strangely mistrust:-/ Oh, hasten!-oh, let us not linger! / Oh, fly!-let us fly!-for we must." / . . . / I replied-"This is nothing but dreaming: / Let us on by this tremulous light! / Let us bathe in this crystalline light! / . . . / We safely may trust to a gleaming / That cannot but guide us aright, / Since it flickers up to Heaven through the night." / Thus I pacified Psyche and kissed her, / And tempted her out of her gloom-/ And conquered her scruples and gloom; / And we passed to the end of the vista, / But were stopped by the door of a tomb-/ . . . / And I said-"What is written, sweet sister, / On the door of this legended tomb?" / She replied-"Ulalume-Ulalume-/ 'Tis the vault of thy lost Ulalume!"*

love with her, on the one hand, and completely resolved that the best way to love her was to get over it and befriend her, on the other! However you would have defined that elusive quality that had drawn me to Helen originally, the rest of her had besieged and redefined my sense of what there was to love a woman for. I loved her for her intellect. I loved her for her wit. I loved her for her generosity. I loved her for her compassion. I loved her for the patience and care with which she tolerated and accepted me, because she had to have known on some level that my interest in her was more than just casual. I loved her for not running away and shutting me out. I loved her for embracing what she had to have seen in me despite my best efforts to conceal it. I loved her for the fact that as abnormal as my feelings for her were, she made me feel so normal in her fearless engagement of me that all of that other would-be nonsense drained away. It was as if there was something in her personality that wicked all of that insanity out of me. Direct engagement was the anchor that kept my passion from drifting away into the irrational. When she and I were together, I was at my most sane. It was in her absence that I was most prone to losing control and letting my feelings for her get out of hand.

It was during those days at Dr. Abbott's house over Thanksgiving that I started to lose control.

I was alone there for the better part of five days. Most of the student population was out of town, and I was relieved not to be in my father's backyard. I took a lot more time walking around an empty town than I was accustomed to – it took Kayo and me forty-five minutes just to walk around the block! – and that left me alone with my thoughts for long hours during which my paper wasn't getting written. *Perhaps it'll be the walk itself*, I consoled myself more than once, *that'll jump-start the process once I get back to work!*

Tragically, alone with my thoughts turned out to be a dangerous place for me to be.

I'm not sure if I knew Helen to be alone that weekend, or whether I just had that impression because her husband was usually away, but I was infuriated by the realization that I was all by myself – I didn't encounter a living soul for two or three long days – and she was just a stone's throw away. I didn't know exactly where she lived; I knew the general vicinity, though, since Davidson's such a small place. And as the days passed I became more and more annoyed by what felt like a distinct, magnetic pull in her direction. Asking Helen out to lunch on a school day was one thing, but reaching out to her when both of us were alone and outside the setting of our professional relationship would have been something else entirely.

The telephones in Dr. Abbott's house agitated me at one point so much that the image of unplugging them and casting them out onto the porch crossed my mind. How easy it would have been to pick one up and dial her number!

How colossal a blunder it would have been!

Is it really better to have loved and lost than never to have loved at all?

That was the question that, with Lissa and Kristen in mind, I'd used to challenge my *carpe diem* creed and leave Helen alone. When I pursued both Kristen and Lissa, I was never out of control. On the contrary, I pursued them because I believed it was my responsibility to live my life for everything it was worth. I wasn't blind to the fact that I could hurt them – certainly I was wide-eyed aware of it with Kristen! Even conventional love hurts, after all. But I'd consoled myself that by loving them, no matter the risk, I'd also be filling their lives in the way that I sought to fill mine. I went forward with open eyes and a clear conscience, because I believed that living life to its fullest was the best answer for everyone.

I'm sure now that I was naïve to think such a thing. I was living that way by choice, but did I really have the right to try to impose it on anyone else?

Dr. Abbott's house was less than one hundred yards from the house my father and mother rented from the college and brought me home to from the hospital when I was born. I lived there for my first three or four years while the log house, just three miles away, was being built, and it was on that same street that I formed my earliest memories. Tera Jacobus's house was right there, as was Thomas and Alice Lyle's, and Michael's across the street. Those were my earliest childhood companions, and my brother and I continued to play in that neighborhood with them even after my parents moved out to the forest. Those ghostlike memories stirred my soul into an almost soup-thick nostalgia as the dog and I wandered ever so slowly around the block – Kayo stopping to smell everything we passed – and I don't doubt that those memories had a lot to do with the change that took place within me during those several days. The peer group I had played with on that block was the first one I was torn from by the original fracturing of my parents' home.

Was not life too short not to embrace the fact that I was in love?

It was too powerful to dismiss. Up until then, I had fought to restrain it. Out of love and respect for Helen, I had struggled to normalize it. I even tried to make it go away. But in the wake of having lunch with her and talking with her about her raising a family of her own – not half a mile from where I had been a child! – it struck me that I could have my cake and eat it too: I could allow myself to revel in my love for her, I could set that building passion free provided I continued to deny myself anything that remotely resembled pursuit. *Carpe diem* came knocking then loud and clear, and I realized that all that mattered with regard to Helen was that I left her alone. Otherwise, I could let out all the stops, I could let the emotion run wild, I could celebrate the fact that I loved her.

After all, who was possibly going to get hurt?

Only me.

For that matter, I wondered if it would kill me, but at least, even then, she'd never know.

And O, what a way to go!

Of course, I was still then too naïve to believe myself to be in any real danger. Something about my past, however, had developed in me a taste for the exhilaration of living life, savoring it for its intensity, either at the joy or heartbreak end of the spectrum. Loving Helen, I already knew, would be both at the same time. She was the most beautiful thing in my world, and I asked myself how it could possibly be wrong to celebrate that.

What greater compliment could there be, I asked myself, *than to let my love for this woman run free while denying myself the pursuit of her, so as not to disrespect her? What greater honor could I pay her than willfully waging that war?*

Such was the argument in which I indulged during the long walks that Dr. Abbott's dying dog and I shared that weekend in Davidson's November. Two opposing forces, Passion and Reason, were battling within me, and it was then that Reason lost the battle to hold Passion in check. Probably I didn't make a conscious decision to give in to the emotional; much more likely, there in my solitude without Helen in the flesh – the anchor I'd come to rely on to normalize what I felt for her – need spilled over and clouded reason to where it seemed like the right thing to do to indulge, safely alone, in letting out all the stops.

And so I walked aimlessly around the town of Davidson, or sat alone in front of food I couldn't eat, paragraphs in my book I couldn't read, or in front a computer screen with nothing on it for hours but a title and an opening sentence, which I kept writing over and over again in search of the creative spark that would ignite the start of a second. I existed there in solitude and I loved this woman, Helen Ecks, for all I was worth. I loved her till I was blind. I loved her till it was hard to breathe. I loved her till I could barely hold myself upright when I walked. I loved her until it felt as if love oozed out of my core like tar to fill the physical spaces I occupied. It filled the first floor of Dr. Abbott's house to waist level before rolling out through the windows, and through the cracks around the doors, to fill the rest of the world. I loved her until it took so much out of me that I'd sit or stand or bathe or lie down and I'd marvel at how much I felt like a shell in the aftermath.

I caught myself rubbing my chest through my shirt, as if the surface warmth might break through and alleviate the dull, unrelenting ache I felt inside.

That Thanksgiving was three-quarters of the way through the most demanding semester of my Davidson experience. I didn't sleep for the six classes I had to pass, and I barely passed a couple of them for the demands of the *Budo Karate Illustrated* project. I was so completely engaged that the work went on without me in my sleep. I had no excess energy even to realize how isolated I'd become. But for those four days that I was alone in Dr. Abbott's house, all of it ground to a sudden, groaning halt. If the vision that drove my endeavors was a locomotive, I'd been shoveling coal into the furnace until my back was breaking and my hands were bleeding, and still I didn't stop. But then, suddenly, during those four days, as if the rails had come to an abrupt end, the beast flew forward momentarily on air and then plowed, cow-catcher first, in an explosion of rocks and then sank into the sand, its wheels no longer turned, the boiler cracked, and there was a sudden stillness.

I was in love, just then that love was the most powerful thing I knew, and life was too short to squander. *My god, it's so incredibly beautiful!* I marveled, and the passion filled my entire existence.

It's no wonder that I was exhausted – and most certainly distracted – as I walked across town to my father's house for the family Thanksgiving dinner I'd been required to attend. At the end of the driveway, I paused to force a deep, controlled breath. I stamped my foot to demand control, and fought my way back down to earth.

Fucking hell! I swore to myself as I walked in through the back door.
"Hello," I called out. "I'm home!"

NINETEEN

MY STEPMOTHER'S VOICE, "Not coming over for Thanksgiving with your family is not an option," rang in my ears, and my stomach turned. Her eyes had done that thing again, like she was congratulating herself for choosing the perfect words to tell me how unwelcome I really was, challenging me, at the same time, to try to prove it.

It was the ultimate hypocrisy.

She wasn't going to be happy until she either wore me down and made me toe the same line as my father, or drove me away as an adult so that she could put on her puppy-eyed display for the world of "he was such an angry young man. We did all we could to make him feel like he was part of the family!"

Not an option.

Her words echoed perfectly my father's attempts to make me feel a way that I didn't in the first few years after he snatched up my brother and me and left Martha behind in the log house. "It's Mother's Day," he'd stand there and tell his 12-year-old son. "Not giving your stepmother a card on Mother's day is not an option."

"But she's not my mother," I'd remind him, and he'd look so wounded for a brief moment before blowing his lid and seething that she was my elder and I had to respect her. Disliking her all the more, I'd go out and buy the Mother's Day card that told the lie he insisted that I tell.

Not an option.

If I had a heart for my father left to break, surely it would have when he used those words after leaving them exclusively to her for six or eight years. They'd become *her* words by then, and they meant something totally different. From him, in the beginning, they'd spoken of his desperation to move on in his life beyond Martha – they'd spoken of his heartbreak. I could see then what my father was feeling, and I'd loved him and pitied him. Now, however, a decade later, my father was still heartbroken at home, and those same words had become the weapon of choice wielded by his wife to throw in my face how I didn't have a family to come home to because *I* was too stubborn to kowtow to her. They'd become a rallying cry in her war to degrade me to where I'd either shut my eyes or go away, and to hear my father use them, in later years and in her tone of voice, was utterly tragic. I was an adult by then – and in no danger of being blinded – but to hear my father speak his wife's words was undeniable and devastating proof that I had lost him.

"Hello, I'm home!" I called out as I stepped in through the back door, still telling the lie I'd always been expected to tell.

My father was there, of course – at least traces of the father I once knew. There was his wife, and their two young children. Besides me, the guests were the two male friends that remained in my father's life from the era when he was married to Martha. Brutally back down to earth after my ghoul-haunted weekend with Helen, I found myself sitting there, a reluctant participant in what felt to me like a sick charade. As far as I could tell my father hadn't developed any new friendships since he had turned his back on all the ones who had been the friends of his marriage to Martha ten years earlier. He saw these two about once a year; they were both UNCC professors who were fairly united in their professional opposition to Martha. Both of them were similarly divorced and either remarried or trying to be.

I wondered if their new wives would be like my stepmother. Younger, shallow, insecure, vindictive. As far as I was concerned, the light in Martha's personality tended to embarrass the whole bunch.

There had been no joy in my father's household for years. When we ate, we often ate in silence, or spoke lies in the form of small talk, either because I was biting my lip to keep from telling my father's wife to go to hell for whatever biting criticism she'd just uttered, or because my father was fighting the urge to blow his top at one of the kids who was misbehaving. He was plainly exhausted trying to keep up with his career – no one was willing to publish his book on Manet – while trying to play father at age fifty-two to two small children. He seemed to me consumed by a useless attempt to force his nontraditional household into the mold of his parents' traditional one, and always on the verge of exploding, if pushed, to deny it.

My father, a graduate of Princeton Seminary and therefore a Presbyterian minister, named the first son of his third marriage Seth. It dawned on me years later that Seth, in the Bible, was Adam's third son, born after Adam's second son Cain killed his first son Abel and was banished by God. Perhaps it was that early – Seth was born when I was thirteen – that my father decided that his first two sons were a total loss, like most of the friends of his marriage to Martha. He turned his back on them, he said, because they wouldn't accept his new wife, but he was lying to himself then too, and I was the last remaining witness who knew the truth: they loved him, and like me, they were heartbroken to watch him close his eyes to all that he'd dared to see during that brief interlude when he was married to Martha. Like me, they believed in him. They believed in his ability to stand on his own two feet in a nonprofessional relationship.

Losing Martha, his link to all that, my father must have decided that he had better focus his energy on starting over. Too bad I didn't even begin to give up on my father until nearly a decade later. There I was at something like the tenth Thanksgiving I'd shared with them since Seth was born, and I looked back and marveled at the abuse I'd suffered over the years for loving my father as much as I did. I marveled at how many times I'd bitten my lip and not stood up for myself out of a twisted notion that it would only hurt "my poor ailing, guilt-stricken dad."

My father asked the blessing at the beginning of the meal and listed all the things we should be thankful for – family, health, and happiness among them – and I sat there and marveled at his fantasy, because his family didn't have any of them. He never once prayed throughout my childhood until he failed in his second marriage and became desperate to rebuild. He'd given me the greatest gift a father could give his son: he was the one who had encouraged me to see the world as I saw it, to ask questions, and to draw my own conclusions. With those seeing eyes that Thanksgiving, I saw my father to be a miserable failure, and the happy, successful family act he put on for those two token friends from a life he'd turned his back on made me want to throw up.

Emotionally drained from that kind of loneliness, and from the kind of solitude I spent at Dr. Abbott's house with Helen, I finished my paper on *Persuasion* in the last sleepless night of my vacation. Duty finally kicked in – I figured I'd be letting Helen down if I couldn't get my act together and get a paper written – and I rode that train back into motion.

Just one more month! I consoled myself.

Classes for the semester would be over, so would my eighteenth-century novel course, and so would my daily exposure to the woman who, for the very first time, I had reason not to look forward to seeing in class.

How can I possibly conceal it now? I asked myself. *How can I possibly endure the charade?*

* * *

Midway through the summer I spent in Martha's house with Lissa, I sat down at the kitchen table, gathered what ego I could to convince myself that "even I can write poetry," and wrote these lines lamenting the loss of the utopian childhood I lived there with my brother:

> I walked down to the creek today
> To hunt crayfish and gold
> Like Aaron and I did when we were kids.
> The wild ginger and the jack-in-the-pulpits
> Still grow down by where the tree-house used to be.
> The dead leaves, ferns, and moss still carpet the gully slopes
> So thickly that I could still slide down
> On the seat of my pants, if I wanted to.
>
> I looked up at the house that Dad built,
> Where he and Mom, Aaron and I lived,
> Where he lived with his second wife,
> Where she lives alone now.
> It still looks the same.
> Dad said he bought this property because of the beech trees
> That grow here among the ferns.
> But that dream must have died
> Because now he lives in town with his new wife
> And their two kids.
>
> Aaron and I recently sat on the trunk of my car
> While his wife marinated the steaks inside.
> It was strange how much we seemed like adults
> And how much it seemed like we were the only family we had.

The other day I dreamed
That he and I were running down the creek bed,
Splashing with our bare feet and cut-offs.
Aaron, ahead of me, jumped over a fallen log
As I ducked under another.
We were too fast for the mosquitoes
And we didn't notice the spiderwebs that we ran through
Because of the flying mud and laughter.
The banks were too high to see over
And the brambles above simply blurred by.

Today as I jumped from stone to stone,
Cautiously,
Afraid that I might disturb a snake,
As I tripped on a poison ivy vine
And had to grab a tree root
To keep from getting my shoes wet,
I realized how little the woods have changed
And how they will never again be like they were
When we were kids.

As an adult I'd realized that the forest was full of peril.

We used to run and play there as if we were indestructible. Without shoes, even, we'd run though the forest with no fear of snakes or sharp rocks. We'd often jump across the creek from a seven-foot-high bank onto the leaf-covered bank below, not knowing if it was going to be soft and cushion our fall, or whether there were rocks hidden by the leaves that would sprain our ankles and skin our knees. The summertime forest was full of spiders, and to run anywhere among the trees would be to collect, face first, all the spiderwebs in our path, spiders and all. Mina, our Labrador-Doberman mix, as a puppy and well into her adolescence, used to run through those woods like there was a devil chasing her, and with complete assurance that there was nothing there that could hurt me, I used to try to catch her as if I believed I might someday be able to.

Once, however, when I balanced on a fallen tree trunk to cross the creek seven feet below me, just as I got out to the middle of its span, a massive copperhead slid off the bank into the water and swam past right under my feet. It caught me off guard, for a moment I lost my balance, and I imagined myself not only falling off, but falling right onto an angry poisonous snake. Another time the top of my scalp brushed under a tree limb overhead, apparently there was a hornet resting on it, and it stung me right on the top of my head and it hurt so bad I thought I would die. I used to not care when I'd come out of the woods with ticks latched onto my ankles and ears, because my parents were there to pluck them off and burn them to death with a match. But I grew up, and I learned what tick-carried Rocky Mountain spotted fever and Lyme disease could do to a man.

By the time I was twenty-two and living in Martha's house with Lissa, I still walked in the forest. But as an adult, I moved through the woods in a totally different way. Even in thick boots, I watched the forest floor under my feet to ensure that my next step wasn't going to put me in danger. I walked cautiously enough to know before I ran into a spiderweb so that I could duck under it, or clear it away with a branch, and even before I picked up that branch I'd roll it over first with my foot to make sure it didn't have something on it – or under it! – that I didn't want to grab. I avoided the creek bed entirely for fear that there were snakes or broken glass discarded by trespassing hunters, and I didn't jump across it because I didn't want to soil my shoes or break my leg. I hesitated when I encountered fallen branches and tree trunks to decide if it would be better to climb over them, or duck under, and even then I'd do so cautiously, as if the unknown was likely to hurt me.

Such is the stuff growing up is made of. We climb trees when we're kids that we wouldn't dream of climbing as adults. As kids we spend hours playing in the surf without a thought for sharks or currents that could whisk us out to sea. In my poem, I lamented this loss of freedom that comes with adulthood.

Little did I know, but by the end of that summer, I was going to get some of it back.

I understand the risk I take by writing about emotional wounds. If I was a *real* karate man, shouldn't I be able to put all that behind me and be the "tough guy," impervious to anything so feminine and weak as affairs of the heart? Perhaps I should, and I've certainly come, more than once, to crossroads in my life when I've seen that option laid out before me. I've seen choices that I could make that would allow my shell to harden over and forever deny all that had remained fluid on the inside. I've seen such opportunities clearly enough to be aware – and to revel in my victories! – as I keep traveling the opposite path with glee.

In the case of tough guys, emotional hardening is a common part of getting older. We age, and just as we become more cautious moving through forests, we become less willing to face the more turbulent aspects of our emotional and psychological composition. Indeed, part of growing up as we define it in America seems to be *letting it all settle*, the good parts and the bad, and moving forward into our future impervious, and therefore better equipped to handle the "more important" things in life, such as making money, developing careers, and raising families that then have to run a gauntlet of whether or not all that we've boxed up will come back and destroy them.

I tell my students that to be the best students possible, they need to make themselves like modeling clay. If, as their teacher, I press my thumb into their side, it's their job to make sure that that thumbprint remains there unchanged until I come along and make an adjustment. In terms of karate technique, that could be something like asking a student to make his stance deeper at the expense of correct hip position, knowing from experience that he won't be able to improve his hip position until his legs get stronger from practicing the deeper stance. Like modeling clay holding a thumbprint, the student must concentrate on that one adjustment, above all else, until such time as I recognize that his legs are now strong enough, his stance is now deep enough and, like pressing a new thumbprint into a lump of clay, I tell him to concentrate on the angle of his hips.

The best student is the one who's most able to assume the shape his teacher asks him to assume, and to hold that shape until it's time to make the next adjustment. In life, however, as we grow up, we tend to gain the ability to do the latter at the expense of the former. We become more and more inclined to hold shapes, and less and less able to either alter them or have them altered for us by the lessons we learn. Using our modeling-clay analogy, we might imagine the worst-case scenario being when the clay is baked in an oven until it becomes brittle and can no longer be adjusted without breaking. This would be analogous to the student growing up, becoming proud of all that he knows, and deciding that he no longer has anything more to learn.

As children, when we fall down, we get up, brush ourselves off, and keep moving forward as if nothing happened. As we get older, we get up a little more slowly, it hurts just a little bit more, and we tend, therefore, to be a little bit more cautious about falling down in the first place.

I have never been one to bemoan the circumstances of my adolescence.⁷¹ I didn't feel sorry for myself because my parents failed repeatedly to keep their families intact, and I didn't walk through life like a victim. After all, nothing in my history could compare to Jacques being shot, starved, and tortured in the Donbas! But neither did I deny the realities of my emotional makeup. I didn't shut my eyes and make myself blind to them. I didn't cease to contemplate the internal forces that drive me. I didn't cease to wonder whether earlier experiences might have a lot to do with how I react to reminiscent situations in the present. I'd been raised, after all, to believe that denying such facts of life was more dangerous than embracing them.

One of the most painful sensations I experienced as a young adult was the heartache I felt when Lissa shut me out. The feeling of loss was as if a vacuum had caused my chest to implode, fracturing my sternum and turning the splintered ends of my ribs inward to slice into my internal organs. I clutched at my chest as if I could pull the broken fragments back into place. Even Lissa's sympathetic embrace in the night didn't ease the suffering. By then she had retreated so far into herself – or at least pulled far enough away from me! – that even the charitable attempt she made with a half-hearted embrace in the night felt more like being held by a corpse than by the woman I had worked into my vision for the future. It was in desperation, therefore, that I reached out during arguments, twice, when Lissa shut me out completely, and grabbed her by the elbows in an attempt to keep her with me. Common sense insists that the intensity of that sensation could only have been something compounded by earlier loss, a reopening of older, deeper wounds causing a disproportionate reaction.

When my still so recently estranged stepmother Martha came home from chasing alligators in Florida's swamps with her camera for the summer, she was in a frenzy to get her life in order for the upcoming semester, and I was reeling from the heartache of having lost Lissa. In the night I clutched at my chest with Lissa turned away, and I couldn't sleep for the ache of it.

My father left Martha when I was eleven. I saw her two or three last times the following year, but it soon became too difficult for my father to bear my brother and me loving his ex-wife while it was increasingly clear that we weren't getting along with his present one. He increased the

---

⁷¹ My adolescence was a victory, after all!

pressure of "your poor, poor ailing dad" until it was no longer possible for us, at twelve and thirteen, to see Martha even though she lived just three miles away.

Finally, having lamented for six years the loss of the warmth and comfort of my childhood, and tracing that loss back to the loss of Martha, I gathered my courage when I was a seventeen-year-old freshman at Davidson, dating Dillon, and drove to the log house in search of Martha, and in search of *home*. I went there in search of whether my suspicions were correct.

And they were.

Once Martha recognized me – and it did take her a moment – she hugged me, and if I'd been a little less proud I would have cried. It was as if it were the first time I'd been held by a parent in half a decade. Parental hugs for seventeen-year-olds are nice, but when parental hugs all but cease for a contact-seeking eleven-year-old, that first one received at seventeen can feel like a rebirth.

It was four years after that reunion that, with such optimism, I moved into my childhood home for the summer with Lissa. Power pooled like primordial soup around me there in the valley of my childhood. I positioned myself at my word-processor in the library, and looked forward to an unprecedented orgy of creative production. Martha and I had been in touch during those past four years, but it had been very much on-again, off-again. I was gone in Japan for two, I'd been fairly withdrawn in the months prior to leaving, and upon returning to Davidson, I went to great lengths to avoid explaining my failure in Japan, which included a shame-born hesitation to seek out anyone to whom I'd have to explain.

Nevertheless, reuniting with Martha was like coming home, and when her father died in October of that first year back from Japan, the cry that I felt from within to rush to her side was rivaled only by the call of duty I had felt to go to Mas Oyama when he visited my country just one month before. It was with pride that I held Martha's hand during her father's funeral, while she held her mother's, because as hard as it was to sit there while my father sat alone in a back row, I knew that if I worked on it, I could overcome the guilt that my father had so carefully carved into me for my continuing to love Martha long after he had left her behind.

It was what was right for me – in my childhood home with Martha was where I belonged. And then, with my rib cage already run through from the loss of Lissa, Martha came home and in effect told me that *she* wasn't so sure I belonged there. To Martha, I had broken my word by neglecting the summer maintenance of her property. For me, it was as if she'd forgotten my hand holding hers at her father's funeral. As if she was unaware of the barriers I'd had to fight through to come home to her in the first place. "You didn't take care of the house and grounds like you were supposed to," she told me. "Pay me rent for the months you've been here," or get out!

Or get out was unspoken and the severity of its impact was, I'm sure, unintended. It was beyond Martha then – she lacked the necessary emotional distance from her own injury – to understand that my paying rent to live there would have betrayed my notion of her house as the home where I was meant to be.

And that I would not abide.

My father left Martha ten years earlier with the house unfinished. Of course, she'd chosen to buy out his half and keep it when he left – but the project they'd started together, renovating a property that included the house, a photography studio, two other outbuildings, and a pool, was enormously incomplete when he left. Alone, Martha set out both to pursue her career and, on a single salary, to complete a construction project that should have required a small army of workers. When I first returned to the log house six years after I'd seen it last, the newest building on the property was the one that blew me away. The house was heated by an enormous wood-burning stove that my father had installed, and until Martha finally converted it to burning oil, one of the property's shortcomings was its lack of a storage facility for the large quantity of wood it took to heat such a house for the winter. With her own two hands, hiring help just to set the largest beams, Martha built a two-story woodshed on a foundation behind the house my father had built for that purpose. And the building was a work of art unto itself.

The real work of art, though, was what I found on the inside.

The main part of the house was a log building made of hand-hewn logs in 1804. When I was three, my father discovered it in a local newspaper and rescued it from demolition. He and a class of his art history students, who got academic credit for the salvaging and restoration of what amounted to a historic North Carolina building, broke the house down board by board and brick by brick, stripped it back to the logs themselves, and loaded the entire house in one piece onto a tractor-trailer. They drove it to the property that my father and mother had purchased, as I wrote in my poem, because of the beech trees that grew there. Lake Norman hadn't been developed, the highway that connected Davidson to Charlotte hadn't been built, and when they drove the house through downtown Davidson, men sat on the highest logs of the cabin's second floor with long wooden poles to lift power lines so the house could crawl by underneath.

The red-brick chimney, eight feet wide at the base and thirty feet high, they'd taken down brick by handmade brick, numbering each one as they went so that they could reassemble it exactly as it had stood for two hundred years.

My father's older brother is an architect, and he designed the modern addition to the house, which quadrupled its square footage. I grew up to the sound of my father on the roof driving nails through thousands upon thousands of handmade cedar-shake roofing shingles, so that even the building's roof would match its original construction. But cedar-shake shingles need to be replaced every decade or so, and the work of art I found inside the work of art that was the woodshed that Martha had built all by herself was the ceiling-high stack of cedar-shake shingles that she'd removed and stacked there, one by one, the last time the house had been reroofed.

A cedar-shake shingle is a plank of dried cedar, sheared off with the grain from a two-foot-long cedar log, half-inch sliver by half-inch sliver, until all that's left of the log is a dozen or so two-foot long, like-sized slices which can then be layered on a rooftop like roofing tiles. The problem with stacking them, however, is that because of the irregularities of the wood, they don't shear off in uniform thicknesses. One end of each shingle is a centimeter or two thick; the other end is often just a millimeter. In other words, they taper down like wedges, and to make a symmetrical stack of them, one has to position them very carefully, one by one, mostly alternating directions so that the thick ends at one side of the stack are balanced out by the thin ones at the other.

Martha's stack of thousands upon thousands of salvaged shingles was a gigantic, ceiling-high monolith, twenty feet long, eight feet deep, and seven feet tall, that was so perfect as to be almost mathematically arranged. Not only were its edges completely square all the way up to the ceiling, but it was so solidly put together that a rugby team couldn't have knocked it down with their best simultaneous concerted effort.

What kind of grief, I marveled, *puts together a stack of shingles like that merely to burn them, one by one, as kindling!*

Beholding that project was the second time I wanted to cry upon reuniting with Martha. At seventeen, I finally saw the evidence of heartache on Martha's side as devastating as my own, and from the same cause, and at the exact same moment! My father had taken Martha from my life, but I realized then that he'd taken her whole family from her, and left her alone in that colossal forest to fight for scraps of the life that she'd shared with her husband and two would-be sons.

During the summer that Lissa and I lived in that basement apartment, just a door away from my childhood bedroom, just a pane of glass therefore away from the nighttime sounds of the forest that had lulled me to sleep in my earliest memories, I most certainly failed to maintain the property as well as I could have. To be sure, I had started the summer with more than a week of morning-to-night labor sealing the leaking basement foundation – frustratingly delaying the resumption of my writing. But after that, writer's block and the problems I was having with Lissa wrought havoc on both creativity and yard work. I was supposed to keep the leaves swept off the walks and netted out of the pool. I had gravel to rake, shrubs to keep trimmed, and a hillside to keep from becoming overgrown. And there is no question that I achieved only a bare minimum in the two months Martha was gone.

I think there can also be no question, though, that Martha's reaction was loaded with far more than the fact that the leaves didn't get raked. Not least of all was that in my red beard I must have been the spitting image of the husband who had abandoned her a decade earlier with endless work to be done.

And Lissa was crying to boot!

I was guilty because I'd reacted physically to being abandoned. I'd grabbed her by the elbows in an attempt to keep her with me. Of course that kind of physical reaction is unacceptable, and in my desperation, I was guilty of that. But somehow the panic Martha saw in Lissa's eyes when Lissa told her – panic that must also have encompassed Lissa's realization that she was setting out into the real world alone after all – combined with the echoes of all my father had put her though, and led her to conclude that I was guilty of far more than I was.

In her defense, I don't think she realized the extent to which the punishment she chose was cruel and unusual.

Tragically for me, it had become the norm for my various fragmented parental units to assume, often incorrectly, that their counterparts were handling all things well in their absence. My parents had fought for me and my brother for the first decade of my life to make sure that we felt fought for, but their struggles to remake their lives yet again, when my father left Martha and my mother left her second husband, somehow inclined them now to barter us away, piece by piece. "Nathan's with his mom," my father would say to himself, "he's being taken care of, so I can afford to put him out of my mind and concentrate on my new family." And I'm sure he never did so intentionally. It was rather that the demands of recreating stability so late in life, and on such a shaky foundation, left him with little energy to spare, those times, for my brother and me.

In my utopian early childhood, each of my separated parents – one in Chapel Hill, one in Davidson – took one hundred percent responsibility for my well-being. How loved I felt as a child! How spoiled I was to have parents who, between them, felt two hundred percent responsible for me! Once their second attempts at families fell through, however, suddenly they both became so desperate to remake their lives yet again, in accordance with what they thought people's lives were supposed to look like at their age, that each dropped down to being just 50% responsible at best, and even to considering themselves not responsible when I was in the other parent's care.

"Out of sight, out of mind," the expression goes.

Martha could not have known that my father had been abandoning me too, not all at once as he had her, but piece by piece, by leaving all matters concerning his sons from his first marriage up to his latest wife. I hadn't even known that woman until she was imposed on me at my life's most traumatic moment, and my father couldn't see that it wasn't in the least bit practical to try to force everyone in his nontraditional family into the mold created by his own parents, who had remained married for sixty years and raised children who believed in pointed-eared demons lurking around corners and hiding in coat closets. Martha couldn't have known that that abandonment had gone so far as my father renovating a building in his backyard that had once been a kitchen or servant's quarters into a room for me – to appease, he'd asserted, his conscience, since he'd created a family home that didn't have a room in it for me – only to bow to his wife's assertion in the end that it was only natural to charge me rent to live there.

Martha swept into town, found me in my childhood home feeling as though I had a fencepost driven through my chest, and she took hold of it with all her might and twisted it till I thought I would die. "You didn't take care of the house and grounds like you were supposed to," she told me. "Pay me rent for the months you've been here," or get out!

White angel of mercy!

It was an inadvertent act of mercy because I was no stranger to how agony and ecstasy can cross over at their extremes. I had been well schooled in that Romantic viewpoint long before I ever read a Romantic poem. Life was indeed made out of those experiences that stamp themselves on your psyche and leave your life feeling as full as it could be, day by day seizing the days for all they're worth, reveling in the heartache as well as the happiness, finding joy even in the beauty of life's pain, and especially in the beauty of the natural world, when it seems that all else is lost.

I drove my father's pickup truck over from his house to move all my belongings out of Martha's. It was the same truck that he'd used to move his own possessions out a decade earlier. I loaded it in silence. Martha was there, but I was too shell-shocked to speak. The last bag of wrinkled laundry tossed into the truck bed, I turned back toward the forest.

I had one last item of business to take care of before I left.

On the top railroad tie of the retaining wall that kept the house from washing down the slope with the seasonal rains, I stood to face the forest for what I then believed would be the last time.

I'd been wrong. Family wasn't there to be found after all. It was time to put that nonsense behind me.

I would never be back.

In accordance with my habit, I paused. I shifted my balance to two feet, rocked my head back, closed my eyes, and drew in a long, deep breath of the forest. I didn't need my eyes to see how beautiful it was. I filled my nostrils with it till I choked. My ears never could escape the unrelenting hum of the summer, but when I paused to actually listen, the gurgle of the creek, the mulling of myriads of insects, and the gentle clicking of thousands upon thousands of tree branches brushing by one another in the breeze rushed in at me in a deafening roar. By the time I opened my eyes to behold the canopy of beech leaves 100 feet above and the valley cut by centuries of running water 100 feet below, chills rippled like electricity down my spine in a way that made my stomach muscles contract with a jolt and left me momentarily weightless. I teetered, there on the edge. For a moment I soared with the hummingbirds and cicadas through the ethereal green that fell away before me, and I had to catch myself when I nearly lost my balance and fell into the abyss.

My god, it's so incredibly beautiful! I told myself.

And that was the extent of my plan. I went there to look at the woods one last time. I went there to say goodbye. I went there to have my breath taken away. I went there to worship one last time before getting into my father's pickup to drive back into town.

What happened next happened all on its own.

I didn't plan it, or scheme it, or make it up. I didn't wish for it.

It dawned on me.

I stepped first out of one shoe and then the other. In a habit formed when entering the dojo, I gathered them up between my thumb and forefinger, made them parallel, and turned the toe-ends outward again so they'd be there to slide into once I was done. I straightened my spine to behold the scene once more from above, and then, steamrolling over a momentary but vicious pang of fear, I stepped, willingly, off that top railroad tie . . .

. . . and fell.

Momentarily weightless, my entire life rushed up at me with the forest floor.

TWENTY

IF ONLY I'D BEEN struck by lightning during that one slow-motion moment as I fell! If only that second sucking in of air as I reached out impatiently with my toes for the forest floor had been my last!

I'd have died believing I couldn't possibly have lived a fuller life.

As if crack cocaine injected had that very instant worked its way though my veins to find its mark, everything that might in my life have resembled pain fell away in a wave of head-spinning ecstasy. If only I could have remained suspended there as my flesh and bones crossed over from what I had been until then to what I was to become from that moment forward!

The last season's dry leaves cushioned my fall, my feet sank into the forest floor more than they struck it, Midas roared his very first roar, and not like a fiery auburn Labrador-Doberman mix but like the ethereal devil that chased her, I took off toward the creek below with an explosion of dry leaves flung up in my wake like that puff of white smoke left behind when a jet fires its afterburners. Single strides covered impossible distances since the valley there fell downwards at forty-five degrees, and Midas took it at as steep an angle as he could and still find purchase on a hillside so slick that a child could have slid down it on the seat of his pants and had his breath taken away by the momentum.

The corners of my mouth twitched in the start of a smile as I realized that a fallen tree branch, four inches thick and already in the early stages of decomposition, blocked at waist level the fourth bound of my berserk flight. I was airborne then, my knees tucked to my chest and my forearms up in the *kumite* position to protect my face from the dogwood branches that cut the flesh like flails as I crashed through. Once clear of the dogwoods, the fallen branch revealed itself – too late to change direction – but Midas smiled when he saw an undeniable truth he'd learned swinging an ax for so many days in that same forest. Like Mas Oyama hanging a stone from a rope outside the door to his mountain cabin, so he would have no choice but to confront it every day until he found its flaw and finally took it down to break it with the edge of his hand, Midas detected that the limb, which at that speed could have folded me over like a towel on a clothesline and broken my ribs, was itself vulnerable and could be broken. In flight, I let my knees down just enough to pass by underneath and with a mere twitch of the muscles in my abdomen crashed through the limb in my path, not merely breaking it in the middle, but actually shearing off a waist-width segment of it at both ends, to be carried across my midsection for a long moment until, the leap complete, it fell away to the forest floor to become compost for the next year's growth.

 Reaching the level ground above the creek's six-foot-wide trench, I turned briefly to accelerate for five or six strides alongside before hurling myself one more time into space, this time towards the opposite bank. I'd never flailed my arms around the way long-jumpers do, but apparently Midas had seen it done, and as athletes are wont to do when as "in the zone" as I was then, I adopted that motion I'd only before that time seen and used it to propel myself farther than I ever could have imagined. The creek's bed was too wide to jump, so I covered the twelve or fifteen feet forward that my long-jump would have taken me, and fell also the six or seven feet deep that the slick red-clay gorge was at that point, and like it was nothing, like I'd done it just yesterday, I lined up my feet to meet the opposite bank at the bottom as fearlessly as I had so many times as a child.

 The bank was soft beneath its thick carpet of last-year's leaves and the bones in my body lined themselves up on their own to absorb the impact. My knees folded into my chest and came so close to smashing into my chin that I'm lucky that I didn't knock myself out cold. Springing to my feet and turning, for a split second I hesitated for the first time as I looked upstream.

 Midas overcame another ferocious wave of fear. The creek was lined by six-foot-high vertical red-clay walls on either side and only intermittent dry, gravelly level ground on which to gain footing should I then continue my rampage up along the course I'd come to run. Midas growled, though, because there was no stopping him, and at a flat-out sprint I took to the creek, barefooted as the day I was born, mud, rocks, broken glass, copperheads and all.

Of course, instinct, training, and childhood experience revealed the best places to let my feet fall to propel me forward without getting hurt. If I had dry level ground to land on, I took that option. If there were flat stones I took to them. At one point the creek banked sharply, however, and there was nothing to stand on in the outside of the curve but slick vertical red clay, and I was moving way too fast to cut to the inside of the curve. As if on cue, like a stock car on a graded track, Midas dashed around the bend with centrifugal force keeping my body near parallel to the surface of the water for those few strides.

How impossible those 3-inch-deep footprints of bare human feet must have looked wrapped around the walls of that crevice!

Not even Midas could defy gravity, of course, and when gravity took command again there was still no dry level ground. And so – deeper still into my childhood abyss – I took my sprint to the sometimes knee-deep but mostly ankle-deep water and ran from that point forward, choosing intentionally with each stride to land on the surface of the water rather than on the gravel and the stones. How soft it was, the surface of that water! Of course my feet found their way through to the rocks and sand unseen below the murky surface, but they splashed down so fast and pulled away so fast that the sensation was as if a millimeter of water remained as a cushion between the soles of my feet and the rocks underneath. I never felt them.

If ever man was capable of unaided flight, surely I achieved it that day.

When on all fours like an animal I finally scrambled out of the creek bed at the opposite end of the property, I was covered from head to toe with spattered red clay. My chest heaving, I paused to look up at the house. It looked the same as it had when I was a child. But there was no point in lingering. It was just a house. It wasn't home. I must have been hallucinating to believe that I'd ever find it again. Another growl and, uphill this time, I resumed my flight. On all fours once again, since the leaf-covered slopes are too steep and slick to climb without sliding, I used my hands as much as my feet, grabbing tree branches, stumps, and even handfuls of delicately rooted ferns to climb at a sprint back out of the valley. When I reached my shoes I attempted the leap back to the top of the retaining wall, and I would have made it but for how spongy the forest floor was with fallen leaves. I was a foot too low, even with my knees brought up to either side of my jaw and my feet above waist level, but it didn't matter. Still running as much with my hands as my feet, I reached out for the nearest vertical railroad-tie post, and *with my claws* took purchase enough that I was able to pull myself back up onto the wall.

Imagine a leap such as these – performed for Bill Giduz's camera in Davidson's gym – clearing the creek bed in the forest gorge behind my childhood home. Here I am (above) breaking boards held by the students on the chairs. The boards are easy to break; the challenge here is the jump and the precision. Facing page: Simply showing off for the camera. This leap originated from a stationary position on the gym floor and went straight upwards to head height. When Helen saw the picture, she told me it looked as if I'd jumped off the bleachers from above.

I'd been in the forest for less than two minutes, but I'd gone back in time twenty years. Anything in my psychological or emotional makeup that had resembled a creativity-blocking hard shell had been crushed, and in that moment, as I reached the top of the retaining wall, I was more fluid than I'd been since I was five.

There was no heartache anymore.

There was no pain.

There was only excitement. Only hunger for life and for what lay ahead in my future.

Once again, I'd transformed emotional pain, and all that remained was a palpable sense of blissful, liberating power.

Utterly careful not to turn back even for an instant towards the forest, I straightened, wiped off the sole of one foot and then the other with the palms of my hands, slid my feet back into my shoes, already pointing away from the ravine, and walked towards the truck. Confidently as a monster I joined Midas, and like twins side by side, we marched back to Davidson, stride for stride. Spattered from head to toe with red clay mud, I moved into the cottage behind my father's house to begin my senior year of college. The vision that I could see for my future had never been so clear.

Myself at about four with Mina, sitting on a stack of beams salvaged from another log building to be used as rafters for the modern addition to the log house. Note the density of the summertime forest in the background.

Of course Dr. Strom was right:
That kind of passion was not sustainable.
Yet I knew from experience that I would be able to find a way to sustain it. That same week I found a letter from Mas Oyama in my post office box, granting me the permission I needed to open the *Budo Karate Illustrated* floodgates. In a state much returned to normal, I called out to new professor Helen Ecks on the ghostly and windowless third floor of Chambers.

How could I have known then why the pull that I felt towards her was so strong?

How could I have known that she was to be life's next instrument for driving me back, just a little more knowingly this time, into that abyss where Midas first roared, where power rolled like lava, and where creativity dripped from my fingertips like blood?

* * *

Training with my ax in the forest eighteen months earlier, I considered whether Conscience would ever allow me *not* to live my life to give back to society all that I'd learned, and yet at the same time, I couldn't deny the terrible premonition that the pursuit just might take from me far more than was healthy for me to give.

The delivery vehicle was simply too huge.

If I was going to give in to Conscience, would not Conscience demand that I go all the way? How could I justify teaching one or two if I could see myself working to improve the lives of thousands?

The problem was that there, in the valley of my childhood, single-handedly dismantling and removing massive tree trunks I'd grown up believing immovable, the image of me teaching entire cross-sections of society came closing in on me from all sides like the weight of the hillside crashing down. Worst of all was what felt to me then to be undisputable: there was sufficient creative power within me to make it all happen *provided I was willing to sacrifice myself to access it.*

It was sacrifice, after all, that lay at the foundation of all that Master Choi and Mas Oyama had taught me.

There had been no creative endeavor in my life greater than the remaking of self that I achieved late in my second decade. Once complete, it became the golden ticket to success that Master Choi promised if I became the first American to graduate from his uncle's thousand-day *uchi deshi* program. I had in fact not completed 1000 days or graduated, but somehow I'd picked up the ticket anyway by pushing so far beyond my limits in the attempt. I was left feeling like I'd already lived one life, and in my newfound freedom, I felt as though I now had a second one to live.

And, piece by piece, Conscience demanded that I give it away.

On some level I must have known where the fuel for that creative fire came from, and I must have known that it was still within me. That berserk run on Sunset Beach with Master Choi when I was eighteen first taught me that power didn't always come from traditional sources. For the Watson interview, I relied on the physical torture of 1000 jumping squats to summon that darker side of me that could better handle the challenge. But then, unexpectedly, at the end of that summer with Lissa, she and Martha unknowingly conspired to show me that the original nonconventional power I'd used to remake myself was still there for me if I only dared to conjure it. The power I found in the valley of my childhood was not born of the physical devastation of a brutal endurance run or 1000 jumping squats. It was born instead of emotional devastation taken to the power of ten, taken so far it flipped over and mutated in the dark reaches of my personality to become euphoric celebration of the power and majesty of life. For those few moments that I'd charged backwards in time, it had felt as if the natural power of the globe was mine to wield as I chose, and for Kyokushin I'd resolved to wield whatever power necessary, no matter the personal cost.

And finally, in Helen, I'd stumbled upon a circumstance that engendered an emotional response the likes of which I'd never before imagined.

I didn't realize it until after I'd let my love for her run free, and it wouldn't be crystal clear to me until years had passed and Helen was completely gone from my day to day, but even as early as when I spent my Thanksgiving holiday simply loving her, something inside me hinted that that celebration, too, was becoming entwined in the creative process that drove the projects I pursued. It's no wonder that Conscience gave me license to let my love for Helen run free in the guise of my *carpe diem* creed!

In an embarrassing journal entry for my American literature professor a year earlier, I'd written of the passion that I felt having Lissa. One year later I realized that I had no idea.

I'd had yet to experience the passion of not having Helen.

I should have known, I suppose, when the schism occurred and the multiple parts of me branched out so masterfully to handle all the simultaneous responsibilities I faced. I should have known when those with whom I shared normal, everyday conversations had no idea that I might as well have been absent since nine-tenths of my attention was so often focused on a vision I could never have shared. I should have known when the *Budo Karate Illustrated* project advanced itself while I was reading Shakespeare or Chinese politics and still somehow managing to absorb the content of what I'd read. I should have realized when I spoke to Mas Oyama on the phone so comfortably because I'd already played out a hundred different Japanese dialogues with Matsui in my head. I should have known when I woke up in the night realizing that I was keeping the creative process going even during the few hours that I slept.

I should have known when the management of the Café started to happen all on its own, and yet I was almost never aware of doing any managing. I should have known when teaching my karate classes became more like popping in the necessary tape and letting it run without me. I should have known when I produced, just after Thanksgiving, the art project that wowed my design professor after struggling through the first four or five assignments alongside much more talented and better-trained Fine Art majors. I should have known that it was Midas smiling when I got an A on one particularly imposing writing assignment on China's Cultural Revolution, having the night before realized not only that it could be handled in a short-story format, but also that such an unprecedented move was likely to be well received by my professor, given my assessment of her personality.

I certainly should have known when I all but achieved unaided flight in the demonstration that I did for Bill Giduz's camera on Davidson's basketball courts. I should have known when it was Helen with whom I first shared those photographs one lunchtime in the Café. I should have known since I was able to share them so naturally and fearlessly, despite my horror as I watched the two of us from above and realized how a third party might have seen me as trying to impress a woman I had vowed not to pursue.

In class with Helen, I certainly should have known.

I'd dreaded the return to her class after Thanksgiving. *How am I ever going to be able to hide it now?* I asked myself. *How can I possibly maintain the charade?* But not only did I manage to hide the passion as well as I ever had, but I also managed to continue – at least on the surface – the development of our friendship where it had left off, albeit at the crawling pace my sense of restraint had set from the start. After all, I couldn't simply have stopped. Helen would have wondered why I'd turned cold, and there were only three students in the class! And yet, to hide what I hid, I should have known, would have only been possible if Midas and I, side by side and stride for stride, handled both tasks simultaneously:

Nathan played the game of student and friend . . .

And Midas lied.

Or was it the other way around?

Sadly, the time I spent with Helen became my classroom for learning too well the art of conscience-driven deceit.

What a masterpiece Midas and I together devised, to lie so perfectly to Helen – to hide the fact that, like removing control rods from a nuclear reactor, I'd pulled out the stops and let my love for her explode! What a game it was for Midas to hide the fact that it was starting not to even matter anymore if I was in her presence, or on the other side of campus, at home, or behind the wheel of my car traveling the back roads of New Jersey to Atlantic City in the wee hours of the morning, or if I was getting my body driven into the dojo floor in Tokyo by full-contact blows. The passion that I felt for her had spilled out and filled my entire world, until walking through it felt like swimming through an electrically charged sludge that slid smoothly in and out of my lungs, feeding me power, keeping the schism open, and invigorating me to the point where I didn't need sleep.

I spent that year of my life in the company of giants, but Mas Oyama, Midas, Matsui, and Jacques Sandulescu didn't compare to the other giant with whom I came to spend my days. Helen Ecks had become the counterbalance that made interaction with all the rest seem routine.

I didn't understand until the end of my semester with Helen why the smell of Lissa's flesh had seemed to me at times so intoxicating. A dozen times or so in a year that we were together, usually in the night just as we fell asleep in each other's arms, I found myself moving my nostrils as close as I could to her neck to draw in a single long breath of her, in much the same way that I took, at other times in my life, single life-worshiping breaths of the natural world. I didn't understand until I caught myself involuntarily flaring my nostrils and sucking in the same slow tantalizing breath in Helen's classroom.

Lissa reads this and shudders at the memory of how, exhausted and wet, we'd lie beside each other in the dark marveling at how powerfully our heartbeats pounded their way into each other's bodies in the aftermath of another of our attempts to outdo the passion of the love we'd made the night before. With my last bit of strength before falling asleep, I would reach out for her neck with my nose and, like a cocaine addict, tear from her a lungful of the microscopic particles of her skin. I didn't realize it until I sat across from Helen listening to her lecture, my eyes and hers dancing the usual dance of my not trespassing beyond where I had been invited, and I caught myself flaring my nostrils in an involuntary, desperate attempt to satisfy my hunger for that which I'd so steadfastly refused to take.

I didn't realize until that moment that, for all the intensity we shared, Lissa had never been enough.

Had the injury I'd sustained as a child left open such a void that even the sexual passion I shared with Lissa fell short of filling the hunger I struggled to fill? Unable to reach out to Helen, as I so desperately wanted by then – just to be held by her, or simply to have my hand held by hers, or to put my head on her shoulder and sob tears of relief at finally telling her the truth, or even to make love to her – it wouldn't have mattered! – unable even to reach out and tell her how badly I wanted simply to befriend her if none of the rest were possible, I found myself involuntarily reaching beyond the mere optical exchange that I'd learned through six years of daily communication with Master Choi. With sensory powers all but lost to the human animal once we leapt forward on evolution's timeline to develop brains capable of language, the thousands of olfactory nerve endings in my nostrils managed somehow to capture and distinguish the handful of floating particles that had most recently separated themselves from Helen's flesh from the thousands that lit on their surface in the course of a single hungry inhale. I realized with self-abhorrence that from the opposite side of the room I'd smelled the flesh of a woman whose scent – God forbid! – was just like everyone else's, at least insomuch as any normal person who'd walked right up to her would only have smelled whatever shampoo, body soap, or perfume she used.

Apparently even that wasn't enough, however, for at the same moment that I realized I had smelled her, the tiniest twitch of light-redirecting movement caught my eye, and I instinctively lowered my gaze to the bare skin just above her collar. I was a physically healthy, hormonal male in my sexual prime who was then not-necessarily-by-choice celibate, and I took pride in the fact that out of my respect for this woman I so admired, I'd never once let even my thoughts venture below her neckline. It was with utter self-loathing, therefore, that I realized that it had been a single course of blood pulsing through her carotid artery that had caught my attention.

What kind of BEAST have you become! I spat at myself.

The impulse to get up, gather my books and get out before I became any more repulsive to myself was quelled only by my never-once-shaken resolve not to reveal myself to Helen, never to let her know that I had crossed that line. If the admiration and friendship she showed me had anything to do with her perceiving the battle I fought against the desire that raged within me, surely she would have seen it then. That pair of devilish perceptions happened in the duration of a single inhale – I smelled her flesh and I watched the blood pulse through her body – and the recovery from them, driven by my sense of duty not to disrespect her, was instantaneous and complete. Inside I stamped my foot and gnashed my teeth to demand control. Externally, I straightened in my chair as if to be more attentive.

And I never so much as lost track of the lecture.

As was my routine, I'd followed flawlessly the reading in class, or at least to the extent of how good a student I was. When my turn came I read the passage aloud that I'd been asked to read. I'd taken the notes that I needed to take all along. To get up and leave to avoid disrespecting Helen as a woman would have been to disrespect her as a teacher, and that I would not do. After all, she couldn't possibly have been aware.

It was all right there to be seen, and yet at that time I still failed to see it. By deliberately letting the love I felt for Helen out of the bottle, by allowing it to intensify exponentially, while at the same time resolving with gnashing teeth and full-contact blows to leave her the hell alone, I'd managed, the way Mozart might have composed a symphony, the way Musashi might have delivered a death blow, or the way Michelangelo might have set chisel to marble, to create a cyclical, ongoing circumstance that replicated the shell-shattering euphoria I felt dropping off of Martha's railroad tie wall into the power that pooled there in my childhood forest like primordial soup.

Every moment I spent in Helen's company became like breaking my heart over and over again. I might as well have remained floating in the ecstasy of transformation between me and the creative monster I'd become before the soles of my feet, bare for the first time in twenty years, impacted the dry-leaf and fern-covered carpet of the forest floor. Ask Freud if it's any surprise that I'd fallen in love with a college professor of the same physical type and age that my stepmother Martha had been when she first entered my life, Martha who, a matter of DAYS before I first accosted Helen in the halls of Chambers, had once again been torn from my life – this time, half by my own doing.

I have to play Freud myself to suggest such a thing, and I never did so until the day I wrote this chapter, thirteen years later, but I do wonder:

could I have set myself up to relive, over and over again, the single most traumatic moment of my life? No matter what force left me so inclined, it was Conscience that drove me to exploit it, to let out all the stops and harness it in the name of creative production, and Conscience sang only one song that year: to do for Kyokushin out of the love and sense of obligation I felt towards Mas Oyama and Master Choi.

Day after day, moment after moment, I sat there in Helen's class and subjected myself to a situation that so closely mimicked my life's most traumatic moment that it could only have been created by design.

"Yes, but is that kind of passion sustainable?"

Yes, Dr. Strom, sadly, it is. I can tell you beyond a shadow of a doubt that that kind of passion is sustainable. I can also tell you that the cost of doing so is nothing to scoff at. Even as the semester ended and I sat there in shock, a complete and total basket case at dinner – at Helen's house! – when she and her husband Jack invited the members of our class over to celebrate the successful end to the semester, I still wasn't done spending.

I sat there – a veritable zombie – and Midas took care of the small talk in what would be the last regular conversation I would have for some time with a woman I'd allowed to shake my world down to its very foundation.

TWENTY-ONE

THAT SAME WEEK I picked up the phone in my tiny one-room cottage and called *Honbu*. Mas Oyama took my call personally and invited me to stay, once again, in the Young Lions' Dormitory for the four days I would be in Japan after New Year's. I hung up the phone to catch my breath and called Matsui, who agreed to meet with me at his Asakusa dojo on the night of my arrival. The floor of my father's backyard cottage was knee-deep with stacks of material that had been submitted by U.S. branch chiefs and dojo operators from across the country. My deadline for submitting the final layout was less than six weeks away. Without breaking my routine of walking the quarter mile across town each morning for classes, I spent my days in the Davidson College Computer Center laying out pages of an eighty-page book that I didn't yet know I'd have to expand to 100 or more to satisfy *Sosai*.

I spent that Christmas holiday with my father's family, longing for it to be the last, but having no clue that it actually would be. In church on Christmas Eve I marveled at how moved I was by the Christmas carols we went there each year as part of our family tradition to hear. I marveled at the hypocrisy imposed on my childhood, and, I presumed, on those of so many other young Americans, for whom Christmas is the celebration of the coming of Santa Claus and expensive gifts and delicious foods, much more so than what we realize one day we'd supposedly been celebrating all along, the birth of the Christian God.

What a tragedy! I thought.

How truly vicious Tradition's bite is when we dare to break away!

Just hearing the music filled my soul with the nostalgic echoes of the childhood Christmas I'd learned to love through years of being bribed with gifts and sweets, with not having to go to school for a month, and with the festive release from responsibility that seemed to take all the world's edges off – all in the name of celebrating the birth of a man who died, or so it would seem, so that humanity would no longer have to be responsible for its own actions.

How spectacular the world would be, I thought, *if all these stupidly jubilant people, high on sugar and eggnog, and on the blind entitlement of believing themselves the world's chosen people, would just for once keep working during the holiday and dedicate the resources otherwise wasted on material display to the betterment of the community!*

Of course I understood how such rapture gave strength to those who barely had the resources to survive. It did seem to give joyous hope to the poor and courage to the sick and dying. But shouldn't there be something like a rule of diminishing returns when you applied the same faith to middle-class Davidson? We were a community of haves, not have-nots. We did have the resources, not merely to survive, but also to spoil our kids at Christmastime. We devoted multiple hours a week to our favorite television shows, we made it to our vacations each year, to our gyms to work on our abs, to our kids' soccer matches, and to our weekly church services to console our consciences that we were living lives that weren't any less righteous than everyone else. Was not the same rapture that gave hope to the have-nots consoling us haves that we didn't have to use our advantaged lives to enact positive change in the world? Were we really doing anything more significant than sitting around, joyously celebrating the fact that someone long dead was going to take care of all that harder stuff so that we wouldn't have to try? Out of some twisted have-not notion that we're all inherently incapable, and inherently evil, it seemed as if all we really had to do in middle-class America was to get on our knees on Sundays to celebrate our faith, and everything would be okay. Even if the world came to an end thanks to our negligence, we'd all be saved to spend eternity in Heaven because of all that time we'd spent impotently waiting around on our knees like drying bacteria, praying for salvation to fall on us from Heaven like so much saline.

"But we do act!" Davidson protested as it sang "Away in a Manger" and – for God's sake! – "Rudolph the Red-nosed Reindeer"! "Hallelujah! We do give money to charity to help feed the starving in Africa! And we do take responsibility when we go to the polls to vote! We do take responsibility when we give money to the church! We do so when we raise our kids to be upstanding Christian adults like us!"

Yes, you do those things, I sang to myself as my lips lied to sing the same songs as the rest . . . *some of you better than others, but are those the things that really need doing to make a difference? If you can write a check to buy off your conscience, but otherwise go right back to striving to live the lives of your favorite prime-time characters, will anything ever change? The work that really needs to be done doesn't seem to be all that costly. It's just a matter of stopping to look again, not only at your own life, but at the direction that our collective life is going, and trying to figure out how you, as an individual, might change the way that you live to help change the whole.*

We humans do seem to run in herds!

Like fish with brains the size of rice grains, we swim in schools, blindly following each other, not the few at the front who can see what's ahead. If enough of us were to realize that, couldn't we change the direction of the entire school?

Oh, you're happy with the direction the school is swimming because your portfolio is doing well and you get to play golf twice a week? The rest of us ought to be ashamed for wasting our lives, working so hard to try and make our lives like yours! If we continue to blindly pursue a high standard of living at the expense of our world and of other people in it who we can pretend *aren't affected by our choices, what good are the lives of our grandchildren going to be?*

"Oh, they'll be fine," you say, "because they'll be Americans and Americans are the world's richest, most powerful people. Even if the world's less fortunate suffer, we'll still be able to sit in our air-conditioned living rooms and watch TV and eat food grown in other countries."

Maybe so. But isn't it about time that we figured out that problems facing the entire world will eventually confront us as well, and that sitting around defending the lifestyle we feel entitled to, because our parents lived it, and because America is the land of the free and the home of the brave, *will only ensure that those problems, as they go critical, will come back to bite us in the most vicious way? Isn't it time we understood that with great power comes great responsibility, and that as privileged citizens of the world's last great superpower, we must each share in being greatly responsible? What if all of us simply made it a practice to stop every once in a while, take a deep breath, and look hard at ourselves and our world? Wouldn't we start to realize the difference between priorities based on social trends — which will allow us to live almost any destructive way that groups of* respectable, upstanding adults *are living — and those stifled priorities that originate in our own conscience?*

Sound like too much work?

Listen to your heart.

Below all that you've learned about how you're supposed to live from watching the people you envy, your conscience is still there, issuing impulses to help you make better choices. Pause to take a deep breath of life and you'll be able to hear. Take pride in listening, and challenge yourself to act on those impulses whenever possible. Believe in your personal ability to enact change. Escape the trap of merely going through life's motions, praying for changes to occur. Make change happen.

"But what change?" Davidson sang.

Listen to your heart, I wept on the inside in response. *The answers are there.*

I didn't wait for my father or stepmother to tell me, "Not going with us to church on Christmas Eve is not an option." I just got ready to go automatically. I was acutely aware that I had no choice, and I felt robbed of my dignity. To say "No, thank you, I don't think I'll go this year. I have work that I'd rather be doing," would have been met with such self-righteous condescension that even someone like me wouldn't have been up to the challenge of trying to break away. I'd once carried a barbell equal to my body weight across my shoulders for seven hours to the top of a mountain, until a ball of fluid the size of a golf ball swelled up on the back of my spine where its weight rested on my failing body, to show that anyone could resolve to sacrifice blood, sweat and tears to try to make a difference, rather than wait to be taken care of by governments or gray-bearded guys on clouds.

And yet here were all these people rejoicing in their freedom from responsibility! All they had to do was follow tradition – and have faith! – and they could continue to rejoice in Heaven after we're all dead. When our children and grandchildren are dying in misery from mass starvation and disease brought on by our own failure to take better care of our planet, or freezing to death in a nuclear winter brought on by our own lust for power, what a tragedy if we look back in our last moments and realize that we could have done something to prevent it, but instead we sat around festive tables celebrating in material excess the belief that someone else had been born and died to save us from ourselves!

Oh, so it's going to be God's will if we all go out that way, because God works in mysterious ways? Sorry, I'd better just sit down and bite my lip . . .

Such were the thoughts that I entertained as I sang "Joy to the World" with all the rest. I wished that there *was* a god so that I might pray to him for the complete destruction of the Christian church, or else for a leader to be born into it who had the courage and insight to preach real-world problem solving, rather than the promise of Heavenly salvation and the righteousness of worldly inaction.

Sure, it's scary to face the world's problems as if there's actually something we can do about them!

How wonderful to have the camaraderie of a mass movement that celebrates choosing the path of least resistance! How happy a world we live in when our religious leaders congratulate us for leaving the really scary problems to a higher power, so that we can concentrate on mundane, lifestyle-improving ones, like not drinking or smoking or fucking our neighbors' wives!

To each their own, sure, but come on!

We live in a society where any impulse we actually might have to do good for anyone other than ourselves is immediately waylaid by strength-negating notions of our forefathers' tradition that we seem powerless to shake. Whether we're churchgoers or not — whether we're aware of it or not! — our national tradition tells us that the greatest works for the common good are the proper domain of an institution that chases the best of our thinkers away. What highly educated person is likely to throw his or her faith in with a church that focuses its entire instructional effort on the largely fictitious *work of saving poor, miserable, uneducated souls for a life other than the one we actually live?*

Sure, it's a great thing to make people spiritually stronger!

Sure, it's great to make miserable people feel enraptured for having nothing!

And sure, if there is a Heaven, it'll be a wonderful thing for those of us who did positive things with our lives to get to hang out there . . . but if our definition of salvation fails to inspire the creativity and open-mindedness it will take to correct the social trends that keep people poor, miserable and uneducated in the first place, what on Earth's the point?

Spiritual strength is great as long as it empowers people to perform great works, but is this so-called **spiritual strength** *that keeps people feeling righteous in their powerlessness really any kind of strength at all?*

Surely this isn't what Christ intended — this American church of the spiritually impotent . . . this man-made church of the willfully blind!

My father held the video camera, as he did every year, while the rest of us decorated the Christmas tree. I knew better than to tell him and his wife to go to hell because I'd rather rot there myself than take part in their charade. I knew my stepmother would only accuse me of being angry and resentful, and express the hope that someday I'd finally grow up and accept that the world's not such a bad place.

But the world, I already knew then, was far from a bad place. On the contrary, the world was a breathtakingly beautiful one. I could think of no greater gift than simply being alive to live in it for just one more moment of one more day. I wondered if she had any experience to compare.

Ironically, I always enjoyed my stepmother's family. Her mother, grandmother, sister and brother came into our lives every Christmas and brought with them hints of the joy that families are supposed to feel when together. I wondered what had happened to my father's wife to make her so different from the rest. I wondered if I would have experienced her the same way if my father hadn't dumped on her the responsibility of being my brother's and my primary parent even though she wasn't, or if she had been secure enough to just let it go when it clearly wasn't working instead of holding on to it out of pride. By that Christmas of 1993, my stepmother's family had become a sad reminder of the failure that I saw my father to be. Aside from those two token friends from his former life who joined us at Thanksgiving, all the people in my father's world were there only because they had come into it along with his wife. It was a tightly closed circle, managed under the self-interested, proud and condescending eyes of my stepmother, and with the exception of me – and the tacit support my older brother offered by mostly staying away – it had become the perfect mechanism for blocking out the truths they didn't want to see.

How hypocritical of my father to pressure me to fit in to his idea of family when it had been his day-in, day-out pressure over the previous decade that had made happy coexistence with my stepmother impossible!

There were times when I felt true pity for her.

If she'd been just a little brighter or a little stronger, she'd have realized that the role he was asking her to play with his sons made no sense. If he'd used his eyes and his heart to figure out how his wife and his sons might have related happily, he'd have saved us all a decade of misery. Sadly, however, he was dead set on misery. It was only his rulebook that he consulted, and he'd written his rules in stone.

If there was any celebration at all for me that holiday season, the pinnacle of it was surely the moment that I found myself alone in the dark, with a fever of 102 at midnight, standing in a snowstorm, holding more luggage than I could carry very far, and staring in disbelief at the YWCA's placard on a deserted Toronto street. I was cold and sick and frustrated and I stood there amazed at how stupid I'd been to misread the advertisement that took me there. And yet, I was the master of my own destiny, and, unlike when I was at my father's house for Christmas, I was in full possession of my dignity as a responsible human being on the planet Earth. I wasn't sitting around waiting to be saved. I was out there in the field developing a real-world vision for positioning myself so that younger people might someday stop and listen to what I had to say – or at least be emboldened by my example.

I didn't feel self-righteous or joyous.

I felt only miserable.

My throat was sore, and my body ached, and I was enough out of my mind, standing there in the snow, to wonder if I wasn't happily passed out in a corner somewhere, having had too many shots of tequila. But, *no*, I told myself, *this is the life you've chosen.*

You've chosen to be the writer of your own destiny.

Moments like this as well are going to be your lot.

* * *

Half a night on the cold carpet of an airport terminal floor, a twelve-hour flight, and a bus ride later, I would find myself sitting in an Asakusa restaurant across from the man who I expected would become Mas Oyama's successor. And I would pitch the sale of the century. I wasn't just going to sell him *Budo Karate Illustrated*; I was going to sell him my entire concept of vision, and how I believed that conscience-driven, self-sacrificial pursuit would in the end reign supreme over the conventions of dollars and business sense. I told him of the fourteen articles generated in North Carolina newspapers during the three months I was home from Mas Oyama's dormitory, carrying barbells up mountains and quadrupling the student body in Master Choi's schools. *"Sugoi!"* he exclaimed ("Great! Wonderful!"). Somehow I convinced him of my vision enough that he agreed to support the project and to believe, as he would tell me four years later in Budapest, that I "have talent."

The next day *Sosai* asked me how many days I'd resided in the Young Lions' Dormitory, and, pleased when I told him "More than 500," he ordered his secretary to prepare a graduation certificate for me. "I've always thought of you as a grandson," he said, "since you were already like the son of my nephew. You should try to be like – what's his name? Cameron! You should try to be like Cameron and publish many books and work for the future of Kyokushin in America."

Judd and I cheated death and a troop of transsexuals that week in Roppongi, and the next morning Midas took a flawless set of photographs of Matsui performing the entire set of Mas Oyama's *kihon*. I sat in *seiza* [72] leaned forward on my elbows on the floor of a Narita departures terminal, typing my story about Jacques in front of a wide-screen television airing sumo wrestling, and a day after that, I was at my father's dining room table in Davidson with my Japanese friend, translating Mas Oyama's history of Kyokushin into English. My friend Lisa and I spent the next nine days of (for me) sleepless nights laying out the book. I sent the proofs off to Annie in New York, and in a whirlwind I found myself sitting in my father's art history survey course, wondering if I'd made a mistake to enroll as I beheld the sad mystery that he'd become, and marveling at the fact that I had only two months to get in shape for twenty consecutive full-contact fights at *Honbu*.

Halfway through my next eight sleepless weeks of training and study, *Sosai's* assistant wrote to tell me I had *"Sosai's* permission to promote to *shodan,"* and it occurred to me then that *Sosai* was prepping me for a branch chief appointment. In that crisp new belt four weeks later, I practiced *kata* on the lawn in front of Yamaguchi *Sensei's* mountaintop temple overlooking Tokyo Bay and Mt. Fuji beyond, and two days after that I survived the beating of my life short of having my neck broken, thanks to Midas, who kicked my legs out from under me not once, but three times, to avoid the *jodan geri* of the Danish kid who tried so hard to kill me. The next day – struck stupider than I'd been at Helen's dinner table with Jack – I spoke the last words I'd ever speak to Mas Oyama in a raspy whisper from the blow I'd taken to my throat the day before, with his wife next to his hospital bed, and Mahashi crying.

---

[72] Formal way of sitting, kneeling with one's shins flat on the floor, and with one's back straight, that can be uncomfortable for adult Westerners who didn't grow up sitting on the floor like the Japanese.

"*Shimpai-yo!*" he told me ("Worry!"), and I didn't understand until after he was dead. That same day I attended the opening ceremony for Matsui's new branch dojo, and the day after that I shot a second several rolls of film as he demonstrated *kumite* applications for me at *Honbu* Dojo for the second volume of *Budo Karate Illustrated*.

It was during the month after that that Nobel laureate Seamus Heaney dropped in on my modern Irish poetry class. I was, for the entire semester, struck so stupid by my quest to borrow creative fire from my love affair with a woman who continued *in her absence* to share every single moment of my life, that I only realized this year, reading the table of contents of a book of W. B. Yeats's poems, that I could recite a couple of them from memory that I hadn't even clearly remembered reading. Each of us was required to prepare a single question for Mr. Heaney, and I asked him a fairly stupid one about large bird imagery that seemed to me to recur in his poems. As I had been in Mas Oyama's hospital room, however, I was so hyped up on the adrenaline of being the new kind of worshiper of the world that I'd become *in Helen's absence* that I failed even to pay much attention to his answer.

Helen, in her presence, had been like the anchor that kept my passion from spinning out of control. Her personality was like the set of carbon rods that keep a nuclear reaction from melting through the walls of the reactor. At Thanksgiving, I'd at least been back in her company the next day. Now, however, I had no daily excuse to see her anymore, and what was worse, I forbade myself to seek her out. It was easy when I had so many responsibilities I wasn't even sleeping. Being at my father's over Christmas and then in Japan, not sleeping for nine days when Lisa and I laid out the book, and finally, training for ten weeks for my *nidan* grading after that, all while battling to keep up with my classes, turned out to be a convenient way of starting to break my habit of seeing Helen regularly.

Of course I longed to see her. When I did run into her by chance in the Café, our exchanges were friendly, and from my side, focused on how busy my endeavors were keeping me, to excuse the fact that I wouldn't be asking her out to lunch anytime soon. Once or twice, when I saw her at the opposite end of a hallway, or on the far side of a wide expanse of campus lawn, I made sure she hadn't seen me and then, bracing myself against a pang of grief, changed course to make sure our paths wouldn't even cross.

It was in the aftermath of sending the first book off to the printer, while week after week the checks for advance purchases continued to roll in, that the vision for what I could achieve beyond the magazine project started to explode. It was one in which the editorship of *Budo Karate Illustrated,* my Davidson diploma, a graduation certificate and a branch chief certificate from Japan, a $10,000 Watson fellowship, and the completion of the book I'd been struggling to write for so long were merely the first few steps. I looked into the future and saw my life's work as amassing the creative capital I'd need to one day deliver the *binta*[73] that would set American society on a course in which the individual took personal responsibility for the direction of the whole.

Of course, I must have been a little psychologically affected by the realization that all my endeavors were succeeding – and certainly by the fact that I barely slept anymore! – but I was not delusional. I was wide-eyed aware that even though I could see it all so clearly, my chances of actually making it happen were slim. I was not so detached from reality that I didn't recognize that I was attempting the impossible. But like giving something your all and then recording the story, so that even if your all turns out not to be enough, your example will perhaps inspire others to pick up the ball you fumbled, I recognized that since I saw a chance of achieving it – no matter how small – it was my responsibility to give everything I had to try to make it come true.

I've described the ecstasy of Midas's first roar, when unrivaled grief ripped open childhood wounds and utterly destroyed any semblance of finality to what I'd become, or what I'd believed I could become, after two decades of society's conditioning that I could only do so much. It wouldn't be until years later that I would come to understand that by letting my love for Helen spin out of control, I'd gone beyond the emotional into the realms of the chemical. I surely should have known during that last semester of my Davidson College experience, when I danced my way though daily endorphin- and adrenaline-fueled visions that would have made heroin addicts run to rehab in wide-eyed terror.

In wide-open spaces particularly, with access to as much of the sky and the natural world as I could take in, it was not unusual for me to walk across brick sidewalks that exploded under my feet as if the weight that I carried was that of Heaven itself. I'd first looked into Lissa's eyes, I'd seen

---

[73] Japanese for "behavior-correcting slap to the face."

the power and beauty of the natural world there, and I'd stumbled away drunk on mere momentary glances of the moon in the night sky. In the valley of my childhood I'd achieved unaided flight, walked on water, and even momentarily defied gravity, hovering in that bliss of relief between Nathan Ligo, buckling with pain one moment, and Midas soaring in ecstasy the next.

But that entire experience lasted less than two minutes.

With Helen gone from my world, with the anchor chain cut and the control rods removed, I crossed over to where I spent more time in Midas's bliss, or struck stupid in the withdrawal from it, than in Nathan Ligo's cold hard truth. In thundering booms the Earth cracked to the core under my feet. Under gray winter skies cut by the silhouettes of college buildings and the naked twigs of Davidson's oaks, I ground my teeth as energy like white-hot lava rolled down my spine and off my shoulders to drip from my fingertips and melt the soil behind me into smoldering trenches of volcanic glass. I was a mediocre student while at Davidson, and people who were there would remember me, but for the most part they would just remember me as "that guy on campus who chased such huge goals but seemed, at least during his last year, kind of lonely and detached." I can tell you with absolute assurance, though, that I was the only student on campus that year to ever glance at the five-foot-thick concrete columns that support the façade and dome of Chambers and watch them explode under the impact of his glance. I was the only Davidson student to congratulate himself for his ability to walk across campus without drawing attention to himself even though on the inside he was staggering through the knee-deep sludge of the melted planet around him. I was the only Davidson college student on campus who could knock all the windows out of a classroom with a twitch of his stomach muscles and then draw the shards back into place with the next inhale.

The hundred steps of my vision were born in the fiery hot plasma that spilled outward to fill my world, and Helen, in her absence, was at the core of the reactor.

Humbert Humbert's sensory spider webs that he spun throughout the house, so that like the spider in the center he could feel Lolita's every move, had nothing on Nathan Ligo's ability to reach out into unseen realms during those few months. It took ever so slight an alteration to the physical sensation of a magnetic pull he felt in the geographical direction where he knew Helen to reside – now he knew exactly where she was because he'd been in her house! – and he could feel her though the earth. If she was indeed a *seer* and he could see into her, if like a wild beast he could smell the particles of her skin from across the room, if he could indeed watch the blood pumping though her arteries, how far-fetched was it that he might learn to feel her through the bedrock beneath Davidson's soil?

Walking across those same wide-open spaces that tended to melt under Nathan's feet, he would lift his chin ever so slightly to the wind and flare his nostrils in a long steady inhale seeking the scent of the woman he loved. When it was nowhere to be found, he would instead welcome the momentary bombardment of surplus oxygen and the smells of the natural world which he had come to equate with the power and majesty of life, and in that euphoric moment when the entire power of the natural world was his to wield as he pleased, he would flare his fingers trailing behind him to project the energy that rolled down his spine into the earth, to search through the planet itself for Helen sleeping, teaching, reading, grading papers, or talking on the phone to her husband in Kansas City. No matter what she was doing or where she was, if Nathan looked, he could feel the life force that sustained her. He drew power from it and Conscience gave him free rein.

And why not?

It was all nonsense, after all! It was fantasy. Helen was completely safe. Nathan had all but removed her from his world, and beyond that loss of a casual friendship, there would be no way that he could hurt her. All the rest was just a harmless psychological gimmick that Nathan created to fight his way through the boring, life-as-college-student challenges that filled his days. Walking alone, it seems, was the primary opportunity, since then he was alone with his thoughts and otherwise powerless to forward the various projects he pursued.

It was a game.

It was harmless.

It was an illusion.

It was so unbelievably powerful.

Spring hit, and so did spring's thunderstorms, and Nathan Ligo was out in them. Everyone else was running for cover to protect themselves from the lightning and the hail, and Nathan Ligo was running like Midas in the valley of his childhood for the widest open area he could find so that he could dare the lighting to hit him. The football field or the wide-open lawn in front of Chambers, either one would do, and Nathan Ligo stood there rolling inside with laughter at how the muscles of his back, shoulders and neck were completely relaxed despite icy rain or torrents of hailstones that would have made even giants hunker down, their heads between their shoulders in an attempt to escape when shelter was unavailable. Ask yourself if you've ever felt hailstones hitting your shoulders and skull. Probably you have, although you were most likely doing your best to get out from under them as quickly as possible. Now ask yourself if you've ever felt them bouncing off your face, turned upwards towards the sky, daring them to hit your open eyes and knowing that they'd melt if they dared try. I would hazard a guess that you have not, but Nathan Ligo did more than once that semester. Milking energy out of the earth at his feet, he laughed aloud at lightning that exploded trees just out of sight. Thunderclaps that sounded like the very sky had torn open didn't engender in him so much as a tremor, because these were sounds that had become so commonplace in his world that it was only the irony of hearing ones that other people could hear as well that moved him.

    Five years earlier, a mysterious screeching winged creature on the winter ridge of Grandfather Mountain had blasted its impression onto Nathan's then so fluid personality, and he'd never again beheld large winged creatures in the same way. [74]

    During his very first morning training in Tokyo, with his eyes closed, he turned his face momentarily skywards to take a deep life-worshiping breath of Tokyo's morning, and before he'd even opened his eyes of his own accord, one of Tokyo's monstrous, chicken-sized ravens shouted angrily down at him from the branch just overhead. Eclipsing Nathan's entire

---

[74] A seventeenth-century book written by Japan's Chozan Shissai, *A Discourse in the Art of Mountain Demons*, was a favorite of mine as a teenager. Shissai's mountain demons, *Tengu* in Japanese, are mythological winged creatures banished to the wilderness for their ugly features who accordingly devote all the hours of their lives to a quest for enlightenment through the mastery of swordsmanship. I spent the eve of my eighteenth birthday shivering myself to sleep alone near the summit of Grandfather Mountain and was visited in the night by a giant bird (eagle, owl, hawk, raven?) that crashed into the limbs of a tree near my tent in a cascade of breaking twigs and falling snow and ice, paused there for a moment to situate himself, screeched like a banshee, and then flew off with thunderous beats of his wings into the subfreezing windless silence, off somewhere I suppose to terrify someone else.

world, he'd spread his wings to show off eagle-like feathers that spread like fingers at the ends of his wings, and with a crackling of branches he'd soared, once again, into Nathan's soul in a way from which he thought he'd never recover.

Hawks swarmed like bees around Yamaguchi *Sensei's* temple on his Tateyama mountaintop and, looking down on the backs of hawks in flight for the first time, Nathan was not at all surprised to find them gathered there.

North Carolina's crows are much smaller than Tokyo's ravens, but how can I possibly describe the soul-shaking shock with which their calls of *Kaw! Kaw!* shook my demeanor when they called out angrily to me from the tops of the fifty-foot pine trees beside the cut-through between my father's East Main Street home and Davidson's fraternity court on the first day that I returned from Japan. *"Baka! Baka!"* they called out to me ("Fool! Fool!"), as if to laugh at me and caution that there'd be no turning my back on karate's icy mountain wind. "Go and see if you want!" they cried, "but *Haw! Haw!* It's in you now! You can try to turn your back, but you might as well accept it because you've gone too *farrr*! Now karate is who you *arrre*!"

And during that semester – when I was struck stupid by the chemical withdrawal from walking through a natural world that routinely exploded around me in thunderous booms, and I asked Seamus Heaney about bird imagery in his poems – I was literally plagued by the larger winged creatures that frequented Davidson's skies.[75] Like a hunter who's spent so

---

[75] My question for Mr. Heaney about bird imagery was a particularly stupid one, because the large bird imagery I remembered from the semester was surely from W.B. Yeats's poems, not from his own, and in my exhaustion, I managed to superimpose them on the wrong poet, right there in his presence for all to see. Locating the actual transcript of the dialogue online (from *Talking with Poets*, Harry Thomas, ed. New York: Handsel Press, 2003), I was relieved to learn that a forgotten attempt to recover I made later in the session was a bit more intelligent. It is also directly pertinent to the action of this story so I include it here:

"You referred a moment ago to a poetic sixth sense," I said to the Nobel laureate, "and you discussed the artistic self and the potential conflict between that self and the world. Do you still feel some conflict arising in your life between the need to hear this inner self and, say, religion, or just people around you who aren't paying heed to it?" I have a hunch that some of my words were *lost in transcription*, but I'm clearly making a reference here to the painful separation I felt from my peers because I was so sure that I routinely saw something about the world than none of the rest of them could see.

many hours in the forest stalking his prey that the sound it makes when it rustles through the leaves still catches his attention years later from half a mile away, there wasn't a crow in the treetops or in the sky during that semester of which I wasn't acutely aware. Eighteen months later, when I crashed my motorcycle – sleepless and in the rain after a double shift on a short-term job I'd then hold – when my motorcycle and I exploded like the space shuttle blowing up across the surface of a freshly furrowed field of North Carolina red clay, I'd leap to my feet and before even stopping to assess the extent of my broken bones, I'd turn my face skyward to behold the red-tailed hawk that at just that moment soared between me and the sun as if to show off his red, translucent tail feathers and the split, finger-like tips of his wings.

Have your eyes ever met with those of hawks, ravens and owls in flight, or, like everyone else, do you just take them for granted and watch the lot of them fly over? As with that hawk that passed between me and the sun, I developed the habit during my last semester at Davidson of looking soaring birds in the eye, and therefore being fully aware whether or not I had become – thanks to my movement, I suppose – the undivided focus of their attention. I found myself not in the least bit surprised that I almost always was. That hawk overhead when I crashed my motorcycle

---

Hungry always for someone who might understand, I was looking for traces of my *vision* in Heaney's *poetic sixth sense*. My reference to "religion" was an allusion to the conflict that existed for me between seeing the world "as *convention* told me I was supposed to see it," and "how I actually, uniquely did."

Heaney responded, "I think that's a need that's in everyone. It's to do with *individuation*, as Jung might have said. It's to do with *coming through*, as Lawrence would have said. It's to do with *integrating*, to do with the problem of *being one person*, as Milosz says. He says in his poem *Ars Poetica?*, 'Our house is open, there are no keys in the doors, and invisible guests come in and out' - but even so we'd like to be one person. But where do we begin this oneness? Where do we start building towards oneness? I think everybody in some intuitive or inchoate or deliberate way seeks answers to those questions. The fact of the matter is that for me the confidence-building and the sense of touching base in myself came from writing poems in my twenties. My first poems were very important to me in grounding some sense of identity. I think the question of faith is separate. You can keep your faith or lose your faith. Those traditional terms mean something. I suppose I lost my faith. That is to say I stopped going to the sacraments and living within the terms of a system of belief and a system of practice, a system of coherence, a system in which everything was ordered. That, perhaps, cannot be replaced. And all the talk and all interviews and so on, they are ways of saying we're making the best of it alone and, we hope, inventively . . ."

was staring right at me, and when our eyes met, his eyes shot through me like twin parallel javelins. Without so much as flinching, I shot the exact same gaze right back at him, and he diverted his eyes and turned up the corner of one wing to alter course in search of a safer field for his hunt.

Crows in Davidson's treetops a quarter of a mile away, which other pedestrians never would have noticed, became at times the focus of my undivided attention. Like spies for Chozan Shissai's mountain demons that visited me on the midnight of my eighteenth birthday on Grandfather's ridge, I often laughed at the sensation that they were watching me, chuckling at my meager efforts, and challenging me to let out all the stops and go all the way.

When I was thirteen or fourteen and in middle school, there was one year during which I missed forty days due to a stomach illness that no one seemed to be able diagnose. Four years of life-altering pain later, a Davidson doctor named Beamon finally ordered the appropriate test and identified a tiny wisp of white on an X-ray image indicating a then little-known condition, well known today as reflux gastritis. The valve at the top of my stomach was failing to do its job, and stomach acid was splashing out of my stomach, backwards, to burn the delicate lining of my esophagus. The resulting sensation was not exactly pain, and it wasn't exactly nausea either. The best way I can describe it is to say that it felt like a shadowy panic. It was like black terror in that it darkened my entire perception of the world and was inescapable. Since the pain was inside, there was no way to soothe it. Rubbing my chest couldn't touch it, I never knew exactly what part of my stomach area it came from, and the result was to render the pain a mysterious one that polluted my whole world and made me question whether it was even real. It would wake me up, particularly in the night, since my digesting dinner was then sloshed to horizontal, and those times I woke up from the deepest sleeps I often carried the subjects of my dreams forward into a shadowy, frightening delirium in which I sometimes couldn't identify what was real and what was dream.

One night at the age of fourteen I woke up from one dream in which a samurai sword had apparently been a predominant prop. It was not uncommon for me even at that late age to run to my mother in the night when hit by fits of such terror that I wanted to leap out of my skin and leave it behind. That night my mother asked me what I thought I'd eaten to make me sick, and I told her, "I think it was the sword I ate." My brain, in that twisted state, had apparently come up with the perfect image to explain the indescribable pain that I felt in my stomach. It did indeed feel as if my stomach was full of shattered fragments of sword blade, at that moment I genuinely believed that it was, and my mother asked, fighting through her own mild delirium of having just woken up, "Nathan, are you saying *sword*? Did you say that you ate a *sword*?"

Even though I haven't seen my biological mother in a decade, it is therefore her voice that comes to me when I imagine my readers' reaction to this description of the euphoric visions I saw during this period of my life. Her voice says, "Are you saying, Nathan, that you actually saw the sky melting, and the earth cracking open under your feet? Are you saying that you actually heard thunderous booms that no one else noticed? Are you saying that the birds spoke to you words that you could hear?"

My answer would have to be, yes and no. No birds ever spoke to me except with the caws, hoots and screeches that birds use to speak to each other or to ward off potential threats. It was rather that certain large birds like ravens and hawks had become symbols for me of a certain type of feeling that I first felt shivering in a frozen February night on Grandfather's ridge on the eve of my eighteenth birthday. It was rather, therefore, that I would encounter these creatures later in life and they would conjure up remnants of the sensation of icy mountain wind. I suppose it was my conscience that added the words, *"Baka! Baka!* (Fool! Fool!) You thought you could just walk away?" With my ears, I only heard *"Kaw! Kaw!"*

I was stunned at the frequency with which I encountered them that year, but that might have been merely because I had started so acutely to notice them, while in other periods of my life I might have simply walked by without paying attention. Right in the middle of campus one two o'clock in the morning, walking home from the Café with my brain just then in overdrive, I encountered a massive owl on a limb, so low and so close to the sidewalk that I stopped and stared with awe. He stared right into my eyes and spread his wings to an awesome four and a half feet, as if to contemplate flight, and then, as if baffled by what he saw, closed them again and stayed there, ten feet from where I stood without moving for the next twenty minutes of my life. Once he rolled his head all the way around as if to show off how magnificently double-jointed his neck was. Another time he made me laugh when he lifted one foot, ruffled all his feathers till he looked like an angry porcupine, and scratched with one of his talons the back of his head.

No, in the case of birds, it was merely that I noticed them, they conjured in me images intricately related to my pursuits and, like a private joke, I therefore chose to revel in the mystery.

The rest, I'd have to say, I very much saw.

I did see the earth cracking, buckling and melting under my feet, but in truth it was more like I felt the thunderous booms reverberating up

Another of my experimental paintings from 1989 (I was eighteen) might as well have been called *Midas and the Mountain Demon*, although the persona I call "Midas" didn't manifest until years later. The painting, one of a series, was inspired by that event which transpired on the eve of my 18th birthday on the ridge of Grandfather Mountain.

from the ground than that I heard them. The key difference between me seeing these things as I did, however, and the type of hallucinations that might have indicated malady, is that I allowed them to occur and intensify – I permitted them! – knowing that of course they weren't real. I could blink and growl and come back to Earth, and my world would reveal itself in its true form.

What's important, though, is that during this period I regularly chose *not* to dismiss them.

The visions that I saw were manifestations of the rapture I felt beholding the beauty of life, and of the natural world, and of love. But I could have put an end to it. I could have stamped my foot and dismissed it as nonsense as everyone else does before such fantasies creep too far forward into the real world. The fact that I could have dismissed them is extremely important to my story – I did, of course, finally dismiss them once and for all. I knew that dwelling in them and allowing them to occur was potentially dangerous to my emotional well-being. I came to know also, however, that they had become an intrinsic part of my creative drive, and Conscience would not allow me to dismiss them until my work was done.

On the Discovery Channel we watch as prides of lions take down and kill water buffaloes, elephants, and other such large prey. We see how it takes quite a while for the cats to kill such big animals, and how towards the end of the struggle, there are often some minutes during which some of the lions have already started feeding on the flesh of an animal that still has light in its eyes and is still trying to escape. "God, can you imagine?" we say to ourselves. "Can you imagine getting eaten alive?" That would be like watching two hungry pit bulls fighting over one of your partially severed legs before the third one, jaws clamped on your throat, cut the jugular or crushed the windpipe to finish you off. Biologists tell us the animal being eaten alive probably doesn't feel much. Sure, it's not happy – it's had better days – but animals, including the human animal, have defense mechanisms for such trauma: the large-scale pumping of various chemicals into the bloodstream, endorphins and adrenaline, so that the wounded animal goes into shock before it feels much actual pain, and is therefore better able to perhaps fend off its attackers and survive should any opportunity to escape present itself.

It didn't occur to me until years later that when Conscience gave me leave to let go my love for Helen, it was in fact giving leave for some part of me to start loosing one of the first mild doses of a potent cocktail of chemicals into my bloodstream, which had first spilled out at the end of that summer when Midas tore though the valley of my childhood. I would have to be a doctor to know exactly what it was – and I can imagine there is a fine line between emotional reactions and chemical ones – so it's possible that what I have interpreted as chemical could have been purely psychological. What was it inside me, though, that took emotional pain and converted it so masterfully into blissful release?

Is it normal for such bliss to be so intrinsically related to the clarity of sight that I was then able to conjure?

It's been only the handful of relapses that I've suffered in the sixteen years since, when similar circumstances evoked similar sensations, that finally convinced me beyond a shadow of a doubt that the situation I faced was indeed a chemical one. Not too long after the events told in this book, I spent six months living like a rat in a tent in a sometimes snow-shrouded winter forest. There were nights when falling asleep there was like falling asleep in my mother's arms. I was never warmer than I was then, I was never as in control of my own destiny, and I never slept better in my life.

Surely, it was then that, through an exercise that most normal people would call crazy, I was locking Midas back into his tomb. I was shutting down production of whatever chemical it was that had kept me high for so long. I was kicking my addiction to emotional overload. I don't think I was aware then of having to put the genie back in the bottle in the name of my future sanity, but it strikes me now that that's exactly what I was doing.

I was letting go of the chemical addiction to endorphins and adrenaline that fueled the creative projects in which I was engaged during the last year of Mas Oyama's life, and I was struggling to let go of the woman that I'd used so masterfully to kick that chemical production into overdrive.

In his book *This is Karate*, Mas Oyama wrote of *chakuriki*, a concept particularly Korean in origin which refers to various means of *borrowing power*. From *medicinal chakuriki*, he wrote, the martial artist can borrow power through the use of herbal and medicinal supplementation, *medicinal* of course referring to the traditional remedies of Chinese Medicine rather than what we might think of as supplementation in the modern era of amino acids and steroids. *Spiritual chakuriki*, the type of borrowed power that I dare say was truly significant to Mas Oyama's life, entailed subjecting himself to the grueling spiritual challenge of isolated mountain training in the frigid loneliness of the wilderness, during which even training more hours a day than he slept paled in significance beside the spiritual battles that he had to face alone, shivering in the night, battling the demons of isolation in the defense of his own sanity.

My own actual strength or weakness aside, my personality was shaped by a physically disadvantaged pre-karate childhood, leading me to at least believe myself fundamentally weak and incapable, particularly in areas of athletic performance. Borrowing strength, therefore, has always been an attractive notion to me, and I have never failed to seize any opportunity to do so if I perceived the chance. I had, and would have been the first to admit that I had, almost no inherent confidence in my own ability to survive Mas Oyama's *uchi deshi* program, and I'm certain that I wouldn't have made it for nearly as long as I did had it not been for the strength that I *borrowed* by vowing that I would succeed at any cost for my first teacher, whom I still credit with having saved my life as a teenager.

It wasn't my own inherent strength that kept me struggling in Japan long past when most sane Americans I knew would have given up. It was, instead, that I had found a way to allow myself no choice but to persevere. When I finally left Japan without completing the program, it wasn't that I underwent any significant change – I was actually far stronger by then than when I first entered the dormitory – it was rather that recent events in my life back home shook the perspective that I'd maintained for so long on how best to fulfill my sense of duty to my first teacher.

I remain conflicted, sixteen years later, over whether the *emotional chakuriki* which I inadvertently discovered could be achieved through my interaction with Helen – or, as the case actually was, my lack of interaction with her! – can fairly be compared to Mas Oyama's *spiritual chakuriki*. Since the Mas Oyama legend was first relayed to me as an early teen, his method has always seemed to me to be fundamentally pure. His training alone on a mountaintop for eighteen months was potentially punishing to the body and certainly terrifying to the soul, but was it not purely creative in terms of spiritual strength? Was not my accidental alternative, on the other hand, potentially spiritually destructive? It did result in the heightened creative energy I sought, but even as a I allowed it to happen, I sensed danger lurking, as if one day it would swoop down from above and take me away.

Koreans who traditionally farmed dogs believed that the meat is much better if the dog is beaten prior to slaughter. Like the water buffalo being eaten alive, the blood of the beaten dog is pulsing with endorphins and adrenaline, and Korean men, who believe dog meat to be an aphrodisiac, want to have high quantities of such chemicals freshly pumped into the meat that they are about to consume. Perhaps in that sense, the practice in which I engaged was some twisted version of Mas Oyama's *medicinal chakuriki*, except that I learned to produce the chemical myself.

When I let myself free for the first time in my life to love someone, Lissa — and have her, too! — and when it became clear that she was shutting me out, it must have brought up deeper feelings of loss from my childhood, and the sensation was a physical pain that conjured images of having a fencepost driven through my chest. In the choices she made, my stepmother Martha unknowingly took up that post with both hands and twisted it until I thought I would die. And Midas was born. And Helen came along. And Conscience somehow allowed me to let my love for her run free. I'd figured out how to take hold of the fencepost myself and twist it, and turn it, and drive one end of it into the soil in an effort to keep Midas's golden touch alive so that I might achieve for Kyokushin, for Mas Oyama, and for Master Choi, for my future students, and for my future readers.

I have at times in my life shaken my head with pity and wonder at drug addicts who introduce foreign chemicals into their bodies to achieve effects that life and the human body are capable of achieving all by themselves.

Perhaps if you consider *medicinal chakuriki*, and the difference between employing something pure such as Chinese herbal remedies and something synthetic such as anabolic steroids, the difference between Mas Oyama's *spiritual chakuriki* and my *emotional chakuriki* might be revealed. That is, if his *spiritual chakuriki* might be likened to the use of herbal remedies, I wonder if my own accidental alternative might not be likened to using steroids.

Perhaps the answer lies in whether or not I would go back and live that year again if I could. Certainly there were mistakes I would correct, but allowing the situation to happen the way I did — and I did allow it! — isn't one of them. It was Conscience that let it happen and it is conscience that I rely on.

After all, I wasn't hurting anyone but myself. And so be it!

I was expendable.

TWENTY-TWO

ONE MONTH AFTER MY GRADING in Japan, my blind sense of duty to do for Kyokushin drove me alone by car from North Carolina to Montreal. André Gilbert was hosting his annual tournament, the biggest one in Eastern Canada, and with a second volume of *Budo Karate Illustrated* already planned, I felt compelled to be there with my camera.

In the form of dojo-wide group photographs, I'd included the faces of fifteen hundred American Kyokushin Karate students in my coming first volume. I'd known from the beginning that it was the students' appearance in the books that would sell copies until the magazine became established, and the development of Kyokushin Karate in French Canada, certainly in terms of its sheer numbers, made U.S. Kyokushin look like something out of the stone age. Looking to the future, I already wondered if I might gain similar support from the Canadian branch chiefs and dedicate a later issue – perhaps even the second one! – to Canadian Kyokushin.

The first volume's advance sales had covered the $20,000 down payment, and it was clear that I would soon be seeing the fruits of my labor in print. It wasn't yet clear, however, that I'd be able to sell enough copies soon enough to pay off the entire $40,000 invoice by the time it was due. I was counting on advance sales of the second volume, therefore, to pay off the remainder of Volume One's printing cost. Sales of the first volume would of course go on. In fact, it was a pretty safe bet, I thought, that a second volume would make buyers want to own the first one to complete their set, and vice versa. There had always been enough of a scarcity of Kyokushin media in North America so that those books and magazines that were published tended rapidly to become coveted, and therefore collected. I was very strongly drawn, therefore, to the notion of a *Canadian Kyokushin Yearbook*. If I was lucky, sales could be so much bigger by comparison that they'd not only cover the leftover cost of Volume One but also cut way into the printing cost of Volume Two.

Midas was all riled up over that idea because of the project's darker, hidden motive.

Remember that from the beginning I'd believed that such a book would throw America's stone-age Kyokushin into the sudden company of the international standard, and in so doing, induce improvement. The other side of that coin, though, had been from the beginning a notion that some of the supporters of the first volume – the ones closer to the *Mickey Mouse karate* end of the spectrum – would become disenfranchised. In that sense, I'd figured that some of the supporters of the first book wouldn't be quite so enthusiastic about the second one. Midas was thrilled, therefore, to already know the solution: the ongoing project wouldn't be completely, or even mostly, dependent on those who were featured in the first volume.

Of course, when it came right down to it, all that really mattered was that *Sosai* supported the continuation of the project. If *Sosai* supported it, it would go on. The North American branch chiefs controlled the purse strings for now, but what better way to protect the project from anyone who was less than motivated by the content of Book One than to base the success of Book Two on an alternate purse? With the project ongoing, supporters of Book One would have no choice but to get with the program, and that had been Midas's intention from the beginning. Once they were on board, and three or four issues had been produced, the project would be well enough established to win over even those who had been stung by the first one.

By the time of Gilbert's tournament, I had already missed the maximum number of classes I was allowed to miss in my father's art history course before my grade – by college policy – would start to be affected. I had a very limited window, therefore, in which to make a round-trip drive to a Saturday tournament in Montreal. I couldn't leave Davidson until after my art history class on Friday got out at 10:00 a.m., and I'd have to be back in Davidson in time to make it to that same class at 9:00 Monday morning. The Chinese history class that I had Friday afternoon could be sacrificed. It would be the last one I could miss, but I could miss it without failing the course.

Such was another of the games I played, pushing to the limit what was possible to achieve in a semester of college. I never missed class because I was tired or hung over or because I lacked motivation. But if I had to miss a class to be in Japan or Atlantic City or Rochester or Montreal – or if I absolutely had to get a layout to the printer by a deadline – I considered a class session now and then a worthy sacrifice.

I was well accustomed by then to Davidson students' semester-end routine of cramming to learn material presented either in class or, much more often, in readings that wound up not getting done during the semester. Even students far less burdened than I routinely played the cram game at semester's end. The key difference for me that year, though, was that I played the game to compensate for classes missed or chapters neglected due to the demands of other responsibilities I had no choice but to take care of as well.

Most other students that I knew played the game to support their social lives.

One of the reasons I have so much love for Davidson is because of how serious a study environment it was. It was also a college, though, and part of what college students do is play. The difference between Davidson and the larger University of North Carolina at Chapel Hill, where I spent my sophomore year, for example, was that at the larger state school students didn't have to work quite as hard to make up material sacrificed to social activities. Davidson students were study animals – those that weren't didn't pass their classes – but part of the reason why they had to be so motivated was because, like all college students, they enjoyed themselves at the same time.

Isn't part of a college education, after all, the growing-up type of lessons we learn by being outside of our parents' home for the first time in our lives?

Exploiting that fact turned out to be one of the avenues by which Midas and I were able to get ahead. I'd learned well the posture and attitude of the Davidson *study machine*. What better bed partner could there have been for Midas?

Everyone else crammed to keep up with their social lives. I crammed for Kyokushin.

* * *

As expected, my father's art history survey was the hardest class of my semester.

It was also the saddest.

I don't know what had so changed my father's demeanor at the front of a classroom since I took his Modern Architecture course as a freshman five years earlier. That course had been one of the best I took at Davidson. It was with utter pride that I attended, knowing that the man at the front of the classroom was my dad.

It was disconcerting, therefore, to behold my father at the front of this survey course, seeming predominantly scatterbrained and unprepared. Was it that he lacked motivation? He was certainly less than passionate. I wondered if it was my perception that had changed. I'd aged five years since my freshman year – and had my life-altering Japan experience for two of them! Perhaps it was a combination of that, and the fact that *my father* had aged in the meantime. I wondered if he'd aged beyond his years under the strain of having two small children in the house while daily losing the battle to fit the two sons of his first marriage into such an impossible mold.

I was still then riding out the tail end of the decade I'd spent believing that my father's free, fun-loving, and open-eyed nature had fallen victim to his third wife's overbearing, insecure, and one-dimensional personality. I'd regarded him for most of that decade as being miserable because of it, and therefore in need of rescue. It was as if his new wife exploited his guilt – guilt that he himself declared for failing in two earlier attempts at family – to dictate the only acceptable way for him to be.

Either way, I spent most of my time that semester beholding my father as a sad mystery, and imagining that his ailment had everything to do with me. I was losing him, but he was very definitely losing me as well. Far from thinking him a bad person, I still struggled to believe that he was a genuinely good and well-intentioned one at heart, and that it must have been just as heartbreaking for him to lose his sons as it was for me to lose a father. The difference, of course, was that my losing him meant losing my entire family. His losing me only meant losing one member of his, and he seemed to be doing his best to show me daily that I was its most expendable member.

Midway through eleventh grade, I brought home a report card showing five A's and one C. The C was in my fifth year of French, and resulted from cumulative difficulties I'd had in the second and third years when I was living in Chapel Hill and still so sick. Already by the end of tenth grade I had become a machine of production in terms of training and study. My impassioned charge into remaking myself through karate and making it to Japan to become Mas Oyama's student had made me an animal of self-improvement. As a tenth grader, I removed the furniture from my room and studied at night kneeling in *seiza* in order to keep myself alert while I strove to fulfill Master Choi's grade point average requirements.

"Get at least a 3.5 GPA this semester," he'd tell me, "join the track team to improve your speed, and, if possible, find a gymnastics class to work on your balance. Continue your karate training and read *Musashi* again. If you do these things, perhaps I'll recommend you to my uncle when you get a little bit stronger."

In caring only about Japan, I'd reduced all of my endeavors to the black-and-white of success versus failure, and I punished myself bitterly for my failures. My father, however, never figured out that my being so driven was a positive thing. Perhaps he saw my single-minded, *barrel ahead at all costs* nature and concluded that it was somehow connected to what must have seemed to him like steadfast resistance to his wife. For a decade he treated me as if I'd made a one-time, stubborn decision not to like her, when in actuality I had no choice but to try – I was a child in her household after all! – but every day gave me some new reason why I didn't.

"I can't see how you can congratulate yourself," he told me, "if you got a C in French. I hope that it won't prevent you from studying harder the next time." The "you should be ashamed" tone that he employed – the all-pervading one that told me there was nothing about me that I had any right to be proud of – was one he'd acquired from his latest wife. It was crystal clear when I heard it coming from him that he had replaced so much of his personality with hers, and it was heartbreaking to hear. Simply criticizing me for the C, and not congratulating me for the A's – not to mention all the strides I was making to remake myself athletically at the same time! – would have been one thing.

Parents will be parents, after all.

It was the "there's no excuse for you" tone tacked on that was so heartbreaking. It was as though he had forgotten the love and confidence with which he'd raised me, as if he'd woken up one day and decided that it hadn't been enough, and that my personality needed to be eradicated and replaced with one based on shame rather than one based on conscience.

Shame, of course, is imposed from the outside and tells you how you're supposed to feel. Conscience comes from within and reveals the way that you actually do.

By eleventh grade, my father and stepmother had come to shame me as if I was guilty of some unspeakable crime. That treatment was decade-long and relentless, and ranged from "you got a C in French? You should be ashamed," to "you left the milk out on the counter? You should be ashamed," and "you don't feel inclined to give a Mother's Day card to your stepmother? You should be ashamed!" My stepmother was quick to tell me that I smelled bad, that some ambition I'd expressed was foolish, or that I should be ashamed for leaving some personal possession in one of the house's common areas. I'd look around and see *a family's* personal belongings: there were things of my father's and my stepmother's, and of course the house was knee-deep in the kids' toys, but I was supposed to be ashamed for the one piece of evidence that got left behind in the TV room that might have suggested that I, too, was a member of the family?

It was as if my stepmother especially, from the beginning, did everything in her power to erase me, because I didn't fit into the mold of the traditional family she and my father wanted to have.

And the guilt trip was her favorite eraser.

My father ultimately joined in that cause as well; I was older then, though, and I didn't see it as him. I saw it as the way he had been changed by her, and my respect for him started to waver. By shaming me for a C in French, he was closing his eyes to the fact that just three years earlier I'd barely escaped failing out of school entirely and having to repeat eighth grade. That was when I'd missed forty days of school out of a single year's 180 due to the vicious onset of the stomach illness that reduced me to half of myself during the day, and had me running delirious and terrified to my mother in the night. The physical rebellion my body mounted began the year it became clear how dramatically my father's household had changed after he'd left Martha – into one that didn't have much of my father in it, after all! – and here he was three years later, shaming me for fighting with everything I had to recover!

In eleventh grade I was still managing meds and diet to cope with illness, but that illness didn't have a name yet that my father could believe:

there was no diagnosis, and I could see my father dismissing it as if it were "all in my head" and therefore invalid. All he could see was the C — because, I suppose, I so selfishly exposed the farce of his closing his eyes to the life he'd lived before his third marriage. "I was never married to Martha," he'd assert, and I was supposed to respect his shaming me for getting a C?

"Selfish," my father learned from my stepmother, along with her other favorites, "stubborn" and, of course, "angry," were the best words to describe my personality, presumably because I wouldn't shut my eyes and let him go through his life with his half-shut.

It was with such confusion that he still beheld me at twenty-two, and I could only imagine that his sad demeanor at the front of the classroom had to do with the fact that he felt like he had lost me and he couldn't figure out how. He didn't understand why I had gone to Japan in the first place, he didn't understand why I was so fanatical about karate, and then, after I'd failed in Japan, he certainly didn't understand why I seemed so dead set on fighting my way back. "Dad, it's the structure in my life that repaired the damage that I suffered when you couldn't keep your act together," I could have told him — and I did try on occasion — but because it didn't fit into his mold of how kids my age were supposed to be, he could never figure it out.

One day that spring I came into his classroom before the hour began and showed him an envelope that I'd received in the mail containing nearly two thousand dollars in twenty-four-dollar checks for advance purchases of *Budo Karate Illustrated*. That's a stack of about eighty checks, and I saw in his eyes a glimmer of understanding that there was some value to the work I was pursuing after all. What a pity that it was dollars — the thing I cared about least — that had resulted in that glimmer of comprehension!

I suppose he was still caught up in his "I work my fingers to the bone to support your college education" fantasy — although my tuition was free as a faculty dependent, and he may have felt that I was disrespecting him by not giving my courses at Davidson undivided attention. The rest had no value, in his view, because it wasn't leading me to the family with the regular paycheck, the two point five grandkids, and the dog that had become the only valuable picture for my future, because it was the one that he could drop in on twice a year in his retirement and feel like he'd done as good a job as *his* parents had done, pounding tradition home.

"I'm driving to Montreal after class today," I'm sure I told him, still waging my ceaseless battle to get though to him and make him understand. Giving up on him entirely was still, at that late date, the farthest thing from my mind. "I have to take pictures of the fights at tomorrow's tournament for the second issue of my book. I'm going to do everything in my power to be back in class Monday morning. If I drive straight through, I ought to be able to make it."

Of course my father was baffled and dismayed. "I thought your car wasn't working," were the words with which he tried to veil his disapproval. His eyes were melting with disappointment, or conflict, or grief.

"Yeah, it's not," I told him, "Rafael's lent me his car for the weekend."

"Isn't that a long drive to make in someone else's car?" ("Don't you think you should be ashamed to abuse a friendship like that?" was the unspoken undertone.)

"I suppose," I said. "But it's his knock-around car that he doesn't plan to drive anymore after this year." I left unspoken "That's what friends are for," since I was talking to a man who didn't seem to me to have any.

The following year, one of Rafael's brothers would die in a car accident, and that sad occurrence started a chain of events that ultimately led to my putting life and limb on the line in a full-contact fight for my friend and student, Rafael. He called me to tell me of his brother's death, and that it had made him want to be sure he lived his dreams, because it could happen to any one of us any day. His dream, he told me, was to fight in a Kyokushin tournament, and he wanted to know if I could make it possible.

I did make that tournament possible for him – I made the phone call that got him admitted even though he had no Kyokushin rank – but I also sensed four weeks out that his training wasn't sufficient, and that he was going to be so caught off guard by the intensity of his first bare-knuckle fight that his result would fall short of what he hoped it would be. It was one hundred percent out of love for him, therefore, that I arranged to fight with him myself one night in Davidson's soon-to-be-retired Johnson Gym. I was out of training, in no condition just then to fight safely with someone as naturally big, strong, and confident as he was. Talk about conquering a vicious pang of fear! Yet I set that personal risk aside, played the teacher that I knew Mas Oyama would expect me to be, and took my best friend, with two minutes of full-contact blows, to a limit that he hadn't known existed.

"That's wasn't . . . . anything like . . . I thought . . . it would be!" he panted at the end, white as a sheet, and having given up in exhaustion just short of breaking a handful of the ribs on my left side. Staggering with his hands on his knees, trying to see again after a mere two minutes – the adrenaline rush of which had taken away not only his breath but also, for a moment, his ability to see – he loved me more than he had at the start, and he set his training onto the correct course that took him to 4th place in Henri Orlean's Atlantic City tournament four weeks later.

That's what friends are for, I knew already when he gave me his car to drive to Montreal – I'd had just a few really close ones in my life – and I had zero illusion that my father might have any experience upon which to rest any common understanding.

* * *

I have very little recollection of the tournament in Montreal, other than being so sleepy I could barely function. One can drive nonstop to Montreal from Davidson in seventeen or eighteen hours; I made it in twenty. It was an all-day Saturday tournament, and I rolled into the arena parking lot about an hour before the earliest tournament organizers began to arrive.

I would have slept if it hadn't been so cold.

Sadly, Midas wasn't with me that weekend, and although I came home with several hundred photographs, it was not a successful shoot. Exhausted and alone, I put my foot in my mouth, telling Annie, the Harvard-educated writer, that I had unspoken ulterior motives for the magazine project, the admission of which could only have made such an avid supporter feel betrayed.

The first book was less than a week away from being printed, and I was already beginning to take some heat – starting with Annie – for the extent to which I, personally, had appeared in the layout.

My strong presence in a book that was, after all, the product of my own blood, sweat, and tears might have been excusable if I'd explained that *Sosai* had required me to increase the length of the book by 20 pages just nine days before my deadline, and certainly if I admitted that, at twenty-two, I truly did lack the experience to pull off such a trial run perfectly. In my conversation with Annie at the tournament that day, however, I failed to use those arguments to defend what could so easily be perceived as an out-of-control, ego-based compulsion to announce to all of North American Kyokushin that Nathan Ligo was now on the scene, the only American to have been a personal student of Mas Oyama for a substantial period of time since Jacques, thirty years earlier, and that, as a result, things in the American karate world were never again going to be the same.

Photograph taken from above during the opening ceremony of *Shihan* André Gilbert's Montreal tournament the weekend I drove up from Davidson, and back again in time for my father's class.

Living then as I did on the fine line between fantasy and reality – *vision,* for me, had become the melding of the two! – I foolishly chose to rely on the forgone conclusion of my vision's success, and on its hidden motives, to defend my choices rather than what might have come across as more humble under the circumstances. "Ten or fifteen years from now, most of these U.S. branch chiefs supporting my project are going to be irrelevant to the future of Kyokushin anyway," I stupidly told Annie that day. "Even Jacques, since he's the oldest, is going to die the earliest and be out of the picture. Fifteen years from now, I'm just going to be getting started, and all the rest will be fading away into obscurity."

"Well, that's a pretty cold and obnoxious viewpoint," Annie told me dismissively and turned away, to a large extent for the rest of the weekend. It's a sign of the degree to which I'd been living in a separate world from everyone else that I felt stung by her response. As if it was unheard of for someone to respond the way she had to something as cold-blooded and tasteless as I'd said!

"What's wrong? Can't you see the future the way I can?" I might have argued. "Doesn't everyone else look at the world and see it, past, present and future, in snapshot summary like I do?" Sadly, though, Midas wasn't with me to handle the social niceties, and Annie's criticism caught me off guard and left me feeling humiliated.

In that sense, I suppose her criticism had had its intended effect.

Jacques and Annie, Tom Flynn and his wife Toni, and Michael Monaco and the rest of us all went to the dojo of a Montreal area branch chief named Roman Sjyrajev after the tournament for pizza, and I raised an eyebrow at that, since our tournament host, André Gilbert, was having a *sayonara* party of his own and we were all invited. In order to go to Roman's, all of America's top brass were apparently boycotting *Shihan* Gilbert's reception, and the only answer I got when I asked why, was that Roman had invited Jacques for pizza and Jacques wanted to eat pizza. Everyone else simply followed Jacques.

Katsuhiko Horai was there in Montreal that day – it was the second North American tournament he'd blessed with his presence since *Sosai*, less than overbrimming with optimism, had appointed him branch chief in Manhattan – and I couldn't help but wonder if boycotting Gilbert's party had anything to do with that sour scent on the wind.

Change was most certainly in the air.

* * *

I slept a very short night on the floor in my Rochester friend Michael Stopani's hotel room – it had been on his sofas that my student Dave and I crashed in Rochester eighteen months earlier – and the next morning I had breakfast with his teacher Michael Monaco and the rest of his students before getting back on the highway for the twenty-hour return drive. I sat across from Michael Monaco at the same table while a dozen or so of his students were scattered about the dining room.

Shihan Monaco asked me how *Sosai*'s health had been when I'd seen him a month earlier at the time of my grading. To my surprise, I had to excuse myself to go to the restroom to hide the tears that filled my eyes upon telling him that *Sosai* had looked fine to me. Something about the way *Shihan* Monaco asked me, some sleeping suspicion awakened, suddenly made me contemplate the world for the first time without *Sosai* in it. I washed my face in the bathroom sink and checked myself in the mirror to make sure it didn't look like I'd been crying. I was so unbelievably tired, having slept just half a night in sixty hours, and it was with something like dread that I faced the twenty-hour return drive, alone, down to North Carolina in time for my father's art history class Monday morning. *That must be what it's all about,* I told myself. *You're just worn out . . . and anyone would be. Don't be silly.* Sosai's *going to be fine.*

After four hours of driving, my first dose of caffeine wore off on a particularly bleak stretch of Canadian or upstate New York highway, and I pulled over on the narrow shoulder next to the guardrail to sleep. Thirty minutes later when my watch alarm beeped I opened the door and – delirious – fell outward onto the concrete, half upside down, in an effort to regain consciousness. I almost suffered a heart attack when the raven that was perched in the lowest limb right over the roof of my car shrieked at me as if to say, "Wake up! Wake up! There's no time! You have to be in class in just eighteen hours!"

There were no trees around except for the one I'd pulled up next to, and slithering the rest of the way out of my seat onto the concrete, I arched my spine to reach up for the guardrail so that I could look straight upwards at the squawking beast. I wasn't at all surprised to find him there, of course. He spread his wings and shouted down at me as if angry that the sudden movement of my falling out of my car woke him when he was trying to sleep.

I laughed at him then. I laughed at the irony of him being there. "What are you so upset about?" I asked aloud. "There's not much more of me I can give."

At that I ignored him and got to my feet and flared my nostrils to take in a deep breath of the pre-spring decay. The grass that stretched out before me to the trees on the horizon was white like snow, and beaten down like it had spent most of the winter covered in it. The raven took to the air when I cranked the engine, and in my rearview mirror I watched for that familiar silhouette of finger-like split wing feathers as he soared off across the field.

I arrived at ten minutes before nine the next morning at the art building at Davidson, still wearing the same clothes I'd had on when I left seventy-two hours earlier. Since then I'd slept six hours on a hotel-room floor, had one shower, and had a half dozen or so thirty-minute naps in the reclined driver's seat of Rafael's car.

Fifteen nonstop hours later, at midnight, on my way home from the Café on foot, I stopped in my tracks next to the small, ancient cemetery two lots down from my father's house when my friend, that massive barred owl, shouted at me so loudly that I almost jumped out of my skin. I couldn't see him at first in the dark. He was perched on the lowest limb of an ivy-covered oak at the back of the cemetery next to the long concrete walk. Apparently I'd pissed him off by disturbing his silence, and he hooted at me to express his discontent.

"What's *your* problem?" I said aloud as I let go of the cemetery gate and resumed my trek. "What are you guys all riled up about lately?" I was only a hundred yards from my bed in the one-room cottage in my father's backyard, and I wanted nothing more than to collapse.

The next morning my father knocked uncharacteristically on my door. Tom Flynn had called.

He'd left the message that *Sosai* had died of stomach cancer, that Matsui was to be the IKO's new chairman, and that a memorial service had been planned for sometime in June.

* * *

Damning it all, in my *dogi* I staggered out of my room ninety seconds later, barefooted and carrying my folded black belt at my side. I was aware of my father nervously watching me walk down the driveway past his living room window, but I didn't stop.

Struck dumb, walking like the dead myself I floated in white across campus in the direction of my dojo. The old Johnson Gym was slated to be refurbished into the new Student Union, it was all but empty already except for the Davidson Outdoors Club offices and all of their boats and tents and other gear, and it was to the former wrestling room there, my first dojo at Davidson, that I went, because I knew the dance studio in the new athletic gym where I'd been teaching that year would likely be occupied.

I was aware of the Davidson Outdoors staff glancing up as I walked past their open door and down the subterranean tiled hall.

Entering the wall-to-wall matted room where I'd done a thousand jumping squats five months earlier in advance of my Watson interview, I bowed twice and shouted "Osu!" in the customary way. At the back of the dojo, facing the back, I straightened my uniform and tied my belt so tight it burned my skin. My face was already burning for the tear tracks that cut their way down from my eyes, but I bared my teeth then and wiped them away. Just like my shoes that I'd positioned on the top tie of Martha's retaining wall so that I could step back into them without turning back towards the forest for even an instant, I resolved never to shed another tear for my teacher, Mas Oyama.

Sitting in *seiza* at the front of the dojo with my back straight and my fists on my hips, I placed my right fist on the floor in front of my right knee and then my left to bow in the traditional Japanese fashion. *Sosai's* picture was no longer there on the wall, but it didn't matter. I hadn't come there to bow to a picture.

"Osu!" I saluted and the voice that emanated from somewhere so deep down within me was one that I'd never before that moment heard. Having been completely absent for several weeks, Midas was suddenly back with all his ferocity, and unlike when he'd shaken the Chambers conference-room walls during my Watson interview, Nathan Ligo was there too. The two of us swore in unison the words of the Dojo Oath in Japanese in such a voice that there is no doubt in my mind that the departing ghost of Mas Oyama heard me straight through the center of the Earth.

Like Midas's flight in the valley of my childhood, the recitation was flawless. Not only did I not miss a single syllable, but the tension in my diaphragm and the air in my lungs was so perfectly regulated as to ensure that not a single syllable of the oath went unheard beyond the grave. The volume made the folks in the Davidson Outdoors office at the other end of Johnson look up from their desks in wonder, and the motorists driving by on the street, two stories down behind the wrestling-room windows, wondered what kind of sporting event had drawn such a crowd to what was supposed to be a retired athletic facility. There was no cracking or melting of the Earth then. It was all voice, but the power and majesty of the entire planet came upwards through the ground beneath the dojo floor and filled me with a sense of power and creativity I'd never before that day rivaled.

And what a transformation occurred that day in the life of Nathan Ligo!

It was almost as if *Sosai* had known that if he'd died at that particular moment, when I was at my most physically, mentally, and emotionally extended – having had one normal night's sleep in five days of raw production for Kyokushin, and actually only a few in the whole semester – I would be forever locked at that level of production.

How blessed I was, I would realize with growing wonder over the weeks, months, and years to come, that at the time of *Sosai's* death I was so incredibly engaged in doing the work for Kyokushin's future that I had even resorted to such potentially self-destructive, creativity-birthing means! Not only had *Sosai* died leaving absolutely no doubt in my mind that he approved of me, that he loved me, that he was proud of me and optimistic that I might achieve something of value for Kyokushin and for the world; but he had died at the climax of a year of my life in which I was maxed out to superhuman levels in the name of Kyokushin and what might be accomplished through it. Having been the only American *uchi deshi* of Mas Oyama he'd ever recognized with a graduation certificate from his Young Lions' Program had already filled me with a sense of responsibility to spill every drop of my own blood if necessary for Kyokushin. But now that Sosai had left me as he had, not only was I ultimately responsible, but I had proven to myself that I was also ultimately able.

Adult men all over the planet were collapsing that day in despair at the loss of that pillar of strength who had redefined the lives of so many, and the making of me alone on the North American continent into a machine of production for the future of Kyokushin was locked in stone.

I would come to realize that, in a way, there was so little change in my world upon the passing of Mas Oyama that the weight of those last few tears that I shed over his passing was more significant. As cold-blooded as it might seem, I never experienced a shred of grief for my personal loss of

Mas Oyama. I never felt grief because I never for a second lost him. Mas Oyama was in me already. Long before this moment, he had already been watching over my shoulder each and every move that I made, and as if he was still just over there in his office in Tokyo, concentrating his energy on more important matters, my path in the world was unaltered.

The tears were more at the shock of the sick, twisted image of the world without Mas Oyama in it. Make fun if you choose, but I was a literature major and a Romantic, and a stanza of Coleridge's "Rime of the Ancient Mariner" leapt out at me that day. I looked it up later, and I had to grit my teeth and hiss to stifle the impulse to cry.

> Alone, alone, all, all alone,
> Alone on a wide wide sea!
> And never a saint took pity on
> My soul in agony.
>
> The many men, so beautiful!
> And they all dead did lie:
> And a thousand thousand slimy things
> Lived on; and so did I.

I thought immediately of Jacques. I knew that since he was the oldest, he would indeed die before the rest, and it was with a horror akin to that of the mariner that I contemplated a future without such giants in the world.

Over my dead body! I swore to myself then.

The world needs its giants, and over my dead body will the world cease to have them!

* * *

In a sad, twisted irony, not two days later I held in my own two hands the first copy of *Budo Karate Illustrated* to roll off the press. With violent insistence, I'd demanded that the printer in Montgomery make an exception to their rule and send me a single copy of the book before the entire order was printed. Instead, they'd printed the entire order and sent me a single, coverless binding of the book's actual 104 pages, so that I could give final approval before they attached the covers.

And I'm glad that they did.

There was an entire six pages, three two-page spreads, the very ones that displayed Bill Giduz's photographs of me breaking baseball bats, leaping to new heights, and splitting apples like William Tell, where they'd somehow, catastrophically, printed the backgrounds in a God-awful hot pink, rather than the jet black that I'd ordered.

What a nightmare for the ego of a twenty-three-year-old Beta who would have to fight to fend off repeated accusations that ego had played too heavy a role in the layout of the *Budo Karate Illustrated* book! What a nightmare to find out by phone in the last minutes of the business day, with all the management gone home, that they'd already printed all 2000 copies of the book, and all that remained in their production process was to attach the bound pages to their hard covers and package them for shipping!

When the plant opened the next morning, in Montgomery, Alabama – so close to America's Gulf of Mexico – I'd already parked Rafael's car and was standing there at the door with piss and blood in my eyes, ready if necessary to fight to make them reprint the entire order. Three and a half days earlier I'd been in Canada. There I was with the upper- and lowermost extremes of the North American continent bracketing the death of Mas Oyama, and, stride unbroken by either calamity, I was ready, still, to fight for Kyokushin.

And to the printer's credit, they relented.

I came straight out and told a team that until then had only been voices on the phone that the man the book was dedicated to, the man on the cover, had died less than two days earlier, and that I wouldn't sell a single copy in an attempt to pay off the rest of my bill if they didn't reprint the entire thing, at what turned out to be, for them, a near $20,000 loss in paper, ink, labor, and machine hours.

Oh, they started to tell me that it couldn't be done.

They told me that mistakes happened sometimes and buyers had to deal with it. I showed them the proofs – and they pulled out their copies that I'd signed – and showed them that the background color code typed clearly in the spot designated for it was correct. I showed them on their color chart that the number code corresponded to their jet black.

"How could this have happened?" I asked. "What kind of people do you have working down here that they could make a mistake like that? That's six whole pages, for heaven's sake!"

The most sensible one of the three that sat across the table from me finally heaved a heavy sigh — she was the boss — and I knew that one of mine would soon follow.

"It'll be moved to the bottom of the production schedule," she said, deadpan, like her cat had died. "It'll likely take four weeks. We can't get it in before then."

"I understand," I said. "So be it. We don't have a choice.

"All we can do is keep fighting forward."

I had to be home the next morning, again, for my father's art history class.

I hadn't slept.

At the Gulf of Mexico, before getting back behind the wheel to head north once again, I hissed:

"Over my dead body will the world cease to have its giants."

PART IV

TWENTY-THREE

THE LAST FINAL EXAM of my college experience happened at the end of May, and I was fighting my way to Japan two weeks later. Mas Oyama's memorial service was scheduled for June 26th, and Duty demanded my attendance. Midas was mostly absent from my day to day by then – I was still so wiped out from the demands of the semester – and the two weeks that I spent in Japan remain somewhat jumbled in my memory.

I will give them to you as best I can.

I felt myself already then to be a freakish exception to the rule. Stride unbroken, I would be in Japan for the fourth time in eighteen months simply to continue. I might have been left behind in terms of anticipating *Sosai's* death, but I more than made up for it in terms of recovery. So many of my overseas compatriots in the Kyokushin world seemed lost without the pillar of strength that had been our leader.

For me, the future was never so clear.

I'd had such a strong sense already that *Sosai* was watching my every move that it was only natural that I go on as if he still were. Perhaps on some level that was why I'd been momentarily blindsided. In a sense it was only on a personal, selfish level that his being alive was even relevant. For the focus of my life's work, his presence didn't matter. I knew that if anything, his death had hardened that path in stone and made me stronger. *Sosai* had always been an external power that I went to if I needed something. When he died he became part of me. He became part of my strength and confidence, thanks to how strongly he'd let it be known in our final encounters that he approved of me. He'd done it so masterfully that I couldn't help but feel that he'd planted that seed of confidence in me intentionally, perhaps even knowing that he was going to die and choosing the ones he wanted to touch before he died.

As my two weeks in Japan droned by and *Sosai's* memorial service happened, my impression of a general confusion within the Kyokushin ranks continued to build. *Sosai's* overseas followers, particularly, seemed to be in Japan either to buck for position under Matsui, and therefore had their eyes fixed too desperately on an uncertain future, or to despair in the absence of *Sosai's* guidance, and were therefore preoccupied with a past that would never again be. *Sosai* would have been honored by the show of devotion as 10,000 of his Tokyo-area students lined up around the block to pay their final respects at his memorial service – up to a point he would have been touched by the tears – but I believed also that he would have preferred to see us all that day in sweat-soaked white rather than in black pressed suits and ties.

Perhaps I was insane to think it, but I felt as though I hadn't been out of my *dogi* in more than a year. I slept in it. I wore it to class. In it I'd fought through the challenges of the previous eighteen months, ever since I'd reconnected with *Sosai* in Rochester. Like a second skin that I wore between my own and the actual clothes on my back, I felt as though it would be mine forever.

I carried two cases of *Budo Karate Illustrated* with me to Tokyo in hopes of selling them. The entire Kyokushin world would be there in the days leading up to Mas Oyama's funeral, and I didn't have any qualms about selling copies to that crowd, since selling them was *Sosai's work*, after all.[76] There was no question that my finances were tight, with an enormous balance due to the printer in Montgomery, and that trip to Japan became the first of several overseas trips in which I would carry with me more books than cash, and rely – fairly successfully – on sales to keep food on the table, while at the same time struggling to amass funds and pay off debt.

Anticipating some difficulty making ends meet for two weeks in Tokyo – and knowing that I couldn't be sure until I got there if I could count on Judd for a place to stay – I opted for the cheapest ticket my travel agent could find. That left me flying out of Toronto again, despite the hardship that always seemed to haunt me every time I got near that city. I would have had to pay more than the cost of my plane ticket from North Carolina to Toronto in excess luggage fees for the two sixty-pound

---

[76] As *uchi deshi* we often referred to work for Kyokushin or *Honbu* as *Sosai's work*.

boxes of books I carried with me, so on the recommendation of my travel agent, I opted to go that far by train. In Washington, DC, I would switch to a sleeper car that would arrive at about midnight at Grand Central Station in Manhattan and remain there for five hours before an early-morning departure for Toronto. After Washington, I'd be able to stretch out and sleep straight through the night.

There was a relatively new Kyokushin branch chief outside of Toronto named Wade Stogran – I knew him from tournaments in Rochester, Atlantic City and Montreal – and he was more than happy to put me up for a couple of days so that I could train in his dojo and sell some books to his students. I was still eyeing a *Canadian Kyokushin Yearbook* for volume two of *Budo Karate Illustrated*, and he was one of the branch chiefs who would have to buy in to the project.

Given my history of bad luck associated with Toronto, I wasn't at all surprised that someone banged on my sleeper-car door at 2:30 in the morning, parked there under Madison Square Garden, to tell me that the train was on fire and that I had to get off immediately.

I'd removed the frame of a long-distance trail pack and figured out how to use a collection of my students' old white belts to tie the two sixty-pound boxes of books to it, so that I could carry them and still have my hands free for my luggage. When I carried that barbell equal to my body weight across my shoulders to the top of Grandfather Mountain, I'd weighed 165 pounds, and this 120 pounds of books plus luggage was certainly reminiscent. The only way I could fit it all into my tiny sleeper compartment had been to break the pack down, and I took a quick look out into the hallway to judge whether the threat looked imminent enough to abandon my cargo.

Happily, I saw no flames.

The hallway was full of a bitter smoke, though – the train car's batteries were suffering an electrical meltdown – and so, trying not to breathe, I took the time to pull everything together, and spent the rest of the night in the Amtrak VIP lounge with the others who'd been in my sleeper car. The rail company booked us coach seats the rest of the way to Toronto, and even gave us cash refunds for the entire cost of our journeys. I thought of *Sosai* in the 1960s, performing one of the first ever demonstrations of Japanese karate in America in the Garden[77] over my

---

[77] I.e. the Madison Square Garden arena.

head, and I smiled to myself at the fact that the rude awakening in the middle of the night was so well worth the crisp new cash bills that I added to the insufficient few in my wallet.

David Bunt, my one-time *sempai* at *Honbu*, the same one who'd helped to interpret for *Sosai* in Rochester eighteen months earlier, came over and met me in the lounge during the breakfast hour. His job on Wall Street was the reason why he had *not* opened a dojo for *Sosai* right away despite his branch chief appointment, but he'd ordered a stack of books anyway, and I'd made arrangements to meet him there and hand deliver them.

Come to think of it, I know that I didn't break into the two cases of books that I carried with me until I got to Japan, so I must have actually left North Carolina with closer to a hundred books than just eighty.

Bunt *Sempai* was happy to see the books, and his initial impression was favorable. He complimented their professional appearance and told me that he looked forward to reading one. He confessed that he hadn't been at all disappointed to see his name in my article about *Sosai* in *Black Belt* Magazine, which had finally come out around that time. I'd included a photo of many of us at *Honbu* with *Sosai*, David was in the photo, and since he was an American and it was an American magazine, I'd mentioned his name in the caption.

Wade Stogran picked me up at the train station in Toronto, and I spent the next two nights on a cot in his basement guest room. His dojo was actually in that same basement – it was a big basement – and we had a surprisingly great training there with about thirty of his students. I was starting to get my first taste of the VIP treatment I would receive in the Kyokushin world, and particularly in eastern Canada, after the publication of my book. Just as all Western Kyokushin people were hungry for Kyokushin media, the eastern Canadians also seemed hungry for Kyokushin celebrities, and my having published a book – and having been a personal student for two years of a man that most of them had only dreamed of one day having a chance to meet – apparently made me fit the bill in a still-a-junior kind of way. I taught part of the class that night, and it was a very successful training in spite of the mortifying fact that I inadvertently broke two of *Sensei* Stogran's wife's toes. We were sparring lightly as part of a rotation, and I lifted my knee to block as Mrs. Stogran – a blue or yellow belt – kicked my shin and snapped two toes. I was very embarrassed, of course, but they were very understanding because it was an accident that had been more attributable to the unusual trajectory of her kick than to the way that I blocked. I sold a dozen more copies of my book that day, and didn't know quite what to make of it when the students all wanted me to sign their copies as if I was some kind of celebrity.

The 1991 group photograph, showing all of us together at *Honbu*, that my *sempai* David Bunt was happy to find in my *Black Belt* Magazine article. The occasion is the graduation ceremony of three of my *uchi deshi sempai*, two years ahead of my class. Those mentioned by name in this book: 1. *Sosai* Mas Oyama seated at center. 2. My Algerian-French *Sempai* Mocaram is immediately behind *Sosai*. 3. That's me to his right in grey sweater. 4. *Ryoobo-san* is the second female face from the left, standing. 5. My *Sempai* Ulrika is the fifth female face from left, in the back row, with blonde hair. 6. Judd is just over my left shoulder. 7. Komukai is just over my right. 8. Yamakage is just over Mocaram's left shoulder, and 9. Suzuki is over Yamakage's left. 10. David Bunt is bearded, standing near the right edge of the photo. 11. That's Hayashidani-*san*, face cut by the right edge of the photo, and finally, 12. that's Yokomiso *Shihan*, seated in the same row as *Sosai*, all the way at the right.

Like the last time I'd been in Tokyo, for my grading five weeks before *Sosai's* death, I had a detailed agenda *and* some long hours to look forward to, knowing that it was going to be a challenge to fill them, half-broke in a foreign capital.

I traveled to Japan early enough so that I could get to Kyokushin's annual weight category tournament in Osaka, provided I could find a place to stay and make affordable arrangements to get myself there. I was not yet ashamed to be attending a tournament as a journalist. I had only just turned twenty-three, and as a late bloomer in a body that felt like it was twenty, I believed myself to have all the time in the world to gain the fighting experience that I imagined necessary to my future of teaching karate in America. I'd fought in the Osaka tournament myself three years earlier, and I compared myself to other Americans of my generation and knew that that experience alone put me well ahead of the game.

I'd already shot those two earlier photo essays of Matsui on my two prior trips to Japan, and I wondered if this time I might be so lucky as to arrange a third with Kyokushin's most recent world champion, Midori Kenji. I'd watched in person as he foolishly allowed overconfidence to get the better of him in 1990's All-Japan Tournament when, still minutes before his final fight against Masuda Akira was finished, he started to sport a celebratory smile of "I've won already" since he knew he had the ten-kilogram weight disadvantage that would give him the fight by default if he could just go the distance. Moments later, Masuda – the same Masuda Akira who I'd fight in his 100-man *kumite* later that year – stunned him with a *jodan mawashi geri* to the head, and Midori reeled in shock as his victory slipped away. A year later, however, at *Sosai's* last world tournament in 1991 – the one I'd worked to support as a 20-year-old *uchi deshi* – the Japan champion Masuda and his runner-up Midori Kenji faced each other once again in the final, and Midori had learned his lesson.

This time he didn't stop fighting until he'd won.

The most important mission of my trip, however, was meeting with *Budo Karate Illustrated's* technical advisor, Kyokushin's new chairman, Matsui *Kancho*. *Honbu* would be a madhouse a week later as Kyokushin people started to roll in from all over the world, and I came to *Honbu* two weeks early exactly in order to avoid that chaos. I met with Matsui in *Sosai's* office soon after my arrival, and he was very friendly and encouraging, just as he'd been in all of our meetings thus far. "You must wait until after the memorial service and until after the international branch chief meeting," he told me concerning my magazine. "After that you should write me a proposal telling me how you plan to manage the magazine's proceeds, and then we can talk about your project's future."

Even though Matsui had chosen *Sosai's* sofa rather than his desk, I had been trained by *Sosai* how to interact with the man that occupied that office, and I answered accordingly with an "Osu!" in which there was no "but. . ." At that time I did not sense any danger to my project, and the fact that Matsui's primary interest had been in "the magazine's proceeds" didn't then raise for me any flags of concern.

My *sempai* from when I was at *Honbu*, Ulrika, a blonde-haired, blue-eyed Swede who had been married to Yuhi *Sempai* [78] for some time, translated for us that day. I was interested that, although Matsui seemed very much his straitlaced self, Ulrika made no effort to sit up straight during our meeting. She slumped all the way down in the armchair in which she sat to the point where it was more her neck that was bent by the back of the chair than her waist. She was wearing a pullover sweatshirt and had her hands hidden in the bottom of its pouch-like uni-pocket. She mentioned something about how hard they'd been working without sleep. I was certain that she would never have been so relaxed in *Sosai's* presence, and I wondered what that meant for Matsui.

Ulrika told me how Peter Chong, *Sosai's* oldest friend and student in Singapore, had called up sobbing on the phone, how he had kept calling and how he hadn't been able to stop crying.

Matsui gave me permission to train at *Honbu* while I was in Japan, and he did not object to my plans to photograph the Osaka tournament. The only recollection I have of Matsui's reaction to my photo shoot with Midori is that, after the fact, I read in his eyes that he disapproved. Retrospectively I wonder if trouble was already starting to brew between the two of them. Yuhi *Sempai* would wind up being a supporter of Midori's splinter Shin-Kyokushin Organization, and Matsui's interpreter in those first few weeks following *Sosai's* death, Yuhi *Sempai's* wife Ulrika, would presumably have gone with him.

I can't remember how I made contact with Midori, although I must have gained some assistance at *Honbu* to arrange a meeting. My former roommates Suzuki and Kuruda were both working in the office at *Honbu*, and one of them probably helped me to make the connection. Unlike when I had first made contact with Matsui, I now had copies of my book in hand, and it would have been much easier to convince Midori to

---

[78] Yuhi *Sempai*, who graduated like Ishida *Sempai* some four or five years before we entered the dormitory, was very kind to all of us foreigners while in the dormitory. Paradoxically, he was also the ringleader of *Honbu*'s mafia-style hierarchy during my first year in the dormitory, the one that *Sosai* ultimately disapproved of and moved to break, the one that led to the dormitory's atmosphere of fear and intimidation during my first year there.

participate, since I was able to show him a quantitative measure of success. The pictures that I shot of Midori in *Honbu's* second-floor dojo were not as successful as the ones Midas had taken of Matsui — my film speed was too fast and the pictures came out grainy — but there were certainly a handful that I'd be able to use. I'd hoped to include, alongside the photos, an interview that would reveal how Midori had trained for his victory at the world tournament, and he invited me to accompany him across Tokyo by train so that we could talk.

This grainy photograph was taken by the author in 1994 of 5th World Open Karate Tournament champion Midori Kenji, right. The photo was taken in *Honbu* Dojo ten days before *Sosai's* memorial service. The *uchi deshi* posing with Midori was one of the *koohai* of my *koohai*, Nick and Mahashi. This is the dojo where I trained for 500 days of my life.

Midori told me he'd trained at least eight hours per day before the tournament, and I revealed my naïveté by asking him how many of those eight hours had been all-out hard training and how much of it had been — I imagined — stretching and drilling techniques at something less than the intensity of so much of what we'd done in Japan, which took us each time to our cardiovascular limits.

"Oh, all eight of them were all-out full-intensity training," he told me. "Of course. What did you think?"

I was stunned, because for the entirety of the time I'd been an *uchi deshi* at *Honbu*, our average was only three and a half hours of training per day. There were certainly times when we did five or six, and periods when we averaged four or five (certainly after we started to add our own self-training), but many of those times felt only barely survivable, because the intensity of the training was so extreme and because we *uchi deshi* almost always trained though the haze of having not yet recovered from the ass-kicking we'd received the training before. And at least in the beginning, ALL of our trainings had been ass-kickings, i.e. we'd been on the receiving end of such. Whether it was our *sempai* deciding we needed to do several hundred more jumping squats than we thought we could, whether it was training so hard in front of *Sosai* because not doing so when he was watching was unthinkable, or whether it was actually getting beaten up beneath the blows of our bigger, stronger *sempai*, nearly all the trainings that I did at *Honbu* could be counted as ass-kickings.

That was why I couldn't even imagine eight hours of intense training, day in and day out. I wouldn't be able to until years later, when, closer to the age Midori was then, I'd train myself for eight intense hours a day under the guidance of my third teacher, Sandor Brezovai in Hungary.[79] At my then still so green age of FOUR in the world of Japanese Kyokushin, however, when Midori said he trained eight hours a day, I was clueless enough to be stunned, because I could see in his expression that he was telling the truth.

I knew that *Sosai* had aspired to train more hours per day than he slept during his seclusion in the mountains. But that was *Sosai*. His story was the stuff of legends. Midori was a tiny little guy whom I'd thrown around on the beach in a sumo wrestling bout at *Honbu's* summer camp at Tateyama. Of course, the referee gave the bout to him when we both went down and out of bounds at the same time. I had been a wrestler in high school, though, and felt fairly confident, and although he was strong, wrestling with him had felt like wrestling with someone two weight classes down, since he was so small. I humored myself then to

---

[79] Sandor and I were both first-year *uchi deshi* at the same time. He was only in Japan for ninety days, from my third day in the dormitory to my ninety-third, but he was already a *shodan* then, and he had already become lightweight champion of Hungary. He is four years my senior and he become my third teacher when I lived in Hungary for two years, from 1996 to 1998.

believe the match had been called in his favor because of his celebrity.

If there was revenge to be had, though, Midori certainly had it the day of our photo shoot, because he decided to show me the intensity of his training rather than simply telling me about it. In the true spirit of my earliest *sempai* at *Honbu*, when the young Yuhi *Sempai* and his gang were operating more like a terror squad than like respected elders, Midori took me to his gym and thanked me for my hard work for Kyokushin by all but humiliating me soundly, not letting me stop long past the point when it was clear that I couldn't keep up with his workout.

The training was a brutal power-stamina workout, done in the gym with weights and body-building machines. The purpose of the exercise, I would understand very clearly years later when I trained with Sandor Brezovai, was to develop explosive muscular power that didn't diminish with repetition. Before that, weight lifting for me was what it had been in my high school gym class and again as an *uchi deshi*, when Judd and Nick and I had trained together in the basement of *Honbu* with the intention of "getting huge" – making ourselves as monstrous as possible to be able to take more punishment in fights without being beaten. We'd trained for bulk: a maximum of five sets per exercise with heavy weight, and a maximum of ten repetitions per set. Midori that day gave me my first taste of doing several tens of sets of several tens of repetitions each of the same exercises over and over again – tens of hundreds of reps in all – with weight that after one or two sets I could barely move anymore.

Four years later, Sandor would teach me to lift weights by the ton, emphasizing that the most important muscle to work during the training was the heart and lungs. On my heaviest day of training in Hungary, at least on the bench press, I pressed 100 kilograms (225 pounds) five hundred times in a single workout (56 tons in about forty sets). Reaching that point, however, took six months of day-in and day-out, carefully prescribed training that began with very high repetitions of very light weight, and eventually built up to eight hours per day. For my first several weeks of power-stamina training with Sandor, he had me press between two and three hundred reps of only 40 kilograms, for a total of only about five tons. Day by day after that, Sandor guided my training upwards until I was doing more like 40-ton workouts twice a day, after morning trainings of six-kilometer runs and 500 push-ups, sit-ups, and jumping squats, and before evening karate or heavy bag training in the dojo.

I was twenty-seven then, and had grown up quite a lot, having trained for two years in Korea before that.

Midori invited me to join him for just such a workout, however, without the benefit of those years of preparation – I had been mostly a full-time college student for the past two – and, much like when our *sempai* would offer us beer and we were required to drink, he would not let me stop following him in a frenzy around his gym, even long after my body could no longer do what he was doing. It seemed to me that it was funny to him, like it had been for Yuhi *Sempai's* gangsters when we were beginners and couldn't keep up. The image that stayed with me from my encounter with Midori that day was of him as he walked me back to the train station, pointing out a massage parlor and telling me that it was a whorehouse by imitating – since I didn't understand the Japanese word – the act of giving a blowjob, complete with his using his tongue to poke out the inside of his cheek as he moved his fist back and forth in front of his mouth. Of course he then rocked his head back and laughed, and I laughed with him, and it was nothing out of the ordinary. Boys will be boys, and Judd's and my idle conversations, for example, were certainly rarely publishable without a great deal of editing. What was remarkable about my exchange with the 27- or 28-year-old world champion, however, was that although he had shown me beyond a shadow of a doubt how strong he was – and more than that, how out of shape *I* was! – he made no effort whatsoever to show me why I should respect his character.

I had never seen Matsui so much as slump in his chair!

Fifty of us from *Honbu* went out drinking together that night, and Matsui didn't even have a sip.

* * *

I find it strange that my recollection of my trip to Osaka is so vague. Jet lag must have combined with the exhaustion of my previous year of working at such a breakneck pace without regular sleep. Midas was gone from my world then – I was back in Japan, where such nonsense never applied – and Midas's surging chemicals weren't there to veil the fatigue.

I traveled by car with a one-time *Honbu* office worker and dojo friend of mine named Hayashidani, and my *uchi deshi* classmates Yamakage and Suzuki. Kuruda was there too – he and Suzuki fought in the light- and middleweight categories – or was he? I find myself doubting that Kuruda was with us on the way south, as the trip was fairly vacation-like, he and I had fought together in the same tournament three years earlier, and Kuruda tended to be more serious before a tournament. In Osaka we stayed in the home of Hayashidani's parents, and it was the first time that I was ever in a private Japanese home. Hayashidani trained at *Honbu*, and although he was a few years older, he was at the same level in the dojo as me and my roommates, and he made friends particularly with the Japanese members of my class.

Hayashidani-*san* had a one-room apartment, so small that it didn't even have its own shower, about halfway between the dormitory and the public bath that we all frequented a kilometer or so away. Although I only stopped there once, I got the impression that his home had became something of a refuge for several of my roommates, where they could go to relax when our *sempai* in the dormitory were making it impossible to do so at home.

Hayashidani's parents were very kind – I imagine I was the first American ever to enter their home – and his father instructed me in the proper etiquette of sword viewing. He owned two vintage swords, squirreled away, I imagine, from before the war, and he showed me how to keep the blade facing myself as I held the sword vertically, and how to follow its edge with my gaze from the hilt end upwards to the tip. He was embarrassed that the swords were not in better shape, and he told me how expensive it was to have them polished. I felt very grateful for his hospitality.

One night we made an outing to a mountaintop overlook from which we could look down on the lights of Osaka. I was exhausted, and not very good company. On top of the sleepless semester and the jet lag, the beating my body had taken in Midori's gym left me feeling quite reduced, and even in some physical pain. I had almost forgotten how severely my brain's ability to process Japanese could shut down after a certain point. It took near total concentration to keep up with a Japanese conversation, particularly one among several people, and as much as I loved those guys as brothers, by the time I'd spent four days with them with no opportunity to speak English, I was quite miserable.

Hayashidani parked at an automated pay-parking lot during the tournament, the meter was apparently broken, and when the day was done we came out to find one of those heavy iron locks bolted onto his front left wheel. With some difficulty we tracked down someone who was acquainted with the parking-lot owner – he was a piglike fat *yakuza* underling wearing boxer shorts and an obvious rug – and for a few tense moments I wondered if there was going to be a fight. Hayashidani became desperate as he calculated how much money he would owe by morning, and I could feel Yamakage beside me gearing up to bash the fat man. In the end, though, we realized that the *yakuza* wasn't responsible for the parking lot, or for the guy who owned it, and we went home by taxi and returned the next day to bail out Hayashidani's car. The trip's motto became for us, "*Osaka debu ki o tsukete!* (Beware the Osaka fat guy!)", since when Yamakage, Suzuki and I parted ways with Hayashidani and boarded a train for Tokyo, one of my former roommates told Hayashidani to be careful of the "Osaka fat guy," and we all laughed.

Shooting photos at the tournament through that same haze of fatigue, I longed for a return to the blissful release of the Midas level of intensity. I was learning action photography the hard way, and I was lucky to walk away with three or four usable shots out of every roll of high-speed film. I chose two fighters, my former roommates Kuruda and Nick, to photograph throughout the tournament from start to finish, because I had best access to them and I figured I'd be able to attach interviews to the photos I hoped to include in *Budo Karate Illustrated*'s second issue. The tournament was too huge to hope to get a representative set of photographs for the whole event, so I resolved to follow those two fighters, one Japanese and one *gaijin*, as illustrative examples. Win, lose or draw, documentation of their experience would be eye-opening to a North American readership that had never even been to a tournament in Japan.

I chose Kuruda over Suzuki because Kuruda was so serious about his training and because he had trained so hard, not only for three years, but for this particular tournament. But in the end he was unlucky, and was defeated fairly early on. I should have been taking pictures of Suzuki, because although he made fun of himself – and we joined him – for doing nothing but *tobakko kekko* ("cigarette training") for the weeks prior to the tournament, he won fight after fight in the middleweight division, making it all the way to the best sixteen (if I remember correctly) before being defeated. I joined my friends and shouted encouragement until I thought my vocal cords would rupture – of course I did! He'd acted as my second at my *nidan* grading! I knew Suzuki well enough to be able to tell, from his color and the look in his eye, that he was at his body's limit, but he stubbornly refused to be beaten, as only our dormitory's Batman could have done.

He too had been working without sleep for weeks in *Honbu's* office after *Sosai* died, and on beer and cigarettes he had made it through. His body must have fought on sheer muscle memory, drilled into him over three years of training as an *uchi deshi*.

My one-time *uchi deshi koohai*, Japan's future K-1 champion, Nicolas Pettas, in a photograph that I took of him missing his target and failing to break a relatively huge stack of boards during the *tameshiwari* round of 1994's Osaka Tournament.

Nick had a real shot at winning the heavyweight division, at a time when foreigners didn't yet win Japanese tournaments, and I remember being a bit annoyed at his "Have no doubt. I'm going to win," attitude. There was no humility about Nick then, certainly not around me. He was so clearly so much stronger than I could ever imagine myself becoming. I think he actually came straight out and told me around that time that "You're not a *sempai* for me, Ligo," and I let it roll off my back because, after all, what could I say? I had failed to graduate, and he'd gone all the way. He was a contender to become the strongest fighter in Japan. Twenty mediocre guys had just that year mopped *Honbu* Dojo's floor with my carcass, and one of his *koohai* from Denmark, who wouldn't even have caused Nick to break a sweat, came that close to sending my head flying off into the crowd. I was in awe of how strong Nick had become, and there would come a time in my own training when what he and Judd accomplished would become an inspiration to me, because I could remember a time when the three of us were all on the same track.

I don't recall what place Nick took that year, but I remember watching him warm up through the lens of my camera, and his *jodan mawashi geri*, which arced up, over, and down to where he'd drop the front center of his massive shin bone on his opponent's jaw from above, was terrifying to behold. Forget about the knockout! I could imagine myself getting hit by one of those kicks and spending the rest of my life in a wheelchair.

When Nick fought, I cheered encouragement for all that I was worth. I cheered for my friend and roommate who came into the dormitory as a gawky kid rapping Ice-T rhymes and reading Spiderman comic books in Danish, I cheered for my *koohai* whom I taught his very first lessons in Japanese, who broke two toes in his very first training at *Honbu* and then went back to training six weeks later and broke the same two on his other foot in his second.

I was also, though, content that he didn't win. I did *not* cheer for the Nicolas who told me with such cocksureness that he was going to win, and that "You're not a *sempai* for me, Ligo." I had never once put on any kind of airs of being superior to him, and I wondered why was it even necessary for him to tell me that I was not?

During the tournament's opening ceremony, the new Matsui *Kancho* stood silently beside the triple pillars of his authority over Mas Oyama's *International Karate Organization*: Yoshiaki Umeda, Yuzo Goda, and Hatsuo Royama. He held a framed photograph of *Sosai*, who had been dead for less than six weeks. When I took a picture of Kyokushin's future spiritual leader I had no idea that it was Hatsuo Royama, one of the men standing patiently beside Matsui, who was ultimately destined to become that leader instead.

All eyes were then focused on the one in the middle: Matsui Shokei, proudly displaying an image of Mas Oyama's death as if he'd pulled the trigger himself and wanted to show the world all that he'd gained.

The new *Kancho* (Chairman) Matsui Shokei, holding a framed picture of the recently deceased Mas Oyama during the opening ceremony of 1994's Osaka Weight Category Tournament, a matter of days before Mas Oyama's memorial service. To his right is Dr. Yoshiaki Umeda, the vice-chairman of the nonprofit foundation Mas Oyama founded to protect the Kyokushin legacy from those who would use it after his death for financial gain. Flanking the photograph, at extreme left, is Yuzo Goda, perhaps the earliest of Mas Oyama's students still associated with Kyokushin at the time of Mas Oyama's death, and at the extreme right, Hatsuo Royama, future chairman and co-founder of Kyokushin-kan International.

TWENTY-FOUR

BACK IN TOKYO, I met Mas Oyama's youngest daughter Kikuko at *Honbu*, and we struck up a friendly conversation. Although she and I hadn't spent a lot of time together, I knew her from when I was an *uchi deshi*, and I considered her a friend.

She was, after all, Mas Oyama's daughter.

I had been fascinated with Kikuko from the first time I met her as an *uchi deshi*, because she was Master Choi's cousin – Master Choi's father was *Sosai's* oldest brother – and the friendly acquaintance that she and I shared was left over from that time. "I've always been curious about the Korean side of my family," she told me when we first spoke. Apparently *Sosai's* Japanese family had not been afforded the opportunity to meet his Korean one, and Kikuko had never met any of her father's many Korean relatives, let alone her first cousin, Master Choi.

The youngest of *Sosai's* three daughters, Kikuko was my age minus a year or less, and since she'd spent several years of her schooling in New York City, she spoke English like an American. She was somewhat less than fluent, but having learned to speak English from Americans, she tended to talk a million miles per hour without much effort to restrain whatever was on her mind. I experienced most Japanese people as somewhat reserved. In stark contrast, the young Miss Oyama seemed almost to want to come across as shocking, from the way she openly discussed personal issues such as boyfriends and experiences she'd had in America, particularly those of which her father surely would not have approved.

When I was an *uchi deshi* and she was eighteen or nineteen like me, it was almost as if she wanted to emphasize, "My father might be the god of modern karate, but I'm just a normal girl, see?"

Me with *Sosai's* youngest daughter Kikuko (my first teacher Master Choi's first cousin) a decade after the 1994 encounter described in this chapter.

I mentioned in an earlier chapter how once Kikuko sat next to her father on the *shinzen* at the front of *Honbu's* second-floor dojo during a brown- and black-belt class that I attended, and how I found myself, for the first time, more interested in impressing someone in the dojo other than *Sosai*. We were practicing a *kata* called *pinan sono go ura* for about forty-five minutes nonstop, and I was in good form that day. There's a leap in *pinan sono go*, about halfway through, in which we used to try to jump as high as we could, and I remember performing each *kata* like it was my last in a quest to make myself visible to *Sosai*, yes, but also to Master Choi's pretty young cousin Kikuko. There were twenty of us in the dojo that night, and I jumped higher than all the rest, landed with better balance, and focused my techniques so that the soaked sleeves of my *dogi* popped louder than anyone else's. *Sosai* pointed me out to his 18- or 19-year-old daughter, and I was all the more encouraged to continue to make a spectacle of myself.

I suppose that at nineteen, Kikuko and I were about matched in terms of maturity.

"That's Ligo from America," I heard *Sosai* say. "He was one of my nephew's students." Kikuko followed with a question that I didn't hear, but imagined might have been "Oh, I see. Which nephew are you referring to, Father?" She had leaned her ear towards him with a poise beyond her years. In stark contrast to the way she behaved when she was speaking English to either me or Judd, she kept herself very poised when she was in her father's company. She sat with her back straight and – certainly there at the front of the dojo – she didn't engage in idle conversation. Her father answered her, and she half-bowed acknowledgement that she'd understood. There was no follow-up discussion, but I watched her eyes out of the corner of mine, and I could tell that she'd gotten the clarification she sought.

She always struck me as remarkably dignified in her father's company, but that was no great surprise, because so of course were we.

I would realize in later years – and comment frequently to my own students – how much I had cheated myself in many of my trainings at *Honbu*, by holding back in an effort to conserve energy and postpone as much pain as possible. Training at *Honbu*, all of it for me for nearly two years, hurt. If I wasn't literally being beaten, I was often being pushed to the limits of my endurance and not allowed to stop when it felt as though I couldn't possibly do another repetition. As a result, I often held back, in an effort both not to hurt during the current exercise and to have the energy in reserve to be able to do the next one . . . and there was always a next one. It was largely due to the training that I did in front of *Sosai* that I even knew I had a higher gear. In front of *Sosai* I was always on fire. It seemed so silly not to do every single movement in front of the creator of Kyokushin Karate with every single scrap of power that I could muster, and I almost always did. I got beat up in *kumite* all the time in the dojo, but when *Sosai* was watching I was like an animal possessed, and that was when I won my most significant victories.

I wonder if *Sosai* had a different impression of me altogether than my peers did. Among them, I was mediocre at best. *Sosai* often sang my praises, however, in a "you should try to be like Ligo" kind of way that must have baffled my roommates. It was in much the same way that *Sosai* complimented the vigor with which I trained that day to his daughter.

I was in good form that evening, but the same certainly couldn't always have been said, not even a majority of the time.

It might have been that same weekend that Kikuko joined her father when he came to eat with us in the dormitory. *Sosai* emphasized in his teaching – and he was as serious as a heart attack – that only half of our fighting strength would come from the dojo, and that the other half would come from the dining room. Every Saturday night when he ate with us in the dormitory was a testament to that fact. He insisted that we eat until our bellies burst, and once we were beyond full, he'd often send one of the third-year guys out to buy watermelons, and give each of us sometimes an entire half all to ourselves. Consuming that watermelon was always a test of will, because it was essentially like drinking a half-gallon of water on an already bursting stomach. There was that one night when, again bucking for *Sosai's* recognition in front of Kikuko, I scraped my watermelon rind with my spoon deep into the green to remove every single cell of edible fruit, just as I knew *Sosai* expected. "*Soo yo! Takusan tabete*, Ligo!" *Sosai* said. "That's it, eat a lot!" I was immediately ashamed, as *Sosai* went on in Japanese to use me as an example of how we should fight to develop our spiritual strength even in the dining room, by making sure we didn't leave even a morsel of food uneaten.

One afternoon, sitting on the curb in front of *Honbu*, where Kikuko and I shared the only conversations we had when I was an *uchi deshi* – she wasn't allowed in the dormitory, and I was barely allowed out of it – she told me she remembered eating with her father in the dormitory when she was a little girl, and that it was a majority who had to excuse themselves to throw up before returning to eat more, rather than just one or two every once in a while, as was the case when I was in the dormitory. She told me, in fact, that as a girl she'd brought buckets for my long-graduated *uchi deshi sempai* to throw up in. The word she actually used was that she'd "held" the buckets for them while they threw up, and the impression she conveyed with her eyes was that she cared for her *uchi deshi* brothers so much that she would make even such a sacrifice as that. "I felt so sorry for them!" she said, and I could see in her eyes that her sympathy was genuine.

In my weaker moments as an *uchi deshi*, I tended to feel kind of sorry for us too! – and so we certainly had at least that in common.

As bold as it might seem to my readers who are familiar with Mas Oyama's fame, I considered myself to be as close to a son as any American could be to my first teacher, Master Choi, and I looked at Kikuko even then as if she were something like my second cousin. My heart broke to see her again during the week of her father's memorial service, because not only had she just lost a father, but (at least as I saw it) that grief seemed likely to be compounded by her having had less access to *Sosai* as a father during his lifetime than she must have wished. Certainly to all outward appearances *Sosai* had been "Karate first! Karate second! Karate third! And karate fourth!" and it was a common impression, discussed as far back as when I was an adolescent student of Master Choi, that *Sosai's* wife and daughters suffered to some extent from his single-minded dedication to karate.

From as early as when I was fourteen, long before I'd ever met Kikuko, Master Choi spoke of how Mas Oyama had dreamed of being like a modern-day Musashi – married to the sword and no other – and how he had always had to struggle to care for his family while setting the example of single-minded devotion to karate first, second and third in the eyes of his students. Master Choi spoke of Mas Oyama's daughters as "spoiled" because their father could often afford to take care of them financially more than he was ever accessible to them emotionally, and I knew that impression to have come from a firsthand dialogue with his uncle.

In the kind of conversation that two adults might have about one of their children who had not yet matured, *Sosai* himself described his daughters as spoiled, and he expressed regret both for that fact and for the fact that he could not be there more for them due to his dedication to karate. Jacques and Annie had helped *Sosai* keep an eye on both Kikuko and at least one older sister when they'd lived and studied in New York, and I'd heard them both echo the same sentiment. Meeting Kikuko this time in June of 1994, it was therefore with some self-congratulation that I chose to give her the benefit of the doubt and trust that she was less spoiled and wayward than I'd been told. To me, she was the charming flesh-and-blood child of the father of modern-day karate, and the flesh-and-blood cousin of the man whom I had come into adulthood crediting with saving my life. I wasn't one to pass judgment without seeing for myself.

On this particular afternoon in Ikebukuro, less than six weeks after her father's death, Kikuko had a yoga class to go to across Tokyo, and she asked me to accompany her as a bodyguard.

I was a little taken aback, of course, by the reason she gave for wanting an escort, and I thought at first that she was appealing to my sense of duty as an *uchi deshi* to care for and protect *Sosai* and his family, as if I might not otherwise have wanted to spend the afternoon with her. I couldn't imagine why she felt the need for protection, but her putting the invitation in those terms made my going with her obligatory even if I hadn't wanted to accompany her simply because I had free time and I considered her a friend. It became clear as we spent the afternoon together traveling across Tokyo, however, that she was in fact genuinely afraid for her own personal safety, and that her inviting me to join her as a bodyguard had nothing to do with any kind of social insecurity.

She believed – of all things! – that her father had been murdered, and that she was in danger as well for daring to suggest it.

Her father's cancer had started in his stomach, she told me, and then moved later into his lungs, and that's presumably what had been finally killing him when last I'd met him in the hospital three months earlier. But Kikuko went into detail that day about how she believed her father to have been given a lethal dose of medication in his final hour – nearly ten times what had been prescribed, she said – and how she had called from New York and made a specific request that his body not be cremated so that an autopsy could be performed, but that he had been cremated anyway. Apparently Dr. Umeda (*Sosai's* longtime associate and ranking member of the *Kyokushin Shogakukai* nonprofit foundation that he'd founded with the intention that it preserve and protect everything that was positive about Kyokushin) had signed the cremation order – or otherwise exerted some kind of influence on her mother to convince her to sign the order before the autopsy could be done. Kikuko went on to tell me that an *uchi deshi* who had been stationed at *Sosai's* bedside (presumably one of Nicolas and Mahashi's *koohai*; I didn't recognize the name) had disappeared from the face of the Earth from the time of *Sosai's* death. The implication, of course, was that his body was in a landfill somewhere because he'd been either party or witness to *Sosai's* murder, and that the cremation had been rushed to hide the evidence.

"Surely someone can locate him?" I said, referring to the missing *uchi deshi*. "Are the police involved?" I was struggling with a grain of salt to comprehend all that she was telling me. "Surely he's got to be around somewhere. Japan's not such a big place."

"No, he's vanished completely," she said. "And don't you think it's strange that my father didn't sign his own will?"

"Why? Did he not?"

"No, and the reason that we were told was that he was too weak to hold a pen. But I know for a fact that on the day he died he signed five of his books to be given away as gifts."

"But why would anyone want to murder your father?"

Although I had never perceived Kikuko as anything but a genuinely sweet, innocent girl who liked to talk a little too much about personal matters and who sometimes seemed to be trying to get herself into trouble in a bid for attention, I struggled hard just then with the warnings I'd gotten from a significant few of my elders that this sweet, innocent girl shouldn't be completely trusted. While Kikuko was a student in New York, Jacques' wife Annie had told me how the then 17- or 18-year-old had boasted of working in a club of less than admirable repute, and of being regularly exposed to illegal drug use by her peers. (Kikuko had mentioned as much to me, and she was not referring to substances as harmless as marijuana.) Annie confessed a suspicion that Kikuko had been part of the club's onstage entertainment, rather than merely a waitress as she'd claimed.

18-year-olds in America can take off their clothes on stage in adult clubs, but they have to be at least twenty-one to serve alcohol.

I didn't know what to believe – and it was none of my business – but the fact that Kikuko might have led Annie to believe such a thing made total sense to me . . . even if it wasn't true. Kikuko always seemed to be trying to make herself more noticed by her father; no one in America was in as regular and intimate contact with *Sosai* concerning his family as Jacques and Annie, and Kikuko would have known that. Kikuko at times seemed to be trying to shock me into giving her the attention she hungered for. Giving her the benefit of the doubt that day, however, I told myself that it would be pretty easy for her to shock an audience such as Jacques and Annie by hinting that she'd had exposures and experiences that she might never actually have had.

Dating a guy who uses drugs, for example, is not necessarily the same thing as using them yourself.

Whatever the truth of Kikuko's involvement in scenes her father wouldn't have approved of, it was clear that she had a penchant for inviting at least the suggestion of trouble upon herself. Given her position as one of Kyokushin's "first daughters," it was easy for me to forgive her and overlook it. I flattered myself that I was a fairly good judge of character, particularly of women when I had them to myself and could look them in the eye. I had Kikuko and her eyes to myself that day, and if I didn't unquestioningly believe what she was telling me, I at least believed beyond a doubt that she believed it. And that made me extremely nervous. If what she was telling me was true, it could turn my entire world upside down.

There was no question that Kikuko was devastated by the sudden loss of her father. I could personally attest to the fact that he'd looked healthy and high-spirited just five weeks before his death. He'd looked so well, in fact, that I couldn't believe that he could possibly be dying. I didn't have any direct experience with lung cancer until years later, when I saw firsthand how quickly it could reduce a man from vibrant and optimistic to right within the inescapable clutches of death. I can't remember exactly how long Kikuko told me it had been since she'd seen her father – she'd been in New York – but since *Sosai's* health apparently went downhill so fast toward the end, I can imagine that even a short time could have passed with almost unbelievable changes. If Kikuko's eyes didn't fill with tears when she talked of curling up on her father's lap and being held by him like a child, as recently as that same year, it only revealed the extent to which she was still in shock that her father was dead.

"People never saw us together being father and daughter," she told me, "but he was a wonderful father and an amazingly gentle man, and he held me like he wanted me to feel held like that forever."

At that, *I* wanted to cry. And I was one hundred percent of the impression that even though she seemed to be suffering more from shock than grief, the young Kikuko Oyama was in no condition to be deliberately untruthful. That was why, in the end, I would take what she told me as at least somehow grounded in truth. "Behind even every lie," the expression goes, "there's always some glimmer of the real story."

Among all the things she mentioned that day, Kikuko talked of her father's love life. I can't remember the name of the pretty young assistant that the 70-year-old *Sosai* had working in his office whom Kikuko told me her mother had fired because she'd suspected that she'd been *Sosai's* lover. "People might be surprised," Kikuko told me, "because he was seventy, but my father's libido was apparently still very much intact, and we believe that not only was this young assistant his lover, but she also had an allegiance to someone with less than admirable intentions towards us and my father." This made me think immediately of Yuhi *Sempai's* wife Ulrika having been brought in at the last minute as an interpreter for Matsui – apparently to fill a vacancy! – when it was well known to me that she wasn't even training at *Honbu* anymore by the time of *Sosai's* death. My mind was racing for evidence to either support or dismiss as nonsense what Kikuko was telling me. For a fleeting moment, my mind brushed by the recollection of calling *Honbu* at Christmastime. *Sosai's* assistant had said to me, "Why don't you ask him yourself?" and handed him the phone so fast that there wasn't even time for her to ask him first if he wanted to talk directly to me.

Could that earlier Japanese interpreter have been the assistant to whom Kikuko had referred?

How healthy and vibrant he'd seemed, how at ease, and how easy to talk to! And he hadn't always seemed that way to me.

Jacques and Annie, *Sosai's* oldest and closest friends in America, welcoming *Sosai* (center) to New York in 1992. Bill Scott, left, was a U.S. branch chief under Mas Oyama at the time, and a U.S. Marshal.

Could Sosai *have been murdered? And if so, why on Earth would anyone want to hurt him?*

"Come on, Ligo," Kikuko said. "My father was an extremely powerful man. You loved him and I loved him, but you have to realize that powerful people make powerful friends, but they make powerful enemies as well. He didn't get where he was merely by making everyone love and respect him."

"But what on Earth would anyone have to gain?" I asked, doing my best to defeat what I hoped was a paranoid overreaction on her part.

"Kyokushin!" she said. "And who owns the rights to the most famous name in Japanese karate! *Sosai's* will left everything he owned to Matsui. He didn't even leave enough money to my mother so that she'll able to keep the house we live in together!"

"Karate first! Karate second! Karate third! And karate fourth!" I could hear *Sosai* saying.

"He didn't leave his family anything?" I asked, confused.

"Not according to the will that was presented," she said. "It says he left everything to Matsui and asked him to take care of my family, but set aside no money for him with which to do so. We don't even believe that the will reflects my father's actual wishes. We don't believe that he wrote it."

"But come on! How is that possible, Kik'ko? Your father was the chairman of a twelve-million-member organization in 130 countries around the world. How could there possibly be any confusion over what his intentions were for his organization after he died?"

"Well, we don't believe that he knew he was going to die when he did. It was as if he hadn't yet decided. He may have been sick, but his head was clear, and I'm certain that if he was sure he wanted to leave everything to Matsui, he would have made it completely clear that that's what he wanted. He would at least have signed his will."

"But how can a will even be legal in the first place if it's not signed?"

"According to Japanese law, he can dictate his will to five witnesses, whose job it is to record it for him, and that's what we were told he did. We're investigating, but we believe the will to be illegal. According to the law, the five witnesses have to be completely unrelated. If it can be shown that any two of the five had any kind of preexisting relationship, even if they just met once, it's enough to make the will illegal."

"And?" I said.

"And we believe that at least two of the five knew each other," she said, "and we believe that we can prove it."

"You mean you plan to fight it?" I asked, and a wave of fear hit me in my midsection. *How easy it is,* I reasoned, *that Mas Oyama died and left everything to Matsui, if Matsui goes right on into the future playing the exact same role that Sosai played! It's so simple. It's so convenient. But what if it's not going to be so simple? What would that mean to me? What would it mean to my vision for the future? What impact would it have on the work that Sosai entrusted to me to do in America?*

"It's hard to believe that the will was even dictated by my father," Kikuko continued. "It can't have been. It speaks of the foundation that my father established in the present tense, as if it still exists. But my father knew that its registration had expired. He knew that it no longer existed, and yet the will speaks of it as if it was still a legal entity. The words in his will cannot be his. Not everyone knew that the foundation was dormant, but *Sosai* did, and the words of his will, therefore, cannot have been his." [80]

I was becoming lost. I didn't know anything about a foundation. I had never considered the role that the ownership of the Kyokushin name might have in a post-*Sosai* world. In typical Kikuko fashion, she was talking a million miles per hour, and her English wasn't quite up to the challenge of discussing legal topics of inheritance. My mind raced to keep up.

"And is this why you felt like you needed a bodyguard?" I asked as we stepped out of the train station into the street. I opened her umbrella and held it out from my side so that she could take my arm beneath it.

"If my family and I fight against people who were willing to kill my father to put the ownership of Kyokushin in Matsui's hands, do you think they would think twice about coming after me?"

Jesus! I all but looked over my shoulder, suddenly feeling as if *I* was being watched. As if on cue, Kikuko went on to tell me how she believed that she'd been under surveillance ever since she came back from New York. "Someone's been following me," she said. "I go out and use pay phones instead of using my own."

---

[80] Kikuko used the word "sleeping" to describe how the foundation's charter (Articles of Incorporation, perhaps) had not been correctly renewed by the appropriate deadline. "Dormant" is my word.

"Oh come on, Kik'ko! Are you serious? Do you know how crazy that sounds?"

"Yes, but Ligo, do you know who Matsui worked for those two years after he won the world tournament and then quit Kyokushin? People say that he went to work as a *companyman*, but do you know who owned the company? He worked for one of the most powerful *yakuza* in Japan. He carried money back and forth for him from Korea and became one of his most valuable assets. Who do you think sponsored Matsui, Ligo, while he was training for the tournaments that he won? He's got a Korean passport! What better person could the *yakuza* use to conduct business with their counterparts in Korea?"

"You mean the whole thing is a coup, and you believe that the Japanese mafia stepped in to take over Kyokushin?" I asked incredulously.

"Who else?" she said. "Matsui is only 32 years old! And he's such a great fighter. Everyone loves him and puts him up on a pedestal. He's got great charisma. What better person to place in charge as a puppet leader so that the *yakuza* can control a twelve-million-member international organization? Do you know how much money the name 'Kyokushin' generates every year in Japan alone?

"Anyway, thank you, Ligo," she said, "We're here."

"You mean that's it?" I asked, confused by the feeling that I was suddenly being dismissed.

"Yes, I'll be okay now. I can make it home on my own."

"What about the people who are following you?"

"I'll be okay, Ligo. Do you know the way back?"

"Yeah, I can find it," I said. "Are you sure?"

"See you again before you go home, okay? Bye!" Kikuko turned and disappeared into her class. It took me, on the other hand, an excruciatingly long moment to turn to go. If I hadn't already been shocked speechless by what she'd been telling me, I was doubly shocked by the way I'd been dismissed.

Had it all been a childish game, after all?

TWENTY-FIVE

Helen Ecks would be relieved to know that I became embroiled in a momentary romance during those two weeks in Japan. It was to become the first of several that would set me on a decade-long path away from her and back in the direction of normalcy.

Normalcy.

What was normal in a world without *Sosai* in it?

Already, on my way to Japan, I felt myself a freakish exception to the rule: My life would continue, stride unbroken, just as it had when *Sosai* was alive. I already knew that my two weeks in Tokyo would be occupied with tasks for the *Budo Karate Illustrated* project and with Mas Oyama's memorial service. But there would also be lots and lots of free, open hours during which I'd have very little to do.

That combination led me to turn some of my thoughts, during those long days alone, towards that city's unique opportunities to mingle with the opposite sex, for no other reason, perhaps, than the need to keep my mind off the more frightening realities that might otherwise have assailed me.

For the year since I'd left Lissa behind with Martha in the log house, I'd been as celibate as I was for two years in the dormitory in Japan, with the exception of one bizarre adventure that I also imagine would have given Helen hope – had she known enough to be concerned in the first place. At least, it probably would have given her hope right up to the moment the adventure was over, and it became clear that it had affected me emotionally about as much as if I had smoked a cigarette and then paused for a moment to smile about it.

During the semester I spent in Helen's class, pursuing women was the farthest thing from my mind for several reasons besides the fact that I was in love with her. The same was true of the next semester, when I was all but making love to Mother Earth and had nearly forgone sleep in the name of my creative endeavors. One night, however, an insecure but far from innocent young female friend of mine from the Café called me up on a Saturday in what turned out to be a bid to seduce me.

I was in my cottage in the backyard of my father's house, it was late, and when the phone rang I could only assume that there was some problem at the Café. My fears intensified when I recognized Erica's voice on the line, but I was a little bit baffled when she asked me what I was up to, instead of immediately launching into some tale of fast-food crisis.

"I'm reading *Henry V*," I told her. "Why? Have you finished it already?"

"No, I'm going to read it tomorrow," she said. "I was just curious what you were doing." There was something about her tone that made me raise an eyebrow.

"Aren't you at the Café?" I asked.

"No, I'm off," she said. "I traded shifts with Mike. I'm home. I've been lying here looking at a *Playboy* magazine and masturbating." She said it so matter-of-factly that my cardiovascular system forwent an entire cycle.

"Oh," I said, recovering quickly and assuming she was pulling my leg. "And why *Playboy*?"

"I subscribe to it," she said, "for the articles, and so I can see what it is that men find attractive in women."

"And that's why you look at pictures of naked women while you masturbate?" There was a long moment of silence on the other end of the line.

"And were you calling because you wanted to come over?" I added finally to break the silence.

The suggestive tone that I used was mostly a joke, although Erica had been one of the several young ladies I'd pursued two years earlier when I was working for the college dining service just after coming back from Japan. Even though I'd never managed to catch up with her because of her emotional entanglement with someone else, we had maintained somewhat of a flirtatious relationship since then.

"Okay, I'll come over," she said with so little hesitation as to imply, "Of course I want to come over, you dolt! Why did you think I was calling to tell you I was masturbating?"

"Which house is it?" she asked. I swallowed hard and understood for the first time that she was absolutely NOT joking. I suppose I was still in shock when I gave her directions, and I'm afraid that I don't have the option of making a long story short because there's not really any kind of long story to tell:

Erica came over and used me for the evening like something she might have bought at an adult novelty store, we showered together both times we thought we were done, and she spent the rest of the night sleeping peacefully but detached beside me. The next morning, she walked home while my parents were at church with the kids. Although I had battled with a myriad of second thoughts during the twenty minutes it took her to walk over from her apartment, in the end I didn't mind.

That's what friends are for, I thought. *Maybe it'll break the spell of all this other nonsense.*

Obviously, the Erica adventure did not break the spell that Helen had unknowingly cast. Although Erica was a friend and would become a closer one in years to come, the act at that time to me, too, meant little more than masturbation would have, and there were no repeat performances.

I suppose that as a one-time hedonist I'd been pretty much ruined by love in the case of Lissa, and whatever it was I was doing with Helen was on yet another plane altogether. Thoughts of the physical act still of course struck me as appealing enough to pursue whenever I had the energy, but even as I marveled that I might rather *not have* Helen for the rest of my life than ever once make love to another woman, I realized that I could be ruining myself for future chances of anything but sex at the most impersonal end of the spectrum.

It was in that kind of emotionally untouchable state that my experiment with a young woman named Akiko in Tokyo six months later started as an attempt not to be outdone by Judd, moved onwards towards an attempt to find out if I was still even capable of a Lissa-type romance in the aftermath of Helen, and finished as something entirely different.

* * *

Six months after the last time we'd survived Roppongi together, and eighteen months after his graduation, blond-haired, blue-eyed, built-like-a-bull Judd had become quite the Casanova of Tokyo. He wore a tailored tuxedo to work at his new upscale club in Roppongi, and he got paid enough to live fairly comfortably. He'd stayed on in his shitty little two-futon apartment to at least contemplate a return to training for the 1995 world tournament eighteen months later, and — like me, I suppose — he figured he just might as well make the most of all the idle time he had there in the interim. Except for the few days I was in Osaka with the Japanese, I spent the rest of my nights there in Judd's apartment.

Almost as soon as I arrived, we worked out a system in which he'd hang a towel outside his front door on the doorknob if he was inside with a woman and didn't want to be disturbed. That certainly got to be a bit of a drag. More than once that first week I sat out on his steps with my elbows on my knees and my face buried in my hands, battling thoughts of *Sosai's* death — alongside jet lag and general fatigue — and wishing that Judd would "hurry the hell up and send her home!" so that I could go in and sleep.

The women that emerged each time after he was through were never the same ones as the time before.

Halfway through the week, Judd brought one woman home who, he said, was "one of his repeats" and wouldn't care if I was inside. Faced with the option of the hard concrete for another hour — or two! — I chose to park myself in front of Judd's television, watching back-to-back episodes from the complete first season of *Seinfeld* (the only thing he had on tape), while he screwed this girl on his futon next to me with so little inhibition as to periodically engage in jovial conversation with me about his sexual performance or, as time passed, approaching lack thereof.

Towards the end of the third miserable twenty-five minutes spent that way, Judd, on his knees, offered me the other end of this "repeat" girlfriend of his by lifting her clear off the futon by her shins in the near fetal position she was in and turning her hindquarters towards me with a "Here, Ligo, have a go! I can't keep this up much longer!" His date was a bit surprised, but went right back to work on Judd once she figured out what was going on.

God only knows why it seemed like a good idea to me at the time. It was either that, I suppose, or another episode of *Seinfeld!*

Happily, though, after a few embarrassing but mirthful moments of fumbling unsuccessfully with a condom, I found that my body had more sense than I did, and I failed to do the deed, while butt-naked, red-faced and laughing Judd continued to do a different version of it an appealingly curved but by then unappealingly clammy backbone's length across from me.

Alpha Judd couldn't have cared less, of course, whether I screwed that girl with him or not – he was simply starting to run out of stamina himself and, playing the good host to both her and me, probably just realized with a private joke that made him roar on the inside with laughter that he could kill two birds with one stone and hook us up with each other. I suppose that on another level, though, he could have been disappointed in his short-term Beta roommate from America.

Last time I'd been out with him in Tokyo I'd kissed a transsexual on the cheek rather than be rude and tear myself away when she wouldn't let me leave the table. Later that same night I had not had sex with the girl I brought back to that same futon when I learned that she was either too young or too inexperienced to want me to be her first. I was the one who had stopped short of bashing the teeth out of his countryman Rod's head that day in the street behind the dormitory, I had been the one that cried one night on my hands and knees in *Honbu's* basement showers after being beaten so badly in the dojo that I couldn't stand, and this time, six months later, I found myself not up to the challenge presented by Judd's sloppy seconds, mostly due to the hilarity of having to do it right in front of him.

We laughed about it later, of course, and forgot about it soon after that. I would be a liar, though, to suggest that my pride wasn't affected by the fact that Judd always seemed to score and I never did.

He must have thought me a little lacking in testosterone.

Judd and I both saw Akiko at the same time in a coffee shop in Ikebukuro's broad daylight two days later. We both noticed her at exactly the same moment as the greatest possible catch of the day, and I am ashamed to recall that I was, at that moment when I first saw her, doing my absolute Beta best not to be outdone by Judd's high conquest, *Japanese woman as object* mode. I'm ashamed because I would come to know the overbrimming beauty of Akiko's spirit, and I realize now that I embarked on the first romantic relationship I would have with a Japanese woman – fleeting though it was – from the mutually degrading standpoint of beholding her, in that very first instant, as an object of sexual conquest.

Judd and I had spent the day together in a jovial, post-dormitory, *Tokyo owes us* mindset, walking together freely around the streets of a city that we hadn't before been allowed to frequent, playing a rude, juvenile game in which we discussed the women that caught our attention in the basest terms imaginable. We discussed the women we saw on the trains, or passed on the sidewalks, in a way that seemed funny at the time, but that makes me cringe to imagine anyone I know today having witnessed. As if trying to outdo each other with our "smart" commentary, we pointed out the beautiful ones, the sexy ones, the cute ones, the older ones, the ones that were too young – but would be of age soon enough – the less than pretty ones, the ones with hot bodies and the ones without, the ones that were still virgins, and the ones that looked like they'd been married long enough to probably wish they could spend a night out with one of us.

Every once in a while, a young Japanese woman would notice that she'd been noticed and glance back and smile innocently. One or two from the thousand or so we saw that hour even smiled back suggestively, in a "maybe another time, in another place" kind of way, and then, of course, Judd and I would look at each other in surprise and laugh knowingly. But even when they didn't notice us at all, our reaction was the same. We'd comment, laugh, and humor ourselves to believe how easy it would be to seduce them and how badly they wished we would try.

More than a decade later in Chapel Hill, I had lunch with one of my Japanese language professors, and she told me how as a student in Tokyo she'd once overheard a couple of Western men on a train talking completely unashamedly about the Japanese women around them in blatant sexual terms and in a shockingly degrading way. "The worst part," she said, "was they either took for granted that no one understood English or, worse, they didn't care if anyone did. They made no effort to muffle their tones, or hide what or who they were talking about. It was as if they were calling us all stupid at the same time they were treating us like animals."

She told me that story – she told me how hurt she had been, and how it made her question why she was studying English if the only reason was to communicate with people from "a culture like that!" I didn't tell her then, but I felt her story deep in the pit of my stomach. I'd like to believe I was less guilty than the pair of *gaijin* men she described, because Judd and I weren't quite so obvious – and because our behavior that afternoon was somehow a result of the combination of the two of us, and otherwise out of character for either of us alone. I did, however, know the other side of the coin my Japanese professor described a bit better than I could ever be proud to admit.

I'd run with that exact class of Western men before in the carnival-like atmosphere of some parts of Tokyo – if only for just moments in a lifetime – and I knew it to be an all too real phenomenon.

Over nearly two decades spent in and out of Japan, I've failed to count the number of times – somewhere between three and five, I think – that I've forced my way through sardine-packed commuters on Tokyo trains at rush hour, or on the last trains of the day, to squeeze myself between Japanese women traveling alone, and men – Japanese men! – who were taking advantage of those unbelievably inescapable close quarters to molest them in plain sight of half a dozen other commuters. How difficult it is for us to understand why a Japanese woman would not call out for help, and why trainloads of Japanese commuters are more inclined to pretend not to notice than to let the victim know that they're bearing witness to her shame!

That was one situation in Japan when I did have to suppress impulses to throw elbow strikes that would have broken the jaws and smashed the Adam's apples of such assholes. Doubting for a few minutes that I was actually seeing what I was seeing, and then finally taking the several minutes more that it took to squirm my way through the crowd, gave me ample opportunity each time to weigh the pros and cons of wrapping my generally stronger, larger *gaijin* hands around the scrawny neck of one of those little perverts to choke the life out of him, rather than simply pushing between him and his prey, which was all I ever actually did. I always figured that the same throngs that pretended not to notice while one of their number felt up some poor woman would most likely have felt obligated to report *me* to the police for knocking the teeth out of one of their fellow commuters' heads.

Of course, such a chivalrous inclination fails to excuse the two or three times in my life that I myself was guilty of transforming Tokyo into a sexual hunting ground – in each case with Judd at my side – and pursuing Japanese women for little more than the hormone-driven animal struggle not to be outdone. Mob violence, I realize, occurs even in mobs of two, and for all of my reliance on conscience to guide me, I can admit now with a strong sense of disappointment in myself the extent to which the call of the Alpha has influenced this Beta's choices in directions that I likely would never have gone on my own.

I shudder to think what might have become of me if I'd stayed on in Tokyo with Judd after moving out of the dormitory. Judd's two- or three-year predatory diversion in the dives of Tokyo following his three years as an *uchi deshi* was out of character for him, too: I know his heart to be a kind one. I saw relief pervade his entire demeanor once he'd finally gone back to Australia for some fresh air and realized that, for him, Tokyo was a place he should have escaped long before.

Judd's transgression and mine, the afternoon we met Akiko, was to allow the attitude of the Roppongi night, the brazen blurred-line predation we'd learned from the nonstop Mardi Gras of the place, to spill over into Tokyo at large.

When the two of us, therefore – Alpha Judd, egged on by Beta Nathan's competitive unwillingness to be outdone yet again, and Nathan, as desperate for diversion as anything else – entered an Ikebukuro coffee shop that afternoon and scanned the establishment's interior with predatory eyes, our gazes both, at exactly the same instant, fell on the one female present who was, hands down, the most beautiful woman either of us had seen in Tokyo, maybe ever. We made a beeline for the fatefully empty table next to her, nearly shoving each other in an effort to get there first, in unabashed mutual understanding that we were heading there specifically to see if we couldn't chat up that particular female, secure her telephone number and a chance, therefore, at a later sexual adventure.

How happy for your narrator – daring to be honest, but, I fear, roundly humiliating himself in the process – that in the case of Akiko, it quickly became apparent that Judd's Roppongi-style predation was no match for the better side of Nathan's character, given this particular Japanese woman's infinitely superior level of personal class!

Akiko was the farthest thing imaginable from one of Judd's Roppongi women, and despite a dangerous run or two through the trenches, Nathan was learning, encounter by encounter, that he was farthest thing imaginable from the American rapist that had so shocked and disgusted him that earlier night in Roppongi. Like carbon rods inserted into a reactor to cool a completely different kind of fire, all Akiko needed to do was make eye contact with Nathan, and every shred of a tendency towards sexual predation slipped away into the undercurrent that for Nathan it generally was. Where there had been only lust on the surface a moment before, Nathan managed, in spite of himself, to replace it on every level that could be seen through the eyes – or conveyed by chemicals on the currents of the air! – with his much more natural propensity for admiring and respecting one worthy of admiration and respect.

And, lo and behold!

As if by some miracle as far as Nathan was concerned, the Beta, who'd never once in his life successfully picked up a woman when it was his conscious intention to do so, turned out to be the one that this stunningly beautiful woman warmed up to. Judd undoubtedly made the mistake of treating her like a Roppongi girl, if only with his tone or body language, and in retrospect I wonder whether Akiko may have warmed up to me at first primarily to evade the embarrassing charge so aggressively mounted by Judd. Either way, Akiko, for me, in the duration of little more than a first glance, metamorphosed from the object of a competition with Judd into an honest attempt to find out if I was still even capable of romance in the wake of Helen.

And why not?

It felt so surreal to be on the loose in carnival-like Tokyo, with its neon lights, and so much free time on my hands, and what was *normal* in the world now, anyway? What was *normal* in Tokyo now that there was no longer a *Sosai* Mas Oyama in it?

Two whole weeks in Tokyo!

If I wasn't careful, I'd find myself bored – if not in fact trapped – in a foreign land with nothing to do but face the vacuum created by *Sosai's* death – and *bored*, I knew, was an unacceptable way to spend a week of memorial for the one man in my life who had broken the mold and shown me how completely a life could be lived.

And what a worthy partner in that endeavor Akiko was!

What a worthy companion with whom to wage my first deliberate attempt to leave Helen behind and so celebrate how full a life could be lived!

Might as well, I thought.
Life is too short to surrender.

* * *

Akiko was definitely a crowd stopper.

In fact, several of the American branch chiefs were among the crowds she stopped, once they and their counterparts from all over the world started to roll in towards the beginning of that second week. I have distinct memories of encountering groups of them on at least two separate occasions on the busy, neon-lit sidewalks of the more cosmopolitan side of Ikebukuro Station, as I walked the other way with china-doll-like Akiko, glowing on my arm with such undeniable beauty and grace. "Good God, who is that?" Rochester's Michael Monaco said with his eyes, once she'd turned to shake the hand of his companion that night, Florida's Michael Lorden.

He said it, in fact, a second time later, when he got me alone, with actual words that so appealed to my ego that I would never forget them. "Good God, Nathan, I think you've somehow found yourself with one of Japan's most beautiful women!" and then, as a joke, "Maybe sometime you can give the rest of us some pointers . . ."

I've known a couple of *Sosai's* other American branch chiefs to be critical of Michael Monaco over the years, but when all was said and done, I imagine that much of that criticism was based on the fact that things weren't going particularly well for them. Surely it was by virtue of Michael Monaco's character that he managed to develop a multigenerational following of students, huge by the standards set by other U.S. branch chiefs, and when you saw them interact with their teacher, you could feel how much they loved and respected him. Was it not telling that, at home in Kyokushin's unconquerable country,[81] not only had *Shihan* Monaco managed to develop the largest branch of devoted students on America's East Coast, but he was also the one of Mas Oyama's branch chiefs who was the least condescending towards me, an ambitious karate student who wasn't his own?

Just like Michael Monaco's spontaneous compliment of me with Akiko, his compliments on the book I had produced that year were among the most heartfelt and unadulterated I heard from the American Kyokushin community. And it wasn't that he went on and on about it; it was just that there were no strings attached to the one or two praises

---

[81] *The Unconquerable Country* is the title of another work in progress by Nathan Ligo. Kyokushin Karate has repeatedly failed to catch hold in America. Even the "golden age" Kyokushin of the 1970s instilled by Shigeru Oyama and Tadashi Nakamura ultimately failed because, after all, where is it now? Thirty years later, where has it gone? Why have the students of these early greats failed to surpass the example set by their own teachers in terms of organizational development, as has occurred in other countries around the world?

he chose to bestow. As time passed, I would talk with *Shihan* Monaco about my book, and about those controversial and inexperience-revealing elements of its presentation that would get me into trouble with those in America who saw me as overstepping my bounds in a *too big for his britches* kind of way. I would have that same conversation in fact, one by one, with all the US branch chiefs who had supported the project originally – but unlike several of the others, Michael Monaco never revealed a need to beat me up in the face of the lessons I was plainly learning anyway.

Printed sixteen years later from a damaged negative, the author with Akiko in Ikebukuro the week of Mas Oyama's memorial service, June '94. (I was clean-shaven at the time of my classmates' graduation March '93, and again in December '93 when I visited *Sosai* at *Honbu*. Midas's beard came and went in the nine months in between.)

Master Choi used to beat the crap out of us with his *shinai* [82] during my first six years of training, and, as I think back, it is with the greatest amount

---

[82] Nonlethal split-bamboo training sword designed for use in *kendo*.

of love – simple love! – that I remember the entire sum of everything that he did for me. If I visited the dojo of some other Kyokushin instructor, however, particularly one that I'd never met until after I'd already spent six years as Master Choi's student and two more years as Mas Oyama's, and that instructor started beating me with his *shinai,* and if he acted like he was entitled because he had more stripes on his belt, I would probably say "Osu" and try to learn what he was so desperate to teach, but in the end, I would probably respect that teacher less unless the lesson turned out to be that good.

I didn't need anyone showering me with compliments to boost my ego, and I repeatedly listened to the advice of my seniors in America outside of my *Honbu* family unit, exposing my choices to them so that I might benefit from the same kind of devil's-advocate criticism I got from Annie. Surely it's telling, though, that Michael Monaco is the one American from whom I would most welcome the welts of his falling *shinai* should he ever find himself inclined to whack me with it.

Today I wonder if his relationship with his own teacher, the Japan-born Korean Shigeru Oyama, wasn't similar to the one I had with Master Choi. Mas Oyama's *sempai-koohai* (senior-junior) system is based on the Confucian family system, and we in the West fail to understand that that system is based on how one feels towards others in the family unit thanks to experiences shared, rather than on how one is supposed to feel based on rules.

Supposed to feel.

How *was* one supposed to feel in Tokyo with Mas Oyama dead?

Once Akiko entered the drama of my second week in Japan, Judd mostly moved offstage. I still spent my nights in his condom-littered, two-futon apartment – except for the two nights I spent out with Akiko right at the end – but when it became apparent, to Judd's initial dismay, that Akiko was open to meeting up with me later and not at all interested in meeting up with him, he shrugged his shoulders, slapped me on the back with a wink that said "Good on ya, Ligo!" and went back to his same old haunts.

I embarked on a journey of a completely different sort.

Sixteen years later, I find a partially damaged set of negatives from that trip to Japan, photographs of Akiko and me together. I scanned to disk and, viewing them for the first time in a decade, I behold the young couple standing there, nearly glowing in each other's company. They exude an aura that could easily be mistaken for love. If the photographs had captions, one might read, "So this is what life is all about! My God, it's so unbelievably beautiful, this life, this love that we share!"

I study one photograph in particular: Nathan and Akiko stand together holding the dozen long-stemmed red roses he'd just given her. I struggle to sort out what could have been going on with that guy who looks so carefree on the eve of the funeral of the man who, after Master Choi, had most redefined his life.

My mind's eye lights on a single massive tear, the summation of five or six normal ones, that gathered at the inside corner of Akiko's right eye as we said our goodbyes five days later, knowing – but not saying – that there was a good chance we would never see each other again. I can see that tear still today, finally breaking free from its eyelash prison and falling like a crystal marble to skip intact off her cheek before shattering into five individual tears again upon impact with her blouse. I remember that moment above all others because it wasn't until right then, at the very end, that Akiko became the first woman in my world to cut through to a heart that had so walled itself into a yearlong love affair with a woman who might as well no longer even have been human. It was as if Akiko and her eyelashes had conspired to catch those tears and hold them there, one after another, desperate to understand how anyone could move into her life with such intensity, the practiced romantic intensity of life with Lissa, compounded by months of abstaining from acting on the passion that I felt for Helen, and then disappear again, so apparently untouched. It was as if Akiko sensed that letting those tears fall one by one wouldn't have been enough to show me how impervious I'd become.

Nathan kissed her then and turned away with the icy resolve of a familiar "Don't love me, Akiko. I'd only hurt you in the end. I have to go where you can't possibly follow, and I have no choice but to go." And it wasn't until I physically turned away and was swallowed up by the crowd that her tear hit its mark. *Beast!* I spat at myself then. *How can you trample on a life like that? How can you tempt her with so much and then take it all away?*

I heard my own words from a time long past: *Don't love me, Dillon. You can't possibly follow where I have to go.*

It was a return full circle to the pre-*uchi deshi*, pre-Lissa Nathan. It was a return to my more familiar icy cold achievement-oriented balance, the same with which I'd held Dillon at bay during my first year at Davidson. It was the one I'd obliterated so completely for the first time when, with gnashing teeth and full-contact blows, I'd fought day after day for a year of days to live so freely with Lissa.

Icy cold, emotionally untouchable, achievement-oriented balance.

Apparently it was exactly that that with wide-open eyes I'd chosen, through my infatuation with Helen, to take back on in exchange for the power I felt I'd need to pursue my creative endeavors as I fought my way back to Kyokushin.

TWENTY-SIX

MASTER CHOI was in Tokyo for two or three days that week, and it might be best through a description of an exchange between the two of us that I can describe how the dynamic between me and Akiko left me at once so emotionally untouchable and so God-awful joyous.

Two years earlier, Master Choi had concluded his twelve-year sojourn in North Carolina and assumed a post as Professor Choi, performing research and teaching physics at the university in Korea where he remains today. Although he and I had not been in close contact ever since I failed in Japan and returned to Davidson, I did have some contact with what was left of his Carolina Martial Arts Club. I had sold books there, and even once recently traveled to Chapel Hill again to give his remaining students the training of their lives before informing them, once it was through, that Mas Oyama had died.

"When I heard that you would go to Tokyo" (for the memorial service), I remember Master Choi's words clearly, "I knew that I had no choice but to attend."

Perhaps he wouldn't otherwise have felt obliged. Matsui's highly politicized funeral was a purely Japanese affair, and Mas Oyama had always kept his Korean family at arm's length in a classic demonstration of his *karate first, karate second, karate third* philosophy. He needed his identity to be as purely Japanese as possible in order to build up his *budo* karate in a country that had in such recent history essentially enslaved Korea. Most histories of Mas Oyama published in Japan even list Japan as his birth country, although the flesh-and-blood boy who was to become Mas Oyama was most certainly born in Korea.

I knew that Master Choi blamed himself for my failure in Japan, because he'd told me that he did. "It would be my fault," he told me, "because I interrupted your training at Tokyo and asked you to come home to help me."

My failure in Japan *was* intimately tied to Master Choi and his deteriorating situation at home, but it goes a step too far that he bear the responsibility. My failure towards Mas Oyama was far more complicated than that. It was mine and mine alone, and I told Master Choi that then. The nephew, whom I still referred to as "my teacher" the entire time I was in Japan as the student of the far greater Mas Oyama, *had* asked me to come home in the middle of my *uchi deshi* training, to help him rescue the two dojos he had opened and then came so close to losing when he could not keep the two black belt assistant instructors who'd signed on to help him.

His appeal for help was one that I couldn't possibly have denied.

The entire reason I was in Japan in the first place was to do *for* my first teacher. It wasn't until my collapse occurred and I fled the dormitory in the night a matter of weeks after returning from three months home in North Carolina helping to resurrect Master Choi – his midlife crisis had reduced him to that extent – that in the shattering explosion of a pair of breaking hearts (his and mine), my loyalty finally shifted from Master Choi to his uncle Mas Oyama, where perhaps it should have been long before. How perplexing it must have been for *Sosai*, as the personal teacher of only a handful of students from all of the world's twelve million, that I alone continued, in the daily journal entries that I wrote to him throughout my time in the dormitory, to refer to his nephew as "my teacher"!

Even when Mas Oyama loved me sometimes more than the rest, in the end he summarized the relationship by confessing that he thought of me as a grandson rather than a son, due to my unshakable loyalty to Master Choi. "In a certain sense," Master Choi had told me, "you cannot think of me as your teacher anymore. You are the student of my uncle now, and my uncle is far greater than I. Remember what you see in the eyes of my uncle and it will be more than I can ever possibly teach you."

At Master Choi's invitation, I was present that weekend for a meeting, in a hotel lobby a long taxi ride from any part of Tokyo I'd visited before, between the 32-year-old Matsui and a delegation of cigarette-smoking businessmen in drab suits. Apparently they'd come from Korea to offer – or barter for – some kind of support that, I had the impression, was about maintaining a Korean foothold in the world's largest karate organization following the death of its Korean founder. Matsui was Korean too – his family was North Korean, in fact – but he had been born in Japan, and unlike Mas Oyama, he did not speak the language. Master Choi's uncle, a newspaper ink company president, and another of Mas Oyama's brothers, was there, and I knew him from a handful of days that I had spent under his care in Seoul in 1990.[83] At Matsui's bidding, I stood at a distance in *fudo dachi* throughout, and did not hear any of the meeting's content. Despite Master Choi's invitation, my role as *uchi deshi* made me much more a part of the Japanese family, and from the Japanese side, the meeting was none of my business.

Of course I watched Matsui with different eyes than ever before. He was wearing Mas Oyama's shoes and sitting in his chair at the head of the table – he was to be the new spiritual head of Kyokushin. I was a *Honbu uchi deshi*, and it was, I realized, now his *Honbu*. Matsui was now the one who, by default, I was supposed to take a bullet for, should one ever fly in his direction when I was close enough to catch it.

I thought of Kikuko's assertion that he was in league with the mafia.

Is there a mafia connection? I wondered. *If so, is it a tool that's going to help him hold Kyokushin together? Is it going to make it stronger? Can he use it to fortify Kyokushin while, at the same time, keeping it enough at bay that it doesn't swallow him whole?*

If so, then so be it!

Mas Oyama was no stranger to the *Yakuza* during parts of the IKO's development, either. Could they have killed him to establish Matsui as the heir to all of Kyokushin?

Only that, to me, would have been intolerable, as long as Matsui otherwise did better than anyone else for Kyokushin. Only Mas Oyama's murder would be too much to bear, because that would imply that *Sosai* had had different intentions for the future of Kyokushin, and that I would not have been able to abide.

---

[83] Mas Oyama and his siblings, from oldest to youngest: 1. Il Un Choi (Master Choi's father, a university president, poet, and Doctor of Western Philosophy from Japan's Wasuda University), 2. Young Myung Choi, 3. Young Bum Choi, 4. Yong-I Choi (who changed his name to Masutatsu Oyama after immigrating to Japan as a teenager), 5. Yong Jung Choi (the newspaper ink company president), and 6. one other, the youngest. Master Choi and his siblings, oldest to youngest: 1. Seh Hyong Choi (economist), 2. Seh Young Choi, 3. Seh Keun Choi, 4. Seong Soo Choi (this is Master Choi), and 5. one other, the youngest.

There's nothing I can do, I knew then, about the darker possibility Kikuko suspected, other than watch and listen, give Matsui the benefit of the doubt, and watch to see if he'd indeed be able to fill *Sosai's* shoes. I beheld him then as the epitome of power – in *Honbu's* gangster-like hierarchy, he always had been anyway. There was no question in my mind that he possessed the "master's figure" to which Master Choi always referred.[84]

Despite not being permitted to listen to the meeting – I wouldn't likely have been able to understand much if I had! – watching it from a distance worked to broaden my view of the Kyokushin world. That man next to Matsui was Mas Oyama's brother! He was Master Choi's newspaper-ink-company-president uncle, and another of Mas Oyama's Korean family members named Choi that even his own daughter Kikuko had never met. The others, I realized, did look to me like gangsters, although reason told me that they couldn't have been, given that Master Choi and his uncle were there too. The impression, I figured, was just the suspicion planted in me by the mischievous Kikuko.

Damn her, I thought, *if, through her wiles, she's managed to plant suspicions in my perception of the Kyokushin world that aren't based on fact!*

And damn me, I thought next, *if they are!*

Those Koreans *did* look like gangsters to me then, with their cigarettes, their drab suits, and their aloof manner. They were gangsters of the business world, I realized, potential sponsors who would maintain a Korean hand in the ownership of one of Korea's all-time greatest exports into Japanese culture.

Just three months after moving into Mas Oyama's dormitory, I'd gone to *Sosai* through his assistant to explain that my visa was going to expire and that I'd learned that the law required me to leave the country to extend it. *Sosai* called me to his office and asked me if I planned to complete three years in the dormitory. When I told him unequivocally that I did, he bought me a round-trip plane ticket to Seoul without batting an eye, handed me 700 U.S. dollars in cash from his office safe, and delivered me into the charge of his newspaper-ink-company-president brother for a week so that I could extend my visa. More than a year later, Master Choi wrote to me in Tokyo and asked me

---

[84] "Master's figure," in Master Choi's book of broken-English definitions, referred to the outer appearance of a master resulting from the undisguisable inner qualities of one.

to return to North Carolina to help him save his dojos, and I went to Matsui to ask his advice.

"Leave the dormitory now, and you can never come back to Kyokushin," *Sosai* had told me.

In that, my second Japanese-language conversation with Matsui, in the dormitory one afternoon when he dropped in for a meal, he advised me to make sure that returning to America for a temporary period to help Master Choi was what I wanted to do, wait for a week or two to be sure, and then ask Mas Oyama one more time.

"If you ask him for a third time," Matsui told me, "he'll let you go."

Three years later, I stood there in Tokyo and watched Matsui sitting at the same table with my first teacher and another of his uncles, the brother

The author in 1990, 19 years old and just three months into his *uchi deshi* training, in front of Seoul Tower with Mas Oyama's younger brother, Master Choi's newspaper-ink-company-president uncle, Yong Jung Choi. Mas Oyama sent me into his brother's care for one week in Korea to extend my Japanese visa.

of Mas Oyama I knew from 1990 in Korea. I thought of the first time I'd watched the video of Matsui's 100-man *kumite* at Master Choi's summer camp at Sunset Beach. And I was awed at how the separate, varied parts of a focused life seemed, like converging roads, to ultimately intersect. It had been nearly ten days since Matsui and I met in *Sosai's* office so that I could ask him about the future of my *Budo Karate Illustrated*.

Our paths had crossed again, of course, briefly, at the tournament in Osaka.

It can only work to my advantage, I reasoned, *that Matsui would be reminded at this juncture of my roots in the Korean family of Mas Oyama. Perhaps it will give me the edge I need, since the future of my project seems for some reason to have been called into question.*

"You must wait until after the memorial service and until after the international branch chief meeting," Matsui told me. "After that, you should write me a proposal telling me how you plan to manage the magazine's proceeds, and then we can talk."

Still I didn't sense any danger.

* * *

I spent the night in an Ikebukuro hotel room making love to Akiko, and the next morning, in a poorly fitted black suit, I met Master Choi to escort him by train to the memorial service.

"I had great sex last night," I told him matter-of-factly ten minutes into our cross-Tokyo train ride, somehow choosing that incredible announcement to break our usual words-aren't-necessary silence. I volunteered the information without inhibition, and Master Choi shot me a glance loaded with a thousand nails, as if to crush the impudence of what I'd just dared to utter. But then his eyes met mine, and *in the second part* of that impromptu optical exchange lies the rest of the Akiko story.

If I were to use Master Choi's own words to summarize his teaching for the first three years of my karate experience, it would have to be the broken-English command he'd used with me time and time again when I was a teenager. "Shut up your mouth!" he'd say.

"Shut up!" it seemed he constantly told me when I was young, once he'd seen that I was learning with my heart rather than my head and that I wasn't likely to be chased away. "You ask too many stupid questions! Think three times before you speak! Ask yourself three times if it's important and probably, by then, you will have already figured out the answer!"

Another time he'd snap, "Don't ask so many stupid questions! In Korea, I'm not allowed to ask my father or older brother personal questions at all! If they don't tell me, I don't know it. That's it. Learn to use your own eyes and ears to answer your questions and then you won't have to ask."

I am one hundred percent certain that I was the only one of Master Choi's students during his twelve years in America who stayed put and listened to him saying "Shut up!" as many times as he did. The others, the older ones, the less desperate, all of them, would have quit. I hadn't seen Master Choi for the better part of two years when we met in Tokyo – it was the longest we'd ever been separated – but there was no question that I knew him, or at least believed myself to know him, better than any other person on the planet. Of course there were thousands of things I didn't know about Master Choi, because I was never allowed to ask him personal questions, and he didn't talk much about personal matters. Our history had been lifetime-long, however, during the mere eight years we knew each other, because for much of it we were living at a different pace than all the rest. Through his eyes, Master Choi had shown me what he was at the core, and I knew what I'd seen in a rare glimpse or two to be a far more complete picture than I could have garnered from a lifetime of studying the externals.

I knew well the near tyrannical strictness of the Korean system of etiquette through which he'd been raised by his father, Mas Oyama's oldest brother, a poet and university president who had been the first Korean to hold a doctorate in Western philosophy; and by his own older brother, who was, when I met him in 1990, vice president of the Korea Foreign Trade Association. I knew well that Master Choi didn't dare smoke a cigarette in front of his father or brother, let alone initiate conversation in many situations where we in America would take it for granted. He'd demonstrated for me more than just once how he wasn't allowed to tip the bottom of his glass towards his father, uncle, or brother when sitting at the same table, sharing the same meal. With his back bolt upright, he would rotate his full torso on his chair at the tailbone to ninety degrees away from the elder male members of his family before even thinking about raising his own glass with two hands to his lips to drink.

Although Master Choi spent much of his later years in America, dangerously lost between this Korean personality and an experimental and precarious emerging Americanized one, and I was around him many times to see him relax, it was exceedingly rare that he would ever relax even a little in his interaction with me. "Shut up your mouth!" therefore, was the summary of all that I learned from him from the age of thirteen to sixteen, and I realize now, with the greatest awe and admiration, that I didn't really start learning from Master Choi until I finally figured out how to actually do so.

My first karate teacher, Professor Seong Soo Choi, PhD in Physics from UNC–Chapel Hill in North Carolina, the youngest son of Mas Oyama's oldest brother, a university president and poet.

As bold a thing as it might be to say – and Master Choi would snap at this juncture, "Then why say it at all?" – I'm fairly certain that he never had another American student who learned the greatest lesson he taught during his twelve years in America. I wasn't anything special. I was just in the right place at the right time. I was the only student he had that started his training so desperately, and at such an early age.

It was that strict, my interaction with Master Choi, and yet, that morning, crossing Tokyo by train en route to his uncle's and my teacher's memorial service, "I had great sex last night," I told him, and he shot me a glance loaded with a thousand nails in dramatized shock at what I'd just dared to utter.

Master Choi's eyes met mine then, however, and in that instant he saw so deep into me that he understood that what I had chosen to share with him had very little to do with sex. He saw, and just as I presumed they would, his eyes abruptly softened to their more usual embracing charcoal black. He chuckled then like a father, beheld me in a rare case as an adult, and with a twinkle in his eye allowed the fragments of broken ice to drift away, with "And was she a Japanese girl?" inserted like a punctuating afterthought.

One shouldn't underestimate the terror-like grief that permeated the entire world for all of us in Kyokushin during those days. Mas Oyama was dead – it was, with a grain of salt of course, as if God himself were dead – and for those of us who had grown up with the inspiration of Kyokushin's founder at our core, the temptation was to behold the world that was left without Mas Oyama in it, and collapse as if under a thousand tons at the horror of facing a future without him. For most of us, Japan wasn't even Japan without Mas Oyama. Since long before I'd even set foot on that rock, it was as if he was standing confidently in a waist-deep Pacific off the coast of Korea, balancing the entire archipelago in an all-loving, all-powerful, and all-protecting embrace.

That's how much Mas Oyama had come to love Japan.

There were more than a handful of moments between that day in my Johnson Gym dojo six weeks earlier, when I spoke to Mas Oyama beyond the grave, and the week of his memorial service in Tokyo when all it took was to pause and embrace the fact that he was dead, and I'd have to stamp my foot and snarl to prevent my eyes from filling with tears. And I did stop the tears from flowing for many years – I knew that I must from that first instant – because my heart told me that Mas Oyama would himself have stamped his foot, growled, and burned the back of my skull to singe them from my eyes.

Tears blur sight, and as Mas Oyama's *uchi deshi*, it was my responsibility to keep my eyes opened wide and clear-seeing. I had too much work to do, and the work was too important. Nevertheless, the temptation to succumb to panic during those first six weeks should not be underestimated. I was far from Mas Oyama's strongest student, and I sensed that it was only for the time being that the gnashing teeth and the snarls would suffice in the battle to fend off despair.

And that wasn't good enough for the Nathan Ligo of 1994, living those volcanic days of his life.

I had grown spoiled by the rules not applying to me. Every day I was finding more and more ways to smash down walls to insure that nothing would stand in my way in any strength- or creativity-limiting fashion, and facing the fear of life without Mas Oyama in it was no exception.

In my case, the work was too important.

Focus was too important.

The oath that I'd taken was too important, and – horrible as it may sound to some – by making love to Akiko on the eve of his funeral, I was eyes-wide-open aware of having found a way to convert grief into celebration, and, in one fell swoop, obliterate any future temptation to betray *Sosai* by succumbing to despair. Remember, I was quite certain that Mas Oyama would have preferred to see the ten thousand of us in attendance that day dressed in sweat-drenched white rather than wrapped four abreast around the city block in despairing black, and my determination to celebrate life with Akiko at the time of his memorial – my attempt to out-*carpe diem* even the *carpe diem* I'd been living by both loving Helen and leaving her the hell alone – became like an *ichigeki-hissatsu* [85] straight punch thrown in a battle to win balance worthy of Mas Oyama's expectation.

Mas Oyama, more than any other person on the planet, was for me the epitome of one who'd gnawed the marrow out of the very core of life.

The man fought barehanded bouts against angered bulls, for God's sake!

He'd suffered being kicked around by the Japanese as a teenage Korean immigrant, and then somehow over the next decade developed a punch that earned him the nickname "God Hand." With the crack of their breaking bones he showed opponent after opponent the folly of their attempts to stand up against it. There is no question that Mas Oyama fought through dark times in his rise to the top – times that he wouldn't have been proud of, but that nevertheless made him who he became once he emerged – and at the end, at seventy-one, he was still working from his

---

[85] One strike, certain death.

hospital bed to promote the legacy of what he had made into the world's strongest karate and the world's strongest karate organization.

His early student Hatsuo Royama told me years later that when he last saw Mas Oyama in the hospital, just days before he died – and just a month after I saw him for the last time – he was shocked at the extent to which the cancer had eaten his body away. He lay there a mere shell of himself, *Kancho* Royama said, and yet when he entered, *Sosai* was lying there staring at his right hand, opening and closing his fist as the last bit of training he was, in his life, able to perform. "Royama!" he confessed, "After all of it, I'm still not sure that I've even mastered the correct fist."

He told the future *Kancho* Royama then, just as he told several of his closest students, to make sure that Kyokushin was carried proudly into the future, and to ensure that Kyokushin's achievements thus far pale in comparison to its achievements to come.

How does one commemorate a life like that?

With tears and a whore?

Never.

That's the way one would succumb to despair.

One commemorates a life such as *Sosai's* by living life to the bursting point in honor of one who redefined how completely a life could be lived!

Because of how it could be misconstrued, and for that reason only, I am sorry to say that on the eve of his memorial it was by making love to a woman as stunningly beautiful inside and out as Akiko that I chose to live my life, on that particular day too, to the fullest extent I was able.

"*Baka!* (Fool!)" one or two of my Japanese compatriots would have sworn, but only because they didn't know anything about the days of the life I was living surrounding that particular day. Outside all of life's rules, I was the one person of the several hundred who'd come to Japan from Mas Oyama's overseas branches who was there not to commemorate Mas Oyama's life, but to continue unbroken the work that I'd set out to do for him. Crazy though it may seem, I believed even then that the work I was doing would not only change the course of history in American Kyokushin, but that it would set Kyokushin on a course to change the history of America itself.

And wouldn't affecting the history of the world's last great superpower affect the course of history beyond even America's borders?

"Careful!" my elders of that era protest. "The lunacy of that youthful ambition set aside – because you'll grow out of having such dreams, like we all did! – we were *all* in Tokyo that week to continue *Sosai's* work! We were all there to make sure the pieces got picked up properly."

And of course I would give them that. They were there, too, to continue their work.

But just as I'm sure there have been times in their lives when they were more engaged than I in a do-or-die frenzy to achieve for Kyokushin, I suspect still today that none of them then could have held a candle to the effort that I was expending in a concentrated war waged to achieve for the future during those days of my life.

They were mere tourists!

They were tourists come to gawk at holy Kyokushin on a pedestal, as for all of them – with their handful of annual weekend trips to Japan in search of inspiration and a chance, maybe, to shake Mas Oyama's hand – it had always been!

And I was so totally engaged that I'd taken my engagement to another level altogether, beyond which I wondered if man was even meant to venture. I was living entire lifetimes in mere years of my life, I was living years in individual weeks, and weeks in individual days. I was completely insane based on anyone else's standards, since none of the rules applied to me. I'd figured out a way to live outside them in order to do for Kyokushin, and I was engaged to the bursting point. I was engaged to the point where my effort had consumed so much of my energy that it had started eating away at me as well.

I was so unbelievably exhausted.

And I was so high on life that I couldn't feel it.

And that *high on life* was the key.

It kept me blasting through the fatigue, it kept my eyes seeing in spite of all the rest, and, as far as I was concerned, it was the ultimate tribute to Mas Oyama. Staggering around a city block dressed in black, I believed, would have been a betrayal both of my teacher and of the ten thousand others who staggered around that block that day. Can anyone tell me that Mas Oyama himself wouldn't have trained one last time with his most beloved students – and made it the training to end all trainings! – put a couple of papers in order, spent some quality time with his family, and then gone out to get laid himself on the eve of his own funeral, had he the strength?

His own daughter seemed to think that it was within his power to have done so!

One of the few personal stories I knew of Master Choi's life was that once, when he was much younger and in the army in Korea, one of his seniors beat him so badly that he coughed up blood, bled from his ears and nose, and even peed blood once he could finally pee at all. He told me how a kind, father-like friend took him out that night to spend the night with an older woman – a prostitute, I imagine – paid in this case in an unlikely capacity, merely to take care of him that night, nurse his wounds, and comfort him as he tried to sleep.

Master Choi in Korea prior to 1982, demonstrating the spiritual strength necessary to allow a car to drive over his unprotected abdomen. Master Choi was always quick to point out that it was through "breathing" and "*chi* energy" training that he developed this strength, not bodybuilding.

Master Choi knew that I knew that story. He knew, more than anyone else on the planet, the love that I felt for Mas Oyama, because it was a love that was shared equally between us, towards each other, and from each of us towards his uncle, my teacher. It was a love that was unrivaled in each of our lives, because for us there could never be another Mas Oyama. Master Choi knew these things, and he must have seen them in my eyes, and I have a hunch that it was on that foundation that he interpreted the absolute calm and guiltless self-assurance that he saw in my eyes on that cross-Tokyo train once he'd smashed his way in with his thousand nails.

I know students of Mas Oyama who were torn to pieces by guilt, feeling that they didn't work hard enough for him during his lifetime, as if they never showed him how much they loved him. I was far from Mas Oyama's strongest student; I was the one in my class that had failed to graduate; I was the one that sobbed on my hands and knees in *Honbu's* basement showers after I'd been beaten in the dojo so badly I couldn't stand. When last we met he'd extended his hand and asked me to show him the book that I was producing in America, the one that hadn't finally been printed until a month after he was dead. But still, I would hazard the guess that I was the one student of Mas Oyama that week who was the flawless antithesis of the one consumed by guilt for feeling like he hadn't done enough in Mas Oyama's final days.

I was on fire during that last year of Mas Oyama's life. That fire burned so hot that it melted the planet around me and, for lack of fuel, turned its hungry attention towards parts of me that would bear the scars of that burn for years to come. I was on fire, that fire filled my entire world, and it was that fire with which I dared to commemorate the life of Mas Oyama by making love to such a worthy partner as was the stunningly beautiful Akiko.

Despite the occasional temptation to allow my eyes to fill with tears for the loss of my teacher, I was shocked by the extent to which I was unchanged by his death. He died and he became part of me. I wondered if I wouldn't live the rest of my life feeling that while I continued his work in America, he was just over there in his office continuing his work for the world, trusting me to carry on in America while he turned his attention to larger concerns.

Mas Oyama was dead, but I knew already in the deepest recesses of my being that I would never be alone for the want of him, and if there was celebration in Nathan Ligo's eyes in photographs taken of me that weekend with Akiko, it was the realization of that inheritance that I celebrated by living life so fully during those few days with her.

Master Choi had only to look into my eyes, and the maelstrom of nails softened to warm charcoal black. He chuckled like a father, beheld me in a rare case as an adult, and asked, "And was she a Japanese girl?"

TWENTY-SEVEN

THE WEEKEND of the memorial service turned out to be heart-breaking for reasons far separated from the loss of Mas Oyama.

Our very own Katsuhiko Horai from New York City finally came into his own that weekend, feeling his way into the shoes that he would wear for the next decade as one of the least-liked men in all of Kyokushin. Of course nobody knew that then – no one knew where he was heading – and I wonder if I wasn't one of the first to feel the bite of the lapdog role he would so eagerly play for Matsui in the years to come.

It was only natural that the young Americanized Horai help the new, young chairman with organizational matters: he was ambitious and bilingual. Just like all the other international Kyokushin events in Japan, *Sosai's* memorial service had two sides, a Japanese one and a "foreign" one. There were over 200 international branch chiefs there that day, from I'd guess half of the 133 countries around the world to which Kyokushin had spread, and they had to be told how to find their way from the Metropolitan Hotel in Ikebukuro to the shrine where the service was to be held. They had to be told where to gather and how to line up to move in single file into the hall. And that chaos would wind up being but a taste of the fiasco the domestic and international branch chief meetings would become at the Metropolitan Hotel on the morning of the following day.

Kyokushin in Japan had suddenly become a blank slate, and although all the international branch chiefs would tell you that they'd come to Japan to honor Mas Oyama, there wasn't one of them who didn't also possess the ulterior, desperate motive of discerning what was to become of Kyokushin and to what extent each one of their individual worlds at home would be turned upside down by Mas Oyama's death. I'd be surprised, in fact, if many of them weren't so preoccupied with the unknowns of their political futures under Matsui that by the time they boarded their planes to return to their countries, they would have had very little energy left over to contemplate what Mas Oyama himself would have wanted.

Perhaps that was Matsui's intent.

Matsui was taking over Kyokushin, and the memorial service was the perfect venue for him to bring all the leaders of Kyokushin together under one roof so that he could get that first crack at them, and show them who was going to be boss.

Nobody flinched when I entered the memorial hall with my camera.

My former roommates, and my current *uchi deshi koohai*, were the ones positioned on the doors and directing traffic. Although there was no chair inside designated for me, because I was not a branch chief, no one batted an eye because I knew, at least by face, everyone associated with the event's operation. As was the norm for Japan's largest Kyokushin events – the World Tournament, certainly – Mas Oyama's *Honbu* was at the core of the production. We did all the work behind the scenes that kept the gears turning, and although I had been home by then in America for more than two years, all of the stationary faces I saw that day – as opposed to those that simply filed by – were like a Who's Who of all those I'd trained with at *Honbu*. All my *sempai* were there, Judd and Nick were there, all of my former Japanese roommates were there, and all of my *koohai*, from both inside the dormitory and out, were there, all just a little bit more grown up in the years that I'd been away.

I had taken myself to the memorial service first and foremost as a journalist, and the work I had come to do was for *Sosai*.

I could already see the contents page of 1995's coming second issue of *Budo Karate Illustrated*. There beside my second photo essay of Matsui, and the first one of Midori, coverage of the Osaka Weight Category Tournament, and material submitted this time not only by all of the U.S. branch chiefs for the second time but also, I hoped, all of the Canadian branch chiefs as well – beside all of that would be some kind of tribute to Mas Oyama. That tribute would include some humble coverage of his memorial service, including especially a choice photograph or two of American and Canadian branch chiefs in attendance.

Although I was told that ten thousand of Mas Oyama's students would file through the funeral hall that day, there were only seats inside for several hundred to watch the actual presentation. The room was split down the middle, one side for foreigners and the other for Japanese. Master Choi and his uncle sat in the front row of the Japanese side in a block of seats designated for *Sosai's* family, and although I recognized all the Japanese branch chiefs, there was quite a long list of dignitaries and older associates of Mas Oyama on the Japanese side with whom I was not acquainted.

It was particularly interesting to see a handful of faces from Kyokushin's ancient history, including those I knew well but had never met, such as the earliest of Mas Oyama's close personal students, Shigeru Oyama and Tadashi Nakamura. They were the two that *Sosai* cited in his letter to Jacques introducing Horai who had made Kyokushin so huge in the U.S. in the seventies before each in turn broke away so destructively.

I had taken several pictures in and around the courtyard and then moved inside, positioned myself in a corner – the proper place for an *uchi deshi* – and waited not too far from some actual journalists for everyone to take their seats. There was to be a showing of a short film that paid tribute to Mas Oyama and a Shinto ceremony to commemorate his passing. It was during those fifteen minutes or so of waiting that I had an opportunity to reflect, and despite the intensity of my life celebration the night before, I considered again the fact that Mas Oyama was dead, and I had to grit my teeth to keep my eyes from welling up with tears.

When I focused them again, the first thing I saw was Katsuhiko Horai.

He was watching me with an annoyed look on his face from across the room, and when our eyes met, he strode over towards me like an angry rooster. I stood as he approached, and without any attempt at nicety, he said, "Branch chiefs only. You get out."

I was caught off guard because I was so much at ease there – within, of course, the bounds of decorum expected of me as a former *uchi deshi*. It was my family running the show, after all, not his. He had been associated with Shigeru Oyama's New York-based splinter Kyokushin organization for several years, and had come on the U.S. Kyokushin scene only after I had. Horai had only just been appointed, evidently with some degree of hesitation, by Mas Oyama in the last months before he died.

"Osu," I said in English, "I understand, but I have to take a photo or two for the next issue of our American magazine."

"It is not important here," he said. "Hurry up, get out."

"Osu," I said, and had no choice but to leave. I'd just taken a full-power whack from the *shinai* of a Kyokushin *sempai* with whom I shared absolutely none of the kind of past that would have made me welcome such a blow. Suffering flashbacks to *Honbu's* old gangster-style hierarchy – the one that *Sosai* so disapproved of and had taken deliberate steps to break – I told *Sensei* Horai then, "*Osu, wakarimashita. Shitsurei shimasu* (I have understood. Excuse me now, please, for leaving)," and I moved out of the hall thinking, but not revealing, *What an asshole! I wonder what his problem is!*

If only that exchange had been the day's greatest source of heartbreak!

Nothing could have prepared anyone for the scene that was to unfold in the parking lot.

Mas Oyama's long black car had arrived.

As usual, it was driven by the oldest Japanese *uchi deshi* still currently living in the dormitory, in this case one of Nick and Mahashi's *koohai*, and today it was carrying the wife and daughters of Mas Oyama. They'd ordered the driver, apparently, to park as close to the memorial hall as he could, and there they'd gotten out, and in bitterly painful-to-see protest of the will that had established Matsui as Mas Oyama's sole heir, they held their ground with pale, tear-streaked faces. Not only were they refusing to enter the hall, but they held up high on their shoulders, balanced by the roof of the car and an opened passenger-side door, the heavy silk-wrapped box that held the cremated remains of Mas Oyama!

And there they stood for hours, in direct sun, with *Sosai* in the parking lot held up high for all to see, or at least for all to see that he wasn't inside with Matsui.

"He is not in there!" was the gesture's unspoken but earth-shaking implication. "You are all in there paying homage to a man whose remains are right here, with the family! You are participating in an event sponsored by a usurper!" For hours they held their ground while the service's thousands of visitors filed by to clap twice, bow, and light their incense before a shrine that did not hold the remains of Mas Oyama.

And that wasn't even the full extent of the spectacle.[86]

I'm still curious to know if an order was given (and by whom), or whether the demonstration of solidarity was a spontaneous one, but the entire Who's Who of virtually everyone I'd trained with at *Honbu* – many of them my roommates and *sempai* – formed a wide circle of black suits, four abreast, around *Sosai's* wife, car, and boxed remains, and turned their backs inwards to shield them from the view of the constant stream of well-wishers who came to pay their respects.

Talk about burying the pharaoh's family alive with him in his tomb for all eternity!

---

[86] Two years after writing this passage, I was frustrated to find a photograph (in the form of the negative of a picture I took but never had printed) of *Sosai's* wife and family *inside* the funeral hall with Matsui. I am one hundred percent sure that the described protest occurred, but sadly do not know how to reconcile that memory with this undeniable proof that the family was indeed present inside the hall for at least part of the ceremony. *Sosai's* widow can be seen here next to Matsui, and Tsura *Shihan* who was the husband of one of Kikuko's two older sisters. The next chair, between Tsura *Shihan* and Kikuko (seen here leaning forward between the camera and Master Choi's newspaper-ink-company-president uncle) is empty, and I wonder if it wasn't one of the older sisters who remained in the parking lot, only to be joined later by her mother and sister, who would have participated in the ceremony to pay their respects to those who came to pay *Sosai* theirs. (Not to mention the fact that they were on edge to see if Matsui would pay

their next month's expenses!) My apologies to the family for any divergence from the truth in this account of what has to be a painful memory for them anyway. This book was written (16 years later) during an era when Kikuko, one of only two surviving daughters from *Sosai's* immediate family, is still battling in court, against all of *Sosai's* followers, for control of the Kyokushin trademarks, and she was not available (to the author) for comment.

The simultaneous double, triple, or even quadruple implication of that human wall stumped even me.

First there was the undeniable expression of solidarity with Matsui. All of *Honbu*, indeed all of Kyokushin, had been told that *Sosai's* last wish was that Matsui take over Kyokushin as the new *Kancho* after his death. Mas Oyama's entire life was a demonstration of "karate first, karate second, karate third," and it was therefore that that human wall drowned out the protest mounted by Kikuko, her mother, and her older sister Grace. All of Kyokushin had turned its back on *Sosai's* family, and then, at the memorial service, they did it literally, with that imposing wall of black, encircling the family's feeble display, there for all to see.

On the other hand, though – on a starkly opposite hand! – that wall was also, it seemed to me, protecting *Sosai's* family, as we at *Honbu* had always been entrusted to do. Being the foreigner that I was – I had always been *the American* – I found myself the exception to the Japanese rule. There was always some *Honbu* business that was protected by the Japanese as personal business, even from the *gaijin uchi deshi* who became in so many other ways such a close-knit part of the whole. That night when the Batman Suzuki came so close to bashing Komukai in the street, and the Gangster Yamakage wound up doing it instead, the American Ligo read them the riot act, and they stood there stoically and listened. They didn't fight me, they didn't agree with me, they didn't ignore me. But it was clear that they considered the altercation theirs, it was one hundred percent their business, and they did not invite me into the fray.

All one had to do was look into the eyes of that outward-facing mob, and it was clear that they were so not conflicted about their choice of action that they believed themselves to be one hundred percent supportive of Kyokushin, which they loved and which at that time was represented by Matsui, and at the same time one hundred percent supportive of *Sosai's* family, whom they also loved as the flesh and blood of their teacher. Like commuters on a Tokyo train choosing not to notice the shame of a woman being accosted by a drunk in plain sight, they were protecting the honor of *Sosai's* family, by shielding them from being seen by the public in such a reduced state.

And what a reduced a state it was!

So reduced that their grief would cloud their judgment to the point where they'd dishonor *Sosai* by putting his ashes on top of a car in a parking lot, when people had come from all over the world to pay their respects!

How confidently, therefore, did *Honbu's* wall of black hold their ground there, in yet a third dimension to their silent but powerful demonstration of loyalty: they stood there to protect *Sosai* himself! His place was the place of honor inside, where everyone had come to pay tribute. They couldn't very well go in and physically remove his remains from his grieving widow, but at the very least they could use their bodies to protect him, one more time, now from the dishonor of being left outside in the parking lot.

For God's sake, that was *Sosai* in that box!

I was ashamed even to consider the camera hanging heavily by its strap around my neck! I could barely even look inwards at *Sosai* in that box, let alone dare to point my camera at him.

Of course, I'm quite certain that most of the people in *Honbu's* great human wall would have known the nature of the family's complaint against Matsui. They would have known of the family's accusations. But what were *Honbu's* soldiers to do? On the one hand, it was so unlikely that Matsui's takeover of Kyokushin had been a coup, and on the other hand, even if it had, there was nothing to be done about it until it could be proven. Either way the soldiers in that circle were Kyokushin, they were *Honbu*, and no matter what, their role was to support Kyokushin and *Honbu,* as they understood it to be, until such time as its definition changed.

And what were the chances of that?

Everyone knew that *Sosai* favored Matsui. Everyone knew that he was the most likely candidate to succeed him. He was the one with the charisma. He was the one with the master's figure. He was the favorite son.

From the outside, next to Judd and not far from Suzuki, I looked inward at Kikuko. Nick's *koohai*, the driver *uchi deshi*, was doing his duty, holding an umbrella over *Sosai's* widow with a concerned look on his face, and Kikuko, with tear-streaked cheeks, was taking turns with her sister fanning their mother with a paper fan. Mrs. Oyama did not look well.

At one point I moved towards my confidant Suzuki.

"What the hell is going on?" I asked him, looking then into his eyes for answers beyond words, since my Japanese might not have been sufficient anyway.

In his eyes was the same knowing, feeling, icy refusal to act any other way that I'd seen in his eyes that night when I lectured them about bashing Komukai in the street.

In Suzuki's eyes I could see that he felt for the Oyama family. I could see that the gesture of holding his place in that circle was for him, at that moment, about protecting *Sosai's* family. I could see also, though, that the other was true. *Sosai* had left Kyokushin to Kyokushin. He didn't leave it to his wife and daughters, and although Suzuki might have loved *Sosai's* family as an extension of *Sosai*, he was first and foremost Kyokushin. He was therefore, like me and the rest, an inheritor of Kyokushin, and what else could he have done?

When *Sosai* died, Kyokushin became Matsui, and Matsui was Kyokushin like Caesar had once upon a time been Rome. There was only one possible course of action.

Nevertheless, I remember feeling brutally conflicted, and in that circle I did not remain for long. I invoked my privilege as *gaijin* – because being a *gaijin* was a privilege at *Honbu* as much as it was a handicap – and stepped to the outside with the greater throngs to try to see from a wider perspective.

I thought of an uncomfortable standoff that had occurred in *Sosai's* office one midday late in my first year as an *uchi deshi*, involving a similar circle of unyielding *Honbu* soldiers.

Mas Oyama called all of us to his office in a rage. In accordance with the prevalent *sempai*-as-gangster atmosphere at *Honbu* my first year, someone had posted a sign in the basement gym stating that the training equipment (weights, punching bags, sandbags, etc.) was for use by black belt *sempai* only. The sign, I believe, said that lower ranks could use the equipment, but only when no *sempai* were around.

It was completely contrary to Mas Oyama's teaching to do anything whatsoever to impede the desire to train of any student, particularly beginners – not to mention that it was bad for business! – and when one of *Honbu's* nonresidential dojo population anonymously wrote a letter to *Sosai* complaining about the policy, he went through the roof.

"Who was it?" he demanded, over and over again. "Who put up that sign?" Mas Oyama all but slammed his fist down on his desk. For that was how angry he was, both about the sign and because no one in the fifteen-man circle squeezed into his office that day would answer his question.

If I'm not mistaken — and I could be, because as a foreigner I was an outside observer so much of the time — that was how thoroughly fear permeated the atmosphere in the dormitory then. We all knew that Yuhi *Sempai* had put up the sign. I was only a half year into my training at *Honbu*, and I didn't consider it my role to jump out and answer a question that everyone else seemed to have a very good reason not to answer. But I knew damn well that it had been Yuhi *Sempai* who'd created the policy.

We were foreigners, and there was a feeling that the Japanese must know better than we did. They knew the Japanese system, so it wasn't our place to speak up. I think that at that point I attributed everyone's refusal to speak to something tough and admirable, like no one wanting to be the rat who reports the wrongdoing of one of his *sempai*. But I wondered in retrospect if it wasn't just cowardice, plain and simple.

Whoever ratted was going to get his ass kicked in the dojo, if not by Yuhi *Sempai*, then by those who shared his worldview. That's all there was to it.

And yet I was on the edge of my toes, millimeters away from stepping forward and saying, "Osu, *shitsurei shimasu!* It was Yuhi *sempai*."

For god's sake, it was Mas Oyama asking the question that we all knew the answer to and that we were all refusing to answer!

Mas Oyama, himself, and we refused him!

I just figured that it wasn't my place, since I was a foreigner, and a weak one at that. How appropriate would that have been, that the weakest foreigner in the dormitory was the one to go against the grain? Somehow, I thought that my stepping forward would have been weak. I only realize now — wishing that I could go back — that on the contrary, it might have actually been the stronger choice.

I had been afraid to speak up after all.[87]

Standing outside *Sosai's* memorial looking in at that immovable circle of *Honbu* warriors, I realized that it was possible that history would show them to be in the wrong. If history unfolded a certain way, it could show

---

[87] Years later, I would ask Kyokushin-kan Chairman Hatsuo Royama, and he would explain, in no uncertain terms, that the important point to consider was that I, and my *uchi deshi* roommates, had *sempai* present. In the Japanese system, he explained, it would have been incorrect to speak up because our *sempai* had chosen not to. "But that was *Sosai* there, demanding an answer!" I protested, but *Kancho* Royama had *not* misunderstood the scenario I described. "It doesn't matter," he said. "Your *sempai* didn't speak up and therefore you had no choice but to stay silent."

them once again to be misguided – if not in fact cowards! – in the face of *Honbu's* outdated gangster-style hierarchy.

But my God, *Sosai* was dead!

The entire world was turned on its ear. Who was to say at that point what was right and what was wrong?

Me?

Surely not. I was pretty big, I thought, in America, because my Japan experience – and my Choi family experience – gave me a significant edge in terms of perspective when compared to the rest. But in Japan?

It was so often the opposite! As a foreigner I was the fish out of water, and I could only do the best I could.

I did suppress an urge to break through that circle like a linebacker and go, particularly, to Kikuko. Not only was she *Sosai's* daughter, not only was she something like my step- second cousin by way of my unspoken adoption by her first cousin Master Choi, not only had she been at one (fleeting) time in my life the object of my more-than-just-friends attention, but she was also my friend!

And as if the whole damn circle had been a windmill, and I was a lunatic on a horse with a lance, I had to shake myself to dismiss an almost irresistible impulse to mount my steed and charge into it to do battle.

Of course I wouldn't have thrown any blows. Like a chivalrous intervention on a crowed Japanese subway train, I'd have merely pushed my way through the crowd, approached the Oyama family, and asked if I could do anything to ease their pain.

"Can I bring you some water?"

"Can I work the fan for awhile?"

The world was on its ear, and I can only find refuge in that fact for failing to know the right course of action that day.

TWENTY-EIGHT

SADLY, THE DISAPPOINTMENT of the weekend, for me, didn't end at the memorial service.

It was that weekend that I started to feel, for the first time, the bite of opposition to the work that I was doing in America, opposition to my raw ambition, and – as best as I could comprehend then – opposition to the fact that I was daring, as a 23-year-old Beta non-branch chief, to be the only person on North American soil to attempt to do something for all of American Kyokushin, not just for myself or for the Kyokushin of my own local area.

Of course Michael Monaco's tournament in Rochester, Henri Orlean's in Atlantic City, and André Gilbert's in Montreal were admirable attempts at continent-wide Kyokushin events. I could only hope that someday I would be able to organize events such as those. But Michael Monaco, Henri Orlean and André Gilbert were branch chiefs, and tournaments were an accepted part of the Kyokushin routine.

North American Kyokushin had never had its own publication before, and control of Kyokushin's English-language media – and certainly the fact that I wanted to share that control with *Honbu* far more than with the Americans – was turning out to be a touchy subject.

I was also beginning to feel that maybe I had done something wrong in my editorial choices for the first book. It was beyond me at first why I should be criticized for including some self-generated material; the entire thing was a product of my own labor, after all, and it was clear that *Sosai* had intended to make me a branch chief.

The one choice I had made that I would probably go back and reverse if I could was that in the heat of the sleepless, nine-day period when the entire 104-page book was laid out, I chose to use its rear cover to announce the autobiographical book that I was still in the throes of writing. Of course, like the other hundred steps of my vision, I could already see that finished product too. I hadn't yet realized that when I looked into the future, I was looking farther than almost anyone else I'd ever met, and when I beheld my own works in the light of a foregone conclusion of success, what was to me as if it had all already happened must have seemed, to almost everyone else, so far-fetched that it made me look presumptuous indeed. I hadn't yet realized how painfully it would separate me from the rest if I continued to make choices based on that unusually far-reaching vision. I certainly lacked the experience as a writer to have any conception at all of how truly far I was from actually having the book written that I'd so audaciously (according to my critics) advertised on the back cover of *Budo Karate Illustrated*.

Indeed, sixteen years later, that greater book is still not finished as I apply the finishing touches to this one.

Ironically, it would be one of my greatest critics of that year, my editor, Jacques's wife Annie, who would finally be instrumental in leading me away from my embarrassment for having blundered to the extent that I did. It would be she, in the end, who would lead me towards an ability to finally assert, "So what? It was my first attempt, and it couldn't have been perfect. There'll be future books in which to make up for any damage done. If I collapse under the weight of my mistakes, won't it impede my ability to keep moving forward?"

Unfortunately for my morale that weekend, however, there were others in the international Kyokushin community who weren't as forgiving.

Cameron Quinn's criticism was gentle, and because of that I welcomed the fall of his *shinai*. Cameron Quinn was the author of the well known *Budo Karate of Mas Oyama*, and he was the fighter/writer/teacher that *Sosai* had encouraged me to emulate in my future. Thanks to stories Judd had told me in the dormitory, my earliest impressions of Cameron were not ones that I wanted to emulate, but Judd's stories were from a long time ago, and in 1994 I valued Cameron's opinion more than most English-speaking others because of his close ties to *Honbu*.

Unlike the rest, he at least knew what the hell he was talking about, having spent some time there, too, in Tokyo at the heart of it all.

"You broke the cardinal rule of journalism, mate," he told me in an Ikebukuro bookstore in the days leading up to the memorial. "You wrote about yourself. The article that you wrote about Jacques was about Jacques, but it also had a lot of you in it, and you're liable to take some heat for it alongside your photos. But, you know," he paused to smile reassuringly, "we live and we learn. I look back at my own book that I did ten years ago, and am embarrassed by some of it myself! A lot of it is good, but all that material that I included about the significance of the belt colors that seemed like such a good idea at the time, I realize now shouldn't have been included. It was just filler to make the book bigger so that it would feel more important. But that's how we learn, and I wouldn't be who I am today without the experience."

"Osu," was all that I could say, but the gentle criticism had hit its mark, and I started to be concerned.

My *sempai* David Bunt's criticism was harder to swallow given an element of our history, and given the way he would, within that same hour at the Metropolitan Hotel, jump down my throat on an unrelated issue for which I was not at fault. Despite his compliments on the book's general appearance two weeks earlier in Amtrak's V.I.P. lounge at Grand Central Station, David had begun to change his tune. "Yeah, Ligo, I was impressed by the book's overall appearance," he said, "but then I looked at it a little closer and realize that there are some problems there. But we don't have to talk about that now. There'll be plenty of time for that later."

Like Cameron's criticism, his words were fairly benign.

But then there was the fact of our early history together at *Honbu*. And there was the tongue-lashing.

David Bunt had been in Japan during my first year there. He'd tested for his *nidan* finally, and returned to New York with a branch chief certificate, but had never gone on to establish his own branch. Although I considered him a likable guy when I was nineteen at *Honbu*, I wound up not liking him much as my first year as an *uchi deshi* drew on, because he fit himself so comfortably into *Honbu's* gangster-like hierarchy that was so unfriendly to a less-than-tough Beta like me.

Judd Reid and Sandor Brezovai were both Kyokushin black belts when they arrived in Japan. They were both already lightweight champions in their respective countries. I was a white belt. The *nidan* that I'd earned during six years of training with Master Choi was somehow less because his system of instruction was slightly outside of Kyokushin's; he taught a different set of *kata*, ones he'd learned in Korea. And my personal toughness did not compare to Judd's and Sandor's. It only made sense to me at the time that they keep their black belts, and that I start over from the beginning. It's what I'd always been told I would have to do anyway once I finally entered the dormitory. Yet there was another key level in our world in which the three of us were equals: We were all foreign, first-year *uchi deshi,* and in terms of the dormitory hierarchy of first-, second- and third-year students, we were all treated the same.

From left to right, Sandor Brezovai, Judd Reid, Nathan Ligo, and our *uchi deshi sempai* Yuhi at *Honbu's* summer camp at Tateyama the same weekend I met the Zen monks, Yamaguchi Sensei and Nagare-*san*. It was the summer of 1990 and the three of us foreigners had been *uchi deshi* for less than three months.

We were all *gaijin* after all, foreigners in a foreign country that was sometimes not very hospitable to foreigners. At least we had that in common: We all had the language barrier; we were all occasionally mistreated by the Japanese.

I hadn't forgotten Bunt *Sempai's* cold indifference towards me during the late part of that year we were in Japan together. He'd shared laughs and funny stories with Judd, Sandor and the brown-belt-wearing Frenchman, our *uchi deshi sempai* Mocaram, while to me he seemed unnecessarily exclusive and condescending. That exclusion felt particularly biting given that we were the only two Americans there. Yet I found myself forgiving him later, back in the U.S. He was a likable guy, after all, and he finally treated me like an adult in Rochester. Maybe he had just been caught up in the tough-guy attitude of it all.

He was a New Yorker, and I was raised in the South, where we tend to be a bit more delicate in our demeanor.

Bunt *Sempai* told me how respectable I looked in my suit when I met with *Sosai* in Rochester, and like Michael Monaco's, his compliment had no strings attached. I had valued his advice when I was first trying to garner support for the *Budo Karate Illustrated* project, so I was starting to warm up to him even though in the back of my mind I remembered the condescending New Yorker who had been a bit too big to talk to me much while at *Honbu*.

But that darker side of him showed itself again the day before *Sosai's* memorial.

I had already made two one-hour trips on foot from the Metropolitan Hotel to the *Kimi Ryokan* – about eight blocks across Ikebukuro to that cheaper traditional Japanese travelers' inn[88] – to guide American branch chiefs who had reservations there but who wouldn't have been able to find it on their own. And I didn't mind. I enjoyed the walk with *Shihan* Monaco and Tom and Toni Flynn, and on one of the return trips I was invited to sit down in a sushi place with Montreal's André Gilbert for a beer. I'd given him a copy of my book, and he was not only complimentary, but also welcoming of the idea of doing a second issue that included content generated in his Montreal branch. After that chance encounter, however, by the time I got back to the Metropolitan where David Bunt was schmoozing with a group of big-shot international branch chiefs, I was only fifteen minutes away from an appointment I'd made with Akiko on the other side of the train station. David chose that inopportune moment to bark an order at me to take a third group, and their luggage, over to the *Kimi*. He barked it like I was a white belt *uchi deshi* again – and I had the distinct impression that his tone had more to do with the company he was with than with any need for him to be, towards me, personally condescending. How uncomfortable for me that I had no choice but to tell him I was not available. "Osu, I'm sorry, I can't. I have a date," I said.

That pissed him off, as you can imagine, even though I was polite and far more frustrated – as the Beta – than angry or confrontational.

---

[88] Where I'd stayed during the weekend of my *nidan* grading, just four months earlier.

Nevertheless, I could see him thinking, "What's this punk kid doing having a date when there's luggage to be carried for Kyokushin?" As I excused myself, I could see him gearing up to vocalize his dissatisfaction to his tablemates.

I've always been sorry that that third group he'd asked me to guide to the *Kimi Ryokan* was Brooklyn's Randy James and his wife Rose, and that I was further put in the uncomfortable position of having to deny David's request in front of the two of them, fresh off a 13-hour flight in from America. But there was nothing else I could have done. I had a beautiful young woman waiting for me across town in the street, and those were still the days before everyone had cell phones.

The third in the triple whammy of increasingly biting criticism I suffered that evening came from Stuart Corrigal of Vancouver.

Although I'd met him in Rochester once before and corresponded with him briefly about my project, he was the other avid supporter that I acquired that day. Corrigal jumped down my throat within that same half hour as David there in the lobby of Metropolitan, and he did so in the company of Hawaii's Bobby Lowe.

In this last case, I made the mistake that warranted it.

Shihan Corrigal paid me for the one copy of my book that I'd mailed him from North Carolina, but told me – in some kind of unspoken huff, I thought – that he wasn't interested in selling any more to his students. More than any other in North America I associated him with *Shihan* Lowe. It had been from Corrigal's tournament in Vancouver that *Shihan* Lowe had boasted about his students bringing home trophies in his original letter to me denying *Budo Karate Illustrated* his support. It was clear that the two of them were pretty tight, and I figured that they just shared the same kind of personality, and therefore the same blanket opposition to anyone trying to do anything ambitious or creative of which they themselves were not at the helm.

In retrospect, I wonder if they weren't simply feeling a bit threatened by the strong organizational work being done on America's East Coast by *Shihan* Jacques and Annie, Tom Flynn, Michael Monaco and the rest. I wasn't part of the East Coast group, but from all the way out west – certainly from as far west as Hawaii – I must have looked like I was.

I wasn't too worried, though. Even *Shihan* Lowe had had no choice, in the end, but to get on board, since *Sosai* supported the book. And during the weekend of Mas Oyama's memorial, I had no reason to suspect that Matsui wouldn't provide the same kind of backing. *Shihan* Corrigal, too, I figured, would have no choice but to become a supporter. I was still confident that even the project's less-than-eager contributors would support the project wholeheartedly once they realized that I was only making waves to make all of North American Kyokushin stronger for them too.

Anyway, I had Montreal's André Gilbert. I had Toronto's much smaller Wade Stogran. Stuart Corrigal had a huge branch – he was the primary west coast guy in Canada – but with most of the U.S. branch chiefs on board for a second go-round, I'd have plenty of material even if, worst-case scenario, he chose to boycott the project entirely.

The mistake I made that resulted in *Shihan* Corrigal's jumping down my throat – and it *was* my mistake – was that I addressed him as "Stuart," rather than as "*Shihan* Corrigal."

What a catastrophe!

It was an honest mistake because all of the American Kyokushin people that I had come to associate with – Michael Monaco, Michael Lorden, David Bunt, Jacques and Annie, the Jameses, all of them – referred to him as "Stuart."

It was about the only thing I'd ever heard him called!

Yet I was not a branch chief. No one had even seen me in my black belt, since the only time I'd worn it outside Davidson was at my grading at *Honbu*. I was in the wrong; it was a breach of the code. Nevertheless, *Shihan* Corrigal's *shinai* fell on my back there in the lobby of the Metropolitan Hotel in a particularly brutal fashion.

Unfortunately, I wasn't as humble as I probably should have been in my apology.

Frankly, I was pissed off, and I didn't care. I had a date with a beautiful woman, *Budo Karate Illustrated's* momentum had not yet been shaken, and Mas Oyama was dead.

I expected some significant fallout.

Leaving the Metropolitan that evening, I thought of *Shihan* Jacques and Annie. Jacques was *Sosai's* oldest friend in America, and fearing that Matsui's public display would belittle the enormity of his personal experiences with *Sosai,* Jacques had opted to steer clear of the memorial service. For him, the notion of it was just too heartbreaking.

I missed Jacques and Annie during that hour because of the hits my morale had just taken. I wished for *Shihan* Jacques when Stuart Corrigal slapped down my well-intentioned mistake with such venom. Jacques would have winked, reassured *Shihan* Corrigal of my good intentions, and cautioned me in a way that would have made the discomfort go away.

Even without Jacques there with me to say it, *Fuck this guy Stuart anyway!* I thought as I walked alone away from the Metropolitan Hotel. *He's pushing what? Fifty? In fifteen years he'll be old and gray, ten years after that he'll be senile or dead, and the future of North American Kyokushin will be in my hands and the hands of my students anyway.*

* * *

Purely by chance, I found myself on the same return flight to Toronto as Michael Monaco, Michael Lorden, and Tom and Toni Flynn. We spent that night together in the same airport hotel before going our separate ways the next morning, and I received the benefit of their briefing on the branch chief meetings that I hadn't been allowed to attend.

Fucking Horai! I thought to myself. *Twins! He and Stuart Corrigal.*

For the first of two times, I had gone to him with a question that would have been better asked of Matsui, thinking that it would be diplomatic to do so, and that I would get to do what I wanted AND make a friend in a new *sempai* at the same time. How silly it was, I know now, to go to the elitist Horai and ask him for permission to attend the international branch chief meeting for the sake of the magazine!

Of course he scoffed at the suggestion.

I lamented missing the history that happened in the Metropolitan Hotel that day, and I thought of *Sosai's* asking me one more time, from his hospital bed the last time we met, if there was anything else he could do for me. How disappointed he seemed when I told him that he looked so fine that I would wait until after he was out of the hospital to ask him about business matters!

I humored myself to believe that I might eventually receive the same kind of blanket support from Matsui that I had once enjoyed from *Sosai*, but it was plain, that particular weekend in Tokyo, that Matsui had his hands full, and it would behoove me to stay out of his way.

According to what the Flynns and *Shihan* Monaco told me, the branch chief meetings could virtually have been summed up by single names: the Japanese meeting by the name Takagi, and the international one by *Shihan* Bobby Lowe.

Kaoru Takagi was one of *Sosai's* fifty-two Japanese branch chiefs. It was my understanding that he was a highly respected one, with a large number of students. On the Japanese Kyokushin map, his photo was the only one pasted on the entire island of Hokkaido, while the other fifty-one faces were scattered densely about the rest of Japan. He was also well known as a biographer who had worked closely with Mas Oyama on a recent biography. Apparently he stood up in protest of Matsui that day at the Metropolitan, and his head was the first one on the Japanese side to bounce. A starry-eyed Tom Flynn told me that Matsui hadn't even flinched.

"No problem," he said, "If you don't want to support Kyokushin, get out, and good luck. We will go on without you."

I don't know what the dispute was about – perhaps he came out in support of the family – but in the overall context, it wasn't important. Matsui was at the helm, and he was powerful enough, at least for the time being, that even a wave such as Takagi's didn't in the slightest affect his course.

Apparently the International Branch Chief Meeting was a bit of a zoo, with overseas branch chiefs from all over the world raising their hands and asking, over and over again, what to do and whom to contact in various situations. "*Shihan* Bobby Lowe, *Shihan* Bobby Lowe, *Shihan* Bobby Lowe," was apparently the answer to all questions.

Shihan Lowe was the only active non-Japanese member of *Sosai's* IKO who wasn't Jacques's *koohai*. His had been the first overseas branch that *Sosai* established, in Hawaii in the fifties, and he was the natural choice for Matsui to have all the international branches funnel their correspondence through any time they needed to contact *Honbu*. For a time it looked like *Shihan* Lowe was getting a huge promotion, but as time passed it would become apparent that it was more of a smokescreen.

Matsui's most important concerns immediately following the death of Mas Oyama were domestic ones. He had to hold the Japanese side together – and fend off the attacks mounted by the family and by a growing number of Takagis, and it must have been oh so convenient! for him to have 133 countries' worth of correspondence filtered through

Shihan Lowe's fax machine in Hawaii. His only two interpreters, after all, were temporary fill-ins!

The most interesting piece of news from the American side to come out of the meetings that weekend was that *Shihan* Lowe told Tom Flynn that he would be putting Tom forward as the chairman of the IKO in America sometime within the next year. So far we hadn't had a chairman, but assuming the right man could be found, it only made sense that we should. Although I suffered an initial pang of fear – the notion of any American standing between me and *Honbu* was an unattractive one – in the end I didn't mind.

Tom Flynn was probably the best man for the job, that is, if there *was* a good man for such an undesirable job.

My relationship with Tom Flynn was closer than with most of the other US branch chiefs. He had been a powerful supporter of my book efforts, and I didn't have much concern about being able to work with him. I certainly had no designs or ambitions of my own for any kind of leadership role in U.S. Kyokushin in the foreseeable future – of course, by that I mean foreseeable for other people, since *foreseeable* for me was lifetime long – and even in that long a term, I only had such designs in a *maybe someday* situation where the majority of the Kyokushin *karateka* in America were either my own students, or the students of my students. I didn't have the slightest bit of desire to ever be the boss of Kyokushin in America, unless – and this I *could* imagine – the majority of American Kyokushin someday came to be by the fruits of my own labor. What a nightmare mistake it would be, I realized, for anyone to try to be the boss of Kyokushin in America without a far stronger claim to that position than a rubber-stamp designation from *Honbu*!

If any one person can make a 100,000-member multistate organization of both his own students and his own students' students, as Shigeru Oyama came so close to doing in the seventies, I thought, *that's the man who will one day be the spiritual leader of American Kyokushin!*

Of course, I was certain then that there was no other American who had a better shot than I did at one day building an organization that would surpass Shigeru Oyama's of the 1970s. I had always considered the chance that I might one day do so my birthright as the prodigal student of Mas Oyama's nephew and the only American personal student of Mas Oyama.

On my more demented days, I even considered it my destiny. On those days it was part of the future that I could see so clearly.

But I was not stupid.

I could see it happening, but that was something like thirty years in the future, and I knew that so much could change in thirty years that I was far more likely to lose sight of it. I knew that I'd have to be dreadfully careful if I wanted to keep such a vision alive, and I considered being that careful my responsibility. It wouldn't work without throngs of my own students, and only the future would tell if I'd ever be able to get there. We have a saying in karate that it's far better to have one student who learns the true way than thousands who call us *sensei* but stray into something less. Building an organization of thousands, I knew, would depend on being able to make a key first few who really understood.

And that, I knew, could take decades.

In the meantime, Tom Flynn could have it. *Far better him than Horai!*

* * *

Virtually broke, I slept that night on the floor of a hotel room between Michael Monaco in the bed to my left and Michael Lorden in the bed to my right. I slept like a baby after having huge beers with Tom and Toni Flynn, who were in their own room down the hall. The next morning I got up early to go running before meeting with Michael Lorden over breakfast.

Sensei Lorden had asked if he could meet privately with me the day before, but would not tell me what it was about. I was afraid that I was in for another round of criticism.

"I met with Matsui *Kancho* the day before yesterday," Michael Lorden began, leaning forward from the creaking plastic of a molded fast-food restaurant chair, "as we all did. You know that he had agreed to meet with all the foreign branch chiefs, but that since there were so many of us, he met with us in pairs, and only gave us about five minutes each. Anyway, I just wanted to tell you that when I was in there with Henri Orlean, he proudly showed *Kancho* one of his magazines – you know, those flimsy paperback things that he prints in his dojo for distribution to his own students that only have pictures of himself? – Well, he showed *Kancho* a copy and told him he hoped to distribute it in all of the U.S. branches. He was clearly trying to move in and compete with your project."

I held my breath.

"The interesting thing that I wanted to talk with you about," Sensei Lorden went on, "was that Matsui told him flat out no. 'Small, inferior magazines will make Kyokushin look small and inferior,' he said and I thought Henri was going to crawl under the table in shame. 'You should make an effort to support Nathan Ligo's magazine,' *Kancho* told him. 'If there's to be a magazine for Kyokushin in the U.S., it will be Nathan Ligo's.'"

You can imagine my relief as he went on.

Sensei Lorden, second in a line of international branch chiefs, entering the memorial hall at *Sosai's* memorial service.

"So, the reason I wanted to talk with you was because I believe there's going to be a really big future for your magazine, and I thought that maybe I could help in some way. I have some money saved up, my pension from the government following my accident . . ."

Sensei Lorden had been some kind of commando with an elite fast-response anti-terrorist team – one that could supposedly be anywhere in the world in less than twelve hours – until he'd fallen out of a parked 747 onto the tarmac during a training exercise, and broken his back. The doctors told him he would never walk again, and he credited his Kyokushin training for his near 100% recovery.

"I thought that I might buy into your project," he went on. "I thought that you could use a partner."

Midas wouldn't have been in the slightest bit surprised, since such a future was his playground, but Nathan Ligo was next to speechless. As if the news that Matsui had voiced such strong support of my book wasn't enough, here was one of the U.S. branch chiefs, one of the book's original supporters, wanting to buy into it and make part of it his own!

How confidently insane I was to all but tell him no!

I needed some time, I told him. "I want to see how things unfold in the next several months. I'm very grateful. I'll keep your offer in mind and we'll see. For now, I've been frankly worried whether or not my magazine is even going to have a future. When I met with *Kancho* two weeks ago, he was nowhere near as supportive.

"He told me to send him a proposal concerning the magazine's proceeds. I feel like I ought to work that out with *Kancho* first, and then you and I can talk about what comes next."

PART V

TWENTY-NINE

As MY CONNECTING FLIGHT from Toronto crossed the Blue Ridge Mountains, I pulled my lips back against my teeth and drew in a sharp breath to brace myself against a perception of coming cold. I was suddenly aware of Helen, and it was with that physical reaction that I denied the magnetic pull that I once again felt so acutely in what I perceived to be her general direction. It had been so easy to put all of that out of my mind in Japan. I never had any choice but to be brutally sane in my second home country, where from the first day I set foot on Japanese soil, grueling physical training had been there to pound away any such nonsense.

I thought of that single massive tear that gathered in the inside corner of Akiko's eye, and smiled a smile of regret that slipped away to the frown of cold acceptance to which my facial muscles were becoming more accustomed. *What a beautiful woman!* I thought. *I don't deserve such a partner. Maybe someday my life's work will take me to where I can stop for long enough to see what would come of such a pursuit!*

For other reasons, too, I couldn't help but feel I was moving into a storm. Sadly, it wasn't one of Davidson's spring thunderstorms that had so complemented Midas's rampage.

In this storm there was no power.

It was simply dark.

It swirled around Davidson and drew energy towards it like a whirlpool churning in slow motion.

I realized then that I had cause to be afraid.

I thought of Katsuhiko Horai bouncing me and my camera from *Sosai's* memorial service, and scoffing at my request to attend Matsui's first international branch chief meeting. I saw once again *Sosai's* ashes in that heavy silk-wrapped box held high on the straining shoulders of his wife and daughters in the parking lot outside. Michael Lorden's description of the meeting he'd had with Matsui gave me a glimmer of hope, but I realized then that it was only a glimmer, and I shuddered at how precarious my situation had become.

Just half a year earlier, I looked into the future and could see a diploma from Davidson College, the completion of my first autobiographical book, a branch chief appointment in Mas Oyama's IKO, a Watson Fellowship that would allow me to spend one more year in Japan, and the editorship of an English language periodical publication on Kyokushin Karate that would rival the leading martial arts magazines on newsstands in North America.

It's difficult to pinpoint exactly when all of that started to slip through my fingers.

It was on my final approach into Charlotte, however, that it dawned on me how much of my future was suddenly hanging on the success of *Budo Karate Illustrated*. All my eggs were in that one basket. Starting with *Sosai's* death and my failure to ask him for the branch chief appointment I'd been sure he was grooming me for, the other benchmarks of my vision's success slipped away, one by one, in the face of the increasing demands of that one all-important project.

It should be no surprise that in a world where I'd used the titan that Helen had become in her absence to normalize my relationships with giants like Jacques Sandulescu, Midas, Matsui, and Mas Oyama, that *Sosai's* death turned out not to be the greatest shock my system sustained during my final semester in college.

Helen's pregnancy, in and of itself, hadn't fazed me in the least. I was only happy for her.

How incestuous tiny little Davidson could be! – so small that an eighteenth-century-novel classmate of mine named Kelly had started dating my friend and student Rafael, and it was she that gave me the news. Apparently she'd had lunch with Helen once during those final weeks before Mas Oyama died, and "Dr. Ecks is pregnant," she told me. "Can you believe it? She's going to have twins!"

Good for her! I thought. *Good for them! Good for all of them!*

My voice was just then finally coming back after the punch I'd taken to my throat by that psycho Russian at my *nidan* grading two weeks earlier. The red welts on my arms and torso had long since darkened to the standard black and blue of bruises and begun their slow fade to brown. I had just gotten to where I could walk normally again after the blows I'd taken to my legs, and the pain of that long-lost but oh so familiar post-*kumite* shuffle had helped to keep Midas at bay. Less than two weeks before Kelly told me that Helen was pregnant, I spoke my last words to Mas Oyama, and I still had no clue that those words were going to be my last.

I hungered to see Helen, of course. I longed to join her for the moment of celebration we'd share when I congratulated her on her news. I longed for the fleeting moment when her eyes softened and welcomed mine as both friend and student absent from her life for too many weeks already. She'd respond with warmth because she'd see that my congratulations were genuine. For months already by then, I was sure that I'd be able to protect her. For months, I'd resolved to let myself be in love with her and, at all costs, leave her safely the hell alone.

And I'd almost been able to prove it.

Several months passed during which I made seeking her out impossible. By welcoming the distractions of my trip to Japan to meet with *Sosai* in January, the final *Budo Karate Illustrated* compilation in the days that followed, the ten weeks of training for my *nidan* grading after that, and finally my second trip to Japan in March for the grading itself, I'd succeeded in keeping Helen safely out of reach for nearly three months. The collateral damage that I never could have foreseen, however, had been the desperate, accidental alternative of reaching out to her *in her absence* in that way that so powerfully opened the doors to Midas's ability to turn everything he touched into gold.

Surely, I reasoned, *if we met now and shared that warm, congratulatory moment, Helen would see in my eyes all that I don't want her to see. Perhaps she'd even see the extent to which I've reached into her life without her knowing it.*

How could she not *see that I love her?*

How could she not see the extent to which I've tied the absence of her *to creative endeavors that are of such earthshaking importance? How could she not see, though I'd struggle with everything I have to conceal it, how badly I want her to know that like Leonardo DaVinci, Miyamoto Musashi, or Wolfgang Amadeus Mozart, I've managed to craft, specifically for her, the compliment to end all compliments? How could I hide from her that I've been wielding* the absence of her *like a sword to cut through all that's threatened to harden in my personality, to* unleash all that's left of the creative monster I was when I was a child?

Would she not look into my eyes as Lissa did once, and realize that what she saw there was insatiable need? Would she not recognize how hard I've struggled to shield her from it? Would compassion not put her in jeopardy as it had Lissa, and my cousin Kristen before that?

Of course it wouldn't!

What kind of insanity is that, anyway!

What kind of fantasy!

How far off the deep end you've gone, Nathan! This woman that you barely even know couldn't possibly have the slightest clue! She probably wouldn't even know if it were written on your face and you were standing right in front of her. She'd have no clue because there's nothing there! It's a fantasy. It's just another hallucination self-propagated to mask what is harder to face. Give it up, Nathan! Let it go. Grow up, for God's sake! Shut down the machine and live a normal life like everyone else!

Get a freakin' grip!

Two weeks after hearing the news of Kelly's lunch date with Helen, however, the blow came that was to be the really earthshaking one of my twenty-third year. Another of Davidson's trio of new young English professors, Shireen Carroll – the same one who had once caught Rafael's attention before it fell finally on Kelly – contacted me and asked me if I could stop by her place twice a day during a weekend that she was going to be away to feed Thor and Toto. And of course I didn't mind. It was the other piece of information I learned in the course of that conversation, however, that altered the course of more than just my semester.

"I was going to leave them with Helen," Dr. Carroll explained, "because she's got that fenced-in backyard. But that became impractical because of the complications she's having with her pregnancy."

I'm sure she wasn't aware, but my world stopped spinning then, the way it had when my student mentioned sixteen months earlier that he'd seen an advertisement for a tournament in Rochester and that Mas Oyama was going to be there.

"Complications?" I asked. "What kind of complications?" I felt as exposed then as I had in my Shakespeare professor's car when I'd broken the silence to call out the name "Helen," when of course I'd meant to call out my professor's name, "Sarah."

"She's having twins, you know," Dr. Carroll said. "And her doctor wants her to stay in bed for safety's sake. Apparently there is some danger."

I'd been so desperate for so long to conceal the truth, I felt myself so dangerously near the threshold beyond which the façade would have cracked that I dared not ask what I so desperately needed to know.

"Danger to whom?" I would have asked. "Do you mean she could lose the babies, or did you mean there was danger to her too?"

The notion of anything bad happening to any of them was more than I could process. The rest of my day passed as if I was frozen in place, and everything else blurred by like a movie played in fast forward.

At one o'clock in the morning as I walked towards home from the Café under Davidson's moon, I took a deep breath of life there on the bricks in front of Chambers as was my norm. I let the oxygen and the scents of spring's coming glory bombard my system. I welcomed the subsequent pulse of energy that rippled down my spine and caused me to convulse once at the midsection. For a moment I felt with my feet downward into the earth and reached through the bedrock in Helen's direction. Such was the extent of my routine.

What happened next happened all on its own.

I stopped in my tracks and dropped to one knee as if pausing to tie my shoe. I sank ten fingertips into the bricks in front of me, looked forward into space parallel to the planet, and took in a second deep breath of life. I felt the power then, but this time it came from quite a different direction. I was suddenly aware of the sky, not just that part of it that was over my head but the entire sky, curved over me like a dome from unseen horizon to unseen horizon in all directions. It glowed with a blue fire of the type I was accustomed to drawing out of the earth beneath me, and with my third inhale, like a collapsing star I drew it all in an instant through my nostrils, downwards into my low belly, and channeled it past my elbows, through my ten fingertips, and into the earth.

I channeled it in the direction where I knew Helen to be.

I reached out for her as I was so accustomed, and imagined or not, I sent that energy with an earth-shattering boom in her direction. Where up until then I'd only drawn it from her, consoling myself that the whole practice was so much nonsense as to be completely harmless to anyone but myself, this time I sent it back for all that I was worth.

Of course, I was more powerless than I'd ever been. Without a God, I wasn't capable of prayer. I believed it to be such a waste. *Get off your ass and do something!* had become my mantra. *Don't just sit there waiting for help to fall on you from above! Figure out how you can make a difference and, for God's sake, have the balls to try!* In terms of helping Helen – repairing damage that my conscience told me I must somehow have caused – there really wasn't much I could do.

But that wasn't enough for me.

In the closest thing to a prayer that nonpraying me could muster, I chose the active, though likely imaginary, course. I reached out into the world for power I'm sure I couldn't really touch, conjured up a supernova, and sent it in the form of healing, life-giving energy in Helen's direction. She was in bed, in that tiny brick house across town with the fenced-in backyard, two tiny versions of her and her husband Jack were forming within her, and whether I could really do it or not – whether it was vision or fantasy – I gave all of them my own personal supernova's worth of blue healing energy, through my ten fingertips, through the melting bricks into the bedrock beneath them, and upwards again into the body of the woman I loved.

"Be at ease, Helen," the gesture would have said could it have been put into words. "Sleep peacefully. Don't worry. Everything's going to be okay. Sleep peacefully now and you'll see that everything will start to be on the upswing when you wake up in the morning."

During the course of just two inhales, my body weight had shifted forward to increase the pressure on my fingertips. The earth spun for a moment laterally around the axis created by the area of brick where my fingertips touched the ground. I realized then that my fingers were bent backwards as far as they could go, the tendons burned to let me know they could take no more, and with that I rose to my feet, shook them once, and continued my trek as if nothing had happened.

Nothing had, right?

The duration was that of three casual breaths. I'd dropped to one knee as if to tie my shoe, and anyone who'd borne witness would have seen no more than that. Yet without my realizing it, the entire course of my life had changed. I still reached out into the world whenever I was alone to inhale the power and beauty of the natural world. I still paused to worship life, love, and the world around me. I still allowed myself to be moved by the thunderstorms. But from that day forward I stamped my foot, gnashed my teeth, and denied myself the euphoric bliss in which Midas had roared his first roar. Whereas before, the earth had melted under my feet and split open in thunderous booms as I drew power out if it, now, if there was any power to be found, I drew it innocuously out of the atmosphere and sent it back down into the earth instead. What before could have been likened to a volcano came instead to resemble a slow swirling gloom that churned like a whirlpool in slow motion, drawing heat and energy out of the sky, back downwards into the earth where it was meant to be.

The next day at Davidson's computer center where Lisa and I had compiled the first issue of *Budo Karate Illustrated*, my work and my world having groaned to a halt once again like a freight train run out of track, I wrote more drafts of a single paragraph than I'd ever written before in an attempt to convey what I already knew I'd be unable to say.

"Dear Helen," was what I finally wound up with. "Long time, no see! And here I thought you were just being antisocial. I just spoke with Shireen. She asked me to walk her dogs a couple times this weekend. She told me that they were going to stay in your yard but that that had turned out to be inconvenient because of the complications you were having with your pregnancy. I had no idea. *Complications* is a big word, isn't it? So is *pregnancy*. God, you must be scared to death! I was really excited for you when Kelly told me a couple weeks ago that you were expecting twins. I ran into her just after you and she had lunch together. I also felt pretty stupid. I'd seen you only a week or so earlier and I didn't even notice. And here you were, how many months pregnant? Wow, they really must be tiny! Don't worry too much, Helen. There's too much life and too many things coming to life right now in this part of the world for anything to go wrong. Have you noticed? If you haven't, step outside or open a window and take a deep breath. You can smell it, the life, I mean. There's plenty to go around . . ."

Step outside and take a deep breath, I wanted to tell her. *Stop in your tracks for just one second. Straighten your spine, rock your head slightly back, and contemplate the wonder of this rock upon which we float through space. Draw in a slow, deep breath and drink from this stunningly beautiful world in which we live, and any possible thing that ails you will fall away to nothing.*

That's what I wanted to say.

I wanted to show her how.

But to do so would have been to give myself away, and that, I believed, would do more harm than good.

What right do I have to so trample on someone else's life?

"I'd be doing the same," I continued in my next line, backtracking to dumb down that which I'd come so close to saying, "but unfortunately as soon as I do my eyes start running, and I start sneezing uncontrollably because of the pollen. Other than that, everything's going well for me. My book rolls off the press in ten days. I haven't forgotten that I said I'd give you a copy. I just turned in the second to last paper of my Davidson career. I've only got one more to write (on Seamus Heaney!), that and two final exams, and it'll all be over. It makes me feel so old! Helen, Dr. Ecks . . ."

I wasn't sure even then what the hell I was supposed to call her!

". . . please let me know if there's anything you need. If Jack's too busy or stressed keeping you company, tell me and I'll come cut the grass or something. Really, I mean it. Just let me know. Hang in there and don't worry. Women have babies all the time."

I realized, of course, that I was putting myself at risk as I finally came to this finished draft, printed and folded it and mailed it inside a card I found at the bookstore on Main Street. What if the complications weren't as serious as I feared them to be? I really didn't know, after all. And in tiny little Davidson, why would I put my well-wishes in writing and mail them rather than picking up the phone, or dropping by her office to see if there were some days that she made it in?

I was in more danger of giving myself away, I think, than ever before, with my pitiful "Helen, Dr. Ecks."

But I didn't care.

Nonsense or not, I couldn't stand to sit by and do nothing. It was against my religion. Of course, all I really did was to send her a card to let her know that I cared. And there is undeniable healing power in letting other people know that they're not alone. The rest, I'm sure, my stupid sapping of power out of the planet Earth, the empty naturalist's prayer I composed wasn't worth the energy it took to conduct.

We don't live in fantasy novels, after all.

In exactly the same way, the reason why all my vision's benchmarks of super achievement started, one by one, to slip though my fingers towards failure was that I simply wasn't equipped. Without Mas Oyama's backing, I lacked the necessary experience and creativity – I lacked the simple time and energy! – to pull all of it off, all at the same time. All of it together was simply too much for the 23-year-old me. I was exhausted! – I hadn't slept normally for the better part of a year – I'd flown though that year on bursts of creative energy that pulsed though my body like chemicals . . . and in the end, I didn't even have the strength to conjure up the chemicals.

Midas was just a fantasy, after all. He was just another reflection of me in a mind shaped by the most fundamental of lessons I'd learned as an adolescent. My peers had taught me that weak, insignificant Nathan Ligo would never be able to achieve anything more than the mundane, and my parents had done their best to second that lesson by teaching me that I was selfish, angry, and maladjusted, and that I ought to be ashamed. The vision, and the creative energy that I conjured up to make it as far as I did, was, of course, simply mine. It was just the way I experienced them that made them seem to be something more. The fact that, on learning of Helen's "complications," I locked Midas back into his tomb was irrelevant. The endeavors were simply too great. They were destined to go down for that reason and that reason alone.

I am amazed when I think back to my psychological preparation for my second and final Watson interview. I compare it to the first one, in which, with one thousand consecutive jumping squats, I woke a demon that I hadn't yet learned to wake through the purer kind of torture I was soon to discover through Helen.

The four of us selected as finalists from Davidson were to meet with a single representative of the Watson Foundation, one by one, in the plush sitting room in the Alumni Building. I spent the entire hour beforehand standing alone in my suit in a rainstorm under an umbrella in the middle of Davidson's football field. It wasn't an earthshaking thunderstorm, like the ones that had shown Midas that the world was his. This one was a slow churning, relentless and monotone deluge that dropped water from above at an unchanging rate for the entirety of the hour that I stood there, my shoes sinking into the turf and my socks soaked through. One of the two largest open areas on campus, the place was one I'd gone to many times before, alone, in search of access to as much of the world at one time as I could find. I had stood there so many times in silence, mostly in the night, to take deep breaths of life and immerse myself in the glory of mostly star-packed skies.

It was there that, foolishly, I took Dillon one night during my freshman year to try to show her, and to try to show her why it would have been a mistake to become attached to me then. "I have to go and see,"

I told her, indicating that wide open sky with a gesture that couldn't have been anything but futile, since, with it, I was indicating not just the entire planet, but also the entirety of the universe around it.

It was all so clear to me then that I was willing to risk letting Dillon believe I'd lost my mind. But this time, it was as if the rain drained away all of that clarity. It brought the boundaries of my world, which were meant to stretch all the way beyond the trees to the unseen horizons, right up to within inches of my flesh. I was accustomed to being able to close my eyes and reach my arms all the way out to feel the curvature of the world, but this time I dared not even reach my arms out beyond the radius of my umbrella for fear I'd soil my suit. In the standing water that gathered there, I was more melted into the planet than I'd ever been on the bricks in front of Chambers, but for some reason that I didn't yet understand, I lacked the heart to reach down into it in search of the power that had seemed so close just a few weeks earlier.

In my interview, I told a geeky little guy in a bowtie of all that I hoped to do in Japan in the year following my graduation. I told him of the aging Mas Oyama and, unaware of the tragic irony of my words, I pointed out that even Mas Oyama wouldn't live forever. I told him how I'd spent the previous months conceiving of and creating a magazine for Kyokushin Karate that I hoped to expand first into Canada and later into South America, to tap into the much larger numbers of Kyokushin *karateka* that populated those countries. I expressed regret that the first issue hadn't been printed yet, because if it had, I told him, "it would be easier for me to show you the scope of the project."

Something must have been missing from my presentation.

One of the Watson Foundation's first priorities is giving money to applicants who couldn't possibly do what that they propose to do without their sponsorship. Perhaps the success I had achieved made him believe that I was set up enough as it was, or that my primary interest was the magazine and opening a dojo in America, and that either I didn't need another year in Japan interviewing Mas Oyama for a future book, or that I would be able to do it anyway, without the Watson. I think more than that though, it was the passion that was missing. I was simply too tired to share with him the same kind of fire that I'd shared with Davidson's exploratory committee six months earlier.

I didn't have the energy.

Perhaps by then it was more the frown of cold acceptance that he saw on my face than any kind of fire in my eyes to go out and achieve the impossible.

The foundation's answer was to come by mail, and it was promised by the end of the semester. I certainly maintained hope for the final weeks of school, but my suspicion that I'd blown my interview was strong enough that it was only hope, and nothing more. Of course, I didn't know how the other three candidates had done in their interviews, or how strict the standard was.

In the end, though, I wasn't at all surprised that I didn't get it.

Midas wasn't with me when I drove to Montreal to photograph André Gilbert's tournament either. My recollection of the entire experience is submerged in a haze of vertigo-like exhaustion, like what I felt when, inverted, I tumbled out of the driver's seat of Rafael's car to look upwards at that angry raven that shrieked down at me the day that Mas Oyama died. The two recollections I have of the tournament were being so sleepy that I couldn't even focus my eyes through the lens of my camera, and putting my foot in my mouth by telling Annie that I was already looking forward into a not-so-distant future when the other supporters of my *Budo Karate Illustrated* project would either be dead or irrelevant.

Of course Midas was back again briefly in all of his glory when he and I together swore our last oath to Mas Oyama beyond the grave. There's no question that Midas helped me then, but then there was the grief of Mas Oyama's loss to call him to the front. I didn't need Helen then and I didn't use her. I didn't need the image of her – or the conglomeration of all she had come in my twisted psyche to represent – to take me where Mas Oyama's death took me so summarily.

Two days later, back in the car again, this time driving to within a stone's throw of America's southern border, it was by sheer force of will that I kept the front wheels of Rafael's car between the lines painted on the concrete. I drove on blind exhausted duty reminiscent of that which had lured me, beyond my control, to Rochester eighteen months earlier to welcome Mas Oyama and support what would become his final visit to my country.

The book had come out PINK, for God's sake!

Mas Oyama was dead, and if my final tribute to him was going to come out pink, it was going to be over my dead body!

Yet among his last requests had been that I show him a copy before he died, and in that, one more time, I'd failed.

From his hospital bed, Mas Oyama extended his open hand towards me in a gesture to accompany his request that I bring him *Budo Karate Illustrated,* and in the end there simply hadn't been time, and I'd left that beseeching hand empty.

Surely, the timing of all that collapsed in Nathan Ligo's life during the exact period when Helen's *complications* were uprooting Midas was little more than coincidence.

It almost had to have been in the case of my father . . .

For even as Mas Oyama died, even as I dropped the ball so miserably in my final Watson interview and failed to arrange for the branch chief certificate that Sosai had been grooming me for, even as I realized the hard truth that my autobiographical writing would be better put into a decade-long time frame than a year-long one, even, as it became more and more apparent that the life of the *Budo Karate Illustrated* project was hanging by a thread – with pieces of my life crumbling all around me – my father made the choice that delivered the death blow to the long-ailing relationship that he and I shared.

THIRTY

DILLON FOUND OUT for sure that she was pregnant on her twenty-first birthday. She told me later that night from the edge of her bed that she'd kneeled with her elbows on the toilet seat in the bathroom at the College Infirmary and prayed that the test result would come back negative. I marvel today at the realization – because I don't remember being aware of it when Helen and I spent our semester together there – that when Dillon kneeled and prayed on her birthday five years earlier, it was in the exact same building across the street from the Student Union, converted to offices and classrooms, that would house Helen's eighteenth-century novel class.

Dillon and I left it unspoken, but we had already known for several weeks by then that she was pregnant. Every night we shared her bed and the air was thick with the knowledge of it.

It's hard for me to imagine today what could have possessed us to be as careless as we were. We both knew better, and all I can say other than simply admitting that we were careless is to add that it was my first experience – I was only seventeen! – and I was essentially doing as I was told. Dillon, perhaps, hadn't yet driven a final self-destructive tendency out of her life from the trauma of her own unique childhood and adolescence.

Both of us knew better, but somehow neither one of us stepped up to the plate to employ common sense.

"What are we going to do?" I asked her that night. I was confident to the point of being self-congratulatory that at least for that instant my eyes and voice conveyed 100% support and zero percent fear, even though it was clear that neither of us was prepared to bring a child into the world.

All I could think about then was Japan. All I could think about were the countless innocent souls I'd have been willing to hack my way through if necessary just to make it there.

"I can't have a baby," Dillon said. "I know it's supposed to be one of the cardinal sins in my church. That's why my sister had a baby when the same happened to her . . ." Her eyes conveyed the greatest dismay when it dawned on her at that moment that she'd made the exact same mistake she'd watched her sister make. "She carried it for nine months," she went on, "and by the time it was born the adoption papers had already gone through and she never even saw the child. I supported her in the beginning, but then I watched what it did to her. I'm 100% sure that I would be doing all of us a disservice to bring a child into the world under those circumstances. It would be wrong. There's no way. I can't have a baby, and there's no way you and I can raise a family. It's my choice, I'm not going to have a baby, and I'll just have to live with the consequences."

My heart spilled out onto the floor then, and I loved Dillon with a passion I hadn't felt before, because of what I knew she was telling me. She didn't say it in so many words — you can't read it in the actual words she spoke — but what she was telling me was that she was going to do whatever she could to take full responsibility, because it was hers, and that she was going to shield me to the extent that she could from sharing it with her.

"Are you sure?" I had indeed asked her the times that we made love without protection. She said something about the time of the month it was and told me that it would be okay. Neither of us brought up those words then, but I could see that it was there behind the words that she spoke.

"It's mine," she said with her use of "I" in "I can't have a baby."

"It's my choice and there's nothing you could say to take it from me. I was supposed to be the experienced one! The responsibility is mine. The choice is mine. Stay with me if you want, but on this particular issue, butt out!"

Today I wonder if she was protecting my dreams of Japan. I know that she was protecting me. I suspect that she was protecting me at her own expense.

Six weeks later, I had turned eighteen and — as incomprehensible as it seems — I involved my parents, out of spite.

My father and his wife had gone away for the weekend, and I spent forty-eight hours with Dillon on their sofa in front of their television. One of Dillon's girlfriends drove her to the clinic for her surgery on Saturday morning and dropped her back off at my father's house that afternoon. By Sunday she was well enough to go back to her dorm room.

My stepmother returned later that night in classic form.

She had zero reason to suspect that I'd broken her rule about having women over to their house while they were away. Just as when we were teenagers, and my brother and I used to be amazed at how we would come home from being out with friends and she'd accuse us of smoking in a "Don't lie to me. I know you were smoking" way, she came home that night, tired from the road, and said, "Don't lie to me. I know you had a girl over here while we were away." My brother and I were always amazed as teenagers because the times she accused us of smoking we never were, and the few times that we did, she had no clue. My brother used to sit out on the roof outside his window, thirty feet from their bedroom, to smoke, and they had no idea. At sixteen he took to extinguishing those cigarettes on the inside of his forearm out of a tough-guy notion that he was training himself to deal with pain and, of course, then too she had no clue.

I alone knew that if that pain was bearable for him, it was only because of the greater pain that he and I shared, being locked in a home with an impotent father dominated by the sightless woman he'd married, and neither of them had any idea.

But in the case of my being in the house with Dillon while they were away, she was right, if only superficially.

My father's third wife came home, tired from the road, and accused me of breaking their rules in the same arrogant "I know you're guilty" tone, and I hated her more than I'd ever hated anyone. I never would have had Dillon over to sleep with her, which was what she was accusing me of. What would have been the point? We had Dillon's dorm room, and we had my own whenever my roommate was away. I did indeed have Dillon over, but it wasn't to break their rules. I was there to take care of a friend in pain. Dillon had made her choice. I was there to be as supportive as I could of her right to live the life she wanted to live. And I was there to care for someone I believed to be making a painful personal sacrifice, at least in part to take care of me in the face of what was so plainly my mistake too.

That was the semester I was enrolled in my father's Modern Architecture class. It was an eight a.m. class and I went to it every single day of the semester straight from Dillon's bed. That bed was very likely a surrogate for the one that I no longer had at home, but again my father and his wife had no clue.

They'd forfeited the right for it to be any of their business.

"Yes, actually Dillon *was* here this weekend," I told them as my hatred for my father's wife spilled over into a resolute calm of "now I'm holding the upper hand."

"She was here recovering from the abortion she had Saturday morning."

As was the norm, my father, the impotent one, fell silent while my stepmother lost control.

"You murdered your child!" she told me in resounding confirmation of what I'd known all along: she didn't possess even a shred of character worthy of my respect. I held my breath, waiting for my father to intervene. Although he would have lectured me for being careless – and we would have discussed the abortion issue – he'd raised me to know that it was the far greater sin to be so self-righteous. I'd made my choice, and the consequences were between me and my conscience. I might have been willing to discuss it with my father. It was absolutely no business of the woman he was married to.

I could count on three fingers the times that my father contradicted his wife in front of me in the decade they'd been married. Each time, she made it clear that such contradiction was unacceptable, and finally he never did it again. He fell silent, and she spoke always with his authority, words that he never would have spoken before he met her. Now I waited for my father at least to ask his wife to excuse us so that he could talk to his son alone. Instead he added his silent support to this woman as she called me a murderer for an affair of the heart that was no affair of hers.

When Mina died – the dog who ran with me as a puppy in the valley of my childhood – I was sixteen, and my stepmother had successfully facilitated my brother's going overseas as an exchange student. My father would say how guilty he felt for confining Mina to the backyard. "She was born to run," he said. "She was meant to have all that space that she had in the country. I can't help but feel like this arthritic stiffness that's killing her is a result of my confining her to this small backyard where she can no longer run."

It was winter when Mina died, and she was old, gray and stiff. Like me, banished to the backyard cottage, Mina lived in the shed way back at the end of the yard, and no one had time for her. One of the two neighbors closest to the cemetery knocked on our door one afternoon to tell us that a dog had come onto his back porch to curl up and die in the night, and that he thought it might be ours. My father and I walked over together, brought Mina's frozen body back, and buried her in the backyard, much as we'd buried several other family pets in earlier years in the forest behind the log house.

When my stepmother met us at the gate carrying Mina wrapped in a blanket, her immediate reaction was to accuse me of leaving the gate open with a "You should be ashamed!" implication: "The dog froze to death because you left the gate open!" My father stood by silently, and I cried on the inside for the loss of my father as much as for the loss of my childhood dog, which was never in the slightest bit hers. The neighbor recognized her attack and, in the void of my father's silence, volunteered that it's normal for animals to wander away and find a distant place when it's their time to die, and it wouldn't have mattered if the gate was open or not.

Ken Wood, whom I'd known since I was born, like Tony Abbott and everyone else my father's age in Davidson, came to my defense, tactfully asserting that it was inappropriate to blame a boy for murdering his dog when it dies. My father stood by, impotent and silent, and I was grateful to the man who stood across from him.

Maybe I *had* left the gate open. Maybe the dog *had* wandered out, couldn't find her way back, and froze to death. That was unlikely, since Ken Wood's house was just one yard away, but in any case that was between me and my conscience. Standing by silently while his wife accused me of killing my dog, that I'll leave to the conscience of my father. As for his wife, conscience in her world seemed to have very little to do with how she felt and everything to do with how she had learned she was supposed to feel in predefined situations. And she'd long since predefined any situation when anything in her world didn't go as it was supposed to as one in which her stepson Nathan should be chastised.

Two years after Mina's death, my father sat by silently while his wife called me a murderer for Dillon's abortion. What I didn't know then was that he and Martha had aborted an unintended pregnancy seven years earlier, and that my father came to resent Martha for that decision because he'd initially believed that they should have that child.

But that was his life, and this was mine. It was he who had raised me to know beyond a shadow of a doubt that personal choice without fear of persecution is the right of every individual. The father who raised me would have insisted that the one who overstepped those bounds and told another how he or she was required to feel was the one who should be ashamed.

My senior year at Davidson, when Mas Oyama died and Helen was pregnant, was seven years after Mina died and five years after Dillon's abortion.

Dillon and I had remained in touch, and we'd remained friends. I'd never stopped loving her for who she was, for the time that we'd spent together and for the way she'd protected me. During my hedonistic stage right after coming back from Japan, I'd even saved up my money and gone to visit her while she was on a study assignment in England. My father and his wife "disapproved," they said, of my "spending my money that way," but I went anyway. Dillon and I rode the bus together to Scotland and visited Linlithgow, the township near Linlithgow Castle, from where the first Linlithgows left for America two or three hundred years earlier, to change their name to Ligo, supposedly because there wasn't room in the blank in the ship's log.

Dillon was romantically involved, and I remember being frustrated that she was less free to love me than I was to love her. I felt one hundred percent in love with her then.

But we'd remained friends nevertheless — we'd exchanged a few letters — and towards the end of my senior year at Davidson, she wrote to tell me she wanted to come to my graduation. She was completing her doctorate and would be job hunting at colleges and universities in the States. She wouldn't at all mind, she told me, taking her first teaching position at Davidson.

"Wonderful," I told her. "Davidson would be lucky to have you, and I'd be delighted to see you! You can stay with me, of course, if you don't have a place to stay."

My father was all gung ho about his role in the church by then. He was singing in the choir, he'd preached once or twice as a substitute, and he'd taken an active role in helping to make design decisions for the new sanctuary being built. That he and his wife still harbored enough of a grudge to actually refuse to let Dillon enter their home, five years after what was for us ancient history, was inconceivable.

Wasn't forgiveness supposed to be one of the key tenets of my father's Christianity?

Dillon had come up in conversation maybe once or twice in those five years between me and my father or his wife. My stepmother had at least once in the meantime taken advantage of something that came on TV or showed up in some magazine on the kitchen counter to tell me, "It's amazing how perfectly formed fetuses are at two months! They're just like complete little people with all of their fingers and toes! Isn't it easy to imagine one of them growing up into a child like your little brother or sister?"

"Yeah, whatever," I wanted to say. "Bitch! What the fuck right do you have to say such a thing to me with 'You murdered your child' still ringing in my ears?"

I let it roll off my shoulders, though. I was older by then and had more important things to worry about. I'd mostly given up by then on ever finding cause to feel the respect for that woman that I still mostly showed in the name of sparing my father the grief of telling her to go to hell.

I was completely stunned, however, two or three years later when I told my parents that I'd invited Dillon to stay with me for my graduation, and my stepmother told me she wasn't welcome in our house, and my father stood by silently, impotently, and said nothing.

How naïve I was to say in protest, "Oh, I can stay in here on the sofa if it makes you more comfortable, and I'll give Dillon my bed in the cottage." How naïve I was to think that the reason they didn't want her to stay with us was because of their same old "We don't want you sleeping with women at our house because of the kids" idea. That it was, rather, that my stepmother was still intent on punishing us for Dillon's abortion five years earlier was beyond my comprehension.

"You've got to be kidding!" was all I could say when it finally hit me. "That was five years ago! We were younger and stupider. That's ancient history now!"

That was the night the bottom fell out of what was left of the relationship I had with my father. My stepmother went upstairs to bed, and I had some minutes alone with him. I forced him to talk, even though he clearly would have preferred to be left alone. That exchange of words ironically wound up being the most valuable minutes we'd spent together in years.

"Are you going to support this?" I asked him, and, "Are you serious?" when he told me that he was.

"This is my wife's house," he told me. "Yes, of course I'm going to support it."

"But it's your house too," I told him. "And it's wrong! I'm not saying what Dillon and I did was right, but it was five years ago, and you're still going to punish her for something that isn't even yours? Don't you think that's wrong?"

"Well, it may be," he said. "But still. This is my wife's house. And I'm going to support her."

There was no element of fighting. My father didn't raise his voice and I didn't raise mine. I was in shock, and if I remember correctly, I embraced my father that night as we parted.

I was less than a month away from taking the final exam in his art history survey course.

I recalled the first Christmas I spent with my father's family one month after returning from Japan, and just one month before I turned twenty-one. My parents planned to spend Christmas at my stepmother's grandmother's house in Florida.

"Being alone on Christmas is not an option," my stepmother told me, all the while making it clear how miserable she was going to be having me in the car with them for the twelve-hour drive to Florida with the kids. Such was my stepmother's M.O. She would tell me how much she cared about me – presumably because she knew that's what was socially expected of her – at the same time as she would do everything in her power to make me go away. I am extremely grateful to her for helping to arrange for me to enter Davidson a year early, so that she wouldn't have to share a house with me for another year. It was truly a valuable year to me in terms of the education I began, and, quite frankly, I didn't want to share a house with her, either.

We spent four or five days together in Florida that were delightful because of her family – who are surprisingly delightful, given that they're related to her – and on the twelve-hour return drive, we passed the scene of a fresh accident on the highway. My stepmother was driving, and had been for some time, and we must have been among the first two or three cars to come on the scene of a multiple-car crash, complete with blood and broken glass, smoke, and at least one flipped-over car clear off the road by the tree line. A young, bleeding lady had crawled out of the upside-down car and was screaming for help with such terror that she could barely stand. Her hands were on her knees, and she cried out to us as we pulled alongside.

Her eyes and mine met as we coasted past, and I could see that the terror she felt was for whoever it was who hadn't yet managed to crawl out of her mangled, upside-down car.

My stepmother slowed down, but drove right on by without stopping.

"Stop the car!" I said. "Jesus Christ! We need to help those people!"

My stepmother, biting her nails, said something about not wanting to expose her kids to such a traumatic scene.

"Someone else will stop," my father said, unwilling even then to cross his wife. "Look, someone already is . . ."

I am ashamed to this day that I didn't do what I should have done: force her to stop by opening the car door in motion and starting to crawl out over one of the child safety seats on either side of me. I was too stunned.

At the rest area up the road fifteen minutes later, my father suggested that it might make me feel better if I used the pay phone to call the emergency number and make sure the accident had been reported. I made the call, and it had been reported, but I wondered mostly about my father.

"What about you?" I wanted to ask. "How do *you* feel? You just allowed your wife to coast past bleeding people on a desolate highway screaming for help! She could have dropped us off and pulled on ahead with the kids. You raised me to be better than that! You raised me to be stronger than that! What has happened to you that you would live so much of your life behind the skirts of this woman you're married to, who is so clearly so much less than you are?

"It's your Christmastime, for God's sake!"

It wasn't until that night two years later, as my graduation approached, that I finally realized my father wasn't a victim at all. For a decade I'd been trying to rescue him from his wife. I didn't need them to break up – although I surely wouldn't have complained! – I just wanted him to stand up for himself, and for what was right. I wanted him to be able to say, "Hold on a second! Nathan didn't kill the dog, even if he did leave the gate open. And whether what he did about Dillon's pregnancy was right or wrong, we don't need to be calling him a murderer. It's inappropriate."

For a decade, I thought that if I held true to myself, he would find his voice again. The third of the only three times he'd dared to contradict her in front of me had occurred the same year Mina died. I was learning to drive then and had shown a tendency to swerve when I reached down to adjust the radio dial. My stepmother had a brilliant idea, and told me, in front of my father, that I would be required to sit in the parked car blindfolded in the driveway and pass a test in which I'd be asked to reach out and touch all the controls in the car from memory before they'd consider letting me get my license. My father pointed out that that notion was silly, because I wouldn't ever, after all, be driving blindfolded; I just needed to practice more and learn not to swerve. His wife, far more embarrassed than she needed to be, had no choice but to concur. Ever since then, I realized, I'd been holding my breath, waiting for my father to dare to speak up again, since so much of what his wife told me day in and day out was either similarly nonsensical or unnecessarily hurtful. Not only was I was supposed to be ashamed for simply existing, but I was also supposed to keep my mouth shut as my stepmother's assertions continued to spiral towards lunacy. When I was a child, she accused me of disagreeing with her no matter what she said. Now, however, half a decade had passed, I was an adult, and it was clear that *she* was doing just that. "Look at that red building," I'd say, simply wanting to make conversation and point out something of interest. "It's not red," she'd respond, "it's orange." Everything was a fight for her, and I waited endlessly for my father to step up to the plate and help her to deal with her misery in some way that wasn't abusive of me. Surely this time – if I revealed her to him so blatantly – if I could lure her out into calling me a murderer in front of a man whose integrity, I believed, wouldn't stand for it! – surely then he'd realize that he was selling himself out.

That night when my stepmother refused to have Dillon in their house, I realized that my father *wanted* to be subordinate to his wife. He wanted to leave all affairs of the heart up to her. He wanted to leave the raising of his children up to her. He wanted to have her make those decisions for him that he'd come to seem so powerless to make for himself.

I was amazed to the point of being speechless.

How can a man live with himself? I thought. *Where is the dignity?*

I hugged him goodnight with a dumb smile on my face because I realized that I was not hugging him goodnight.

I was hugging him goodbye.

The man who had raised me was no more.

"Oh my God, I feel ill!" Dillon said when I told her. She must have thought I was insane when I tried to explain the bright side.

"Don't you see?" I told her. "Don't you see that I finally understand my father?

"After a decade, I finally see that he wants to be the way he's been with his wife all this time. She *is* his conscience! She *is* his personality. And I always thought he was a victim, and that he could break free, because I know my father. I know the man that raised me. I've seen him be so much of a better, stronger, more independent person than that. But now I realize that he wants to be subordinate to her so he no longer has to be bothered!"

Dillon couldn't understand what I was so excited about, and I can't blame her, because I couldn't yet explain why I felt so utterly relieved. It was because my father had set me free. He'd finally made me understand that he didn't want me fighting for him. He was reconciled to his station in life, and he wasn't going to change, not because he couldn't, but because he didn't want to. The man who had established in me my faith in conscience as a life-governing force was no more . . . because he'd chosen not to be.

Although it took me another eight or ten months to finally walk away, I realized finally that night that I could.

Five years earlier I had supported Dillon as she aborted my child, and although she was the experienced one, and she took the responsibility and shielded me from it, there is no question that I battled for the best course of action. There is no question that there are consequences of that year of my life that are purely mine to deal with. I never blew it off as nothing. I didn't take it lightly. I came to what I believed was the correct decision under the circumstances – at least, I did the best I could at the time – and I trusted my ability to judge that, to learn from my mistakes, and to move forward in such a way as to live life better in the future.

My father, on the other hand, had decided to confine himself to rules of right and wrong – and to allow his wife to define all the rules. He'd decided to deny the inner conflict that in the human heart leads both to the creation of the rules we follow and to the constant testing of those rules in search of better ones. He'd decided to mistrust his own ability to judge, to close his eyes and throw himself on the mercy of a woman who was 100% rules, and zero percent creative or confident enough to recognize when one of those rules didn't apply.

My father's decade-long support of my stepmother as she did everything in her power to erase me from his life is deplorable.

It's shameful!

I wonder to this day how he shares a home with her, looks at her every day, looks at himself in the mirror, and realizes that their socially prescribed desire to have a perfect family with two point five kids, and a dog, and a yard to mow on Saturdays, church to go to on Sundays, and an SUV in the driveway, was so important that they'd be willing to hack their way through more than just one innocent soul in the process.

I ask my father to consider the cigarette burns on the inside of my brother's forearm.

I invite him to return to the time in the final days before my brother's first wedding when I told him the marriage would fail. It was Christmas during Lissa's and my year together, the Christmas after I reunited with *Sosai* in Rochester. It was one year after his wife drove past the bloody accident scene on the way back from Florida.

My father became, that afternoon, one of the only people ever to confront an early manifestation of my life-worshipping, teeth-gnashing Midas. He encountered him in the flesh, my father with his blinders knocked suddenly lopsided to the verge of falling off, and his graying mustache quivering with faltering rage. That mere sneak preview of the Midas to come didn't have to glare. He didn't have to attempt a deliberately piercing look. He certainly didn't have to raise his voice. He merely strolled with his eyes into the heart of my shouting and composure-lost father and snapped the tirade's back like a toothpick by asking him calmly whether he might finally try to correct the damage he'd done before my brother walked into a marriage that was destined to fail. All my normally self-righteous and reality-denying father could do was stammer, reveal in his eyes the wave of panic that had so suddenly dashed his rage, and issue an embarrassing appeal for his 21-year-old second son to please explain what he was missing.

"Listen to your heart," I should have told him. Perhaps I even did.

I can't recall exactly how I responded to his feeble effort to pick up the pieces of his dignity – I was shaken too. My father's tantrum had been so decisively crushed by all that Midas could see that I was taken aback too, for it had all but happened without me, thanks, perhaps, to something planted in me by Master Choi, or by his uncle Mas Oyama.

I knew then that there was no point in trying to explain, because one doesn't make up for a decade of what my brother and I had endured in the few days we had left before the wedding. I could have told my father of the doubts that my brother's beautiful and brilliant fiancée, Traci, had expressed in my brother's ability to love himself enough to see a marriage through. I could have told him how a few months before the wedding, Traci left my stomach tied in knots I wanted cut out of my body when she spoke of a side of my brother that no one else knew. She had no idea, as she spoke of what she saw inside of him, that she was so perfectly describing parts of me, too. She described me perfectly the way I was BEFORE I lucked into six years with Master Choi, and started methodically to remake myself through my love for him as the father figure that had been so painfully lost from my life.

Traci responded simply, "Ask your father!" in a "Duhhh" sort of way when I asked her where she thought the injury came from. "I mean, my God," she said, "look at what that woman does to him while your father stands by and does nothing!"

My own vocal cords got a workout that day as, all but crushed by grief – for my brother! – I drove alone back to Davidson from Chapel Hill where, as in that passage in my poem, my brother and I had "sat on the hood of my car while his wife marinated the steaks inside." I nearly succeeded in ripping the steering wheel out of my moving car that day as I considered for the first time my brother in the suddenly undeniable context of what my father and his bitch wife had done to him, too. It was one thing that they continued day in and day out to try to stamp me out, but on that day for the first time I had evidence to support what I'd suspected to be true all along, and I knew that they'd been fucking with my always-so-thick-skinned brother, too. I loved my brother like life. I loved him like my twin – he was the only one who knew, because, born only thirteen months apart, he and I had shared the exact same childhood – and with my Ford Fairmont's engine still sputtering and the driver's door open in a ditch by that lone oak where Concord Road splits off towards Davidson, on my hands and knees in the dirt I did my best to vomit out what was for me the oh so happy image of burning my father's house to the ground with him and his cunt wife still in it.

I ask my father why he thinks it is today that my brother, with his rock-solid, oh-so-mature, and extremely capable professional shell, is married this second time around to a woman with adult children his own age – my brother who failed to look for the pieces of his lost childhood in Martha years later the way I did, my brother whose substitute for the teachers who fell on me like so much manna from Heaven was the United States Marine Corps! I ask my father why he thinks it is that my brother handles his professional relationships so perfectly but goes through long periods when he fails to return phone calls when his own brother calls him, or when his few real friends from his teenage years leave message after message on his machine, and then run into his little brother in town and ask him why his brother never returns their calls.

I ask my father to consider why it is that every wife, girlfriend or lover that either my brother or I ever had, especially Traci and my brother's current wife, so often referred to my stepmother as "that woman" rather than by her name. I ask him why he thinks it is that any girlfriend or wife of ours always hated his wife and shook their heads at the blinders he proudly wore when it came to his adult sons.

Blinders.

It was Lissa who coined the phrase, Dillon who had the most cause, Traci who had been the most vocal, and my brother's current wife who shared with me the devastation of her first visit to meet her would-be in-laws. My stepmother laid into my brother right in front of her! – viciously attacking any notion that the two of them could be an *acceptable* couple because of her age, while my father sat by, silent and glassy-eyed in the background.

In case my father needs it spelled out, they all hated her because they loved us! – they were having to love us on most days to levels beyond their normal ability, and it didn't take any kind of seer to figure out why.

I ask my father to remember that my brother would never tell him where the burns on his forearm came from, my father who relies on his "poor wounded animal" routine to keep people pitying and protecting him rather than holding him responsible. I ask him whether hacking his way through these two innocent souls, as he and his wife did, day by day, for a decade of days, to trim their lives to fit their parents' tradition, could possibly have been worth it.

My father wouldn't let Dillon in his house?

For having an abortion?

No matter what you believe about an eight-week-old embryo with a brain the size of a pea, its mere potential for one day knowing what pain was would have been scraped away in an instant!

My brother and I, children already, were innocent souls too at the ages of eleven and twelve, were we not? But we were long since alive, we knew a lot of things, and it was about the time that my father's third wife came into our lives that we most certainly came to know pain.

And thanks to our father who stood impotently by for a decade as his wife scraped us out of his life, we most certainly came to know abortion.

My father the hypocrite!

It wasn't your failure to stay married to Martha, Dad. It wasn't your leaving her. It was your leaving yourself behind when you left her. It was how much you seemed to be in love with her for those years we were together, and how you seemed so heartbroken, blind, and loveless after you lost her. It was your abandoning us, piece by piece, to the mercy of the selfish and simple-minded woman you then married that was so – nearly literally – heartbreaking.

My father's wife excuses herself by saying how unfortunate it was that I could never get past my anger and resentment at the loss of Martha, how sad that I came into her household with too much emotional baggage ever to integrate into the perfect family she'd managed to create. It's all my fault for her to this day, and she's self-congratulatory enough to put on a sad, puppy-eyed expression at my loss. My father stands by silently, grateful that she's so thoroughly helped him to abandon that part of himself that once had the strength to look at the world with original, seeing eyes, and the courage to put himself at risk in search of the truth.

And yet, that decision was his to make: if that's the man he wanted to be all along, all the power to him!

Of course, it's unfortunate – and tragic for me. I lost a father – and yet another family! – to forces beyond my control.

But I'm not going to go up to him and tell him, the way his wife would, "You abandoned your sons! You should be ashamed!"

I am sure my father doesn't feel that way.

I'm sure he did the best he could under the circumstances.

I'm sure he finds fault with me too.

All I knew then, though — eighteen months after my brother's wedding, when I heard my own voice telling Dillon that she wasn't going to be welcome in my father's house — was that I was free. I didn't have to fight for my father anymore. As soon as the opportunity presented itself, I would be better off fulfilling his own prophecy by simply leaving him and his wife and their kids to go on with their lives, while I go on with mine.

Until that day, I would have felt morally conflicted about walking away.

After that day, there was nothing holding me back.

I'd mourned my father for a decade, and now it was time to stop mourning.

It was time to concentrate my energy on more important things.

It was time to look, with that energy too — and with that energy especially! — towards the future.

In the future that I could see, I would need every scrap of energy that I could muster.

THIRTY-ONE

I FAILED TO GRADUATE from college in the very last hour of my last year at Davidson.

I spent a week's worth of sleepless nights in the slide-viewing room in the art building, ensuring that if I was to fail a class that semester, it wouldn't be my father's. Those days of last-minute work were enough to make my performance on his exam a passing mediocre, and after it was over, I still had a full day and night to prepare for what would be the last final exam of my college experience:

Dr. Job Thomas's History of China.

Like the History of the Western World survey I'd taken at UNCC over the summer, my Chinese history class had been one of the most delightful I'd taken. How spoiled I felt just to sit there, day after day, and listen while such an educated man told me in detail the story of China's history! Even though I'd sacrificed significant swaths of the coursework during the semester to all my other responsibilities, I wasn't intimidated by the exam because I felt I had a relatively firm grasp of the subject matter. Unlike economics, or conlaw – or Chaucer! – I hadn't had to struggle to absorb the material. I didn't have to force it down. It was quite frankly delicious. I was thirsty for it, and when I was in class I gulped it down.

I spent those last sleepless twenty-four hours in the College Union, and I had plenty of company. The Union, the Library, Chambers, the art building, all were unlocked around the clock during exam week, and every corner was occupied by studying students. Aside from pausing to go down to the Café to get a bite to eat – or for another cup of coffee – I studied for twenty-four hours straight, and when the time came, I walked across to Chambers for my exam, sleepy but high on caffeine. The daylight looked a little strange, as it tends to do when one's been staring at printed pages under artificial light for so many nighttime hours in a row, but I was confident that I was just two hours away from completing the requirements for graduation from Davidson College. I was sure I would add at least that feather to my cap beside my *nidan*, the honorary graduation certificate that Mas Oyama had given me, and of course *Budo Karate Illustrated*. Who needed the Watson or the branch chief certificate? I'd still make it back to Japan, I'd still become a branch chief, I'd still have my own dojo . . . and there would be plenty of time to finish writing my book later.

Sadly, however, once I opened my exam envelope, I couldn't even comprehend the questions. There were six, and I had to choose four. Each one was a paragraph meant to engender an essay that would draw on the core of all that we'd spent the semester learning. I had all that information in my head. But try as I might, I couldn't for the life of me figure out where my professor wanted me to begin.

I was so unbelievably tired.

With the lines of text blurring on the page in front of me, I stared into my future and faced more than just that one exam. If I put karate completely aside and did nothing but work a job like the one I'd had at the dining service before starting back to school, in half a year I could probably make enough money to pay for one more class.

I knew that passing my Chinese history exam was a requirement for passing the course, and that passing the course was all that stood between me and graduation. In most classes at Davidson, a student who'd done A work all along could fail a final and still wind up with something like a D. Dr. Thomas, however, was one of the strictest professors I had while at Davidson,[89] and he'd made it crystal clear from the moment he'd handed me a syllabus on the first day of class that passing his final was a requirement for passing the entire course.

What if I have to earn tuition for one more class when I still owe nearly $20,000 to the printer in Montgomery? I wondered.

That was the balance still outstanding for the first book. And I wasn't particularly intimidated by it at that time; I could still see the coming success of Book Two and its all-important proceeds from the larger Canadian market. Once the book project went forward into that second

---

[89] Not to be confused with my Brit lit. and modern Irish poetry professor, Harry Thomas.

stage, taking one more class at Davidson would be within easy reach.

Maybe it won't be such a big deal . . . even if I do fail this exam, I thought.

Mas Oyama was dead, though. He'd been dead for nearly a month, and I was beginning to suspect that in his absence my situation might have become precarious. I knew that as long as he was supporting my project it didn't matter so much whether I pleased the U.S. branch chiefs who'd supported the first issue. If Mas Oyama was supporting it, it would go on. I didn't, however, need the several critics that had risen up in protest to feel a bit uncomfortable with the rear cover advertisement I'd designed. But even that mild embarrassment wouldn't endanger the project as long as Matsui stepped up to the plate and filled even half the role in my life that Mas Oyama had left vacant.

I had been counting on Mas Oyama's being critical of my first book. I was looking forward to his guidance to tell me the parts that he liked and the parts that he didn't. I had hoped and believed that when it came time to design Book Two, he would be there, alongside Jacques and Annie, to tell me how to make the project better.

"Look at what I've made for you," I wanted through my work to tell *Sosai*. "I've built an avenue through which *Honbu* can disseminate the needed information to our branches to bring the North American standard closer to the international norm. Let's get some U.S. fighters who won't get defeated in the first round back into the world tournament! Let's use this project as a springboard for unifying the scattered U.S. branches into one stronger, better-informed, and better-motivated front!"

I thought of Matsui as I sat there in that third-floor Chambers classroom, realizing that I couldn't even read the lines on the page in front of me. I had involved him in the first book, right from the beginning, because he had been my choice, too, as the most likely successor to Mas Oyama. He was the only one I knew at *Honbu* who had the charisma to carry forward the legacy that Mas Oyama had brought to life.

Of course I failed miserably to anticipate just how soon that transition would occur. In something like shadowy panic, I wondered if *Budo Karate Illustrated* really would survive the transfer of power.

It has to, I thought. *There's been no stopping it all along. It has a life of its own. I'll push it through two weeks from now when I go to Japan for the memorial. I'll make sure to get there early enough to get a first crack at Matsui before the international throngs start to roll in. What's one more Davidson class next year? It's not like I have any reason to give a damn about my GPA. I'll publish Book Two, and then I'll come back and complete one more class.*

I wrote several lines of apology to Dr. Thomas on my mostly blank exam paper and sealed the envelope. I wanted to be sure he understood that I'd given it my best shot, considering all that I had on my plate that semester. I'd thoroughly enjoyed his class and I wanted him to know that my blowing his exam wasn't a reflection on him.

Job Thomas was an Indian man with a thick accent and a strict nature who scolded students for wearing shorts or flip-flops to class, and he'd scolded me severely once too, about two-thirds of the way through the semester. I'd missed a few of his classes and, like my father, he had been unable to reconcile that with the fact that the rest of the time I seemed so genuinely interested and motivated. I could have explained to him that I was enrolled in six classes rather than four, and that during that semester I had prepared for and passed my *nidan* grading; had been to Japan twice and to Atlantic City, Montreal and Montgomery once each by car; and had almost single-handedly written, compiled, published and marketed a 104-page hardcover book. I could have told him that in the aftermath of my loss of Lissa and Martha I was losing my father, too. I could have told him that Mas Oyama had died . . . but that would have meant about as much to him as if I'd told him that Midas was dead too. I could have told him that I'd managed the Café nights and weekends on top of all of the rest; at least that part he'd have understood. I could have told him all that – but because it was his nature, he still would have seen, first and foremost, that my performance in his class was less that it should have been.

I didn't tell him, too, because it was in *my* nature not to try to explain myself for shortcomings that others perceived in me, as long as I knew that I was justified by that which those around me couldn't see. I never did understand why *Sosai* had spoken to me in Rochester of stealing. All I knew was that I had failed by leaving the dormitory early, and there was no appropriate answer other than "Osu, I will struggle to do better in the future."

Dr. Thomas scolded me that one time halfway through the semester for coming into class fifteen minutes late without my notebook and without even so much as a pen to write with, and there was no way I could have explained to him what I had gone through to make it to class at all that day, so I kept quiet and apologized, said "Yes, sir," a number of times, and just took my seat as soon as I was given leave. I'd been in Charlotte during the hours between my father's class and his that day, shopping for the camera I would take to Montreal that weekend. I'd been working with the salesman-photographer who was helping me understand how to use it, and I left Charlotte in plenty of time to make it back home to change clothes and prepare for class. But my god-awful shitty Ford Fairmont died on the interstate halfway to Davidson – that was the last time it ever moved without a tow truck – and I'd sprinted the quarter mile to the nearest ramp, and another quarter mile to the nearest pay phone.

I called everyone I could think of, but that was in the days before cell phones, and everyone I knew was in class.

All I could think about was that I was going to miss yet another Chinese history class, and knowing that I might miss another one or two before the semester was through, I wasn't about to give up on that one! With less than a half hour to spare, I sprinted back towards the highway and onto the northbound ramp. I was still five miles from the Davidson exit. With all my pride sprawled out on the grimy, trash-littered shoulder beside me, and with no other option, I stuck out my thumb and prayed that someone would stop and give me a ride.

Five or six cars passed, and – lo and behold! – a traveling vacuum-cleaner salesman stopped and drove me to Davidson. That was 1994, and people in my part of America didn't really hitchhike anymore. They certainly didn't safely. Hitchhikers were generally undesirable types, and those who picked them up were usually fairly undesirable themselves. Somehow I lucked into the right guy, though. I told him how important it was that I make it to class, and he drove me right up to the front doors of Chambers. I sprinted the two flights of stairs, paused outside our classroom to catch my breath, and then walked in to face Dr. Thomas's wrath, fifteen minutes late, sweaty, and without my notebook or a pen.

When I met with Dr. Abbott in his office after my exam – after sleeping with my phone off the hook for most of two days straight – he told me that Dr. Thomas had searched the campus for me, high and low, trying to contact me to give me another chance. Although I was already resigned to my fate, Dr. Abbott told me that I should go see him, so I went by Dr. Thomas's office to at least thank him for trying to track me down.

"I'm so very sorry," he said. "I tried to find you. I would have given you another chance. But now it's past the deadline. I had no choice but to turn in the F for you. If only I'd been able to find you! What on earth happened?"

The brief dialogue that followed revealed the philosophy that I'd adopted for driving myself in my pursuits, not only that year, but also into the future of my life. Dr. Thomas's response exemplified the opposition that I would face time and again.

At last I explained how much I'd had on my plate that semester, starting with taking six courses instead of four. I admitted that common sense had told me from the beginning that it was likely more than I'd be able to pull off perfectly. "But won't trying 150% of what I might be able to achieve flawlessly," I asked, "insure that I achieve the maximum that I can? Sure I'll probably only be 85% successful, but 85% of 150 is more than I would have achieved if I just safely bit off what I knew I could chew."

The concept wasn't clear enough in my mind then to explain better, but it's crystal clear to me now that Mas Oyama's teaching – my entire *uchi deshi* experience in Japan – had shown me beyond a shadow of a doubt that the human animal is capable of far more than our experiences train us to believe. We might think we couldn't possibly do 1500 consecutive jumping squats, for example, but then one day someone might threaten to beat us if we don't give it our best shot, and then and only then would we find out that in fact we could. The jury was still out on whether or not I'd be able to single-handedly create a successful periodical publication to rival those on American newsstands, but if I wasn't brave enough to give in to the foregone conclusion that I could, I'd never know how far the wholehearted attempt might take me.

It was that philosophy that had come to me in the valley of my childhood two years earlier, when, with an ax, I'd fought my way back to the training I believed myself to have left behind forever.

Is it vision that drives me, or is it fantasy? That had been the question that plagued me.

But *It's up to me,* the answer always came back. *I decide whether it's going to be vision or fantasy. The deciding factor is how far I'm willing to push myself to the extremes of exhaustion in the pursuit.*

Is it far-fetched? Is it crazy? Is it more likely to fail than succeed?

Of course. But what chance is there of success if I don't try? Who else is going to take the risk?

Dr. Thomas was not convinced.

"But look at your success rate," he told me.

"If you bite off only as much as you know you can chew, you can be sure of 100% success. In your method, you will condemn yourself to something less than that. Do you want to be 100% successful in life, or do you want to live in such a way that some percentage of your life will be a failure?'

I didn't have the clarity of mind then to counter his point as well as I could now. I was living it, though, and I was undaunted.

"I know, but it's my duty to move forward the way I am," was all I could tell him.

To HELL with my diploma from Davidson College! I would exult quite a few times before I finally went back, beyond the timeline of this book, to complete one more course and graduate for the sake of the degree.

What difference is a piece of paper on the wall going to make in the end?

None!

It's just a means, after all, of getting ahead in a society that celebrates the blind eye turned to painful truths! It would merely help me to integrate into a status quo where individuals coast past injured people bleeding on the side of the highway, and then come home and pass themselves off as upstanding, valuable members of society, because they keep their lawns mowed and make it in to church on Sundays! A diploma would help me to fit in, and to be more successful as just another wheel in society's economic machine. But since the machine is so clearly failing to serve the people of the present, never mind the future, isn't the willingness to step outside its workings more important?

Who else has been shaped by his life up until this point into one who can not only see the path but also dare to take it?

What right do I have to turn my back and cower?

I've got just this one life. Not only that, I've already lived the one I was entitled to. What right do I have not to let myself go to the experiment?

To hell with it!

Push forward.

Never quit.

Be willing to let it kill you and you might have a chance.

Are you willing?

Hell, I'm half dead already.

THIRTY-TWO

Less than one month after Matsui hosted Mas Oyama's memorial service in Tokyo, his new assistant typed the words that dealt the death blow to *Budo Karate Illustrated*.

It was midsummer, and I was in Florida. I'd taken Rafael up on his invitation to ride down with him so that I could visit Michael Lorden's Orlando dojo while Rafael visited his father's family. I'd exchanged a flurry of correspondence with *Honbu* since the memorial service, and I'd left instructions for Matsui's assistant to contact me through Jacques and Annie in New York if they needed to reach me while I was away.

It was Annie, therefore, who read me Matsui's fax when I called her from Rafael's in Florida.

"Dear Mr. Nathan," the earthshaking and ridiculous fax began. "Herewith to inform you to freeze all your activity on your magazine, *Budo Karate Illustrated*. This means you have no authorization to issue *Budo Karate Illustrated* in the name of Kyokushinkaikan neither to in any other represent Kyokushin Karate. I discussed about this with the Chairman of the International Committee, *Shihan* Bobby Lowe, and we can not agree with the statements which you have been sent to *Honbu*." It was signed, "Matsui Shokei, Director, *International Karate Organization*, Kyokushinkaikan."

Insult added to injury, I was dumbstruck by the words with which I'd been informed that Matsui was prepared, just like that, to throw away all the work I'd done over the previous year of my life for what was now his Kyokushin. The English his interpreter used was so ridiculous that, in my initial shock, it was next to impossible to see even past the language to start to make sense of what had happened.

I was sure that there must have been some kind of misunderstanding.

"We can not agree with the statements which you have been sent to Honbu," it said.

What in the hell does that mean? was the question that echoed in my ears for days as I tried to make sense of it.

What statements? I didn't issue any statements!

I had always been aware that my attempt to make a magazine was precocious. Thanks to some of the criticism I'd received, I also had more of a sense of *it's all my fault* than was probably healthy. Perhaps I should have chosen one or two branch chiefs and pursued the kind of material that would make them stand out – that's exactly what I did with Jacques. As the book turned out, however, it's true that from one perspective, it could have appeared that there was American Kyokushin on one hand, and Nathan Ligo, American *uchi deshi* of Mas Oyama, on the other. Certainly it would seem that way in the eyes of anyone who was biased to see it that way already. Annie came to accuse me of being blinded by ego – she would excuse me in the same breath, because of my youth – but I've always disagreed, because on that particular issue I was far from blind.

Of course, Midas's very existence could be read as sheer, unadulterated ego. When Midas moved to the fore to take over whenever Nathan Ligo didn't feel up to the challenge at hand, the world was his to do with as he pleased and he wasn't much ashamed to let it be known. As for Nathan Ligo, he was at least aware that he risked getting under the skin of the personalities that made up the American status quo whenever he set Midas free. Putting Mas Oyama's only American uchi deshi forward as an example, Midas had in fact gnashed his teeth and dared the establishment to outdo him by the time the second issue, featuring the Canadian Kyokushin Yearbook, rolled around.

If I get burned in the process, so be it! are the words that perhaps best describe the strategic choice I made. *Just so long as the magazine makes the best demonstration it can, to serve as a launching pad for a second issue. I'll chalk up the heat I take for this one to acceptable risk once Book Two comes out.*

Of course I was aware, too, of the impact that the project's successful first step did have on my fragile ego.

All my life, I'd been the smallest, weakest member of any peer group I'd ever been part of. Yet there I was in those photographs, breaking baseball bats with my shins and carrying barbells up mountains in the name of a cause beyond myself, and I definitely felt some satisfaction. "Martial art creates the super ego," Master Choi cautioned in my youth. I understood later that his assertion was based on the substandard American martial-arts model, and that "martial arts in the absence of full-contact fighting creates the super ego" would have been a more accurate statement in a martial arts world that includes Kyokushin: it's not possible, after all, to have too elevated a sense of one's own abilities when getting pounded into the floor by full-contact blows.

I certainly took a few good licks that year after the book had already been sent off to the printer, but when I was first laying it out, there wasn't anyone around to put me in my place. Far from being blinded, however, I had never forgotten Master Choi's warnings. Just as I was probably more aware than most of the battling forces within me of Reason and conscience-born vision, I was also wide-eyed aware of how ego could present itself as a tantalizing counterbalance to the sometimes-crippling sense of insecurity that was for me a fact of life.

It was, after all, exactly because I doubted my ability to achieve what my conscience demanded that I resorted to such desperate measures. I believed myself capable . . . but never inherently. I had no sense whatsoever that I could just buckle down and employ my God-given talents to create a magazine and do all the other things that I simultaneously set out to achieve. I was extremely confident, but it was in my own unique form of borrowed power, and in my conviction that Conscience would drive me to the reaches necessary to tap into it, that I found confidence, not in any sense that I was the prodigy that could have done it alone. Flying on Midas's endorphins, I was king of the world, and those in my way might better have served themselves by stepping aside. But that was Midas, never Nathan Ligo. Midas didn't need to see his picture up in lights to know what he could do. Nathan Ligo wouldn't have dared.

Ultimately, it was the work that was important; Nathan Ligo had been expendable from the start.

I alone looked at the book in a long-term future context and saw it as an insignificant forerunner of a magazine that would eventually have far greater resources than the blood, sweat and sleepless nights I'd used to generate the first one. Accordingly, I saw it as more important to show what the book could achieve in terms of presentation than to protect myself from criticism. When I designed the rear-cover announcement of my autobiographical book in progress, I saw it as *What a great model for a future advertisement!* rather than, *How important Nathan Ligo is!* As for my *tameshiwari* demonstration, there simply weren't better action photos in the pool from which to choose, and I saw them first and foremost as a demonstration not of what I could do, but what Kyokushin karate could do, and what the magazine could do in the future.

But then there was also that other dimension to Midas's vision. There was the darker one.

I *wanted* to show the American status quo what I had achieved and all that I could do. I wanted to show them because I was in so many ways far less than the rest of them – a weak, insignificant 22-year-old Beta who couldn't even graduate from Mas Oyama's program. I'd been on the American Kyokushin scene for less than two years, but I had one or two significant one-ups on all of them, and I wanted them to know it, because I believed those advantages to be within reach of the status quo as well.

From the very first moment I stepped on the scene, American Kyokushin had looked to me like a stairway going steadily down, and *Budo Karate Illustrated* jumped out at me as a potential remedy. Through it, I would bring Japan to America, and America to Japan. I would expose the gap and the truth of the diverging trends. Some of the U.S. instructors would surely catch on; the others would be left by the wayside.

And if they were all left by the wayside?

So be it!

If those at the top were holding back what should have been the next booming generation, still hung up on their own disenfranchisement by those early instructors who had left Kyokushin, then to hell with them! – they needed to be replaced anyway.

When Bobby Lowe first declined to support *Budo Karate Illustrated*, Jacques roared, "Who needs him? His idea is that if you never try anything, you'll never fail! Use my name like a battering ram! Tell everyone I'm behind you. You're just a kid but you have the energy to do what no one else is willing to try! If only we could bottle the stuff, we could make a fortune."

Surely it was egotistical of me to know exactly what kind of energy Jacques was referring to.

When I was just barely seventeen, the summer before I entered Davidson a year early as a freshman, I was living in Chapel Hill with my mother so that I could train with Master Choi. One night, after Master Choi scolded me sharply for overstepping my bounds in the dojo, I walked forty miles to his house in Raleigh to demonstrate the sincerity of my intention to do better in the future. That was before I had a choice, it was survival for me then, and Master Choi told me to fix my attitude or never come back to the dojo. He didn't know then — I probably didn't know it yet then either! — the extent to which I was banking my very survival on being the first American to succeed in Japan as Mas Oyama's *uchi deshi*. My getting there depended on Master Choi's recommendation, and his suggestion that he might throw me away struck so deep at the core of my survival instinct that, still in my *dogi*, I started walking after training in Chapel Hill and didn't stop until I reached his apartment, ten hours later, on the far side of North Carolina's capital city.

I arrived at his door and did not ring his bell, because I would not disturb him uninvited at that hour of the morning, but an hour later, when he emerged to start his day, I was there to bow to him deeply and apologize for overstepping my bounds and to assure him that I would try harder in the future.

I had not intended to show him the three-inch-round, deep-purple blood blisters on the soles of my feet. I didn't know they were there. I hadn't taken my slippers off since I'd left the dojo the night before, and when I stooped to take them off upon entering his apartment, something felt funny about the bottom of my foot as I exposed it to the air. I turned it skywards to inspect it, and in doing so I inadvertently revealed that the soles of my feet had been rubbed away into a bloody mess.

It was then that Master Choi wrote of me to his uncle for the first time.

"I have a student," he wrote, "who wants to become your *uchi deshi* in Japan when he's old enough. Just this week, he walked forty miles to apologize for a mistake he made in the dojo. Perhaps when the time comes, you will consider him."

As a teenager under Master Choi's tutelage, I emerged from a sense of despair so dark that I vowed to become the first American to succeed in Japan, at any cost, to bring honor to my teacher. It was a particularly weighted gesture because Master Choi believed himself to have missed that exact opportunity when his own father, the poet and university president Il Un Choi, denied his younger brother Mas Oyama's request to send his fourth-born to Japan, as a boy, so that he might adopt him and raise him as his own son.

I was an unlikely candidate to succeed. I came into the world ten weeks premature, spent the first two months of my life in an oxygenated box, and had been disadvantaged ever since. It was fate that put me in Master Choi's dojo within eighteen months of my father's leaving Martha — and somehow leaving the father that I knew behind too! Simple luck, nothing else. And I was also somehow able to identify Master Choi, and the future under his uncle's wing that he represented, as my only chance to pull out of a dive that felt as though it was destroying me.

My karate training — Musashi's *pen and sword in accord* creed that Master Choi had instilled in me — came from the very beginning, therefore, right from the core of my being. It was primal for me from the start. It came from a place beyond the physical, beyond where people find themselves inclined to take up hobbies; it came from some dark recess beyond that, where, thanks to the instinct to survive, more of me became gathered up in its pursuit than any American I'd ever met could have imagined.

And of course it was impossible to reside there.

That kind of passion too, Dr. Strom, is unsustainable.

If I could have sustained it, if I could have spent my every day there, I'd have become a champion despite all my athletic disadvantages.

Yet certain situations in life — like Master Choi threatening to expel me from his dojo — would push me, and something in me would split wide open, releasing a concentrated, self-sacrificing insistence upon success at all costs. It was an attitude readily accessible among Japanese who were only one generation removed from one of which literally thousands opened their own bellies with their daggers or dropped themselves on their bayonets because they believed death to be a better fate than surrender. It was an attitude so foreign to the American personality of the late twentieth century that Mas Oyama had given up on ever finding it on American soil.

I didn't luck into a glimpse of that kind of spirit because I was great. I didn't discover it because I was stronger than the rest. I found it because I was weaker, and because my disadvantages were so pronounced that I felt my very life to be in danger. Nevertheless, somehow, fate put me in the right place at the right time. I saw it — mere glimpses of it, mind you! — and I was forever changed.

I would never suggest that we are in need of American citizens slicing open their own bellies when they fail in their endeavors, but I would stamp my foot and growl to assert that we are in desperate need of American citizens willing to pursue endeavors for the common good, even at the expense of themselves, as if failure would mean their own ultimate undoing. American society teaches us that someone else will take care of life's more difficult concerns, and that we're entitled to grind along on the road to social and economic advancement, reaping the benefits of someone else's sacrifice.

Indeed, such thinking is at the core of our very religion.

And so, with the first issue of *Budo Karate Illustrated*, far from being blinded by ego, I *willfully* showed the supporters of the status quo what could be done by one willing to sacrifice himself in the process. My presentation of self in the first issue stepped on toes because on some level I wanted it to. At least, Midas wanted it to. Midas, the primal part of me that worked from as close to the survival instinct as I could drive myself, stamped his foot, growled, gnashed his teeth, and roared to the best of his ability, "Get with the program, or get out of the way! It's the dawn of a new day!"

And how did such an oath end up falling on deaf ears?

Simple.

I failed to anticipate the death of Mas Oyama.

Mas Oyama was often critical of my mistakes and shortcomings, just as he was with all his students. He didn't spoil me. Once early on, to my shame and embarrassment, he even called me to his office and asked me directly if I was sure I wanted to continue on as his *uchi deshi*. I knew he was asking me because he could see how close I was to crumbling under the demands of the program that was so much easier for my Alpha peers. There were times when he worried about me and times when he scolded me – and I know I disappointed him to the core on at least one occasion – but he always supported me, and in the early summer of 1994, just after he died, there was no question in my mind that of all the things I'd done that he'd been there to see, my ambition for *Budo Karate Illustrated*, and for the future of Kyokushin in North America, was the one that he most approved.

What if Mas Oyama had not died when he did?

Probably he *would* have been critical of the content of my first book. After all, he was critical of it before it was even laid out.

"How many pages is it going to be?"
"Osu, eighty pages."
"No good, make it at least one hundred."
"Osu!"
"Have you included the history of Kyokushin?"
"Osu, no, I didn't think to."
"Well, you better include it, then!"
"Osu!"

I think it's likely that *Sosai* would even have expressed concern over the precocious risks I took with some of my editorial decisions. But by then I would have piqued the interest of the French Canadians in a second issue, and the project would have gone on. My presence would have been toned down in the second book. Mas Oyama would have insisted on it, and the supporters of the American status quo would see what could be achieved with a little daring to try. With Mas Oyama's support of the second issue, they would see the book becoming an institution, and some of them would rise to Midas's challenge.

What I truly hoped to inspire, of course, went far beyond stunts such as breaking baseball bats and carrying barbells up mountains. The ones who tried to imitate such feats for photo-ops of their own would be missing the point. Just as you'd be underestimating me to believe that the eye-contact communication I've described was something so trivial as making snarling faces of "Now I'm going to beat you" or puppy-eyed expressions of "I love you," you'd be missing the point if you thought Midas merely hoped to break baseball bats and inspire others to do the same.

Beyond the physical feats, beyond the book project, beyond the dojos I'd open and the autobiographical books I'd write, it was my self-transformation that was the challenge.

It was the life I was living that was the challenge.

The vision was the challenge.

The willingness to sacrifice myself in the process was the challenge.

Somehow that year, Nathan Ligo picked up a bloody scourge that had been wielded by forces beyond his control as an adolescent, and not only created, but also did his best to aggravate, a situation that kept him right there within the jaws of that same kind of emotional devastation. The mother of his second childhood home returned in 1993 from a summer away in the Everglades and found him suffering the dull relentless ache of the loss of the first woman that he'd let himself completely free to love. That pain lingered like a fencepost driven through his chest, and unknowingly and unintentionally, her reaction to what she found when she returned had been as if to grasp that post with both hands and twist it until Nathan thought he would die.

That was when Midas first gnashed his teeth, because, for Nathan, surrender was never on the agenda.

But what then did Nathan so summarily do?

He grabbed that post himself, with his own two calloused hands, and used Helen to create a situation that would continue to twist it, as if the splinters that cut his flesh were the only thing keeping him alive:

Twist, Nathan!

Bleed!

You know that you can, and you know that you can survive it. For someone else, for the world this time, go back and see! Do it one more time!

Could I actually have stopped?

Was it really that I willfully chose to let it go on?

Reason told me daily that I should have just let it go as the nonsense that it was. As crazy as some of it seems, I was never unaware that it seemed crazy. I let myself go with open eyes, and I was aware of passing milestones where I knew for certain I could have shut it down. Every time I paused to take that deep breath of life under a star-packed sky, every time I reached out to Helen in her absence, every time I noticed the eyes of the hawk on the wind and welcomed the resultant euphoric, creativity-instilling release . . .

Every time, I knew that all I had to do was stop.

Don't take that breath, Nathan! Don't pause to revel in it. Don't feed the beast. It'll only tear you apart. Grow up and pull yourself together! Get a freakin' grip before it's too late!

But in a certain sense it was too late.

The years that followed would testify that I suffered real, quantifiable damage at my own hands as I so resolutely made the choices that kept the machine roaring along at its breakneck pace, right up to the moment I learned of Helen's *complications* and steered it off its tracks and into the dirt. I know because I've spent more than a decade now living the withdrawal. Like sunlight through a magnifying glass, I used Helen to focus all of my life's lost love until it became the fire of creative energy that fueled the conscience-driven projects I pursued. Through her I continued day after day to rip open old wounds, until I swam through my world in the blissful release of the body's most toxic chemicals. I know because from the moment I shut down that machine, and for the years of my life that followed, I have, to gradually diminishing degrees, felt the withdrawal of those chemicals. I have matured to accept their absence, and a set of certain, mostly uncomfortable physical symptoms associated with it, as a permanent part of my adult life.

If what I was doing that year for Kyokushin, and for what Kyokushin could do for the world, was not self-sacrificial, what was it? I took the name of a friend who was the most beautiful person in my world and gave it with open eyes to the monster of painful withdrawal that *Helen* became. Midas turned everything that he touched to gold, and for him that included the people he loved. Who in the end is the biggest loser as the beautiful ones go on into the future to live and to love, and cold ugly Midas remains behind, robbed of that which could have been?

It is in that context that all decisions I made that year, including the editorial ones, have to be considered. I designed the *Budo Karate Illustrated* forerunner in a nine-day sleepless marathon right in the middle of the time when I was literally swimming in the endorphins of self-sacrifice. I'd willfully cast myself to a pride of lions, knowing that they would eat me alive, and I reveled in the knowledge that lingering there carried me daily closer to my goal.

"But what about your success rate?" Job Thomas asked.

"Don't you want to be 100% successful in life, and in order to do so, shouldn't you attempt only what you know you can accomplish?"

I smiled when I confessed that I understood his point. I smiled because I was undaunted. *You've already lived once,* I had told myself already. *Why not burn up all that remains in an attempt to do for the world?*

But Mas Oyama died, and as if Midas really had been able to see the future, the status quo rose up against *Budo Karate Illustrated*.

Matsui froze the project.

And Nathan Ligo burned.

THIRTY-THREE

Indeed, NATHAN LIGO returned to North Carolina from Japan emboldened by Michael Lorden's description of the exchange he'd witnessed between Matsui and Henri Orlean, and he pressed Matsui for an answer on whether or not he could proceed with the production of Book Two. And in the irony to end all ironies, Matsui sent him back into the heart of the status quo of America's Kyokushin – the very status quo that Midas had challenged to get with the program or step aside! – to ask them to yea or nay the continuation of the project.

It was clear that Matsui didn't have the energy to give to *Budo Karate Illustrated*. The 32-year-old chairman had inherited the 133-nation IKO, and just when Nathan needed a green light to avoid the financial damage of *not* producing Book Two, Matsui had concerns that were far more pressing.

"Ask the U.S. branch chiefs if they support the project," he instructed. "Have them contact the Chairman of the International Committee, *Shihan* Bobby Lowe in Hawaii, to express their support, and if he tells me that they want you to continue, I will look at your proposal."

I should have been more concerned than I was.

Matsui's "You should make an effort to support Nathan Ligo's magazine. Small, inferior magazines will make Kyokushin look small and inferior" was still ringing in my ears, and I wasn't yet afraid. *Shihan* Lowe in Hawaii had never eagerly supported my project, but he was never up in arms against it, either. Mainly, though, it was because of the other U.S. branch chiefs that I wasn't concerned.

As high, mighty and condescending as I may sound discussing the shortcomings of American Kyokushin, those impressions of mine were still among Midas's most deeply guarded secrets. Aside from tipping my hand in Montreal in one particularly ill-fated conversation with Annie, I wasn't aware of even the slightest reaction from the U.S. branch chiefs that might suggest that they suspected me of any such mischief.

The momentum the project had maintained from the beginning had still not been shaken.

The U.S. branch chiefs that I had become closest to – Tom Flynn in Massachusetts, Michael Monaco in Rochester, Michael Lorden in Orlando, and Bill Richards in Binghamton – hadn't so much as flinched. Tom Flynn had expressed some concern – he was the one likely in closest contact with Jacques and Annie – but when it came directly from him to me, it came only as the advice of an older, wiser instructor of Kyokushin who, in Mas Oyama's image, cautioned me about my self-presentation. Midas and I had my youth to fall back on, as an excuse, if all else failed. There was always my willingness to repent, accept criticism, and make the necessary adjustment in the next book. It wasn't an absence of friends among the North American branch chiefs that should have scared me . . .

It was the absence of Midas.

It had only been Nathan Ligo ever since I'd locked Midas back into his tomb, and Nathan Ligo was far less prepared to handle the heat than he would have been with Midas by his side.

I'm not sure exactly when it was that my favorite devil's-advocate critic, Jacques' wife Annie, became the most vocal of those who had spoken up about my self-presentation in *Budo Karate Illustrated's* first book. She had copyedited the entire book minus the cover pages, and it was the cover pages that must have left her feeling betrayed. I hadn't shared with her my plans for a rear-cover advertisement for my autobiographical book-in-progress – I frankly hadn't considered it consequential! – and when the status quo started to murmur about a work that she had edited, that omission gave her the grounds she needed to join hands with several of the others who expressed concern.

Annie was a book critic, and all of a sudden I was getting my first negative review.

The fact that that criticism came from Annie – at a time when the whole world had been turned on its ear by the death of Mas Oyama – became particularly important, because she and Jacques were the ones with whom I shared the most camaraderie. They were the project's grandparents, and Jacques' broad battering-ram-like support had been there to embolden me from the start. When Mas Oyama sat the three of us down together in Rochester, the introduction was not, "Oh, by the way, Jacques, this is Nathan. Nathan, this is Jacques." Instead, it had been an introduction heavily laden with unspoken intent. "Jacques, you crawled out of Stalin's Russia, and Ligo, well, you obviously crawled out of some other kind of shithole. You should be there to take care of one another. Jacques, take care of Nathan. Nathan, take care of Jacques. You are the ones that I rely on in America. Therefore you must rely on each other."

It was the Annie Gottlieb half of that pair, however, with whom I connected in a more conventional way.

Jacques was a man of few words and, like Sosai, the words that he uttered were often bone-splitting. The day after I met him in Rochester, he sat behind Sosai against the wall in our North American branch chief meeting while Sosai invited anyone present to stand up and voice any concerns. One poor guy from Chicago stood up and launched into this diatribe about how he'd been wronged by some other Kyokushin instructor who shared his same geographical location. It wasn't the venue to discuss his personal issue in such detail, and I shifted uncomfortably in my seat to watch how Sosai figured out both the situation and the guy in about the first fifteen seconds of his speech, just by watching his eyes and the way he stood. And yet the Chicago instructor wouldn't shut up. Sosai sighed heavily and shifted his own position impatiently from one side of his seat to the other, not wanting to cut the speaker off.

That's when Jacques, who had been silent up until that moment, intervened. "Get to the fucking point!" he roared.

Even Sosai jumped before breaking into a torrent of belly-shaking laughter.

"This guy comes all the way here from Japan!" Jacques went on, just half of his volume easily carrying over the laughter that had broken out from various other quadrants of the room. "Tell him what the problem is and sit down! If you keep this up they're going to have to reschedule his flight!"

The unfortunate recipient of Jacques's correction had been shaken to the core, and, his knees already softened, he lost the battle with gravity and dropped into his chair with a weak, disheartened "Osu."

"Okay, okay," Sosai said reassuringly, stifling his laugher and addressing the fellow Jacques had just flattened. "That's okay. Don't worry." One of the interpreters told him that they could talk about it later. The point was, though, that there wasn't another man in America who could sit there in silent support of Sosai and then break into someone else's speech and have the kind of effect that not only shook the recipient's entire world, but also met with Sosai's full approval.

That's when Jacques, who had been silent up until that moment, intervened. "Get to the fucking point!" he roared. Even Sosai jumped before breaking into a torrent of belly-shaking laughter. (This is the last of the substitutions for Kobayashi Yo images. The intended photo showed Sosai and Jacques, with David Bunt and Cameron Quinn translating, at the 1992 meeting in Rochester. This one, from Jacques's own collection, shows him standing behind his friend and teacher in an earlier era. Jacques stood, in fact, behind Mas Oyama for the better part of five decades.)

And I was no stranger to that kind of intensity coming from Jacques.

Jacques used the very same tone to shake me to the core on occasion as well. "I read your book *Donbas*," I told him on my first visit to New York. "I've been writing one of my own, and once I read yours, I became ashamed. I've always believed hardship and suffering to be a large part of the book I'm writing about my adolescence, but now I've read *Donbas* and I realize that the hardship that I experienced doesn't even in a thousand years compare . . ."

"Nathan!" Jacques roared more then with his eyes than with his tone, since we were in a public place. "Growing up in the Donbas could have made me dead! But growing up in this country can make you WISH you were dead! Write the book!"

"Osu," I said feebly, every bit as chopped off at the knees as that fellow had been in the meeting in Rochester. When I was sixteen or seventeen, my stepmother told me that I should be ashamed when I told her that I wanted to teach karate to try to unravel some of the problems in American society. "How dare you suggest that American society has problems!" she said. "In other places in the world governments torture women for daring to seek education, or imprison people for daring to speak their mind. Children are massacred by government policy . . ." And like most of what she told me, since it was all negative – all carping and condescending – it tended to accumulate, and to ring in my ears for months, and even years. Jacques' simple, ingenious "growing up in this country can make you WISH you were dead!" silenced that key portion of my stepmother's complaint once and for all, and I only realized over the months and years to come the extent to which I'd finally been set free.

"Osu!" I always stood up and saluted every time Jacques entered and left the room during my earliest trips to Greenwich Village to stay with him and Annie, and Jacques would swear at me in the same soul-shaking tone.

"Nathan, I told you to relax! You're my FRIEND! Why do you jump up and down like that all the time? Relax, will you! Take it easy!"

"Osu!" I'd answer at full volume and he'd roll his eyes. He was my *dai-sempai*, it was in my bones to treat him in the fashion I'd learned in Japan, and Jacques had to shake my very bones in an attempt to make me relax.

In much the same way that I was with Sosai, therefore, I was always on eggshells around Jacques. I loved him, he was one of the giants around whom my world revolved, but there's no question that it took me years before I was able to relax in his company. I was always too much in awe.

Annie, on the other hand, writer, *New York Times* book critic, and graduate of Harvard with a degree in history and literature – and my *sempai* too, as she'd been training in Kyokushin since I was an infant! – was always there to be much easier for me to talk to. Jacques's average sentence was only about three words long, and they were often words that shook the floor under my feet. Annie, on the other hand, could spit out a thousand well-crafted ones without ever once repeating herself, and without ever once leaving any doubt as to why she'd made Jacques a worthy match. That was probably why I got myself into trouble a number of times in conversations with her. She was easier to talk to – she was more on my wavelength intellectually – and more than any other Kyokushin-related party that year, I tended to use her as a sounding board for thoughts that I didn't dare broach with anyone else. She came closer to talking with Midas – directly to Midas – than anyone else, at least insofar as once or twice I found myself uttering statements to her that had been planted by him. It's no wonder, then, that she became so vocal in her protest. Whereas Nathan might have admitted errors, Midas was utterly unrepentant, and although she never knew Midas – no one did – on occasion I let my words with Annie sway in the direction of honesty, and during that period honesty meant bringing Nathan Ligo and Midas together into one. As a result, I must have come across as too self-assured for my own good.

Once it dawned on the Corrigals, the Bunts, and the Cameron Quinns that support of the project was no longer something to be taken for granted as it had been before *Sosai* died, Annie's criticism started to get to me. I no longer had access to Midas's fire, Jacques was temporarily muted by the death of his lifelong friend Mas Oyama, and I failed to differentiate Annie's criticism from Jacques' opinion.

I was so unbelievably exhausted, and without Midas there to turn my exhaustion into unaided flight, my morale suffered, and my ability to stand up for myself took a serious blow.

And that's why I should have been concerned.

* * *

I realize now that I did it to myself.

I had help, surely, from others who, unlike Annie, did not want me to succeed, but when I made two dozen phone calls that week to branch chiefs in two dozen corners of America, I must have come across as being a little bit more threatened than I should have. I brought up the fact that I'd taken some criticism about my self-presentation.

And that's important, because a good half of them hadn't even flinched.

The ones whose toes Midas had stepped on noticed – the ones who were themselves ambitious to extend their influence beyond their own branches — but most of them were only congratulatory, complimentary, and happy about my coming second volume. The majority of them didn't bat an eye to see me in my own book, and they were surprised to hear that there had been any criticism. The general reaction among the branch chiefs was, if anything, "Sure, it's not perfect. He's only 23 years old! But wow, look what he was able to accomplish!"

Far from being critical, Michael Lorden wanted to join me!

And yet I must have done myself some harm as I volunteered the topic with all of them by phone, repented perhaps even where repentance wasn't necessary, and then asked them to send faxes anyway to *Shihan* Lowe on my behalf. I must have done myself harm as I broached the subject with *Shihan* Lowe in Hawaii, assured him that the whole thing was a learning experience for me, and that I'd be sure to steer clear of the same trap the next time. "It's all my fault," were the unspoken words behind the tone I'd employed. Midas wasn't there to roar like Jacques, "To hell with those bastards! You were right to do as you did! It's *your* book, after all. Except for Michael Monaco and his tournament, what the hell are those guys doing for the development of Kyokushin in America anyway?"

The seeds of doubt had once again been planted, however: I'd failed to graduate from college; I'd not gotten the Watson or the branch chief appointment that I'd been sure would be on the way. I blamed myself for more than I was guilty of, and, unable to figure out exactly what I had done wrong, I handed those elements of the American status quo who were threatened by Midas's ulterior motive exactly what they needed to bury *Budo Karate Illustrated*.

Shihan Lowe told me to write the statement that I wanted him to send to Matsui, and I wrote:

> Nathan Ligo has informed me that before you look at his draft of an agreement concerning the future of his magazine, you want to hear whether or not the American branch chiefs support his efforts. I directed Nathan to call all the U.S. branch chiefs and ask them to fax me a simple statement of support. Within 24 hours, I received positive, supportive messages from almost all of the U.S. branch chiefs. Their only criticism was that in the future the magazine should be focused more on *Honbu* and less on Nathan. They want to hear what Matsui *Kancho* has to say, not what Nathan Ligo has to say. Nathan has told me that this is what he wants as well. Therefore, if

you are supportive of Nathan Ligo's magazine, I recommend that you look at the agreement that he has to show you. I believe Nathan when he says he truly wants to make Kyokushin his life's work.

I shudder today to realize that it was I who delivered into *Shihan* Lowe's hands the language that he might best use to galvanize the status quo's self-defensive bias against the project.

How truly tired I must have been!

I didn't even see then the extent to which *Shihan* Lowe axed my project with the rewritten statement he sent to *Honbu* instead. The branch chiefs had all told me that they supported the magazine's continuation. Tom Flynn and David Bunt were the most critical in an advisory sort of way, but there wasn't one of them who I believed to be such a good liar as to be so supportive with me on the phone and then turn around and write opposite statements to *Shihan* Lowe.

But it didn't matter, really.

The project was in *Shihan* Lowe's hands.

It was up to him. He could take the comments he received and spin them however he chose.

In the image of Mas Oyama, he could even have acknowledged the value of my project to North American Kyokushin, acted as an older, wiser, impartial advisor and teacher, and advised me how to avoid such a situation in the future. He could have said, "Look, Nathan, it's plain that *Sosai* wanted this book, and it's plain that you have the ambition to continue it, but you've absolutely got to tread a little more lightly, so as not to bias these *sempai* of yours against you." He could have said that, but he didn't. He could have welcomed and helped to guide a project that promised to help American Kyokushin emerge from the dark ages.

He could have . . . but perhaps *Shihan* Lowe felt more comfortable leaving us there.

Maybe he felt I'd already proven myself too willing to disregard his advice. I'd asked him for help on the very first day of the project, and he'd told me that it was too much of a challenge for me. He advised me not to try. Perhaps he didn't like being proved wrong – he had his own copy of my book with his own submitted material in it to prove it. How ironic that a year later he held the fate of my project in those same two hands!

He told me that it was too much for me, and then a year later he found himself in a position to make it so.

To Matsui, he wrote:

> Dear Matsui *Kancho*, Nathan Ligo has informed me that before you look at his draft of a contract agreement between you/*Honbu* and him, concerning the future of his United States magazine, that you wanted to hear whether or not the American branch chiefs support his efforts. I told Nathan Ligo to call all the U.S. branch chiefs and ask them to fax me a statement of support. Within a day or so, I received supportive messages from most of the American branch chiefs. However, they all indicated that the focus of the magazine should not be on himself, Nathan Ligo. Sincerely, *Shihan* Bobby Lowe.

Maybe I should have gone back to him as soon as *Honbu* faxed me what he wrote. Maybe I should have established whether he really meant to be as unsupportive as he sounded, or whether, as I naïvely suspected at the time, it was merely his poor choice of words that had made it sound so much less supportive. I read his fax today and am immediately reminded of the letter *Sosai* sent to Jacques earlier that same year, asking him to support Katsuhiko Horai, with so much hesitation in his language that it sounded more like a warning not to do so.

It's ironic, therefore, that it was Katsuhiko Horai who was to deliver the *two* of the one-two attack that undid *Budo Karate Illustrated*.

And once again, I'm sure it was my fault.

Matsui asked me to have all the U.S. branch chiefs contact *Shihan* Lowe to express their support, and I had taken that to mean all the branch chiefs who had supported the first book. And all of them had. Only Katsuhiko Horai didn't appear in the first volume because he hadn't been appointed branch chief by *Sosai* until after the book had already been sent off for printing.

Honbu's next fax was a telling one:

> Dear Ligo,
>
> We received your letter yesterday. And I also received the fax from *Shihan* Bobby Lowe concerning about your activity. But he said that all the branch chiefs in America said that the focus of the magazine should not be on yourself. I do really think so and I also want to say that do not forget that you work for that magazine only by the name of Kyokushinkaikan and remember the spirit of our organization. I just curious, you wrote you have gotten all the branch chief's agreement

for your activity but I talked to Mr. Horai branch chief in New York about that and he said he does not know about that. WHY???

Sincerely yours, Miyatomi Yoshie, Secretary.

Three days after that, on the road to Florida with Rafael, I awaited the end of our 12-hour drive with bated breath so that I could call Jacques and Annie in New York and ask them if a response from Japan had arrived. I'd responded to the above fax with one final message to Matsui, and now, once more, I could do nothing but wait for *Honbu* to respond.

It would take the better part of a decade, after Matsui and his new right hand in the international branches, Katsuhiko Horai, had committed the stunning crimes they would commit against Mas Oyama's Kyokushin, for the pieces to fall into place enough for me to realize that the mistakes I made during those weeks of negotiation after *Sosai's* memorial were not even relevant. Even if I hadn't been exhausted, even if I hadn't been plagued by doubt, even if Midas had been right there beside me, I know now that the project couldn't possibly have survived with Matsui and Horai at the helm of the new IKO.

My performance as a negotiator unquestionably left something to be desired. I did, in fact, come close to proving *Shihan* Lowe right: Perhaps I'd never been up to the challenge.

I was twenty-three years old, I'd made it as far as I had, and all of a sudden, I found myself dreadfully confused. I was one hundred percent sure that Midas's choices had been the right ones, but without him there to sort out the new, altered political environment, I couldn't square my conviction that I had been right all along with consequences that suggested I'd been wrong to try it at all.

It's all my fault. It's all my fault. I know that it's all my fault . . . but what the hell did I do wrong? My choices were all so right, why am I suffering all this heat?

It was in that frame of mind that I sent my last fax to *Honbu* concerning *Budo Karate Illustrated*. In it, I explained the pressure that I'd been under to lay out a 100-page book in nine days that weren't enough for the 80 pages I already planned to design. I apologized and explained that I hadn't contacted *Sensei* Horai because he hadn't been one of the original supporters of the book. I went on to assure Matsui that it was never my intention to use the book to promote myself. I told him that, on the contrary, it had always been my intention to work for *Honbu* directly, so that I would have the daily guidance that had been missing on the trial run. I even suggested that I relocate to Tokyo to work on the next several issues, so that *Honbu* could make the editorial choices and I'd just do the work. I explained how I envisioned the book moving forward into Canada, and that I believed there was potential for moving beyond that into South America as well.

Matsui's response, when it came a few days later, was such a shock because the "statements which I had been sent to *Honbu*" were written in the form of a proposal. I didn't send any kind of ultimatum that said "This is the way it has to be, or to hell with you." I just said, "This is what I propose." At the very least, I expected a response that suggested why my proposal wouldn't work, and a counterproposal of how my work might be redirected to better serve *Honbu's* purposes as well.

The response when it came, however, was biting and ridiculous.

It was a non sequitur.

"Herewith to inform you to freeze all your activity on your magazine, *Budo Karate Illustrated*," was the statement that Matsui signed into law. "This means you have no authorization to issue *Budo Karate Illustrated* in the name of Kyokushinkaikan neither to in any other represent Kyokushin Karate. I discussed about this with the Chairman of the International Committee, *Shihan* Bobby Lowe, and we can not agree with the statements which you have been sent to *Honbu*."

PART VI

Nor happiness, nor majesty, nor fame,
Nor peace, nor strength, nor skill in arms or arts,
Shepherd those herds whom tyranny makes tame;
Verse echoes not one beating of their hearts,
History is but the shadow of their shame,
Art veils her glass, or from the pageant starts
As to oblivion their blind millions fleet,
Staining that Heaven with obscene imagery
Of their own likeness. What are numbers knit
By force or custom? Man who man would be,
Must rule the empire of himself; in it
Must be supreme, establishing his throne
On vanquished will, quelling the anarchy
Of hopes and fears, being himself alone.

— P.B. Shelley

THIRTY-FOUR

PERHAPS IT WAS the painful memory of running away from Mas Oyama's dormitory.

Perhaps it was the oath I swore to him beyond the grave when he died.

Maybe it was the echo of that terrible voice in which I swore it.

But I would be DAMNED if I was going to quit again so easily!

"Go and hide under a rock and don't talk to anyone!" Jacques told me. "Give it some time to die down and see what happens. Give it some time and I'll talk to Matsui."

It wasn't much to hold on to, but I did hold on.

None of us knew then the extent to which even Jacques Sandulescu's wings had been clipped from the moment Matsui moved into *Sosai's* office at *Honbu*. Matsui established Katsuhiko Horai in his new Fifth Avenue dojo just four blocks down from the Empire State Building in New York, and it wouldn't take half a decade before they'd whittled down *Shihan* Lowe's authority as International Committee Chairman and delivered it piece by piece into the waiting, ambitious hands of Horai himself, the IKO's newly created International Secretary. Just as Matsui depended on his *dai-sempai* Yuzo Goda and Hatsuo Royama as the twin pillars of his authority over the branches in Japan, he positioned *Shihan* Bobby Lowe behind Horai as the pillar of *his* authority over the Kyokushin organizations of 133 nations around the globe.

Jacques was there too, on the International Committee beside Bobby Lowe, Singapore's Peter Chong, and three or four others of *Sosai's* oldest and most trusted students. But it took Jacques less than three years to realize that, like the rest, he was only there to validate Matsui, and he sent Kyokushin's young chairman a full-power *binta* in the form of a fax message that he sent not just to the North American branch chiefs, but to all of the IKO branch chiefs around the world. In it he condemned Horai's alienating totalitarianism and Matsui's blatant disregard for those senior members who were meant to be his advisors. He cautioned that the decisions they were making stood to undo all that *Sosai* had spent his life building.

Hatsuo Royama – one of Mas Oyama's earliest students and thus *sempai* to nearly every active Kyokushin *karateka* in Japan – bit his lip out of loyalty to *Sosai* and did his best to guide Matsui. It was nearly ten years before he knew for sure that Matsui had no intention of ever listening and that the greater loyalty to *Sosai* was to move to break Matsui's hold on Kyokushin.

By five years after *Sosai's* death, only five of the twenty U.S. branch chiefs who had supported *Budo Karate Illustrated* remained with what had been Mas Oyama's organization. Guam's Paul Alfred, Chicago's Leslaw Samitowski, and Hawaii's Bobby Lowe were the only ones I've mentioned by name who remained. *Shihan* Lowe, with his "If you don't try, you won't fail!" philosophy, must have been the perfect match for Matsui's demand for puppet pillars of authority-validating support.

I myself waited for a decade.

Matsui could have stepped up to the plate and, in the image of his teacher and mine, scolded me for what he perceived to be my shortcomings. He could have used the energy that I cast at his feet to achieve his own ends. All he'd have needed to do was tell me how he wanted me to change course, and out of loyalty to Mas Oyama, I'd have changed.

Instead, he and Horai threw me away in the most destructive way imaginable.

With near-total disregard for my own safety, I'd never entertained the slightest impulse to take the simple but time-consuming steps required to form a corporation that would have served as a firewall between *Budo Karate Illustrated* and my own personal finances. Why would I have? Deciding that the project would succeed at all costs – my giving in to the foregone conclusion of success – had been where I'd drawn the creative energy to make it as far as I had.

But now, the project frozen, I found myself in danger of staggering away with a level of personal debt that I couldn't possibly pay off. In accordance with my *uchi deshi* training, in which there was never any element of *but* in *Osu*, I took Matsui's decree that I "freeze all activity" regarding *Budo Karate Illustrated* to mean that I wasn't even to sell additional copies of Book One. The eleven hundred books I'd already sold paid for just over half of Montgomery's $40,000 balance. But without permission to sell what was left, I would be condemned to carry nearly $18,000 of debt on the salary of a dining service manager.

And yet, for ten long years, I put myself aside.

I left myself in the bitter cold where Matsui had cast me – and I waited for him to mature into the leader that *Sosai* had apparently expected him to become. Even as the shrinking membership of Mas Oyama's single massive organization broke up into three, then six, and then even more squabbling international Kyokushin organizations, I bit my lip and waited for Matsui, the man who had come so close to destroying me in 1994.

I waited because *Sosai* had pointed at him and said, "He's the one."

He had been my choice too.

I chose Matsui because it was clear to everyone – it had been clear for many years – that his destiny was to take over when *Sosai* died. Even Jacques all but told Matsui to go to hell with his last-resort fax to the world's branch chiefs, but in my self-enforced exile, I insisted on giving Matsui the benefit of the doubt. Overnight I found myself condemned to having to share my home country with Katsuhiko Horai – Matsui's young International Secretary, who never would tolerate anyone who possessed a shred of their own creative initiative – and yet for years I refused to join another organization. For ten years, I waited for Matsui to prove beyond a shadow of a doubt that there was in fact no method to his madness, and that what everyone perceived as a total loss of control was in fact exactly that.

In a sense, he and Horai were carrying out one of Midas's contingency plans for America, after all. They were destroying the status quo. All that was important to me at the time was that sustainable, authentic Kyokushin come to America. I'd always known that the status quo might have to be broken in order to achieve that end. Maybe Matsui and Horai were going to open the doors to a new generation that would finally make Kyokushin in America what it was meant to be. I was willing to put myself aside, give Matsui the benefit of the doubt, and credit him with most likely knowing something that I didn't know.

But it was not to be.

For ten years Matsui proved that he was only taking Kyokushin downwards, and for ten years I proved that my desire to do for Kyokushin had never been about me.

They've grouped you, too, into the status quo that they're destroying, but give them the benefit of the doubt anyway, I told myself. *Don't fight like the rest. Don't join the fickle masses who so easily hand over their allegiance to rival factions. Stand on the sidelines and burn if necessary! You know well your ability to endure on the fringe as Family's black sheep. Watch and listen. Maybe in the end they'll achieve what hasn't been achieved in America since Shigeru Oyama came so close. Hide under a rock and don't do anything to step on Matsui's toes. Maybe the pieces will eventually settle, and then you can go back to work.*

Of course, I never forgot Kikuko's assertion that Mas Oyama had been murdered by the *yakuza* in order to create a forged will that favored Matsui. In the end, though, I wasn't willing to buy into the theory of Mas Oyama's brat kid, given that she was so nearly alone in her belief. I'm sure people get away with murder all the time, but Mas Oyama was one of the most famous men in Japan! Surely someone beyond his 22-year-old daughter would have noticed if there had been anything more to it than the paranoid theory of a girl who found herself, from one day to the next, not only fatherless but also excluded from her father's will. I believed in Kikuko as a friend. I believed in her good intentions. I looked into her eyes and I trusted that she believed what she was telling me. And I did leave my encounter with her during the week of her father's memorial service with a vague but nagging impression that something wasn't quite right about Matsui's succession.

But even that I set aside.

So be it, I told myself. *Give Matsui the benefit of the doubt! He's the one that everyone idolized. He's the one with the energy and the charisma. He's the one that seems most likely to be able to mature to fill Mas Oyama's shoes. He must be supported if he's the one who's going to be the best for Kyokushin.*

For a decade, I waited to see if he was.

* * *

Jacques told me to lie low and wait.

"Hide under a rock and don't do a fucking thing!" had been his exact words. "Let some time pass and I'll talk to *Kancho* for you. Go shack up with a beautiful woman, and have some fun," he roared, "but DON'T DO A FUCKING THING!"

For a time, there was nothing I could do.

My brother's new wife Traci offered me their spare bedroom in Chapel Hill, and when my brother suggested that he could finagle a job for me at the property management company where he worked, I jumped at the opportunity. I was broke, my hands were tied by Japan, and doing whatever it took to get out of my father's backyard cottage was, for me, a no-brainer. What was left of Master Choi's Carolina Martial Arts Club was still at the university, and out of loyalty to my first teacher, I resolved to see what I could do to clean up the mess he'd left behind. As for Jacques's suggestion that I "find a beautiful woman and have some fun," my entire world had been flattened by Helen, and I could only wince in a way that left me relieved he couldn't see my face as we spoke on the phone.

One year after I became the only child member of Master Choi's CMAC in 1984, Master Choi promoted five students to *shodan*. Although he'd made black belts before, this group of five at once was a milestone, since five at one time indicated the growing strength of his organization as a university institution. A decade later, those five black belts were all long gone except for the most unlikely of the bunch. Steve Hobson, the club's new head instructor, was unlikely because he had always been so awkward. Forget about Master Choi's lessons from the more esoteric end of the spectrum; Steve was the one who always struggled to grasp the obvious ones! He was the one who always made the rest of us cringe when he punched boards that didn't break in attempts at *tameshiwari*.

A decade had passed since I was thirteen, however, and I had begun to give Steve some credit for remaining committed to the CMAC out of loyalty to our teacher. I wasn't much surprised that the karate he was teaching wasn't very good: whatever Steve's strengths, he was not the ideal channel for conveying Master Choi's teaching.

The broader fact of the matter was that the CMAC had never been introduced to Kyokushin by an authentic source. Master Choi was Mas Oyama's nephew, of course, and in a certain sense one can't get any more authentic than that; I was often in awe at how much the two men shared in terms of personality, character and spirit. But the physical aspect of Kyokushin that Master Choi incorporated into his Korean martial arts background was substantially less than the real thing, since he'd never actually trained with his uncle. Even though when I first arrived in Japan I was likely ahead of several of my athletically talented peers in some of the spiritual and philosophical nuances of karate, it was only fitting that I leave behind the *nidan* that Master Choi had given me.

Spiritual and philosophical nuances don't protect skinny little 19-year-olds from getting their asses kicked at Mas Oyama's world headquarters dojo.

Steve was busy when I arrived in Chapel Hill with my head still spinning from Matsui's about-face. He was recently remarried, if I remember correctly, and he was apparently having to put a lot of effort into making the new one work. For whatever reason, he seemed more relieved than anything to have me take over the instruction of the CMAC's entire Monday, Wednesday, Friday, Sunday schedule.

And I did so with a passion.

There were a dozen regular students training there when I arrived, and it was only natural that I pour my energy back into the recruiting process that had been my responsibility in years past. With a small team that I inspired to help me, I dusted the entire campus with flyers, and hosted the introductory meetings in the College Union that we'd used since I was a boy to recruit new members at the beginning of each semester. As a result, our class size increased to sixty members within about two months. It was the largest it had ever been, and it was with pleasure that I announced the addition of Tuesday and Thursday classes for all the beginners, to bring them up to speed so they could better follow the regular class.

For the first time in the CMAC's history, its members started practicing the authentic *kihon*, *iddo*, *kata* and *kumite* of Mas Oyama's Kyokushin. I exulted as day by day I broke down even the preexisting students' misconceptions about what the human body could take in the way of hard training and hard blows. One evening, I paired up two advanced students and challenged them to trade powerful uppercuts to the midsection, as my Davidson students had done, punching harder and harder until one of them gave up. Steve's senior students stubbornly refused to go beyond a certain point – believing it was somehow unnatural since they'd never been asked to hit each other that hard before – but my disappointment all but fell away when I watched the new class jump eagerly into the exercise and outdo their *sempai*, as if to join me in shouting from the rooftops,

It's the dawn of a new day! Some of the old guard may fade away, but this fresh generation will bring at least this tiny corner of America closer to the goal!

For the CMAC, at least, it did look like the dawn of a new day. After nearly fifteen years, authentic Kyokushin was finally combining with the indomitable spiritual elements of Master Choi's teaching that had been missing ever since he returned to Korea. The excitement in the students' eyes overflowed, and I knew that I was successfully channeling both the small part of Kyokushin that I'd acquired under Mas Oyama's tutelage, and the spirit that Master Choi's teaching had once inspired in me.

Sadly for the CMAC, however, trouble was brewing behind the scenes, and I'm ashamed to admit that it took me most of three months to realize it.

Starting well before my relocation to Chapel Hill, when I myself made the announcement to the members of the CMAC that Mas Oyama had died, Steve began to press me for ways that he could ally his group with what I have so tirelessly referred to as the status quo of American Kyokushin. For him, the Bobby Lowes and the Tom Flynns represented the promised land, offering the hope of finally bringing his ailing club in closer contact with the karate of its founder's renowned uncle. And since what Steve had was so much less than even that status quo, I saw no harm in lending him a hand. He sold my books to his students, and I wrote the letters that introduced him to Bobby Lowe and Tom Flynn.

Steve made plans for himself and several other senior members to visit the seminar hosted by Bobby Lowe in Hawaii that I'd volunteered to advertise in *Budo Karate Illustrated*.

Inwardly, I cringed at the notion of Steve and his students training in the same room as established Kyokushin members. Their karate was, by that time, so much deteriorated from what even Master Choi had given them that I feared they would jeopardize his reputation. Nevertheless, I supported the strengthening of those ties between Steve and the IKO because Steve convinced me that he wanted only to ensure the survival of the CMAC for the protection of Master Choi's legacy.

About ten weeks into my tenure at the unofficial helm of the CMAC, however, Steve matter-of-factly dropped a bomb that made it impossible for me to continue.

In the eyes of some, Master Choi had left North Carolina two years earlier in shame. In the wake of a failed marriage and two failed dojos in

Raleigh and Cary – and a failed *uchi deshi* student of Mas Oyama to boot! – he had finally bowed to his father's pressure and returned to Korea to take a post as a professor at a university there. Some of us knew that the failed marriage and the failed dojos were the products of another set of personal failures indicative of the all-too-human midlife crisis that he was then suffering. Steve left me virtually speechless when he told me that he had brought up some of that ancient history and shared it with new student populations who had no business knowing. It was Master Choi's personal business regarding specifically a period of his life of which he, too, was deeply ashamed.

And to disclose it, as Steve had, was to betray Master Choi.

Struggling to process, my mind lit on an incident that occurred in the dojo just a few weeks before that, when Steve was teaching one of our novice students how to break a board. He had that one board correctly supported between two concrete blocks, and after demonstrating the downward punching motion a couple of times, he decided, appropriately, that it would be easier to have the young lady punch the board with her knuckles parallel to the grain rather than perpendicular to it. Instead of rotating the student ninety degrees to stand in line with the two blocks, however, he rotated the board ninety degrees so that its grain spanned the distance between the blocks. I couldn't believe it! Steve had been at the CMAC since what for me was the dawn of time, and I watched in awe as he asked this poor girl to punch a board that Mas Oyama himself wouldn't have been able to break, unless he'd smashed a fist-sized hole straight through the middle of it!

Thankfully, I recovered quickly and saved the student from breaking her hand, by correcting Steve as humbly as possible in front of the class.

It was my decade-long experience with that somewhat confused Steve that saved him from personal injury the evening he told me across the table in a Chapel Hill restaurant what he had told his students about Master Choi's past. Suppressing a powerful impulse to stand up and knock the teeth out of his head, I realized that he was simply living up to his clueless norm. His intentions were genuine, but he was still the one, after all, who had always missed the point of what his teacher had tried to teach him.

No wonder Steve had been so eager to tie into the U.S. Kyokushin organization!

He had been trying to shore up his own shaky authority by finding a replacement for Master Choi. I knew then that Steve's intentions were more about him and his own position than about our teacher. He was using me as an instrument to worm his way out from under the man who had made me what I am, and that I could not abide. If he truly felt he couldn't strengthen ties with the IKO without discrediting our teacher, his duty would have been to express regret to his twelve students and shut down the club entirely, rather than continue under such a shadow.

Could I have stayed on and fixed it?

Perhaps.

But then there was the fact of my own shifted loyalty: my first responsibility was now to Mas Oyama, not Master Choi, and the CMAC was simply not on the path that I saw myself following for *Sosai*. Helping Steve would have been one thing; having to fight him to replace him would have been something entirely different. I simply could not commit to staying on in Chapel Hill.

Don't pin me down, Dillon! I could hear, six years later, my own voice echoing in my ears. *Not yet, CMAC! I'd only hurt you in the end. I have to go where you can't possibly follow, and I have no choice but to go.*

* * *

Coincidentally, it was exactly then that permission came down from above for me to at least resume sales of *Budo Karate Illustrated's* Book One.

Permission came through Jacques and Annie, and exactly how it was obtained is unclear. Given what I now know about Matsui and Horai, it's hard to believe that they would have supported my further book sales; Horai was calling the shots in more than just North America, and Horai seemed intent on standing in my way at any cost. I had expressed dismay more than once on the phone to Jacques: I couldn't possibly get out from under my book debt without at least selling the books that had already been printed. I wonder today if Jacques didn't just say, "To hell with these two Japs! Sell the books!"

It wouldn't have been out of character.

But on the other hand, that early in the deterioration of his own relationship with Matsui and Horai, Jacques was intentionally treading lightly as well, doing his best to give them the benefit of the doubt. "I hope that you can support him fully," *Sosai* had written regarding Horai.

("But I'm not sure that you'll be able to.") The world was on its ear, and like the rest of us, Jacques could do little other than wait and see what would come of Matsui's efforts. Annie made the point that they might as well let me sell the books, since preventing me from doing so merely insured that they would never get any money out of it. Any profits beyond the printing cost were promised to *Honbu*, after all.

Perhaps it was in that light that Jacques had convinced *Honbu* to allow me at least to sell the books that were already printed. However it was obtained, Jacques and Annie informed me that I had "the green light," and I immediately turned my eyes towards Canada.

Spending half of all the money I had on shipping, I sent two cases of books to the dojo of my friend Joe Addesso in Montreal and four more to Tom Flynn's dojo in Massachusetts. I'd have shipped them all to Canada, because I had no doubt that I'd be able to sell them there, but I couldn't afford it. I'd go up to Canada and generate some capital selling the first two cases of books first, and then send *Shihan* Flynn money to ship me some more from that closer location. I owed him money too, of course, and besides being a stalwart supporter who wanted the best for me, he would have known that helping me to sell books in Canada was the best way to get his own money back.

If only I could have shipped myself to Canada!

My Ford Fairmont had been resting in peace in my father's driveway in Davidson ever since that vacuum cleaner salesman had driven me to my Chinese history class, and when I'd needed a car, I'd borrowed Rafael's. Rafael and his car were in Florida now, however, and in Chapel Hill I'd been using only my brother's. Now I would be forced to improvise.

My brother, who had been trained to ride a motorcycle by the Marine Corps, had noticed one in the parking lot of one of the apartment complexes our company managed, and learning that it had been standing there, neglected and exposed to the weather, for longer than a year, we knocked on the tenants' door one afternoon to find out if it was for sale. Its owner turned out to be a CMAC student of Master Choi's from the time when I was in Japan, and when I promised him one of my books, he told us that he had no objection to our at least trying to get it started.

My brother taught me to ride that motorcycle over a period of several weeks, on our lunch breaks, going round and round in the apartment complex parking lot. My situation had become fairly desperate by then

– I had no money, no car, no college diploma, no home, no job, and all of a sudden no CMAC. Somehow, however, in the diminishing echoes of Midas's growls, I held to my vow.

"Challenge me in the name of Sosai's work and I will do whatever it takes!"

The bike was a Yamaha 400, although Yamaha 400s, I learned, only have 390-cc engines. It was not, its owner told me, the bike that he would choose for riding any significant distance. It had been stationary and exposed to the weather for nearly two years; its wires, tires, and rubber fittings were all rotten. It had no windshield or fairing to block out the weather. "Montreal?" he said, "You better hurry up and go, if you're gonna go! It's gonna be winter up there pretty soon. And on this bike, you'll take all that weather right in the face . . . It ought to be fairly quick . . . with a tune-up and an overall. Right now, I doubt you'll even make the Virginia border."

Thirty-six hours after I turned my back on the CMAC, I took the motorcycle out on public roads for the very first time and had my first experience with turn signals and a helmet, with using third, fourth, and fifth gears, and with speeds greater than fifteen miles per hour. I had a new set of tires put on that first day, and rode three hours southwest to Davidson to evaluate the bike mechanically, and simply to find out if I could. (Steering way clear of my father's house, of course, I spent that night on a friend's sofa.) The helmet I'd borrowed was a size too big, and any time I turned to look over my shoulder, the wind threatened to spin it around sideways. It took me well into my third day of traveling towards Canada to figure out how to look over my shoulder without feeling like I was going to lose control. Before that, if it hadn't been for the side mirrors, I'd have been running blind to any traffic behind me, and I was barely brave enough to change lanes.

I was acutely aware of how dangerous it was to do what I'd set out to do. My exploratory overnight to Davidson set aside, I'd never ridden a motorcycle faster than fifteen miles an hour before, and yet I strapped my *dogi* and several changes of winter clothes in a dry bag to the rack behind my seat and set off for Canada. I spent my first night in Washington, DC at my mother's brother's house, and the next night in New York City with Jacques and Annie. The motorcycle suffered an electrical meltdown when I cranked it the morning I set out from Washington – corroded fuses started blowing, wires started melting, lightbulbs started failing – and my first stop before leaving town was a salvage yard, where I borrowed tools from some real bikers who were amazed I was riding that piece of junk to Canada in the face of approaching November.

I was next to frozen by the time I crossed under the Hudson River through the Holland Tunnel, but visions of Jacques' lentil soup and southern fried chicken kept me pushing forward. A passerby on the West 4th Street sidewalk just beside Washington Square Park held the door open for me as I unscrewed my side mirrors and pushed my motorcycle right in through Jacques' building's front door and down the hallway to park it in the courtyard with the garbage cans.

Five floors up, I took a hot shower to wash away the windburn, and confessed over dinner with Jacques and Annie that an ulterior motive for my trip had come up.

There were two or three Canadian branch chiefs I knew I would encounter in Montreal that I would tell straight out that a misunderstanding had occurred between me and Matsui, and that as far as I knew then, there would be no second volume of the book I'd visited their dojos to sell. "But if *Shihan* Jacques turns out to be able to reverse Matsui's thinking on the issue," I would explain, "or if by some chance I myself am able to, I was wondering if you might be willing to support a second volume that focuses on Canadian Kyokushin?"

"Don't you think it's possible," I told Jacques and Annie, "that a positive, open-arms response from the French Canadians, suggesting ready access to a pool of potential profit, could be the key that unlocks the door to the project's continuation when we finally go to Matsui?"

It's interesting that already as early as that, we in the international Kyokushin community were beginning to associate Matsui and Horai with dollars and profit. Annie and I read the faxes that I had exchanged with *Shihan* Lowe and *Honbu*, and the unenthusiastic one that *Shihan* Lowe had sent to Matsui instead. Jacques blasted the way *Shihan* Lowe had moved to stamp out a kind of "youthful energy" that "we could make a fortune if we could learn to bottle." Annie thought that in my final fax to *Honbu*, I'd "conveyed a sense of my own importance for the future of Kyokushin that lacked humility" and that "it was not surprising that Matsui and Horai responded the way they did."

Annie and I argued – I was still less willing to face my shortcomings than I should have been – and Jacques finally put an end to it: "To hell with 'em all, Nathan! I'm behind you! You're my friend! If anyone in Canada gives you any trouble, just give me their name, and I'll straighten them out!

"Don't quit fighting, Nathan!

"Go as far as you can with the energy you have. You'll only be young this once!"

THIRTY-FIVE

I SET OFF EARLY the next afternoon on what was intended to be the final leg of my trip, and nearly crushed my booted ankle between my right motorcycle peg and a four-inch raised manhole cover on a badly potholed Greenwich Village street. Five hours later, my foot was still throbbing. It was pitch dark as I ran north along one of Vermont's most barren mountain highways. My headlight went out when I blew another fuse, and I barely escaped getting arrested by a state trooper who stopped to see if he could be of any assistance.

I had no driver's license to operate a motorcycle, and the bike itself was illegal three times over, since I had no insurance, it hadn't been inspected for years, and the license plate on it was registered to someone else from years past. I was on the side of the highway with only my charcoal-red taillights and instrument panel lights burning – I had been unable to start the bike earlier that day, and I was afraid to shut it off while I fiddled with fuses – and the Vermont trooper just happened to be passing by during the five minutes I was on the side of the road so nearly engulfed in darkness. "Oh hell, here we go!" I thought as he pulled over behind me and his blue strobe lights came on.

Once the officer established that I was not hostile, he took his hand off his pistol grip and asked me for my driver's license.

I was exhausted from five straight days of riding with all the muscles of my body clenched, either against the cold or against the realization of how much danger I was subjecting myself to by using the highway, at seventy miles per hour, as my motorcycle-riding classroom. In Delaware I'd laughed at the irony of a yellow caution sign warning of gaps in the road ahead as it crossed over a giant suspension bridge: the black silhouette on the sign was that of a motorcyclist flying off his cycle, upside down. In Vermont I laughed aloud as a similar series of caution signs warned of potential MOOSE CROSSINGS! – we don't have moose in North Carolina – and I was forced to imagine what would happen if a six-hundred-pound motorcycle and driver collided at seventy miles per hour with a half-ton moose.

Including the two days it had taken me to ride back and forth to Davidson, I'd been on a motorcycle for the first five days in my life, and I wasn't yet ready to relax enough to let my mind wander to happier subjects on long hauls of barren highway. Instead, I focused nearly constantly on the motorcycle and the sound of its engine, on its balance and my control over it, on the traffic around me and on the road ahead of me. Although I would become a lot more practiced over the five weeks of travel to come, it was a miracle that I made it all the way to Montreal in one piece.

The entire experience had been somewhat dreamlike, and it was through a haze of fatigue-induced delirium that I tried to lie my way out of my predicament with the Vermont Highway Patrol. The officer left me standing on the side of the highway next to my bike, blinded by his headlights, for what seemed like an eternity while he returned to his car with my license to look me up on his computer. When he finally returned, he confessed confusion:

"I don't understand," he said. "I don't see anything on this North Carolina license of yours about you having any kind of certification to be riding a motorcycle."

"Yeah, I know," I said, "I should have told you. I don't. I had to get to Canada to see a family member of mine who's sick. I didn't have any other way to get there, so I borrowed this bike."

"And what about the registration?" he asked. "I ran that plate and nothing came back on it at all."

"I know," I said, "that's the plate that was on it when I borrowed it."

"You mean it's not your plate?" he asked. "Do you even have insurance?"

"Insurance?" I asked, playing dumb.

I volunteered the location of my pocket knife when the officer frisked me a minute later, spread-eagled with my hands on the hood of his car, and I complied politely and nonthreateningly when he invited me to come back and join him "for a chat" in his squad car.

"I feel for you in your predicament," the trooper finally told me, after doing some more research to make sure my motorcycle hadn't been reported stolen. I rolled my eyes inwardly at how silly it seemed that he "felt bad" about a predicament I'd made up.

"I really ought to take you to jail," he went on, "but let me tell you what I'm going to do: I'm going to write you tickets for having no insurance and no license. I've got to write you some kind of ticket; I'd look like an idiot if I didn't. I'll let the inspection and the registration slide, but I'm going to have to call you a wrecker and have them come up here and pick up you and your bike and take you back to the nearest city. From there you'll have to find another way to get where you're going. You can't ride this motorcycle anymore in Vermont."

"Thank you officer, I do appreciate it," I told him, "but . . . and you're going to think I'm a criminal . . ."

The trooper looked at me sideways out from under his brow as I went on, "What's really to stop me from getting right back on the motorcycle again once the tow truck driver drops me off, and getting right back on the highway to Canada?" I knew perfectly well that there was nothing I could do, grounded in a random small town alongside the highway in Vermont. I had very little money and no access to more. Stifling a pang of fear in the pit of my stomach, I knew that the decision was already made: I'd have no choice but to press on as soon as the officer turned his back.

It was thus physically that I felt my determination to make it to Canada barreling over my ingrained sense of what was right and wrong in the eyes of the law. I was acutely aware of not only breaking the law, but also resolving to do so after expressly being warned not to by a police officer.

"You're making this really difficult for me, son," the officer said sternly, "but the answer to your question is that nothing's going to stop you . . . except me. If I see you on this bike again – and now I *am* goin' to be lookin' for you – I'm going to arrest you. You can be sure of that."

"Yes, sir," I said. "I understand. You don't have to worry."

The tow truck driver wound up not charging me for the tow, because he failed to strap down my motorcycle adequately, and when he did his U-turn on the grassy median, it fell over and broke one of the turn-signal lenses. The state trooper, who'd been long gone by then, pulled us over ten minutes later. "Uh-oh, what now?" I muttered to myself when the blue lights came back on behind us, but I was pleasantly relieved when he walked up to the tow truck's window beside me, handed me my pocket knife, and apologized for forgetting to give it back. I'd forgotten, too. Two hours later, at eleven o'clock at night, I found myself in a 24-hour diner on the outskirts of Montpelier, sitting across from an out-of-work American Indian truck driver – named Dave! – leaning over a Vermont highway map interrogating him on the best way to get north across the Canadian border without crossing paths with the Highway Patrol.

Dave advised me to just risk it and go right back on the same highway that night, since I was only ninety minutes from the border anyway, but as it turned out, I couldn't start my motorcycle, and I wound up sleeping on his sofa. He and his 16-year-old daughter – and her 16-year-old girlfriend – smoked about an ounce of pot and passed out at about three in the morning in various other corners of their grimy mobile home. I drank a beer or two and shared in the cost of the pizza to try to be sociable, but as grateful as I was for the free sofa, it was hard for me to relax. I'd developed a loathing for marijuana when I smoked too much of it as a teenager, and, with a beer buzz and a contact high, I fell asleep fearing that I would arrive in Canada with my *dogi* smelling like pot.

Happily, I was able to roll-start my motorcycle the next morning once Dave gave me a ride back to the diner, and ninety nail-biting minutes later I was out of the frying pan and into the fire, being interrogated at a Canadian border checkpoint by a four-and-a-half-foot-tall, Napoleon-like French-Canadian hunchback of a border patrol guard who took one look at me and assumed I was up to no good. In the thickest French accent imaginable, he asked me how much money I had and what my business was visiting Canada. I told him that I was going to visit my friend for karate training, but declined to mention the book sales because I didn't know if that would make me liable for any kind of import tax. I only had about sixty dollars in cash left at that point, and no credit card, and I sat there for nearly ninety minutes while this demonic Quasimodo did everything he could to poke holes in my story. He couldn't understand how I planned to survive in Canada even for a day with only sixty dollars, unless I planned to work illegally while I was there.

In the end he let me go – the criminal background check and the near body cavity search that he'd done of my person and motorcycle didn't reveal anything damning, and I thanked my lucky stars that Canadian immigration apparently had no interest in matters of motor vehicle legality. The hunchback did take down all my information, and he did fill out a report. He entered all my information into the computer and warned that a warrant would be automatically issued for my arrest in two weeks if the system didn't show that I had crossed the border back into the U.S. by that time. "You have fourteen days, monsieur!" he told me with a sinister smile.

"Welcome to Canada!"

* * *

I let go of my handlebars while traveling at speed, straightened my back, and relaxed with my arms outstretched for the first time as I crossed one of Montreal's massive suspension bridges over the St. Lawrence River. I took what felt to me like a deep breath of freedom. An hour after that I was unloading my saddlebags into the garage of Joe Addesso's family home in Montreal's Little Italy.

Joe was a young Italian-Canadian fighter whom I knew as one of the more spirited lightweights to frequent the North American tournaments I'd been to in Rochester, Montreal and Atlantic City. He and I knew each other by name and reputation, and he'd bought a copy of my book, but my staying with him for a week must have been arranged by Jacques and Annie, since they knew him a lot better than I did. A year or so later they would drive to Montreal to attend his wedding to the young lady who was his girlfriend in that October of 1994.

The two weeks that I spent in Montreal commuting from dojo to dojo by motorcycle passed like a lifetime. I spent the first week with Joe's family, surrounded by Italian speakers, and the second one brushing up on my French with a French-Canadian assistant instructor of André Gilbert's named Michel and the two young French-Canadian women who were his flatmates. In all, I visited nine Kyokushin dojos, trained in seven, and taught classes as a guest instructor in four. As I'd suspected, my books and I quickly became hot items. Hands down, the highlight of the trip was a class I taught at the Lamarre Dojo: one of its full-time instructors – a well-known former women's champion of Canada named Sylvie – put out the word and brought in a staggering 120 adult black belt members to attend my class with just one day's notice.

I'm not ashamed to admit that I stifled a significant pang of fear as I took my position at the front of that mob, with the knowledge that they were mine for the next two hours and that I would be representing Mas Oyama. I had never stood at the front of a class of 120 adult black belts before. I was amazed that there were so many who were members of the same dojo in a city where the Lamarre Dojo was only one of more than a dozen. My nine-member class at Davidson had represented the total interest in karate out of Davidson's 1500-member student body. The sixty-member CMAC had similarly represented the 30,000 students at UNC, and its three or four black belts represented the five to ten percent of any established dojo that's normally achieved that level of seniority. I could only imagine what kind of total student body at that single dojo 120 adult black belts might represent, and what that said about the local population's interest in Kyokushin. I could easily imagine five or six hundred active students at that one dojo alone. In the American South, you'd be lucky to find more than one percent of the population interested in practicing martial arts daring to join a Kyokushin dojo, where the level of contact makes the average American Tae Kwon Do school look like day care.

Sylvie introduced me to the class as the author/editor of the book, which she held up and explained would be available for purchase after training. She described me as a former *uchi deshi* of Mas Oyama who had trained at *Honbu* for two years, and explained with a smile that I had ridden the tiny little motorcycle that they might have seen on the sidewalk out front all the way from North Carolina to visit dojos in Montreal. In spite of my fear, I found myself enjoying the fact that I understood her French, thanks to my high school foreign-language experience.

Somehow, it was with something like Midas's power over that group of professors at my Watson interview that I came to own that mob of 120 from the moment I began teaching, and without any help from the netherworld. I started by acknowledging that I was younger than many of them and had been training in Kyokushin karate for fewer years – I was still wearing the *shodan* belt that Michael Monaco had arranged at *Sosai's* behest – and that "while there are many things that I'm sure some of you could teach me, I do have one or two things I can share with you simply because I lucked into an experience in Japan that none of you have had." The fact that I didn't presume myself to be somebody great was extremely well received.

I was on fire that night, and I gave that mob of 120 a two-hour workout that I doubt they'll ever forget. It was a very simple one in terms of content. I took them through the standard thirty-six repetitions of the thirty-two techniques of Mas Oyama's *kihon* as taught at *Honbu*, followed by about a million repetitions of *iddo kekko* techniques, just as we'd done day after day in Japan. I didn't presume to do much teaching of how to do the techniques better. I didn't stop to talk much. They were all black belts at the higher end of the international competency spectrum, after all. If I did in fact manage to leave an impression, it was with the tempo, volume, and ferocity of the training.

In the eighteen years since I was an *uchi deshi* at *Honbu*, I've trained in dojos all around the world, and I've never once experienced the level of intensity, in terms of hard training day in and day out, that we did at *Honbu*. *Sosai* was there – if not in the dojo, we knew he could hear us through the floor from his office upstairs – and more than anything else, *Sosai* stressed hard, hard training. He believed that correct technique would reveal itself with a minimum of explanatory guidance simply by repeating the movements with their intent in mind, hundreds and hundreds of times each, with a ferocity that suggested our lives depended on it.

I have a hunch that the students at the Lamarre Dojo that day, at the very least, learned that their practice of karate basics could be taken up a notch. As technically proficient as that Canadian group was, I'm certain that none of them had ever done so many repetitions of so many techniques with the fervor I managed to draw out of them that day. I never had an opportunity to teach classes while at *Honbu* – I was gone by the time my roommates began teaching in their third year – but if there was one thing I'd learned just by following the classes at *Honbu* every day, it was how to put more energy into my movements and more volume into my voice than I ever would have thought possible. It was like that time when, in front of *Sosai* and his teenage daughter, I made my *kiai* the loudest in the room, and my jumps the highest, in a successful bid for their attention. I had two gears, low and high, and the higher gear was seared into our personalities as *uchi deshi* early on, when our *sempai* made it clear under threat of violence what level of performance was expected of us. During those classes when we couldn't escape training that hard – and we often did try to escape those particular classes! – we executed every technique as if our intention was to rupture our vocal cords, tear our muscles, and wring the sweat out of our limbs like water from canvas. I'd learned to convey that same intensity through my voice and my body movements to my students at Davidson and in the CMAC, and it was that intensity that I managed to inspire at the Lamarre Dojo. Sweat trickled off the dojo floor in streams. The windows and the wall of mirrors were so fogged over with condensation that water rolled down them as if it was raining. I didn't need the embarrassingly long standing ovation they gave me at the end of the training to know that I'd left an impression.

I sold fifteen hundred dollars worth of books that night almost as an afterthought. Their buyers wouldn't let me go until I'd signed every single copy – I suppose they all expected me to make something of myself someday – and that kind of experience, I'm ashamed to say, does threaten to forever change a person. I was a celebrity for a day – I was for a good part of those two weeks in Canada – and I forced myself to imagine *kumite* with the stronger members of the mob to keep my ego in check.

If those 120 had been the first-round fighters in an open tournament, if I was lucky in the draw I might have made it to the second round.

Joe took me out on the town that last night I spent with him in Little Italy, and with nostalgic visions of Judd's and my foreign-capital rampages, I was intrigued that it was to an adult entertainment club that he proposed to take me. For three months in Chapel Hill, I'd been picking up trash on the grounds of low-rent apartment complexes, and spending my nights alone at home with my sister-in-law's Norton Anthology of English Literature. I'd been hiding under Jacques' proverbial rock without even the beautiful woman he'd advised me to shack up with, and – immature though it certainly was! – the excitement of that momentary stardom I found at the Lamarre Dojo got to me, my chemical genie made his first significant progress in months towards edging the cork out of his bottle, and I stepped out into the city, hungry to claim what I felt was surely mine by right.

I'd never been to such a club before – the whole concept had always seemed so ridiculous! – and it turned out that I couldn't have ever been to a club like that in America because the show in that particular foreign capital was a little bit more risqué than it would have been in the States. What was the point, I'd always wondered, of getting all bent out of shape watching something that you only want to touch, but are never allowed to?

In the end, however, I found myself pleasantly surprised with what I found.

Nicole was seventeen – French! – and physically flawless. She was a first-year university student there in Montreal, living with her parents, and working nights with their tacit approval to pay tuition that they otherwise wouldn't have been able to afford. After losing an inner battle *not* to watch her perform on stage – I had no qualms watching the others, who seemed like they might have been my age or a bit older – I asked our waitress to bring her to a private table and, for the cost of a lap dance, I at once fed my curiosity and appeased my conscience by inviting her to close and tie shut that tiny little silk robe–like thing she was wearing and sit down with me for a song-length conversation.

I was completely fascinated, I confessed, because I'd never been to such a club before and because Nicole wasn't at all the type of person I expected to find taking her clothes off in one. When I learned that she was a student and that her night job was paying her tuition, that admission allowed me to make better sense of the mismatched pair that was that club and what I saw in the eyes of that particular stripper. I was a foreigner, both in North America's most European city and in a nightclub such as that one, and in a bid to better understand, I dared to watch the light in Nicole's eyes to ensure that she hadn't felt disrespected when I asked her if she ever went home with any of the club's patrons. Trusting that I'd be able to see in her reaction if her night job pushed her towards prostitution, I was quite sure from what I saw that she lived a pretty normal life for a 17-year-old girl, aside from taking off her clothes on stage for a living.

It cost me three more songs after that one, and an abbreviated version of my life story told like it hadn't been since I sat on the Chambers lawn with Lissa, to amass the courage to ask Nicole for her phone number, and I was convinced by her reaction, as she clearly overcame some inner qualms to give it to me, that doing so for a club patron was way out of the ordinary for her. The bat-size butterflies in my stomach when Joe and I finally took our leave left me sure that I'd be seeing more of Nicole before my stay in Montreal was through.

* * *

André Gilbert's Centreville Dojo was the oldest one in Montreal, and the one on the most expensive piece of real estate. The more time I spent in Montreal investigating the Kyokushin scene, the more it became clear that André Gilbert had his hand in the development of most of it. The Lamarre Dojo was just one of his branch dojos; he had six or eight others in Montreal. Intermingling with the instructors of nine dojos that week, several of whom were affiliated with Gilbert and several who weren't, it was clear that although he was not loved by all, he was indisputably the father of the largest IKO family on the North American East Coast. I'd never been to Western Canada, but if Gilbert's organization was bigger than Stuart Corrigal's – and I had a hunch that it was – it was the largest IKO branch in North America.

Tom Flynn had his dojo in Massachusetts, Michael Lorden had his in Orlando, Leslaw Samitowski had his in Chicago, Randy James had his in Brooklyn, but though several of those U.S. branch chiefs had been around for nearly as long as Gilbert, none of them had established organizations beyond the confines of their own individual dojos as Gilbert had. None of them had managed to create students who went on to become instructors in their own right, as Gilbert so clearly had many times over. It was interesting that *Sosai* always bemoaned the United States as *the unconquerable country* when it came to propagating budo karate. The frustration in his eyes would boil over when he cited the repeated tragedies that were his attempts to popularize Kyokushin in the U.S. It was extremely telling for me, therefore, to behold the monster of branch development that André Gilbert had become. Just half a day's drive from New York City, he had developed the kind of organization that led to the booming popularity of Kyokushin all over the globe.

Is it that he's French? I wondered. *Is there truly some element of the American personality that gets in the way of our achieving what so many non-Americans have done so successfully all over the world?* Whatever the cause, I was impressed by André Gilbert's operation, and it was clear that if there was to be a successful Eastern Canadian issue of *Budo Karate Illustrated*, it would have to be with his support.

I was a little disappointed that I was not invited to teach a class in *Shihan* Gilbert's dojo. The applause from the Lamarre Dojo was still ringing in my ears, and although I surely had less to offer as an instructor in my wildest dreams than André Gilbert did on his worst day, I did believe I had something of value to offer, and I desperately wanted to share it. Instead, I wound up feeling marginalized – I was just one of the mob – and that led me to worry during the training that he was not going to offer me the support that I hoped for.

There were thirty students in class that night, and when it was over, I wasn't surprised that I sold only three books to students who forgot to ask me to sign them.

Shihan Gilbert and I had shared that beer four months earlier in Ikebukuro the week of Mas Oyama's memorial service, I had given him a book and signed it for him then, and he seemed genuinely pleased. It was he who had invited me to join him for a beer. I told him then that I hoped to expand my yearbook project into Canada, and with a twinkle in his eye and a thickly-accented "Superb!" he'd confirmed the fact that still then at that point – five days before Matsui told Henri Orlean at *Honbu*, "You should make an effort to support Nathan Ligo's book" – *Budo Karate Illustrated's* incredible momentum was still unbroken.

That night in Montreal, *Shihan* Gilbert knew that I wanted to meet with him to discuss business, and I hoped that opportunity would come when he invited me, with that same twinkle in his eye, to share another beer with him after training. He sent Michel out for a couple of liter-sized bottles, and, dehydrated and drenched in sweat as I was, the liter of beer I had to myself while *Shihan* Gilbert polished off one of his own was one of the best I'd ever had.

"How long are you going to be in Montreal?" *Shihan* Gilbert asked.

"Osu, just three more days," I told him. "I have to leave Canada by November first." I was never too far from the image of that sinister hunchbacked border control guard eagerly crossing the days off his calendar and waiting for his computer screen to tell him that I hadn't crossed back south over the border.

"And you'll still be staying on with Michel?"

"Osu," I said, "thank you for arranging it."

"Excellent!" he said, "Then you should come down to the dojo one morning before you leave and we'll discuss your book over coffee."

"Osu," was all I could say, thanking *Shihan* Gilbert for the training, for the beer, and for agreeing to meet with me before I left. I was worried that he didn't seem too impatient to meet with me. I feared that it might mean he wasn't going to be receptive after all.

I was amazed at how drunk I was, though I shouldn't have been surprised. It was with beer that I'd so uncharacteristically replenished all of my body's water reserves lost during training, and I've never been much of a drinker. I was thankful that my conversation with *Shihan* Gilbert was over and I'd have a little more control over my world when we sat down to talk business the next time. Likewise, I was relieved that Michel's flat was so close by, since I rode home by motorcycle and I was drunk.

Michel's apartment was up on the mountain above Centreville. A good portion of the streets between the dojo and his place were cobblestone and straight up a massive slope, and I laughed to myself at how surreal it was to climb into the hills with the blackness of the river visible behind me like a night sky in my rearview mirrors.

THIRTY-SIX

THE ENDLESS STRETCHES of North American highway that I covered by motorcycle during those five weeks on the road were enticingly reminiscent of the wide open spaces of my past, in which I allowed myself to embrace more of the natural world than was likely good for my health. Of course, then I had no idea that I was doing so in an attempt to fill internal wide open spaces that couldn't possibly be filled by such a mismatched surrogate. I certainly had no idea how dangerous the game I'd played with passion during the previous year had been.

For a year's worth of months the image of Helen Ecks had never been further than a single thought away from whatever subject my conscious mind embraced, and those long hours alone under North America's wide-open skies were no exception. The way that I beheld her, however, had changed.

I was utterly ashamed.

In the beginning I'd tried to stamp out the love that I felt for Helen in order to befriend her. Now I fought to stamp her out of my head altogether so that I might go on with my life without dwelling in realms that struck me, too, as so inappropriate. I'd made the choices I'd made with open eyes – I wasn't sure I'd have made them any differently if I could go back and do it all over again – but at least now I knew unequivocally that it was time to leave the nonsense behind and move forward on a more stable foundation.

I was glad to be done with Davidson.

Home had not been in the log house with Martha after all, and for the first time I was sure enough that my father was no longer the man who raised me that I felt no obligation whatsoever to even try to salvage what remained. I was one course credit away from a diploma, but I told myself, with a hint of a sharp-toothed smile with which Midas might have torn a bleeding chunk of marrow from one of life's bones, that the diploma was just paper and that, like a bandit, I'd made off with the education, which was all that would matter in my future anyway.

I'd once complained to Helen in the Café during the lunch hour, "Why is it that we devote all this time to literary criticism and so little energy to creating literature? How can we go though four years in college, studying English lit, and hardly ever be encouraged to write it? Shouldn't students be taught that they might actually create works of literature themselves, rather than spending all this energy searching for more and more clever ways to read other people's work?"

Helen laughed with me at my frustration, but didn't attempt an answer. For a millisecond I feared that I might have been misunderstood, but I reached an eyelash depth deeper with my gaze and saw that, no, she'd understood my question to be a rhetorical one. She knew that I meant no disrespect. Only a fragment of what any generation writes becomes lasting literature, and writing has to come from within to be worth a damn. It doesn't really make much sense to try to plant it, although reading, and learning to read better, may help to inspire some students to write someday. Thanks to my father, I was well aware of the inherent conflict between the artist and the art historian, but that was the first time I'd applied my understanding to the subject I'd been studying for the past two years. The art historian sits at a desk and employs carefully constructed rules to interpret the eccentricities of the artist and his work. The artist lives to create works of art, and often finds himself compelled to break a rule or two in the process.

Emily Dickinson supposedly didn't leave her second-floor bedroom for a large portion of her life, and we can assume that she wasn't entirely unaffected. Edgar Allan Poe was an opium addict and sometimes lunatic, Walt Whitman was a grey-bearded fag who reportedly liked to run naked through the wilderness, and on the other side of the Atlantic, a similar collection of yahoos whooped and hollered around Percy Shelley's funeral pyre before one of them tore Shelley's heart from his smoldering carcass, and his widow Mary, the author of *Frankenstein,* kept its charred remains with her for the rest of her life.

Academics dissect all of these freaks posthumously through the works they've left behind, and they need their diplomas to do so. The better the diploma, the better their access to academic exchanges in which their own theories are likely to develop and gain acceptance. As grateful as I was for the field — without it I never would have read the handful of literary masterpieces that I have — I was sure that I would have no need for a diploma myself. My future was in living life in accord with my conscience and writing it all down in an attempt to make a difference in a world that I could see desperately needed a difference made. My future was in Kyokushin, and for Kyokushin I didn't need any kind of document to validate the education that I knew I would daily exhaust every effort to broaden and employ. It was never, after all, Mas Oyama's graduation certificate that mattered; it was the spirit-fortifying stamp of *Sosai's* approval that came with it.

I was relieved because I could really, once and for all, be done with Davidson. I wouldn't have to set foot back in that town in which I was so god-awfully aware of the presence of a woman that I could feel the magnetic pull of her all the way from the Canadian border.

Ever since I'd driven Midas into the ground, Helen had ceased to be a woman I was in love with. Helen, the woman, was still someone I dared to care for. She was still someone I admired. She was certainly someone who has caused me to long for a second chance at friendship as I never had before. But from the moment I learned of Helen's *complications*, I knew I would have no choice but to stamp out the nonsense that was the passion I felt for her, and the distance from Davidson did seem to be having the desired effect.

"Helen" was then, and was until I wrote it down for the first time in this book more than a decade later, a name that I never dared to utter. The only time in a decade I ever spoke the name "Helen" in reference to Dr. Ecks was that day I'd done so accidentally in my Shakespeare professor's car.

"Helen, Dr. Ecks . . ." I did indeed write that time I wrote to her, but I'd never before spoken the name that had so shaken my world.

The only time the story has ever been told was six years after the fact, when I wrote to Helen and confessed the whole thing, in an apparent bid to humiliate myself and so drive her presence from dreams that had once again begun to tear me painfully from the deepest sleep. Already by the time I was in Canada looking south, *Helen* the name was well on its way to leaving Helen the person behind, and becoming the best word in my vocabulary to describe a diminishing force of my past that I can still only recall with a terrible awe. *Helen* became, for me, the best word to describe an uncomfortable set of physical and emotional symptoms that would plague me for years, not the least of which was the shame I felt for having allowed myself to fall victim to such abominable weakness.

I was Mas Oyama's *uchi deshi*, for heaven's sake!

After Akiko, I spent those three months in Chapel Hill training, and in hard physical training there is no room for such nonsense. My soul was mostly still then. My mind was numb at the shock of having my work frozen by Matsui, and I was able to fill the rest with my duty to do for Master Choi's CMAC. Next to my bed in my brother's spare bedroom, I kept the Norton Anthology of British Literature that I'd borrowed from my sister-in-law's shelf, and I read myself to sleep each night, my mind apparently free of the altered state of consciousness in which I'd once kept two or three separate lines of thought advancing all at once. By keeping my newly single mind thus focused, I was able to leave Helen in the past at times when I might otherwise have fallen victim. Heading north without a windshield into the waning October, I was similarly free; the mere act of making it in one piece around the next bend, or alive as far as the next horizon, required every shred of my concentration.

But oh, how convenient it would be! – if Conscience would simply allow me to omit the embarrassing events of my second week in Montreal among André Gilbert's French. How horrible to once again have to confess the extent of my lingering immaturity in order to remain true!

I left Nicole in her club and did not see her again, but I can't help but wonder if what she did to me by getting me all riled up hormonally didn't have something to do with what happened when, one day later, I moved into Michel's flat with his roommates Isabelle and Caroline.[90] As during my first week with Joe, I had lots of free time when I wasn't visiting dojos, and while Michel was at work it was rare that either Isabelle or Caroline wasn't home and feeling social. My experience in Japan had made me disrespect tourists – the only way to truly experience a foreign land, I knew, was to interact on a personal level with the population – and it was because I became romantically entangled with BOTH of Michel's

---

[90] *Michel, Isabelle* and *Caroline* (*Nicole, Sylvie* and *André*) with French pronunciations, please!

roommates that I lost the battle to the butterflies and decided not to call Nicole.

Isabelle was my age or a bit younger, and she had apparently been Michel's girlfriend when she first moved in. She was my *koohai*, since she was a green-belt student at André Gilbert's dojo. She was more than a little bit eligible, certainly for a week's diversion; she seemed to think the same of me or more, and by the end of the week I was fending her off when she crawled half-naked into my bed because I didn't feel right having sex with the ex-girlfriend of the guy who was letting me stay in his apartment, even though he'd told me that their relationship was long since over. The other roommate, Isabelle's SISTER Caroline, was four or five years older than me; she had apparently moved in later when Michel and Isabelle had put the extra room up for rent. She was more than a little bit eligible herself, and I am ashamed to say that I would be crawling into *her* bed by the end of the week, only to have her fend *me* off because she didn't feel right having sex with the guy her sister had flipped for.

By the end of the week, Isabelle almost wouldn't let me go, and, virtually crushed by Caroline's rejection, I came close to making a terrible mistake. Isabelle wanted to go south with me on the back of that tiny motorcycle that would barely carry me alone, and although I was one hundred percent certain that she wouldn't be able to follow me beyond the short term, I bowed to her suggestion that she at least ride with me for a day or so, so that we could spend a final couple of days together. I reasoned that I could then put her on a bus back to Montreal once we found out, as I knew we would, that there was no point.

How weak I was to bend to her tearful insistence!

In the end, Isabelle rode with me for less than one of the two hours to the American border before I snapped out of it, realized the folly of what we were doing, and pulled over to explain that I couldn't possibly take her with me, if for no other reason than that my motorcycle wouldn't survive it. As it turned out, that hour on the highway with the wind in her hair and the St. Lawrence at her back was the time she needed to snap out of it too. By the time I pulled over to tell her it was hopeless, she didn't put up much of a fight, and we parted fairly painlessly.

Caroline, on the other hand, left my heart stretched out on the highway like that possum I'd run over with a *SWOOSH!* at 3 a.m. on the way to Rochester to meet *Sosai* two years earlier.

To this day I am amazed at how gentle, how generous, and how confidently strong Caroline was in the face of my advances!

On her bed, surrounded by the playing cards that we'd forgotten, she let me kiss her, she kissed me in return, and with her palms ever so gently placed on my chest between us, she let me know that she wasn't going to be seduced. I tried again, and she kissed me again — she kissed me out of unadulterated friendship and compassion — but again she held me ever so gently at bay. Again I tried, and again, like the control rods in a nuclear fire, her steady resolve let me know that she wasn't going to have me until, try after try, she finally rendered me powerless to try again.

It's hard to pinpoint exactly when my reaction to her left me feeling so carved out from within, in a way that would only become more and more familiar as the years of my life took me further and further from Helen. Caroline was most certainly a *seer*. I didn't know it yet for several days living with her and her sister and Michel, and I'm not sure just when she let it be known. Perhaps it wasn't so much that she was a seer as that at one point in our interaction, partway though the week, she, for whatever reason, decided *to look*.

It must have been the night before Isabelle climbed into my bed the next morning.

The four of us were on Caroline's bed playing cards — three of us had been to training at Gilbert's dojo — and it dawned on me: making love to Isabelle couldn't possibly hold a candle to the intellectual, and even unrequited, pursuit of Caroline. It must have started hormonally with Nicole, and playing romantic games with Isabelle for the days that followed hadn't helped. But by the time I spent that entire night awake longing for Caroline, cursing the fact that Michel was just on the other side of the wall and Isabelle was at the other end of the hall, the sensation of chemical overload had migrated away from the sexual and lodged itself in a part of me of far greater consequence.

Half awake in the night on Michel's sofa, more than once I sprang upwards into a sitting position and reached for my chest, half expecting to find a warm, sticky void. *My God! How is it possible to want someone so badly?* I thought. It felt as though the contents of my rib cage had been scraped out. I kept seeing what was left of me crawling down the hall in Caroline's direction, clutching my belly as one might crawl towards a desert horizon in hopes that there might be water just over the next rise. Something made me know that Caroline would exhaust herself in the attempt to make me whole again – I'd seen it in her eyes! – and to resist the pull that I felt in her direction felt to me like dying a slow death.

Of course, I had endured similar sensations in the past, and I did not succumb to the impulse to flee, barefooted and naked, onto Mount Royal's moonlit cobblestones. It was not the stomach-burning delirium I had endured as a teenager, but that experience was there in my history to assure me that whatever this new nightmare was, it too would certainly pass. Besides, I'd felt something like it before: turned away in the night from Lissa, I'd clutched at the front of my T-shirt and longed for the amputation of everything from my neck down. But that sensation was only a fraction of what Caroline conjured in me now, for the first time unprotected since Midas's bliss had so mercifully veiled what would have been so much worse, day after day, in the absence of Helen.

The next morning, a nearly naked and all the more beautiful Isabelle climbed on top of me beneath the sheets with Michel just on the other side of the wall. How else could I possibly have resisted her except by having spent the entire night longing to he held by her sister?

I was relieved when the others stirred and Isabelle started to pull herself away, but that relief couldn't compare to the relief I felt an hour later when she followed Michel out to begin her job for the day, leaving me alone in the apartment with Caroline. On her bed surrounded by the playing cards that we'd cast aside, she kissed me, and with her palms only ever so gently placed on my chest between us, she let me know that, beyond that point, she wasn't going to be seduced.

A moment later I had her eyes.

Sitting there in each other's arms with our knees bent, Caroline leaned on my thighs and I leaned on hers. Our arms wrapped around each other kept us comfortably locked in that twin fetal position that Lissa and I had discovered, and from there I locked her eyes to mine and used every bit of what I'd once used to conquer my own flesh-and-blood cousin to reach into Caroline and make her mine. It was as if my rib cage had split open at the sternum, wrapped around hers, and mended again behind her. How humbled I am today to realize that through her eyes she'd opened herself up as if to mend her own ribs back together the same way behind me! – her ribs with my own like the fingers of two hands interlocked. I am amazed that she let me linger there, that she never once made me feel small for what could only have surprised and baffled her, and yet, without disrespecting me, she held me at bay.

She must have felt when my resolve fell away, because in a movement that felt to me like the gentlest possible of all caresses, she let her hands slide past the front corners of my rib cage where they'd been for one more round, and wrapped them instead around me. She joined me – joined me as an equal! – as I pulled her heart as close to mine as our bodies would allow. How kind, patient and perceptive she was to handle me as she did! With my nose at her neckline, in a long steady inhale, I drew in the first lungful of flesh I'd drawn off the skin of a woman since I had inhaled molecules of Helen from the other side of our conference-room table. With a jolt, I felt it in my midsection as the particles of Caroline's flesh bombarded my system. I was aware of having further exposed myself when a tear tickled its way down the crevice formed between the bridge of my nose and the warmth of Caroline's neck.

When she gasped, I realized I was holding her so tightly that my fingertips had reached my own shoulder blades on either side of her, and still she didn't push me away. To hold her like that, to hold her so tightly as to move her just next to actually being inside me, was almost all that I could bear, because still, I realize now, I couldn't fill the void.

I had all of her then, more than I possibly could have had through the simple act of sex, and still I wanted more. I needed more. I was dying for more. I kissed her again with a passion that I hadn't yet, and for a moment Caroline reciprocated. For a moment I thought that finally she'd have me, but I'm amazed to recall that Caroline's steady resolve kicked back in and ever so gently, she invited me to let it pass. If her hands on my chest had been words, they'd have said, "Take a deep breath, Nathan. It's clear that I can't fill whatever it is that you're trying to fill. I'm not the answer. Let me help you to take that deep breath. Give it a couple of minutes and it'll pass."

* * *

The ulterior motive for my trip to Montreal was accomplished during fifteen minutes over coffee with *Shihan* André Gilbert on my last morning in Canada. I marvel today at how several of my recent choices had reached out as if without me to tap into those particular chemicals I'd so completely left behind since Helen. In a coffee shop beneath the

Centreville Dojo, I maintained unbroken, warm, humble and optimistic eye contact with *Shihan* Gilbert, holding a business conversation that had the power to make or break my future, and it was easy, since it was the storm that raged within me, just under the surface of the dialogue, that actually dominated so much of my attention.

Shihan Gilbert agreed wholeheartedly and without hesitation to do everything in his power to support a second volume of *Budo Karate Illustrated*, provided I could resolve my situation with Matsui. He would encourage all the dojo operators in his branch to submit photographs and articles, and he would help to ensure that they all marketed the books through advance sales to their students in plenty of time to help me with the printing cost. "Of course!" he told me, he had no objection to my including material from other competing Canadian branch chiefs, even though he clearly regarded one or two of them as something less than friends.

I can't remember what percentage of the proceeds I promised him as an afterthought. It was probably a dollar or two per book, and I could tell by the way he embraced the idea after he'd already agreed to support the project that I'd made the sale of the century.

"Superb!" he exclaimed. "Perfect! We will work together and sell many books!"

Almost immediately upon fulfilling that portion of my mission to Montreal, I turned my eyes towards Florida. Three months earlier, when I'd visited his dojo in Orlando, Michael Lorden had offered to invest up to $20,000 towards the continuation of my project in exchange for an editorial partnership. Now, for the first time, I was interested in his offer, and I wondered if it still stood.

How perfect a demonstration of *Budo Karate Illustrated's* potential for success, I realized, if I could go back to Matsui not only with Jacques' endorsement, but also with André Gilbert all but guaranteeing the advance book sales required to fund a second issue, and even better still, Michael Lorden, an older, wiser partner who was not only going to help guide the project, but who was willing to invest such a large chunk of his own pension!

I would have made it to Canada in just three days, I told myself, *if it hadn't been for the cop who grounded me in Vermont.*

Surely I can make it to Orlando in five!

* * *

I let go of Caroline alone, in the park near the summit of Mount Royal, looking south over the St. Lawrence River towards home. My shoulders were hunched forward again, as if staggered by the weight of the rock on which I stood, the corners of my mouth pulled back into a grimace, and my teeth held just a millimeter short of clenched, already cutting the first traces of the permanent lines that would entrench themselves at the outside corners of my eyes over the decade to come. My fingers twitched in the beginning of a reflex that would have failed anyway to catch my heart, liver, lungs, and entrails as they spilled forth and slipped hopelessly through my grip had my belly been sliced open in a vertical slit, as for one more instant I felt like it had.

A moment passed, and I took a deep breath.

The image of my belly slit reminded me I was still a viable force: I still had my life to give, and I still had the same work to do. I raised my eyes towards the world stretched out before me.

I allowed my spine to straighten and my shoulders to roll back into place. My weight shifted from my heels forward onto the balls of my feet as they pivoted to parallel, facing south. I forced a long, deep breath. I could see all of the American continent stretched out before me, and I knew that as wonderful a woman, as wonderfully perceptive and generous as Caroline was, what I felt for her couldn't possibly have had so much to do with her.

Beyond an impression, I didn't even know who she was!

It couldn't possibly have been Helen either, and, in a flood, I knew that then, so well that it was as if it had been mine all along. *Well I knew, then,* that the whole thing was a consequence of so much more, so many years before Helen! *Well I knew, then,* that Helen had simply been the mechanism by which I'd pried all of that out of its hiding place behind the hardened shell that had grown to shield it![91]

---

[91] "Well I know, now . . ." from the end of Poe's "Ulalume" (The "she" referred to is the poet's walking companion, *Psyche,* his soul): *And I said - "What is written, sweet sister, / On the door of this legended tomb?"/ She replied – "Ulalume – Ulalume –/ 'Tis the vault of thy lost Ulalume!"/ Then my heart it grew ashen and sober/ As the leaves that were crispéd and sere, / As the leaves that were withering and sere, / And I cried – "It was surely October/ On this very night of last year/ That I journeyed – I journeyed down here, / That I brought a dread burden down here: / On this night of all nights in the year, / Ah, what demon has tempted me here? / Well I know, now, this dim lake of Auber, / This misty mid region of Weir: / Well I know, now, this dank tarn of Auber, / This ghoul-haunted woodland of Weir."*

I felt the burn of broken blisters on the palms of my hands and the almost intolerable numbness of fatigue as I so nearly failed to support the weight of twin axes that in that instant hung once again in their phantom forms at my sides. I felt the sweat roll off my brow and its salt burn my eye, I smelled the sap of freshly opened hardwood, and I remembered the vow I'd sworn in the forest of my childhood when, a thousand days earlier, I dared myself to set Nathan Ligo aside one more time and use all that I'd learned in an attempt to do for the future.

My God, it could kill you! I told myself then. *To go back means to face that which in your life has hurt you the most. To give in to Conscience, to catch the impulse that beckons you to really, actually set yourself aside and exhaust yourself for the future . . . have no doubt that it could kill you in the end!*

Is it vision that drives me, or is it fantasy? Throughout my life that question would plague me.

But, *It's up to me*, the answer always came back.

I can decide whether it's going to be vision or fantasy.

Is it far-fetched? Is it crazy? Is it more likely to fail than succeed?

Sure it is. Of course it is. But what chance is there of success if I don't try?

Who else is going to take the risk?

I stared down at America from the top of the continent, and my path had never seemed so clear.

I knew that giving in to Conscience had opened a channel to achieving so much more than I ever could have envisioned through conventional means. I recalled the pull that I'd felt to the log house the summer before, to move in with Lissa and find the mother that I'd lost in Martha, already a year after I'd vowed with my axes in that same forest to give myself over to Conscience's twisted experiment. I considered the extent to which I myself – perhaps even by choice! – had walked headlong into the conflicts that had led to the crushing collapse of those relationships and, in so doing, torn open Midas's shell.

My God! I swore when I realized that my decision to give in to Conscience had preceded Lissa entirely. It had preceded my opening myself up so far. It had preceded my refusing to be shut down by Lissa's on-again, off-again resistance, even after I began to know how much danger I was in.

Had the vision been working without me all along?

Was Lissa coincidence, or did Conscience simply need a Lissa in order to set the monster free?

Had Midas simply needed a Helen to bottle Jacques's priceless youthful energy?

I recalled the most powerful of the earth-shaking visions I'd faced in the wide-open spaces of Davidson the year before. I thought of my love for Master Choi, my first teacher, and for Mas Oyama, my second. I thought of my loss of the parents of my childhood, and I remembered how painfully disenfranchised socially I'd been as an adolescent because of it. I thought of the solution I'd found, not for fixing my family, because day by day it had become more and more clear that my family was beyond repair.

No, it'll be the world that I'll fix instead! I'd sworn. *So help me, I'll make the planet one on which an adolescence like mine, a need like I spent last night feeling for Caroline, might never again happen in the life of another!*

"Could it be," I asked aloud, "that I'm actually the sanest person I know?"

Well I knew, then, that the driving force that had moved me for the last two years of my life had come from the core of what I was. It had come from *Heart*, one not in the least tainted by society's droning call to run with the herd.[92] *Surely all of mankind's suffering,* I reflected, *must derive from the ease with which we, as rational beings on an overcrowded planet, allow alternate lesser sources of guidance to impede natural sight, and cloud the directives that flow from the innate heart of man!*

How truly treacherous the alleys are that impulses to do right must wander before we find the willpower to set them free in the form of deliberate action! [93]

---

[92] Chozan Shissai, in his 17th century *Discourse in the Art of Mountain Demons*, describes an understanding of three key components as central to achieving enlightenment through artistic pursuit – *Heart*, *Life Force* and *Form* – and, in so doing, joins hands with the 17th century Zen monk Takuan, who may or may not have actually influenced the teaching of Miyamoto Musashi. *Heart*, the Zen monk's "beginner's mind," represents the childlike innate ability in man to utilize and unite all of his senses at once with thoughtless or intuitive thought to create the ideal execution of action, movement or application in art. Mastering *Form*, the sword stroke in the case of Musashi, or the brush stroke in the case of Da Vinci, is only achieved through a clearing of the natural impediments that occur in the minds of rational beings that inhibit the flow of *Life Force*, the energy with which we strive to enact the vision of *our purest mind's eye*, a.k.a. Chozan Shissai's *Heart*. For both of these philosophers, enlightenment is the result of training ones *Life Force* until it flows so readily that *Heart* and *Form*, and thus *Heart* and *Art*, become one.

[93] The "alleys through which our impulses must wander," from Poe's "Ulalume": *Here once, through an alley Titanic, / Of cypress, I roamed with my Soul - / Of cypress, with Psyche, my Soul. / These were days when my heart was volcanic / As the scoriac rivers that roll, / As the lavas that restlessly roll / Their sulphurous currents down Yaanek/ In the ultimate climes of the pole, / That groan as they roll down Mount Yaanek/ In the realms of the boreal pole. / Our talk had been*

I marveled at the genius born, in my own recent experience, of the mere impulse to let myself go to the experiment.

As a human being, it's my birthright, after all!

It's all of our birthright!

There's nothing special about me! It was only my profound personal weakness — my injury! — that made it so imperative for me to access that which is right here for the taking, in front of us all. It's those who don't consider themselves disenfranchised who will face the real challenge. Society's Alphas, traveling in such beautiful cadence with the herd, have no idea there's so much work to be done — but is it not they who are destined to become the true heroes once the survival instinct pushes them, too, to dare to listen to their hearts? Once they, too, learn to stare down Convention's bitter resistance, and act on what they know, rather than on what they've been trained to see?

It doesn't matter, I told myself, *if Horai and Matsui stand in my way. Fuck them! They will render themselves irrelevant.*

No matter what the sacrifice, I told myself, *live the life that allows you to hear the voice of Conscience! Live the life that allows you to catch the impulses that come from the heart, the ones that ask you to sacrifice for the future, the ones that show you the way, and there will be opportunity after opportunity to make — in both big* and *small ways — the difference you've been already this year so impatient to make.*

You're only 23 years old, for heaven's sake! You've lived only a quarter of your life, and just look what you've managed to squeeze into it!

Sure it could kill you in the end, but what a beautiful day it is to embark on the next chapter!

What a life!

My God, it's so unbelievably beautiful!

---

serious and sober, / But our thoughts they were palsied and sere, / Our memories were treacherous and sere, / For we knew not . . .

THIRTY-SEVEN

THE STORM THAT STRUCK on that first afternoon after I crossed the Canadian border struck with the wrath of God. It was the first day of November, and the rain fell in icy torrents that shouldered most *four*-wheeled vehicles and reduced the rest to a blind crawl in the slow lane. By the time the afternoon waned in the southern part of New York, I'd burned the fingertips and part of the palms out of both of my leather gloves by placing them alternately on the engine block for thirty- or forty-second intervals. In this way, I managed to keep my hands from becoming so numb with cold that I could no longer squeeze my clutch or brake levers when I needed to. When I smelled burning leather, I knew that it was time to switch hands.

I couldn't always feel it when my fingertips started to burn.

Beneath my high school letter jacket, which I'd chosen because of its thick leather sleeves to protect myself from the road if I were to crash, I wore a black plastic trash bag through which I'd torn holes for my head and arms, in an effort to block out the rain. Within minutes of the thunderous boom that split the clouds overhead, however, my clothes were so wet that I might as well have just crawled out of a briny sea. The plastic layer kept the water from soaking my wool sweaters, and the polypro long underwear below, for all of fifteen minutes before I felt the first trickles of icy water dripping past my collar. It was as if someone had opened a tap at my neckline.

The best investment I'd made all year, at an army surplus store before leaving Chapel Hill, was a vintage pair of trousers, made for the armed services of one of the Scandinavian countries. They had a layer of crinkly wind-blocking foil sewn between inner and outer layers of thick wool. I'd bought them to save me from the road, but I realized that they were now saving me from the cold. In minutes, the rain found its way inside that foil as well, but at least it was thick enough that the wind chill was sufficiently blocked. By the time one hour had passed of the six that I rode in the rain that day, I was shivering so hard that I had to clutch the seat with my thighs to keep myself from shaking into a lethal loss of control.

It was as if the entire world stood in my way, blocking me from where I had no choice but to go.

"Oh, so it's the martyr you'll make yourself then?" America at large sneered in knee-jerk self-defense at the entire concept of my vision, and of the life that I knew it would drive me to pursue. And in my stepmother's shaming voice this time, "How DARE you presume to make yourself some kind of sacrificial lamb for our benefit!"

"How dare *I*?" I said aloud to the roar of the highway, and a flash of white-hot fire cut through the cold and came close, even in that icy deluge, to convincing me that I might yet survive the day.

"How dare WE!"

"How dare we, as members of the human race on this straining planet, NOT be willing to sacrifice ourselves to protect either that race, or this rock that sustains it!"

I opened my visor to bare my own teeth this time at the blinding cold, and saw my parents at home in front of the TV in their warm, quiet living room. I thought of the American Kyokushin status quo . . . the students I'd gone to school with who had no idea where to go from there, the multitudes who lacked ambition to do for anyone but themselves.

"The new, improved American dream," I thought. "Sitting at home on warm, comfortable sofas, taking the easy way out!"

"Freeze, Nathan!" America cried. "Crash and burn! Give it up! Find a warm place – for god's sake conform! – and leave life's harder problems up to someone greater than you. You're a fool to think you can make a difference!"

But I smiled, because at least for the moment I knew that I was free.

I knew that far from being a threat to anybody, all that I could see – the vision enacted – would work to make all people stronger, to reveal the man-made flaws that had crept into the American mix, rendering *these truths we hold to be self-evident* less than they were meant to be. Everyone had to be aware of it on some level . . . our relentless pursuit of a higher standard of living, and the blind eye we turn towards the consequences. But I also knew that unless through some subtle shift it became the new heroic ideal for individuals to rise up and try to make a difference on their own, no real change would ever come.

In the muffled stillness of my motorcycle helmet, against the roar of the engine and the driving rain, it wasn't clear whether I spoke the words aloud as I asked, "Is it anti-American to criticize American patriots – fallible humans, after all! – for fooling themselves that making so much patriotic noise is ever going to make a difference? Is it anti-Christian to criticize an American status quo that's made the tenets of Christianity-done-badly one of its cornerstones?"

I knew that my impatience for change wasn't as controversial as all that, but I also knew that I would be heard that way before all was said and done. My successes – the barbells I'd carry up mountains, the books I'd write, the dojos I'd open, other risks I'd take – all would challenge apathy and passive inaction in a largely Christian, patriotic nation, and my efforts would be felt as attacks on worldviews that some would fight bitterly to defend.

But "So be it!" I reveled, lifting the toe end of my right boot to downshift into fourth while cranking the accelerator with my right wrist to roar out into the fast lane. I marveled at how my life experience had accustomed me to weathering attacks born of such knee-jerk self-defensiveness.

Was that not exactly what Kyokushin's American status quo had done?

They rose up against the *Budo Karate Illustrated* vision because they couldn't see all that I saw. And that response was old hat for me, because of the decade-long storm I'd weathered at home, my father and stepmother rising up against the truths that my mere presence had always exposed.

"Oh, someone else is going to solve all the big problems?" I asked. "We can't, because we're weak, evil, and incapable? Our elected officials are supposed to take care of all that? Our religious leaders? God?"

"What a cop-out!"

"Soo da yo, Ligo!" I heard Mas Oyama's voice, roaring. "Yes, that's it! *Amerika no michi, sore!"* I saw him shaking that finger which he often lifted to scold us, and *Honbu's* floors shook with his complaint, echoing deep into the howl of storm.

"That's the *American* way!" he'd shout, one more time criticizing the all-about-me personality that had proved time and time again so inhospitable on the North American continent to his attempts to introduce the self-sacrificial core of *budo* karate. He'd shout it, not because he had any hope left for America, but because he saw a new generation of Japanese young people so eagerly buying into what he called "the American way" that they were selling out their ability to give their hearts and souls to karate.

"Such willful ignorance and apathy!" I imagined him saying in Japanese words I couldn't yet understand, and "Osu!" that day in the rain, I shouted in reply. "Is it not born of our wealth and comfort? We're so content, here, to ride these social freight trains to the economic gain that we as competitive beasts all want to have, never mind if it's at the expense of future generations!"

"Never quit, Ligo! Never close your eyes!"

I felt *Sosai's* hand on my shoulder as, in my mind's eye, I conjured the day I'd finally have a voice that the whole world would hear. I could see it already. It was as though I was already there, on a stage somewhere, perhaps on television or in print, in front of millions who were afraid to listen, but had no choice but to hear.

"Oh, I'm just as human as the rest of you," I would say, and I spat rainwater out from between my teeth. "But I'm quite certain that to be able to sacrifice myself for my brothers is more than just my birthright; it's my responsibility! It's as human as it comes. It's only when we stray from our humanity and start to run in competitive herds that we come to think it unnatural!

"Would I have us sacrifice ourselves at the expense of others? Would I have us hack our way through innocents in the process? Do you think I'd have us charge blindly off cliffs to dash ourselves on the rocks like lemmings, wasting our creative energy before it can be spent on works for the human community?

"I certainly have no intention of thus throwing mine away!

"What do you think I'm doing out here anyway . . . in the cold? I'm fighting to survive! Sure, it's dangerous, but I'm living a life in which your kids and their futures are more important than me. And *their* kids, and all the children of the future!

"Is there any other way? Is living to get rich, and comfortable and personally successful, really even living? Not for me, it's not. And so help me, it won't ever be! This is the only way to truly live, and here I have no choice but to fight!"

I came up on a row of shouldered cars, their hazard lights flashing out of time. All I could see was dancing red, and I had to lift my visor to see. *I can sit here and wait in the rain on the side of the road like an idiot,* I told myself, *or I can keep moving and hopefully ride out from under the storm.*

It was raining so hard that the only way I could even see was to lie completely down on my gas tank and rest my chin on the gas cap in front of the instrument gauges. My visor fogged up so badly that the only way to keep it transparent was to leave it open an inch at the bottom, and the only way I found that I could tolerate the bitter cold blasting its way through my helmet was to try to shelter that inch of exposed flesh behind my handlebars. *I can stay in the slow lane and travel at thirty-five like everyone else,* I told myself, and I tried it for a while, but it seemed so hopeless to be traveling so slowly – like such a waste! – so I hugged my fuel tank like a life preserver one more time, swerved through standing water into the fast lane – and roared myself! – as I kicked it up to the rigid, muscle-clenching sixty that I would maintain for the rest of the day.

Just once, early that afternoon, the sun broke through the clouds as I was passing an exit with some civilization. "*Dekiani!*" I caught myself muttering as I pulled in, "I can't keep it up any more!" I was that close to broken by the cold, and I wished for a *second*, like Suzuki had been at my grading, to slap me on the back and shove me back into combat. Instead, I located a laundromat, and stripped down to my long underwear and then the rest of the way behind a counter while I threw everything I was wearing except the trash bag into one of those industrial hot-air dryers. Setting out again forty minutes later – since I had no choice! – I watched the clouds nervously.

Three minutes after that, thunder shook the planet one more time, and in less than four more minutes – I know because I timed it with my watch! – I was soaked so completely through to the bone that a standing three-inch-deep lake had already formed between my thighs, the vinyl of my motorcycle seat, my crotch, and the seat of my pants.

A white Mercedes blasted past, throwing additional bucketfuls of water in my face. "Bitch!" I swore, even though it was impossible for me to see the driver. Throwing my visor open one more time, I saw how jealous my stepmother would be: a woman with diamond earrings in a brand new Mercedes. All of that hate! Ten years of abuse, the decade of it that I suffered at home for daring to interfere with her chances of having all that she felt entitled to have!

"Behold!" I said aloud. "*Amerika no michi da!* (That's the American way!) That's what we fight for! The white Mercedes, the sense of entitlement it takes to sail through life like an idiot because the other guy doesn't matter!"

I laughed when I realized that there was one of those self-righteous little fish glued to the hundred-thousand-dollar white, just next to the license plate.

"Oh . . ." I said. "Sorry!

"But have no fear, I mostly agree with you!

"That teacher of yours had to be one hell of an inspiration to kick off such an enduring commotion! I certainly wouldn't mind having met him; I'm sure there was a lot I could have learned! Never mind that nothing strikes me as more ridiculous than an old bearded guy on a cloud wielding lightning bolts and floods . . .

"Isn't it funny, though, that the choice I've made – all by myself! – of how to live my life comes far closer to the course of action your savior allegedly chose than yours does, waiting around on your knees to be saved?

"But to hell with you anyway!

"You render yourself irrelevant. Careful, or you'll render your entire movement irrelevant when it comes to finding the solutions that'll one day have to be found to save us all from extinction! Problem solving requires creativity, creativity stems from sight, sight requires seeing eyes, and teaching your children the only thing that's morally acceptable for them to see is the fastest way to ensure that they won't be able to see what's right in front of them to be seen just when it matters most![94]

---

[94] I.e. It is a dangerous precedent to teach young people – our clearest seers, after all! – what they're supposed to see and how they're supposed to see the world, in this case through the Christian filter of *God made this, God made that*. My complaint, however, is not with Christianity itself – unless this human, and therefore fallible, status quo is actually practicing it exactly as Christ intended. If it is, I would have to assert that there's a major flaw in the belief structure. If the flaw is in human interpretation and application, however – as it surely must be! – then I would assert that today's Christian majority has some damage to repair, lest they render the entire movement historically more relevant to the world's coming disasters than to its salvation. Would Christ

"My concern is not with you . . .

"My concern is with this social standard that *we the people* inherited from devout Christian predecessors, whose world was so much smaller than ours that the guidance they left us is no longer enough.

"My concern is with this American personality that doesn't seem to be able to rise above.

"Has not the teaching that man is both inherently incapable and inherently evil wormed its way to the core of our national personality in exactly the way it was never supposed to? It was meant to teach us humility and make us work harder, but hasn't it backfired, since so many have taken it instead to mean that we're not capable of solving problems beyond the ends of our own driveways?

"Go ahead, though, if you really want fallible man to authorize your faith![95] Hide behind the skirts of a man long dead! Wait passively on your knees to be saved! *I'm* going to face life like a man of far greater faith than yours . . .

"Because my faith is in me!

"I'll learn from the mistakes I make — because I am a man and, like you, I will make mistakes! — and then I'll be far likelier to make better

---

have wanted his followers to have their sight clouded to the blank-slate reality and immediacy of the world that would best help them to live for the love and protection of others? Surely not. My complaint, therefore, is with the human stewardship of the faith, not with the tenets of the faith itself. Correct stewardship, in this case, would be teaching young people how to find clear sight through the worldview that's unique to Christianity, and critical to that end would be an emphasis on the moral responsibility of being open to new ideas, and embracing horizon-expanding multilateral education. Since the American Christian majority is clearly failing here, it's also failing to provide proper stewardship of Christ's teaching. Ironically, my father, who taught me to see the world with my own two eyes, may have taught me to see God far more clearly than the Christian status quo would have. In that sense, my Christian education might have actually been far above average.

[95] Was man so God-awful evil and incapable in the Gospels According to All the Others? Was Christ even divine in all the accounts? Was he resurrected at all, or was he only divine in Mark, Mathew, Luke and John? What about the gospels of the other disciples, recorded from oral traditions in the same era, in which the mortal Jesus comes across as more of an Eastern philosopher, guiding his disciples towards enlightenment? Was it God who brought the early church in Rome so very close to succeeding in their book-burning campaign, as they labeled those other gospels heresy to shore up their political power? Or was it God who ensured that they would fail by preserving rolls of papyrus buried in the Egyptian desert for 1700 years so that we would find them, finally today, just when we are so clearly in such need?

choices the next time. What are you going to do when you make mistakes? REPENT, so you won't have to learn anything, and take advantage of your faith's automatic forgiveness?" Just then, a gust of wind struck from the left and nearly blew me off the road. I ground my teeth and hissed involuntarily as I compensated, leaning hard into the wind, all the way to forty-five degrees, to fight back into the middle of the lane. "Son of a bitch!" I swore as I sat up, and threw my visor open once I could breathe again. The blast had subsided as quickly as it kicked up, and my bike had righted, as if on its own. I'd let go of the accelerator, and now I allowed the resistance of the engine to slow my speed, waiting to see what would come next. "Where the hell did that come from!"

I'm on a mountain ridge, I realized. *Halfway down New York. Nothing beside the highway at this elevation for miles to block the wind. The heart of the storm.*

"Fucking hell!" I swore as another gust just about took my bike out from under me. Again, I was able to right myself, but for the next thirty minutes, gusts of wind kicked up laterally across my direction of travel, and the storm was so violent that years later I went back to see if that November first wasn't the date the "Storm of the Century" hit America's Northeast. The storm was truly a monster, and I can virtually prove how violent it was by describing the bizarre physical reaction when wind that powerful strikes the side of a motorcycle traveling at speed through standing water.

Four-wheeled vehicles turn when their drivers angle their front wheels to one side or the other, and the friction between the tire rubber and the road pulls the vehicle in that same direction. I almost didn't believe my brother when he explained that to turn a motorcycle *left* you have to pull the handlebars *right*, but I understood by the time I'd spent my first day on the highway. Want to change lanes on a motorcycle traveling at speed? You have to *lean* in the direction you want to turn, which means pulling on the opposite handlebar. That part's no secret. Anyone who rides a motorcycle knows it. But what that dynamic means to a motorcyclist traveling through gusts of lateral wind powerful enough to blow both motorcycle and cyclist off the highway tends to baffle those to whom I try to describe it.

On that mountain ridge exposed to the weather, intermittent roaring gusts of wind struck me from the left like tidal waves. Buckets of rain slammed into my left side at forty and fifty miles per hour, threatening for several seconds at a time to knock me completely off the road, before dropping off again instantaneously to shock me by the sudden stillness as I was once again struck only by the more constant onslaught from the front. It was instinct by then, developed after three weeks of riding, that when those torrents slammed into me from the left, I had to lean proportionately hard *to the left* in order to keep traveling in a straight line. I compensated automatically by pulling my right handlebar, sometimes all the way to my thigh, to lean far enough into the wind that I wouldn't be blown off the highway. During the intermittent gusts I found myself traveling straight down the highway while leaning sometimes for seconds at a time to a forty-five-degree angle. To this day, I have no idea how my tires possibly maintained enough friction with the road to keep my bike from skipping sideways out from under me.

At least I was able to forget about the cold for a time in the heat of both battles that I was by then fighting simultaneously.

"We don't even differentiate as a people, anymore, between morals and morality!

"Morals are LAWS made by fallible man, for God's sake! Morality is the natural ability to discern the difference between right and wrong on our own! If we reduce our confidence in ourselves until we doubt our own ability to tell right from wrong, and instead automatically buy into the laws handed down by the herd, how will we ever muster the creativity to find answers to the real problems that threaten us all?

"Perhaps it's just in my blood to try and save the children that I encounter drowning in wells into which the unseeing have cast them.[96]

"I do come from such stock, after all! Even my mother's father was born among the ghosts of Japan, a missionary's son, there to carry Christianity to that country in the first quarter of the last century.[97]

---

[96] The Confucian scholar Mencius uses the image of a child drowning in a well to argue that the purest original human impulse is the benevolent one. I.e. everyone's first spontaneous response is to try to rescue the drowning children that they happen upon in life.

[97] See *Japanese Customs, their Origin and Value* by my great-grandfather William Hugh Erskine (Tokyo: Kyo Bun Kwan, 1925). My mother's grandfather lived in Japan for 30 years, and her father, who was born in Japan along with his siblings, didn't come to America for the first time until college. I had no idea of the depth of my family history in Japan until after the first draft of this manuscript was already finished. I knew only that my grandfather was born there, the son of a missionary. I was shocked to learn recently the true extent of his history in Japan because my own Japan connection had already,

"Who would I be to deny that call? Who's to say that God's will won't reveal itself through the work of a nonbeliever?

"He is supposed to work in mysterious ways, is he not?

"There are Muslim extremists in the world today who believe that it's the duty of man to speed up apocalypse so that the savior will hurry up and come save us . . . but by doing so little to prevent Earthly apocalypse, is America's status quo doing any better? Is closed-minded pro-afterlife at the expense of open-minded pro-planet any better than Mullah-minded pro-apocalypse?"

I all but welcomed the distraction when I was waylaid once again by the highway patrol. For some thirty minutes already, a state trooper had been following me in the fast lane. Like me, he didn't want to be traveling at twenty-five with the motorists who'd slowed because they couldn't see the road in front of them, and I had no idea he was behind me. With my chin on my gas tank and all my muscle-clenching concentration facing forward, it was impossible to see in my side mirrors. The trooper merely wanted to pass — he wouldn't have been able to see my license plate — and he had been wanting to for some tens of minutes already before he finally got frustrated and turned on his blue lights. I couldn't see those either in the gray downpour, and he finally had to turn on his siren to let me know he was there.

"Motherfucker!" I swore as I sat up and saw the flashing blue.

* * *

Before the officer had even pulled on his rain slicker and climbed out into the rain, I'd raised my bike up onto its center stand, removed my helmet, and slung my jacket down onto the concrete like a drowned cat. As the officer approached, I stood there in my black plastic trash bag in all its glory, with my numb to nearly frostbitten — and smoking! — fists on my hips, a scowl on my face, and the start of an unspeakable oath in my throat.

---

coincidentally, occurred and matured. I was not surprised to learn that my great-grandfather had a reputation in the family as more a student of Japanese culture than a Christian proselytizer. In his own introduction, he cites how when he first went to Japan he tried to Americanize the Japanese in order to make them Christians, but, by the end of his third decade there, he was working more to understand Japanese culture so that he might incorporate those Christian tenets that the Japanese might more readily accept.

My stomach muscles were shivering so violently with cold that my trash bag rain slicker shuddered and popped like a sail torn free in a storm.

"Is everything okay?" the trooper asked, glancing downwards nervously at the violence with which the black plastic shook on a human frame that didn't shake at all. I'm afraid I may have merely glared as he explained that the only reason he pulled me over was because he'd been trying to pass me for the previous thirty minutes.

"Yes sir," I said, wiping the rain from my face with the charred palm of my right hand, and drilling the back of the policeman's skull with my gaze. "And, officer, I've got to be completely honest with you . . . There is absolutely nothing legal about me being on this motorcycle whatsoever. I don't have a license to ride one. This motorcycle hasn't been inspected in years. I don't have insurance. And the bike's not registered. That license plate isn't even mine." *Take me to jail if you must. I am the master of my own destiny and I would hardly be intimidated by the likes of you!*

"Well, all right then," the officer said. "Do you have any identification at all?"

"Help yourself," I said as I withdrew my license from a drab green thigh pocket and extended it towards him with two steady hands. In my head, I went over how I would bail myself out of jail, how I would get home without my motorcycle, and whether or not I had enough cash. For a moment, as the officer turned to go back to his car, I glanced back down at my bike and saw the exact *mae-geri* [98] that it would take to send it sprawling into an explosion of its own shattered glass and plastic lenses across the shoulder and into the dynamite-scarred sheer rock face next to it.

For ten minutes I stood there in the rain and held my ground while the highway patrolman, to his credit, seemed to be hacking away fairly quickly at his computer in an effort to minimize my suffering. Like an ice sculpture I stood, daring far more than just the rain and the cold to daunt me. With long, steady breaths I battled to bring my shivering under control, and the patrolman finally returned.

"I ran your license," he said, "and I couldn't find any warrants outstanding. I couldn't find anything on that plate whatsoever, so I have no reason to assume that your motorcycle's been stolen. You look like you're having a hard enough day as it is." He handed me my license. "So why don't

---

[98] Front snap kick.

you just be careful, and get where you're going in one piece, okay?"

"Yes sir," I said, stunned beyond those two syllables speechless when the policeman tipped his hat and turned to go.

I was still standing there, frozen, when the trooper pulled back into traffic and sped into the fast lane.

THIRTY-EIGHT

I DIDN'T QUITE MAKE IT to Bill Richards's place in Binghamton that first day south of the border, although that had been my goal. The darkness had come, and it got to where I couldn't see at all. I spent the night in a motel, uncomfortable and alone, and set off the next day for my uncle's place in DC. The rain had ushered in a cold front, and I drove for most of that second day through constant drizzle and bitter cold. I was so enraged by the sheer misery of it that halfway through I swore not to spend another day like that. It was dark by the time I reached the DC Beltway, but I kept on south and made Chapel Hill five and a half hours later. My brother, proud of his creation, stared at me in wide-eyed wonder when I pulled up on my motorcycle the next morning. He slapped me on the back to welcome me home, and I realize today that it was the exact approval of me that I hadn't seen in my father in nearly a decade.

I spent the next night in Davidson on my way south, and then opted to stay on for one more when my stepmother went through the roof over the motorcycle and convinced my father of the wisdom of purchasing an accidental death insurance policy in my name and listing themselves as the beneficiaries. "How else are we going to pay for his funeral," she asked, "without jeopardizing the comforts that the kids enjoy?"

My father brought the idea out to me in the cottage like an errand boy.

He always looked like he was straining under an enormous weight in such situations. In the past I had tended to interpret that strain as conflict, as if he was using every scrap of willpower he had to conquer his own character and enact his wife's will. This time, however – the first time since I'd watched him support his wife in refusing to have

Dillon in their house – I questioned my decade-long interpretation.

Maybe it was him after all.

Maybe he'd changed that much. Maybe he'd matched his character to the woman he was married to, just as perhaps he'd matched his character to Martha up until ten years earlier. Perhaps the strain that I saw in him was just his battle to conquer the guilt that he regularly admitted to experiencing when confronting his sons.

That my father felt guilty made sense to me, but I was routinely exasperated by the reason he'd give. He felt guilty, he said, for subjecting me and my brother to a second divorce. He never understood that it was his decade-long, daily casting of us at the feet of his third wife that was so hurtful. Of course it was a great tragedy for me to lose Martha, but I was no stranger to divorce, and I forgave my father as a matter of course.

I was only eleven, after all, and I never bore any ill will towards my father for what to me was just a fact of life:

Parents divorce. Parents remarry.

Sadly, however, my father could never see the truth. "See?" he always suggested, "I finally married a woman who's charitable enough to be willing to act like a mother to you."

Act *like a mother? What difference does it make if she* acts like a mother *if she doesn't love me? What difference does it make, since my disrespect* for her act *keeps me from ever looking for anything in her I might like?*

Of course, for my little brother and sister, I didn't have any objections to signing my name on an accidental death policy to pay for my funeral, and I didn't argue. My father explained that I would have to stay in town for one more day so that I could sign the form my stepmother was taking a morning off from work to prepare. I was beyond caring, so I only agreed.

Besides, if Canada hadn't killed me, Florida sure as hell wasn't going to!

How dare I threaten their attempts to create a perfect family by dying in a motorcycle accident! I thought as I fell asleep that night. *They've made it so clear that I frustrate that prospect simply by existing! Now I'm to understand that even by dying in an accident I would be in the way?*

My half brother and sister, born into a household in which I was a young teenager, *are* my brother and sister. One doesn't spend the kind of time I spent with them – as infants, as toddlers, and as preschoolers – without developing that kind of bond. But then, they were also always my stepmother's instrument for demanding that I roll over and play dead. My brother's wife Traci in Chapel Hill would get off the phone with my stepmother and exclaim, "If *that woman* EVER wants me to come visit them again, she's going to have to learn how to ask me!" – her mother-in-law having just used the children, one more time, to try to guilt-trip her into bringing my brother over to visit on a weekend when they'd already explained they likely wouldn't be able to. "Not being with your family on this holiday weekend is not an option," my stepmother would suggest. "The kids are going to be sooo disappointed," my father's wife using even her own kids to make visiting her household so unappealing that her older stepson and his wife would come round as seldom as possible.

I wondered sometimes if she wasn't losing her mind. Her actions made her seem so incredibly intent, so much of the time, on achieving the exact opposite of the words that came out of her mouth. A feminist-era pro-choicer, she wouldn't let Dillon in her house for having an abortion? Of course she wouldn't! The greater priority was to make sure that I was eradicated.

Her words were like lies told even to herself.

In the same way that *because of the kids* she wouldn't stop at a fresh accident scene to see if the bleeding people needed our help, my brother and I had had to play her twisted game of presentation to the outside world so that her kids would grow up believing that there was no strife in the world, and so that they would grow up into the status quo's version of *respectable, upstanding adults*. For my brother and sister "with all their perfectly-formed little fingers and toes," as their mother had so eloquently put it, I had been asked to roll over and play dead ever since they were born. They were my stepmother's number-one guilt-trip, her number-one stepson eraser. They, my parents' moral excuse for leaving my brother and me bleeding on the side of the highway.

I imagined my stepmother crying tears at my funeral, if I had died in a motorcycle accident, that would have further endeared her to my father while she secretly retired her stepson eraser. "Finally! I got rid of the second one," she'd say to herself as she celebrated how she'd managed to pay off their mortgage twenty years ahead of schedule. *In that case, there truly would be,* I laughed, *a fine line between tragic loss and ecstatic celebration!*

How relieved she'd be to have merely to comfort my father for the loss of me!

With new cause after Mount Royal to look again at the falling-out I'd had with Martha and wonder whether Midas had set me up for it, I had no doubt that while I might recently have been hurt by Martha's underestimating me, she'd only otherwise ever made me feel unconditionally loved.

What a tragedy! I thought. *I'll eventually have to go away to ensure even that my little brother's and sister's education is complete!*

They have to see my success, they have to understand how it all happened, and maybe then they'll grow up and be able to understand all that they must have picked up on anyway — kids being the perfect little seers that they are!

"No matter what you've been told," I would tell them today, "remember that while I might have been an adult during the action of this story – and an older, hopefully-wiser adult when I wrote it! – I was most certainly a child when your mother and father threw me away."

* * *

Cruising south towards Charleston, I took a deep breath of the exact sort I'd taken when Helen and I were finally alone that day after lunch. It was a breath that made me feel human again, like I could finally be myself, and quit playing a game that somebody else expected me to play. I thought of the books that already existed in my mind's eye, in a finished form so complete that chapters of them had already been written in the voice they would retain, and I managed a smile. A warm, ocean-scented breeze blowing up from Florida blasted its way in through my open visor. Florida was Martha's state. I thought of her and knew unequivocally that I was free. I'd never again have cause to bite my lip in the face of my stepmother's abuse. I'd never again be a victim of my father's willful blindness, his cold, impotent silence.

How does the Mencian man[99] abandon his own father?

Of course, it's easy to abandon someone who seems hell-bent on hurting you, but what happens as the years pass and the parent becomes the one who needs protection? How does the child, raised to be a particularly sentimental and conscience-driven adult, abandon his father as he starts to decline into a time of his life when he needs his children's support? How does the child commit the crime that much of

---

[99] i.e. one guided, first and foremost, by conscience.

our society today would condone — certainly knowing the particulars of the treatment he'd suffered! — when the child, in spite of himself, knows the crime to be a crime because his heart reveals it to him as such?

How does he walk away from the parents who gave him two of the four greatest gifts he's been given?[100] They gave him, first, life, and they gave him, next, the full benefit of a utopian childhood for his first ten years.

How does he walk away from those who gave him that?

How does he distance himself from those who continue so relentlessly to hurt him, given that his love for them is so deeply ingrained? How does he extricate himself, knowing that those from whom he must escape are far from intrinsically, or even willfully, harmful? How does he abandon them when he knows, in spite of himself, that they hurt him only as a side effect of fateful choices of their own, never out of any kind of malicious intent?

"It's so simple!" I told myself when I realized the genius of all that the vision had collaterally achieved.

"I should have known! It only makes sense that something so primal would have been working behind the scenes to achieve a set of entirely unintended results as well!"

"I simply had to find a greater cause!

"I had to find a higher call of conscience!

"In my case, in fact, I found one that's so great that even the most basic of personal relationships became expendable. I turned even to desperate means, when necessary, in pursuit of a vision so ambitious that most men would dismiss it from the outset!

"And how do I keep at bay the extreme potential for the same kind of guilt that ruined my father?

"Simple!

"I work my knuckles till they bleed! I drive myself till I can drive myself no further. I ensure that my efforts to pound the vision into the here and now are greater than all that I've left behind!"

I was distracted by an American flag–flying motorist in a pickup

---

[100] My biological mother, although still living in Chapel Hill, and present enough to give me the last of the money she'd set aside for my education the summer I moved into Martha's house with Lissa, was largely absent from my life already by the time the action of this story began.

truck with a gun rack and a deer rifle. I realized that I was composing lines of future books as I rode, and turned my attention to the world at large.

"Oh have no fear, my untraveled, uneducated compatriot!

"Even if the vision does come true, and our country does mature by degrees, have no fear — even then! — for these *truths we hold to be self-evident.*

"Fear for those truths, instead, if a revolution of sight and perspective FAILS to overtake us!

"But if such a shift does occur?

"If we, the American people, DO stumble into the sense of personal responsibility that we were meant to have, before it's too late?

"Fear then for blindness!

"Fear for apathy, ignorance, and bigotry!

"Fear for our herd-like tendency to follow the paths of least resistance at the expense of harder, wiser choices! Fear for the social approval of closing our eyes to real-world consequences to gain the false comfort of not knowing! Fear for this bitter defense of conformity, when conforming so often means living to support society's economic machine, and fooling ourselves that doing so is somehow wholesome!"

I laughed at the juxtaposition when I came up on a VW bug with a New York license plate, and a bumper sticker that read "Peace is Patriotic."

"None of that applies to you?" I asked, considering middle-class America, and my "highly educated" parents at home. "You condescend, and shake your head at the redneck whose version of patriotism is to whoop and holler and pine for war? Oh, but it's precisely you that needs to open your eyes! You who are in the majority! You who have a better chance of seeing what's right before you than those who have already irrevocably closed their minds.

"If only we could open the floodgates of transcendental wisdom with the flip of a switch! Then we wouldn't have to work to fill the shoes of the enlightened!

"But since we can't, since it's instead left to us to earn our birthright as Americans, bestowed on us by Jefferson, Hamilton, Franklin, and the rest, we have no choice but to recognize that they didn't give us enlightenment when they gave us freedom; they merely gave us the world's most advantageous conditions for achieving enlightenment IF we muster the courage to do the necessary work!

"Of course we should celebrate democracy!

"But what right do we have to act as if being the proud inheritors of an enlightened system is enough to make us enlightened without having to do any of the work? How dare we go through our lives with the complacency of the enlightened, when the enlightened who gave us our freedom and security – the foundation upon which our complacency rests! – would have resisted with gnashing teeth and full-contact blows had anyone called them enlightened!

"Have we been so far reduced that we can't see that they were fighters?

"They were revolutionaries, for God's sake!

"Their wisdom, their enlightenment, was born in the trenches of hardship!

"Are we to listen to the wisdom of one who crawls out of frozen Russia and then spends his life trying to inspire others to live deliberately heroic lives? Or are we to listen to those who build up what they believe to be wisdom along with their grotesque bellies watching Sunday afternoon football games?

"What happens when more and more of us crave that kind of 'wisdom' because the freedom to put our feet up is what we've come to value more than anything else?

"What happens if we reach a point where the majority of our fathers are the fat guys on the sofas? The ones who'll drive past injured people on the side of the highway, knowing they'll be judged at home only by whether or not their front lawns are kept mowed?

"What happens – God forbid! – when those types of fathers become our teachers?

"What if fathers with true integrity and wisdom – born of experiences such as the Great Depression, wars, and the struggle for equal rights – are becoming fewer and farther between, thanks to our affluence, and to the cruise missiles and laser-guided bombs that keep more and more of us out of the trenches?

"What happens when the books and newspapers we read, and the television shows and movies we watch, are written and produced by the fat guys on the sofas instead of by the survivors of the foxholes?

"Individual character worthy of the personal responsibility that upholds democracy is far from inherent!

"It's far from automatic.

"It's far from hereditary.

"We have to work our fingers to the bone through training, and study, and character-deepening life experience to draw it out! Through our individual choices, each and every one of them, we either uphold American enlightenment or, through our complacency, we betray it, and cast it wasted and broken upon the rocks.

"Hold this truth to be self evident!

"The disasters we face today won't hold a candle to the disasters we'll face in the future as we continue to push the limits of the population this ecosystem can sustain . . . and if we don't improve our average so that our majority becomes a *seeing* majority, we WILL eventually be responsible for our own apocalyptic demise!"

Suddenly one hundred percent of my attention was back on the road.

I wondered for a moment if I'd run out of gas; my motorcycle was still running, but I was steadily losing speed.

I cranked the accelerator.

The pitch of the engine changed, but to no avail.

That's lucky! I thought, realizing there was an offramp just ahead. I checked my rearview mirrors. My speed had already fallen below 40, and I felt sure I'd draw the attention of the highway patrol if I broke down.

At the top of the ramp I pulled over and leaned out, first to the left and then to the right, to inspect my motor. There was no evidence of anything wrong. I removed the gas cap; I had plenty of gas. Making sure I was in neutral, I released my brake lever, dismounted, and raised my bike up onto its center stand. Finally, squatting beside the sputtering motorcycle and cranking the accelerator, I found the culprit: hot air was hissing out through a crack in the dry rubber of the right-side carburetor boot.

"Dammit!" I checked the other side.

It was both of them.

I couldn't believe that I'd made it all the way to Canada and then back as far as South Carolina before losing a fairly critical set of my bike's various dry, cracked rubber parts.

It must have been the heat, I figured. *Those days of extreme cold and rain, followed by this South Carolina sun . . .*

At 20 mph I pulled up around the bend and parked out of sight of the highway, pulled out the highway map that I carried in my right thigh pocket, and began to search for a back road into Charleston. My motorcycle still ran, but with the loss of engine compression, its maximum speed was reduced to twenty-five, and I was certain that to ride any significant distance on the highway at that much less than the speed limit would finally get me arrested. I'd already pressed my luck, and I figured that the third strike would surely land me in jail.

Happily, I found a suitable two-lane road and spent the noon hour that day riding on the side of the road, doing my best to impersonate a bicyclist.

Half a set of yellow pages hanging from a cable below a pay phone, an hour later, led me to a motorcycle salvage yard, and I spent two hours there waiting nervously for a fat, tobacco-chewing mechanic who told me he'd show me how to replace carburetor boots when he got done with the bike he was working on.

While I was waiting, nervous about how much it would cost, a tall, gaunt black man who looked like he wasn't much of a regular bather came in angrily. He pointed a bony finger at the mechanic and told him he'd been attacked and robbed by the man's dogs. I'd watched just five minutes earlier as the mangy, decrepit pair – elderly, overweight, coats matted into globs with fleas, ticks, and motor oil – staggered arthritically out into the yard. Apparently the German shepherd, who could still run, trotted out through the open gate and grabbed the passerby by the heel of his boot. The obese Rottweiler then staggered up behind him and pushed him over to rid him of the bag of fast-food fried chicken he was carrying under his arm towards the neighborhood beyond.

The mechanic winked at me with a brown-toothed smile and said, "I told you dey was good dogs."

"All right, all right," he said, turning back to the black man, who was muttering curses. "Hold on to yer britches!" Reaching for the till, he removed the greasiest five-dollar bill he had, handed it to him and said, "Make sure next time yer carryin' fried chicken, you don't take it down my street! I ain't got no say over what my dogs do. They's too old and they was raised not to like niggers. Now get on home! And stay clear of my yard!"

The black man, content with the five-dollar bill, turned to go without further protest.

Amazing, I thought. *Home sweet South! America, the Beautiful!* The combination of poverty, heat, ignorance and oil-soaked sand took the wind right out of me. I watched as the Shepherd and the Rotty came back into the shade of the garage, flopped down in front of the fan, and neatly divided and consumed a bag of Kentucky Fried Chicken — paper bag, chicken bones, plastic coleslaw cup and all.

Late that afternoon, halfway down Georgia in a T-shirt with my sweaters, polypro, and letter jacket all bungee-corded to the rack behind my seat, I realized that my body had finally thawed. Overcome by drowsiness in the blinding sun, I pulled into a campground, parked my motorcycle under a tree, made sure that there were no ants, and lay down on a bed of dry, prickly grass, with my head propped up on the saddlebag that held my *dogi* and belt.

"Of course freedom must be protected," I mused. "If someone attacks us, of course we have to have the strength to defend ourselves!

"But what if the next attack, when it comes, comes from within?"

I curled onto my left side and wrapped my arms tightly to sleep. I shivered despite the warm afternoon sun.

* * *

Michael Lorden arranged for me to spend the first half of the week at the home of one of his students, and I spent the second half in his own guest room. About midweek I knocked another of his students out cold with a high roundhouse kick when he got a little too spunky with me during *kumite*. I was as surprised as he was, and even thought that he was faking when he fell to the ground with his eyes rolled up into his skull after such an insignificant smack to the jaw. I finally did believe it, though.

When he picked up his glass jaw to continue fighting, he'd lost all of his spunk.

Sensei Lorden was extremely receptive when I belatedly accepted his offer to partner with me in the continuation of *Budo Karate Illustrated*. "Of course I'm still interested!" he said. "Let me talk to my accountant, and we'll see how it can all be worked out."

I wasn't at all surprised.

Since Canada, the project's momentum was back on track, and I could see, once again, how close I was to positioning myself so that one day my own efforts might make a real difference. That roaring momentum had been the project's natural state from the beginning; it was the stillness that followed Matsui's freezing the project in June that had seemed out of place.

Puzzle piece number one would be the continued support of the giant, Jacques Sandulescu, and the influence that I still allowed myself to believe he could find with Matsui. Puzzle piece number two was the support of André Gilbert and the army of French Canadian buyers his endorsement would ensure. And number three, the final piece of the puzzle, would be Michael Lorden, an older, wiser coeditor who would both divert attention from the *young, impulsive* editor who'd designed the first book, and kick in $20,000 of his own pension towards getting the project back on its feet. The third piece fell into place as smoothly as the second one had, and I wonder that Midas didn't claw his way out of the earth one more time for the sheer bragging rights.

See? he'd have exulted, *It's unstoppable! Its foundation was in the vision, and the vision was born in my own backyard! You and I have seen the future, and there will be no stopping it! So what if Mas Oyama died when he did! The vision has a life of its own. Matsui himself won't be able to stop it!*

It's a pity that Midas did *not* clamber once more to my aid. Maybe then I'd have come just a little closer than I did to pulling off the impossible.

To Jacques from Michael Lorden's office, by fax, I wrote:

> Dear Jacques,
>
> I can not think of anything I would not give if somebody could magically remove from my personality either the willingness to believe that I am capable of achieving literally anything as long as I am willing to make literally any sacrifice, or that part of my conscience that prevents me from not making that sacrifice, from not taking that risk, if my heart tells me that through it I can ultimately someday, in some way, make a difference in society in which I believe a difference so desperately needs to be made. If somebody could take this from me, I could live my life in the way that society demands that I live; I could end the punishment that society deals me for daring not to conform, for daring to listen to my heart. I can not even begin to relay what it's like to give everything I know how to give and in return to hear that I'm crazy or that I do "stupid things." This is why your faith in me, why what I have perceived to be a common understanding, why your camaraderie, has meant so much to me. Perhaps I am wrong to live the way I do. Only the future will tell.

> This is the last chance for me on this book project. I can no longer justify waiting with my hands tied. If, for whatever reason, this project is truly dead, that's okay. It was never really an important part of my plans. It was just a freak opening that I saw as a way to get ahead, to improve my odds in ultimately making the impossible possible. I need to be training. I need to be writing. *Sensei* Lorden will make this possible if we are allowed to work together. He is willing to share the commitment, to help direct a project that is really much too big for one person to handle. He will give me the time for doing what I need to do. Who knows? Maybe if Matsui *Kancho* says no, it'll be for the best. Then I'll have all the time in the world.
>
> Bottom line, if your faith in me survives, I will indeed be grateful if you would ask *Kancho* one last time on my behalf. If he again says no, it will be the last time.
>
> I will not ask again.

I've always been a terrible reader of my own writing, and I read those words today and wonder if the exhaustion I felt as I wrote them shows through. It was certainly through a haze of fatigue that I wrote them. "I need to be training. I need to be writing," I told Jacques. "I need to be free of having to fight these godforsaken political battles to achieve what my conscience demands I pursue!"

Canada had been a last-ditch effort to save the magazine. There was no *but* in *Osu*, and yet with that gargantuan effort I'd tried to insert one in protest of Matsui's axing my project. *Maybe it is beyond saving,* I told myself, *but so what? What I have already done – gathering the support to print even the first book – was beyond achieving too!*

But this insane Canada to Florida road trip?

This time, I really could have been killed!

For five weeks I'd been on a motorcycle I had started out not even knowing how to ride. I was exhausted by the cold. I was exhausted by the storm. I was exhausted by Caroline. I was exhausted by Midas. And I was of course so unbelievably exhausted by Helen. I was exhausted by Conscience's call to believe the impossible possible, and I was exhausted by surviving the sacrifice of self in its service, even though I knew I could survive it again. *My god, Jacques!* I swore. *If only there were a way I could continue, and not have to subject my creative energy to those from whom I have to ask permission! Asking for guidance is one thing. Subjecting my choices to the scrutiny of the life-experienced is another! But permission?*

That's another thing altogether!

My guts have been ripped out, Jacques, and spilled on the floor! Sometimes it's all I can do to crawl *to my next destination while struggling to contain all of that inside me and keep the work moving forward at the same time.*

Conscience demands it, because I can see the result. I can see the end product, and I have no choice.

And yet, I have to ask permission to do what I know is right?

I have to bear the consequences of being told no by those who can't see?

To hell with them all, Jacques! You crawled out of Russia. You've got to understand. You had no choice but to keep going forward. To stop meant the end for you, and it's the same for me.

Sure, I could shut it down. It would be so easy for me to close my eyes and follow in my father's footsteps to comfortable blind acceptance of the status quo. I could find someone less than me, like he did, to manage the affairs of my heart. I could celebrate my escape when I give myself over to a creed that would allow me to stop fighting for this life and hope that there really is going to be another world so wonderful that it will justify my failure to give my all for this one!

But how, Jacques, could I live with myself?

Knowing what I know, seeing what I've seen, how could I lie on my deathbed and look back at my life — how could I look into the eyes of my children's generation — knowing that I turned a blind eye and took the easier course just because it's the one everyone else takes?

* * *

Michael Lorden's accompanying letter read:

Dear *Shihan* Jacques,

Osu!

I hope that you and your lovely wife Annie are in good health and that all is fine for both of you. The support that you have shown Nathan is heart-felt, you are truly friends in every way. Nathan, as you know, is energetic and at times can be impulsive. These traits are not necessarily demeaning, but he tells me that they have gotten him into trouble in the past. One thing that I believe I can offer this project is life experience and, perhaps, a more delicate and diplomatic approach to things. Since the beginning of Nathan's first book I have offered him my support and I intend to continue this support. In the event that approval, for the next book, is received from *Honbu* and Matsui *Kancho*, I intend to offer my support and the commitment of both time and shared financial responsibility. I enter into this venture without hesitation, for I believe in the project and Nathan, as well as a need for this project as a communication avenue, long overdue in North American Kyokushin. I believe with your endorsement we will achieve the needed approval from *Honbu*, at which time Nathan and I will push forward 100% with the book. If you require any additional information or I can be of any assistance, please feel free to contact me.

Sincerely, Michael Lorden

I didn't hear an answer for a day.

And then I didn't hear an answer for another.

On the third day, I was momentarily baffled when *Sensei* Lorden handed me a fax addressed to me from Annie which, he told me, had arrived *two days before,* there on his fax machine in the house in which I, too, had just spent most of the past forty-eight hours.

Why didn't he give it to me when it arrived?

But in almost the same breath, *Sensei* Lorden went on to explain that he'd learned from his accountant that the penalty for drawing on his retirement plan early was going to be too great to make it possible, and suddenly I understood. My head would have spun as I read Annie's fax from the realization that *Sensei* Lorden was withdrawing his support, even if what Annie wrote hadn't been enough to rock my world on its own.

Something had clearly rocked Sensei Lorden's.

THIRTY-NINE

BY HAND, Annie had written:

Dear Nathan,

I know my nit-picking is not as gratifying as Jacques' big broad support, but it might be worth listening to as a counterpoint. What happened was not that you threw yourself into this heart and soul and got shot down by a cruel world demanding that you conform, be mediocre, and run at 33%. What happened was very simple: you did not keep your word! You wrote to all Branch Chiefs, 1) "This is not my book, it's your book" and then you put yourself on the back cover; and 2) you wrote, "I will get the approval of all of you before I print the book, or (since that's unrealistic) at least of my advisors," and then you didn't seek advice until it was too late. Time and space problems notwithstanding, this made you appear insincere and more ambitious for yourself than for Kyokushinkai. Simple!

There's nothing wrong with being ambitious, but when you are young, it's strategic to keep a lower profile. No one would have objected to your putting in a couple of pictures of your demonstration or some of your own story, but you overdid it, and then in your faxes to Honbu, you betrayed a sense of your own importance that is disproportionate to your experience (and that, in fact, a more experienced person would have tempered out of them). In your vision of this book/magazine, its role in Kyokushin, and your role in it, you were running on sheer fantasy.

There's a delicate balance, because Jacques is right: that ability to dream big and to give your all to realize the dream, is precious, and it would be a terrible waste for Kyokushinkai to throw you away. What you should do, maybe, is recognize — really recognize, not just pretend — that there's a lot you don't know yet about the world and other people — and that's okay, that's even an advantage, because it doesn't clutter up the purity of your energy. So leave that to us — the older folks, Mike Lorden, Bobby Lowe, Jacques and me. Just recognize that you've got to run stuff by us, like running it through a filter. We will provide that perspective and tempering and balance that you can't possibly have yet — just as we can't have your incredible drive!

Jacques will read your fax and tell you if he needs a proposal.

Love, Annie

Annie's letter read like the dropping of a guillotine blade.

Please, Jacques! I'd written. *I need you to use your influence like a battering ram like you told me you would. I need you to understand!*

I need someone to understand!

But it had been Annie's letter that came instead, and no matter the intent, Annie's particularly pointed criticism joined hands with Michael Lorden's ominous delay in letting me know his plans had changed, and had the opposite effect. "In your vision," Annie wrote, "you were running on sheer fantasy," and — the loss of Michael Lorden set aside! — it was that uncannily perceptive challenge that flipped the switch to the OFF position on *Budo Karate Illustrated*.

The doors simply closed.

The blade fell, and I could no longer see even the slim chance of success I had managed until that moment to hold on to. Not only had I lost my *older, wiser* co-editor, but somehow the Nathan-be-damned opinion of the status quo had crept into my innermost camp as well.

I felt like I'd also lost Jacques.

What the hell happened during the past forty-eight hours? I wondered. *What discussions occurred that I wasn't privy to? Why would I want to work with a partner who would sit on a piece of my personal mail like that for forty-eight hours, anyway?*

I read Annie's letter and the look in *Sensei* Lorden's eye like the flipping of a switch through which the electrical current of my vision flowed. Leave that switch untouched, and the current would have kept right on following the same path, uninterrupted and without resistance. Flip it the other way, however, and with an innocuous spark, the current leapt its tracks onto a parallel course and kept right on flowing at the speed of light, leading me along a different route, but to the exact same destination.

It ran, in fact, so much towards the same goal that on many levels it was as if there had been no change at all.

I didn't blink. I didn't lose balance for an instant.

Of course, those around me might have been shocked by the spark.

Within half an hour I was on the road again, heading north towards a Davidson that had suddenly taken on a whole new significance. The doors closed that quickly on the magazine project, but in snarling defense of the future I could still see, another set had opened wide. The picture of *Budo Karate Illustrated* as a shortcut to achieving my life's work was gone, but another one in a millisecond came to take its place, and Plan B stretched out before me in high definition like some bizarre twisting of fame's long red carpet, and the final steps of a condemned man.

I would need to make use of unknowing Davidson just one more time.

* * *

My *uchi deshi dai-sempai* Kenji Fujiwara pointed out recently on a cross-Pacific flight that according to my birth date and the Chinese zodiac, the Chinese would consider me a Wild Boar. "Like *Sosai*," he said, "the same. *Sosai* was born under the Sign of the Boar too."

The Boar's nature is to charge forward relentlessly, pigheadedly even, never quitting until he gets where he intends to go; he's going to smash his way through everything in his path until he hits walls that he can't break through. "But the boar doesn't care even then," *Shihan* Fujiwara said, "He's just going to shake his head to regain balance, turn toward the nearest opening in the wall, and just keep right on blasting forward."

How ironic! that it was with Annie's help this time, rather than with the help of her husband, that I'd found myself, once again, at just such a strength-doubling crossroads. In place of Jacques' battering-ram-like support, Annie's suggestion that "in my vision" I had been "running on sheer fantasy" came at me like a wall of solid granite, and – stone-headed do-or-die student of Mas Oyama that I was! — I shook my head once to regain balance, snorted like an angry pig, and charged off for the nearest opening towards where I was still — so help me! — going to go.

Roaring north on a motorcycle that, with new carburetor boots, had finally started to run like the rocket it was meant to be, I took even more risk than I had before in terms of how confidently I rode it. Somewhere along the way I'd acquired a collarless, sleeveless terrycloth sweatshirt of the type body builders wear to show off as much chest and arms as possible; the warm Florida air whipped delightfully through it that day, and I might as well have been shirtless. I shudder to think of how much skin I'd have lost had I gone down in an accident.

Beyond my impatience to be done with the highway, I felt like I had wasted an entire eighteen months of creative drive, and I was desperate to be home. Florida's warm ocean breeze, although delightful to the touch, struck me like insult added to injury, because I knew that where I was going was far from warm. It was far from delightful. Plagued by images of Mas Oyama's solitary mountain training — and, in my own experience, that meant the snow- and sleet-packed torrents that whipped past Grandfather's peaks in the moonlight — I carried with me the abject horror of knowing that my path was irrevocably set.

At least there would be no political battles. Where I was going, I wouldn't have to ask anyone's permission.

And that was exactly the point.

In my own personal training, there would be no opposition. No one could take away the strength I would gain, or the lessons I would learn. In writing, too, there would be no opposition. No one could tell me what to write, and pen and sword, used in accord, would be mightier than either wielded alone. In teaching, too, I would need no one's approval. My students would either follow or they wouldn't. But some of them *would* learn, in small ways if not always in the big ones I envisioned; and those that did would carry what I taught onward into America's future.

Of course I was numb, powerless, still, for the time being, to process the *detail* of what was to come. I would need a job; that much was clear. I would need to maximize earning for awhile, and minimize expense, in order to move my training back into line with what it had been as an *uchi deshi*. I would file for bankruptcy to eliminate the *Budo Karate Illustrated* debt. Perhaps I would see Dr. Abbott and arrange to complete one more course credit along the way. One more independent study in writing would do the trick.

The book still needed to be written, after all!

Training, writing, and teaching. That path had been with me all along. Until that morning, though, I had no idea how far the vision would drive me to pursue it.

With eyes wide open, I knew that I'd have to stray even farther from the herd than the past three years had taken me. To sharpen the pen and the sword I'd need to take my efforts to a level worthy of my ambition, I would have to move even further out into the cold. It was as if I could see two possible sets of my own footprints leading off into the future. The first led off into the Florida sand in pursuit of a failing *Budo Karate Illustrated*. It led towards Matsui and his new IKO, towards Annie's "filters of the more experienced," and towards the sacrifice of my vision as "fantasy." Those footprints were man-sized like my own size 9s. They led towards what had become, for me, an uncertain future.

Perhaps I *could* have revived *Budo Karate Illustrated*.

Perhaps I should have walked forty miles to *Matsui's* doorstep to show him the sincerity of my apology.

Maybe that was Kikuko Oyama's doing. Perhaps she had planted the seeds of doubt. Maybe it was something that I, myself, had seen in Matsui. Maybe it was something that I *hadn't* seen — because, in Matsui, maybe it wasn't there to be seen! — something vital that I had become accustomed to seeing in Mas Oyama. Maybe Matsui's willingness to set aside his own instinct in favor of Bobby Lowe's or Katsuhiko Horai's had led me to doubt whether life- and limb-jeopardizing support of his IKO was going to be worth the effort.

But the second set?

The other set of footprints I could see, the one that steered even farther clear of the herd?

That set led off towards the vision realized. The feet that left them were numb, aching and frostbitten, and the snow into which they led was streaked with blood. And that one, Annie! that set of tracks were the size of *Jacques'* 14 quadruple wides! They were the shape of those stonelike archless BLUDGEONS that had carried *Sosai* down from his mountain, and fifty years onward to his death at the age of seventy-one, a teacher of millions. They were the footprints of giants, and I saw them clear as day, and terrifying as dying a meaningless death after a wasted life.

Sosai was behind me, and I knew that I had no choice.

"Over my dead body!" I'd sworn in my dojo when he died. "Over my dead body will the world cease to have its giants."

My God! I swore, roaring north towards Charleston and Davidson beyond. *You thought that last harebrained plan could kill you?*

This *could be the one that'll make you* wish you were dead![101]

Talk about death by obscurity if you fail!

* * *

Impulsive?

Yes, but nobody had any idea just how impulsive I had become.

"Listen to your heart!" Master Choi told me when I was barely nineteen and standing at a crossroads that would either lead me to Japan, or ruin my chances of making it there forever. Like a scalpel, his command cut into me with a surgical precision that enacted what felt like an actual, physiological change: From that day forward, I did listen to my heart. Real or imagined, from that day on I could in fact hear what Master Choi ordered me to hear – and my life was forever changed by that man, one more time.

It wasn't something that I always heard. It wasn't there to confuse my day-to-day. But certain circumstances would cut into me, conjuring what Master Choi had revealed at my core, and Conscience's voice, like a cathedral bell, would toll, and precise and often terrifying courses of action would reveal themselves so clearly that it was as though there was no choice but to follow. By degrees, I got better at catching the impulses that rang from that source, and experience showed me, day by day, that doing so would only be rewarded by the most positive results, even – and especially! – when they weren't the ones I had foreseen.

Don't let Mas Oyama set foot on American soil without being there to greet him! Follow him to your former roommates' graduation ceremony in Tokyo. Love this woman, Lissa, at all costs, and don't quit no matter the personal risk. Don't quit

---

[101] Jacques's words: "Growing up in the Donbas could have made me dead; but growing up in America can make you *wish you were dead!* Write the book, Nathan!"

even when she quits: *find another way to leave yourself exposed. Don't publish in an existing magazine. Make your own for Kyokushin.*

At all costs, be in the front row of Helen's class.

Do a thousand jumping squats before your Watson interview and shake the interviewers in their chairs with Japanese they won't understand. At your own risk, embrace those volcanic visions of the natural world melting at your feet. Run barefooted into thunderstorms and stare upwards into the falling hail. Allow your eyes to meet with those of hawks on the wind and embrace the emotions of your past that those visions instill. Lend voices to the caws of the crows and the screeches of owls. Go to Tateyama for strength before attempting the nidan *exam for which you're so dramatically unprepared. Drive Midas into the ground the instant it feels like he's threatening innocents. Swear the dojo oath at the top of your lungs to Mas Oyama beyond the grave. Make love to Akiko on the eve of his funeral. Take this decrepit motorcycle to Canada to win André Gilbert's support. Michael Lorden is the puzzle's last piece. You made it to Canada in four days . . . Good!*

You can make it to Orlando in five.

All of it was impulse, all of it came from the same source, that source was the core of what I was, and all of it, every single directive, came so close to passing me by! How close I came, each time, to dismissing them, one by one, out of the learned habit of choosing the safer course! But somehow, time and again, I realized on the brink what was about to be lost and, with gnashing teeth, I grabbed hold.

"Listen to your heart!" Master Choi told me, and he unknowingly gave me a name for the schism that had already been revealing itself to me for years: the rift between what was surely human impulse at its most basic, and those contradictory impulses born of competitive human interaction. It was the latter that left me so painfully alienated by those from whom I'd so desperately longed for acceptance. My father, for one, clearly loved me. He clearly meant well. The impulse was there at his core. Yet he'd chosen, time and again, to fight to protect a line of reasoning that had no basis in such original impulse. He was going to use force if necessary – Nathan be damned! – to create his own tradition-based vision of the life he wanted, even if there was no place in it for several of the people he loved.

Clearly, Martha had refused to play the game. She wouldn't be the mother that he wanted her to become, because of course she was *my stepmother* and could never magically become my mother from the outset by trying to impose a bond that wasn't there. My father wanted to marry a mother for me who would allow him overnight to be a backstage father only – like *his* father had been while his mother raised the kids – but Martha, who was nothing but real – nothing, so help her, but honest! – recognized that it couldn't possibly work that way, and she wasn't about to fake it.[102]

Socially, it had been the same. All my life I'd been the outsider, the newcomer – the freak! added to each and every new peer group to whom I was introduced, and I had no doubt – I could see it in the eyes of every single individual member of those groups, those times when I had them alone – that none of them, individually, possessed even a shred of an original impulse to cast me aside, and hurt me, simply because I was new, or different, or appreciated by my teachers, or smaller than most, or smarter. It was in their interaction where that new set of impulses was born, in their social combination, and as an adult, as a student of Master Choi, and later of Mas Oyama, I'd come to know that it was exactly that type of born-of-society, learned impulse that was leading all of us, as a people, into peril as men and women on a drastically overburdened planet.

---

[102] Sources of guidance we have to choose from, when making the decisions that govern our lives, include *conscience* of course, *learning*, *law*, and *habit*. In the case of *conscience* we employ compassion to do what we feel is right. In the case of *learning*, we make choices based on how we've been taught to choose. We choose to follow *laws*, whether our legal codes, religious laws, or the laws of tradition (or even our *perceived* laws of personal limitation!) because there are generally undesirable consequences to breaking them. In the case of *habit*, we make choices because we made them that way the last time and it seemed to carry us through. All of us make the choices of our lives based on the combined influence of all of these sources of guidance. There are instances where conscience reinforces what we do out of habit, or affirms what we do because it's what we were taught. And there are instances where habit trumps conscience when we lack the willpower to make the stronger decision. The *law* of one's family tradition and the *learning* that one acquires from one's parents are very deeply ingrained, but not quite so deep as the benevolent impulse of *conscience,* born in one's very first moments when first held, protected and fed by one's mother (and father). *My* father, already approaching his 50's, chose to rely on his family tradition when deciding how to govern his new family, and effectively ignored the greater source of guidance at his core. Conscience within him wouldn't have stood – and didn't stand! – for making both his wife and his first two sons so miserable by forcing them to combine so unrealistically. Here I cite my father's paralyzing guilt and the conflict that I saw in his eyes whenever he had to suppress conscience to uphold the decision he'd made. This type of inner conflict is what makes people unhappy, and can result in people being truly unhappy, as I believe my father was in 1994, that fumbling mess at the front of his classroom.

For me, disenfranchised, cast out into the cold, trained by titans, shown by giants like Jacques, Master Choi and Mas Oyama that I could endure it, I'd come to know that schism so well that I could identify, and pick and choose the impulses I felt based on their source. "That one," I would say, "came from within; that one came from the core of what I am. That one, on the other hand, that one's tainted. That one came from society's teaching me by example the easy way out. That's the choice everyone else makes, and that one, therefore, I will ignore."

And for me, of course, the loudest one of all – the impulse that had came to ring clearer to me than any other – was the impulse that told me that if I gave my all, I could alert some significant cross-section of the young people I would encounter in my future to the truth of that schism. I could teach them to hear the impulses and differentiate the source. I could empower them, starting with the spiritual strength gained through hard physical training, to make a better set of choices that just might lead enough us towards fixing some of the world's most significant problems.

Was I ambitious?

God almighty, was I ever ambitious! I'd never met another who was even a fraction as ambitious as I was.

But was I ambitious for myself, as I'd been accused of being?

How could I have been? In my vision for the future, I rarely survived the effort!

Far from wanting to build myself up, I looked into the future and saw myself burning myself up in the effort to do something for the children of my generation, so important that it was worth the attempt even if only a tiny fraction of it would succeed. Far from seeing myself up on a pedestal looking down over my minions, I looked into the future and saw myself *DEAD*. I saw myself wasting away under the strain of pounding the vision into the here and now. I saw myself beaten to the dojo floor, staggering to my feet, and being pounded down again. I saw myself crawling down titanic corridors as if dying to reach what was at the other end while at the same time struggling to contain the bloody mess spilling outwards from my open belly.

Reason was fine as far as it went. Reason could benefit from prudent advice. Reason might show me how to pace and preserve myself to achieve some realistic fraction of the vision. But to make it all the way? To make it far enough that Conscience might be appeased, and allow me some moments of peace before I die?

That would take something more.

I was coming to realize that like Leonardo Da Vinci, Mozart, or Miyamoto Musashi, I just might have stumbled upon a life equation for a runaway reaction to generate great works for the common good. By making my very survival dependent on fulfilling the demands of Conscience, I'd have no choice but to struggle to my utmost to do exactly that. And at the same time, to dedicate my life to that struggle, I'd have to make choices that would keep me on the brink of survival. They were opposing forces that, like a pair of caged lions battling for dominance, would daily strive to surpass one another in the ferocity of their attacks.

We're all familiar with the balance of yin and yang, if only as the twin teardrop symbol in which two equal and opposing forces form the unity of a perfect circle. If only the twin forces at the core of the Nathan Ligo reactor had formed such a balance! And maybe they will approach balance in the end, but if you asked me to draw a diagram of the forces that drove me as I moved into my twenty-third year, yin would slightly overreach yang, yang as an equal and opposing force would then have to slightly overreach yin, the cycle would repeat, and the balance would come to resemble a double helix spiraling upwards toward theretofore unimaginable reaches of achievement. One strand of the helix was my giving in to my animal nature, which insisted upon survival at all costs. The other was my insistence on listening to the voice of Conscience, the voice that so clearly distinguishes us from beasts, even when the costs of doing so threatened my survival. The bond that held the two strands together was the conviction that the combination was bringing me closer, choice by choice, to a goal that even Reason told me was too valuable to dismiss.

Was I "running on sheer fantasy"?

Perhaps.

But that's always been up to me.

I can decide whether it's going to be vision or fantasy. The deciding factor is how far I'm willing to push myself towards the extremes of exhaustion in the pursuit of artistic creativity.

Do what it takes to keep your eyes seeing eyes. When in doubt, drive yourself to the point of collapse where everything is so clear. Maintain like this and you can pound the fantasy into the here and now.

Vision, Annie!

It will be vision at any personal cost.

If it kills me, it will be vision.

So long as Conscience's voice rings true, it will be vision.

* * *

In 1993 and 1994, I combined all that I'd ever loved and lost in my life, and found it again in Helen – she became the embodiment of all the rest! – and, like a monster, I burned it all away like so much rocket fuel!

And I burned away far more than just Helen.

I burned away any chance of having, for many more years to come, even smaller degrees of what I'd found in her, and would have been so content to find, even in those lesser degrees, in someone else. My heart breaks at the thought of it . . .

But look at what was achieved as a result!

With Helen in mind I mobilized all of Midas's armies in what I believed to be the spirit of my teacher Mas Oyama, because it was only through such an all-encompassing mobilization that I could possibly have mounted an attack on the twin towers of America's weakness worthy of Mas Oyama's expectation. With Helen in mind, I launched a thousand ships and charged off, torch in hand, to burn America's topless towers of weakness before weaker people come along from other nations to burn down the towers of our strength![103]

It was all that I was, and I couldn't have changed if I'd wanted to.

There was no other Troy for me to burn.[104]

Those *were* days when my heart was volcanic, and the odds of days like those coming for me again are slim. From this point onwards, certainly, my life will be all about moving back into sync with the herd, because I've always known that that's where I'd ultimately have to be to enact change.

But sixteen years ago I stood at the brink of my choice to move even further out into the cold, against the herd, to pursue training, and

---

[103] From *Doctor Faustus* by Christopher Marlowe: *Was this the face that launch'd a thousand ships, / And burnt the topless towers of Ilium? –/ Sweet Helen, make me immortal . . .*

[104] *Troy*. Sinéad O'Connor. The Lion and the Cobra: Capitol Records, 1987.

writing, and teaching, in the tradition of the giants that went before me.

And the choice that I made to follow that set of footprints was the ultimate tribute to my teacher, Mas Oyama.

My parting gift to you, *Sosai*!

My tribute! – because there can be no fraud in hard physical training.[105]

My tribute to you, Jacques! – because I'll never stop fighting. *Fighter* is in my blood now just like *writer* is, it's what I am, and I don't think I could stop fighting if I wanted to.

There's too much to be fought for and won! There's too much to be written and read.

There's too much at stake.

My love and gratitude for you, Master Choi! – how could I ever possibly find the words?

My awe at what you gave me, Davidson! – because now I'll never stop learning.

My celebration! – of the open-minded education my parents bestowed upon me when I was a child, because the generations of the future will know how wonderful the wonderful things were that they gave me.

My oath! – that I will do everything within my power – I will spill every drop of my own blood if necessary! – to deliver into the hearts of my children's generation the best that all of my teachers gave me, and the best that my teachers in the future have yet to give me, in an ongoing education that – God willing! – will never cease developing my strengths and my understanding into realms I am as yet powerless to imagine.

Has it all been a product of injury?

Will telling the story repair the damage I suffered as my own parents strove to teach me that *I* was broken when they could no longer compute what actually was?

The tightly-managed closed circle of my stepmother's home was the

---

[105] Earlier I wrote "there can be no such *nonsense* in hard physical training." The Chinese characters used to write Sosai's name "Oyama" are: "O", *great*, and "yama", *mountain*. Of course, there's no connection to Shelley's *Mont Blanc* except for the uncanny coincidence as Shelley uses that exact phrase, "great Mountain," and cites its potential to "repeal" society's "codes" (I.e. laws) of fraud and woe: *The wilderness has a mysterious tongue / Which teaches awful doubt, or faith so mild, / So solemn, so serene, that man may be, / But for such faith, with Nature reconcil'd; / Thou hast a voice, great Mountain, to repeal / Large codes of fraud and woe; not understood / By all, but which the wise, and great, and good / Interpret, or make felt, or deeply feel.*

perfect machine for blocking out truths they did want to see, but it was also the perfect mechanism for hiding from the world the truth of their abysmal treatment of me and my older brother. We were the children that were thrown away in order to make room for fresh starts at family; can this quest of mine really ever fill the void, and make – at least in my case – the pain of that abandonment go away?

Surely that's where it all has to have begun. I truly would be broken not to acknowledge the possibility. I would be far less a man to deny it!

But why leave it at that?

Why not embrace the possibility, celebrate it, and use it to be the best man I can be? Why not exist at the brink, because I know that, there, I'll have the best chance to achieve the greatest good for the people that walk beside me on this godforsaken rock?

And if the pursuits fail?

Or if success costs me everything, and I find myself, in the end, friendless, homeless, cold, and alone?

What did *Sosai* have at the end?

Empty hands.

Only karate.

How can I possibly hope for more?

EPILOGUE

IN THE IRONY TO END THEM ALL, one of the first faces I beheld, in almost the first instant I set foot back in Davidson, was that of Helen Ecks.

I rode into town at the end of the five hundred miles from Orlando, stopped first at what had been my Café the year before, and at the first table, the only one visible from the door off the patio where I parked my motorcycle, sat my advisor Tony Abbott, Shireen Carroll, and, "Oh my God," I would have sworn had I not been too afraid I'd give myself away, "that's Helen!"

I hadn't even recognized her. She looked exactly like herself, of course, but that was exactly the point.

It had been months since I'd seen Helen in her flesh-and-blood humanity, and it wasn't until that moment that I realized the extent to which I'd elevated her in my mind's eye to something more. The knowledge of it ran over me like one of those icy blasts that had tried so hard to knock me off the highway at the top of the continent. Just like the "*Sosai* as God trap" that we used to fall into during weeks or months separated from him, I realized how far I'd fallen into a "Helen as Goddess trap." I curled my toes, hard, into the insoles of my boots.

What have I done? How could I have taken someone so beautiful and allowed her to mutate into such a monster?

Helen was so completely innocent and unknowing of the whole ordeal, and, once again, I felt like a rapist.

Dr. Abbott, Dr. Carroll, and Dr. Ecks all seemed happy to see me, and they all at least feigned curiosity about what had transpired since last we met, if for no other reason than that I was one of the more colorful seniors to fade away from the English department at the end of the previous year.

"I wonder what's next in the Nathan Ligo saga?" I read as the average of those three sets of bright, intelligent eyes. "I wonder how long he'll hold out before he realizes how much more comfortable his life will be if he can move it into better sync with the rest of the world?"

I probably failed to hide my dismay when someone asked me about my book project. I don't remember whether it was Dr. Abbott or Dr. Carroll – Helen was perceptive enough, I think, not to ask – and I had no choice but to report that I was quite certain that my project would have no future in a Kyokushin world dominated by Matsui.

"No, unfortunately it's dead," were the words that I used. My further attempt to make that trio understand the events that had transpired in Florida faltered after a feeble line or two that would have served only to expose, if not my crushing disappointment, then at least the backbreaking fatigue I'd suffered from far more than just the highway. I was blown away by the irony of running into Helen in my first second back on campus after six months away. It was as if the Helen-pointing magnetic pull that I'd come to feel so acutely during the previous year had actually drawn me to that exact point in space and time. I hadn't seen her since I'd written to her before her babies were born.

I saw her see it when I diverted my eyes.

How heartbreaking it was to find myself lying all over again simply by standing there!

Like my same old runaway train but onto a parallel set of tracks, I'd already moved onward to the next creative endeavor. Yet I was powerless to tell anyone, least of all Helen, the extent to which I'd made her an unknowing participant in the one I'd finally now put to rest. How disappointing to realize that the new track onto which Conscience had taken me was one that – yet again! – I couldn't possibly share . . . this time with anyone!

Oh, I was done with the unique and dangerous means I'd discovered for stealing creative power. I was done downing lost love's blissful cocktail of endorphins. If the subsequent sixteen years could be shown as evidence, I would never again be so careless with the safety of innocents.

I've even, for the most part, managed to shut down the gaze.

Thanks to my experience with Helen, I find myself today, for better or for worse, far more inclined to divert my eyes when I encounter those who might see than to succumb to what was once my natural tendency to search inside them for that for which I have been in my life the most desperate.

This time, it was the lunacy of the new track on which Conscience had set the vision, and the consequences that following it could possibly have *for me*, that prevented me from sharing what lay ahead. To expose it then would have left people that cared about me unnecessarily concerned. I was one of the sanest people I knew – I had a firm grasp on that then – but I also wasn't stupid, and I knew that anything short of a book-length attempt to explain would make people who cared think me unbalanced.

I found myself there in front of three people whom I really would have wanted to make understand, and I was crushed to find myself, still, so desperately disenfranchised. With no other course than to excuse myself awkwardly, I walked away with more than just one set of concerned eyes burning into my back.

* * *

I don't remember exactly when I knew that Helen's babies were fine, but I know that I already knew by the time I came back from Canada, because I was long since no longer afraid for them. I finally met them on the lawn in front of the College Union one afternoon – one infant boy and one infant girl with blatantly literary names – blond, chubby, and vibrantly healthy. Helen was sitting with them in the grass next to a stroller built for two, and I was finally able to congratulate her.

How convenient it would be for my story if I could tell you that I looked over my shoulder for one last glimpse as I walked towards Chambers and smiled to myself as I realized how much the three of them resembled my own mother, brother, and me. My brother was born just a few months before my mother moved to Davidson to join the Music Department faculty, and I was born in Davidson, like Helen's kids, in my mother's first year there. I think of Helen's *complications* and recall how I was born ten weeks premature.

My English professor Dr. Holland told me on the first day of his class two years earlier – on the same day that I read Chaucer aloud in Middle English and scared that freshman girl half to death – how his first memory of me was actually of my mother pregnant with me while she performed in a solo voice recital at the church, and how he was sure that I was partially responsible for how beautiful both she and her voice were then.

"Hauntingly beautiful," he said.

I recall his words and the window to his soul through his eyes that confirmed them, and I marvel at how moved I still was then by how beautiful Helen was, and now by the beauty of her children as well. They were beautiful to me like life. They were beautiful like a life that I doubted then that I'd risk ever having for myself.

It's probably just not in the cards for you, I told myself. *Having a family, I mean. In your case it'll be students and books, first, second and third. Work first, work second, work third and, if you're lucky, a little rest once it's through.*

Had I indeed been strong enough to look over my shoulder, back towards Helen, perhaps my eyes would have fallen on the old Infirmary building across the street where, a lifetime-long six years earlier, Dillon had knelt on the cold tile floor with her elbows on the toilet and prayed that she wasn't pregnant with my child.

I'd have been looking at the exact same building where, fifteen years before that, Didi Bevon had her part-time job – one of my babysitters, the one above all the others with whom I shared a beyond-words affinity. Had I turned to look over my shoulder, and had I been able to see magically through that same building and through the narrow strip of trees beyond, I'd have been looking straight at Ann White's house, the wife of Davidson physics professor Locke White, and my first preschool teacher, who'd played such a powerful role alongside our parents in making my earliest childhood about love, and an attempt to lay the foundations for adult enlightenment.

If you had a ruler and a map of Davidson, you could see whether I wouldn't in fact have been looking straight at Tony Abbott's new house, where I let my love for Helen run free, and at the Lorimar Street neighborhood where my parents first brought me home from the hospital, and where I had my earliest childhood memories with my earliest companions! Within about fifteen degrees of that same line, you would find the tiny house with the fenced-in back lawn where Helen lived, sometimes alone and sometimes with her husband Jack, and finally with her whole family once the kids were born. Is it any wonder that when I drew in deep breaths of Davidson's spring in search of Helen, I turned in the exact same direction of all the rest?

Is it any wonder that my internal compass pointed towards Helen all the way from the Canadian border!

I would remain in Davidson for exactly eleven more months before leaving the country for the subsequent four years of my life, to pursue training in Korea and in Eastern Europe on a level I hadn't attempted since I was an *uchi deshi* in Japan. Those eleven months included Helen's last months in Davidson before moving out west to join Jack, and she and I had one final encounter halfway through that year.

The occasion was the English Department's end-of-year banquet.

Phillip Levine had won a Pulitzer for his poetry halfway through the semester, and he did his first public reading after receiving the news in our very own College Union 900 Room[106] over the Café. It was the kind of event that an entire English department the size of Davidson's shows up for, and I had gone there to find Helen.

Downstairs on the loading dock across from the old Infirmary building, with a shaking hand that made Mas Oyama's only American *uchi deshi* laugh out loud at the irony, I smoked a rare cigarette in an attempt to find balance in the half hour before the event. I'd come to understand that during those volcanic days on the lawn in front of Chambers, when the planet melted around me and the vision was born, Midas had made my reaction to the absence of Helen a chemical one, and although Midas was long gone and Helen was moving farther and farther away from my world, it was in an effort to drive that demon side effect from my life that I went to a public event in search of Helen. I went there in the hope that meeting her would reexpose the nonsense of it all. I went there for the control rods of Helen's flesh and blood. I went there, conflicted but finally compelled, longing for the stabilizing anchor chain of her friendship.

Unfortunately, Helen was the department's only faculty member absent that evening for Levine's reading. She was still on leave that semester, still apparently home with the children.

The rest of my class had already graduated by then – members of my freshman class had graduated three whole years earlier! – and I was happy to have Erica still in town two months later, finishing up her last class, so I'd have someone to lean on as my date for the English Department banquet. I felt sure Helen would be there, and I panicked momentarily

---

[106] Davidson's Student Union building was the Davidson College library in an earlier era, and "the 900 Room" retained its name from when it housed library books numbered in the 900s.

when Erica backed out, feeling herself I think a little too distanced from her former English Department family.

Sara was back in town, though, after her Watson — working for the college as an intern — and in the end she and I became, arm in arm, the last two members of our class to attend that year's banquet.

I was surprised to see so clearly in Helen that she had become a bit estranged from Davidson, too. Her leave, taken during the two years that she taught at Davidson, must have limited her exposure to much of the younger crowd that was gathered there that day. Maybe Shireen Carroll wasn't there for some reason, and maybe Dr. Strom and Sarah Beasley were already gone. Dr. Abbott must have been busy running the thing.

Of course I knew the moment Helen walked into the room because there ceased to be a rest of the room, and there ceased to be anyone else in it. The five or eight minutes that Sara and I mingled with other English majors while Helen's presence burned a hole through my spine were among the longest of my life.

How sure I must have been of the safe distance I'd achieved from Helen to kiss her like a gentleman as she embraced me!

With unadulterated pleasure Helen embraced her friend and student too many months absent from her life, and confident as Midas reborn I kissed her on the cheek to punctuate a careful return embrace. Somehow I was confident enough not to be afraid as my lips fell an inch closer to her ear than I'd intended, due to the unexpected fever of her embrace. They'd fallen a mere six inches above the collarbone from where, just eighteen months earlier, I'd stolen that desperate lungful of her flesh from across the room. With Helen finally there beside me, such abomination was the farthest thing from my mind.

I had all of her then, for those few moments. What was the point of trying to take more?

An old familiar anchor had caught hold, the chain pulled taut as the bow swung round with the storm, and the next breath I took was the easiest of my year.

If Helen's managed to fight her way through to the end of what I imagine has been something of a horror story for her, and if she's managed to find any humor in it at all, I have a hunch that she'd smile to remember and understand for the first time what was going on with me when the call came for us to find seats for dinner. I whisked Sara away, momentarily abandoning Helen to the crowd out of a lingering notion that I shouldn't give away how badly I wanted HER beside me during dinner! That's when I saw the disenfranchisement in Helen's eyes: the rest of the faculty was engaged in other corners of the room, and she all but physically reached out to catch hold of me with optical grappling hooks that said, "For God's sake, Nathan, don't leave me alone! I don't know anyone here either!"

Happily, I came back to Earth then, before too much damage was done, and found myself surprised – by the unlikely reversal of my having rescued Helen! – and I placed her safely beside Sara and me for dinner, and for the presentation that followed.

Of course I didn't hear a lick of the presentation.

I don't even remember who was at the podium.

Helen was so unbelievably beautiful to me then – "How can this woman just have given birth to twins!" I remember thinking, and beyond that I can only remember being so completely relieved that she was once again one hundred percent real, and that there was absolutely nothing there of the chemical monster I'd made her in her absence.

How shocking it would have been to everyone present had I spent the rest of the presentation on my knees, with my forehead in Helen's lap, crying tears of relief at having found her at once again human, and once again still so much my friend!

That night, after the dinner was over, I smiled to myself at the diminished, barely even audible echoes of long-lost thunder as, arm in arm, I walked beautiful, brilliant, and highly literary Sara across the bricks in front of Chambers to her car parked across the lawn on Main Street. Sara and I hugged each other goodnight like one-time lovers who'd become better friends because of it, and "Remind me to tell you a story someday," I told her.

Sara straightened, having already started to climb in behind the wheel of her car. She turned to look at me again, both eyes glowing like the moon for that moment – maybe it was the wine – and, smiling, said, "Why not now? I've got time if you do."

I could only laugh.

"I know. I'm sorry," I said, "It'll have to wait for another time. I'm not quite ready to tell it."

I spent my first two years abroad in Master Choi's Korea, training for the first year on a level that did indeed surpass my *uchi deshi* training.

During the second year I pounded out my first book-length manuscript. Two very different women in Korea awoke in me the same kinds of feelings of loss that Caroline had in Montreal, but I suspected it mostly to be the remnants of the chemical, and in both cases I let it go.

Work first, work second, work third! I consoled myself. *There's barely enough time as it is. Keep the vision on track. Pound it into the here and now, so there'll be peace once it's done.*

After one more year in Hungary, training on a level that blew away everything that had gone before, I spent a final year in Budapest training, writing – no less than three more book-length exercises this time! – teaching English to Hungarians, and living with the woman who would, by the end of that year, become my wife.

Halfway through the year, in an advanced English class I taught to a dozen nearly conversational adult professionals for ninety minutes three times a week, my single-mother, office-assistant student Zsuzsa came up to me after class and asked me if I knew what kind of eyes I had.

"Brown?" I said, smiling naïvely, relieved that it would be the last question of the day.

"No, that's not what I meant," she said, and I inadvertently rapped the backs of my knuckles on the tabletop between us so hard that it broke the skin as I snatched out for control.

"See?" she said.

My God, did I ever at that moment see!

"You shouldn't block it out," she went on as if it were nothing. "It's a gift that not many people have. You can see what other people can't. Mostly in the eyes of certain people. Not all of them. Not all the time. If you don't let it happen, though, maybe you'll forget how. Whoever she was, you shouldn't be so hard on yourself."

"*Boszerkany!* (Witch!)" I muttered under my breath in Hungarian, once she'd smiled with her seeing eyes and turned to go.

LIGO DOJO OF BUDO KARATE
A 501.c.3 Public Charity Nonprofit

Readers who want to know more, or wish to make a tax-deductible contribution to Ligo Dojo, can find information about The Society for the Betterment of the Human Condition through the Training, Instruction, and Propagation of Budo Karate (d.b.a. Ligo Dojo of Budo Karate) online at:

www.budokaratehouse.com

Contributions go directly to make self-esteem- and discipline-instilling karate training available to young people who might not otherwise be able to participate. At the dojo, we teach karate and karate alone. In accordance with Mas Oyama's teaching, it is best through hard physical training that the greater truths of life will emerge; we provide the hard physical training, and hope that each individual will discover those greater truths that will be important for his or her own life in the future.